EXPLORING
MEDICAL
LANGUAGE

A Student-Directed Approach

EXPLORING MEDICAL LANGUAGE

A Student-Directed Approach

Myrna LaFleur Brooks, R.N., B.Ed.

Founding President
National Association of Health Unit Coordinators

Former Director
Health Services Management Program
GateWay Community College
Phoenix, Arizona

Fourth Edition

 Mosby

A Harcourt Health Sciences Company

St. Louis   London   Philadelphia   Sydney   Tokyo

A Harcourt Health Sciences Company

Publisher: Don Ladig
Senior Editor: Jeanne Rowland
Developmental Editor: Winnie Sullivan
Project Manager: Mark Spann
Production Editor: Julie Eddy
Book Design Manager: Yael Kats
Book Designer: Lee Goldstein
Manufacturing Supervisor: Karen Boehme

FOURTH EDITION

Printed in the United States of America

Mosby, Inc.
11830 Westline Industrial Drive
St. Louis, Missouri 63146

0-323-01718-5

01 / 9 8 7 6 5 4

To
Danielle, Michael, Brian, and Andy
who bring joy, fun, and fulfillment to my life.

PREFACE

Welcome to the fourth edition of *Exploring Medical Language*. Medical terminology, like any living language, is not static. It has become the common currency not only of those in medical professions but also of insurers, lawyers, equipment suppliers, pharmaceutical representatives and others who interact with health care providers and consumers. To keep apace of medical science and to communicate medical knowledge effectively, medical language must expand and change. The goal of this fourth edition is to reflect those changes with a presentation that is up to date, sound in its approach to language instruction, and that visually supports the learning process.

New to this Edition

The most apparent change in the fourth edition of *Exploring Medical Language* is its extensive redesign, use of color, and inclusion of new illustrations. These modifications were implemented to increase both the instructive value of the book and its ease of use, consistent with our student-directed approach.

In addition to style, this edition has improved in substance. Dated medical terminology has been replaced with terms (and their abbreviations) that convey the most recent advances in medical knowledge. An end-of-chapter review now allows you to test your retention. Appendixes have been added, anticipating your need to know terms specific to certain medical areas. Finally, a new interactive computer program on disk will reinforce what you have learned in the text. Our intent is that you, the student, in response to these changes, will develop an appreciation for the language of medicine and a curiosity about medical terms that will linger long after your medical terminology course is completed.

Building Your Medical Vocabulary

Exploring Medical Language is designed to assure your mastery of the language of medicine. This is accomplished by categorizing related terms into easily learned units and by introducing you to the structure of medical language. In this way you will be equipped to understand the terms included in this text, as well as the new and unfamiliar terms you may encounter in a clinical setting.

Many medical terms are constructed from language elements known as word parts. The word parts, each with its own definition, combine to form specific medical terms. Retaining a proven aid to learning, this edition of *Exploring Medical Language* distinguishes medical terms that can be translated literally (or built) from word parts from those that cannot and provides a variety of exercises to help memorize the word parts and their meanings. Because the language of medicine is incomplete without them, terms not built from word parts are included in separate sections with their own exercises. These sections, if not part of your course of study, can easily be omitted.

Organization

Introductory Chapters

Chapters 1-3 provide a foundation for building medical vocabulary. Chapter 1 introduces the word part method of learning medical terminology and explains how prefixes, word roots, combining vowels, and suffixes are used to form terms. Chapter 2 establishes a base for the body system chapters that follow by providing information about body structure and by helping you to build the terms related to color and oncology that apply to all body systems. Chapter 3 covers directional terms and anatomical planes and regions. All chapters are enhanced with many new four-color illustrations, providing clarification of terms and procedures. Each chapter ends with a review, offering you, the student, an additional opportunity to evaluate your knowledge.

Body System Chapters

Chapters 4-16 present medical terms organized by body system. Each of these chapters opens by introducing the relevant anatomy. This section may either acquaint you with body structure and function or, if you have studied anatomy in a separate course, can serve as a review.

Body system word parts precede the medical terms, which are divided into four categories: disease and disorder terms, surgical terms, procedural terms, and complementary terms. Each category of terms is further divided into terms built from word parts and those not built from word parts. Considerable attention has been given, in this edition, to updating these terms, ensuring that they reflect current usage and include the newest techniques and procedures. Abbreviations have been added, and boxed information throughout the chapters amplifies definitions and describes the derivation of specific terms. Exercises follow each group of terms, giving you the opportunity to review and rehearse new vocabulary immediately after it is presented.

Appendixes

Helpful appendixes supplement the information provided in the chapters. Appendixes A and B list, in alphabetical order, all the combining forms, prefixes, and suffixes from the entire book by word part and by definition. Appendix C lists less commonly used word parts not presented in the chapters. Appendixes D and E provide abbreviations and plural endings to medical terms.

Appendixes F through I present medical terms that are not related to a particular body system, but that are frequently used in the day-to-day health care environment. These terms that have a more general application fall into the categories of pharmacology, health care delivery/managed care, alternative medicine, and psychiatry.

Learning Aids

The fourth edition of *Exploring Medical Language* comes with a variety of learning aids intended to make your study of medical terminology as efficient and enjoyable as possible.

Diskette with Extra Exercises

Your copy of *Exploring Medical Language* includes a complimentary program on disk that provides additional opportunities for word building and definition, plus the application of language skills. This interactive program presents terminology in various medical documents to help you get accustomed to seeing medical terms as they will be used in actual health care settings. A variety of exercises will help you memorize the word parts and their definitions, then combine the parts to form medical terms.

Flash Cards

480 flash cards printed on card stock come with *Exploring Medical Language*. Each flash card has a word part, a combining form, suffix or prefix on one side, and the definition of the word part on the other side.

Audiotapes with Pronunciations and Definitions

The audiotapes that accompany *Exploring Medical Language* include pronunciations and definitions. You will find the audiotapes an aid to learning not only the pronunciations of the medical terms but also their definitions. Because the audiotapes include definitions, they are an additional tool for learning and reviewing terms. The tapes are especially helpful at times when using your book is impractical, such as when you are driving in the car. You may purchase the audiotapes separately or packaged with the book for a small additional cost.

To The Instructor

Instructor's Manual

The Instructor's Manual to accompany *Exploring Medical Language* will assist you in effectively and efficiently planning and teaching your medical terminology course. The instructor's manual will provide a suggested course outline, chapter objectives, classroom activities, additional terms not included in the text, transparency masters, and a wealth of multiple choice questions that you can use for quizzes and exams. If you have adopted *Exploring Medical Language* for your course or are considering it for adoption, you may request the Instructor's manual by contacting your sales representative.

Computerized Testbank

This testbank offers 1200 multiple choice questions that you can sort and compile into chapter tests, midterm exams, and final exams. Please contact your sales representative to request a copy.

ACKNOWLEDGMENTS

I am grateful to many individuals who assisted me in revising this text. They shared with me their imaginations, their intuition, and their enthusiasm for the changes that are reflected in this fourth edition of *Exploring Medical Language.*

First I would like to recognize Jeanne Rowland, Senior Editor, for obtaining the resources needed to publish this text on schedule, for her dedication to quality, and for her pursuit of a meaningful and substantial revision. Without the expert, supportive, and friendly assistance of Winnie Sullivan, who assisted me through the writing, development, and production stages of the manuscript, publication of the text may not have been realized. Her contribution to this edition was invaluable. Thanks to Sharon Tomkins Luczu, RN, MBA, Director, Health Sciences Management Program, Gateway Community College, Phoenix, Arizona, for contributing Appendices G and H, Health Care Delivery/Managed Care Terms and Alternative Health Care Terms.

I especially appreciate the contributions of Richard K. Brooks, M.D., who reviewed the chapters and offered expert criticism, and of Danielle S. LaFleur, who was instrumental in moving the revision forward during a period when I was sidelined by an unexpected surgery. I am grateful to all those listed below who reviewed the manuscript. They played a major role in updating the content of this edition. A special thanks goes to Bernice D. Stiansen whose involvement, both in the review and proofreading of the text, made an important contribution to its production.

Thanks to the adept production staff at Mosby—Mark Spann and Julie Eddy—for their participation in this project. I am also grateful to artists May S. Cheney, Jeanne Robertson, and Nadine Sokol and to designers Lee Goldstein and Yael Kats; together they breathed new life into the book's appearance.

Finally, my appreciation to the faculty who have adopted the text to use in their classes and to the students who, over the years, have worn thin the pages of previous editions to acquire the language of medicine.

MYRNA LaFLEUR BROOKS

Reviewers

JOANNA BARNES, RN, MSN
Instructor
Associate Degree Nursing Program
Grayson County College
Denison, Texas

KAREN L. BAUER, DA
Assistant Professor
Department of Natural Sciences
Dixie College
St. George, Utah

ANNE T. CAMPBELL, RHS, RT(R)(T)
Leader
Radiation Oncology Department
Central Baptist Hospital
Lexington, Kentucky

ELIA CHACON, RDH, MED
Faculty Member
Associate Degree Nursing Program
El Paso Community College
El Paso, Texas

CHRISTINE COSTA
Maricopa Integrated Health System
Phoenix, Arizona

WANDA HANCOCK, MHSA
Associate Chair and Associate Professor
Director of Alumni Affairs
Clinical Services Department
College of Health Professions
Medical University of South Carolina
Charleston, South Carolina

JOYCE C. HONEA, RN, BSN, MSA
Program Director
Nurse Refresher/Medical Assisting
    Program
Front Range Community College
Fort Collins, Colorado

SUSAN MAXWELL, RN, CNOR, BSN
Assistant Professor
Surgical Technology
Tarrant County Junior College
Fort Worth, Texas

BETTY MITCHELL, RRA
Assistant Professor and Clinical
    Coordinator
Health Information Technology
    Program
Baltimore City Community College
Baltimore, Maryland

JOAN PIERSON, BS, RT(R)(T)
Program Director
School of Radiation Therapy
    Technology
Henry Ford Hospital
Detroit, Michigan

DIANE PREMEAU, RRA, ART
Health Information Technology
    Program
Chabot College
Hayward, California

ELLEN RAINIER, MS, RN, C
Lecturer, Adult Health Nursing
School of Nursing
Indiana University
Indianapolis, Indiana

SCOTT SECHRIST, MS, CNMT, RT(N)
Program Director
Nuclear Medicine Technology
School of Medical Laboratory Sciences
    and Environmental Health
Old Dominion University
Norfolk, Virginia

BERNICE D. STIANSEN, RN, BScN
Instructor
Medical Terminology
Grant MacEwan Community College
Edmonton, Alberta

JAMES B. TEMME, RT(R), FASRT,
    FAERS
Program Director and Associate
    Professor
Radiography Program
University of Nebraska Medical Center
Omaha, Nebraska

CAROL A. THOMAS, MSEd
Professor
Sciences for Allied Health
Santa Fe Community College
Gainesville, Florida

JOAN VanOSTEN, MBA, RT(R)(M)
Program Director
Radiologic Technology Program
North Iowa Mercy Health Center
Mason City, IA 50401

MARY WEIS, DVM
Professor of Biology
Math and Natural Sciences
    Department
Collin County Community College
Plano, Texas

CONTENTS

HOW TO USE THIS TEXT

To the newcomer, the language of medicine is like a vast, uncharted frontier. *Exploring Medical Language* systematically guides you along a path of vocabulary development that is interesting, enjoyable, and that thoroughly prepares you to communicate as a medical professional. While using this text, you will become familiar with the structure of medical language and with the most effective strategies for learning medical terms. A variety of learning activities will allow you the practice to grow confident in your use of the terminology. Follow the guidelines below to get the most from this textbook as you embark on your journey of acquiring a new language.

Understand the content of Chapter 1 before moving on to Chapter 2.

Chapter 1 is the most important chapter in the text because it is here that you are introduced to word parts—combining forms, prefixes, suffixes, and combining vowels—and the rules for combining them to build medical terms. You will use this information in each of the subsequent chapters to analyze, construct, define, and spell terms built from word parts.

Use each chapter section fully to help you master the medical terms presented.

Objectives

1. *Read the objectives* before you begin the chapter. Objectives state what you can expect to learn as you progress through the chapter.

2. *Refer to the objectives when you have completed a chapter* to evaluate whether you have learned all of the material presented.

Anatomy

1. *Read the content,* using the illustrations to clarify the structure, location, and the relationship of parts of the anatomy.

2. *Complete the exercises.*

3. *Check your answers* with the answer portion of the text. If you have previously studied anatomy, you can easily omit this section or use it as a review.

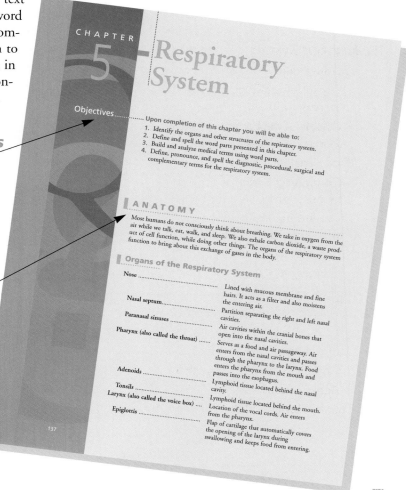

CHAPTER 5 — Respiratory System

Objectives

Upon completion of this chapter you will be able to:
1. Identify the organs and other structures of the respiratory system.
2. Define and spell the word parts presented in this chapter.
3. Build and analyze medical terms using word parts.
4. Define, pronounce, and spell the diagnostic, procedural, surgical and complementary terms for the respiratory system.

ANATOMY

Most humans do not consciously think about breathing. We take in oxygen from the air while we talk, eat, walk, and sleep. We also exhale carbon dioxide, a waste product of cell function, while doing other things. The organs of the respiratory system function to bring about this exchange of gases in the body.

Organs of the Respiratory System

Nose	Lined with mucous membrane and fine hairs. It acts as a filter and also moistens the entering air.
Nasal septum	Partition separating the right and left nasal cavities.
Paranasal sinuses	Air cavities within the cranial bones that open into the nasal cavities.
Pharynx (also called the throat)	Serves as a food and air passageway. Air enters from the nasal cavities and passes through the pharynx to the larynx. Food enters the pharynx from the mouth and passes into the esophagus.
Adenoids	Lymphoid tissue located behind the nasal cavity.
Tonsils	Lymphoid tissue located behind the mouth.
Larynx (also called the voice box)	Location of the vocal cords. Air enters from the pharynx.
Epiglottis	Flap of cartilage that automatically covers the opening of the larynx during swallowing and keeps food from entering.

137

Word Parts

1. *Read each word part and its definition.*

2. *Complete the exercises.* Each list of words is followed by exercises that help you to recall the definition of the word part and to retrieve the word part when the definition is provided.

3. *Label the anatomical diagram* with the correct combining forms.

4. *Compare your answers* on both the diagram and the exercises with the answer portion of the text.

5. *Use the flash cards to help memorize the word parts.* Group the combining form flashcards separately for each body system. Gather the prefix and suffix flashcards from all of the chapters because you will be using them throughout the text; keeping them together provides the opportunity for frequent review.

6. *Read the information boxes* to enrich your understanding about the derivation of the word parts.

WORD PARTS

Combining Forms of the Respiratory System

Study the word parts and their definitions listed below. Completing the exercises that follow will help you to learn the terms.

Combining Form	Definition
adenoid/o	adenoids
alveol/o	alveolus
bronch/i, bronch/o	bronchus
[Note: Both *i* and *o* combining vowels are used with the word root *branch*.]	
diaphragmat/o	diaphragm
epiglott/o	epiglottis
laryng/o	larynx
lob/o	lobe
nas/o	
rhin/o	nose
pharyng/o	pharynx
pleur/o	pleura
pneum/o	
pneumat/o	
pneumon/o	lung, air
pulmon/o	lung
sinus/o	sinus
sept/o	septum (wall off, fence)
thorac/o	thorax (chest)
tonsill/o	tonsil
[NOTE: Tonsil has one *l* and the combining form has two *l*.]	
trache/o	trachea

Learn the anatomical locations and meanings of the combining forms by completing Exercises 3 and 4.

Medical Terms

1. *Become familiar with the presentation of terms.* The medical terms are divided into four categories: *disease and disorder* terms, which are used to diagnose conditions; *surgical* terms, which are used to describe surgical procedures; *procedural* terms, which are used to describe diagnostic procedures and equipment; and *complementary* terms that complete the vocabulary presented in a chapter by describing signs, symptoms, medical specialties, specialists and related words. Understanding that the terms are categorized will assist you in the overall comprehension of medical language and how it is used. For example, you will soon learn that the suffix indicates if a term is surgical, diagnostic, or procedural.

2. *Become familiar with the organization of terms* into those "built from word parts" and those "not built from word parts." All of the medical terms in the text are arranged into one of these two categories that determine the learning

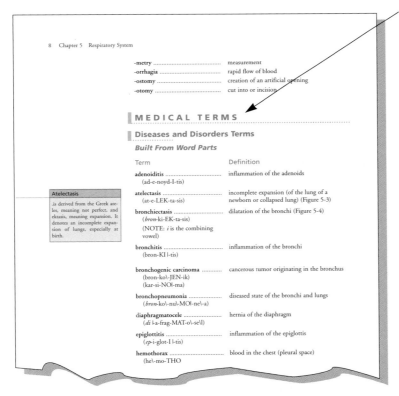

8   Chapter 5   Respiratory System

-metry	measurement
-orrhagia	rapid flow of blood
-ostomy	creation of an artificial opening
-otomy	cut into or incision

MEDICAL TERMS

Diseases and Disorders Terms

Built From Word Parts

Term	Definition
adenoiditis (ad-e-noyd-I-tis)	inflammation of the adenoids
atelectasis (at-e-LEK-ta-sis)	incomplete expansion (of the lung of a newborn or collapsed lung) (Figure 5-3)
bronchiectasis (*bron*-ki-EK-ta-sis) (NOTE: *i* is the combining vowel)	dilatation of the bronchi (Figure 5-4)
bronchitis (bron-KI I-tis)	inflammation of the bronchi
bronchogenic carcinoma (bron-ko\-JEN-ik) (kar-si-NOI-ma)	cancerous tumor originating in the bronchus
bronchopneumonia (*bron*-ko\-nu\-MOI-ne\-a)	diseased state of the bronchi and lungs
diaphragmatocele (*di* l-a-frag-MAT-o\-se\l)	hernia of the diaphragm
epiglottitis (*ep*-i-glot-I l-tis)	inflammation of the epiglottis
hemothorax (he\-mo-THO	blood in the chest (pleural space)

Atelectasis

...is derived from the Greek ateles, meaning not perfect, and ektasis, meaning expansion. It denotes an incomplete expansion of lungs, especially at birth.

strategy you will use. Terms built from word parts are constructed from specific language elements, through application of certain rules. Learning the rules for analyzing and combining word parts will help you to master this set of terms. Terms not built from word parts may contain some of the word parts you know, but you cannot literally translate the term to arrive at its meaning; memorization is used to learn these terms.

3. *Read each of the terms and its definition.* If more information is necessary for comprehension of the term, it is included in parentheses following the definition.

4. *Use the pronunciation guide and the audiotape to practice pronouncing the medical terms.* Because it is impractical to use all of the markings of an unabridged dictionary in a medical terminology book, the pronunciations provided in the text are approximate. In respelling for pronunciation, the words have been distorted minimally to indicate phonetic sound. Diacritical marks are used over vowels to show pronunciation. The macron (⁻) is used to indicate long vowel sounds; unmarked vowels have a short vowel sound. An accent mark is the stress on a certain syllable. The primary accent is indicated in this text by capital letters, and the secondary accent (which is stressed, but not as strongly as the primary accent) is indicated in italics.

5. *Complete all the exercises for each word list.* The exercises may seem repetitive, but they are provided to allow the practice needed to master the terms.

6. *Read the information boxes;* they contain information on the origin of terms and the distinguishing features of the words.

7. *Use the appendixes* to assist you in building and defining terms built from word parts. Use Appendix A for a fast, alphabetical listing of the meanings of word parts; use Appendix B to find the word part to match a definition.

8. *Label the diagrams* placed throughout this section by filling in the blanks with the correct word part. Check your answers against the answers provided at the end of the text.

9. *Review the abbreviation list.*

Chapter Review

1. *Complete the review exercises.* Use this as an opportunity to evaluate your comprehension of the content of the chapter. Some questions will require you to recall terms from previous chapters.

2. *Compare your answers* with the answers provided in the text.

3. *Review the list of terms* presented in the chapter. Highlight terms that need more practice.

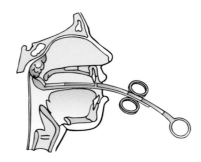

Fill in the blanks: ADENOID / EXCISION **performed with** ADENOID / SURGICAL INSRUMENT

4. *Use the pronunciation tape* with the review list to evaluate and practice your pronunciation.

Appendixes

Use the appendixes to locate alphabetically listed word parts, definitions, and abbreviations quickly. The appendixes also will introduce you to less commonly used word parts and to the plural endings of medical terms. Four additional appendixes have been provided to help you develop a familiarity with terms specific to the areas of psychiatry, pharmacology, alternative medicine, and health care delivery/managed care.

After you've worked through a chapter, completing all the exercises and correcting errors, you will have met the chapter objectives and will feel confident and eager to move on to the next chapter. I wish you the best as you begin your discovery of the language of medicine.

EXPLORING MEDICAL LANGUAGE

A Student-Directed Approach

Introduction to Word Parts

Objectives .... **Upon completion of this chapter you will be able to:**

1. Identify and define the four word parts.
2. Identify and define a combining form.
3. Analyze and define medical terms.
4. Build medical terms for given definitions.

Medicine has a language of its own. Medical language, like the language of a people, also has a historical development. Current medical vocabulary includes terms built from Greek and Latin word parts, some of which were used by Hippocrates and Aristotle 2000 years ago; *eponyms* (words based on the personal names of people); and terms from modern language (Figure 1-1). With the advancement of medical and scientific knowledge, medical language changes. Some words are discarded, the meanings of others are altered, and new words are added.

Still, the majority of medical terms in current use are composed of Greek and Latin word parts. There are two ways to learn these terms: one is to memorize them, the

Greek and Latin Terms
such as femur (L)
and hemorrhage (G)

Eponyms
such as
Parkinson's disease

Modern language
such as laser (acronym for
light amplification by
stimulated emission of radiation)

Fig. 1-1
Origins of medical language.

other is to learn word parts and how they fit together to form medical terms. Because memorization can be monotonous and because learning word parts and how they fit together provides the key to learning scores of medical terms, the word part method is used to learn terms composed of Greek and Latin word parts. The memorization method is used to learn other terms not built from word parts, such as *Alzheimer's disease* or *coronary artery bypass*.

FOUR WORD PARTS

Most medical terms built from word parts consist of some or all of the following components:

1. Word roots
2. Suffixes
3. Prefixes
4. Combining vowels

1. Word Root

The word root is the word part that is the core of the word. The word root contains the fundamental meaning of the word.

Examples:

In the word	play/er, *play* is the word root.
In the medical term	arthr/itis, *arthr* (which means *joint*) is the word root.
In the medical term	hepat/itis, *hepat* (which means *liver*) is the word root.

Because the word root contains the fundamental meaning of the word, each medical term contains one or more word roots.

Complete the Following: A word root is _____

_____

Answer: the word part that is the core of the word.

2. Suffix

The suffix is a word part attached to the end of the word root to modify its meaning.

Examples:

In the word	play/er, *-er* is the suffix.
In the medical term	hepat/ic, *-ic* (which means *pertaining to*) is the suffix.

As mentioned on p.3, *hepat* is the word root for liver; therefore *hepatic* means *pertaining to the liver.*

In the medical term . . . .   hepat/itis,
-itis (which means *inflammation*) is the suffix.

The term *hepatitis* means *inflammation of the liver.*

> The suffix is used to modify the meaning of a word. Most medical terms have a suffix.

Complete the Following: The suffix is _____

_____

Answer: a word part attached to the end of the word root to modify its meaning.

▍ 3. Prefix

The prefix is a word part attached to the beginning of a word root to modify its meaning.

Examples:
In the word . . . .   re/play,
re- is the prefix.
In the medical term . . . .   sub/hepat/ic,
sub- (which means *under*) is the prefix.

Hepat is the word root for *liver,* and *-ic* is the suffix for *pertaining to.* The medical term *subhepatic* means *pertaining to under the liver.*

In the medical term . . . .   intra/ven/ous,
intra- (which means *within*) is the prefix, *ven-* (which means *vein*) is the word root, and *-ous* (which means *pertaining to*) is the suffix.

The word *intravenous* means *pertaining to within the vein.*

> A prefix may be used to modify the meaning of a word. Many medical terms do not have a prefix.

Complete the Following: The prefix is _____

_____

Answer: a word part attached to the beginning of a word root to modify its meaning.

▍ 4. Combining Vowel

The combining vowel is a word part, usually an o, and is used:

- **Between two word roots**
- **Between a word root and a suffix to ease pronunciation**

The combining vowel is not used between a prefix and a word root.

Examples:

In the word	therm/o/meter,
	o is the combining vowel used between two word roots.
In the medical term	arthr/o/pathy,
	o is the combining vowel used between the word root *arthr* and the suffix *-pathy* (which means *disease*).

GUIDELINES FOR USING COMBINING VOWELS

Guideline One:
When connecting a word root and a suffix, a combining vowel is usually not used if the suffix begins with a vowel.

Example:

In the medical term	hepat/ic,
	the suffix *-ic* begins with the vowel *i;* therefore a combining vowel is not used.

Guideline Two:
When connecting two word roots, a combining vowel is usually used even if vowels are present at the junction.

Example:

In the medical term	oste/o/arthr/itis,
	o is the combining vowel used, even though the word root *oste* (which means *bone*) ends with the vowel *e,* and the word root *arthr* begins with the vowel *a.*

> The combining vowel is used to ease pronunciation; therefore, *not all medical terms have combining vowels.* Medical terms introduced throughout the text that have combining vowels other than *o* are highlighted at their introduction.

Complete the Following: A combining vowel is _____

_____

Answer: a word part, usually an o, used between two word roots or between a word root and a suffix to ease pronunciation.

When connecting a word root and a suffix, a combining vowel is usually

_____ if the suffix begins with a _____ .

Answer: not used, vowel

When connecting _____ a combining vowel is usually used even if vowels are present at the junction.

Answer: two word roots

COMBINING FORM

A combining form is a word root with the combining vowel attached, separated by a vertical slash.

Examples: arthr/o
oste/o
ven/o

The combining form is not a word part per se; rather it is the association of the word root and the combining vowel. *For learning purposes word roots are presented together with their combining vowels as combining forms throughout the text.*

Complete the Following: A combining form is _____

_____

Answer: a word root with the combining vowel attached, separated by a vertical slash.

Learn the word parts and combining forms by completing exercises 1 and 2.

Exercise 1

Match the phrases in the first column with the correct terms in the second column. Check your answers with the correct answers at the end of the book.

_b_ 1. attached at the beginning
of a word root

_a_ 2. usually an o

_d_ 3. all medical terms contain
one or more

_e_ 4. attached at the end of a
word root

_c_ 5. word root with combining vowel attached

a. combining vowel

b. prefix

c. combining form

d. word root

e. suffix

Exercise 2

Answer *T* for true and *F* for false.

_F_ 1. There is always a prefix at the beginning of medical terms.

_F_ 2. A combining vowel is always used when connecting a word root and a
suffix.

_T_ 3. A prefix modifies the meaning of the word.

_T_ 4. A combining vowel is used to ease pronunciation.

_F_ 5. *I* is the most commonly used combining vowel.

_T_ 6. The word root is the core of a medical term.

_F_ 7. A combining vowel is used between a prefix and a word root.

_F_ 8. A combining form is a word part.

ANALYZING AND DEFINING MEDICAL TERMS

Analyzing

To analyze a medical term divide it into word parts, label each word part, and label the combining forms. Follow the procedure below:

1. **Divide the term** into word parts using vertical slashes.

   EXAMPLE: oste/o/arthr/o/pathy

2. **Label each word part** by using the following abbreviations.

WR	WORD ROOT
P	PREFIX
S	SUFFIX
CV	COMBINING VOWEL

            WR   CV   WR   CV   S
   EXAMPLE: oste / o / arthr / o / pathy

3. **Label the combining forms.**

            WR   CV   WR   CV   S
   EXAMPLE: oste / o / arthr / o / pathy
               CF   CF

Analyze the following medical term: osteopathy

         WR CV S
Answer: oste / o / pathy
           CF

Defining

To define medical terms apply the meaning of each word part in the term.

> A helpful rule: *Begin by defining the suffix, then move to the beginning of the term to complete the definition.* (Does not apply to all medical terms)

Apply this rule to find the definition of oste/o/arthr/o/pathy. Begin by defining the suffix -*pathy*, then move to the beginning of the term. Use the box to find the meaning of the word parts. oste/o/arthr/o/pathy means _____

_____

_____

Answer: disease of the bone and joint.

Practice analyzing and defining medical terms by completing exercise 3.

Combining Forms	Definition
arthr/o	joint
hepat/o	liver
ven/o	vein
oste/o	bone

Prefixes	
intra-	within
sub-	under

Suffixes	
-itis	inflammation
-ic	pertaining to
-ous	pertaining to
-pathy	disease

Combining Vowel	
-o-	

Exercise 3

Using the box on p. 7 to identify the word parts and their meanings, analyze and define the following terms.

                WR CV WR CV S

EXAMPLE: oste/o/arthr/o/pathy   *disease of bone and joint*
              CF   CF

1.   arthritis   *inflammation of the joint*
2.   hepatitis   *inflammation of the liver*
3.   subhepatic   *pertaining to under the liver*
4.   intravenous   *pertaining to within the vein*
5.   arthropathy   *disease of the joint*
6.   osteitis   *inflammation of the bone*

BUILDING MEDICAL TERMS

Building medical terms means using word parts that match a given definition.

Using the box on p. 7 as a reference, complete the following steps to build the medical term for

disease of a joint

Step 1: Find the word part for *disease*. Write the word part in the correct space below.
Step 2: Find the word part for *joint*. Write the word part in the correct space below.
Step 3: The suffix does not begin with a vowel, so a combining vowel is needed. Insert the combining vowel *o* in the correct space below.

                   arthr / o / pathy
                        WR   CV   S

Answer: arthropathy

Complete the Following: Building a medical term means _____

_____

Answer: using word parts that match a given definition.

Practice building medical terms by completing exercise 4 and Exercise Figure A.

> Keep in mind that the beginning of the definition usually indicates the suffix.

Exercise 4

Using the box on p. 7 as a reference, build medical terms for the following definitions.

EXAMPLE: disease of the joint   arthr / o / pathy
                               WR   CV   S

1.   inflammation of the joint   arthr / itis
                                    WR   S

2. pertaining to the liver

$\dfrac{\text{h epat / ic}}{\text{WR} \quad \text{S}}$

3. pertaining to under the liver

$\dfrac{\text{sub / hepat / ic}}{\text{P} \quad \text{WR} \quad \text{S}}$

4. pertaining to within the vein

$\dfrac{\text{intra / ven / ous}}{\text{P} \quad \text{WR} \quad \text{S}}$

5. inflammation of the bone

$\dfrac{\text{oste / itis}}{\text{WR} \quad \text{S}}$

6. inflammation of the liver

$\dfrac{\text{hepat / itis}}{\text{WR} \quad \text{S}}$

7. disease of the bone and joint

$\dfrac{\text{oste / o / arthr / o / pathy}}{\text{WR} \quad \text{CV} \quad \text{WR} \quad \text{CV} \quad \text{S}}$

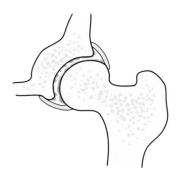

Exercise Fig. A
Fill in the blanks to label the diagram.

$\dfrac{\text{oste / o / arthr /}}{\text{BONE} \quad \text{CV} \quad \text{JOINT}}$

$\dfrac{\text{itis}}{\text{INFLAMMATION of the hip}}$

> In a term that has more than one word root, there is no rule as to which goes first. The order is usually dictated by common practice. You will eventually become accustomed to the accepted order.

CHAPTER REVIEW

To complete this chapter successfully, you do not need to know what the word parts, such as *arthr,* mean. You will learn these in subsequent chapters. **It is important that you have met these objectives:**

1. Can you identify and define the four word parts?
2. Can you identify and define a combining form?
3. Can you use word parts to analyze and define medical terms?
4. Can you use word parts to build medical terms for a given definition?

If you answered yes to these questions, move on to Chapter 2, and begin to build your medical vocabulary so that you will be better prepared than Grimm in Figure 1-2 to understand and use the language of medicine.

by Mike Peters

Fig. 1-2
Reprinted by permission of Tribune Media Services.

2 Body Structure, Color, and Oncology

Objectives .... **Upon completion of this chapter you will be able to:**

1. Identify anatomical structures of the human body.
2. Define and spell the word parts presented in this chapter.
3. Build and analyze medical terms using word parts.
4. Define, pronounce, and spell the disease and disorder terms and the complementary terms related to body structure, color, and oncology.

▌ A N A T O M Y

▌ Organization of the Body

The structure of the human body falls into the following four categories: cells, tissues, organs, and systems. Each structure is a highly organized unit of smaller structures.

cell	basic unit of all living things (Figure 2-1). The human body is composed of trillions of cells, which vary in size and shape according to function.
cell membrane	forms the boundary of the cell
cytoplasm	makes up the body of the cell
nucleus	small, round structure in the center of the cell that contains chromosomes
chromosomes	located in the nucleus of the cell. There are 46 chromosomes in all human cells, with the exception of the mature sex cell, which has 23.
genes	regions within the chromosome. Each chromosome has several thousand genes that determine hereditary characteristics.
DNA (deoxyribonucleic acid) ..	each gene is composed of DNA, a chemical that regulates the activities of the cell
tissue	group of similar cells that performs a specific task (Exercise Figure A)

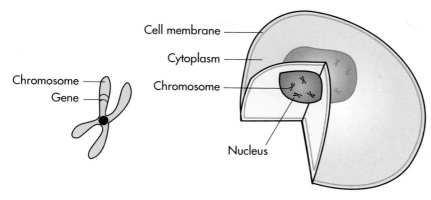

Fig. 2-1
Body cell.

muscle tissue . . . . produces movement

nervous tissue . . . . conducts impulses to and from the brain

connective tissue . . . . connects, supports, penetrates, and encases various body structures. Adipose (fat) and osseous (bone) tissues are types of connective tissue.

epithelial tissue . . . . found in the skin and lining of the blood vessels; the respiratory, intestinal, and urinary tracts; and other body systems.

organ . . . . two or more kinds of tissues that together perform special body functions. For example, the skin is an organ composed of epithelial, connective, and nerve tissue.

system . . . . group of organs that work together to perform complex body functions. For example, the nervous system is made up of the brain, spinal cord, and nerves; its function is to coordinate and control other body parts.

Body Cavities

The body is not a solid structure, as it appears on the outside, but has five cavities (Figure 2-2), each containing an orderly arrangement of the internal organs.

cranial cavity . . . . space inside the skull (cranium), containing the brain

spinal cavity . . . . space inside the spinal column, containing the spinal cord

thoracic, *or* **chest cavity** . . . . space containing the heart, aorta, lungs, esophagus, trachea, and bronchi

abdominal cavity . . . . space containing the stomach, intestines, kidneys, liver, gallbladder, pancreas, spleen, and ureters

pelvic cavity . . . . space containing the urinary bladder, certain reproductive organs, part of the large intestine, and the rectum

Learn the anatomical terms by completing exercises 1 and 2.

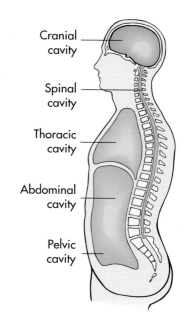

Fig. 2-2
Body cavities.

Exercise 1

Match the terms in the first column with the correct definitions in the second column.

h.	1. chromosomes	a.	type of connective tissue
e.	2. nucleus	b.	regions within the chromosome
d.	3. cytoplasm	c.	tissue found in the skin
k.	4. cell	d.	makes up the body of the cell
g.	5. muscle	e.	contains chromosomes
f.	6. nerve	f.	conducts impulses
c.	7. epithelial	g.	produces movement
a.	8. bone	h.	contains genes
b.	9. genes	i.	chest cavity
j.	10. DNA	j.	a chemical that regulates the activities of the cell
		k.	basic unit of all living things

Exercise 2

Match the terms in the first column with the correct definitions in the second column.

h.	1. spinal cavity	a.	group of organs functioning together
b.	2. thoracic cavity	b.	chest cavity
c.	3. organ	c.	composed of two or more tissues
e.	4. cranial cavity	d.	found in the skin
g.	5. pelvic cavity	e.	space inside the skull
a.	6. system	f.	contains the stomach
f.	7. abdominal cavity	g.	contains the urinary bladder
		h.	contains the spinal cord

WORD PARTS

Begin building your medical vocabulary by learning the word parts listed below. The list may appear long to you; however, the many exercises that follow are designed to help you understand and remember the word parts.

Reminder: the word root is the core of the word. The combining form is the word root with the combining vowel attached, separated by a vertical slash.

Combining Forms for Body Structure

Combining Form	Definition
cyt/o	cell
epitheli/o	epithelium
fibr/o	fibrous tissue
hist/o	tissue
kary/o	nucleus
lip/o	fat
my/o	muscle
neur/o	nerve
organ/o	organ
sarc/o	flesh, connective tissue
system/o	system
viscer/o	internal organs

> **Epithelium**
>
> originally meant **surface over the nipple. Epi** means **upon,** and **thela** means **nipple** (or projecting surfaces of many kinds.)

Learn the anatomical locations and definitions of the combining forms by completing exercises 3 and 4.

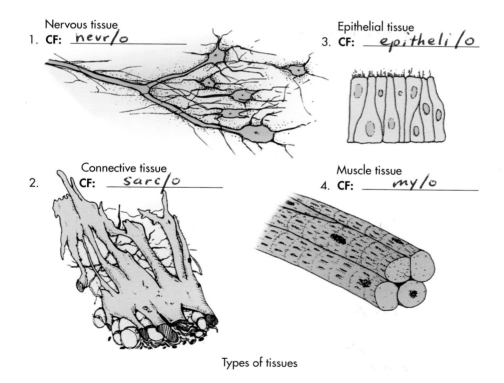

Nervous tissue
1. **CF:** _neur/o_

Epithelial tissue
3. **CF:** _epitheli/o_

Connective tissue
2. **CF:** _sarc/o_

Muscle tissue
4. **CF:** _my/o_

Types of tissues

Exercise Fig. A
Fill in the blanks with combining forms in this diagram of types of tissues.

Exercise 3

Write the definitions of the following combining forms.

1. sarc/o — flesh, connective tissue
2. lip/o — fat
3. kary/o — nucleus
4. viscer/o — internal organs
5. cyt/o — cell
6. hist/o — tissue
7. my/o — muscle
8. neur/o — nerve
9. organ/o — organ
10. system/o — system
11. epitheli/o — epithelium
12. fibr/o — fibrous tissue

Exercise 4

Write the combining form for each of the following.

1. internal organs — viscer/o
2. epithelium — epitheli/o
3. organ — organ/o
4. nucleus — kary/o
5. cell — cyt/o
6. tissue — hist/o
7. nerve — neur/o
8. muscle — my/o
9. fat — lip/o
10. system — system/o

11. connective tissue, flesh ____sarc/o____

12. fibrous tissue ____fibr/o____

Combining Forms Commonly Used with Body Structure Terms

Combining Form	Definition
carcin/o	
cancer/o	cancer (a disease characterized by the unregulated, abnormal growth of new cells)
eti/o	cause (of disease)
gno/o	knowledge
iatr/o	physician, medicine (also means treatment)
lei/o	smooth
onc/o	tumor, mass
path/o	disease
rhabd/o	rod-shaped, striated
somat/o	body

> **Cancer**
>
> Both **carcin** and **cancer** are derived from Latin and Greek words meaning **crab** and originated before the nature of malignant growth was understood. One explanation was that the swollen veins around the diseased area looked like the claws of a crab.

Learn the related combining forms by completing exercises 5 and 6.

Exercise 5

Write the definitions of the following combining forms.

1. onc/o ____tumor, mass____

2. carcin/o ____cancer____

3. eti/o ____cause (of disease)____

4. path/o ____disease____

5. somat/o ____body____

6. cancer/o ____cancer____

7. rhabd/o ____rod-shaped, striated____

8. lei/o ____smooth____

9. gno/o ____knowledge____

10. iatr/o ____physician, medicine (also means treatment)____

Exercise 6

Write the combining form for each of the following.

1. disease _____path/o_____

2. tumor, mass _____onc/o_____

3. cause (of disease) _____eti/o_____

4. cancer   a. ___carcin/o___

   b. ___cancer/o___

5. body _____somat/o_____

6. smooth _____lei/o_____

7. rod-shaped, striated _____rhabd/o_____

8. knowledge _____gnol/o_____

9. physician, medicine _____iatr/o_____

Combining Forms for Terms that Describe Color

Combining Form	Definition
chrom/o	color
cyan/o	blue
erythr/o	red
leuk/o	white
melan/o	black
xanth/o	yellow

Learn the color combining forms by completing exercises 7 and 8.

Exercise 7

Write the definitions of the following combining forms.

1. cyan/o ___blue___

2. erythr/o ___red___

3. leuk/o ___white___

4. xanth/o ___yellow___

5. chrom/o _____ *color* _____

6. melan/o _____ *black* _____

Exercise 8

Write the combining form for each of the following.

1. blue   *cyan/o*
2. red   *erythr/o*
3. white   *leuk/o*
4. black   *melan/o*
5. yellow   *xanth/o*
6. color   *chrom/o*

Prefixes

Reminder: prefixes are placed at the beginning of a word root.

Prefix	Definition
dia-	through, complete
dys-	difficult, labored, painful, abnormal *PLAD*
hyper-	above, excessive
hypo-	below, incomplete, deficient
meta-	after, beyond, change *BAC*
neo-	new
pro-	before

Learn the prefixes by completing exercises 9 and 10.

Exercise 9

Write the definitions of the following prefixes.

1. neo- _____ *new* _____

2. hyper- _____ *above, excessive* _____

3. meta- _____ *after, beyond, change* _____

4. hypo- _below, incomplete, deficient_

5. dys- _difficult, labored, painful, abnormal_

6. dia- _through, complete_

7. pro- _before_

Exercise 10

Write the prefix for each of the following.

1. new   _neo-_

2. above, excessive   _hyper-_

3. below, incomplete, deficient   _hypo-_

4. beyond, after, change   _meta-_

5. abnormal, painful, labored,   _dys-_
   difficult

6. through, complete   _dia-_

7. before   _pro-_

Suffixes

> Reminder: suffixes are placed at the end of a word root.

Suffix	Definition
-al	
-ic	
-ous	pertaining to
-cyte	cell
(NOTE: Cyte ends in an "e" when used as a suffix.)	
-gen	substance or agent that produces or causes
-genesis	origin, cause
-genic	producing, originating, causing
-oid	resembling
-ologist	one who studies and practices (specialist, physician)
-ology	study of
-oma	tumor, swelling
-osis	abnormal condition (means *increase* when used with blood cell word roots)
-pathy	disease _process_

don't think
beginning

> Some suffixes are made up of a word root plus a suffix; they are presented as suffixes for ease of learning. For example, **-pathy** is made up of the word root **path** and the suffix **-y.** When analyzing a word, divide the suffixes as learned. For example, a word such as **somatopathy** should be divided somat/o/pathy and **not** somat/o/path/y.

-plasia . . . .   condition of formation, development, growth
-plasm . . . .   a growth, a substance, a formation
-sarcoma . . . .   *highly* malignant tumor → *not just tumor*
-sis . . . .   state of   ⟶   *form to use with diagnosis, prognosis*
-stasis . . . .   control, stop, standing

Learn the suffixes by completing exercises 11 and 12.

Exercise 11

Match the suffixes in the first column with their correct definitions in the second column.

i   1. -ology   a. producing, originating, causing

l   2. -osis   b. cell

e   3. -pathy   c. specialist

f   4. -plasm   d. new

g   5. -al, -ic, -ous   e. disease *process*

j   6. -stasis   f. a substance, a growth, a formation

h   7. -oid   g. pertaining to

b   8. -cyte   h. resembling

p   9. -genesis   i. study of

c   10. -ologist   j. control, stop, standing

n   11. -oma   k. substance that produces

k   12. -gen   l. abnormal condition

q   13. -sarcoma   m. condition of formation, development, growth

m. 13. -plasia

a. 15. -genic   n. tumor, swelling

0   16. -sis   o. state of

p. origin, cause

q. *highly* malignant tumor

> **Sarcoma**
>
> has been used since the time of ancient Greece to describe any fleshy tumor. Since the introduction of cellular pathology, the term came to be restricted to mean a **malignant connective tissue tumor.**

Ted Small

Exercise 12

Write the definitions of the following suffixes.

1. -ologist _one who studies and practices (specialist, physician)_
2. -pathy _disease process_
3. -ology _study of_
4. -ic _pertaining to_
5. -stasis _control, stop, standing_
6. -cyte _cell_
7. -osis _abnormal condition (means increase when used with blood cell word roots)_
8. -ous _pertaining to_
9. -plasm _a growth, a substance, a formation_
10. -al _pertaining to_
11. -plasia _condition of formation, development, growth_
12. -oid _resembling_
13. -gen _substance or agent that produces or causes_
14. -genic _producing, originating, causing_
15. -oma _tumor, swelling_
16. -genesis _origin, cause_
17. -sarcoma _highly malignant tumor_
18. -sis _state of_

MEDICAL TERMS

Oncology Terms

Built From Word Parts

The medical terms listed below are built from the word parts you have already learned. By using your knowledge of word parts to analyze, define, and build the terms in the following exercises and Exercise Figure B, you will come to know the terms. At first the lists may seem long to you; however, many of the word parts are repeated in the lists of words, and you will soon find that knowing parts of the terms makes learning the words easy. Further explanation of terms beyond literal translation, if needed, is included in parentheses following the definition.

Term	Definition
carcinoma . . . . (*kar*-si-NŌ-ma)	cancerous (<u>malignant</u>) tumor
epithelioma . . . . (ep-i-*thē*-lē-Ō-ma)	tumor composed of epithelium (<u>malignant</u> tumor)
fibroma . . . . (fī-BRŌ-ma)	tumor composed of fibrous tissue
fibrosarcoma . . . . (fī-brō-sar-KŌ-ma)	<u>malignant</u> tumor composed of fibrous tissue
leiomyoma . . . . (lī-ō-mī-Ō-ma)	(<u>benign</u>) tumor of smooth muscle
leiomyosarcoma . . . . (lī-ō-mī-ō-sar-KŌ-ma)	<u>malignant</u> tumor of smooth muscle
lipoma . . . . (li-PŌ-ma)	tumor containing fat (<u>benign</u> tumor)

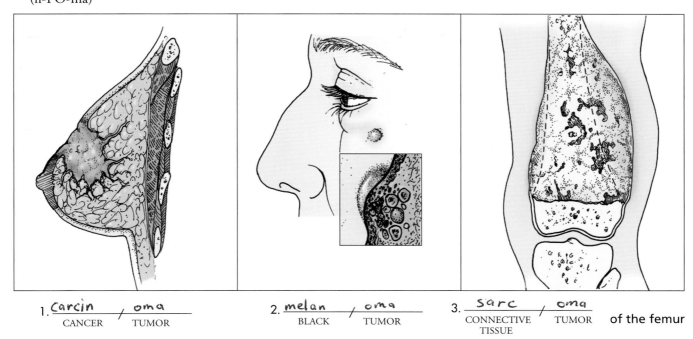

1. <u>Carcin</u> / <u>oma</u>
   CANCER   TUMOR

2. <u>melan</u> / <u>oma</u>
   BLACK   TUMOR

3. <u>Sarc</u> / <u>oma</u>   of the femur
   CONNECTIVE TUMOR
   TISSUE

Exercise Fig. B
Fill in the blanks to label this diagram of types of cancer.

liposarcoma . . . . (lip-ō-sar-KŌ-ma)	<u>malignant tumor</u> composed of fat
melanocarcinoma . . . . (*mel*-a-nō-*kar*-si-NŌ-ma)	cancerous (<u>malignant</u>) black tumor
melanoma . . . . (mel-a-NŌ-ma)	black tumor (primarily of the skin) *malignant*
myoma . . . . (mī-Ō-ma)	tumor formed of muscle *benign*
neoplasm . . . . (NĒ-ō-plazm)	new growth (of abnormal tissue or tumor)
neuroma . . . . (nū-RŌ-ma)	tumor made up of nerve *benign*
rhabdomyoma . . . . (rab-dō-mī-Ō-ma)	(<u>benign</u>) tumor of striated muscle
rhabdomyosarcoma . . . . (rab-dō-mī-ō-sar-KŌ-ma)	<u>malignant tumor</u> of striated muscle
sarcoma . . . . (sar-KŌ-ma) (NOTE: sarc/o also is presented in this chapter as a word root.)	(highly <u>malignant</u>) tumor composed of con- nective <u>tissue</u> (such as bone or cartilage)

Practice saying each of these terms aloud. Refer to "How to Use This Text," in the beginning of this book for explanation of the pronunciation key. To assist you in pronunciation, obtain the audiotape designed for use with this text. Learn the definitions and spellings of the oncology terms built from word parts by completing exercises 13, 14, and 15.

Exercise 13

Analyze and define the following terms. Refer to Chapter 1, pp. 7 and 8, to review analyzing and defining techniques. **This is an important exercise; do not skip any portion of it.**

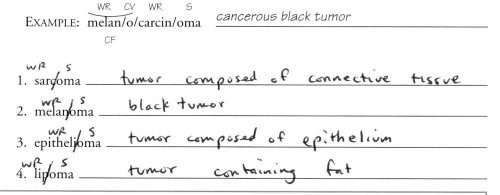

EXAMPLE: melan/o/carcin/oma   *cancerous black tumor*

1. sarcoma _____ tumor composed of connective tissue
2. melanoma _____ black tumor
3. epithelioma _____ tumor composed of epithelium
4. lipoma _____ tumor containing fat

Note: when you are analyzing terms that have a suffix containing a word root, it may appear, as in the word **neoplasm,** that the word is composed of only a prefix and a suffix. Keep in mind that the word does have a word root but that it is embedded in the suffix. S(WR) indicates the WR is embedded in the suffix.

P, S(WR)

5. neoplasm _____ new growth

WR, S

6. myoma _____ tumor formed of muscle

WR, S

7. neuroma _____ tumor made up of nerve

WR, S

8. carcinoma _____ cancerous tumor

WR CV WR CV S

9. leiomyosarcoma _____ malignant tumor of smooth muscle

CF WR CF WR CV S

10. rhabdomyosarcoma _____ malignant tumor of striated muscle

CF CF WR S

11. leiomyoma _____ tumor of smooth muscle

CF CV WR S

12. rhabdomyoma _____ tumor of striated muscle

WR S

13. fibroma _____ tumor composed of fibrous tissue

WR CV S

14. liposarcoma _____ malignant tumor composed of fat

CF CV S

15. fibrosarcoma _____ malignant tumor composed of fibrous tissue

Exercise 14

Build medical terms for the following definitions by using the word parts you have learned. If you need help, refer to p. 8 to review word-building techniques. **Once again, this is an integral part of the learning process; do not skip any part of this exercise.**

EXAMPLE: a tumor containing fat $\dfrac{lip}{WR} / \dfrac{oma}{S}$

1. black tumor $\dfrac{melan}{WR} / \dfrac{oma}{S}$

2. cancerous tumor $\dfrac{carcin}{WR} / \dfrac{oma}{S}$

3. new growth $\dfrac{neo}{P} / \dfrac{plasm}{S(WR)}$

4. tumor composed of epithe-
   lium $\dfrac{epitheli}{WR} / \dfrac{oma}{S}$

5. tumor composed of connec-
   tive tissue $\dfrac{sarc}{WR} / \dfrac{oma}{S}$

6. cancerous black tumor $\dfrac{melan}{WR} / \dfrac{o}{CV} / \dfrac{carcin}{WR} / \dfrac{oma}{S}$

7. tumor made up of nerve
   cells $\dfrac{neur}{WR} / \dfrac{oma}{S}$

8. tumor formed of muscle

_____ my _____ oma _____
WR   S

9. malignant tumor of striated muscle

_____ rhabd _____ o _____ my _____ o _____ sarcoma _____
WR   CV   WR   CV   S

10. tumor of smooth muscle

_____ lei _____ o _____ my _____ oma _____
WR   CV   WR   S

11. tumor of striated muscle

_____ rhabd _____ o _____ my _____ oma _____
WR   CV   WR   S

12. malignant tumor of smooth muscle

_____ lei _____ o _____ my _____ o _____ sarcoma _____
WR   CV   WR   CV   S

13. malignant tumor composed of fat cells

_____ lip _____ o _____ sarcoma _____
WR   CV   S

14. tumor composed of fibrous tissue

_____ fibr _____ oma _____
WR   S

15. malignant tumor composed of fibrous tissue

_____ fibr _____ o _____ sarcoma _____
WR   CV   S

Exercise 15 ....

Spell each of the oncology terms built from word parts. Have someone dictate the terms on pp. 21 and 22 to you, or say the words into a tape recorder; then spell the words from your recording. Think about the word parts before attempting to write the word. Study any words you have spelled incorrectly.

1. _____   9. _____
2. _____   10. _____
3. _____   11. _____
4. _____   12. _____
5. _____   13. _____
6. _____   14. _____
7. _____   15. _____
8. _____   16. _____

Oncology Terms

Not Built From Word Parts

The oncology terms in this list are not built from word parts. The terms are commonly used in the medical world and you will need to know them. In some of the words, you may recognize a word part; however, these terms cannot be literally translated to find the meaning. New knowledge may have changed the meanings of the terms since they were coined. Some terms are eponyms and have no apparent explanation for their names. Memorization is used in the following exercises to learn the terms.

Term	Definition
benign (bē-NĪN)	not malignant, nonrecurrent, favorable for recovery
cancer chemotherapy (kē-mō-THER-a-pē)	treatment of cancer by using drugs
cancer in situ (in SĪ-too)	cancer in the early stage before invading surrounding tissue
cancer radiotherapy (CaXRT) (rā-dē-ō-THER-a-pē)	treatment of cancer using radioactive substance (x-ray or radiation)
encapsulated (en-KAP-sū-lā-ted)	enclosed in a capsule, as with benign tumors
idiopathic (id-ē-ō-PATH-ik)	pertaining to disease of unknown origin
inflammation (in-fla-MĀ-shun)	response to injury or destruction of tissue. Signs are redness, swelling, and pain *heat*
in vitro (in VĒ-trō)	within a glass, observable within a test tube
in vivo (in VĒ-vō)	within the living body
malignant (ma-LIG-nant)	tending to become progressively worse and to cause death, as in cancer
remission (rē-MISH-un)	improvement or absence of signs of disease

Practice saying each of these terms aloud. To assist you in pronunciation, obtain the audiotape designed for use with this text. Learn the definitions and spellings of the oncology terms not built from word parts by completing exercises 16 and 17.

Benign

is derived from the Latin word root **bene**, meaning well or good, as used in **benefit** or **benefactor**.

Situ

is from the Latin term **situs**, which means **position** or **place**. Think of **in situ** as meaning "in place" or "not wandering around."

Idiopathic

is derived from the Greek word **idios** meaning "one's own" and "path" or disease. The term probably originated from the idea that disease of unknown origin comes from within oneself and is not acquired from without.

Inflammatory and Inflammation

are spelled with two "m's." Inflame and inflamed have one "m."

Malignant

is derived from the Latin word root **mal** meaning bad, as used in **malicious**.

Exercise 16 ....

Write the definitions for the following terms.

1. benign *not malignant, nonrecurrent, favorable for recovery*

2. malignant *tending to become progressively worse, and to cause death, as in cancer*

3. remission *improvement or absence of signs of disease*

4. idiopathic *pertaining to disease of unknown origin*

5. inflammation *response to injury or destruction of tissue Signs are redness, swelling, pain, heat*

6. cancer chemotherapy *treatment of cancer using drugs*

7. cancer radiotherapy *treatment of cancer using radioactive substance*

8. encapsulated *enclosed in a capsule, as with benign tumors*

9. in vitro *within a glass, observable within a test tube*

10. in vivo *within the living body*

11. cancer in situ *cancer in the early stage before invading surrounding tissue*

Exercise 17 ....

Spell each of the oncology terms not built from word parts. Have someone dictate the terms on p. 25 to you, or say the words into a tape recorder; then spell the words from your recording. Study any words you have spelled incorrectly.

1. _____   7. _____

2. _____   8. _____

3. _____   9. _____

4. _____   10. _____

5. _____   11. _____

6. _____

Complementary Terms

Built From Word Parts

The following terms are built from the word parts you have already learned. By analyzing, defining, and building the terms in the exercises that follow, you will come to know the terms.

Term	Definition
cancerous .... (KAN-ser-us)	pertaining to cancer
carcinogen .... (kar-SIN-ō-gen)	substance that causes cancer
carcinogenic .... (*kar*-sin-ō-JEN-ik)	pertaining to producing cancer
cyanosis .... (*sī*-a-NŌ-sis)	abnormal condition of bluish discoloration of the skin caused by inadequate supply of oxygen in the blood
cytogenic .... (*sī*-tō-JEN-ik)	pertaining to producing cells
cytoid .... (SĪ-toid)	resembling a cell
cytology .... (sī-TOL-ō-jē)	study of cells
cytoplasm .... (SĪ-tō-plazm)	cell substance
diagnosis (Dx) .... (*dī*-ag-NŌ-sis)	state of complete knowledge (identifying a disease)
dysplasia .... (dis-PLĀ-zhē-a)	abnormal development
epithelial .... (*ep*-i-THĒ-lē-al)	pertaining to epithelium
erythrocyte .... (e-RITH-rō-sīt)	red (blood) cell (RBC)

> An essential part of a word, such as the word root for **blood,** may be omitted from a medical term, as in **erythrocyte,** by common consent. The practice is called **ellipsis.**

erythrocytosis .... (e-*rith*-rō-sī-TŌ-sis)	increase in the number of red (blood) cells
etiology .... (*ē*-tē-OL-ō-jē)	study of causes (of diseases)
histology .... (his-TOL-ō-jē)	study of tissue
hyperplasia .... (*hī*-per-PLĀ-zhē-a)	excessive development (of cells) (Exercise Figure C)

Erythro

Aristotle noted "two colors of blood" and applied the term **erythro** to the dark red blood.

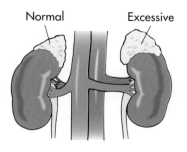

Normal   Excessive

Exercise Fig. C

Fill in the blanks to label the diagram.

<u>hyper   /   plasia</u>
EXCESSIVE / DEVELOPMENT

Red blood cells

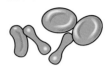

White blood cells

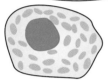

Exercise Fig. D
Fill in the blanks to label
this diagram of blood cells.

erythr / o / cytes
RED / CV / CELL(S)

leuk / o / cytes
WHITE / CV / CELL(S)

**Oncology
and Oncological**

are used to name the medical
specialty and hospital nursing
units devoted to the treatment
and care of cancer patients.

Prognosis

was used by Hippocrates to
mean the same as we use it
now, **to foretell the course of
a disease.**

---

hypoplasia . . . .   incomplete development (of an organ or tis-
(hī-pō-PLĀ-zhē-a)   sues)

iatrogenic . . . .   produced by a physician (adverse condition)
(ī-*at*-rō-JEN-ik)

iatrology . . . .   study of medicine
(ī-a-TROL-ō-jē)

karyocyte . . . .   cell with a nucleus
(KĀR-ē-ō-sīt)

karyoplasm . . . .   substance of a nucleus
(KĀR-ē-ō-*plazm*)

leukocyte . . . .   white (blood) cell (WBC) (Exercise Figure D)
(LŪ-kō-sīt)

leukocytosis . . . .   increase in the number of white (blood) cells
(*lū*-kō-sī-TŌ-sis)

lipoid . . . .   resembling fat
(LIP-oid)

metastasis (*pl.* metastases)
(mets) . . . .   beyond control (transfer of disease from one organ
(me-TAS-ta-sis)   to another as in the transfer of malignant tumors)

myopathy . . . .   disease of the muscle
(mī-OP-a-thē)

neopathy . . . .   new disease
(nē-OP-a-thē)

neuroid . . . .   resembling a nerve
(NŪ-rōyd)

oncogenic . . . .   causing tumors
(*ong*-kō-JEN-ik)

oncologist . . . .   physician who specializes in oncology
(ong-KOL-ō-jist)

oncology . . . .   study of tumors
(ong-KOL-ō-jē)

pathogenic . . . .   producing disease
(path-ō-JEN-ik)

pathologist . . . .   specialist in pathology
(pa-THOL-ō-jist)

pathology . . . .   study of body changes caused by disease
(pa-THOL-ō-jē)

prognosis (Px) . . . .   state of before knowledge (forecast of probable
(prog-NŌ-sis)   outcome of disease)

somatic . . . .   pertaining to the body
(sō-MAT-ik)

somatogenic . . . .   originating in the body (as opposed to mental)
(sō-ma-tō-JEN-ik)

somatopathy . . . .   disease of the body
(sō-ma-TOP-a-thē)

somatoplasm . . . .   body substance
(sō-MAT-ō-plazm)

systemic . . . .   pertaining to a body system (or the body as a
   (sis-TEM-ik)   whole)

visceral . . . .   pertaining to the internal organs
   (VIS-er-al)

xanthochromic . . . .   pertaining to yellow color
   (*zan*-thō-KRŌ-mik)

xanthosis . . . .   abnormal condition of yellow (discoloration)   *jaundice*
   (zan-THŌ-sis)

Practice saying each of these aloud. Refer to "How to Use This Text, in the beginning
of this book, for an explanation of the pronunciation key. To assist you in pronunciation, obtain the audiotape designed for use with this text. Learn the definitions and
spellings of the complementary terms by completing exercises 18, 19, and 20.

Exercise 18 . . . .   *Ted Small*

Analyze and define the following complementary terms.

        WR CV S
   EXAMPLE: path/o/genic   *producing disease*
          CF

1. cytology *study of cells*
2. histology *study of tissue*
3. pathology *study of (body changes caused by) disease*
4. pathologist *specialist in pathology*
5. visceral *pertaining to internal organs*
6. metastasis *beyond control (transfer of disease)*
7. oncogenic *causing tumors*
8. oncology *study of tumors*
9. karyocyte *cell with a nucleus*
10. neopathy *new disease process*
11. karyoplasm *substance of a nucleus*
12. cytogenic *producing cells*
13. systemic *pertaining to a body system*
14. cancerous *pertaining to cancer*
15. cytoplasm *cell substance*

Ted Small

16. carcinogenic _____ producing cancer

17. somatic _____ pertaining to the body

18. somatogenic _____ originating in the body

19. somatoplasm _____ body substance

20. somatopathy _____ disease process of the body

21. neuroid _____ resembling a nerve

22. myopathy _____ disease process of the muscle

23. erythrocyte _____ red (blood) cell

24. leukocyte _____ white (blood) cell

25. cyanosis _____ abnormal condition of blue

26. epithelial _____ pertaining to epithelium

27. lipoid _____ resembling fat

28. etiology _____ study of causes (of disease)

29. xanthosis _____ abnormal condition of yellow

30. xanthochromic _____ pertaining to yellow color

31. hyperplasia _____ excessive development (of cells)

32. erythrocytosis _____ increase in the number of (red) cells

33. leukocytosis _____ increase in the number of white (blood) cells

34. carcinogen _____ substance that causes cancer

35. hypoplasia _____ incomplete development (of an organ or a tissue)

36. cytoid _____ resembling a cell

37. oncologist _____ physician who specializes in oncology

38. dysplasia _____ abnormal development

39. pathogenic _____ producing disease

40. prognosis _____ state of before knowledge

41. diagnosis _____ state of complete knowledge

42. iatrogenic _____ produced by a physician (adverse condition)

43. iatrology _____ study of medicine

Exercise 19

Build medical terms for the following definitions by using the word parts you have learned.

EXAMPLE: producing cells $\dfrac{cyt}{WR}$ / $\dfrac{o}{CV}$ / $\dfrac{genic}{S}$

1. cell substance

$\dfrac{cyt}{WR}$ / $\dfrac{o}{CV}$ / $\dfrac{plasm}{S}$

2. pertaining to yellow color

$\dfrac{xanth}{WR}$ / $\dfrac{o}{CV}$ / $\dfrac{chrom}{WR}$ / $\dfrac{ic}{S}$

3. beyond control

$\dfrac{meta}{P}$ / $\dfrac{stasis}{S(WR)}$

4. new disease

$\dfrac{neo}{P}$ / $\dfrac{pathy}{S(WR)}$

5. study of the cause (of disease)

$\dfrac{eti}{WR}$ / $\dfrac{ology}{S}$

6. substance of a nucleus

$\dfrac{kary}{WR}$ / $\dfrac{o}{CV}$ / $\dfrac{plasm}{S}$

7. study of tumors

$\dfrac{onc}{WR}$ / $\dfrac{ology}{S}$

8. study of (body changes caused by) disease

$\dfrac{path}{WR}$ / $\dfrac{ology}{S}$

9. pertaining to the body

$\dfrac{somat}{WR}$ / $\dfrac{ic}{S}$

10. specialist in pathology

$\dfrac{path}{WR}$ / $\dfrac{ologist}{S}$

11. disease of the muscle

$\dfrac{my}{WR}$ / $\dfrac{o}{CV}$ / $\dfrac{pathy}{S}$

12. body substance

$\dfrac{somat}{WR}$ / $\dfrac{o}{CV}$ / $\dfrac{plasm}{S}$

13. abnormal condition of yellow

$\dfrac{xanth}{WR}$ / $\dfrac{osis}{S}$

14. pertaining to the internal organs

$\dfrac{viscer}{WR}$ / $\dfrac{al}{S}$

15. causing tumors

$\dfrac{onc}{WR}$ / $\dfrac{o}{CV}$ / $\dfrac{genic}{S}$

16. originating in the body

$\dfrac{somat}{WR}$ / $\dfrac{o}{CV}$ / $\dfrac{genic}{S}$

17. disease of the body

$\dfrac{somat}{WR}$ / $\dfrac{o}{CV}$ / $\dfrac{pathy}{S}$

18. red (blood) cell

erythr / o / cyte
WR / CV / S

19. resembling a nerve

neur / oid
WR / S

20. pertaining to a body system

system / ic
WR / S

21. white (blood) cell

leuk / o / cyte
WR / CV / S

22. cell with a nucleus

kary / o / cyte
WR / CV / S

23. resembling fat

lip / oid
WR / S

24. pertaining to cancer

cancer / ous
WR / S

25. study of cells

cyt / ology
WR / S

26. excessive development (of cells)

hyper / plasia
P / S(WR)

27. resembling a cell

cyt / oid
WR / S

28. pertaining to epithelium

epitheli / al
WR / S

29. abnormal condition of blue

cyan / osis
WR / S

30. producing cancer

carcin / o / genic
WR / CV / S

31. producing disease

path / o / genic
WR / CV / S

32. study of tissue

hist / ology
WR / S

33. increase in the number of red (blood) cells

erythr / o / cyt / osis
WR / CV / WR / S

34. incomplete development (of an organ or tissue)

hypo / plasia
P / S(WR)

35. increase in the number of white (blood) cells

leuk / o / cyt / osis
WR / CV / WR / S

36. substance that causes cancer

carcin / o / gen
WR / CV / S

37. physician who specializes in oncology

onc / ologist
WR / S

38. abnormal development

dys / plasia
P / S(WR)

39. study of medicine

iatr / ology
WR / S

40. state of complete knowledge

dia / gno / sis
P / WR / S

41. produced by a physician

iatr / o / genic
WR / CV / S

42. state of before knowledge

pro / gno / sis
P / WR / S

<h2>Exercise 20</h2>

Spell each of the complementary terms. Have someone dictate the terms on pp. 27-29 to you, or say the words into a tape recorder; then spell the words from your recording. Remember to think about the word parts before attempting to write the word. Study any words you have spelled incorrectly.

1. _____   16. _____
2. _____   17. _____
3. _____   18. _____
4. _____   19. _____
5. _____   20. _____
6. _____   21. _____
7. _____   22. _____
8. _____   23. _____
9. _____   24. _____
10. _____   25. _____
11. _____   26. _____
12. _____   27. _____
13. _____   28. _____
14. _____   29. _____
15. _____   30. _____

31. _____   38. _____

32. _____   39. _____

33. _____   40. _____

34. _____   41. _____

35. _____   42. _____

36. _____   43. _____

37. _____

Abbreviations

should be CA

Ca . . . . cancer

chemo . . . . chemotherapy

DNA . . . . deoxyribonucleic acid

Dx . . . . diagnosis

CXR- Chest Xray

mets . . . . metastasis

Px . . . . prognosis

RBC . . . . red blood cell

WBC . . . . white blood cell

XRT . . . . radiotherapy, radiation therapy

CHAPTER REVIEW

Exercises

Exercise 21

To test your understanding of the terms introduced in this chapter, circle the words that correctly complete the sentence. The italicized words refer to the correct answer.

1. Mr. Roberts was diagnosed as having a cancerous *tumor of the bone,* or (sarcoma, melanoma, lipoma). The doctor said the tumor was *becoming progressively worse;* that is, it was (benign, malignant, pathogenic).

2. The blood test showed an *increased amount of red blood cells,* or (erythrocytosis, leukocytosis, cyanosis).

3. (Organic, Visceral, Systemic) means *pertaining to internal organs.*

4. *A tumor containing fat,* or (neuroma, carcinoma, lipoma), is *benign,* or (recurrent, nonrecurrent, cancerous).

5. Many substances are thought to be *cancer producing,* or (carcinogenic, carcinogen, cancerous).

6. *Etiology* is the study of (the causes of disease, tissue disease, the causes of tumors).

7. A *tumor* may be called a (neopathy, neoplasm, karyoplasm).

8. The pain *originated in the body,* or was (somatogenic, oncogenic, pathogenic).

9. Any *disease of a muscle* is called (myoma, myopathy, somatopathy).

10. The term for *abnormal development* is (hypoplasia, dysplasia, hyperplasia).

11. The term that means *produced by a physician* is (diagnosis, iatrogenic, prognosis).

12. The incidence of malignant *black tumor* (fibrosarcoma, fibroma, melanoma) is increasing in the white population. One *study of body changes caused by disease* (pathology, pathogenic, liposarcoma) influencing *state of before knowledge* (cancer in situ, in vitro, prognosis) may be tumor thickness.

13. The term that means *within the living organism* is (in vitro, in vivo, encapsulated).

14. A (liposarcoma, fibroma, myoma) is a *malignant tumor.*

The following exercises are for those who like an extra challenge.

Exercise 22

Unscramble the following mixed-up terms. The word on the left indicates the word root in each of the following.

EXAMPLE: skin | c | y | a | n | o | s | i | s |

 s o n a i s y c

1. tumor | o | n | c | o | l | o | g | y |

 g o n o c l o y

2. body | s | o | m | a | t | i | c |

 m a t o s i c

3. cancer | c | a | r | c | i | n | o | m | a |

 a n c c a r i m o

4. black | m | e | l | a | n | o | m | a |

 n a m o l a e m

5. cell | c | y | t | o | i | d |

 o t c i d y

6. medicine | i | a | t | r | o | l | o | g | y |

 i y t a r g o l o

Exercise 23

The following are medical terms that did not appear in this chapter but are composed of word parts studied in this chapter. Find their definitions by translating the word parts literally. Translate the meaning of the suffix first, and then go back to the beginning of the word.

1. **epithelioid** (ep-i-THĒ-lē-oyd) _resembling epithelium_

2. **neural** (NŪR-al) _pertaining to the nerves_

3. **pathogen** (PATH-ō-jen) _agent that produces disease_

4. **myoid** (MĪ-oyd) _resembling muscle_

5. **leukocytic** (lūk-ō-CIT-ik) _pertaining to white (blood) cells_

6. **iatric** (ī-AT-rik) _pertaining to a physician or medicine_

Combining Forms Crossword Puzzle

Across Clues
- 2. tissue
- 4. nerve
- 7. red
- 8. nucleus
- 9. tumor
- 12. epithelium
- 16. disease
- 17. cancer
- 19. body
- 20. muscle
- 21. blue
- 22. black

Down Clues
- 1. organ
- 3. flesh, connective tissue
- 5. system
- 6. cell
- 7. cause (of disease)
- 10. internal organs
- 11. cancer
- 13. fat
- 14. white
- 15. color
- 18. yellow

Review of Terms

Can you build, analyze, define, spell and pronounce the following terms built from word parts?

Diseases and Disorders

carcinoma

epithelioma

fibroma

fibrosarcoma

leiomyoma

leiomyosarcoma

lipoma

liposarcoma

melanocarcinoma

melanoma

myoma

neoplasm

neuroma

rhabdomyoma

rhabdomyosarcoma

sarcoma

Complementary

cancerous

carcinogen

carcinogenic

cyanosis

cytogenic

cytoid

cytology

cytoplasm

diagnosis

dysplasia

epithelial

erythrocyte

erythrocytosis

etiology

histology

hyperplasia

hypoplasia

iatrogenic

iatrology

karyocyte

karyoplasm

leukocyte

leukocytosis

lipoid

metastasis

myopathy

neopathy

neuroid

oncogenic

oncologist

oncology

pathogenic

pathologist

pathology

prognosis

somatic

somatogenic

somatopathy

somatoplasm

systemic

visceral

xanthochromic

xanthosis

Can you define, pronounce, and spell the following terms not built from word parts?

Complementary

benign

cancer chemotherapy

cancer in situ

cancer radiotherapy

encapsulated

idiopathic

inflammation

in vitro

in vivo

malignant

remission

Directional Terms and Anatomical Planes and Regions

Objectives .... **Upon completion of this chapter you will be able to:**

1. Write the definitions of the word parts included in this chapter.
2. Build, analyze, define, pronounce, and spell the terms used to describe directions of the body.
3. Define, pronounce, and spell the terms used to describe the anatomical planes.
4. Define, pronounce, and spell the terms used to describe the anatomical abdominal regions.

In the description of body directions and planes, a position of reference is used. In the *anatomical position,* as it is called, the body is viewed as erect, arms at the side with palms of the hands facing forward and feet placed side by side. Whether the patient is standing or lying down face up, the directional terms are the same.

WORD PARTS FOR DIRECTIONAL TERMS

Study the following word parts and their definitions.

Combining Forms for Directional Terms

Combining Form	Definition
anter/o	front
caud/o	tail, (downward)
cephal/o	head, (upward)
dist/o	away (from the point of reference)
dors/o	back
infer/o	below
later/o	side

medi/o . . . .   middle

poster/o . . . .   back, behind

proxim/o . . . .   near (the point of reference)

super/o . . . .   above

ventr/o . . . .   belly (front)

Learn the directional term combining forms by completing exercises 1 and 2 and Exercise Figure A.

Exercise 1 . . . .

Write the definitions for the following combining forms.

1. ventr/o _____ belly (front) _____

2. cephal/o _____ head (upward) _____

3. later/o _____ side _____

4. medi/o _____ middle _____

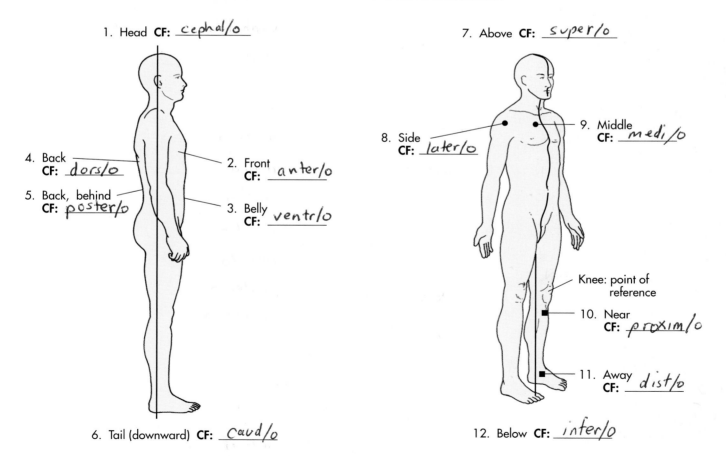

1. Head **CF:** _cephal/o_

4. Back **CF:** _dors/o_

5. Back, behind **CF:** _poster/o_

2. Front **CF:** _anter/o_

3. Belly **CF:** _ventr/o_

6. Tail (downward) **CF:** _caud/o_

7. Above **CF:** _super/o_

8. Side **CF:** _later/o_

9. Middle **CF:** _medi/o_

Knee: point of reference

10. Near **CF:** _proxim/o_

11. Away **CF:** _dist/o_

12. Below **CF:** _infer/o_

Exercise Fig. A
Fill in the blanks with directional combining forms.

5. infer/o _below_

6. proxim/o _near (the point of reference)_

7. super/o _above_

8. dist/o _away (from the point of reference)_

9. dors/o _back_

10. caud/o _tail, (downward)_

11. anter/o _front_

12. poster/o _back, behind_

Exercise 2

Write the combining form for each of the following.

1. side _later/o_

2. above _super/o_

3. head _cephal/o_

4. away (from the point of reference) _dist/o_

5. front _anter/o_

6. middle _medi/o_

7. back _dors/o_

8. belly (front) _ventr/o_

9. tail _caud/o_

10. below _infer/o_

11. back, behind _poster/o_

12. near (the point of reference) _proxim/o_

Prefixes

bi- . . . .   two

uni- . . . .   one

Suffixes

-ad . . . .   toward

-ior . . . .   pertaining to

There are many suffixes that mean "pertaining to." You have already learned three of them in Chapter 2: -al, -ic, and -ous. You will learn more in subsequent chapters. With practice, you will learn which suffix is most commonly used with a particular word root or combining form.

Exercise 3

Match the prefixes and suffixes in the first column with their correct definitions in the second column.

_c_ 1. -ad   a. one

_b_ 2. -ior   b. pertaining to

_d_ 3. bi-   c. toward

_a_ 4. uni-   d. two

Exercise 4

Write the definitions of the following prefixes and suffixes.

1. -ior _pertaining to_

2. -ad _toward_

3. bi- _two_

4. uni- _one_

DIRECTIONAL TERMS

The following list of terms is built from word parts you have already learned. You will learn the terms by completing the analyzing, defining, and word-building exercises.

Term	Definition
anterior (ant) (an-TĒR-ē-or)	pertaining to the front
anteroposterior (AP) (an-ter-ō-pos-TĒR-ē-or)	pertaining to the front and to the back
bilateral (bī-LAT-er-al)	pertaining to two sides
caudal (KAW-dal)	pertaining to the tail
cephalad (SEF-a-lad)	toward the head
cephalic (se-FAL-ik)	pertaining to the head

distal . . . .   pertaining to away (from the point of
   (DIS-tal)   reference)

dorsal . . . .   pertaining to the back
   (DOR-sal)

inferior (inf) . . . .   pertaining to below
   (in-FĔR-ē-or)

lateral (lat) . . . .   pertaining to a side
   (LAT-e-ral)

mediad . . . .   toward the middle
   (MĒ-dē-ad)

medial (med) . . . .   pertaining to the middle
   (MĒ-dē-al)

mediolateral . . . .   pertaining to the middle and to the side
   (mē-dē-ō-LAT-er-al)

posterior . . . .   pertaining to the back
   (pos-TĒR-ē-ōr)

proximal . . . .   pertaining to the near (from the point of refer-
   (PROX-si-mal)   ence)

posteroanterior (PA) . . . .   pertaining to the back and to the front
   (pos-ter-ō-an-TĒR-ē-or)

superior (sup) . . . .   pertaining to above
   (sū-PĒR-ē-or)

unilateral . . . .   pertaining to one side (only)
   (ū-ni-LAT-er-al)

ventral . . . .   pertaining to the belly (front)
   (VEN-tral)

Practice saying each of these terms aloud. To assist you in pronunciation, obtain the audiotape designed for use with this text. Learn the definitions and spelling of the terms used to describe body directions by completing exercises 5, 6, and 7 and Exercise Figure B.

Exercise 5

Analyze and define the following directional terms.

1. cephalad _toward the head_

2. cephalic _pertaining to the head_

3. caudal _pertaining to the tail_

4. anterior _pertaining to the front_

5. posterior _pertaining to the back_

6. dorsal _pertaining to the back_

7. superior _pertaining to above_

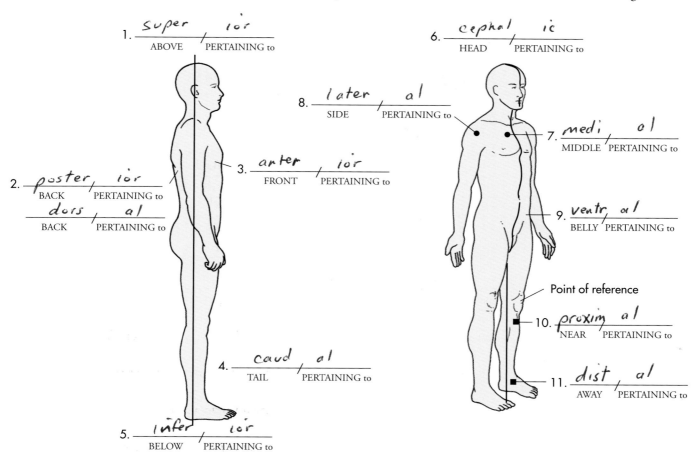

1. super / ior
   ABOVE / PERTAINING to

2. poster / ior
   BACK / PERTAINING to
   dors / al
   BACK / PERTAINING to

3. anter / ior
   FRONT / PERTAINING to

4. caud / al
   TAIL / PERTAINING to

5. infer / ior
   BELOW / PERTAINING to

6. cephal / ic
   HEAD / PERTAINING to

8. later / al
   SIDE / PERTAINING to

7. medi / al
   MIDDLE / PERTAINING to

9. ventr / al
   BELLY / PERTAINING to

Point of reference

10. proxim / al
    NEAR / PERTAINING to

11. dist / al
    AWAY / PERTAINING to

Exercise Fig. B
Fill in the blanks to label the diagram with directional terms.

8. inferior   pertaining to below
9. proximal   pertaining to the near (from the point of reference)
10. distal   pertaing to away (from the point of reference)
11. lateral   pertaining to a side
12. medial   pertaining to the middle
13. mediad   toward the middle
14. ventral   pertaining to the belly (front)
15. posteroanterior   pertaining to the back and to the front
16. unilateral   pertaining to one side (only)
17. mediolateral   pertaing to the middle and to the side
18. anteroposterior   pertaining to the front and to the back
19. bilateral   pertaining to two sides

Exercise 6 ....

Build directional terms for the following definitions by using the word parts you have learned. Also label the diagram in Exercise Figure C.

1. toward the head

   $\underline{\text{cephal}}_{\text{WR}} / \underline{\text{ad}}_{\text{S}}$

2. pertaining to the head

   $\underline{\text{cephal}}_{\text{WR}} / \underline{\text{ic}}_{\text{S}}$

3. pertaining to the tail

   $\underline{\text{caud}}_{\text{WR}} / \underline{\text{al}}_{\text{S}}$

4. pertaining to the front

   $\underline{\text{anter}}_{\text{WR}} / \underline{\text{ior}}_{\text{S}}$

5. pertaining to the back

   $\underline{\text{poster}}_{\text{WR}} / \underline{\text{ior}}_{\text{S}}$ $\underline{\text{dors}}_{\text{WR}} / \underline{\text{al}}_{\text{S}}$

6. pertaining to above

   $\underline{\text{super}}_{\text{WR}} / \underline{\text{ior}}_{\text{S}}$

7. pertaining to below

   $\underline{\text{infer}}_{\text{WR}} / \underline{\text{ior}}_{\text{S}}$

8. pertaining to the near

   $\underline{\text{proxim}}_{\text{WR}} / \underline{\text{al}}_{\text{S}}$

9. pertaining to away

   $\underline{\text{dist}}_{\text{WR}} / \underline{\text{al}}_{\text{S}}$

10. pertaining to a side

    $\underline{\text{later}}_{\text{WR}} / \underline{\text{al}}_{\text{S}}$

11. pertaining to the middle

    $\underline{\text{medi}}_{\text{WR}} / \underline{\text{al}}_{\text{S}}$

12. toward the middle

    $\underline{\text{medi}}_{\text{WR}} / \underline{\text{ad}}_{\text{S}}$

13. pertaining to the belly

    $\underline{\text{ventr}}_{\text{WR}} / \underline{\text{al}}_{\text{S}}$

14. pertaining to the back and to the front

    $\underline{\text{poster}}_{\text{WR}} / \underline{\text{o}}_{\text{CV}} / \underline{\text{anter}}_{\text{WR}} / \underline{\text{ior}}_{\text{S}}$

15. pertaining to the middle and to the side

    $\underline{\text{medi}}_{\text{WR}} / \underline{\text{o}}_{\text{CV}} / \underline{\text{later}}_{\text{WR}} / \underline{\text{al}}_{\text{S}}$

16. pertaining to one side (only)

    $\underline{\text{uni}}_{\text{P}} / \underline{\text{later}}_{\text{WR}} / \underline{\text{al}}_{\text{S}}$

17. pertaining to the front and to the back

    $\underline{\text{anter}}_{\text{WR}} / \underline{\text{o}}_{\text{CV}} / \underline{\text{poster}}_{\text{WR}} / \underline{\text{ior}}_{\text{S}}$

18. pertaining to two sides

    $\underline{\text{bi}}_{\text{P}} / \underline{\text{later}}_{\text{WR}} / \underline{\text{al}}_{\text{S}}$

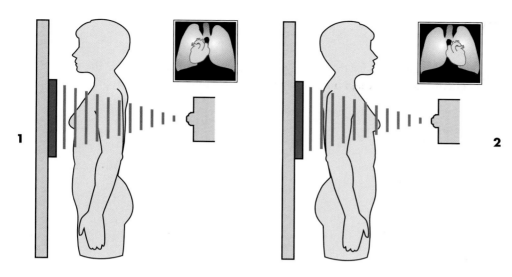

Exercise Fig. C

Fill in the blanks to label the diagram. 1, BACK / CV / FRONT / PERTAINING TO beam

poster / o / auter / ior

from an x-ray machine. 2, FRONT / CV / BACK / PERTAINING TO beam from an x-ray machine.

auter / o / poster / ior

Exercise 7 ···

Have someone dictate the terms on pp. 41 and 42 to you, or say the words into a tape recorder; then spell the words from your recording as often as necessary. Think about the word parts before attempting to write the word. Study any words you have spelled incorrectly.

1. _____   11. _____

2. _____   12. _____

3. _____   13. _____

4. _____   14. _____

5. _____   15. _____

6. _____   16. _____

7. _____   17. _____

8. _____   18. _____

9. _____   19. _____

10. _____

ANATOMICAL PLANES

Planes are imaginary flat fields used as points of reference to identify the position of parts of the body (Figure 3-1). These terms are not built from word parts. Memorization is the learning method used in the exercises that follow.

Term	Definition
frontal or coronal (ko-RŌN-al)	vertical field passing through the body from side to side, dividing the body into anterior and posterior portions
sagittal (SAJ-i-tal)	vertical field running through the body from front to back, dividing the body into right and left sides. *Midsagittal* divides the body into right and left halves.
transverse (trans-VERS)	horizontal field dividing the body into upper and lower portions

Learn the definitions and spellings of the terms used to describe the anatomical planes by completing exercises 8 and 9 and Exercise Figure D.

Exercise 8

Fill in the blanks with the correct terms.

1. The plane that divides the body into superior and inferior portions is the _____*transverse*_____ plane.

2. The plane that divides the body into right and left halves is the _____*Sagittal*_____ plane.

3. The plane that divides the body into anterior and posterior portions is the _____*Frontal*_____ or _____*coronal*_____ plane.

Exercise 9

Spell each of the terms used to describe the anatomical planes. Have someone dictate the terms above to you, or say the words into a tape recorder; then spell the words from your recording as often as necessary. Study any words you have spelled incorrectly.

1. _____   3. _____

2. _____   4. _____

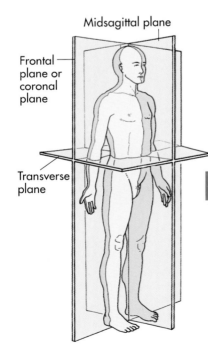

Midsagittal plane

Frontal plane or coronal plane

Transverse plane

Fig. 3-1
Anatomical planes.

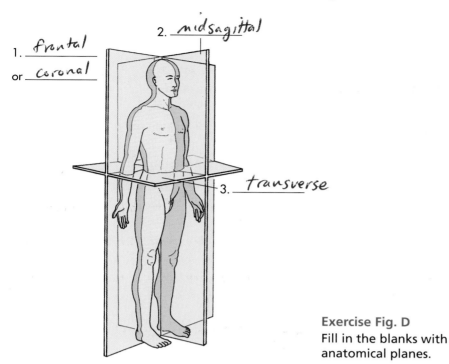

1. _frontal_
or _coronal_

2. _midsagittal_

3. _transverse_

Exercise Fig. D
Fill in the blanks with anatomical planes.

ANATOMICAL ABDOMINAL REGIONS

To assist medical personnel to locate medical problems with greater accuracy and for identification purposes, the abdomen is divided into regions (Figure 3-2). These terms are not built from word parts. Memorization is the learning method used in the exercises that follow.

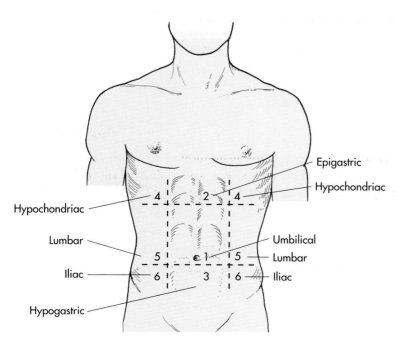

Epigastric

Hypochondriac

Hypochondriac

Lumbar

Umbilical

Lumbar

Iliac

Iliac

Hypogastric

Fig. 3-2
Anatomical abdominal regions.

Term	Definition
umbilical region . . . . (um-BIL-i-kal)	around the navel (umbilicus)
epigastric region . . . . (*ep*-i-GAS-trik)	directly above the umbilical region
hypogastric region . . . . (*hī*-pō-GAS-trik)	directly below the umbilical region
hypochondriac regions . . . . (*hī*-pō-KON-drē-ak)	to the right and left of the epigastric region
lumbar regions . . . . (LUM-bar)	to the right and left of the umbilical region
iliac regions . . . . (IL-ē-ak)	to the right and left of the hypogastric region

Practice saying each of these words aloud. To assist you in pronunciation, obtain the audiotape designed for use with this text. Learn the definitions and spellings of the terms used to describe the anatomical abdominal regions by completing exercises 10, 11, and 12 and Exercise Figure E.

Exercise 10

Fill in the blanks with the correct terms.

1. The regions to the right and left of the hypogastric region are the <u>iliac</u> regions.

2. The <u>epigastric</u> region is directly above the umbilical region.

Umbilicus

is a term derived from the Latin **umbo,** which denoted the boss, or protuberant part, of a shield. Around the first century the term was used to designate either a raised or a depressed spot in the middle of anything.

Epigastric

is a term composed of the Greek **epi,** meaning **upon,** and **gaster,** meaning **belly.** In the first century the term referred to the area between the breast and the umbilicus. The term designates only the upper middle portion of the abdomen.

Hypogastric

is composed of the Greek **hypo,** meaning **under,** and **gaster,** meaning **belly.** It literally means **beneath** or **under the belly.**

Hypochondriac

is derived from the Greek **hypo,** meaning **under,** and **chondros,** meaning **cartilage.** This ancient term was used by Hippocrates to refer to the region just below the cartilages of the ribs. In 1765 the term was first used to refer to people who experienced discomfort or painful sensations in this area but had no organic findings. Now, a person who has an imaginary illness is referred to as a **hypochondriac.**

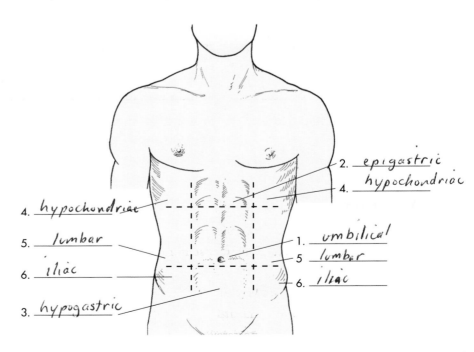

Exercise Fig. E
Fill in the blanks with anatomical abdominal regions.

3. Inferior to the umbilical region is the ___*epigastric*___ region.
4. The ___*hypochondriac*___ are the regions to the right and left of the epigastric region.
5. Superior to the hypogastric region is the ___*umbilical*___ region.
6. To the right and the left of the umbilical region are the ___*lumbar*___ regions.

Exercise 11

Match the terms in the first column with the correct definitions in the second column.

___*b*___ 1. epigastric   a. inferior to the umbilical region

___*d*___ 2. hypochondriac   b. superior to the umbilical region

___*a*___ 3. hypogastric   c. right and left of the umbilical region

___*e*___ 4. iliac   d. right and left of the epigastric region

___*c*___ 5. lumbar   e. right and left of the hypogastric region

___*g*___ 6. umbilical   f. below the hypogastric region

                                 g. inferior to the epigastric region

Exercise 12

Spell each of the terms used to describe the anatomical abdominal regions. Have someone dictate the terms on p. 48 to you, or say the words into a tape recorder; then spell the words from your recording as often as necessary. Study any words you have spelled incorrectly.

1. _____   4. _____

2. _____   5. _____

3. _____   6. _____

Abbreviations

ant . . . . anterior

AP . . . . anteroposterior

inf . . . . inferior

lat . . . . lateral

med . . . . medial

PA . . . . posteroanterior

sup . . . . superior

CHAPTER REVIEW

Exercises

Exercise 13

To test your understanding of the terms introduced in this chapter, complete the sentence by filling in the blank with the term that corresponds to the definition provided.

1. A polyp was found in the colon __*distal*__ to the splenic flexure. (pertaining to away from the point of reference)

2. The drainage catheter is placed over the right __*anterior*__ pelvis. (pertaining to the front)

3. The patient's diagnosis is left __*medial*__ atelectasis. (pertaining to the middle)

4. The incision was made at the __*superior*__ pole of the lesion. (pertaining to above)

5. A(n) __*anteroposterior*__ chest x-ray is taken in the __*frontal*__ plane. (pertaining to the front and to the back) (dividing the body into anterior and posterior portions)

6. The patient complained of __*epigastric*__ pain. (directly above the umbilical region)

7. A __*sagittal*__ plane is used to take a __*lateral*__ chest x-ray. (divides the body into right and left sides) (pertaining to a side)

8. The patient was scheduled for an ultrasound-guided __*bilateral*__ thoracentesis. (pertaining to two [both] sides)

Exercise 14

The following terms did not appear in this chapter but comprise word parts studied in this or previous chapters. Find their definitions by translating the word parts literally.

1. **anterolateral** (an-ter-ō-LAT-er-al) __*pertaining to the front and the side*__

2. **anteromedial** (an-ter-ō-MĒD-ē-al) __*pertaining to the front and the middle*__

3. **anterosuperior** (an-ter-ō-sū-PĒR-ē-ōr) __*pertaining to the front and above*__

4. **cephalocaudal** (sef-a-lō-KAW-dal) __*pertaining to the head and tail*__

5. **dorsocephalad** (dor-sō-SEF-a-lad) __*toward the back and head*__

6. **superolateral** (sū-per-ō-LAT-er-al) __*pertaining to above and the side*__

7. **ventrodorsal** (ven-trō-DOR-sal) __*pertaining to the belly and back*__

Terms Crossword Puzzle

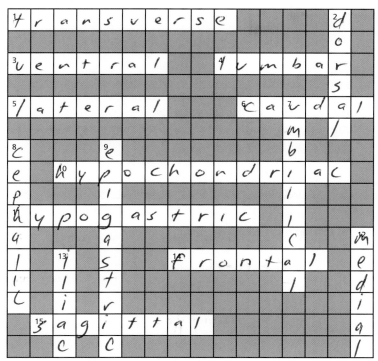

Across Clues

1. plane that divides the body into upper and lower portions
3. pertaining to the belly (front)
4. regions to the right and left of the umbilical region
5. toward a side
6. toward the lower end of the body region
10. regions to the right and left of the epigastric region
11. region directly below the umbilical region
14. plane dividing the body into anterior and posterior portions
15. plane dividing the body into right and left sides

Down Clues

2. toward the back of the body
7. region around the navel
8. toward the top of the body
9. region directly above the umbilical region
12. toward the midline or middle
13. regions to the right and left of the hypogastric

Review of Terms

Can you define, pronounce, and spell the following terms?

Body Directional Terms

anterior (ant)   mediad

anteroposterior (AP)   medial (med)

bilateral   mediolateral

caudal   posterior

cephalad   proximal

cephalic   posteroanterior (PA)

distal   superior (sup)

dorsal   unilateral

inferior (inf)   ventral

lateral (lat)

Anatomical Planes

frontal or coronal

sagittal (midsagittal)

transverse

Anatomical Abdominal Regions

umbilical

epigastric

hypogastric

hypochondriac

lumbar

iliac

Integumentary System

Objectives .... **Upon completion of this chapter you will be able to:**
1. Identify organs and structures of the integumentary system.
2. Define and spell the word parts presented in this chapter.
3. Build and analyze medical terms using word parts.
4. Define, pronounce, and spell the disease and disorder, procedural, surgical, and complementary terms for the integumentary system.

ANATOMY

The term *integumentary* is derived from the Latin word *tegere,* meaning *to cover.* Part of the integumentary system is the skin, our body's covering, which serves as a defense against germs; regulates body temperature; excretes wastes through sweat; and acts as a sensor for pain, touch, heat, and cold. Hair, nails, sweat glands, and oil glands are also part of the integumentary system (Figure 4-1).

The Skin

[handwritten annotations: sloughs off every 30 days; 4 layers; non vascular]

epidermis	outer layer of skin
keratin	horny, or cornified, layer composed of protein. It is contained in the hair, skin, and nails.
melanin	color, or pigmentation, of the skin *[handwritten: , eyes]*
dermis (also called the *true skin*)	inner layer of skin
sweat glands (also called *sudoriferous glands*)	tiny, coiled, tubular structures that emerge through pores on the skin's surface
sebaceous glands	secrete sebum (oil) into the hair follicles where the hair shafts pass through the dermis

[handwritten annotations: none in lips; 2-4 million deeper; more superficial; hypodermis — subcutaneous; fat; blood vessels; nerves]

skin functions: control body temp, has sensors, excretes waste (sweat), first line of defense unless there is a break in the skin

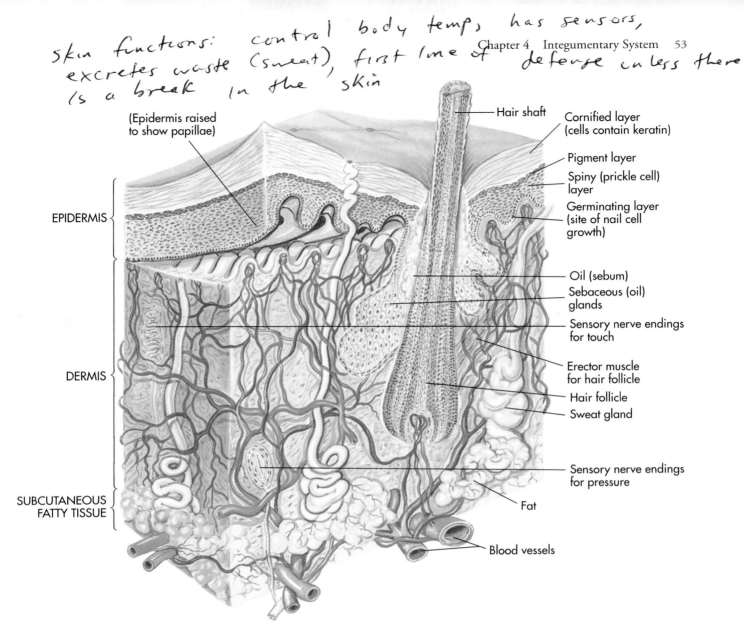

Fig. 4-1
Structure of the skin.

Labels (clockwise from top):
- Hair shaft
- Cornified layer (cells contain keratin)
- Pigment layer
- Spiny (prickle cell) layer
- Germinating layer (site of nail cell growth)
- Oil (sebum)
- Sebaceous (oil) glands
- Sensory nerve endings for touch
- Erector muscle for hair follicle
- Hair follicle
- Sweat gland
- Sensory nerve endings for pressure
- Fat
- Blood vessels
- (Epidermis raised to show papillae)

EPIDERMIS

DERMIS

SUBCUTANEOUS FATTY TISSUE

Accessory Structures of the Skin

beatification

hair . . . .   compressed, keratinized cells that arise from hair follicles; the sacs that enclose the hair fibers

nails . . . .   originate in the epidermis. Nails are found on the upper surface of the ends of the fingers and toes. The white area at the base of the nail is called the *lunula*, or *moon*. (*little*)

Learn the anatomical structures by completing exercise 1.

0.5 in every month
grows back
2-5 years - hair
3-5 months - brows

grasping, beutification, protection

Exercise 1

Match the terms in the first column with the correct definitions in the second column.

_C_ 1. dermis
_d_ 2. epidermis
_g_ 3. hair
_b_ 4. melanin
_f_ 5. nail
_h_ 6. sebaceous glands
_a_ 7. sweat glands

a. coiled, tubular structures
b. responsible for skin color
c. true skin
d. outermost layer of the skin
e. white area at the nail's base
f. originate in the epidermis
g. composed of compressed, keratinized cells
h. secrete sebum

WORD PARTS

Combining Forms for the Integumentary System

Study the word parts and their definitions listed below. Learning will be made easier by completing the exercises that follow.

Combining Form	Definition
cutane/o, derm/o, dermat/o	skin
hidr/o	sweat
kerat/o . . . . (NOTE: *kerat/o* is also used to refer to the cornea of the eye; see Chapter 12)	horny tissue, hard
onych/o, ungu/o	nail
seb/o	sebum (oil)
trich/o	hair

Learn the anatomical locations and meanings of these combining forms by completing exercises 2 and 3 and Exercise Figures A and B.

Exercise 2

Write the definitions of the following combining forms.

1. hidr/o _____ sweat _____

2. derm/o _____ skin _____

3. onych/o _____ nail _____

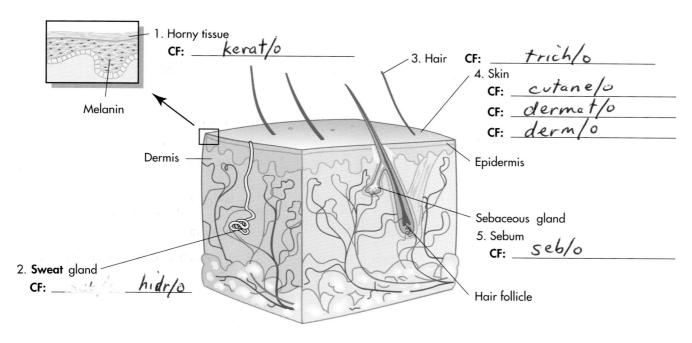

1. Horny tissue
CF: _____kerat/o_____

3. Hair   CF: _____trich/o_____
4. Skin
CF: _____cutane/o_____
CF: _____dermat/o_____
CF: _____derm/o_____

Melanin

Dermis

Epidermis

Sebaceous gland

5. Sebum
CF: _____seb/o_____

2. **Sweat** gland
CF: _____hidr/o_____

Hair follicle

Exercise Fig. A
Fill in the blanks with combining forms in this diagram of a cross section of the skin.

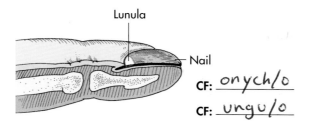

Lunula

Nail
CF: _____onych/o_____
CF: _____ungu/o_____

Exercise Fig. B
Fill in the blanks with combining forms in this diagram of a cross section of the finger with nail.

4. trich/o _____hair_____

5. kerat/o _____horny tissue, hard_____

6. dermat/o _____skin_____

7. seb/o _____sebum (oil)_____

8. ungu/o _____nail_____

9. cutane/o _____skin_____

Exercise 3

Write the combining form for each of the following.

1. hair   _____trich/o_____

2. sweat   _____hidr/o_____

3. nail   a. _____onych/o_____

               b. _____ungu/o_____

4. sebum   _____seb/o_____

5. skin   a. _____cutane/o_____

               b. _____derm/o_____

               c. _____dermat/o_____

6. hard, horny tissue _____kerat/o_____

Combining Forms Commonly Used with Integumentary System Terms

Combining Form	Definition
aden/o	gland
aut/o	self
bi/o	life
coni/o	dust
crypt/o	hidden
heter/o	other
myc/o	fungus
necr/o	death (cells, body)
pachy/o	thick
rhytid/o	wrinkles
staphyl/o	grapelike clusters
strept/o	twisted chains
xer/o	dry

Learn the combining forms by completing exercises 4 and 5.

The prefix **bi-,** which means **two,** was presented in Chapter 3. The word root **bi** means **life.**

Exercise 4

Write the definitions of the following combining forms.

1. necr/o _____ death (cells, body) _____
2. staphyl/o _____ grapelike clusters _____
3. crypt/o _____ hidden _____
4. pachy/o _____ thick _____
5. coni/o _____ dust _____
6. myc/o _____ fungus _____
7. bi/o _____ life _____
8. heter/o _____ other _____
9. aden/o _____ gland _____
10. strept/o _____ twisted chains _____
11. xer/o _____ dry _____
12. aut/o _____ self _____
13. rhytid/o _____ wrinkles _____

Exercise 5

Write the combining form for each of the following.

1. fungus _____ myc/o _____
2. death (cells, body) _____ necr/o _____
3. other _____ heter/o _____
4. dry _____ xer/o _____
5. thick _____ pachy/o _____
6. twisted chains _____ strept/o _____
7. wrinkles _____ rhytid/o _____
8. grapelike clusters _____ staphyl/o _____
9. self _____ aut/o _____

10. gland _____ aden/o _____

11. hidden _____ crypt/o _____

12. dust _____ coni/o _____

13. life _____ bi/o _____

Prefixes

Prefix	Definition
epi-	on, upon, over
intra-	within
para-	beside, beyond, around
per-	through
sub-	under, below

Learn the prefixes by completing exercises 6 and 7.

Exercise 6

Write the definitions of the following prefixes.

1. sub- _____ under, below _____

2. para- _____ beside, beyond, around _____

3. epi- _____ on, upon, over _____

4. intra- _____ within _____

5. per- _____ through _____

Exercise 7

Write the prefix for each of the following.

1. within _____ intra- _____

2. under, below _____ sub- _____

3. on, upon, over _____ epi- _____

4. beside, beyond, around _____ para- _____

5. through _____ per- _____

Suffixes

Suffix	Definition
-coccus (*pl.* -cocci)	berry-shaped (form of bacterium)
-ectomy	excision or surgical removal
-ia	diseased or abnormal state, condition of
-itis	inflammation
-malacia	softening
-opsy	view of, viewing
-orrhea	flow, excessive discharge
-phagia	eating or swallowing
-plasty	surgical repair
-tome	instrument used to cut

Learn the suffixes by completing exercises 8 and 9.

Exercise 8

Match the suffixes in the first column with the correct definitions in the second column.

_C_ 1. -coccus

_e_ 2. -ectomy

_a_ 3. -itis

_j_ 4. -malacia

_i_ 5. -opsy

_h_ 6. -orrhea

_d_ 7. -phagia

_b_ 8. -plasty

_f_ 9. -tome

_k_ 10. -ia

a. inflammation

b. surgical repair

c. berry-shaped

d. eating or swallowing

e. excision or surgical removal

f. instrument used to cut

g. thick

h. flow, excessive discharge

i. view of, viewing

j. softening

k. diseased or abnormal state, condition of

Exercise 9

Write the definitions of the following suffixes.

1. -plasty _Surgical repair_

2. -ectomy _excision or surgical removal_

3. -malacia _softening_

4. -itis _inflammation_

5. -tome _____ *instrument used to cut* _____

6. -phagia _____ *eating or swallowing* _____

7. -orrhea _____ *flow, excessive discharge* _____

8. -coccus _____ *berry shaped* _____

9. -opsy _____ *view of, viewing* _____

10. -ia _____ *diseased or abnormal state, condition* *of* _____

MEDICAL TERMS

The terms you need to learn to complete this chapter are listed on the following pages. The exercises at the end of each list will help you to learn each word well enough to add it to your vocabulary.

Disease and Disorder Terms

Built From Word Parts

Term	Definition
dermatitis . . . . (*der*-ma-TĪ-tis)	inflammation of the skin
dermatoconiosis . . . . (*der*-ma-tō-kō-nē-Ō-sis)	abnormal condition of the skin caused by dust
dermatofibroma . . . . (*der*-ma-tō-fī-BRŌ-ma)	fibrous tumor of the skin
hidradenitis . . . . (*hī*-drad-e-NĪ-tis)	inflammation of a sweat gland
leiodermia . . . . (lī-ō-DER-mē-a)	condition of smooth skin
onychocryptosis . . . . (*on*-i-kō-krip-TŌ-sis)	abnormal condition of a hidden nail (ingrown nail)
onychomalacia . . . . (*on*-i-kō-ma-LĀ-shē-a)	softening of the nails
onychomycosis . . . . (*on*-i-kō-mī-KŌ-sis)	abnormal condition of a fungus in the nails
onychophagia . . . . (*on*-i-kō-FĀ-jē-a)	eating the nails or nail biting
pachyderma . . . . (paki-DER-ma) (NOTE: the *a* ending is a noun suffix and has no meaning.)	thickening of the skin

paronychia . . . .   diseased state around the nail (Exercise Fig-
(par-ō-NIK-ē-a)   ure C)
(NOTE: the *a* from para- has
been dropped. The final vowel
in a prefix is dropped when the
word to which it is added begins
with a vowel.)

seborrhea . . . .   excessive discharge of sebum
(*seb*-ōr-Ē-a)

trichomycosis . . . .   abnormal condition of a fungus in the hair
(*trik*-ō-mī-KŌ-sis)

xeroderma . . . .   dry skin
(zē-rō-DER-ma)
(NOTE:the *a* ending is a noun
suffix and has no meaning.)

Practice saying each of these terms aloud. To assist you in pronunciation, obtain the
audiotape designed for use with this text. Learn the definitions and spellings of the
terms used to describe diseases and disorders of the integumentary system by completing exercises 10, 11, and 12.

Exercise Fig. C
Fill in the blanks to complete the labeling of the
diagram.

paro / nych
AROUND / NAIL
i a

DISEASED STATE; **also called
"run around" because the
infection runs around the
nail.**

Exercise 10

Analyze and define the following terms used to describe integumentary system diseases and disorders. If you need to, refer to p. 7 for a review.

EXAMPLE: onych/o/myc/osis   abnormal condition of a fungus in the nails

1. dermatoconiosis __abnormal condition of the skin caused by dust__
2. hidradenitis __inflammation of a sweat gland__
3. dermatitis __inflammation of the skin__
4. pachyderma __thickening of the skin__
5. onychomalacia __softening of the nails__
6. trichomycosis __abnormal condition of a fungus in the hair__
7. dermatofibroma __fibrous tumor of the skin__
8. paronychia __diseased state around the nail__
9. onychocryptosis __abnormal condition of a hidden nail__
10. seborrhea __excessive discharge of sebum__
11. onychophagia __eating the nails__
12. xeroderma __dry skin__
13. leioderma __condition of smooth skin__

Exercise 11 ....

Build disease and disorder terms for the following definitions by using the word parts you have learned. If you need help, refer to p. 8 to review word-building techniques.

EXAMPLE: abnormal condition of a fungus in the hair   <u>trich / o / myc / osis</u>
                                                        WR / CV / WR / S

1. thickening of the skin

   <u>pachy | derm a</u>
          WR / WR / S

2. abnormal condition of a
   fungus in the nails

   <u>onych   / o / myc / osis</u>
        WR / CV / WR / S

3. excessive discharge of sebum

   <u>seb | orrhea</u>
          WR / S

4. inflammation of the skin

   <u>dermat | itis</u>
        WR / S

5. fibrous tumor of the skin

   <u>dermat / o / fibr / oma</u>
        WR / CV / WR / S

6. softening of the nails

   <u>onych   / o / malacia</u>
        WR / CV / S

7. inflammation of a sweat gland

   <u>hidr | aden | itis</u>
        WR / WR / S

8. abnormal condition of a
   hidden nail

   <u>onych   / o / crypt / osis</u>
        WR / CV / WR / S

9. abnormal condition of the
   skin caused by dust

   <u>dermat / o / coni / osis</u>
        WR / CV / WR / S

10. eating the nails

    <u>onych   / o / phagia</u>
         WR / CV / S

11. diseased state around the nail

    <u>par   pnych / ia</u>
          P / WR / S

12. dry skin

    <u>xer   / o / derm a</u>
         WR / CV / WR / S

13. condition of smooth skin

    <u>lei   / o / derm / ia</u>
         WR / CV / WR / S

Exercise 12

Spell each of the terms used to describe integumentary diseases and disorders. Have someone dictate the terms on pp. 60 and 61 to you, or say the words into a tape recorder; then spell the words from your recording as often as necessary. Think about the word parts before attempting to write the word. Study any words you have spelled incorrectly.

1. _____   8. _____
2. _____   9. _____
3. _____   10. _____
4. _____   11. _____
5. _____   12. _____
6. _____   13. _____
7. _____   14. _____

Disease and Disorder Terms
Not Built From Word Parts

Term	Definition
abrasion .... (a-BRĀ-zhun)	scraping away of the skin by mechanical process or injury
abscess .... (AB-ses)	localized collection of pus
acne .... (AK-nē)	inflammatory disease of the skin involving the sebaceous glands and hair follicles
actinic keratosis .... (ack-TIN-ik) (ker-a-TŌ-sis)	a precancerous skin condition of horny tissue formation that results from excessive exposure to sunlight
basal cell carcinoma (BCC) ..... (BĀ-sal) (sel) (kar-si-NŌ-ma)	epithelial tumor arising from the epidermis. It seldom metastasizes but invades local tissue. Common on the face of elderly individuals.
candidiasis .... (kan-di-DĪ-a-sis)	an infection of the skin, mouth (thrush), or vagina caused by the yeast-like fungus *Candida albicans*. *Candida* is normally present in the mucous membranes; overgrowth causes an infection. Esophageal candidiasis is often seen in AIDS patients.
carbuncle .... (KAR-bung-kl)	skin infection composed of a cluster of boils caused by staphylococcal bacteria
cellulitis .... (sel-ū-LĪ-tis)	inflammation of the connective tissue caused by infection, leading to redness, swelling, and fever

Abscess

is derived from the Latin **ab**, meaning **from**, and **cedo**, meaning **to go.** The tissue dies and goes away, with the pus replacing it.

Acne

may be derived from **akme**, meaning **point.** Thus it was named for the point on a pimple.

Candida

comes from the Latin **candidus**, meaning **gleaming white**; albicans is from the Latin verb **albicare**, meaning **to make white.** The growth of the fungus is white, and the infection produces a white discharge.

contusion . . . .
(kon-TŪ-zhun)

injury with no break in the skin, characterized by pain, swelling, discoloration (also called a *bruise*)

eczema . . . .
(EK-ze-ma)

noninfectious, inflammatory skin disease characterized by redness, blisters, scabs, and itching

fissure . . . .
(FISH-ūr)

slit or crack-like sore in the skin

furuncle . . . .
(FER-ung-kl)

painful skin node caused by staphylococcal bacteria in a hair follicle (also called a *boil*)

gangrene . . . .
(GANG-grēn)

death of tissue caused by loss of blood supply followed by bacterial invasion

> **Herpes**
>
> is derived from the Greek **herpo,** meaning to **creep along.** It is descriptive of the course and type of skin lesion.

(handwritten: (L) girdle =shingles)

herpes . . . .
(HER-pēz)

inflammatory skin disease caused by herpes virus characterized by small blisters in clusters. There are many types of herpes. *Herpes simplex*, for example, causes fever blisters and *herpes zoster*, also called *shingles,* is characterized by painful skin eruptions that follow nerves inflamed by the virus (Figure 4-2)

impetigo . . . .
(im-pe-TĪ-gō)

superficial skin infection, characterized by pustules and caused by either staphylococci or streptococci (Figure 4-2) *(handwritten: highly contagious)*

Kaposi's sarcoma . . . .
(KAP-ō-sēz) (sar-KŌ-ma)

a cancerous condition starting as purple or brown pimples on the feet, which spreads through the skin to the lymph nodes and internal organs. Frequently seen in AIDS (acquired immune deficiency syndrome).

laceration . . . .
(*las*-er-Ā-shun)

torn, ragged-edged wound

lesion . . . .
(LĒ-zhun)

any pathological change in the structure or function of tissue resulting from injury or disease

pediculosis . . . .
(pe-*dik*-ū-LŌ-sis)

invasion into the skin and hair by lice

psoriasis . . . .
(so-RĪ-a-sis)

chronic skin condition producing red lesions covered with silvery scales

scabies . . . .
(SKĀ-bēz)

skin infection caused by the itch mite, a minute animal whose relative is the tick. The infection causes severe itching with red papules.

scleroderma . . . .
(skle-rō-DER-ma)

a disease characterized by chronic hardening (induration) of the connective tissue of the skin and other body organs

squamous cell carcinoma (SqCCa)
(SQWĀ-mus) (sel)
(kar-si-NŌ-ma)

a malignant growth that develops from scale-like epithelial tissue. On the skin it appears as a firm, red, painless bump. It also is found in other body sites (Figure 4-2).

(handwritten: worse than BCC not as bad as melanoma)

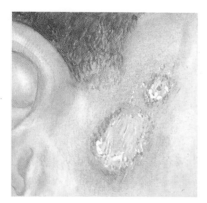

Tinea corporis (ringworm)

Squamous cell carcinoma

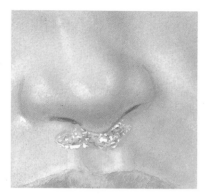

Impetigo contagiosa

Herpes zoster (shingles)

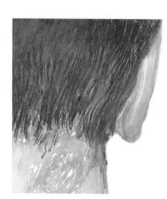

Dermatitis

Fig. 4-2
Common skin disorders.

[handwritten notes: discoid DLE - skin; also; more dangerous; organs]

systemic lupus erythematosus (SLE) . . . .
(sis-TEM-ik) (LŪ-pus)
(er-i-thē-ma-TŌ-sus)

inflammatory disease of the joints and the protein in the white fibers (collagen) of the connective tissue of the skin. It also may affect other organs.

[handwritten note: death is usu. heart-related]

tinea . . . .
(TIN-ē-a)

fungus infection of the skin, commonly called "ringworm" (Figure 4-2)

urticaria . . . .
(ūr-ti-KA-rē-a)

an itching skin eruption composed of wheals of varying size and shape

[handwritten notes: circumscribed area white in center, red around perimeter; hives]

Practice saying each of these terms aloud. To assist you in pronunciation, obtain the audiotape designed for use with this text. Learn the definitions and spellings of the terms by completing exercises 13, 14, 15 and 16.

Ted Small

Exercise 13 ....

Fill in the blanks with the correct terms.

1. An inflammatory disease affecting joints and the collagen of connective tissue is ___systemic___ ___lupus___ ___erythematosus___.

2. A(n) ___abscess___ is a localized collection of pus.

3. A crack-like sore in the skin is called a(n) ___fissure___.

4. The scraping away of the skin by mechanical process or injury is called a(n) ___abrasion___.

5. ___Psoriasis___ is a chronic skin condition characterized by red lesions covered with silvery scales.

6. An inflammatory skin disease characterized by small blisters in clusters is called ___herpes___.

7. ___Pediculosis___ is the name given to the invasion of the skin and hair by lice.

8. A fungus infection of the skin, also known as *ringworm*, is called ___tinea___.

9. An injury with no break in the skin and characterized by pain, swelling, and discoloration is called a(n) ___contusion___.

10. ___Gangrene___ is the name given to tissue death caused by a loss of blood supply followed by bacterial invasion.

11. Any pathological change in the structure or function of tissue, resulting from injury or disease is called a ___lesion___.

12. ___Kaposi's___ ___sarcoma___ is a cancerous condition starting as purple or brown pimples on the feet.

13. A horny tissue formation that results from excessive exposure to sunlight and is precancerous is called ___actinic___ ___keratosis___.

14. A cluster of boils caused by staphylococcal bacteria is a ___carbuncle___.

15. An inflammatory skin disease that involves the oil glands and hair follicles is called ___acne___.

16. ___Laceration___ is the name given to a torn, ragged-edge wound.

17. A painful skin node caused by staphylococcal bacteria in a hair follicle is called a(n) ___furuncle___.

18. A malignant growth that develops from scale-like epithelial tissue is known as ___squamous___ ___cell___ carcinoma.

19. Inflammation of the connective tissue caused by infection and creating redness, swelling, and fever is called ___cellulitis___.

20. __Impetigo__ is the name given to a superficial skin infection characterized by pustules and caused by either staphylococci or streptococci.

21. __Eczema__ is a noninfectious inflammatory skin disease characterized by redness, blisters, scabs, and itching.

22. A skin infection caused by the itch mite is called __scabies__.

23. __Urticaria__ is an itching skin eruption composed of wheals.

24. An epithelial tumor commonly found on the face of elderly individuals is __basal__ __cell__ carcinoma.

25. __Schleroderma__ is a disease characterized by induration of the connective tissue.

26. __Candidiasis__ an infection of the mouth, skin, or vagina caused by *Candida albicans.*

Exercise 14   *Ted Small*

Match the words in the first column with their correct definitions in the second column.

f 1. abrasion	a. death of tissue caused by loss of blood supply and entry of bacteria
j 2. abscess	b. crack-like sore in the skin
g 3. acne	c. cluster of boils
l 4. actinic keratosis	d. induration of connective tissue
m 5. basal cell carcinoma	
c 6. carbuncle	e. noninfectious inflammatory skin disease having redness, blisters, scabs, and itching
i 7. cellulitis	f. scraped away skin
k 8. contusion	g. involves sebaceous glands and hair follicles
e 9. eczema	h. painful skin node caused by staphylococci in a hair follicle
b 10. fissure	i. inflammation of connective tissue with redness, swelling, and fever
h 11. furuncle	j. localized collection of pus
a 12. gangrene	k. injury characterized by pain, swelling, and discoloration
d 13. scleroderma	l. precancerous skin condition caused by excessive exposure to sunlight
	m. epithelial tumor commonly found on the face of elderly individuals
	n. red lesions with silvery scales

Exercise 15 ....

Match the words in the first column with the correct definitions in the second column.

_d_ 1. herpes

_i_ 2. impetigo

_f_ 3. Kaposi's sarcoma

_h_ 4. laceration

_l_ 5. lesion

_k_ 6. pediculosis

_c_ 7. psoriasis

_a_ 8. scabies

_m_ 9. squamous cell carcinoma

_e_ 10. systemic lupus erythematosus

_b_ 11. tinea

_g_ 12. urticaria

_j_ 13. candidiasis

a. skin infection caused by the itch mite

b. fungus infection of the skin

c. red lesions covered by silvery scales

d. inflammatory skin disease having clusters of blisters

e. inflammatory disease of joints and collagen of the connective tissue of the skin

f. a cancerous condition that starts as brown or purple pimples on the feet

g. composed of wheals

h. torn, ragged-edged wound

i. superficial skin condition having pustules and caused by staphylococci or streptococci

j. infection of the skin, mouth, or vagina caused by a yeast-like fungus

k. invasion of the hair and skin by lice

l. pathological change in tissue structure or function resulting from injury or disease

m. a malignant growth that develops from scale-like epithelial tissue

n. crack-like sore in the skin

Exercise 16 ....

Spell each of the terms, not built from word parts, which are used to describe integumentary diseases and disorders. Have someone dictate the terms on pp. 63 and 65 to you, or say the words into a tape recorder; then spell the words from your recording. Study any words you have spelled incorrectly.

1. _____

2. _____

3. _____

4. _____

5. _____

6. _____

7. _____

8. _____

9. _____

10. _____

11. _____

12. _____

13. _____

14. _____

15. _____

16. _____

17. _____

18. _____

19. _____   23. _____

20. _____   24. _____

21. _____   25. _____

22. _____   26. _____

Surgical Terms

Built From Word Parts

Term	Definition
biopsy (bx) . . . . (BĪ-op-sē)	view of life (the removal of living tissue from the body to be viewed under the microscope)
dermatoautoplasty . . . . (*der*-ma-tō-AW-tō-*plas*-tē)	surgical repair using one's own skin (for the skin graft [autograft])
dermatoheteroplasty . . . . (*der*-ma-tō-HET-er-ō-*plas*-tē)	surgical repair using skin from others (for the skin graft [allograft])
dermatoplasty . . . . (DER-ma-tō-*plas*-tē)	surgical repair of the skin
onychectomy . . . . (on-i-KEK-tō-mē)	excision of a nail
rhytidectomy . . . . (rit-i-DEK-tō-mē)	excision of wrinkles
rhytidoplasty . . . . (RIT-i-dō-*plas*-tē)	surgical repair of wrinkles

Practice saying each of these terms aloud. To assist you in pronunciation, obtain the audiotape designed for use with this text. Learn the definitions and spellings of the surgical terms by completing exercises 17, 18, and 19.

Exercise 17

Analyze and define the following surgical terms.

EXAMPLE:
WR CV S
dermat/o/plasty   *surgical repair of the skin*
CF

1. rhytidectomy _____ excision of wrinkles _____
2. biopsy _____ view of life _____
3. dermatoautoplasty _____ surgical repair using one's own skin _____
4. onychectomy _____ excision of a nail _____
5. rhytidoplasty _____ Surgical repair of wrinkles _____
6. dermatoheteroplasty _____ surgical repair using skin from others _____

Exercise 18

Build surgical terms for the following definitions by using the word parts you have learned.

EXAMPLE: surgical repair using one's own skin $\dfrac{dermat}{WR}$ | $\dfrac{o}{CV}$ | $\dfrac{aut}{WR}$ | $\dfrac{o}{CV}$ | $\dfrac{plasty}{S}$

1. excision of wrinkles

$\dfrac{rhytid}{WR}$ | $\dfrac{ectomy}{S}$

2. view of life (removal of living tissue from the body)

$\dfrac{bi}{WR}$ | $\dfrac{opsy}{S}$

3. surgical repair using skin from others

$\dfrac{dermat}{WR}$ | $\dfrac{o}{CV}$ | $\dfrac{heter}{WR}$ | $\dfrac{o}{CV}$ | $\dfrac{plasty}{S}$

4. excision of a nail

$\dfrac{onych}{WR}$ | $\dfrac{ectomy}{S}$

5. surgical repair of wrinkles

$\dfrac{rhytid}{WR}$ | $\dfrac{o}{CV}$ | $\dfrac{plasty}{S}$

6. surgical repair of the skin

$\dfrac{dermat}{WR}$ | $\dfrac{o}{CV}$ | $\dfrac{plasty}{S}$

Exercise 19

Spell each of the surgical terms. Have someone dictate the terms on p. 69 to you, or say the words into a tape recorder; then spell the words from your recording as often as necessary. Think about the word parts before attempting to write the word. Study any words you have spelled incorrectly.

1. _____   5. _____

2. _____   6. _____

3. _____   7. _____

4. _____

Complementary Terms

Built From Word Parts

Term	Definition
dermatologist . . . . (*der*-ma-TOL-ō-jist)	physician who specializes in skin (diseases)
dermatology . . . . (der-ma-TOL-ō-jē)	study of the skin

dermatome . . . .   instrument used to cut skin
(DER-ma-tōm)
(NOTE: when two consonants
of the same letter come together,
one is sometimes dropped.)

epidermal . . . .   pertaining to upon the skin
(*ep*-i-DER-mal)

erythroderma . . . .   red skin (abnormal redness of the skin)
(e-rith-rō-DER-ma)
(NOTE: the *a* ending is a noun
suffix and has no meaning.)

hypodermic . . . .   pertaining to under the skin   *[handwritten: subcutaneous subdermal]*
(*hī*-po-DER-mik)

intradermal . . . .   pertaining to within the skin
(*in*-tra-DER-mal)

keratogenic . . . .   originating in horny tissue
(ker-a-tō-JEN-ik)

leukoderma . . . .   white skin (less color than normal)
(lū-kō-DER-ma)
(NOTE:the *a* ending is a noun
suffix and has no meaning.)

necrosis . . . .   abnormal condition of death (cells and tissue
(ne-KRŌ-sis)   die because of disease)

percutaneous . . . .   pertaining to through the skin
(per-kū-TĀ-nē-us)

staphylococcus (*pl.* staphylococci)
(staph) . . . .   berry-shaped (bacteria) in grapelike clusters
(*staf*-il-ō-KOK-us,   (these bacteria cause many skin diseases)
staf-il-ō-KOK-si)   (Exercise Figure D)

streptococcus (*pl.* streptococci)
(strep) . . . .   berry-shaped (bacteria) in twisted chains
(*strep*-tō-KOK-us,   (Exercise Figure E)
strep-tō-KOK-si)

subcutaneous (sc) . . . .   pertaining to under the skin
(sub-kū-TĀ-nē-us)

ungual . . . .   pertaining to the nail
(UNG-gwal)

xanthoderma . . . .   yellow skin (also called *jaundice*)
(zan-thō-DER-ma)
(NOTE: the *a* ending is a noun
suffix and has no meaning.)

Practice saying each of these terms aloud. To assist you in pronunciation, obtain the
audiotape designed for use with this text. Learn the definitions and spellings of the
complementary terms by completing exercises 20, 21, and 22.

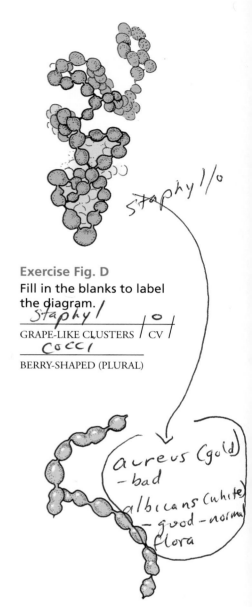

[handwritten: staphyl/o]

Exercise Fig. D
Fill in the blanks to label
the diagram.
[handwritten: Staphyl / o]
GRAPE-LIKE CLUSTERS / CV /
[handwritten: cocci]
BERRY-SHAPED (PLURAL)

[handwritten: aureus (gold) – bad; albicans (white) – good – normal flora]

Exercise Fig. E
Fill in the blanks to label
the diagram.
[handwritten: Strept / o]
TWISTED CHAINS / CV /
[handwritten: cocci]
BERRY-SHAPED (PLURAL)

[handwritten: hundreds of strains; Beta & Alpha strains; strep throat, can damage bicuspid valve, kidneys]

[handwritten: impetigo pustules form — contagious ← flesh eating pyogenes]

Exercise 20

Analyze and define the following complementary terms.

EXAMPLE: intra/derm/al   *pertaining to within the skin*

1. ungual — *pertaining to the nail*
2. dermatome — *instrument used to cut skin*
3. streptococcus — *berry-shaped (bacteria) in twisted chains*
4. hypodermic — *pertaining to under the skin*
5. dermatology — *study of the skin*
6. subcutaneous — *pertaining to under the skin*
7. staphylococcus — *berry-shaped (bacteria) in grape-like clusters*
8. keratogenic — *originating in horny tissue*
9. dermatologist — *physician who specializes in skin (diseases)*
10. necrosis — *abnormal condition of death*
11. epidermal — *pertaining to upon the skin*
12. xanthoderma — *yellow skin*
13. erythroderma — *red skin*
14. leukoderma — *white skin*
15. percutaneous — *pertaining to through the skin*

Exercise 21

Build complementary terms for the integumentary system by using the word parts you have learned.

EXAMPLE: pertaining to under the skin $\dfrac{hypo}{P} / \dfrac{derm}{WR} / \dfrac{ic}{S}$

1. study of the skin   *dermat* / *ology*
   WR / S

2. abnormal condition of death (of cells and tissue)   *necr* / *osis*
   WR / S

3. instrument used to cut skin   *derma* / *tome*
   WR / S

4. pertaining to the nail

ungu / al
WR / S

5. berry-shaped bacteria in grapelike clusters

staphyl / o / coccus
WR / CV / S

6. specialist in skin diseases

dermat / ologist
WR / S

7. pertaining to within the skin

intra / derm / al
P / WR / S

8. pertaining to upon the skin

epi / derm / al
P / WR / S

9. pertaining to under the skin

hypo / derm / al
P / WR / S

10. berry-shaped bacteria in twisted chains

strept / o / coccus
P / WR / S

strept / o / cocci
WR / CV / S

11. originating in the horny tissue

kerat / o / genic
WR / CV / S

12. white skin

leuk / o / derm / a
WR / CV / WR / S

13. red skin

erythr / o / derm / a
WR / CV / WR / S

14. yellow skin

xanth / o / derm / a
WR / CV / WR / S

15. pertaining to through the skin

per / cutane / ous
P / WR / S

Exercise 22

Spell each of the complementary terms. Have someone dictate the terms on pp. 70-71 to you, or say the words into a tape recorder; then spell the words from your recording as often as necessary. Think about the word parts before attempting to write the word. Study any words you have spelled incorrectly.

1. _____   9. _____
2. _____   10. _____
3. _____   11. _____
4. _____   12. _____
5. _____   13. _____
6. _____   14. _____
7. _____   15. _____
8. _____   16. _____

Complementary Terms

Not Built From Word Parts

Term	Definition
adipose . . . . (AD-i-pōs)	fat
albino . . . . (al-BĪ-nō)	white
allergy . . . . (AL-er-jē)	hypersensitivity to a substance
alopecia . . . . (al-ō-PĒ-shē-a)	baldness *atrichia*
cicatrix . . . . (SIK-a-triks)	scar
cytomegalovirus (CMV) . . . . (sī-tō-meg-a-lō-VĪ-rus)	a herpes-type virus that usually causes disease when the immune system is compromised
debridement . . . . (da-BRĒD-mon)	removal of contaminated or dead tissue and foreign matter from an open wound
decubitus ulcer . . . . (de-KŪ-bi-tus) (UL-ser)	bedsore; an open area of skin caused by pressure or irritation
dermabrasion . . . . (*derm*-a-BRĀ-zhun)	procedure to remove skin scars with abrasive material, such as sandpaper
diaphoresis . . . . (*dī*-a-fō-RĒ-sis)	profuse sweating
disseminate . . . . (dis-SEM-i-nāt)	to scatter over a considerable area
ecchymosis . . . . (ek-i-MŌ-sis)	escape of blood into the tissues, causing superficial discoloration; a "black and blue" mark
edema . . . . (e-DĒ-ma)	puffy swelling of tissue from the accumulation of fluid
emollient . . . . (e-MOL-yent)	agent that softens or soothes the skin
erythema . . . . (er-i-THĒ-ma)	redness
induration . . . . (in-dū-RĀ-shun)	abnormal hard spot(s)
jaundice . . . . (JAWN-dis)	condition characterized by a yellow tinge to the skin (xanthoderma)
keloid . . . . (KĒ-loyd)	overgrowth of scar tissue (Figure 4-3)
leukoplakia . . . . (lū-kō-PLĀ-kē-a)	condition characterized by white spots or patches on mucous membrane, which may be precancerous
macule . . . . (MAK-ūl)	flat, colored spot on the skin (Figure 4-3)

Alopecia

is derived from the Greek **alopex,** meaning **fox.** One was thought to bald like a mangy fox.

Decubitus

is derived from **de,** meaning **down,** and **cubere,** meaning **to lie. Decubitus** is a term also used in x-ray terminology to denote the recumbent (lying-down) position.

Diaphoresis

is derived from the Greek **dia,** meaning **through,** and **phoreo,** meaning **I carry.** Translated, it means the carrying through of perspiration.

Ecchymosis

is derived from the Greek **ek,** meaning **out of,** and **chumos,** meaning **juice.** Extended, it means to pour out juice of the body, or blood.

Macule

is probably derived from the ancient Sanskrit word **mala,** meaning **dirt.**

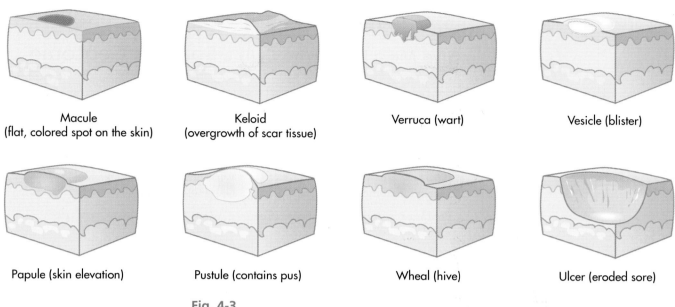

Macule
(flat, colored spot on the skin)

Keloid
(overgrowth of scar tissue)

Verruca (wart)

Vesicle (blister)

Papule (skin elevation)

Pustule (contains pus)

Wheal (hive)

Ulcer (eroded sore)

Fig. 4-3
Cutaway sections of some common skin disorders.

nevus (*pl.* **nevi**) . . . . (NĒ-vus, NĒ-vī)	circumscribed pigmented area present at birth; mole, birthmark
pallor . . . . (PAL-ōr)	paleness
papule . . . . (PAP-ūl)	small, solid skin elevation (pimple) (Figure 4-3)
petechia (*pl.* **petechiae**) . . . . (pe-TĒ-kē-a, pe-TĒ-kē-ē)	pinpoint skin hemorrhages
pruritus . . . . (prū-RĪ-tus)	severe itching
purpura . . . . (PER-pū-ra)	disorder characterized by hemorrhages into the tissue, giving the skin a purple-red discoloration
pustule . . . . (PUS-tūl)	elevation of skin containing pus (Figure 4-3)
ulcer . . . . (UL-ser)	eroded sore on the skin or mucous membrane (Figure 4-3)
verruca . . . . (ver-RŪ-ka)	circumscribed cutaneous elevation caused by a virus; wart (Figure 4-3)
vesicle . . . . (VES-i-kl)	small elevation of the epidermis containing liquid (blister) (Figure 4-3)
virus . . . . (VĪ-ras)	an infectious agent
wheal . . . . (hwēl)	transitory, round, itchy elevation of the skin with a white center and a red surrounding area (hive) (Figure 4-3)

clear liquid

Petechia

is originally from the Italian **petechio,** meaning **flea bite.** The small hemorrhagic spot resembles the mark made by a flea.

Dermatology
or
Give Me a Man Who Calls a Spade a Geotome

I wish the *dermatologist*
Were less a firm apologist
For all the terminology
That's used in *dermatology*

Something you or I would deem a
Redness he calls *erythema;*
If it's blistered, raw and warm he
Has to call it multiforme

Things to him are never simple;
Papule is his word for pimple
What's a macule, clearly stated?
Just a spot that's over-rated!

Over the skin that looks unwell
He chants Latin like a spell;
What he's labeled and obscured
Looks to him as good as cured.

Reprinted with permission from *The New England Journal of Medicine,* © 1977; 297(12):660.

Practice saying each of these terms aloud. To assist you in pronunciation, obtain the audiotape designed for use with this text. Learn the definitions and spellings of the terms by completing exercises 23, 24, 25, and 26.

Ted Small

Exercise 23

Fill in the blanks with the correct terms.

1. Another name for scar is ___cicatrix___ .
2. Profuse sweating is called ___diaphoresis___ .
3. The term for an agent that softens or soothes the skin is ___emollient___ .
4. The medical term for wart is ___verruca___ .
5. ___Macule___ is the name for a flat, colored skin spot.
6. A yellow skin condition is known as ___jaundice___ .
7. The condition of white spots or patches on mucous membrane is called ___leukoplakia___ .
8. ___Petechiae___ are pinpoint hemorrhages of the skin.
9. An eroded sore is called a(n) ___ulcer___ .
10. A(n) ___keloid___ is an overgrowth of scar tissue.
11. Another name for paleness is ___pallor___ .
12. Superficial skin discoloration caused by escaping blood is referred to as ___ecchymosis___ .
13. Another term for white is ___albino___ .
14. A bedsore caused by prolonged lying down is called a(n) ___decubitus ulcer___ .
15. Another term for fat is ___adipose___ .
16. ___Disseminate___ means scattered over a considerable area.
17. Severe itching is called ___pruritus___ .
18. Another name for redness is ___erythema___ .
19. The condition of tissue hemorrhages giving the skin a purple-red discoloration is known as ___purpura___ .

20. ___Nevus___ is another name for mole or birthmark.

21. The removal of dead or contaminated tissue from an open wound is called ___debridement___.

22. The term for baldness is ___alopecia___.

23. Hypersensitivity to a substance is called a(n) ___allergy___.

24. A small, solid skin elevation is called a (n) ___papule___.

25. A transitory, round skin elevation with a white center and a red surrounding area is a(n) ___wheal___.

26. A(n) ___pustule___ is a skin elevation containing pus.

27. A blister is also called a(n) ___vesicle___.

28. ___Dermabrasion___ is the name of the procedure using abrasive material to remove scars.

29. ___Virus___ is an infectious agent.

30. An abnormal hard spot(s) is called ___induration___.

31. ___Edema___ is the swelling of tissue.

32. ___Cytomegalovirus___ is a herpes-type virus.

Exercise 24

_m_ 1. adipose

_o_ 2. albino

_h_ 3. allergy

_a_ 4. alopecia

_j_ 5. cicatrix

_e_ 6. debridement

_n_ 7. decubitus ulcer

_l_ 8. dermabrasion

_g_ 9. diaphoresis

_d_ 10. disseminated

_b_ 11. ecchymosis

_f_ 12. emollient

_k_ 13. erythema

_c_ 14. jaundice

_q_ 15. edema

_i_ 16. induration

a. baldness

b. superficial discoloration caused by blood escaping into the tissues

c. yellow color to the skin

d. spread over a considerable area

e. removal of dead tissue from an open wound

f. agent that softens or soothes the skin

g. profuse sweating

h. hypersensitivity to a substance

i. hard spot(s)

j. scar

k. redness

l. procedure to remove skin scars by using abrasive material

m. fat

n. bedsore

o. white

p. patches

q. swelling of tissue

Exercise 25

Match the terms in the first column with the correct definitions in the second column.

_g_ 1. keloid

_d_ 2. leukoplakia

_j_ 3. macule

_a_ 4. nevus

_l_ 5. pallor

_k_ 6. papule

_n_ 7. petechiae

_b_ 8. pruritus

_e_ 9. purpura

_f_ 10. pustule

_o_ 11. ulcer

_c_ 12. verruca

_h_ 13. vesicle

_i_ 14. wheal

_m_ 15. virus

_q_ 16. cytomegalovirus

a. mole

b. severe itching

c. wart

d. condition of white spots or patches on mucous membranes

e. hemorrhages in tissue giving skin a red-purple color

f. skin elevation containing pus

g. overgrowth of scar tissue

h. small elevation of epidermis containing liquid

i. transitory elevation of skin with a white center and a red surrounding area

j. flat, colored spot on skin

k. small, solid skin elevation

l. paleness

m. an infectious agent

n. pinpoint hemorrhages

o. eroded sore on the skin or mucous membrane

p. profuse sweating

q. herpes-type virus

Exercise 26

Spell each of the complementary terms. Have someone dictate the terms on pp. 74-75 to you, or say the words into a tape recorder; then spell the words from your recording as often as necessary. Study any words you have spelled incorrectly.

1. _____   17. _____

2. _____   18. _____

3. _____   19. _____

4. _____   20. _____

5. _____   21. _____

6. _____   22. _____

7. _____   23. _____

8. _____   24. _____

9. _____   25. _____

10. _____   26. _____

11. _____   27. _____

12. _____   28. _____

13. _____   29. _____

14. _____   30. _____

15. _____   31. _____

16. _____   32. _____

Abbreviations

bx . . . . biopsy

BCC . . . . basal cell carcinoma

CMV . . . . cytomegalovirus

sc . . . . subcutaneous

SLE . . . . systemic lupus erythematosis

staph . . . . staphylococcus

strep . . . . streptococcus

SqCCa . . . . squamous cell carcinoma

CHAPTER REVIEW

Exercises

Use the information you have learned thus far to complete the review exercises.

Exercise 27

Below is a written hospital report. Complete the report by writing the medical terms in the blanks that correspond to the numbered definitions.

> **Case History:** 50-year-old white woman presents in the 1. _____ office with a complaint of changes in 2. _____ located in 3. _____ aspect of left eyebrow. Changes include hair loss, "crusty" surface, and some enlargement of 4. _____. Nevus has been present for approximately 3 years. Hair loss present for 2 years. Patient has history of 5. _____ _____ and current case of nonrelated 6. _____ 7. _____ on both forearms. 8. _____ revealed 9. _____ _____ _____, nodular, transected at base.

> **Operative Report:** Patient's operative site was prepped with Betadine. Xylocaine 1% with epinephrine was used as local anesthesia. Skin was incised at 10. _____ pole of lesion. Lesion was then excised as diagnosed, including a margin of clinical normal 11. _____. Specimen submitted to 12. _____. The superior pole was sutured. Hemostasis achieved with electrocautery. Two **A-T** flaps were then constructed on superior aspect of upper eyelid. Flaps and upper eyelid undermined 2 to 3 mm. Flaps sutured with 6-0 Vicryl, followed by 6-0 nylon for closure. Pressure dressing applied.

1. physician who specializes in skin disease *dermatologist*
2. mole *nevus*
3. pertaining to the middle *medical*
4. pathological changes in the structure of tissue *lesion*
5. precancerous skin condition *actinic keratosis*
6. noninfectious, inflammatory skin disease with redness, blisters, scabs, and itching *eczyma*
7. pertaining to two sides *bilateral*
8. view of life *biopsy*
9. epithelial tumor arising from epidermis *BCC*
10. pertaining to above *superior*
11. inner layer of skin *dermis*
12. study of body changes caused by disease *pathology*

Exercise 28

To test your understanding of the terms introduced in this chapter, circle the words that correctly complete the sentences. The italicized words refer to the correct answer.

1. The physician called *the injury with pain, swelling, and discoloration with no break in the skin* a (fissure, <u>contusion,</u> laceration).

2. *Berry-shaped bacteria in grapelike clusters* are (streptococci, <u>staphylococci,</u> pediculosis).

3. The physician ordered lotions applied to the patient's *skin* to alleviate *dryness,* or (pachyderma, dermatoconiosis, <u>xeroderma</u>).

4. The injection given *within the skin* is called a(n) (<u>intradermal,</u> epidermal, hypodermic) injection.

5. The diagnosis of *onychomalacia* was given by the physician for (ingrown nails, nail biting, <u>softening of the nails</u>).

6. The *pinpoint hemorrhages,* or (nevi, verrucae, <u>petechiae</u>), were distributed over the patient's entire body.

7. The primary symptom of the disease was *profuse sweating,* or (<u>diaphoresis,</u> ecchymosis, pruritus).

8. The patient had an *abnormal condition of fungus in the hair;* therefore the doctor recorded the diagnosis as (onychocryptosis, <u>trichomycosis,</u> onychomycosis).

9. The student nurse learned that the medical name for a *blister* was (verruca, keloid, <u>vesicle</u>).

10. The patient was to receive a *skin graft from her mother,* so the operation was listed as a (dermatoplasty, dermatoautoplasty, <u>dermatoheteroplasty</u>).

11. An *abnormal hard spot* is called (edema, <u>induration,</u> virus).

12. Another word for *jaundice* is (erythroderma, leukoderma, <u>xanthoderma</u>).

13. *Leiodermia* is a condition of (striated, <u>smooth,</u> sweaty) skin.

The following exercise is for the student who likes an extra challenge.

Exercise 29

Unscramble the following mixed-up terms. The word(s) on the left hint at the meaning of the word in each of the opposite scrambled words.

EXAMPLE: SKIN   / d / e / r / m / a / t / i / t / i / s /
t t m i s r e d a i

1. bad habit   / / / / / h / / / h / / / / /
p o n a a g y o i h h c

2. examination   / / / / / / /
s i b y o p

3. skin needs fluids   / / / r / / / / r / / /
m e d o x r r e a

4. face-lift
/ / / / t / / / / / o / / /
m e c t o r t y h i d y

5. hidden nail
/ / / / c / / c / / / / / o / / /
p o t h o s s y c o n c r i y

6. herpes-type virus
/ / / / o / / / / / / / v / / / /
m e a g o l r v i c s o y u t

Exercise 30

The following words did not appear in this chapter but are composed of word parts studied in this or the previous chapters. Find their definitions by translating the word parts literally.

1. **dermatopathic** (der-ma-tō-PATH-ik) _____

2. **fibroma** (fi-BRŌ-ma) _____

3. **keratosis** (kar-a-TŌ-sis) _____

4. **lipocyte** (LIP-ō-sīt) _____

5. **onychoid** (ON-i-koyd) _____

6. **trichoid** (TRIK-oyd) _____

Combining Forms Crossword Puzzle

Across Clues	Down Clues
4. dust	1. horny tissue, hard
5. skin	2. sweat
7. hair	3. dry
11. grapelike clusters	6. sebum
13. death (cell, body)	8. skin
17. wrinkles	9. fungus
19. self	10. thick
20. other	12. twisted chains
	14. hidden
	15. nail
	16. life
	18. gland

Review of Terms

Can you build, analyze, define, pronounce, and spell the following terms built from word parts?

Diseases and Disorders

dermatitis

dermatoconiosis

dermatofibroma

hidradenitis

leiodermia

onychocryptosis

onychomalacia

onychomycosis

onychophagia

pachyderma

paronychia

seborrhea

trichomycosis

xeroderma

Surgical

biopsy (bx)

dermatoautoplasty

dermatoheteroplasty

dermatoplasty

onychectomy

rhytidectomy

rhytidoplasty

Complementary

dermatologist

dermatology

dermatome

epidermal

erythroderma

hypodermic

intradermal

keratogenic

leukoderma

necrosis

percutaneous

staphylococcus (staph)
   (pl. staphylococci)

streptococcus (strep)
   (pl. streptococci)

subcutaneous (sc)

ungual

xanthoderma

Can you define, pronounce, and spell the following terms not built from word parts?

Diseases and Disorders

abrasion

abscess

acne

actinic keratosis

basal cell carcinoma
   (BCC)

candidiasis

carbuncle

cellulitis

contusion

eczema

fissure

furuncle

gangrene

herpes

impetigo

Kaposi's sarcoma

laceration

lesion

pediculosis

psoriasis

scabies

scleroderma

squamous cell carcinoma
   (SqCCa)

systemic lupus erythematosus
   (SLE)

tinea

urticaria

Complementary

adipose

albino

allergy

alopecia

cicatrix

cytomegalovirus (CMV)

debridement

decubitus ulcer

dermabrasion

diaphoresis

disseminate

ecchymosis

edema

emollient

erythema

induration

jaundice

keloid

leukoplakia

macule

nevus (*pl.* nevi)

pallor

papule

petechia (*pl.* petechiae)

pruritus

purpura

pustule

ulcer

verruca

vesicle

virus

wheal

Respiratory System

Upon completion of this chapter you will be able to:
1. Identify the organs and other structures of the respiratory system.
2. Define and spell the word parts presented in this chapter.
3. Build and analyze medical terms using word parts.
4. Define, pronounce, and spell the disease and disorder, procedural, surgical, and complementary terms for the respiratory system.

ANATOMY

Most humans do not consciously think about breathing. We take in oxygen from the air while we talk, eat, walk, and sleep. We also exhale carbon dioxide, a waste product of cell function, while doing other things. The organs of the respiratory system function to bring about this exchange of gases in the body (Figure 5-1).

Organs of the Respiratory System

nose	lined with mucous membrane and fine hairs. It acts as a filter to moisten and warm the entering air (Figure 5-2).
nasal septum	partition separating the right and left nasal cavities
paranasal sinuses	air cavities within the cranial bones that open into the nasal cavities
pharynx (also called the *throat*)	serves as a food and air passageway. Air enters from the nasal cavities and passes through the pharynx to the larynx. Food enters the pharynx from the mouth and passes into the esophagus.
adenoids	lymphoid tissue located behind the nasal cavity
tonsils	lymphoid tissue located behind the mouth
larynx (also called the *voice box*)	location of the vocal cords. Air enters from the pharynx.
epiglottis	flap of cartilage that automatically covers the opening of the larynx during swallowing and keeps food from entering
trachea (also called the *windpipe*)	passageway for air to the bronchi

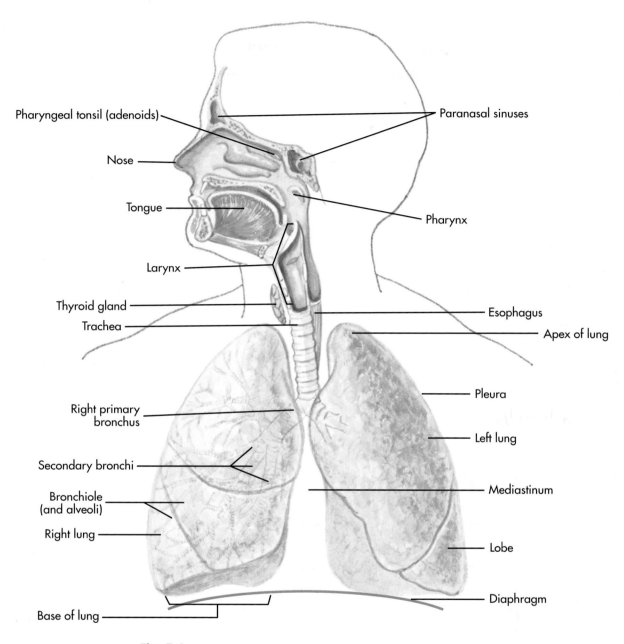

Fig. 5-1
Organs of the respiratory system and associated structures.

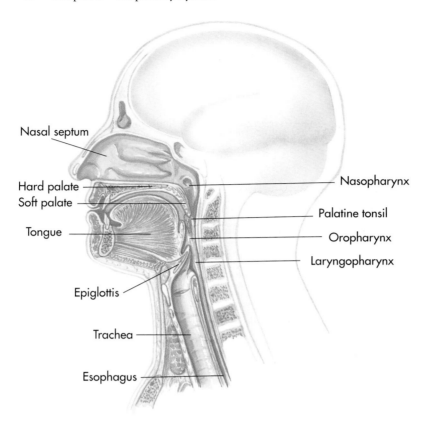

Fig. 5-2
Structures of nasal passages and throat.

Nasal septum

Hard palate
Soft palate

Tongue

Epiglottis

Trachea

Esophagus

Nasopharynx

Palatine tonsil

Oropharynx

Laryngopharynx

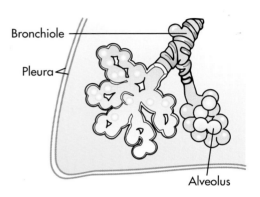

Fig. 5-3
Bronchioles and alveoli.

Bronchiole

Pleura

Alveolus

Bronchi

originated from the Greek **brecho,** meaning **to pour** or **wet.** An ancient belief was that the esophagus carried solid food to the stomach while the bronchi carried liquids.

Adam's Apple

is the largest ring of cartilage in the larynx and is known as the thyroid cartilage (also called the **Adam's apple**). The name came from the belief that Adam, realizing he had sinned when he ate the forbidden fruit, was unable to swallow the apple lodged in his throat.

Mediastinum

literally means **to stand in the middle,** because it is derived from the Latin **medius,** meaning **middle,** and **stare,** meaning **to stand.**

bronchus (*pl.* bronchi) . . . .

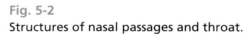

bronchi = brŏng′kī or brŭng′kē

brŏng′kē ōl′
bronchioles . . . .

alveolus (*pl.* alveoli) . . . .

lungs . . . .

pleura . . . .

diaphragm . . . .

mediastinum . . . .

has two branches, which carry the air from the trachea into the lungs, where the branches divide and subdivide. The branchings resemble a tree and therefore are referred to as a bronchial tree.

smallest subdivision of the bronchial tree

air sacs at the end of the bronchioles. Oxygen and carbon dioxide are exchanged through the alveolar walls and the capillaries (Figure 5-3).

two sponge-like organs in the thoracic cavity. The right lung consists of three lobes, and the left lung has two lobes.

serous membrane covering each lung and lining the thoracic cavity

muscular partition that separates the thoracic cavity from the abdominal cavity. It aids in the breathing process.

space between the lungs. It contains the heart, esophagus, trachea, great blood vessels, and other structures.

Learn the above terms by completing exercises 1 and 2.

Exercise 1

Match the terms in the first column with the correct definitions in the second column.

_h_ 1. alveoli

_a_ 2. bronchi

_g_ 3. larynx

_c_ 4. lungs

_f_ 5. pharynx

_d_ 6. pleura

_e_ 7. adenoids

_b_ 8. trachea

a. tubes carrying air between the trachea and lungs

b. passageway for air to the bronchi

c. located in the thoracic cavity

d. membrane covering the lung

e. lymphoid tissue behind the nasal cavity

f. acts as food and air passageway

g. location of the vocal cords

h. air sacs at the end of the bronchioles

i. keeps food out of the trachea and larynx

Exercise 2

Fill in the blanks with the correct terms.

1. The partition that separates the right and left nasal cavities is called the ___nasal___ ___septum___.

2. The ___epiglottis___ is a flap of cartilage that prevents food from entering the larynx.

3. The smallest subdivisions of the bronchial tree are the ___bronchioles___.

4. The ___nose___ serves as a filter to moisten and warm air entering the body.

5. The thoracic cavity is separated from the abdominal cavity by the ___diaphragm___.

6. The space between the lungs is called the ___mediastinum___.

7. The lymphoid tissues located in the pharynx behind the mouth are called the ___tonsils___.

WORD PARTS

Combining Forms of the Respiratory System

Study the word parts and their definitions listed below. Completing the exercises that follow will help you learn the terms.

Combining Form	Definition
adenoid/o	adenoids
alveol/o	alveolus
bronch/i, bronch/o	bronchus

(NOTE: Both *i* and *o* combining vowels are used with the word root *bronch*.)

> **Adenoid**
>
> is derived from the Greek **aden,** meaning **gland** and **eidos,** meaning **like.** The word was once used for the prostate gland. The first adenoid surgery was performed in 1868.

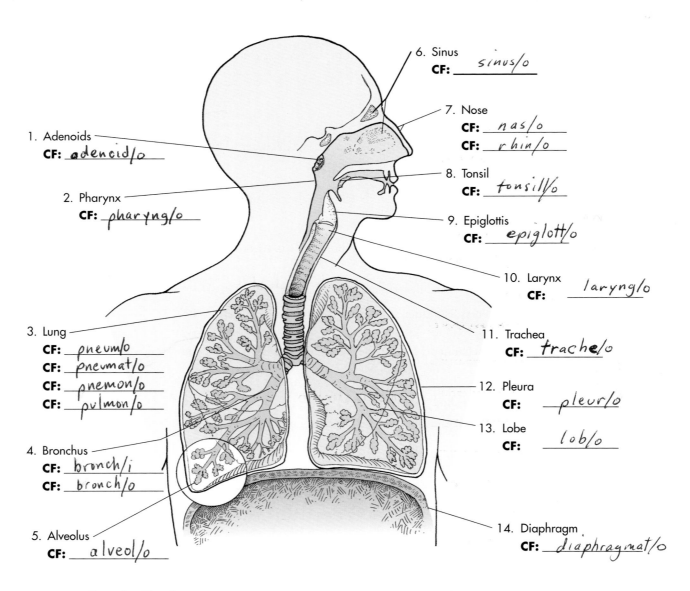

1. Adenoids
   CF: _adenoid/o_

2. Pharynx
   CF: _pharyng/o_

3. Lung
   CF: _pneum/o_
   CF: _pneumat/o_
   CF: _pnemon/o_
   CF: _pulmon/o_

4. Bronchus
   CF: _bronch/i_
   CF: _bronch/o_

5. Alveolus
   CF: _alveol/o_

6. Sinus
   CF: _sinus/o_

7. Nose
   CF: _nas/o_
   CF: _rhin/o_

8. Tonsil
   CF: _tonsill/o_

9. Epiglottis
   CF: _epiglott/o_

10. Larynx
    CF: _laryng/o_

11. Trachea
    CF: _trache/o_

12. Pleura
    CF: _pleur/o_

13. Lobe
    CF: _lob/o_

14. Diaphragm
    CF: _diaphragmat/o_

Exercise Fig. A
Fill in the blanks with combining forms in this diagram of the respiratory system.

diaphragmat/o . . . .   diaphragm

epiglott/o . . . .   epiglottis

laryng/o . . . .   larynx

lob/o . . . .   lobe

nas/o

rhin/o . . . .   nose

pharyng/o . . . .   pharynx

pleur/o . . . .   pleura

pneum/o

pneumat/o

pneumon/o . . . .   lung, air

pulmon/o . . . .   lung

sinus/o . . . .   sinus

sept/o . . . .   septum (wall off, fence)

thorac/o . . . .   thorax (chest)

tonsill/o . . . .   tonsil

    (NOTE: Tonsil has one *l,* and
the combining form has two *l's.*)

trache/o . . . .   trachea

Lobe
literally means **the part that hangs down,** although it comes from the Greek **lobos,** meaning **capsule** or **pod.** Also applied to the lobe of an ear, liver, or brain.

Learn the anatomical locations and meanings of the combining forms by completing Exercise Figure A and exercises 3 and 4.

Exercise 3

Write the definitions of the following combining forms.

1. laryng/o _____laryux_____

2. bronch/o, bronch/i _____bronchus_____

3. pleur/o _____pleura_____

4. pneum/o _____lung, air_____

5. tonsill/o _____tonsil_____

6. pulmon/o _____lung_____

7. diaphragmat/o _____diaphragm_____

8. trache/o _____trachea_____

9. alveol/o _____alveolus_____

10. pneumon/o _____lung, air_____

11. thorac/o _____thorax (chest)_____

12. adenoid/o _____ *adenoid*

13. pharyng/o _____ *pharynx*

14. rhin/o _____ *nose*

15. sinus/o _____ *sinus*

16. lob/o _____ *lobe*

17. epiglott/o _____ *epiglottis*

18. pneumat/o _____ *lung, air*

19. nas/o _____ *nose*

20. sept/o _____ *septum (wall off, fence)*

Exercise 4

Write the combining form for each of the following terms.

1. nose
   a. *nas/o*
   b. *rhin/o*

2. larynx
   laryng/o

3. lung, air
   a. *pneum/o*
   b. *pneumat/o*
   c. *pneumon/o*

4. lung
   pulmon/o

5. tonsils
   tonsill/o

6. trachea
   trache/o

7. adenoids
   adenoid/o

8. pleura
   pleur/o

9. diaphragm
   diaphragmat/o

10. sinus
    sinus/o

11. thorax
    thorac/o

12. alveolus
    alveol/o

13. pharynx   _pharyng/o_

14. bronchus   a. _bronch/i_

             b. _bronch/o_

15. lobe   _lob/o_

16. epiglottis   _epiglott/o_

17. septum   _sept/o_

Combining Forms Commonly Used With Respiratory System Terms

Combining Form	Definition
atel/o	imperfect, incomplete
hem/o, hemat/o	blood
muc/o	mucus
orth/o	straight
ox/o, ox/i	oxygen
(NOTE: The combining vowels *o* and *i* are used with the word root *ox.*)	
py/o	pus
spir/o	breathe, breathing

Learn the combining forms by completing exercises 5 and 6.

Oxygen

was discovered in 1774 by Joseph Priestly. In 1775 Antoine-Laurent Lavoisier, a French chemist, noted that all the acids he knew contained oxygen. Because he thought it was an acid producer, he named it using the Greek **oxys,** meaning **sour,** and the suffix **gen,** meaning **to produce.**

Exercise 5

Write the definition of the following combining forms.

1. ox/o, ox/i _oxygen_

2. spir/o _breathe, breathing_

3. muc/o _mucus_

4. atel/o _imperfect, incomplete_

5. orth/o _straight_

6. py/o _pus_

7. hem/o, hemat/o _blood_

Exercise 6

Write the combining form for each of the following.

1. breathe, breathing   _spir/o_

2. oxygen   a. _ox/o_

                          b. _ox/i_

3. imperfect, incomplete   _atel/o_

4. straight   _orth/o_

5. pus   _py/o_

6. mucus   _muc/o_

7. blood   a. _hem/o_

                          b. _hemat/o_

Prefixes

Prefix	Definition
a-, an- (NOTE: *An-* is used when the word root begins with a vowel.)	without or absence of
endo- (NOTE: The prefix *intra-*, introduced in Chapter 4, also means *within*).	within
eu-	normal, good
pan-	all, total

Learn the prefixes by completing exercises 7 and 8.

Exercise 7

Write the definitions of the following prefixes.

1. endo- _within_

2. a-, an- _without or absence of_

3. pan- _all, total_

4. eu- _normal, good_

Exercise 8

Write the prefix for each of the following.

1. within   _endo-_

2. normal, good   _eu-_

3. without or absence of   a.   _a-_

                            b.   _an-_

4. all, total   _pan-_

Suffixes

Suffix	Definition
-algia	pain
-ar, -ary	pertaining to
-capnia	carbon dioxide
-cele	hernia or protrusion
-centesis	surgical puncture to aspirate fluid (with a sterile needle)
-eal	pertaining to
-ectasis	stretching out, dilatation, expansion
-emia	blood condition
-gram	record, x-ray film
-graphy	process of recording, x-ray filming
-meter	instrument used to measure
-metry	measurement
-orrhagia	rapid flow of blood
-ostomy	creation of an artificial opening
-otomy	cut into or incision
-oxia	oxygen
-pexy	surgical fixation, suspension
-phonia	sound or voice
-pnea	breathing
-scope	instrument used for visual examination
-scopic	pertaining to visual examination
-scopy	visual examination
-spasm	sudden, involuntary muscle contraction (spasmodic contraction)
-stenosis	constriction or narrowing
-thorax	chest

> **Capnia**
>
> is derived from the Greek **kapnos,** meaning **smoke.** It now refers to carbon dioxide.

Learn the suffixes by completing exercises 9, 10, and 11.

Exercise 9

Match the suffixes in the first column with their correct definitions in the second column.

_k_ 1. -algia
_f_ 2. -ar, -ary, -eal
_m_ 3. -capnia
_g_ 4. -cele
_c_ 5. -centesis
_b_ 6. -ectasis
_j_ 7. -emia
_a_ 8. -gram
_l_ 9. -graphy
_h_ 10. -meter
_d_ 11. -metry
_e_ 12. -scopic

a. record, x-ray film
b. stretching out, dilatation, expansion
c. surgical puncture to aspirate fluid
d. measurement
e. pertaining to visual examination
f. pertaining to
g. hernia or protrusion
h. instrument used to measure
i. rapid flow of blood
j. blood condition
k. pain
l. process of recording
m. carbon dioxide

Exercise 10

Match the suffixes in the first column with their correct definitions in the second column.

_c_ 1. -orrhagia
_f_ 2. -ostomy
_a_ 3. -otomy
_i_ 4. -oxia
_k_ 5. -pexy
_e_ 6. -phonia
_j_ 7. -pnea
_b_ 8. -scope
_m_ 9. -scopy
_g_ 10. -spasm
_d_ 11. -stenosis
_h_ 12. -thorax

a. cut into or incision
b. instrument used for visual examination
c. rapid flow of blood
d. constriction, narrowing
e. sound or voice
f. creation of an artificial opening
g. sudden, involuntary muscle contraction
h. chest
i. oxygen
j. breathing
k. surgical fixation, suspension
l. carbon dioxide
m. visual examination

Exercise 11

Write the definitions of the following suffixes.

af

1. -thorax _____ chest

2. -ar, -ary, -eal _____ pertaining to

3. -stenosis _____ constriction or narrowing

4. -cele _____ hernia or protrusion

5. -ostomy _____ creation of an artificial opening

6. -pexy _____ surgical fixation, suspension

7. -meter _____ instrument used to measure

8. -spasm _____ sudden involuntary muscle contraction

9. -algia _____ pain

10. -scopy _____ visual examination

11. -centesis _____ surgical puncture to aspirate fluid

12. -otomy _____ cut into or incision

13. -scope _____ instrument used for visual examination

14. -orrhagia _____ rapid flow of blood

15. -ectasis _____ stretching out, dilation, expansion

16. -gram _____ record, x-ray film

17. -pnea _____ breathing

18. -graphy _____ process of recording, xray filming

19. -metry _____ measurement

20. -emia _____ blood condition

21. -oxia _____ oxygen

22. -capnia _____ carbon dioxide

23. -phonia _____ sound or voice

24. -scopic _____ pertaining to visual examination

MEDICAL TERMS

The terms you need to learn to complete this chapter are listed below. The exercises following each list will help you learn the definition and the spelling of each word.

Disease and Disorder Terms

Built From Word Parts

Term	Definition
adenoiditis . . . . (*ad*-e-noyd-Ī-tis)	inflammation of the adenoids
atelectasis . . . . (at-e-LEK-ta-sis)	incomplete expansion (of the lung of a newborn or collapsed lung) (Figure 5-4)
bronchiectasis . . . . (*bron*-ki-EK-ta-sis)	dilatation of the bronchi (Exercise Figure B)
bronchitis . . . . (bron-KĪ-tis)	inflammation of the bronchi
bronchogenic carcinoma . . . . (bron-kō-JEN-ik) (kar-si-NŌ-ma)	cancerous tumor originating in the bronchus
bronchopneumonia . . . . (*bron*-kō-nū-MŌ-nē-a)	diseased state of the bronchi and lungs
diaphragmatocele . . . . (*dī*-a-frag-MAT-ō-sēl)	hernia of the diaphragm
epiglottitis . . . . (*ep*-i-glot-Ī-tis)	inflammation of the epiglottis
hemothorax . . . . (hē-mō-THŌ-raks)	blood in the chest (pleural space)
laryngitis . . . . (*lar*-in-JĪ-tis)	inflammation of the larynx
laryngotracheobronchitis (LTB) . . (lar-*ing*-gō-*trā*-kē-ō-bron-KĪ-tis)	inflammation of the larynx, trachea, and bronchi; the acute form is called *croup*
lobar pneumonia . . . . (LŌ-bar) (nū-MŌ-nē-a)	diseased state of a lobe(s) of the lung
nasopharyngitis . . . . (nā-zō-far-in-JĪ-tis)	inflammation of the nose and pharynx
pansinusitis . . . . (*pan*-sī-nū-SĪ-tis)	inflammation of all sinuses
pharyngitis . . . . (far-in-JĪ-tis)	inflammation of the pharynx
pleuritis . . . . (plū-RĪ-tis)	inflammation of the pleura (also called *pleurisy*)
pneumatocele . . . . (nū-MAT-ō-sēl)	hernia of the lung (lung tissue protrudes through an opening in the chest)

Atelectasis

is derived from the Greek **ateles**, meaning **not perfect**, and **ektasis**, meaning **expansion**. It denotes an incomplete expansion of the lungs, especially at birth.

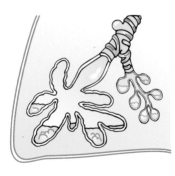

Fig. 5-4
Atelectasis showing the collapsed alveoli.

Exercise Fig. B
Fill in the blanks to label the diagram.

bronch / i / ectasis
BRONCHUS / CV / DILATATION
showing the alveoli

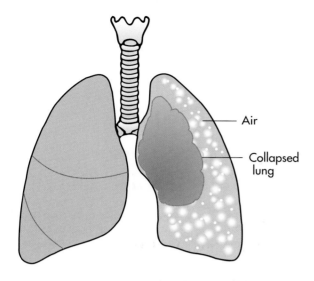

Air

Collapsed lung

Exercise Fig. C
Fill in the blanks to label the diagram.

pneumo / o / thorax
AIR / CV / CHEST

pneumonia . . . . (nū-MŌ-nē-a)	diseased state of the lung (the infection and inflammation is caused by bacteria such as *Pneumococcus, Staphylococcus, Streptococcus,* and *Haemophilus;* viruses; and fungi.)
pneumonitis . . . . (*nū*-mō-NĪ-tis)	inflammation of the lung
pneumoconiosis . . . . (nū-mō-*kō*-nē-Ō-sis)	abnormal condition of dust in the lungs
pneumothorax . . . . (*nū*-mō-THŌ-raks)	air in the chest (pleural space), which causes collapse of the lung (Exercise Figure C)
pulmonary neoplasm . . . . (PUL-mō-nar-ē) (NĒ-ō-plazm)	new growth (tumor) in the lung
pyothorax . . . . (pī-ō-THŌ-raks)	pus in the chest (pleural space) (also called *empyema*)
rhinitis . . . . (rī-NĪ-tis)	inflammation of the (mucous membranes) nose
rhinomycosis . . . . (*rī*-nō-mī-KŌ-sis)	abnormal condition of fungus in the nose
rhinorrhagia . . . . (rī-nō-RĀ-jē-a)	rapid flow of blood from the nose (also called *epistaxis*)
thoracalgia . . . . (thō-rak-AL-jē-a)	pain in the chest
tonsillitis . . . . (*ton*-sil-Ī-tis)	inflammation of the tonsils
tracheitis . . . . (trā-kē-Ī-tis)	inflammation of the trachea
tracheostenosis . . . . (trā-kē-ō-sten-Ō-sis)	narrowing of the trachea

> **Pneumoconiosis**
>
> is the general name given for chronic inflammatory disease of the lung caused by excessive inhalation of mineral dust. When the disease is caused by a specific dust, it is named for the dust. For example, the disease caused by silica dust is called **silicosis.**

Practice saying each of these terms aloud. To assist you in pronunciation, obtain the audiotape designed for use with this text. Learn the definitions and spellings of the disease and disorder terms by completing exercises 12, 13, and 14.

Ted Small

Exercise 12 ....

Analyze and define the following terms.

EXAMPLE: diaphragmat/o/cele   hernia of the diaphragm

1. pleuritis _____ inflammation of the pleura
2. nasopharyngitis _____ inflammation of the nose and pharynx
3. pneumothorax _____ air in the chest, which causes collapse of the lung
4. pansinusitis _____ inflammation of all sinuses
5. atelectasis _____ incomplete expansion
6. rhinomycosis _____ abnormal condition of fungus in the nose
7. tracheostenosis _____ narrowing of the trachea
8. epiglottitis _____ inflammation of the epiglottis
9. thoracalgia _____ pain in the chest
10. pulmonary neoplasm _____ new growth (tumor) in the lung
11. bronchiectasis _____ dilation of the bronchi
12. tonsillitis _____ inflammation of the tonsils
13. pneumoconiosis _____ abnormal condition of dust in the lungs
14. bronchopneumonia _____ diseased state of the bronchi and lungs
15. pneumonitis _____ inflammation of the lung
16. laryngitis _____ inflammation of the larynx
17. pneumatocele _____ hernia of the lung
18. pyothorax _____ pus in the chest
19. rhinorrhagia _____ rapid flow of blood from the nose
20. bronchitis _____ inflammation of the bronchi
21. pharyngitis _____ inflammation of the pharynx
22. tracheitis _____ inflammation of the trachea
23. laryngotracheobronchitis _____ inflammation of the larynx, trachea, and bronchi
24. adenoiditis _____ inflammation of the adenoids

25. hemothorax _____ blood in the chest

26. lobar pneumonia _____ diseased state of a lobe(s) of the lung

27. rhinitis _____ inflammation of the (mucous membranes) nose

28. bronchogenic carcinoma _____ cancerous tumor originating in the bronchus

29. pneumonia _____ diseased state of the lung

Exercise 13

Build disease and disorder terms for the following definitions using the word parts you have learned.

EXAMPLE: inflammation of the tonsils $\dfrac{\text{tonsill}}{\text{WR}} \Big/ \dfrac{\text{itis}}{\text{S}}$

1. pain in the chest

$\dfrac{\text{thorac}}{\text{WR}} \Big/ \dfrac{\text{algia}}{\text{S}}$

2. abnormal condition of fungus (infection) in the nose

$\dfrac{\text{rhin}}{\text{WR}} \Big/ \dfrac{\text{o}}{\text{CV}} \Big/ \dfrac{\text{myc}}{\text{WR}} \Big/ \dfrac{\text{osis}}{\text{S}}$

3. hernia of the lung

$\dfrac{\text{pneumat}}{\text{WR}} \Big/ \dfrac{\text{o}}{\text{CV}} \Big/ \dfrac{\text{cele}}{\text{S}}$

4. new growth (tumor) in the lung

$\dfrac{\text{pulmon}}{\text{WR}} \Big/ \dfrac{\text{ary}}{\text{S}}$ $\dfrac{\text{neo}}{\text{P}} \Big/ \dfrac{\text{plasm}}{\text{S(WR)}}$

5. inflammation of the larynx

$\dfrac{\text{laryng}}{\text{WR}} \Big/ \dfrac{\text{itis}}{\text{S}}$

6. incomplete expansion (of the lung)

$\dfrac{\text{atel}}{\text{WR}} \Big/ \dfrac{\text{ectasis}}{\text{S}}$

7. inflammation of the adenoids

$\dfrac{\text{adenoid}}{\text{WR}} \Big/ \dfrac{\text{itis}}{\text{S}}$

8. inflammation of the larynx, trachea, and bronchi

$\dfrac{\text{laryng}}{\text{WR}} \Big/ \dfrac{\text{o}}{\text{CV}} \Big/ \dfrac{\text{trache}}{\text{WR}} \Big/ \dfrac{\text{o}}{\text{CV}} \Big/ \dfrac{\text{bronch}}{\text{WR}} \Big/ \dfrac{\text{itis}}{\text{S}}$

9. dilatation of the bronchi

$\dfrac{\text{bronch}}{\text{WR}} \Big/ \dfrac{\text{i}}{\text{CV}} \Big/ \dfrac{\text{ectasis}}{\text{S}}$

10. inflammation of the pleura

$\dfrac{\text{pleur}}{\text{WR}} \Big/ \dfrac{\text{itis}}{\text{S}}$

11. abnormal condition of dust in the lung

$\dfrac{\text{pneum}}{\text{WR}} \Big/ \dfrac{\text{o}}{\text{CV}} \Big/ \dfrac{\text{coni}}{\text{WR}} \Big/ \dfrac{\text{osis}}{\text{S}}$

12. inflammation of the lung

pneumon | itis
WR   S

13. inflammation of all sinuses

pan | sinus | itis
P   WR   S

14. narrowing of the trachea

trache | o | stenosis
WR / CV / S

15. inflammation of the nose and pharynx

nas | o | pharyng | itis
WR / CV / WR / S

16. pus in the chest (pleural space)

py | o | thorax
WR / CV / S

17. inflammation of the epiglottis

epiglott | itis
WR / S

18. hernia of the diaphragm

diaphragmat | o | cele
WR / CV / S

19. air in the chest (pleural space)

pneum | o | thorax
WR / CV / S

20. diseased state of the bronchi and the lungs

bronch | o | pneumon | ia
WR / CV / WR / S

21. rapid flow of blood from the nose

rhin | orrhagia
WR / S

22. inflammation of the pharynx

pharyng | itis
WR / S

23. blood in the chest (pleural space)

hem | o | thorax
WR / CV / S

24. inflammation of the trachea

trache | itis
WR / S

25. inflammation of the bronchi

bronch | itis
WR / S

26. pertaining to disease state of lobe(s) of the lung(s)

lob | ar   pneumon | ia
WR / S   WR / S

27. inflammation of the (mucous membranes) nose

rhin | itis
WR / S

28. cancerous tumor originating in a bronchus

bronch | o | genic
WR / CV / S

carcin | oma
WR / S

29. diseased state of the lung

pneumon | ia
WR / S

Exercise 14

Spell each of the disease and disorder terms. Have someone dictate the terms on pp. 96-97 to you, or say the words into a tape recorder. Then spell the words from your recording as often as necessary. Think about the word parts before attempting to write the word. Study any words you have spelled incorrectly.

1. _____
2. _____
3. _____
4. _____
5. _____
6. _____
7. _____
8. _____
9. _____
10. _____
11. _____
12. _____
13. _____
14. _____
15. _____

16. _____
17. _____
18. _____
19. _____
20. _____
21. _____
22. _____
23. _____
24. _____
25. _____
26. _____
27. _____
28. _____
29. _____
30. _____

Disease and Disorder Terms

Not Built From Word Parts

Term	Definition
adult respiratory distress syndrome (ARDS)	respiratory failure in an adult as a result of disease or injury. Symptoms include dyspnea, rapid breathing, and cyanosis.
asthma . . . . (AZ-ma)	respiratory disease characterized by paroxysms of coughing, wheezing, and shortness of breath
chronic obstructive pulmonary disease (COPD) . . . . (KRON-ik) (ob-STRUK-tiv) (PUL-mō-nar-ē) (di-ZĒZ)	any persistent lung disease that obstructs the bronchial airflow, such as asthma, chronic bronchitis, and emphysema
coccidioidomycosis . . . . (kok-*sid*-ē-oyd-ō-mī-KŌ-sis)	fungal disease affecting the lungs and sometimes other organs of the body (also called *valley fever* or *cocci*)

not on test

Adult respiratory distress syndrome

(ARDS) is respiratory failure in an adult. In newborns the condition is referred to as respiratory distress syndrome of newborn (RDS) or **hyaline membrane disease.**

Asthma

is derived from the Greek **astma,** meaning **to pant.**

Fig. 5-5
Emphysema showing the distended alveoli.

Pneumocystis Carinii Pneumonia

Before the 1980s, *Pneumocystis carinii* **pneumonia** was rare. During the 1980s it became the most common opportunistic infection of AIDS patients. Now 60% to 80% of AIDS patients develop *Pneumocystis carinii* pneumonia.

cor pulmonale . . . . serious cardiac disease associated with chronic
(kōr) (pul-mō-NAL-ē)   lung disorders, such as emphysema

croup . . . . condition resulting from acute obstruction of
(krūp)   the larynx, which occurs in children

cystic fibrosis (CF) . . . . generalized hereditary disorder of infants and
(SIS-tik) (fī-BRŌ-sis)   children characterized by excess mucus production in the respiratory tract

deviated septum . . . . one part of the nasal cavity is smaller because
(SEP-tum)   of malformation or injury

emphysema . . . . stretching of lung tissue caused by the alveoli
(em-fi-SĒ-ma)   becoming distended and losing elasticity
  (Figure 5-5)

epistaxis . . . . nosebleed (synonymous with *rhinorrhagia*)
(ep-i-STAK-sis)

influenza . . . . highly infectious respiratory disease caused by
(*in*-flū-EN-za)   a virus (also called *flu*)

Legionnaire's disease . . . . a lobar pneumonia caused by the bacterium
(lē-JE-narz)   *Legionella pneumophila*

obstructive sleep apnea (OSA) . . . repetitive pharyngeal collapse during sleep,
(AP-nē-a)   which leads to absence of breathing (Figure
  5-6)

pertussis . . . . respiratory disease characterized by an acute
(per-TUS-sis)   crowing inspiration, or whoop (synonymous
  with *whooping cough*)

pleural effusion . . . . escape of fluid into the pleural space as a result
(PLŪ-ral) (e-FŪ-zhun)   of inflammation

Pneumocystis carinii (P. carinii)
pneumonia (PCP) . . . . a pneumonia caused by *P. carinii,* a fungus.
(nū-mō-SIS-tis) (car-i-Nē-ī)   Common disease of AIDS patients

pulmonary edema . . . . fluid accumulation in the alveoli and bronchi-
(PUL-mō-nar-ē) (e-DĒ-ma)   oles

pulmonary embolism
(*pl.* **emboli) (PE)** . . . . foreign matter, such as a blood clot, air, or fat
(PUL-mō-nar-ē) (EM-bō-lizm)   clot carried in the circulation to the pulmonary
  artery, where it acts as a block

tuberculosis (TB) . . . . an infectious disease, caused by an acid-fast
(tū-ber-kū-LŌ-sis)   bacillus, most commonly spread by inhalation
  of infected droplets, and usually affecting the
  lungs

upper respiratory infection (URI) infection of the pharynx, larynx, trachea, and
(RE-spi-ra-tō-rē)   bronchi

Practice saying each of these terms aloud. To assist you in pronunciation, obtain the audiotape designed for use with this text. Learn the definitions and spellings of the diagnostic terms by completing exercises 15, 16, and 17.

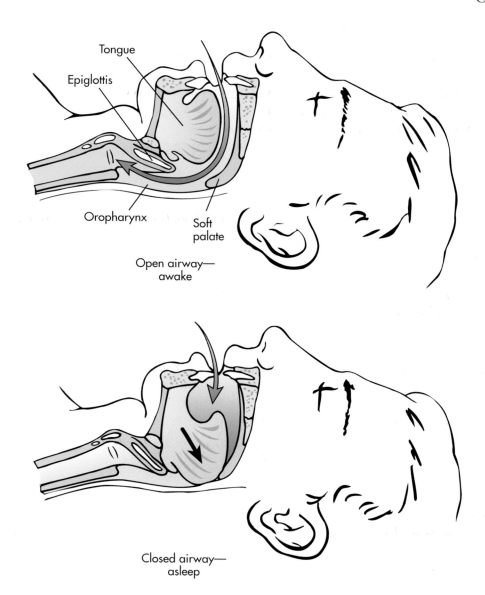

Tongue

Epiglottis

Oropharynx

Soft palate

Open airway—awake

Closed airway—asleep

Fig. 5-6
Obstructive sleep apnea. During sleep the absence of activity of the pharyngeal muscle structure allows the airway to close.

Exercise 15

Fill in the blanks with the correct terms.

1. A disease characterized by lung tissue stretching that results from the alveoli losing elasticity and becoming distended is called *emphysema*.

2. *pleural effusion* is the name given to the escape of fluid into the pleural space as a result of inflammation.

3. A cardiac condition that is associated with chronic lung disorders is called __cor____ __pulmonale____.

4. A fungal disease affecting the lungs is called __coccidioidomycosis__.

5. __cystic____ __fibrosis____ is a hereditary disease characterized by excess mucus production in the respiratory tract.

6. The medical name of the infectious respiratory disease commonly referred to as flu is __influenza____.

7. Any persistent lung disease that obstructs the bronchial airflow is known by the general term __chronic____ __obstructive____ __pulmonary____ __disease____.

8. The medical name for the disease characterized by an acute crowing inspiration is __pertussis____.

9. __Croup____ is a condition resulting from an acute obstruction of the larynx.

10. A chronic respiratory disease characterized by shortness of breath, wheezing, and paroxysmal coughing is called __asthma____.

11. A condition in which fluid accumulates in the alveoli and bronchioles is __pulmonary____ __edema____.

12. A(n) __upper____ __respiratory____ __infection____ generally refers to an infection involving the pharynx, larynx, trachea, and bronchi.

13. Foreign matter, such as a clot, air, or fat carried in the circulation to the pulmonary artery where it acts as a block is called a(n) __pulmonary____ __embolism____.

14. __Epistaxis____ is another name for nosebleed.

15. A lobar pneumonia caused by the *Legionella pneumophila* bacterium commonly is called __Legionnaire's____ __disease____.

16. A pneumonia often found in AIDS patients is called __Pneumocystis____ __carinii____ __pneumonia____.

17. __Deviated____ __Septum____ is one part of the nasal cavity that is smaller than the other because of malformation or injury.

18. The diagnosis for repetitive pharyngeal collapse is __obstructive____ __sleep____ __apnea____.

19. An infectious disease usually affecting the lungs by inhaling small droplets is __tuberculosis____.

20. __Adult____ __respiratory____ __distress____ __Syndrome____ occurs in adults as a result of disease or injury.

Exercise 16

Match the terms in the first column with the correct definitions in the second column.

_h_ 1. asthma

_t_ 2. chronic obstructive pulmonary disease

_o_ 3. coccidioidomycosis

_k_ 4. cor pulmonale

_n_ 5. croup

_e_ 6. cystic fibrosis

_a_ 7. emphysema

_j_ 8. epistaxis

_b_ 9. influenza

_p_ 10. Legionnaire's disease

_g_ 11. pertussis

_d_ 12. pleural effusion

_f_ 13. pulmonary edema

_i_ 14. pulmonary embolism

_l_ 15. upper respiratory infection

_q_ 16. deviated septum

_s_ 17. obstructive sleep apnea

_m_ 18. *P. carinii* pneumonia

_u_ 19. tuberculosis

_c_ 20. adult respiratory distress syndrome

a. alveoli become distended and lose elasticity

b. caused by a virus (commonly called *flu*)

c. respiratory failure in an adult

d. escape of fluid into pleural cavity

e. hereditary disorder characterized by excess mucus in the respiratory tract

f. fluid accumulation in alveoli and bronchioles

g. whooping cough

h. characterized by wheezing, paroxysmal coughing, and shortness of breath

i. foreign material, moved by circulation, that blocks pulmonary artery

j. nosebleed

k. cardiac disease associated with chronic lung disorders

l. infection of pharynx, larynx, trachea, and bronchi

m. common in AIDS patients

n. condition resulting from obstruction of the larynx

o. also called *valley fever*

p. a lobar pneumonia caused by bacterium *Legionella pneumophila*

q. unequal size of nasal cavities

r. narrowing of the trachea

s. repetitive pharyngeal collapse

t. name given to any persistent lung disease that obstructs the bronchial airflow

u. an infectious disease, usually affecting the lungs

Exercise 17 ....

Spell the disease and disorder terms. Have someone dictate the terms on pp. 101-102 to you, or say the words into a tape recorder. Then spell the words from your recording. Study any words you have spelled incorrectly.

1. _____   11. _____

2. _____   12. _____

3. _____   13. _____

4. _____   14. _____

5. _____   15. _____

6. _____   16. _____

7. _____   17. _____

8. _____   18. _____

9. _____   19. _____

10. _____   20. _____

Surgical Terms

Built From Word Parts

Term	Definition
adenoidectomy .... (*ad*-e-noyd-EK-tō-mē)	excision of the adenoids
bronchoplasty .... (BRON-kō-plas-tē)	surgical repair of a bronchus
laryngectomy .... (lār-in-JEK-tō-mē)	excision of the larynx
laryngocentesis .... (lār-in-gō-sen-TĒ-sis)	surgical puncture to aspirate fluid from the larynx
laryngoplasty .... (lar-IN-gō-*plas*-tē)	surgical repair of the larynx
laryngostomy .... (lar-in-GOS-tō-mē)	creation of an artificial opening into the larynx
laryngotracheotomy .... (lar-in-gō-*trā*-kē-OT-ō-mē)	incision of the larynx and trachea
lobectomy .... (lō-BEK-tō-mē)	excision of a lobe (of the lung) (Figure 5-7)
pleurocentesis .... (*plūr*-ō-sen-TĒ-sis)	surgical puncture to aspirate fluid from pleural space
pleuropexy .... (plū-rō-PEK-sē)	surgical fixation of the pleura

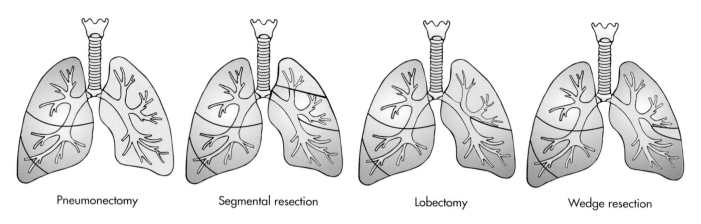

Pneumonectomy   Segmental resection   Lobectomy   Wedge resection

Fig. 5-7
Types of lung resection. The diagram illustrates the amount of lung tissue removed with each type of surgery.

pneumobronchotomy . . . .   incision of lung and bronchus
   (*nū*-mō-bron-KOT-ō-mē)

pneumonectomy . . . .   excision of a lung (Figure 5-7)
   (*nū*-mō-NEK-tō-mē)

rhinoplasty . . . .   surgical repair of the nose (Figure 5-8)
   (RĪ-nō-plast-ē)

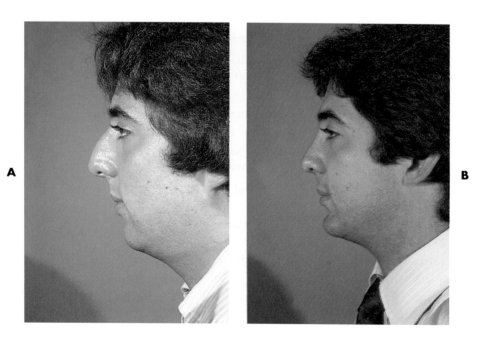

A   B

Fig. 5-8
Side view of patient before **(A)** and after **(B)** rhinoplasty and chin augmentation.

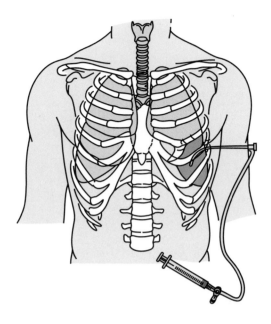

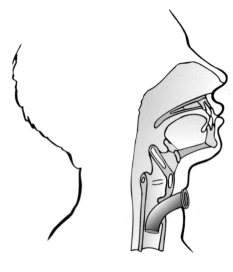

Exercise Fig. D
Fill in the blanks to label the diagram.

thorac / o / centesis

CHEST   /   CV   /   SURGICAL PUNCTURE TO
REMOVE FLUID

is a procedure done to aid in diagnosis or
as a treatment.

Exercise Fig. E
Fill in the blanks to label the diagram.

trache / ostomy

TRACHEA / CREATION OF AN ARTIFICIAL OPENING,
with tube in place.

septoplasty . . . . (*sep*-tō-PLAS-tē)	surgical repair of the (nasal) septum
septotomy . . . . (*sep*-TOT-ō-mē)	incision into the (nasal) septum
sinusotomy . . . . (*sī*-nū-SOT-ō-mē)	incision of a sinus
thoracocentesis . . . . (*thō*-rak-ō-sen-TĒ-sis)	surgical puncture to aspirate fluid from the chest cavity (also called *thoracentesis*) (Exercise Figure D)
thoracotomy . . . . (*thō*-rak-OT-ō-mē)	incision into the chest cavity
tonsillectomy . . . . (*ton*-sil-EK-tō-mē)	excision of the tonsils
tracheoplasty . . . . (TRĀ-kē-ō-*plas*-tē)	surgical repair of the trachea
tracheostomy . . . . (*trā*-kē-OS-tō-mē)	creation of an artificial opening into the trachea (Exercise Figure E)
tracheotomy . . . . (*trā*-kē-OT-ō-mē)	incision of the trachea

Endoscopic thoracotomy

and **thoracoscopy** are current
terms used to describe the use of
an endoscope (thoracoscope) to
perform a **thoracotomy.**

Practice saying each of these terms aloud. To assist you in pronunciation, obtain the
audiotape designed for use with this text. Learn the definitions and spellings of the
surgical terms by completing exercises 18, 19, and 20.

Exercise 18

Analyze and define the following surgical terms.

  EXAMPLE: pneumon/ectomy   *excision of lung*
          WR   S

1. trache/otomy   *incision of the trachea*
2. laryng/ostomy   *creation of an artificial opening into the larynx*
3. adenoid/ectomy   *excision of the adenoids*
4. rhin/o/plasty   *surgical repair of the nose*
5. pleur/o/centesis   *surgical puncture to aspirate fluid from pleural space*
6. trache/ostomy   *creation of an artificial opening into the trachea*
7. sinus/otomy   *incision of a sinus*
8. laryng/o/plasty   *surgical repair of the larynx*
9. pneum/o/bronch/otomy   *incision of lung and bronchus*
10. bronch/o/plasty   *surgical repair of a bronchus*
11. lob/ectomy   *excision of a lobe (of the lung)*
12. laryng/o/trache/otomy   *incision of the larynx and trachea*
13. trache/o/plasty   *surgical repair of the trachea*
14. thorac/otomy   *incision of the chest cavity*
15. laryng/ectomy   *excision of the larynx*
16. thorac/o/centesis   *surgical puncture to aspirate fluid from the chest cavity*
17. tonsill/ectomy   *excision of the tonsils*
18. laryng/o/centesis   *surgical puncture to aspirate fluid from the larynx*
19. pleur/o/pexy   *surgical fixation of the pleura*
20. sept/o/plasty   *surgical repair of the (nasal) septum*
21. sept/otomy   *incision of the (nasal) septum*

Exercise 19

Build surgical terms for the following definitions by using the word parts you have learned.

EXAMPLE: surgical fixation of the pleura $\dfrac{pleur}{WR} \Big/ \dfrac{o}{CV} \Big/ \dfrac{pexy}{S}$

1. surgical repair of the trachea $\dfrac{trache}{WR} \Big/ \dfrac{o}{CV} \Big/ \dfrac{plasty}{S}$

2. incision of larynx and trachea $\dfrac{laryng}{WR} \Big/ \dfrac{o}{CV} \Big/ \dfrac{trache}{WR} \Big/ \dfrac{otomy}{S}$

3. surgical puncture to aspirate fluid from pleural space $\dfrac{pleur}{WR} \Big/ \dfrac{o}{CV} \Big/ \dfrac{centesis}{S}$

4. incision into the chest cavity $\dfrac{thorac}{WR} \Big/ \dfrac{otomy}{S}$

5. creation of an artificial opening into the trachea $\dfrac{trache}{WR} \Big/ \dfrac{ostomy}{S}$

6. excision of the tonsils $\dfrac{tonsill}{WR} \Big/ \dfrac{ectomy}{S}$

7. incision of the trachea $\dfrac{trache}{WR} \Big/ \dfrac{otomy}{S}$

8. surgical repair of a bronchus $\dfrac{bronch}{WR} \Big/ \dfrac{o}{CV} \Big/ \dfrac{plasty}{S}$

9. excision of the larynx $\dfrac{laryng}{WR} \Big/ \dfrac{ectomy}{S}$

10. surgical puncture to aspirate fluid from the larynx $\dfrac{laryng}{WR} \Big/ \dfrac{o}{CV} \Big/ \dfrac{centesis}{S}$

11. surgical repair of the nose $\dfrac{rhin}{WR} \Big/ \dfrac{o}{CV} \Big/ \dfrac{plasty}{S}$

12. incision of a sinus $\dfrac{sinus}{WR} \Big/ \dfrac{otomy}{S}$

13. surgical puncture to aspirate fluid from the chest cavity $\dfrac{thorac}{WR} \Big/ \dfrac{o}{CV} \Big/ \dfrac{centesis}{S}$

or $\dfrac{thora}{WR} \Big/ \dfrac{centesis}{S}$

14. excision of the adenoids

adenoid / *ectomy*
WR / S

15. surgical repair of the larynx

laryng / *o* / *plasty*
WR / CV / S

16. excision of a lobe of the lung

lob / *ectomy*
WR / S

17. incision of a lung and bronchus

pneum / *o* / *bronch* *otomy*
WR / CV / WR / S

18. creation of an artificial opening into the larynx

laryng / *ostomy*
WR / S

19. excision of a lung

pneumon / *ectomy*
WR / S

20. incision into the septum

sept / *otomy*
WR / S

21. surgical repair of the septum

sept / *o* / *plasty*
WR / CV / S

Exercise 20

Spell each of the surgical terms. Have someone dictate the terms on pp. 106-108 to you, or say the words into a tape recorder. Then spell the words from your recording. Think about the word parts before attempting to write the word. Study any words you have spelled incorrectly.

1. _____   12. _____
2. _____   13. _____
3. _____   14. _____
4. _____   15. _____
5. _____   16. _____
6. _____   17. _____
7. _____   18. _____
8. _____   19. _____
9. _____   20. _____
10. _____   21. _____
11. _____   22. _____

Procedural Terms

Built From Word Parts

Term	Definition
Diagnostic Imaging	
bronchogram . . . . (BRON-kō-gram)	x-ray film of the bronchi
bronchography . . . . (bron-KOG-ra-fē)	process of x-ray filming the bronchi
Endoscopy	
bronchoscope . . . . (BRON-kō-skōp)	instrument used for visual examination of the bronchi (Figure 5-9 and Exercise Figure F)
bronchoscopy . . . . (bron-KOS-kō-pē)	visual examination of the bronchi (Exercise Figure F)
endoscope . . . . (EN-dō-skōp)	instrument used for visual examination within a hollow organ or body cavity. (Current trend is to use endoscopes for surgical procedures as well as for viewing.)
endoscopic . . . . (en-dō-SKOP-ic)	pertaining to visual examination of a hollow organ or body cavity. (used to describe the current practice of performing surgeries using endoscopes)
endoscopy . . . . (en-DOS-kō-pē)	visual examination of a hollow organ or body cavity

Scope

is taken from the Greek **skopein,** which means to *see* or to *view.* It also means observing for a purpose. To the ancient Greeks it meant "to look out for, to monitor, or to examine."

Today the suffix **-scope** is used to describe the **instrument used to view or to examine** such as in the term **endoscope** (means instrument used for visual examination within a hollow organ or body cavity). **Scopy** is the suffix, which means **visual examination,** such as in the term **endoscopy** (visual examination of a hollow organ or body cavity). **Scopic** is the adjectival suffix, which means **pertaining to visual examination,** such as in the term **endoscopic** (pertaining to visual examination within a hollow organ or body cavity).

Endoscopic surgery is now a common term used to describe modern surgery performed with the use of endoscopes. Most often the suffixes **-scope, -scopy,** and **-scopic** mean to **visually examine,** and that is the definition given in this text. However, a term included in a subsequent chapter, **stethoscope,** is an instrument used for monitoring and not for viewing.

Fig. 5-9
Fiberoptic bronchoscope.

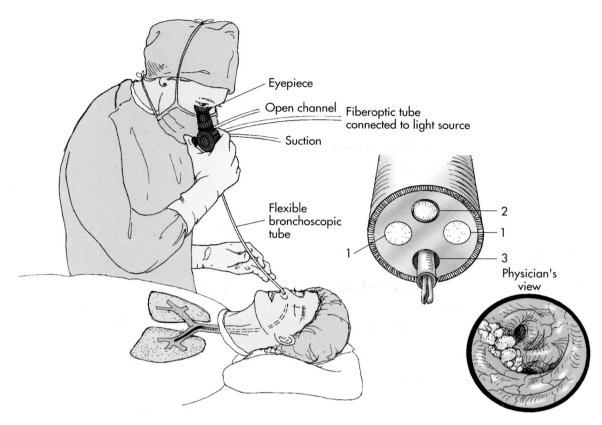

Eyepiece

Open channel   Fiberoptic tube
connected to light source

Suction

Flexible
bronchoscopic
tube

1

2

1

3   Physician's
view

Exercise Fig. F

Fill in the blanks to complete labeling of the diagram. *bronch/o/scopy* BRONCHIS / CV / VISUAL EXAMINATION. The *bronch/o/scope* BRONCHI / CV / INSTRUMENT USED FOR VISUAL EXAMINATION is inserted through the nostril into the bronchi. The tube has four channels: *1*, two light sources; *2*, viewing channel; *3*, channel to hold biopsy forceps and other instruments.

laryngoscope . . . .   instrument used for visual examination of the
  (*lar*-IN-gō-skōp)   larynx

laryngoscopy . . . .   visual examination of the larynx
  (lar-in-GOS-kō-pē)

thoracoscope . . . .   instrument used for visual examination of the
  (tho-RA-kō-skōp)   thorax

thoracoscopy . . . .   visual examination of the thorax
  (tho-ra-KOS-kō-pē)

Pulmonary Function

oximeter . . . .   instrument used to measure oxygen (saturation
  (ok-SIM-e-ter)   in the blood) (Exercise Figure G)
  (NOTE: The combining vowel
  is *i*.)

spirometer . . . .   instrument used to measure breathing (or lung
  (spī-ROM-e-ter)   volumes)

spirometry . . . .   a measurement of breathing (or lung volumes)
  (spī-ROM-e-trē)

> **Diagnostic Imaging Procedures** are diagnostic procedures that produce images, including the following:
>
> *radiography*—x-ray films of internal organs taken using ionizing radiation
>
> *nuclear medicine*—scans using radioactive material to determine functional capacity of an organ
>
> *ultrasound*—sonograms, or echograms, using sound waves to create an image of body organs
>
> *computed tomography*—(CT scans) computerized images of body organs in slices, horizontally.
>
> *magnetic resonance imaging*—(MRI scans), gives information about the body's biochemistry by placing the patient in a magnetic field
>
> **Endoscopy**—endoscopes, which are lighted, flexible instruments are used for visual examination of a hollow organ or body cavity, such as the stomach or larynx
>
> **Laboratory Procedures**—diagnostic procedures performed on specimens such as blood, tissue, sputum, and urine
>
> **Pulmonary Function Tests** (PFT)—diagnostic tests performed to determine lung function

Practice saying each of these words aloud. To assist you in pronunciation, obtain the audiotape designed for use with this text. Learn the definitions and spellings of the procedural terms by completing exercises 21, 22, and 23.

Exercise 21

Analyze and define the following procedural terms.

EXAMPLE: WR CV S
bronch/o/scopy   visual examination of the bronchi
CF

1. spirometer — *instrument used to measure breathing*
2. laryngoscope — *instrument used for visual examination of the* larynx
3. bronchogram — *x-ray film of the bronchi*
4. spirometry — *a measurement of breathing*
5. oximeter — *instrument used to measure oxygen*
6. bronchography — *process of x-ray filming the bronchi*
7. laryngoscopy — *visual examination of the larynx*
8. bronchoscope — *instrument used for visual examination*
9. thoracoscope — *instrument used for visual examination of the thorax*
10. endoscope — *instrument used for visual examination within a hollow organ or body cavity*

11. thoracoscopy _____ visual examination of the thorax
12. endoscopic _____ pertaining to visual examination of a hollow organ or body cavity
13. endoscopy _____ visual examination of a hollow organ or body cavity

Exercise 22

Build procedural terms that correspond to the following definitions by using the word parts you have learned.

EXAMPLE: instrument used to measure oxygen $\dfrac{ox}{WR}$ / $\dfrac{i}{CV}$ / $\dfrac{meter}{S}$

1. visual examination of the larynx

$\dfrac{laryng}{WR}$ / $\dfrac{o}{CV}$ / $\dfrac{scopy}{S}$

2. instrument used to measure breathing

$\dfrac{spir}{WR}$ / $\dfrac{o}{CV}$ / $\dfrac{meter}{S}$

3. x-ray film of the bronchi

$\dfrac{bronch}{WR}$ / $\dfrac{o}{CV}$ / $\dfrac{gram}{S}$

4. instrument used for visual examination of the larynx

$\dfrac{laryng}{WR}$ / $\dfrac{o}{CV}$ / $\dfrac{scope}{S}$

5. visual examination of the bronchi

$\dfrac{bronch}{WR}$ / $\dfrac{o}{CV}$ / $\dfrac{scopy}{S}$

6. measurement of breathing

$\dfrac{spir}{WR}$ / $\dfrac{o}{CV}$ / $\dfrac{metry}{S}$

7. instrument used for visual examination of the bronchi

$\dfrac{bronch}{WR}$ / $\dfrac{o}{CV}$ / $\dfrac{scope}{S}$

8. process of x-ray filming the bronchi

$\dfrac{bronch}{WR}$ / $\dfrac{o}{CV}$ / $\dfrac{graphy}{S}$

9. visual examination of a hollow organ or body cavity

$\dfrac{endo}{P}$ / $\dfrac{scopy}{S(WR)}$

10. instrument used for visual examination of the thorax

$\dfrac{thorac}{WR}$ / $\dfrac{o}{CV}$ / $\dfrac{scope}{S}$

11. instrument used for visual examination of a hollow organ or body cavity

$\dfrac{endo}{P}$ / $\dfrac{scope}{S(WR)}$

12. visual examination of the thorax

thorac / *o* / *scopy*
WR   CV   S

13. pertaining to visual examination of a hollow organ or body cavity

endo / *scopic*
P   S(WR)

Exercise 23 ....

Spell each of the procedural terms. Have someone dictate the terms on pp. 112-113 to you, or say the words into a tape recorder; then spell the words from your recording. Think about the word parts before attempting to write the word. Study any you have spelled incorrectly.

1. _____   8. _____

2. _____   9. _____

3. _____   10. _____

4. _____   11. _____

5. _____   12. _____

6. _____   13. _____

7. _____   14. _____

Procedural Terms
Not Built From Word Parts

Term	Definition
Diagnostic Imaging	
chest CT (computed tomography) scan (tō-MOG-ra-fē)	computerized images of the chest reproduced in sections sliced from front to back horizontally. Used to diagnose tumors, abscesses, and pleural effusion. Computed tomography is used to visualize other body parts such as the abdomen and the brain (Figure 5-10).
chest x-ray (CXR)	an x-ray film of the chest used to evaluate the lungs and the heart. Also referred to as a *chest radiograph* (Figure 5-11).
ventilation-perfusion scanning (VPS) (ven-ti-LĀ-shun) (per-FŪ-zhun)	a nuclear medicine procedure used to diagnose pulmonary embolism and other conditions. Also called *lung scan.*

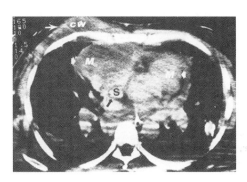

Fig. 5-10
Computed tomographic (CT) scan of the chest.

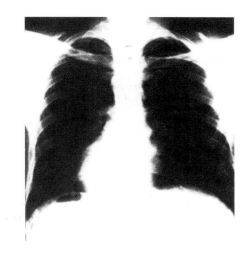

Fig. 5-11
X-ray film of a normal chest.

Clinical Laboratory

NT **acid-fast bacilli (AFB) stain** . . . . .   a test done on sputum to determine the pres-
(AS-id-fast bah-SIL-ī)   ence of acid-fast bacilli, which cause tuberculosis

Pulmonary Function

arterial blood gases (ABG) . . . . . .   a test done on arterial blood to determine levels
(ar-TĒ-rē-al)   of oxygen, carbon dioxide, and other gases
present

pulmonary function tests (PFT) .   a group of tests performed on breathing to de-
(PUL-mō-ner-ē)   termine respiratory function or abnormalities

pulse oximetry . . . .   a noninvasive method of monitoring arterial
(ok-SIM-e-trē)   blood for oxygen levels

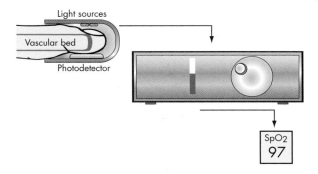

Exercise Fig. G
Fill in the blanks to complete labeling of the diagram. OXYGEN / CV / INSTRUMENT USED TO MEASURE.

Exercise 24

Fill in the blanks with the correct terms.

1. _ventilation-perfusion_ _scanning_ is a nuclear medicine procedure used to diagnose pulmonary embolism and other conditions.

2. Computerized images of the chest, reproduced in sections sliced from front to back horizontally are called a(n) _Chest_ _CT_ _scan_ .

3. _chest_ _x-ray_ is used to evaluate the lungs and the heart.

4. The test done on arterial blood to determine levels of oxygen, carbon dioxide, and other gases present is called _arterial_ _blood_ _gases_ .

5. A noninvasive test to monitor arterial blood for oxygen levels is called _pulse_ _oximetry_ .

6. A test performed on sputum to diagnose tuberculosis is called _acid-fast_ _bacilli_ _stain_ .

7. _Pulmonary_ _function_ _tests_ is the name of a group of tests performed on breathing to determine respiratory function or abnormalities.

Exercise 25

Match the terms in the first column with their correct definitions in the second column.

_f_ 1. ventilation-perfusion scanning

_e_ 2. chest x-ray

_g_ 3. chest CT scan

_d_ 4. acid-fast bacilli stain

_b_ 5. pulse oximetry

_c_ 6. arterial blood gases

_g_ 7. pulmonary function tests

a. computerized images of the chest

b. a noninvasive method used to monitor arterial blood for oxygen levels

c. a blood test used to determine oxygen and other gases in the blood

d. a test for tuberculosis

e. chest radiograph

f. a nuclear medicine procedure used to diagnose pulmonary conditions

g. tests performed on breathing

h. an instrument to measure pulse waves

Exercise 26

Spell each of the terms. Have someone dictate the terms on pp. 116-117 to you, or say the words into a tape recorder. Then spell the words from your recording. Study any words you have spelled incorrectly.

1. _____   5. _____

2. _____   6. _____

3. _____   7. _____

4. _____

Complementary Terms
Built From Word Parts

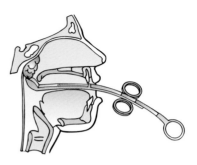

Term	Definition
acapnia . . . . (a-CAP-nē-a)	absence (less than normal level) of carbon dioxide (in the blood)
adenotome . . . . (AD-e-nō-tōm) (NOTE: The word *aden* is used instead of *adenoid* because *adenoid* means resembling a *gland*)	surgical instrument used to cut the adenoids (Exercise Figure H)
anoxia . . . . (a-NOK-sē-a)	absence (deficiency) of oxygen
aphonia . . . . (ā-FŌ-nē-a)	absence of voice
apnea . . . . (AP-nē-a)	absence of breathing
bronchoalveolar . . . . (*bron*-kō-al-VĒ-ō-lar)	pertaining to the bronchi and alveoli
bronchospasm . . . . (BRON-kō-spazm)	spasmodic contraction in the bronchi
diaphragmatic . . . . (*dī*-a-frag-MAT-ik)	pertaining to the diaphragm
dysphonia . . . . (dis-FŌ-nē-a)	difficulty in speaking (voice)
dyspnea . . . . (DISP-nē-a)	difficulty breathing
endotracheal . . . . (*en*-dō-TRĀ-kē-al)	pertaining to within the trachea (Exercise Figure I)
eupnea . . . . (ŪP-nē-a)	normal breathing
hypercapnia . . . . (hī-per-KAP-nē-a)	excessive carbon dioxide in the blood
hyperpnea . . . . (hī-perp-NĒ-a)	excessive breathing
hypocapnia . . . . (hī-pō-KAP-nē-a)	deficient carbon dioxide in the blood
hypopnea . . . . (hī-pop-NĒ-a)	deficient breathing
hypoxemia . . . . (hī-pok-SĒ-mē-a) NOTE: The *o* from *hypo* has been dropped. The final vowel in a prefix may be dropped when the word to which it is added begins with a vowel.)	deficient oxygen in the blood

Exercise Fig. H
Fill in the blanks to label the diagram.

<u>a d e n</u> / <u>o t o m y</u>
ADENOID / EXCISION

performed using a(n)

<u>a d e n</u> / <u>o</u> / <u>t o m e</u>
ADENOID / CV / SURGICAL
INSTRUMENT USED TO CUT.

Anoxia

The literal meaning of **anoxia** is **without oxygen** or **absence of oxygen**. The term actually denotes an oxygen deficiency in the body tissues.

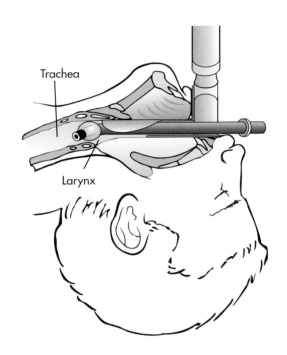

Trachea

Larynx

Exercise Fig. I

Fill in the blanks to label the diagram.
The physician is inserting a

endo | trach | eal

WITHIN / TRACHEA / PERTAINING TO

tube using a

laryng | o | scope

LARYNX / CV / INSTRUMENT USED FOR

_____

VISUAL EXAMINATION.

hypoxia . . . .   deficient oxygen (to the tissues)
　(hī-POK-sē-a)
　(NOTE: See NOTE for hypox-
　emia)

laryngeal . . . .   pertaining to the larynx
　(lar-IN-jē-al)

laryngospasm . . . .   spasmodic contraction of the larynx
　(lar-ING-gō-spazm)

mucoid . . . .   resembling mucus
　(MŪ-koyd)

mucous . . . .   pertaining to mucus
　(MŪ-kus)

orthopnea . . . .   able to breathe only in an upright position
　(or-THOP-nē-a)

nasopharyngeal . . . .   pertaining to the nose and pharynx
　(*nā*-zō-fa-RIN-jē-al)

rhinorrhea . . . .   discharge from the nose (as in a cold)
　(rī-nō-RĒ-a)

Mucus is the noun that means the slimy fluid secreted by the mucous membrane.
Mucous is the adjective that means pertaining to the mucous membrane. Pronunciation is the same for both terms.

Practice saying each of these terms aloud. To assist you in pronunciation, obtain the
audiotape designed for use with this text. Exercises 26, 27, and 28 will help you to
learn the definitions and spellings of the complementary terms related to the respiratory system.

Exercise 27 ....

Analyze and define the following complementary terms.

EXAMPLE: hyper/capnia $\frac{P \quad S(WR)}{\text{excessive carbon dioxide (in the blood)}}$

1. laryngeal _____ pertaining to the larynx

2. eupnea _____ normal breathing

3. mucoid _____ resembling mucus

4. apnea _____ absence of breathing

5. hypoxia _____ deficient oxygen to tissues

6. laryngospasm _____ spasmodic contraction of the larynx

7. endotracheal _____ pertaining to within the trachea

8. anoxia _____ absence of oxygen

9. dysphonia _____ difficulty in speaking (voice)

10. bronchoalveolar _____ pertaining to the bronchi and alveoli

11. dyspnea _____ difficulty breathing

12. hypocapnia _____ deficient in carbon dioxide

13. bronchospasm _____ spasmodic contraction in the bronchus (i)

14. orthopnea _____ able to breathe only in a straight position

15. hyperpnea _____ excessive breathing

16. acapnia _____ absence of CO_2

17. hypopnea _____ deficient breathing

18. hypoxemia _____ deficient O_2 in the blood

19. aphonia _____ absence of voice

20. rhinorrhea _____ discharge from the nose

21. adenotome _____ surgical instrument used to cut the adenoids

22. mucous _____ pertaining to mucus

23. nasopharyngeal _____ pertaining to the nose and pherynx

24. diaphragmatic _____ pertaining to the diaphragm

Exercise 28

Build the complementary terms for the following definitions by using the word parts you have learned.

EXAMPLE: pertaining to bronchi and alveoli $\dfrac{\text{bronch}}{\text{WR}} / \dfrac{o}{\text{CV}} / \dfrac{\text{alveol}}{\text{WR}} / \dfrac{\text{ar}}{\text{S}}$

1. deficient oxygen

$\dfrac{hyp}{P} / \dfrac{oxia}{S(WR)}$

2. resembling mucus

$\dfrac{muc}{WR} / \dfrac{oid}{S}$

3. able to breathe only in an upright position

$\dfrac{orth}{WR} / \dfrac{o}{CV} / \dfrac{pnea}{S}$

4. pertaining to within the trachea

$\dfrac{endo}{P} / \dfrac{trache}{WR} / \dfrac{al}{S}$

5. absence of oxygen

$\dfrac{an}{P} / \dfrac{oxia}{S(WR)}$

6. difficult breathing

$\dfrac{dys}{P} / \dfrac{pnea}{S(WR)}$

7. pertaining to the larynx

$\dfrac{laryng}{WR} / \dfrac{eal}{S}$

8. excessive carbon dioxide in the blood

$\dfrac{hyper}{P} / \dfrac{capnia}{S(WR)}$

9. normal breathing

$\dfrac{eu}{P} / \dfrac{pnea}{S(WR)}$

10. absence of voice

$\dfrac{a}{P} / \dfrac{phonia}{S(WR)}$

11. spasmodic contraction of the larynx

$\dfrac{laryng}{WR} / \dfrac{o}{CV} / \dfrac{spasm}{S}$

12. deficient carbon dioxide in the blood

$\dfrac{hypo}{P} / \dfrac{capnia}{WR}$

13. pertaining to the nose and pharynx

$\dfrac{nas}{WR} / \dfrac{o}{CV} / \dfrac{pharyng}{WR} / \dfrac{eal}{S}$

14. pertaining to the diaphragm

$\dfrac{diaphragmat}{WR} / \dfrac{ic}{S}$

15. absence of breathing

$\dfrac{a}{P} / \dfrac{pnea}{S(WR)}$

16. deficient oxygen in the blood

__hyp / ox / emia__
P   WR   S

17. excessive breathing

__hyper / pnea__
P   S(WR)

18. spasmodic contraction in the bronchi

__bronch / o / spasm__
WR   CV   S

19. deficient breathing

__hypo / pnea__
P   S(WR)

20. absence of carbon dioxide in the blood

__a / capnia__
P   S(WR)

21. difficulty in speaking (voice)

__dys / phonia__
P   S(WR)

22. discharge from the nose

__rhin / orrhea__
WR   S

23. pertaining to mucus

__muc / oid__
WR   S

24. instrument used to cut the adenoids

__aden / o / tome__
WR   CV   S

Exercise 29

Spell each of the complementary terms. Have someone dictate the terms on pp. 119-120 to you, or say the words into a tape recorder. Then spell the words from your recording as often as necessary. Think about the word parts before attempting to write the word. Study any words you have spelled incorrectly.

1. _____
2. _____
3. _____
4. _____
5. _____
6. _____
7. _____
8. _____
9. _____
10. _____
11. _____
12. _____
13. _____

14. _____
15. _____
16. _____
17. _____
18. _____
19. _____
20. _____
21. _____
22. _____
23. _____
24. _____
25. _____

Fig. 5-12
Nebulizer.

Complementary Terms

Not Built From Word Parts

Term	Definition
airway . . . . (AR-wā)	*a,* mechanical device used to keep the air passageway unobstructed; *b,* passageway by which air enters and leaves the lungs
asphyxia . . . . (as-FIK-sē-a)	deprivation of oxygen for tissue usage; suffocation
aspirate . . . . (AS-per-āt)	*a,* to withdraw fluid or to suction; *b,* to draw foreign material into the respiratory tract
bronchoconstrictor . . . . (*bron*-kō-kon-STRIK-tor)	agent causing narrowing of the bronchi
bronchodilator . . . . (*bron*-kō-dī-LĀ-tor)	agent causing the bronchi to widen
cough . . . . (kawf)	sudden, noisy expulsion of air from the lungs
hiccup . . . . (HIK-up)	sudden catching of breath with a spasmodic contraction of the diaphragm (also called *hiccough*)
hyperventilation . . . . (*hī*-per-ven-ti-LĀ-shun)	ventilation of the lungs beyond normal body needs
hypoventilation . . . . (*hī*-pō-ven-ti-LĀ-shun)	ventilation of the lungs, which does not fulfill the body's gas exchange needs
mucopurulent . . . . (*mū*-kō-PŪR-ū-lent)	containing both mucus and pus
mucus . . . . (MŪ-kus)	slimy fluid secreted by the mucous membranes
nebulizer . . . . (*neb*-ū-LĪZ-er)	device that creates a fine spray (used for giving respiratory treatment) (Figure 5-12)
nosocomial infection . . . . (nos-ō-KŌ-mē-al)	an infection acquired during hospitalization
paroxysm . . . . (PAR-ok-sizm)	periodic, sudden attack
patent . . . . (PĀ-tent)	open (an airway must be patent)
pulmonary . . . . (PUL-mō-ner-ē)	pertaining to the lungs
sputum . . . . (SPŪ-tum)	mucous secretion from the lungs, bronchi, and trachea expelled through the mouth
ventilator . . . . (VEN-ti-lā-tor)	mechanical device used to assist with or substitute for breathing when patient cannot breathe unassisted (Figure 5-13)

Sputum

is derived from the Latin **spuere,** meaning **to spit.** In a 1693 dictionary it is defined as a "secretion thicker than ordinary spittle."

Practice saying each of these terms aloud. To assist you in pronunciation, obtain the audiotape designed for use with this text. Learn the definitions and spellings of the complementary terms by completing exercises 29, 30, 31, and 32.

Exercise 30

Fill in the blanks with the correct terms.

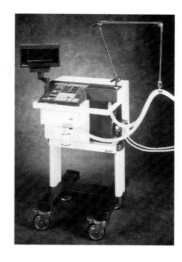

Fig. 5-13
Positive pressure ventilator.

1. Another term for ventilation of the lungs beyond normal body needs is _hyperventilation_.

2. A device that creates a fine spray for respiratory treatment is a(n) _nebulizer_.

3. A(n) _bronchodilator_ is an agent that causes the air passages to widen.

4. A patient who has difficulty breathing may be attached to a mechanical breathing device called a(n) _ventilator_.

5. Another term for suffocation is _asphyxia_.

6. Material made up of mucous secretions from the lungs, bronchi, and trachea is called _sputum_.

7. To suction or withdraw fluid is to _aspirate_.

8. A(n) _airway_ is a mechanical device that keeps the air passageways unobstructed.

9. A sudden catching of breath with spasmodic contraction of the diaphragm is called a(n) _hiccup_.

10. A sudden, noisy expulsion of air from the lung is a(n) _cough_.

11. Material containing both mucus and pus is referred to as being _mucopurulent_.

12. _hypoventilation_ is the name given to ventilation of the lungs that does not fulfill the body's gas exchange needs.

13. An infection acquired during hospitalization is called _nosocomial_.

14. The term that means pertaining to the lungs is _pulmonary_.

15. The term that applies to a periodic sudden attack is _paroxysm_.

16. An airway must be kept _patent_ (open) for the patient to breathe.

17. An agent that causes bronchi to narrow is called a(n) _bronchoconstrictor_.

18. _Mucus_ is the name given to the slimy fluid secreted by the mucous membranes.

Exercise 31

Match the terms in the first column with their correct definitions in the second column.

___b___ 1. airway

___j___ 2. pulmonary

___h___ 3. aspirate

___c___ 4. bronchoconstrictor

___i___ 5. bronchodilator

___a___ 6. cough

___d___ 7. hiccup

___g___ 8. hyperventilation

___f___ 9. asphyxia

a. sudden, noisy expulsion of air from the lungs

b. mechanical device used to keep the air passageway unobstructed

c. agent that narrows the bronchi

d. catching of breath with spasmodic contraction of diaphragm

e. mucus from throat and lungs

f. suffocation

g. ventilation of the lungs beyond normal body needs

h. to draw foreign material into the respiratory tract

i. agent that widens the bronchi

j. pertaining to the lungs

Exercise 32

Match the terms in the first column with their correct definitions in the second column.

___e___ 1. hypoventilation

___h___ 2. mucopurulent

___i___ 3. mucus

___c___ 4. nebulizer

___j___ 5. nosocomial

___a___ 6. patent

___b___ 7. sputum

___d___ 8. ventilator

___f___ 9. paroxysm

a. open

b. mucous secretion from lungs, bronchi, and trachea, expelled through the mouth

c. respiratory treatment device that sends a fine spray

d. mechanical breathing device

e. ventilation of the lungs, which does not fulfill the body's gas exchange needs

f. periodic, sudden attack

g. agent that widens air passages

h. containing both mucus and pus

i. slimy fluid secreted by mucous membranes

j. hospital-acquired infection

Exercise 33

Spell each of the complementary terms. Have someone dictate the terms on p. 124 to you, or say the words into a tape recorder. Then spell the words from your recording as often as necessary. Study any words you have spelled incorrectly.

1. _____
2. _____
3. _____
4. _____
5. _____
6. _____
7. _____
8. _____
9. _____

10. _____
11. _____
12. _____
13. _____
14. _____
15. _____
16. _____
17. _____
18. _____

▌Abbreviations

ABG . . . .   arterial blood gases

AFB . . . .   acid-fast bacilli stain

ARDS . . . .   adult respiratory distress syndrome

CF . . . .   cystic fibrosis

COPD . . . .   chronic obstructive pulmonary disease

CT . . . .   computed tomography

CXR . . . .   chest x-ray

flu . . . .   influenza

LTB . . . .   laryngotracheobronchitis

OSA . . . .   obstructive sleep apnea

PCP . . . .   *Pneumocystis carinii* pneumonia

PE . . . .   pulmonary embolism

PFT . . . .   pulmonary function tests

TB . . . .   tuberculosis

URI . . . .   upper respiratory infection

VPS . . . .   ventilation-perfusion scanning

CHAPTER REVIEW

Exercises

Exercise 34

Complete the hospital report by writing the medical terms in the blanks. Use the list of definitions with the corresponding numbers.

Case History: A 55-year-old Asian man was admitted to the hospital with complaints of recent 1. _coughing_ , 2. _dyspnea_ , and shortness of breath. He denies experiencing hemoptysis, chest pain, or night sweats. Complains of weight loss and chronic cough of 6 months duration. Moderate clubbing of fingers. History of smoking 2 packs of cigarettes a day for 40 years. Referred for 3. _pulmonary_ consult.

Pulmonary Consultation: 4. _Chest x-ray_ reveals a suspicious lesion in the left upper lobe proximal to the left 5. _bronchus_ and diffuse interstitial fibrotic lesions. Indirect 6. _Laryngoscopy_ shows edematous vocal cords with no obvious nodules. However, at entry of the left bronchus, a lesion is observed, which partially obstructs the opening. 7. _Arterial blood gases_ show alveolar 8. _hypoventilation_ of moderate degree and significant 9. _hypoxemia_ for age. Evaluating the overall situation for this man, it is my feeling this patient may have 10. _bronchogenic carcinoma_ . My approach to the workup would be to obtain full 11. _pulmonary function tests_ , including lung volumes and diffusing capacity, and to obtain a biopsy of the lesion in the bronchus. He doesn't seem to demonstrate any overt evidence of 12. _cor pulmonale_ at this time.

1. sudden noisy expulsion of air from the lungs
2. difficult breathing
3. pertaining to the lungs
4. x-ray film used to evaluate the lungs and heart
5. carries air from the trachea to the lungs
6. visual examination of the larynx   _laryngoscopy_
7. test done on arterial blood to determine the presence of oxygen, carbon dioxide, and other gases   _ABG_
8. ventilation of the lungs, which does not fulfill the body's oxygen needs   _hypoventilation_
9. deficient oxygen in the blood   _hypoxemia_
10. cancerous tumor in the bronchus   _bronchogenic carcinoma_
11. a group of tests performed on breathing
12. serious cardiac disease associated with chronic lung disorders

Exercise 35

To test your understanding of the terms introduced in this chapter, circle the words that correctly complete the sentences. The italicized words refer to the correct answer.

1. The patient in the emergency room was admitted with a *severe nosebleed,* or (rhinomycosis, epistaxis, nasopharyngitis).

2. The accident caused damage to the larynx, necessitating *a surgical repair,* or a (laryngectomy, laryngostomy, laryngoplasty).

3. Mr. Prince was *able to breathe only in an upright position,* so the nurse recorded that he had (orthopnea, eupnea, dyspnea).

4. The *test on arterial blood to determine oxygen and carbon dioxide levels* (pulse oximetry, pulmonary function tests, arterial blood gases) indicated that the patient was *deficient in oxygen,* or had (dysphonia, hypoxia, hypocapnia).

5. The physician informed the patient that a heart attack was not the cause of the *chest pain,* or (thoracalgia, pneumothorax, thoracentesis).

6. The patient complained of dizziness brought on by *ventilation of the lungs beyond normal body needs,* or (hyperventilation, hypoventilation, dysphonia).

7. The physician wished the patient to have the medication given by *a device that delivers a fine spray,* so he ordered that the treatment be given by (airway, nebulizer, ventilator).

8. The patient with *blood in the chest* was diagnosed as having a (pneumothorax, pleuritis, hemothorax).

9. Following surgery, the patient developed *a block in the circulation to the pulmonary artery* or (pleural effusion, pulmonary edema, pulmonary embolism).

10. The patient was diagnosed as having *a fungal disease affecting the lung,* or (obstructive sleep apnea, *P. carinii* pneumonia, coccidioidomycosis).

11. The physician ordered an *x-ray film of the chest* (chest x-ray, chest CT scan, bronchogram) because she suspected *an infection acquired during hospitalization,* or (patent, nosocomial, paroxysm) pneumonia.

Exercise 36

Unscramble the following terms. The words on the left hint at the meaning in each of the following.

EXAMPLE: chest, air   / p / n / e / u / m / o / t / h / o / r / a / x /
                          m   o   r   p   u   t   x   a   n   h   o   e

1. nose, fungus   / r / h / i / n / o / m / y / c / o / s / i / s /
                       n   o   c   h   y   s   o   r   s   i   i   m

2. no more tonsils   / t / o / n / s / i / l / l / e / c / t / o / m / y /
                         l   o   m   e   t   y   t   o   n   s   l   i   c

3. collapsed

a	t	e	l	e	c	t	a	s	i	s
t	e	e	l	s	s	i	c	a	a	t

4. all sinuses affected

p	a	n	s	i	n	u	s	i	t	i	s
s	t	u	s	i	i	n	a	p	s	i	n

5. to lose one of the five found in the thorax

l	o	b	e	c	t	o	m	y
t	o	o	m	y	b	e	c	l

6. x-ray film of part of tree

b	r	o	n	c	h	o	g	r	a	m
m	o	o	n	h	x	r	b	g	c	

7. inside the windpipe

e	n	d	o	t	r	a	c	h	e	a	l

Exercise 37

The following terms did not appear in this chapter but are composed of prefixes, word roots, and suffixes that have appeared in this or the previous chapters. Find their definitions by translating the word parts literally.

1. **dermatogenic** (*der*-ma-tō-JEN-ik) _originating in the skin_

2. **erythrocytometer** (e-*rith*-rō-sī-TOM-e-ter) _instrument used for measuring or counting red blood cells_

3. **melanonychia** (*mel*-a-nō-NIK-ē-a) _abnormal state of black nail_

4. **mycology** (mī-KOL-ō-jē) _study of fungi_

5. **myomalacia** (*mī*-ō-ma-LĀ-shē-a) _softening of a muscle_

6. **myonecrosis** (*mī*-ō-ne-KRŌ-sis) _death of a muscle tissue_

7. **tonsillomycosis** (ton-*sil*-ō-mī-KŌ-sis) _abnormal condition of fungus in the tonsils_

8. **viscerosomatic** (*vis*-er-ō-sō-MAT-ik) _pertaining to the body and internal organs_

Combining Forms Crossword Puzzle

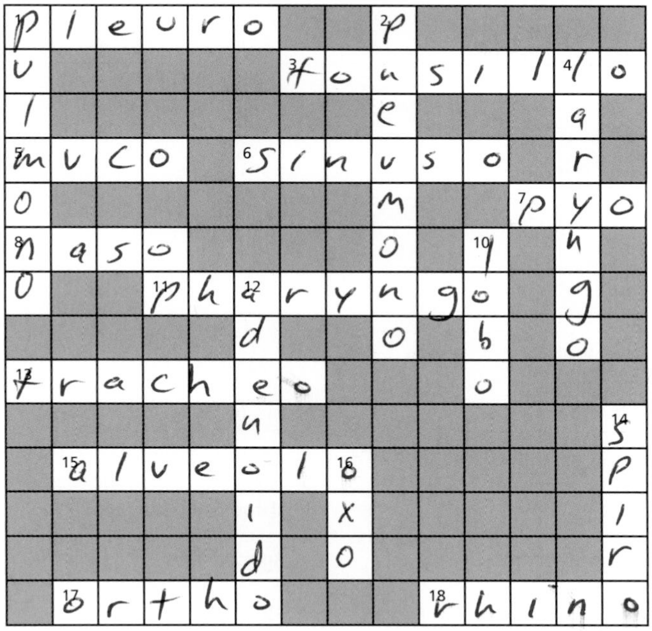

Across Clues

1. pleura
3. tonsil
5. mucus
6. sinus
7. pus
8. nose
11. pharynx
13. trachea
15. alveolus
17. straight
18. nose

Down Clues

1. lung
2. lung, air
4. larynx
10. lobe
12. adenoids
14. breathe
16. oxygen

Review of Terms

Can you build, analyze, define, pronounce, and spell the following terms *built from word parts?*

Diseases and Disorders	Surgical	Procedural	Complementary
adenoiditis	adenoidectomy	bronchogram	acapnia
atelectasis	bronchoplasty	bronchography	adenotome
bronchiectasis	laryngectomy	bronchoscope	anoxia
bronchitis	laryngocentesis	bronchoscopy	aphonia
bronchogenic carcinoma	laryngoplasty	endoscope	apnea
bronchopneumonia	laryngostomy	endoscopic	bronchoalveolar
diaphragmatocele	laryngotracheotomy	endoscopy	bronchospasm
epiglottitis	lobectomy	laryngoscope	diaphragmatic
hemothorax	pleurocentesis	laryngoscopy	dysphonia
laryngitis	pleuropexy	oximeter	dyspnea
laryngotracheobronchitis (LTB)	pneumobronchotomy	spirometer	endotracheal
	pneumonectomy	spirometry	eupnea
lobar pneumonia	rhinoplasty	thoracoscope	hypercapnia
nasopharyngitis	septoplasty	thoracoscopy	hyperpnea
pansinusitis	sinusotomy		hypocapnia
pleuritis	thoracocentesis		hypopnea
pneumatocele	thoracotomy		hypoxemia
pneumonitis	tonsillectomy		hypoxia
pneumonia	tracheoplasty		laryngeal
pneumoconiosis	tracheostomy		laryngospasm
pneumothorax	tracheotomy		mucoid
pulmonary neoplasm			nasopharyngeal
pyothorax			orthopnea
rhinitis			rhinorrhea
rhinomycosis			
rhinorrhagia			
thoracalgia			
tonsillitis			
tracheitis			
tracheostenosis			

Can you define, pronounce, and spell the following terms *not built from word parts?*

Diseases and Disorders

adult respiratory distress syndrome (ARDS)

asthma

chronic obstructive pulmonary disease (COPD)

coccidioidomycosis

cor pulmonale

croup

cystic fibrosis (CF)

deviated septum

emphysema

epistaxis

influenza (flu)

Legionnaire's disease

obstructive sleep apnea (OSA)

pertussis

pleural effusion

Pneuomocystis carinii pneumonia (PCP)

pulmonary edema

pulmonary embolism (PE)

tuberculosis (TB)

upper respiratory infection (URI)

Procedural

acid-fast bacilli stain (AFB)

arterial blood gases (ABG)

computed tomography (CT)

chest x-ray (CXR)

pulmonary function tests (PFT)

ventilation-perfusion scanning (VPS)

Complementary

airway

asphyxia

aspirate

bronchoconstrictor

bronchodilator

cough

hiccup

hyperventilation

hypoventilation

mucopurulent

mucous

mucus

nebulizer

nosocomial infection

paroxysm

patent

sputum

ventilator

6 Urinary System

Objectives .... **Upon completion of this chapter you will be able to:**

1. Identify the organs and other structures of the urinary system.
2. Define and spell the word parts presented in this chapter.
3. Build and analyze medical terms using word parts.
4. Define, pronounce, and spell the disease and disorder, procedural, surgical, and complementary terms for the urinary system.

ANATOMY

The body must have a means to eliminate waste products to sustain life. The kidneys are the main organs of excretion. The kidney, ureters, urinary bladder, and urethra compose the urinary, or excretory, system (Figures 6-1 and 6-2).

Organs of the Urinary System

kidneys	two brownish bean-shaped organs located on each side of the spinal column on the posterior wall of the abdominal cavity. Their function is to remove waste products from the blood and to aid in maintaining water and acid-base balances.
nephron	urine-producing microscopic structure, millions of which are located in each kidney.
glomerulus (*pl.* glomeruli)	cluster of capillaries at the entrance of the nephron. The process of filtering the blood, thereby forming urine, begins here.
renal pelvis	funnel-shaped reservoir that collects the urine and passes it to the ureter
hilum	indentation on the medial side of the kidney, where the ureter leaves the kidney
ureters	two slender tubes, approximately 10 to 13 inches (26 to 33 cm) long, that receive the urine from the kidneys and carry it to the posterior portion of the bladder

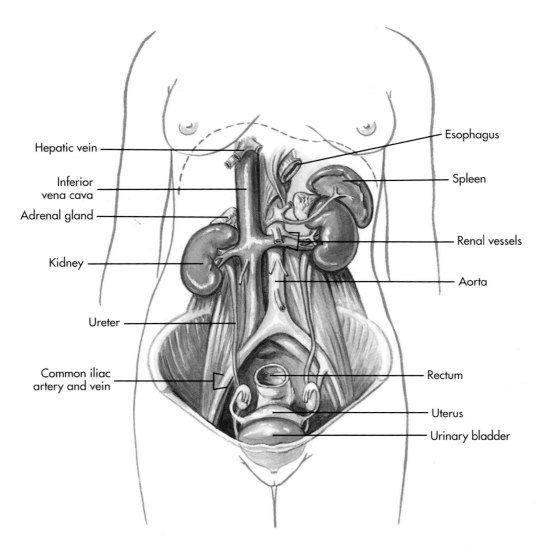

Hepatic vein

Inferior
vena cava

Adrenal gland

Kidney

Ureter

Common iliac
artery and vein

Esophagus

Spleen

Renal vessels

Aorta

Rectum

Uterus

Urinary bladder

Fig. 6-1
The female urinary system and some associated structures.

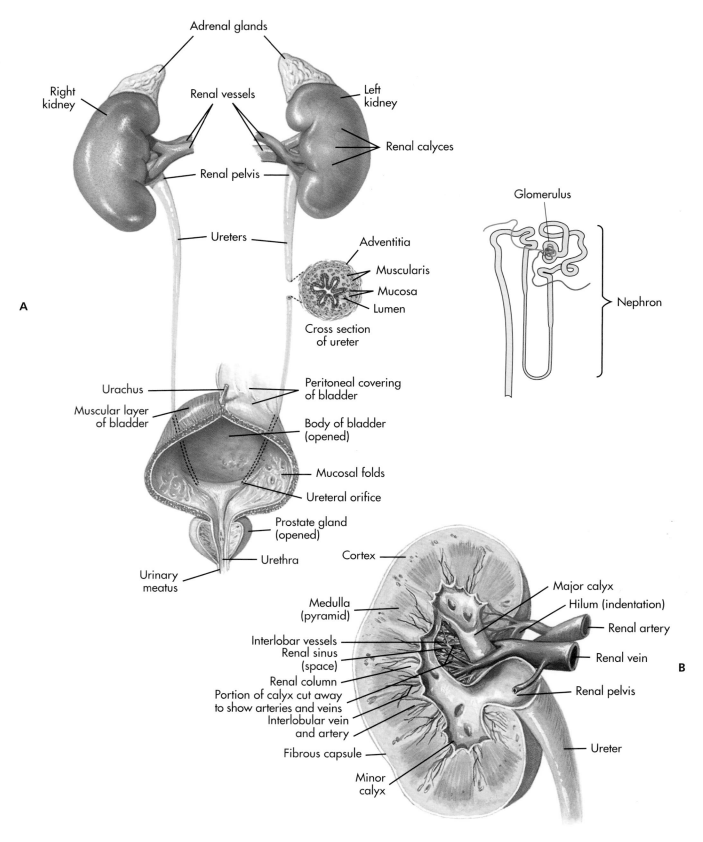

Fig. 6-2
A, Anatomy of the male urinary tract. **B,** Frontal section of the kidney.

urinary bladder . . . .   muscular, hollow organ that temporarily holds the urine. As it fills, the thick, muscular wall becomes thinner, and the organ increases in size

urethra . . . .   lowest part of the urinary tract, through which the urine passes from the urinary bladder to the outside of the body. This narrow tube varies in length in each sex. It is 1.5 inches (3.5 cm) long in the female and 8 inches (20 cm) in the male, in whom it is also part of the reproductive system. It carries the sperm during intercourse.

urinary meatus . . . .   opening through which the urine passes to the outside

urine . . . .   pale yellow liquid waste product made up of 95% water and 5% nitrogenous wastes and mineral salts. Urea, uric acid, ammonia, and creatinine are eliminated from the body in urine.

Bladder
is a derivative of the Anglo-Saxon **blaeddre,** meaning a **blister** or **windbag.**

Learn the anatomical terms by completing exercise 1.

Exercise 1

Match the anatomical terms in the first column with the correct definitions in the second column.

_g_ 1. kidney(s)

_d_ 2. glomeruli

_f_ 3. nephron

_c_ 4. ureters

_a_ 5. urinary bladder

_b_ 6. urinary meatus

_e_ 7. urethra

a. stores urine

b. outside opening through which the urine passes

c. carry urine from the kidney to the urinary bladder

d. cluster of capillaries in the kidney where the urine begins to form

e. carries urine from the bladder to the urinary meatus

f. kidney's urine-producing unit

g. organs that remove waste products from the blood

WORD PARTS

Combining Forms of the Urinary System

Study the word parts and their definitions listed below. Completing exercises 2 and 3 and Exercise Figures A and B will help you to learn the terms.

Combining Form	Definition
cyst/o	
vesic/o	bladder, sac
(NOTE: these refer to the urinary bladder unless otherwise identified.)	
glomerul/o	glomerulus
meat/o	meatus (opening)
nephr/o	
ren/o	kidney
pyel/o	renal pelvis
ureter/o	ureter
urethr/o	urethra

Glomerulus

is derived from the Latin **glomus,** which means **ball of thread.** It was thought that the rounded cluster of capillary loops at the nephron's entrance resembled thread in a ball.

Meatus

is derived from the Latin **meare,** meaning **to pass** or **to go.** Other anatomical passages share the same name, for instance, the auditory meatus.

Pyelos

is the Greek word for **tub-shaped vessel,** which describes the kidney's shape.

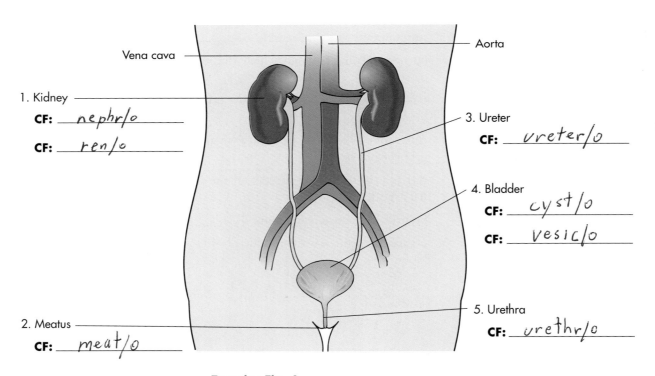

1. Kidney
   CF: _nephr/o_
   CF: _ren/o_

2. Meatus
   CF: _meat/o_

3. Ureter
   CF: _ureter/o_

4. Bladder
   CF: _cyst/o_
   CF: _vesic/o_

5. Urethra
   CF: _urethr/o_

Vena cava

Aorta

Exercise Fig. A
Fill in the blanks with combining forms.

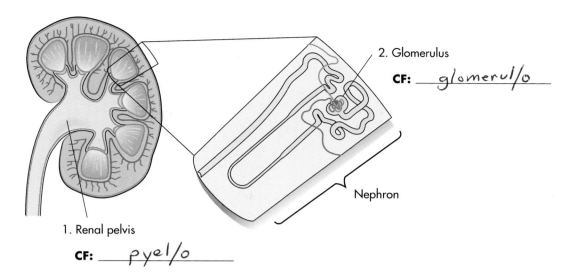

2. Glomerulus

CF: _glomerul/o_

Nephron

1. Renal pelvis

CF: _pyel/o_

Exercise Fig. B
Fill in the blanks to label this diagram of the renal pelvis.

Exercise 2

Write the definitions of the following combining forms.

1. glomerul/o _____ glomerulus _____
2. vesic/o _____ bladder, sac _____
3. nephr/o _____ kidney _____
4. pyel/o _____ renal pelvis _____
5. ureter/o _____ ureter _____
6. cyst/o _____ bladder, sac _____
7. urethr/o _____ urethra _____
8. ren/o _____ kidney _____
9. meat/o _____ meatus _____

Exercise 3

Write the combining form for each of the following terms.

1. kidney   a. _____ nephr/o _____

                 b. _____ ren/o _____

2. bladder, sac

a. _____ *vesic/o* _____

b. _____ *cyst/o* _____

3. ureter _____ *ureter/o* _____

4. renal pelvis _____ *pyel/o* _____

5. glomerulus _____ *glomerul/o* _____

6. urethra _____ *urethr/o* _____

7. meatus _____ *meat/o* _____

Combining Forms Commonly Used With Urinary System Terms

kidney problems (in urine
—girl's pregnant at 9 or a young age

Combining Form	Definition
albumin/o	albumin
azot/o	urea, nitrogen *waste*
blast/o	developing cell, germ cell
glyc/o, glycos/o	sugar
hydr/o	water
lith/o	stone, calculus
noct/i	night
(NOTE: the combining vowel is *i*.)	
olig/o	scanty, few
son/o	sound
tom/o	cut, section
trachel/o	neck, necklike
urin/o, ur/o	urine, urinary tract
ven/o	vein

petro
petros —
nycto —

Learn the combining forms by completing exercises 4 and 5.

Exercise 4

Write the definitions of the following combining forms.

1. hydr/o _____ water _____

2. ven/o _____ vein _____

3. azot/o _____ urea, nitrogen _____

4. trachel/o _____ neck, necklike _____

5. noct/i _____ night _____

6. lith/o _____ stone, calculus
7. tom/o _____ cut, section
8. albumin/o _____ albumin
9. urin/o _____ urine, urinary tract
10. son/o _____ sound
11. glyc/o _____ sugar
12. blast/o _____ developing cell, germ cell
13. olig/o _____ scanty, few
14. ur/o _____ urine, urinary tract
15. glycos/o _____ sugar

Exercise 5

Write the combining form for each of the following.

1. sugar
   a. glyc/o
   b. glycos/o

2. neck, necklike _____ trachel/o

3. sound _____ son/o

4. urine, urinary tract
   a. urin/o
   b. ur/o

5. water _____ hydr/o

6. developing cell, germ cell _____ blast/o

7. cut, section _____ tom/o

8. albumin _____ albumin/o

9. night _____ noct/i, nyct/o

10. urea, nitrogen _____ azot/o

11. stone, calculus _____ lith/o

12. vein _____ ven/o

13. scanty _____ olig/o

Prefixes

Prefix	Definition
poly-	**many, much**

Learn the prefix by completing exercises 6 and 7.

Exercise 6

Write the definition of the following prefix.

1. poly- _____ *many, much* _____

Exercise 7

Write the prefix for the following definition.

1. many, much _____ *poly-* _____

Suffixes

Suffix	Definition
-iasis,	
-esis	condition
-lysis	loosening, dissolution, separating
-megaly	enlargement
-orrhaphy	suturing, repairing
-ptosis	drooping, sagging, prolapse
-tripsy	surgical crushing
-trophy	nourishment, development
-uria	urine, urination

Learn the suffixes by completing exercises 8 and 9.

Exercise 8

Match the suffixes in the first column with their correct definitions in the second column.

_c_ 1. -iasis, -esis   a. nourishment, development

_i_ 2. -lysis   b. urine, urination

_d_ 3. -megaly   c. condition

_f_ 4. -orrhaphy   d. enlargement

_g_ 5. -ptosis   e. surgical crushing

_e_ 6. -tripsy   f. suturing, repairing

_a_ 7. -trophy   g. drooping, sagging, prolapse

_b_ 8. -uria   h. stretching out

          i. loosening, dissolution, separating

Exercise 9

Write the definitions of the following suffixes.

1. -orrhaphy   *suturing, repairing*
2. -lysis   *loosening, dissolution, separating*
3. -iasis, -esis   *condition*
4. -trophy   *nourishment, development*
5. -uria   *urine, urination*
6. -megaly   *enlargement*
7. -ptosis   *drooping, sagging, prolapse*
8. -tripsy   *surgical crushing*

MEDICAL TERMS

The terms you need to learn to complete this chapter are listed below. The exercises following each list will help you learn the definition and the spelling of each word.

Disease and Disorder Terms

Built From Word Parts

Term	Definition
cystitis . . . . (sis-TĪ-tis)	inflammation of the bladder
cystocele . . . . (SIS-tō-sēl)	protrusion of the bladder
cystolith . . . . (SIS-tō-lith)	stone in the bladder (Exercise Figure C)

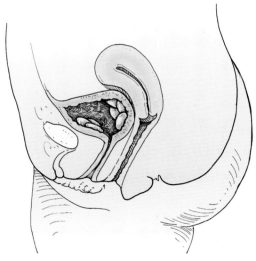

Exercise Fig. C
Fill in the blanks to label the diagram.

<u>cyst</u> / <u>o</u> / <u>lith</u>
BLADDER / CV / STONE

[handwritten: bright's disease]

glomerulonephritis . . . .   inflammation of the glomeruli of the kidney
(glō-*mer*-ū-lō-ne-FRĪ-tis)

hydronephrosis . . . .   abnormal condition of water in the kidney
(*hī*-drō-ne-FRŌ-sis)   (distension of the kidney pelvis with urine because of an obstruction)

nephritis . . . .   inflammation of a kidney
(ne-FRĪ-tis)

nephroblastoma . . . .   kidney tumor containing developing cell (embryonic tissue). Also known as *Wilms' tumor.*
(nef-rō-blas-TŌ-ma)

nephrohypertrophy . . . .   excessive development of the kidney
(*nef*-rō-hī-PER-trō-fē)
(NOTE: The prefix *hyper-* appears in the middle of this term.)

nephrolithiasis . . . .   condition of stone(s) in the kidney
(*nef*-rō-lith-Ī-a-sis)

nephroma . . . .   tumor of the kidney
(nef-RŌ-ma)

nephromegaly . . . .   enlargement of a kidney
(*nef*-rō-MEG-a-lē)

nephroptosis . . . .   drooping kidney
(*nef*-rop-TŌ-sis)

pyelitis . . . .   inflammation of the renal pelvis
(*pī*-e-LĪ-tis)

pyelonephritis . . . .   inflammation of the renal pelvis and the kidney
(*pī*-e-lō-ne-FRĪ-tis)

trachelocystitis . . . .   inflammation of the neck of the bladder
(*trā*-kel-ō-sis-TĪ-tis)

uremia . . . .   condition of ~~urine~~ *[handwritten: urea]* in the blood (toxic condition resulting from retention of by-products of the kidney in the blood)
(ū-RĒ-mē-a)

ureteritis . . . .   inflammation of a ureter
(ū-rē-ter-Ī-tis)

ureterocele . . . .   protrusion of a ureter
(ū-RĒ-ter-ō-sēl)

ureterolithiasis . . . .   condition of stones in the ureters
(ū-rē-ter-ō-lith-Ī-a-sis)

ureterostenosis . . . .   narrowing of the ureter
(ū-rē-ter-ō-sten-Ō-sis)

urethrocystitis . . . .   inflammation of the urethra and the bladder
(ū-*rē*-thrō-sis-TĪ-tis)

Nephroptosis also is known as a **floating kidney** and occurs when the kidney is no longer held in place and drops out of its normal position. The kidney is held in position by connective and adipose tissue and so it is prone to injury and also may cause the ureter to twist. Truck drivers and horseback riders are prone to this condition.

Practice saying each of these terms aloud. To assist you in pronunciation, obtain the audiotape designed for use with this text. Learn the definitions and spellings of the disease and disorder terms by completing exercises 10, 11, and 12.

Exercise 10

Analyze and define the following terms.

EXAMPLE:
WR CV WR   S
glomerul/o/nephr/itis   *inflammation of the glomeruli of the kidney*
       CF

1. nephroma _____ tumor of the kidney _____
2. cystolith _____ stone in the bladder _____
3. nephrolithiasis _____ condition of stones in the kidney _____
4. uremia _____ condition of ~~urine~~ in the blood Urea
5. nephroptosis _____ a drooping kidney _____
6. cystocele _____ protrusion of the bladder _____
7. nephrohypertrophy _____ excessive development of the kidney
8. trachelocystitis _____ inflammation of the neck of the bladder
9. cystitis _____ inflammation of the bladder _____
10. pyelitis _____ inflammation of the renal pelvis _____
11. ureterocele _____ protrusion of a ureter _____
12. hydronephrosis _____ abnormal condition of water in the kidney
13. nephromegaly _____ enlargement of a kidney _____
14. ureterolithiasis _____ condition of stones in the ureters
15. pyelonephritis _____ inflammation of the renal pelvis and the kidney
16. ureteritis _____ inflammation of a ureter _____
17. nephritis _____ inflammation of a kidney _____
18. urethrocystitis _____ inflammation of the urethra and bladder
19. ureterostenosis _____ narrowing of the ureter _____
20. nephroblastoma _____ kidney tumor containing developing cell (tissue)

Exercise 11

Build disease and disorder terms for the following definitions using the word parts you have learned.

EXAMPLE: inflammation of the ureter $\dfrac{ureter}{WR} \Big/ \dfrac{itis}{S}$

1. enlargement of the kidney

$\dfrac{nephr\ \ \ \Big/ o \Big/ \ megaly}{\ \ WR \ \ \ \ CV \ \ \ \ S}$

2. inflammation of the bladder

$\dfrac{cyst \ \ \ \ \ \ \ \ \ \ itis}{\ \ WR \ \ \ \ \ \ \ S}$

3. overdevelopment of the kidney

$\dfrac{nephr \ \Big/ o \Big/ hyper \Big/ trophy}{\ \ WR \ \ \ CV \ \ \ P \ \ \ \ \ S}$

4. inflammation of the urethra and bladder

$\dfrac{urethr \ \Big/ o \Big/ cyst \Big/ itis}{\ \ WR \ \ \ CV \ \ WR \ \ \ S}$

5. protrusion of the bladder

$\dfrac{cyst \ \Big/ o \Big/ cele}{\ WR \ \ \ CV \ \ \ S}$

6. inflammation of the neck of the bladder

$\dfrac{trachel \ \Big/ o \Big/ cyst \ \ itis}{\ \ WR \ \ \ CV \ \ WR \ \ \ S}$

7. abnormal condition of water in the kidney

$\dfrac{hydro \ \Big/ o \Big/ nephr \Big/ osis}{\ \ WR \ \ \ CV \ \ WR \ \ \ S}$

8. stone in the bladder

$\dfrac{cyst \ \Big/ o \Big/ lith}{\ WR \ \ \ CV \ \ WR}$

9. inflammation of the glomeruli of the kidney

$\dfrac{glomerul \ \Big/ o \Big/ nephr \Big/ itis}{\ \ WR \ \ \ \ CV \ \ WR \ \ \ S}$

10. tumor of the kidney

$\dfrac{nephr \ \ \ \ \Big/ oma}{\ \ WR \ \ \ \ \ \ S}$

11. a drooping kidney

$\dfrac{nephr \ \Big/ o \Big/ ptosis}{\ \ WR \ \ \ CV \ \ \ S}$

12. inflammation of a kidney

$\dfrac{nephr \ \ \ \ \Big/ itis}{\ \ WR \ \ \ \ \ S}$

13. condition of stones in the kidney

$\dfrac{nephr \ \Big/ o \Big/ lith \Big/ iasis}{\ \ WR \ \ \ CV \ \ WR \ \ \ S}$

14. protrusion of a ureter

$\dfrac{ureter \ \Big/ o \Big/ cele}{\ \ WR \ \ \ CV \ \ \ S}$

15. inflammation of the renal pelvis

_pyel_____|_itis_____
   WR   S

16. condition of urine in the blood

____ur_____|_emia_____
       WR   S

17. narrowing of the ureter

__ureter__|o|stenosis___
     WR   CV   S

18. inflammation of the renal pelvis and the kidney

_pyel___|o|nephr_|itis___
    WR   CV   WR   S

19. condition of stones in the ureters

_ureter__|o|lith_|iasis___
    WR   CV   WR   S

20. kidney tumor containing developing cell tissue

_nephr___|o|blast_|oma___
    WR   CV   WR   S

Exercise 12 ....

Spell each of the disease and disorder terms. Have someone dictate the terms on pp. 143 and 144 to you, or say the words into a tape recorder; then spell the words from your recording. Think about the word parts before attempting to write the word. Study any words you have spelled incorrectly.

1. _____   12. _____

2. _____   13. _____

3. _____   14. _____

4. _____   15. _____

5. _____   16. _____

6. _____   17. _____

7. _____   18. _____

8. _____   19. _____

9. _____   20. _____

10. _____   21. _____

11. _____

Disease and Disorder Terms

Not Built From Word Parts

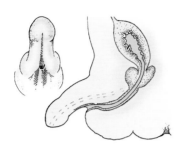

Fig. 6-3
Hypospadias.

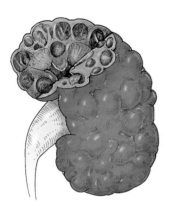

Fig. 6-4
Polycystic kidney.

Term	Definition
epispadias . . . . (*ep*-i-SPĀ-dē-as)	congenital defect in which the ~~urinary meatus~~ *urethra* is located on the upper surface of the penis; a similar defect can occur in the female, ~~urethra~~
hypospadias . . . . (*hī*-pō-SPĀ-dē-as)	congenital defect in which the ~~urinary meatus~~ is located on the underside of the penis; a similar defect can occur in the female (Figure 6-3).
polycystic kidney . . . . (*pol*-i-SIS-tik) (KID-nē)	condition in which the kidney contains many cysts and is enlarged (Figure 6-4)
renal calculi . . . . (RĒ-nal) (KAL-kū-lī)	stones in the kidney
renal hypertension . . . . (RĒ-nal) (hī-per-TEN-shun)	elevated blood pressure resulting from kidney disease
urinary retention . . . . (Ū-rin-*ā*-rē) (rē-TEN-shun)	abnormal accumulation of urine in the bladder because of an inability to urinate
urinary suppression . . . . (Ū-rin-*ā*-rē) (sū-PRESH-un)	sudden stoppage of urine formation
urinary tract infection (UTI)	infection of ~~one~~ *two* or more organs of the urinary tract

Practice saying each of these terms aloud. To assist you in pronunciation, obtain the audiotape designed for use with this text. Learn the definitions and spellings of the disease and disorder terms by completing exercises 13, 14, and 15.

Exercise 13 . . . .

Fill in the blanks with the correct terms.

1. Stones in the kidney are also called _____*renal*_____ _____*calculi*_____.

2. The inability to urinate, which results in an abnormal amount of urine in the bladder, is known as _____*urinary*_____ _____*retention*_____.

3. The name given to a kidney that is enlarged and contains many cysts is _____*polycystic*_____ _____*kidney*_____.

4. The condition in which the urinary meatus is located on the underside of the penis is called _____*hypospadias*_____.

5. Elevated blood pressure resulting from kidney disease is _____*renal*_____ _____*hypertension*_____.

6. Sudden stoppage of urine formation is referred to as _____*urinary*_____ _____*suppression*_____.

7. _____*epispadias*_____ is a condition in which the urinary meatus is located on the upper surface of the penis.

8. Infection of one or more urinary system organs is called _____*urinary*_____ _____*tract*_____ _____*infection*_____.

Exercise 14

Match the terms in the first column with the correct definitions in the second column.

_c_ 1. epispadias

_f_ 2. hypospadias

_d_ 3. renal calculi

_h_ 4. renal hypertension

_a_ 5. polycystic kidney

_e_ 6. urinary retention

_b_ 7. urinary suppression

_g_ 8. urinary tract infection

a. enlarged kidney with many cysts

b. sudden stoppage of urine formation

c. urinary meatus on the upper surface of the penis

d. kidney stones

e. inability to urinate

f. urinary meatus on the underside of the penis

g. infection of one or more organs of the urinary system

h. characterized by elevated blood pressure

i. excessive amount of urine

Exercise 15

Spell the disease and disorder terms. Have someone dictate the terms on p. 148 to you, or say the words into a tape recorder; then spell the words from your recording. Study any words you have spelled incorrectly.

1. _____   5. _____

2. _____   6. _____

3. _____   7. _____

4. _____   8. _____

Surgical Terms

Built From Word Parts

Term	Definition
cystectomy . . . . (sis-TEK-tō-mē)	excision of the bladder
cystolithotomy . . . . (sis-tō-li-THOT-ō-mē)	incision of the bladder to remove a stone
cystoplasty . . . . (SIS-tō-plas-tē)	surgical repair of the bladder
cystorrhaphy . . . . (sist-ŌR-a-fē)	suturing the bladder

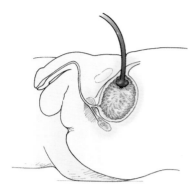

Exercise Fig. D
Fill in the blanks to label the diagram.

cyst / _ostomy_

BLADDER / CREATION OF AN
ARTIFICIAL OPENING

cystostomy . . . . creating an artificial opening into the bladder
(sis-TOS-tō-mē)   (Exercise Figure D)

cystotomy
(sis-TOT-ō-mē)

or vesicotomy . . . . incision of the bladder
(_ves_-i-KOT-ō-mē)

cystotrachelotomy . . . . incision of the neck of the bladder
(_sis_-tō-_trā_-ke-LOT-ō-mē)

lithotripsy . . . . surgical crushing of a stone (Exercise Figure E)
(LITH-ō-trip-sē)

meatotomy . . . . incision of the meatus
(_mē_-a-TOT-ō-mē)

nephrectomy . . . . excision of a kidney
(ne-FREK-tō-mē)

nephrolysis . . . . separating the kidney (from other body struc-
(ne-FROL-i-sis)   tures)

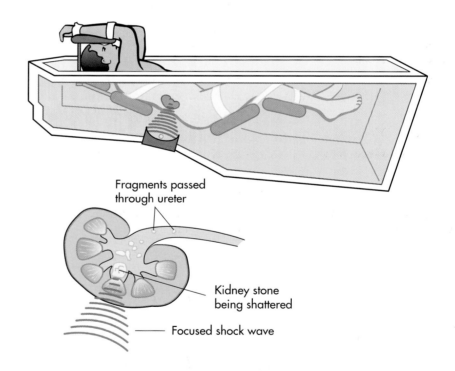

Fragments passed
through ureter

Kidney stone
being shattered

Focused shock wave

Exercise Fig. E
Fill in the blanks to complete labeling of the diagram. Extracorporeal shock wave

lith / _o_ / _tripsy_

STONE / CV / SURGICAL CRUSHING (ESWL). ESWL may be carried out by entering the
body or by noninvasive procedures. ESWL breaks down the kidney stones into tiny
pieces from outside the body. The broken pieces of the kidney stone are then
eliminated from the kidney through the urine. Another lithotripsy procedure is
percutaneous ultrasonic lithotripsy (PUL—not shown). An ultrasonic probe, which
generates high-frequency sound waves, is used to shatter the calculi. PUL is useful
for treatment of radiolucent calculi lodged in the kidney that cannot be treated
by ESWL.

nephropexy . . . . surgical fixation of the kidney
(NEF-rō-*peks*-ē)

nephrostomy . . . . creation of an artificial opening into the kidney
(nef-ROS-tō-mē)   (Exercise Figure F)

pyelolithotomy . . . . incision of the renal pelvis to remove a stone
(pī-el-ō-lith-OT-ō-mē)   (Exercise Figure G)

pyeloplasty . . . . surgical repair of the renal pelvis
(PĪ-el-ō-*plas*-tē)

pyelostomy . . . . creation of an artificial opening into the renal
(*pī*-el-OS-tō-mē)   pelvis

ureterectomy . . . . excision of a ureter
(ū-*rē*-ter-EK-tō-mē)

ureterostomy . . . . creation of an artificial opening into the ureter
(ū-rē-ter-OS-tō-mē)   (Exercise Figure H)

ureterotomy . . . . incision of a ureter
(ū-rē-ter-OT-ō-mē)

urethropexy . . . . surgical fixation of the urethra
(ū-RĒ-thrō-pek-sē)

urethroplasty . . . . surgical repair of the urethra
(ū-RĒ-thrō-*plas*-tē)

urethrostomy . . . . creation of an artificial opening into the ure-
(ū-rē-THROS-tō-mē)   thra

urethrotomy . . . . incision in the urethra
(ū-rē-THROT-ō-mē)

vesicourethral suspension . . . . surgical suspension pertaining to the bladder
(ves-i-kō-ū-RĒ-thral)   and urethra

Practice saying each of these terms aloud. To assist you in pronunciation, obtain the audiotape designed for use with this text. Learn the definitions and spellings of the surgical terms by completing exercises 16, 17, and 18.

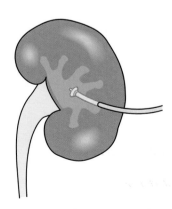

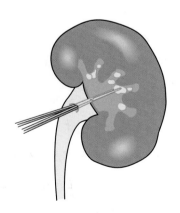

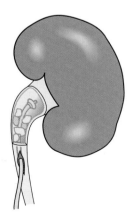

Exercise Fig. F
Fill in the blanks to label the diagram.
nephr / *ostomy*
KIDNEY / CREATION OF AN
ARTIFICIAL OPENING

Exercise Fig. G
Fill in the blanks to label the diagram.
Pyel / *o* / *lith* /
RENAL PELVIS / CV / STONE /
otomy
INCISION

Exercise Fig. H
Fill in the blanks to label the diagram.
ureter / *ostomy*
URETER / CREATION OF AN
ARTIFICIAL OPENING

Exercise 16

Analyze and define the following surgical terms.

1. vesicotomy _incision of the bladder_

2. nephrostomy _creation of an artificial opening in the kidney_

3. nephrolysis _separating the kidney (from other body structures)_

4. cystectomy _excision of the bladder_

5. ureterotomy _incision of a ureter_

6. pyelolithotomy _incision of the renal pelvis to remove a stone_

7. cystotrachelotomy _incision of the neck of the bladder_

8. nephropexy _surgical fixation of the kidney_

9. ureterostomy _creation of an artificial opening in a ureter_

10. cystolithotomy _incision of the bladder to remove a stone_

11. nephrectomy _excision of the kidney_

12. pyelostomy _creation of an artificial opening in the renal pelvis_

13. urethropexy _surgical fixation of the urethra_

14. ureterectomy _excision of the ureter_

15. cystostomy _creation of an artificial opening in the bladder_

16. pyeloplasty _surgical repair of the renal pelvis_

17. cystorrhaphy _suturing the bladder_

18. urethrostomy _creation of an artificial opening in the urethra_

19. cystoplasty _surgical repair of the bladder_

20. meatotomy _incision of the meatus_

21. lithotripsy _surgical crushing of a stone_

22. cystotomy _incision of the bladder_

23. urethroplasty _surgical repair of the urethra_

24. vesicourethral suspension _surgical suspension pertaining to the bladder and urethra_

Exercise 17

Build surgical terms for the following definitions by using the word parts you have learned.

1. incision of the urethra

   <u>urethr / otomy</u>
       WR   S

2. excision of a kidney

   <u>nephr / ectomy</u>
       WR   S

3. incision of the renal pelvis to remove a stone

   <u>pyel / o / lith / otomy</u>
     WR   CV   WR   S

4. surgical fixation of the urethra

   <u>urethr / o / pexy</u>
      WR   CV   S

5. suturing of the bladder

   <u>cyst / orrhaphy</u>
      WR   S

6. separating the kidney (from other structures)

   <u>nephr / o / lysis</u>
      WR   CV   S

7. creation of an artificial opening into the kidney

   <u>nephr / ostomy</u>
      WR   S

8. incision of a ureter

   <u>ureter / otomy</u>
       WR   S

9. surgical repair of the urethra

   <u>urethr / o / plasty</u>
      WR   CV   S

10. excision of the bladder

    <u>cyst / ectomy</u>
       WR   S

11. incision of the meatus

    <u>meat / otomy</u>
       WR   S

12. creation of an artificial opening into the urethra

    <u>urethr / ostomy</u>
        WR   S

13. incision of the bladder

    a. <u>cyst / otomy</u>
           WR   S

    b. <u>vesic / otomy</u>
           WR   S

14. surgical repair of the renal pelvis

    <u>pyel / o / plasty</u>
       WR   CV   S

15. incision of the neck of the bladder

    <u>~~trachel~~ cyst / o / ~~cyst~~ trachel / otomy</u>
         WR   CV   WR   S

16. excision of the ureter   _ureter_ / _ectomy_
                                      WR   S

17. surgical fixation of the kidney   _nephr_ /o/ _pexy_
                                         WR   CV   S

18. creation of an artificial   _pyel_ / _ostomy_
    opening into the renal pelvis   WR   S

19. incision into the bladder to   _cyst_ /o/ _lith_ / _otomy_
    remove a stone   WR CV WR   S

20. creation of an artificial   _ureter_ / _ostomy_
    opening into the ureter   WR   S

21. surgical repair of the bladder   _cyst_ /o/ _plasty_
                                         WR CV   S

22. surgical crushing of a stone   _lith_ /o/ _tripsy_
                                         WR CV   S

23. surgical suspension pertaining   _vesic_ / o / _urethr_ _al_   suspension
    to the bladder and urethra   WR   CV   WR   S

24. creation of an artificial   _cyst_ / _ostomy_
    opening into the bladder   WR   S

Exercise 18

Spell each of the surgical terms. Have someone dictate the terms on pp.149-151 to you, or say the words into a tape recorder; then spell the words from your recording. Think about the word parts before attempting to write the word. Study any words you have spelled incorrectly.

1. _____   14. _____

2. _____   15. _____

3. _____   16. _____

4. _____   17. _____

5. _____   18. _____

6. _____   19. _____

7. _____   20. _____

8. _____   21. _____

9. _____   22. _____

10. _____   23. _____

11. _____   24. _____

12. _____   25. _____

13. _____

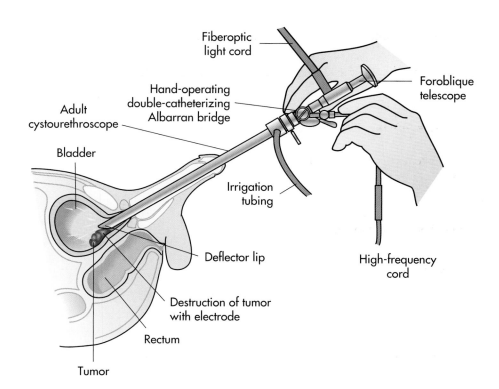

Fiberoptic
light cord

Hand-operating
double-catheterizing
Albarran bridge

Adult
cystourethroscope

Foroblique
telescope

Bladder

Irrigation
tubing

Deflector lip

High-frequency
cord

Destruction of tumor
with electrode

Rectum

Tumor

Fig. 6-5
Bladder fulguration.

Surgical Terms

Not Built From Word Parts

Term	Definition
fulguration . . . . (ful-gū-RĀ-shun)	destruction of living tissue with an electric spark (a method commonly used to remove bladder growths) (Figure 6-5)
lithotrite . . . . (LITH-ō-trīt)	instrument used to crush a stone in the urinary bladder (Figure 6-6)
renal transplant . . . . (RĒ-nal) (trans-PLANT)	surgical implantation of a donor kidney to replace a nonfunctioning kidney (Figure 6-7)

Fig. 6-6
Lithotrite.

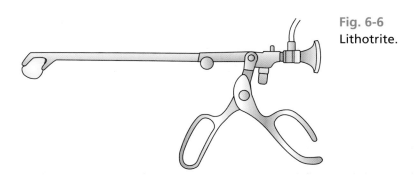

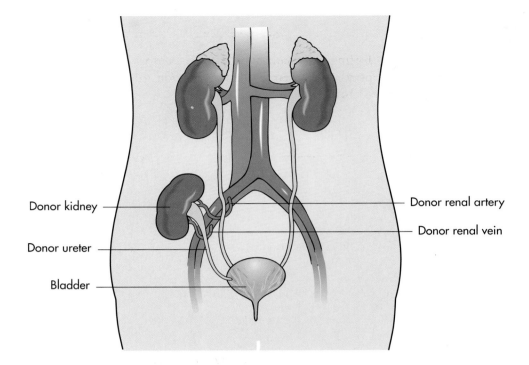

Fig. 6-7
Renal transplant showing donor kidney and blood vessels in place. Recipient's kidney is not always removed unless it is infected or is a cause of hypertension.

Donor kidney
Donor ureter
Bladder
Donor renal artery
Donor renal vein

Exercise 19

1. The surgical implantation of a donor kidney to replace a nonfunctioning kidney is called ___renal___ ___transplant___.
2. A(n) ___lithotrite___ is an instrument used to crush a stone in the urinary bladder.
3. The destruction of living tissue with an electric spark is ___fulguration___.

Exercise 20

Match the terms in the first column with their correct definitions in the second column.

___b___ 1. fulguration
___c___ 2. lithotrite
___a___ 3. renal transplant

a. used to replace a nonfunctioning kidney
b. used to remove bladder growths
c. used to crush stones
d. used to remove tumors

Exercise 21

Spell each of the surgical terms. Have someone dictate the terms on p. 155 to you, or say the words into a tape recorder; then spell the words from your recording. Study any words you have spelled incorrectly.

1. _____   3. _____

2. _____

Procedural Terms

Built From Word Parts

Term	Definition
Diagnostic Imaging	
cystogram . . . . (SIS-tō-gram)	x-ray film of the bladder
cystography . . . . (sis-TOG-ra-fē)	x-ray filming the bladder
cystopyelogram . . . . (*sis*-tō-pī-EL-ō-gram)	x-ray film of the bladder and the renal pelvis
cystopyelography . . . . (sis-tō-*pī*-e-LOG-ra-fē)	x-ray filming the bladder and the renal pelvis
cystoureterogram . . . . (*sis*-tō-ū-RĒ-ter-ō-gram)	x-ray film of the bladder and the ureters
cystourethrogram . . . . (*sis*-tō-ū-RĒ-thrō-gram)	x-ray film of the bladder and the urethra
intravenous pyelogram (IVP) **also called** *intravenous* *urogram* (IVU) . . . . (in-tra-VĒ-nus) (PĪ-e-lō-gram) (UR-ō-gram)	x-ray film of the renal pelvis with contrast medium injected intravenously
nephrogram . . . . (NEF-rō-gram)	x-ray film of the kidney
nephrography . . . . (ne-FROG-ra-fē)	x-ray filming the kidney
nephrosonography . . . . (*nef*-rō-so-NOG-ra-fē)	process of recording the kidney with sound (an ultrasound test)
nephrotomogram . . . . (*nef*-rō-TŌ-mō-gram)	sectional x-ray film of the kidney (a CT scan)
pyelogram . . . . (PĪ-el-ō-gram)	x-ray film of the renal pelvis

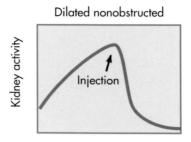

Normal pattern

Obstructed pattern

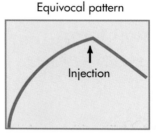

Exercise Fig. I
Fill in the blanks to label the diagram. Normal standard dynamic renal scan and

ren / _o_ / _gram_
KIDNEY / CV / RECORD.

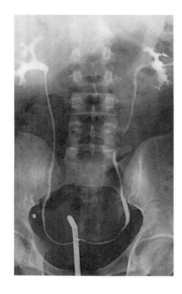

Exercise Fig. J
Fill in the blanks to label the diagram. Retrograde

pyel / _o_ /
RENAL PELVIS / CV /

gram
X-RAY FILM.

A ureteral catheter is passed by means of cysto-scope, and contrast material is injected to show urinary system structures.

renogram . . . . (RĒ-nō-gram)	(graphic) record of the kidney (produced by radioactivity after injecting a radiopharmaceutical, or radioactive material, into the blood) (a nuclear medicine test) (Exercise Figure I)
retrograde pyelogram . . . . (RET-rō-grād) (PĪ-e-lō-gram)	x-ray film of the renal pelvis (*retrograde* means to move in a direction opposite from normal) with contrast medium injected through the urethra (Exercise Figure J)
ureterogram . . . . (ū-RĒ-ter-ō-gram)	x-ray film of the ureters

Endoscopy

cystoscope . . . . (SIS-tō-skōp)	instrument used for visual examination of the bladder
cystoscopy . . . . (sis-TOS-kō-pē)	visual examination of the bladder
meatoscope . . . . (mē-ĀT-ō-skōp)	instrument used for visual examination of the meatus
meatoscopy . . . . (mē-ā-TOS-kō-pē)	visual examination of the meatus
nephroscopy . . . . (ne-FROS-kō-pē)	visual examination of the kidney
urethroscope . . . . (ū-RĒ-thrō-skōp)	instrument used for visual examination of the urethra

Additional Procedural Terms

renal biopsy . . . .   view of portion of living kidney tissue
(RĒ-nal) (BĪ-op-sē)

urethrometer . . . .   instrument used to measure the urethra
(ū-rē-THROM-e-ter)

urinometer . . . .   instrument used to measure (the specific grav-
(ū̄-ri-NOM-e-ter)   ity of) urine (Exercise Figure K)

> A voiding cystourethrogram (VCUG) is a procedure in which x-ray films are taken
> of the bladder and urethra while the patient is expelling urine.

Practice saying each of these words aloud. To assist you in pronunciation, obtain the
audiotape designed for use with this text. Learn the definitions and spellings of the
procedural terms by completing exercises 22, 23 and 24.

Exercise Fig. K
Fill in the blanks to label
the diagram.

_____urin_____ /
URINE (SPECIFIC GRAVITY) /
o/ meter
CV / INSTRUMENT USED TO
MEASURE

Exercise 22

Analyze and define the following procedural terms.

1. urethrometer   *instrument used to measure the urethra*
2. cystourethrogram   *x-ray film of the bladder and urethra*
3. meatoscope   *instrument used for visual examination of the meatus*
4. cystopyelogram   *x-ray film of the bladder and renal pelvis*
5. cystography   *x-ray filming of the bladder*
6. urethroscope   *instrument used for visual examination of the urethra*
7. nephrosonography   *process of recording the kidney with sound*
8. cystoscope   *instrument used for visual examination of the bladder*
9. pyelogram   *x-ray film of the renal pelvis*
10. nephrotomogram   *sectional x-ray film of a kidney*
11. cystogram   *x-ray film of the bladder*
12. cystoureterogram   *x-ray film of the bladder and ureters*
13. meatoscopy   *visual examination of the meatus*
14. nephrogram   *x-ray film of the kidney*
15. ureterogram   *x-ray film of the ureters*
16. cystoscopy   *visual examination of the bladder*
17. nephrography   *x-ray filming of the kidney*
18. urinometer   *instrument used to measure (the specific gravity of) urine*

19. intravenous pyelogram (urogram) _x-ray film of the renal pelvis with contrast medium injected intravenously_

20. (retrograde) pyelogram _x-ray film of the renal pelvis with contrast medium injected through the urethra_

21. cystopyelography _x-ray filming of the bladder and renal pelvis_

22. renogram _x-ray film of the kidney_

23. nephroscopy _visual examination of the kidney_

24. renal biopsy _view of portion of living kidney tissue_

Exercise 23

Build procedural terms that correspond to the following definitions by using the word parts you have learned.

1. visual examination of the bladder

cyst / o / scopy
WR / CV / S

2. x-ray film of the bladder and ureters

cyst / o / ureter / o / gram
WR / CV / WR / CV / S

3. instrument used to measure the urethra

urethr / o / meter
WR / CV / S

4. sectional x-ray film of the kidney

nephr / o / tom / o / gram
WR / CV / WR / CV / S

5. x-ray film of the bladder and the renal pelvis

cyst / o / pyel / o / gram
WR / CV / WR / CV / S

6. x-ray film of the renal pelvis with contrast medium injected intravenously

intra / ven / ous
P / WR / S

pyel / o / gram
WR / CV / S

7. instrument used for visual examination of a meatus

meat / o / scope
WR / CV / S

8. instrument used for visual examination of the urethra

urethr / o / scope
WR / CV / S

9. process of x-ray recording the kidney using (ultra) sound

nephr / o / son / o / graphy
WR / CV / WR / CV / S

10. x-ray film of the bladder

cyst / o / gram
WR / CV / S

11. visual examination of the meatus

meat / o / scopy
WR / CV / S

12. x-ray film of the ureters

ureter / o / gram
WR / CV / S

13. x-ray film of the renal pelvis

pyel / o / gram
WR / CV / S

14. instrument used for visual examination of the bladder

cyst / o / scope
WR / CV / S

15. x-ray film of the bladder and the urethra

cyst / o / urethr / o / gram
WR / CV / WR / CV / S

16. x-ray filming the bladder

cyst / o / graphy
WR / CV / S

17. x-ray film of the kidney

nephr / o / gram
WR / CV / S

18. instrument used to measure (the specific gravity of) urine

urin / o / meter
WR / CV / S

19. (graphic) record of the kidney (produced by radioactivity after injecting a radiopharmaceutical material into the blood)

ren / o / gram
WR / CV / S

20. x-ray filming the bladder and the renal pelvis

cyst / o / pyel / o / graphy
WR / CV / WR / CV / S

21. x-ray filming the kidney

nephr / o / graphy
WR / CV / S

22. x-ray film of the renal pelvis (with contrast medium injected through the urethra in a direction opposite from normal)

retrograde pyel / o / gram
WR / CV / S

23. view of a portion of living kidney tissue

ren / al bi / opsy
WR / S WR / S

24. visual examination of the kidney

nephr / o / scopy
WR / CV / S

Exercise 24 ....

Spell each of the procedural terms. Have someone dictate the terms on pp.157-159 to you, or say the words into a tape recorder; then spell the words from your recording. Think about the word parts before attempting to write the word. Study any words you have spelled incorrectly.

1. _____
2. _____
3. _____
4. _____
5. _____
6. _____
7. _____
8. _____
9. _____
10. _____
11. _____
12. _____
13. _____

14. _____
15. _____
16. _____
17. _____
18. _____
19. _____
20. _____
21. _____
22. _____
23. _____
24. _____
25. _____

▌ Procedural Terms
....
Not Built From Word Parts

Term	Definition
Diagnostic Imaging	
kidney, ureter, and bladder (KUB)	a simple x-ray film of the abdomen. It is often used to view the kidneys and bladder to determine size, shape, and location.
Laboratory Procedures	
blood urea nitrogen (BUN) ..... (ū-RĒ-a) (NĪ-trō-jen)	measures the amount of urea in the blood. Used to determine kidney function. An increased BUN indicates renal dysfunction.
specific gravity (SG) .... (spe-SIF-ik) (GRAV-i-tē)	a test performed on a urine specimen to measure the concentrating or diluting ability of the kidneys
urinalysis (UA) .... (ū-rin-AL-is-is)	multiple routine tests done on a urine specimen

Exercise 25

Fill in the blanks with the correct terms.

1. The x-ray film of the abdomen used to view the kidneys and bladder to determine size, shape, and location is called __kidney__ __Ureter and__ __bladder__.

2. A test performed on a urine specimen to measure concentrating and diluting ability of the kidneys is called __specific__ __gravity__.

3. __Blood__ __urea__ __nitrogen__ measures the amount of urea in the blood.

4. Multiple routine tests done on a urine specimen is called __urinalysis__

Exercise 26

Match the terms in the first column with their correct definitions in the second column.

__c__ 1. specific gravity
__b__ 2. blood urea nitrogen
__d__ 3. urinalysis
__a__ 4. kidney, ureter, bladder

a. an x-ray film of the kidneys, ureter, and bladder

b. used to determine kidney function

c. a test to measure concentrating or diluting abilities of the kidneys

d. multiple routine tests done on a urine sample

e. an x-ray film of the kidneys, urethra, and bladder

Exercise 27

Spell each of the procedural terms. Have someone dictate the terms on p. 162 to you, or say the words into a tape recorder; then spell the words from your recording. Study any words you have spelled incorrectly.

1. _____ 3. _____

2. _____ 4. _____

Complementary Terms

Built From Word Parts

Term	Definition
albuminuria . . . . (*al*-bū-min-Ū-rē-a)	albumin in the urine (albumin is an important protein in the blood, but when found in the urine, it indicates a kidney problem)
anuria . . . . (an-Ū-rē-a)	absence of urine (failure of the kidney to excrete urine)
azoturia . . . . (*az*-ō-TŪ-rē-a)	(excessive) urea and nitrogenous substances in the urine
diuresis . . . . (*dī*-ū-RĒ-sis) (NOTE: The *a* is dropped from dia because the word root begins with a vowel.)	condition of urine passing through (increased excretion of urine)
dysuria . . . . (dis-Ū-rē-a)	difficult or painful urination
glycosuria . . . . (glī-kō-SŪ-rē-a)	sugar (glucose) in the urine
hematuria . . . . (*hēm*-a-TŪ-rē-a)	blood in the urine
meatal . . . . (mē-Ā-tal)	pertaining to the meatus
nocturia . . . . (nok-TŪ-rē-a)	night urination
oliguria . . . . (ol-ig-Ū-rē-a)	scanty urination
polyuria . . . . (pol-ē-Ū-rē-a)	much (excessive) urine
pyuria . . . . (pī-Ū-rē-a)	pus in the urine
urinary . . . . (Ū-rin-*ā*-rē)	pertaining to urine
urologist . . . . (ū-ROL-ō-jist)	physician who specializes in the diagnosis and treatment of diseases of the male and female urinary systems and the reproductive system of the male
urology . . . . (ū-ROL-ō-jē)	study of the male and female urinary systems and the reproductive system of the male

Practice saying each of these terms aloud. To assist you in pronunciation, obtain the audiotape designed for use with this text. Exercises 28, 29, and 30 will help you to learn the definitions and spellings of the complementary terms related to the urinary system.

Exercise 28

Analyze and define the following complementary terms.

1. nocturia _night urination_
2. urologist _physician who specializes in the diagnosis and treatment of diseases of the male and female urinary systems and the reproductive system of the male_
3. oliguria _scanty urination_
4. azoturia _(excessive urea and nitrogenous substances in the urine_
5. hematuria _blood in the urine_
6. urology _study of the male & female urinary systems and the reproductive system of the male_
7. polyuria _much (excessive) urine_
8. albuminuria _albumin in the urine_
9. anuria _absence of urine_
10. diuresis _condition of urine passing through_
11. pyuria _pus in the urine_
12. urinary _pertaining to urine_
13. glycosuria _sugar in the urine_
14. meatal _pertaining to the meatus_
15. dysuria _difficult or painful urination_

Exercise 29

Build the complementary terms for the following definitions by using the word parts you have learned.

1. night urination   noct / uria   WR / S

2. scanty urination   olig / uria   WR / S

3. pus in the urine   py / uria   WR / S

4. physician who specializes in the diagnosis and treatment of diseases of the male and female urinary systems and the reproductive system of the male   urin / ologist   WR / S

5. much (excessive) urine

poly / _uria_
P / S(WR)

6. (excessive) urea and nitrogenous substances in the urine

azot / _uria_
WR / S

7. pertaining to urine

urin / _ary_
WR / S

8. blood in the urine

hemat / _uria_
WR / S

9. study of the male and female
urinary systems and the reproductive system of the male

urin / _ology_
WR / S

10. condition of urine passing
through (increased excretion
of urine)

_di_ / _ur_ / _esis_
P / WR / S

11. absence of urine

_an_ / _uria_
P / S(WR)

12. sugar in the urine

glycos / _uria_
WR / S

13. difficult or painful urination

dys / _uria_
P / S(WR)

14. albumin in the urine

albumin / _uria_
WR / S

15. pertaining to the meatus

meat / _al_
WR / S

Exercise 30

Spell each of the complementary terms. Have someone dictate the terms on p. 164 to you, or say the words into a tape recorder; then spell the words from your recording. Think about the word parts before attempting to write the word. Study any words you have spelled incorrectly.

1. _____   9. _____
2. _____   10. _____
3. _____   11. _____
4. _____   12. _____
5. _____   13. _____
6. _____   14. _____
7. _____   15. _____
8. _____

Complementary Terms

Not Built From Word Parts

Term	Definition
catheter (cath) (KATH-e-ter)	flexible, tubelike device, such as a urinary catheter, for withdrawing or instilling fluids
urinary catheterization (*kath*-e-ter-i-ZĀ-shun)	passage of a catheter into the urinary bladder to withdraw urine (Exercise Figure L)
distended (dis-TEN-ded)	stretched out (a bladder is distended when filled with urine)
diuretic (*dī*-ū-RET-ik)	agent that increases the amount of urine
enuresis (en-ū-RĒ-sis)	involuntary urination (bed-wetting)
hemodialysis (HD) (*hē*-mō-dī-AL-i-sis)	procedure for removing impurities from the blood because of an inability of the kidneys to do so
incontinence (in-KON-ti-nens)	inability to control bladder and/or bowels
micturate (MIK-tū-rāt)	to urinate or void

(handwritten annotations) permanent — connect smaller artery & vein, shunt and provide an entry for dialyzing fluid

(handwritten annotations) not all old people — stroke, altered mental status, CP, alzheimers

Catheter

is derived from the Greek **katheter,** meaning a **thing let down.** A catheter lets down the urine from the bladder.

Micturate

is derived from the Latin **mictus,** meaning **a making of water.** The noun form of micturate is **micturition.** Note the spelling of each. **Micturition** is often misspelled as **micturation.**

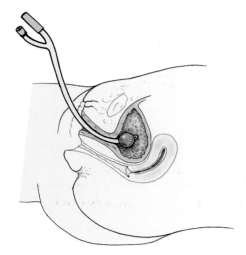

Exercise Fig. L

Fill in the blanks to label the *urin / ary* diagram. URINE / PERTAINING TO catheterization. Catheter has been inserted through the urethra, and urine has been drained. Balloon on the end of the catheter has been inflated to hold the catheter in the bladder for a period of time. This type of catheter is called a *retention catheter.*

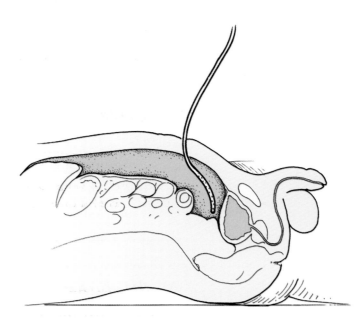

Fig. 6-8

Peritoneal dialysis. A sterile dialyzing fluid is instilled into the peritoneal cavity and dwells there for a time ordered by the physician. The fluid, containing the nitrogenous wastes and excess water that a healthy kidney normally removes, is then drained from the cavity by gravity.

peritoneal dialysis . . . . (par-i-tō-NĒ-al) (dī-AL-i-sis)	procedure for removing toxic wastes when kidney is unable to do so; the peritoneal cavity is used as the receptacle for the fluid used in the dialysis (Figure 6-8)
stricture . . . . (STRIK-chūr)	abnormal narrowing, such as a urethral stricture
urinal . . . . (Ū-rin-al)	receptacle for urine
urodynamics . . . . (ū-rō-dī-NAM-iks)	pertaining to the force and flow of urine within the urinary tract
void . . . . (voyd)	to empty or evacuate waste material, ~~especially~~ urine *only urine*

expell defacate / stool

Practice saying each of these terms aloud. To assist you in pronunciation, obtain the audiotape designed for use with this text. Learn the definitions and spellings of the complementary terms by completing exercises 31, 32, 33, and 34.

Exercise 31

Fill in the blanks with the correct terms.

1. A receptacle for urine is a(n) ____urinal____.
2. The procedure for removing impurities from the blood because of the inability of the kidneys to do so is called ____hemodialysis____
3. A ____distended____ bladder is stretched out.
4. A flexible, tubelike device for withdrawing or instilling fluids is a(n) ____catheter____.
5. The inability to control the bladder and/or bowels is called ____incontinence____.
6. The passage of a catheter into the urinary bladder to withdraw urine is a(n) ____urinary____ ____catheterization____.
7. To remove toxic wastes caused by kidney insufficiency by placing dialyzing fluid in the peritoneal cavity is called ____peritoneal____ ____dialysis____.
8. To void is to ____evacuate____ ____waste____ ____material____.
9. An abnormal narrowing is a(n) ____stricture____.
10. An agent that increases the amount of urine is called a(n) ____diuretio____.
11. Involuntary urination is called ____enuresis____.
12. ____Micturate____ is another word for void, or urinate.
13. ____Urodynamics____ is the name given to the study of the force and flow of the urinary tract.

Exercise 32

Match the terms in the first column with their correct definitions in the second column.

_e_ 1. catheter
_g_ 2. urinary catheterization
_f_ 3. distended
_a_ 4. diuretic
_d_ 5. hemodialysis
_c_ 6. incontinence
_h_ 7. void

a. increases the amount of urine

b. overdevelopment of the kidney

c. inability to control the bladder and/or bowels

d. process for removing impurities from the blood when the kidneys are unable to do so

e. flexible, tubelike device for removing urine from the bladder

f. stretched out

g. passage of a tubelike device into the urinary bladder

h. to evacuate or empty waste material, especially urine

Exercise 33

Match the terms in the first column with their correct definitions in the second column.

_a_ 1. micturate, or urinate
_e_ 2. peritoneal dialysis
_g_ 3. stricture
_b_ 4. urinal
_f_ 5. enuresis
_c_ 6. urodynamics

a. to void liquid waste

b. receptacle for urine

c. force and flow of urine within the urinary tract

d. absence of urine

e. use of peritoneal cavity to hold dialyzing fluid in the removal of toxic wastes

f. involuntary urination

g. narrowing

Exercise 34

Spell each of the complementary terms. Have someone dictate the terms on pp. 167-168 to you, or say the words into a tape recorder; then spell the words from your recording. Study any words you have spelled incorrectly.

1. _____ 8. _____
2. _____ 9. _____
3. _____ 10. _____
4. _____ 11. _____
5. _____ 12. _____
6. _____ 13. _____
7. _____

Abbreviations

BUN . . . .   blood urea nitrogen
cath . . . .   catheterization
ESWL . . . .   extracorporeal shock wave lithotripsy
HD . . . .   hemodialysis
KUB . . . .   kidney, ureter, and bladder
SG . . . .   specific gravity
UA . . . .   urinalysis
UTI . . . .   urinary tract infection
VCUG . . . .   voiding cystourethrogram

C H A P T E R   R E V I E W

Exercises

Exercise 35

Complete the hospital report by writing the medical terms in the blanks. Use the list of definitions with the corresponding numbers.

> **Case History:** This 32-year-old married white man, appearing his stated age, was admitted to the hospital after presenting himself to the emergency department in acute distress. He complained of intermittent pain in the right posterior lumbar area, radiating to the right flank. He has a family history of 1. _nephrolithiasis_ and has been treated for this condition several times in the past 10 years.

> **Discharge Summary:** This patient was admitted to the 2. _urinology_ unit from emergency department, complaining of severe intermittent pain in the back and right flank. His 3. ___KUB___ showed 4. _calculi_ in the region of the right renal pelvis. Laboratory data were all normal except for slight microscopic 5. _hematuria_ . 6. _Intravenous_ _pyelogram_ showed three stones in the right kidney with minimum 7. _hydronephrosis_ 8. _cystoscopy_ with a right retrograde 9. _pyelogram_ confirmed the presence of three stones in the right kidney. Minimal ureteral obstruction was present. 10. _pyelotomy_ was completed with no complication. A ureteral 11. _catheter_ was inserted as was an indwelling Foley catheter. Drainage from the right kidney was pale yellow in 48 hours. The Foley and ureteral catheters were removed 3 days postoperatively. At discharge, the patient is 12. _voiding_ without difficulty. The stones were sent to the laboratory for analysis. The report indicated that they were calcium oxalate. He is discharged to his home on restricted activity for the next 2 weeks. He is advised to drink copious amounts of fluids. He will be examined in the office in 3 weeks.

1. condition of stones in the kidney
2. study of male and female urinary systems
3. x-ray of the abdomen
4. stones
5. blood in the urine
6. x-ray film of the renal pelvis with contrast medium injected intravenously
7. abnormal condition of water in the kidney
8. visual examination of the bladder
9. x-ray film of the renal pelvis
10. incision into the renal pelvis to remove a stone
11. flexible, tubelike device
12. evacuating urine

Exercise 36

To test your understanding of the terms introduced in this chapter, circle the words that correctly complete the sentences. The italicized words refer to the correct answer.

1. The patient was admitted with a *drooping kidney,* or (nephromegaly, nephrohypertrophy, nephroptosis).
2. The patient's x-ray film showed a *stone in the ureter,* or a condition known as (ureterocele, ureterolithiasis, ureterostenosis).
3. The physician ordered an *x-ray film of the renal pelvis,* or a (pyelogram, nephrogram, cystogram).
4. The physician first suspected diabetes when told of the *excessive amounts of urine* voided, or (oliguria, polyuria, dysuria).
5. The physician told the patient with the drooping kidney that it was necessary to put the *kidney back in place* by performing a (nephropexy, nephrolysis, nephrotripsy).
6. The patient experienced a *sudden stoppage of urine formation,* or (urinary suppression, urinary retention, azoturia).
7. The patient was scheduled for an *x-ray film of the urinary bladder,* or a (cystoscopy, cystogram, cystography).
8. The patient informed the doctor of her son's *involuntary urination,* or (diuresis, dysuria, enuresis).
9. The patient was admitted to the hospital for *kidney and ureteral infection,* or (polycystic kidney, urinary retention, urinary tract infection).

Exercise 37

Unscramble the following mixed-up terms. The words on the left hint at the meaning in each of the following.

1. bladder
2. urine

3. renal pelvis

P Y E L I T I S
x̶ i̶ t̶ p e x̶ s̶ i̶

4. kidney

N E P H R O M A
t̶ o̶ p m e n a t̶

uri eam

5. urine

U R E M I A
m e r a u i

6. ureter

U R E T E R O C E L E
x̶ x̶ l̶ x̶ e̶ x̶ e̶ o x̶ e e

Exercise 38

The following terms did not appear in this chapter but are composed of word parts that have appeared in this chapter or the previous chapters. Find their definitions by translating the word parts literally.

1. **hyperlipemia** *more than normal amount of fat in the blad*
   (hī-per-li-PĒ-mē-a)

2. **hypoglycemia** *less " " " of sugar " "*
   (hī-po-glī-SĒ-mē-a)

3. **leukonychia** *condition of white nails*
   (lū-kō-NIK-ē-a)

4. **neurocutaneous** *of nerves and the skin*
   (nū-rō-kū-TĀ-nē-us)

5. **oncotomy** *incision of a tumor*
   (ong-KOT-ō-mē)

6. **phonogram** *record of sound x̶-r̶a̶y̶ o̶f̶*
   (FŌ-nō-gram)

7. **somatalgia** *body pain*
   (sō-ma-TAL-jē-a)

8. **trichology** *study of hair*
   (tri-KOL-ō-jē)

Combining Forms Crossword Puzzle

Across Clues
1. urine, urinary tract
5. glomerulus
6. sound
9. albumin
11. scanty
14. bladder
15. bladder
18. ureter
22. kidney
23. opening
24. sugar

Down Clues
2. cut, section
3. blood
4. night
5. sugar
7. neck, necklike
8. urine, urinary tract
10. urethra
12. stone
13. water
16. urea, nitrogen
17. kidney
19. vein
20. renal pelvis
21. blood

Review of Terms

Can you build, analyze, define, pronounce, and spell the following terms *built from word parts?*

Diseases and Disorders	Surgical	Procedural	Complementary
cystitis	cystectomy	cystogram	albuminuria
cystocele	cystolithotomy	cystography	anuria
cystolith	cystoplasty	cystopyelogram	azoturia
glomerulonephritis	cystorrhaphy	cystopyelography	diuresis
hydronephrosis	cystostomy	cystoscope	dysuria
nephritis	cystotomy	cystoscopy	glycosuria
nephroblastoma	cystotrachelotomy	cystoureterogram	hematuria
nephrohypertrophy	lithotripsy	cystourethrogram	meatal
nephrolithiasis	meatotomy	intravenous pyelogram (IVP)	nocturia
nephroma	nephrectomy	intravenous urogram (IVU)	oliguria
nephromegaly	nephrolysis	meatoscope	polyuria
nephroptosis	nephropexy	meatoscopy	pyuria
pyelitis	nephrostomy	nephrogram	urinary
pyelonephritis	pyelolithotomy	nephrography	urologist
trachelocystitis	pyeloplasty	nephroscopy	urology
uremia	pyelostomy	nephrosonography	
ureteritis	ureterectomy	pyelogram	
ureterocele	ureterostomy	renal biopsy	
ureterolithiasis	ureterotomy	renogram	
ureterostenosis	urethropexy	retrograde pyelogram	
urethrocystitis	urethroplasty	ureterogram	
	urethrostomy	urethrometer	
	urethrotomy	urethroscope	
	vesicourethral suspension	urinometer	
	vesicotomy		

Can you define, pronounce, and spell the following terms *not built from word parts?*

Diseases and Disorders	Surgical	Procedural	Complementary
epispadias	fulguration	kidney, ureter, and bladder (KUB)	catheter (cath)
hypospadias	lithotrite	blood urea nitrogen (BUN)	urinary catheterization
polycystic kidney	renal transplant	specific gravity (SG)	distended
renal calculi	vesicourethral suspension	urinalysis (UA)	diuretic
renal hypertension			enuresis
urinary retention			hemodialysis (HD)
urinary suppression			incontinence
urinary tract infection (UTI)			micturate
			peritoneal dialysis
			stricture
			urinal
			urodynamics
			void

7 — Male Reproductive System

Objectives .... **Upon completion of this chapter you will be able to:**

1. Identify the organs and other structures of the male reproductive system.
2. Define and spell the word parts presented in this chapter.
3. Build and analyze medical terms using word parts.
4. Define, pronounce, and spell the disease and disorder, procedural, surgical, and complementary terms for the male reproductive system.

ANATOMY

The function of the male reproductive system is to produce sperm, the male reproductive cells, and to secrete the hormone testosterone (Figure 7-1).

Organs of the Male Reproductive System

testis, or testicle
(*pl.* testes, or testicles) .... main male sex organs, paired, oval-shaped, and enclosed in a sac called the *scrotum.* The testes produce spermatozoa (sperm cells) and the hormone testosterone.

seminiferous tubules .... a pair of coiled tubes within the testes where the sperm have their beginning

epididymis .... a pair of coiled 20-foot (6 m) tubes atop the testes that carry the mature sperm up to the *vas deferens*

vas deferens, ductus deferens,
or seminal duct .... duct carrying the sperm from the epididymis to the urethra. (The urethra also connects with the urinary bladder and carries urine to the outside of the body. A circular muscle constricts during intercourse to prevent urination.)

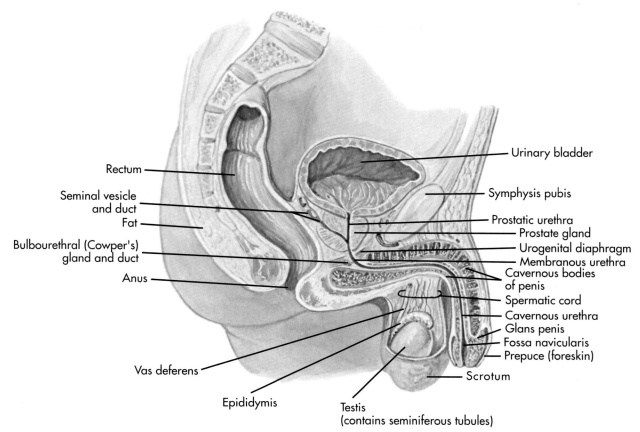

Fig. 7-1
Male reproductive organs and associated structures.

seminal vesicles . . . . two main glands located at the base of the bladder that open into the vas deferens. The glands secrete a thick fluid, which forms part of the semen.

prostate gland . . . . encircles the upper end of the urethra. The prostate gland secretes a fluid that aids in the movement of the sperm and ejaculation.

scrotum . . . . sac suspended on both sides of and just behind the penis. The testes within are each suspended by a *spermatic cord,* which comprises the veins, arteries, nerves, and vas deferens.

penis . . . . male organ of urination or copulation (sexual intercourse)

glans penis . . . . enlarged tip on the end of the penis

prepuce . . . . fold of skin near the tip of the penis

semen . . . . composed of sperm, seminal fluids, and other secretions

genitalia (genitals) . . . . reproductive organs (male or female)

> **Prostate**
>
> is derived from the Greek **pro,** meaning **before,** and **statis,** meaning **standing** or **sitting.** Anatomically it is the gland standing before the bladder.

Learn the anatomical terms by completing exercise 1.

Exercise 1

Match the anatomical terms in the first column with the correct definitions in the second column.

_____ 1. epididymis

_____ 2. glans penis

_____ 3. penis

_____ 4. prepuce, or foreskin

_____ 5. prostate gland

_____ 6. scrotum

_____ 7. semen

_____ 8. seminal vesicles

_____ 9. seminiferous tubules

_____ 10. spermatic cord

_____ 11. testes

_____ 12. vas deferens

_____ 13. genitalia

a. sac in which the testes are suspended

b. area in testes where the sperm originate

c. tube atop the testes that carries sperm to the vas deferens

d. reproductive organs (male or female)

e. male organ of copulation

f. encircles upper end of urethra

g. glands that open into the vas deferens

h. main male sex organs

i. large tip at end of male organ of copulation

j. fold of skin at tip of penis

k. comprises sperm and secretions

l. suspends testes in scrotum

m. engorgement of blood

n. duct that carries sperm to the urethra

WORD PARTS

Combining Forms of the Male Reproductive System

Study the word parts and their definitions listed below. Completing the exercises that follow will help you learn the terms.

Combining Form	Definition
balan/o	glans penis
epididym/o	epididymis
orchid/o, orchi/o **orch/o, test/o**	testis, testicle
prostat/o	prostate gland
vas/o	vessel, duct
vesicul/o	seminal vesicles

Learn the anatomical locations and meanings of the combining forms by completing exercises 2 and 3 and Exercise Figure A.

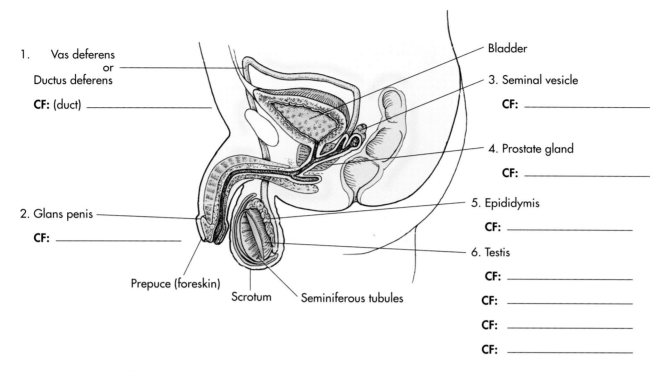

1. Vas deferens
        or
    Ductus deferens
    CF: (duct) _____

2. Glans penis _____
    CF: _____

Prepuce (foreskin)

Scrotum   Seminiferous tubules

Bladder

3. Seminal vesicle
    CF: _____

4. Prostate gland
    CF: _____

5. Epididymis
    CF: _____

6. Testis
    CF: _____
    CF: _____
    CF: _____
    CF: _____

Exercise Fig. A
Fill in the blanks with combining forms in this diagram of the male reproductive system.

Exercise 2

Write the definitions of the following combining forms.

1. test/o _____

2. vas/o _____

3. balan/o _____

4. prostat/o _____

5. orch/o _____

6. vesicul/o _____

7. orchi/o _____

8. epididym/o _____

9. orchid/o _____

Exercise 3 ....

Write the combining form for each of the following terms.

1. vessel, duct   _____

2. prostate gland   _____

3. glans penis   _____

4. seminal vesicle   _____

5. epididymis   _____

6. testicle, or testis   a. _____

                             b. _____

                             c. _____

                             d. _____

Combining Forms Commonly Used With Male Reproductive System Terms

Combining Form	Definition
andr/o	male
sperm/o	
spermat/o	spermatozoon (*pl.* spermatozoa), sperm (Figure 7-2)

Learn the combining forms by completing exercises 4 and 5.

Fig. 7-2
Spermatozoon, or sperm. In normal ejaculation there may be as many as 300 million to 500 million sperm.

Exercise 4 ....

Write the definition of the following combining forms.

1. sperm/o _____

2. andr/o _____

3. spermat/o _____

Exercise 5

Write the combining form for each of the following.

1. sperm   a. _____

                  b. _____

2. male   _____

Prefix and Suffix

Prefix	Definition
trans-	through, across, beyond

Suffix	Definition
-ism	state of

Learn the prefix and suffix by completing exercise 6.

Exercise 6

Write the definitions for the prefix and the suffix.

1. -ism _____

2. trans- _____

MEDICAL TERMS

The terms you need to learn to complete this chapter are listed below. The exercises following each list will help you learn the definition and the spelling of each word.

Disease and Disorder Terms

Built From Word Parts

Term	Definition
anorchism . . . . (an-OR-kizm)	state of absence of testis (unilateral or bilateral)
balanitis . . . . (*bal*-a-NĪ-tis)	inflammation of the glans penis
balanocele . . . . (BAL-a-nō-sēl)	protrusion of the glans penis (through a rupture of the prepuce)
balanorrhea . . . . (*bal*-a-nō-RĒ-a)	excessive discharge from the glans penis

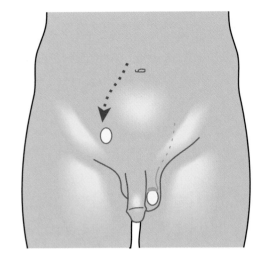

Exercise Fig. B
Fill in the blanks to complete labeling of

the diagram. HIDDEN / TESTIS / STATE OF.
Arrow shows path the testis takes in its
descent to the scrotal sac before birth.

Benign prostatic hyperplasia	
is an increase in the number of cells resulting in **benign prostatic hypertrophy,** which is the **excessive development** (enlargement) of the prostate gland.	

benign prostatic hypertrophy (BPH) . . . .
    (bē-NĪN) (pros-TAT-ik)
    (hī-PER-trō-fē)

nonmalignant, excessive development of the prostate gland (pertaining to) (also called *benign prostatic hyperplasia*)

cryptorchidism . . . .
    (kript-OR-kid-izm)

state of hidden testes (NOTE: during fetal development, testes are located in the abdominal area near the kidneys. Before birth they move down into the scrotal sac. Failure to do so results in cryptorchidism, or undescended testicles.) (Exercise Figure B)

epididymitis . . . .
    (*ep*-i-*did*-i-MĪ-tis)

inflammation of an epididymis

orchiepididymitis . . . .
    (*or*-kē-ep-i-did-i-MĪ-tis)

inflammation of the testis and epididymis

orchitis, orchiditis, or testitis . . . .
    (or-KĪ-tis) (or-ki-DĪ-tis)
    (tes-TĪ-tis)
    (NOTE: the *i* from *orchi* is dropped.)

inflammation of the testis or testicle

prostatitis . . . .
    (pros-ta-TĪ-tis)

inflammation of the prostate gland

prostatocystitis . . . .
    (pros-*ta*-tō-sis-TĪ-tis)

inflammation of the prostate gland and the bladder

prostatolith . . . .
    (*pros*-TAT-ō-lith)

stone in the prostate gland

prostatorrhea . . . .
    (pros-*tat*-ō-RĒ-a)

excessive discharge from the prostate gland

prostatovesiculitis . . . .
    (*pros*-ta-tō-ves-*ik*-ū-LĪ-tis)

inflammation of the prostate gland and seminal vesicles

Practice saying each of these terms aloud. To assist you in pronunciation, obtain the audiotape designed for use with this text. Learn the definitions and spellings of the disease and disorder terms by completing exercises 7, 8, and 9.

Exercise 7

Analyze and define the following terms.

1. prostatolith _____

2. balanitis _____

3. orchitis, orchiditis, or testitis _____

4. prostatovesiculitis _____

5. prostatocystitis _____

6. orchiepididymitis _____

7. prostatorrhea _____

8. epididymitis _____

9. benign prostatic hypertrophy _____

10. balanocele _____

11. cryptorchidism _____

12. balanorrhea _____

13. prostatitis _____

14. anorchism _____

Exercise 8

Build disease and disorder terms for the following definitions using the word parts you have learned.

1. inflammation of the prostate gland and urinary bladder

   _____
   WR / CV / WR / S

2. stone in the prostate

   _____
   WR / CV / S

3. inflammation of the testis

   a. _____
      WR / S

   b. _____
      WR / S

   c. _____
      WR / S

4. a nonmalignant, excessive development of the prostate gland (pertaining to)

(benign)

_____ / _____   _____ / _____
WR   S   P   S(WR)

5. State of hidden testes

_____ / _____ / _____
WR   WR   S

6. inflammation of the prostate and seminal vesicles

_____ / ____ / _____ / _____
WR   CV   WR   S

7. State of absence of testis

_____ / _____ / _____
P   WR   S

8. protrusion of the glans penis

_____ / ___ / ___
WR   CV   S

9. inflammation of the prostate gland

_____ / _____
WR   S

10. inflammation of the testis and the epididymis

_____ / _____ / _____
WR   WR   S

11. excessive discharge from the glans penis

_____ / _____
WR   S

12. inflammation of an epididymis

_____ / _____
WR   S

13. inflammation of the glans penis

_____ / _____
WR   S

14. excessive discharge from the prostate

_____ / _____
WR   S

Exercise 9

Spell each of the disease and disorder terms. Have someone dictate the terms on pp. 179-180 to you, or say the words into a tape recorder; then spell the words from your recording. Think about the word parts before attempting to write the word. Study any words you have spelled incorrectly.

1. _____   5. _____

2. _____   6. _____

3. _____   7. _____

4. _____   8. _____

9. _____

10. _____

11. _____

12. _____

13. _____

14. _____

Disease and Disorder Terms

Not Built From Word Parts

Term	Definition
erectile dysfunction (ē-REK-til)	the inability of the male to attain or maintain an erection sufficient to perform sexual intercourse
hydrocele (HĪ-drō-sēl)	scrotal swelling caused by a collection of fluid along the tubes within the testes (Figure 7-3)
impotent (IM-pō-tent)	lack of power to have an erection or to copulate
phimosis (fi-MŌ-sis)	narrowing, or constriction, of the opening of the prepuce (foreskin) of the glans penis (Figure 7-4)
priapism (PRĪ-a-pizm)	persistent abnormal erection of the penis accompanied by pain and tenderness

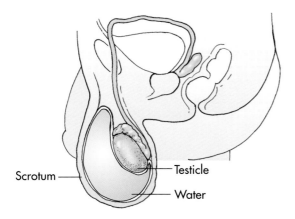

Scrotum — Testicle

— Water

Fig. 7-3
Hydrocele.

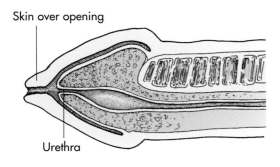

Skin over opening

Urethra

Fig. 7-4
Phimosis. Cross section of the penis showing foreskin covering the opening.

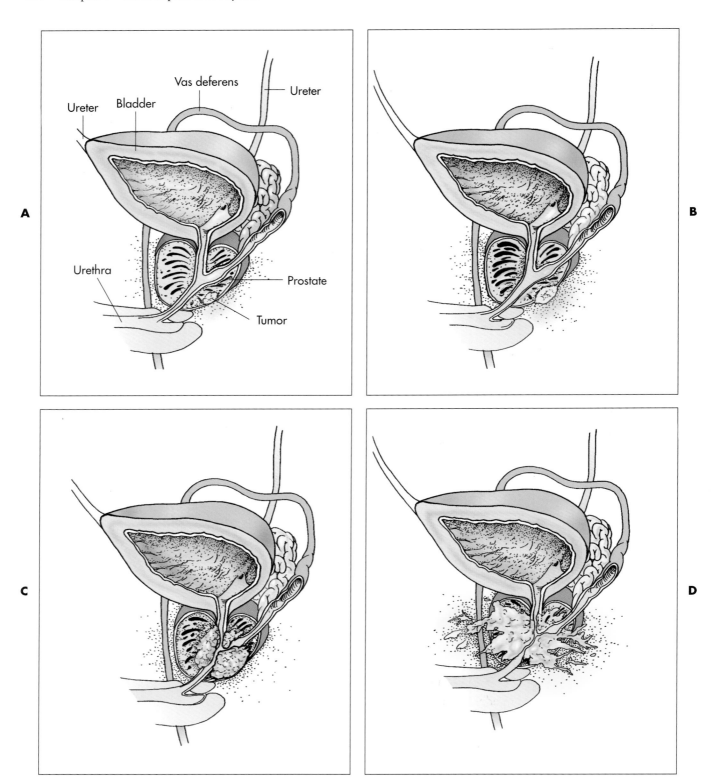

Ureter　Bladder　Vas deferens　Ureter

A

Urethra

Prostate

Tumor

B

C

D

Exercise Fig. C

Fill in the blanks to complete labeling. Four stages of PROSTATE GLAND / PERTAINING TO cancer.

prostatic cancer . . . .   cancer of the prostate gland (Exercise Figure C)
(prō-STAT-ik) (CAN-ser)

varicocele . . . .   enlarged veins of the spermatic cord (Figure
(VĀR-i-kō-sēl)   7-5)

testicular carcinoma . . . .   cancer of the testicles
(tes-TIK-ū-ler) (*kar*-sin-Ō-ma)

testicular torsion . . . .   twisting of the spermatic cord causing de-
(tes-TIK-ū-ler) (TOR-shun)   creased blood flow to the testis. Occurs most
often during puberty. Because of lack of blood
flow to the testis, it is often considered a surgical emergency.

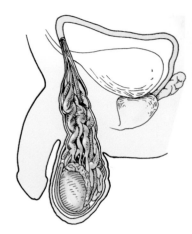

Fig. 7-5
Varicocele.

Prostatic cancer is the second most common cause of cancer deaths among American males and typically occurs after the age of 40 years. Procedures used for detecting prostatic cancer are as follows:

1. digital rectal examination

2. prostatic specific antigen (PSA)

3. transrectal ultrasound

Treatment includes prostatectomy and/or radiation therapy. For stage C prostatic
cancer, hormonal therapy may be used or an orchidectomy may be performed to reduce the production of testosterone, which fuels the prostatic cancer.

Practice saying each of these terms aloud. To assist you in pronunciation, obtain the
audiotape designed for use with this text. Learn the definitions and spellings of the
disease and disorder terms by completing exercises 10, 11, and 12.

Exercise 10 . . . .

Fill in the blanks with the correct terms.

1. Another way of referring to cancer of the testicles is   *testicular*
    carcinoma.

2. A constriction of the opening of the foreskin of the glans penis is called
    phimosis.

3. Lack of power to copulate or have an erection is to be   *impotent*   .

4. The condition of having enlarged veins of the spermatic cord is known medically
    as a(n)   *varicocele*   .

5. A scrotal swelling caused by a collection of fluid along the tubes within the testes
    is called a(n)   *hydrocele*   .

6. Cancer of the prostate gland is called   *prostatic*   *cancer*   .

7. Inability of the male to attain erection is called   *erectile*
    dysfunction

8. Persistent abnormal erection is called   *priapism*   .

9. *testicular*   *torsion*   is the twisting of the spermatic cord.

Exercise 11

Match the terms in the first column with the correct definitions in the second column.

_____ 1. varicocele

_____ 2. phimosis

_____ 3. testicular carcinoma

_____ 4. impotent

_____ 5. hydrocele

_____ 6. prostatic cancer

_____ 7. testicular torsion

_____ 8. erectile dysfunction

_____ 9. priapism

a. scrotal swelling caused by a collection of fluid along the tubes within the testes

b. lack of power to have an erection or to copulate

c. narrowed opening of the foreskin of the glans penis

d. enlarged veins of the spermatic cord

e. cancer of the testicles

f. cancer of the prostate gland

g. stone in the prostate gland

h. persistent abnormal erection

i. inability to attain an erection

j. twisting of the spermatic cord

Exercise 12

Spell the disease and disorder terms. Have someone dictate the terms on pp. 183 and 185 to you, or say the words into a tape recorder; then spell the words from your recording. Study any words you have spelled incorrectly.

1. _____   6. _____

2. _____   7. _____

3. _____   8. _____

4. _____   9. _____

5. _____

Surgical Terms
Built From Word Parts

Term	Definition
balanoplasty (BAL-a-nō-plas-tē)	surgical repair of the glans penis
epididymectomy (_ep_-i-_did_-i-MEK-tō-mē)	excision or surgical removal of an epididymis
orchioplasty (ŌR-kē-ō-plas-tē)	surgical repair of a testis

orchidectomy, orchiectomy . . . . .
(ōr-kid-EK-tō-mē)
(or-kē-EK-tō-mē)

excision or surgical removal of one or both testes (castration)

orchidopexy, orchiopexy . . . .
(ŌR-kid-ō-pek-sē)
(ŌR-kē-ō-pek-sē)

surgical fixation of a testicle (performed to bring undescended testicle[s] into the scrotum)

orchidotomy, or orchiotomy . . . .
(ōr-kid-OT-ō-mē),
(ōr-kē-OT-ō-mē)

incision into a testis

prostatectomy . . . .
(*pros*-ta-TEK-tō-mē)

excision of the prostate gland

prostatocystotomy . . . .
(pros-*tat*-ō-sis-TOT-ō-mē)

incision into the bladder and prostate

prostatolithotomy . . . .
(pros-*tat*-ō-li-THOT-ō-mē)

incision into the bladder prostate gland to remove a stone

prostatovesiculectomy . . . .
(*pros*-tat-ō-ves-*ik*-ū-LEK-tō-mē)

excision of the prostate gland and seminal vesicles

transurethral resection of the prostate gland (TURP) . . . .
(*trans*-ū-RĒ-thral)
(re-SEK-shun)

pertaining to resection (cutting back) through the urethra (performed through the urethra to cut back with a resectoscope the prostate gland when the enlargement of the gland interferes with normal urination) (Figure 7-6)

vasectomy . . . .
(va-SEK-tō-mē)

excision of a duct (actually the surgical removal of a portion of the vas, or ductus, deferens; male sterilization) (Exercise Figure D)

vasovasostomy . . . .
(vas-ō-va-SOS-tō-mē)

creation of artificial openings between ducts (the severed ends of the vas deferens are reconnected to restore fertility in men who have had a vasectomy)

vesiculectomy . . . .
(ve-*sik*-ū-LEK-tō-mē)

excision of the seminal vesicle(s)

Practice saying each of these terms aloud. To assist you in pronunciation, obtain the audiotape designed for use with this text. Learn the definitions and spellings of the surgical terms by completing exercises 13, 14, and 15.

Exercise 13

. . . .

Analyze and define the following surgical terms.

1. vasectomy _____

2. prostatocystotomy _____

3. orchidotomy, orchiotomy _____

4. epididymectomy _____

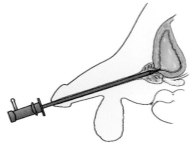

Fig. 7-6
Transurethral resection. Resectoscope is inserted through urethra to the prostate. The end of the instrument is equipped to remove small pieces of enlarged prostate gland.

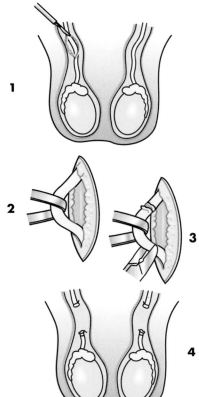

Exercise Fig. D

DUCT / EXCISION OF
1, Incision is made into the covering of the vas. **2,** Vas is exposed. **3,** Segment of vas is excised. **4,** Vas is replaced and skin is sutured.

5. orchidopexy, orchiopexy _____

6. prostatovesiculectomy _____

7. orchioplasty _____

8. vesiculectomy _____

9. prostatectomy _____

10. balanoplasty _____

11. transurethral resection of the prostate gland _____

12. vasovasostomy _____

13. orchidectomy, orchiectomy _____

14. prostatolithotomy _____

Exercise 14

Build surgical terms for the following definitions by using the word parts you have learned.

1. excision of one or both testes

   a. _____ / _____
                        WR   S

   b. _____ / _____
                        WR   S

2. surgical repair of the glans penis

   _____ / ___ / _____
             WR   CV   S

3. incision into the bladder and prostate gland

   _____ / ___ / _____ / _____
       WR   CV   WR   S

4. excision of the seminal vesicle(s)

   _____ / _____
                        WR   S

5. incision into the prostate gland to remove a stone

   _____ / ___ / _____ / _____
       WR   CV   WR   S

6. incision into a testis

   a. _____ / _____
                        WR   S

   b. _____ / _____
                        WR   S

7. cutting back (the prostate)
   through the urethra

   _____ / _____ / _____   resection
   P   WR   S   of the
                               prostate
                               gland

8. excision of the epididymis

   _____ / _____
   WR   S

9. surgical repair of a testis

   _____ / ___ / _____
   WR   CV   S

10. excision of the prostate gland

    _____ / _____
    WR   S

11. excision of a duct (surgical
    removal of a portion of the
    vas, or ductus, deferens)

    _____ / _____
    WR   S

12. excision of the prostate gland
    and seminal vesicles

    _____ / ___ / _____ / _____
    WR   CV   WR   S

13. surgical fixation of a testicle

    a. _____ / ___ / _____
       WR   CV   S

    b. _____ / ___ / _____
       WR   CV   S

14. creation of artificial openings
    between the severed ends of
    the vas deferens

    _____ / ___ / _____ / _____
    WR   CV   WR   S

Exercise 15

Spell each of the surgical terms. Have someone dictate the terms on pp. 186 and 187 to you, or say the words into a tape recorder; then spell the words from your recording. Think about the word parts before attempting to write the word. Study any words you have spelled incorrectly.

1. _____   8. _____

2. _____   9. _____

3. _____   10. _____

4. _____   11. _____

5. _____   12. _____

6. _____   13. _____

7. _____   14. _____

Surgical Terms

Not Built From Word Parts

Term	Definition
circumcision (*ser*-kum-SI-zhun)	surgical removal of the prepuce (foreskin) (Figure 7-7)
hydrocelectomy (*hī*-drō-sē-LEK-tō-mē)	surgical removal of a hydrocele
penile implant (PĒ-nīl)	surgical implantation of a penile prosthesis to correct erectile dysfunction
suprapubic prostatectomy (*sū*-pra-PŪ-bik) (*pros*-ta-TEK-tō-mē)	surgical excision of the prostate gland through an abdominal incision made above the pubic bone
transurethral incision of the prostate (TUIP) (trans-ū-RĒ-thral)	a surgical procedure that widens the urethra by making a few small incisions in the bladder neck and the prostate gland. No prostate tissue is removed. TUIP may be used (instead of TURP) when the prostate gland is less enlarged.
transurethral microwave thermotherapy (TUMT) (trans-ū-RĒ-thral) (mī-crō-WĀVE) (ther-mō-THER-a-pē)	a treatment that eliminates excess cells present in benign prostatic hypertrophy using heat generated by microwave (Figure 7-8)

Surgical Treatment for Benign Prostatic Hypertrophy (BPH)

Suprapubic prostatectomy

Transurethral resection of the prostate gland (TURP)

Transurethral microwave thermotherapy (TUMT)

Transurethral incision of the prostate (TUIP)

Various laser procedures are also being used in the treatment of benign prostatic hypertrophy.

Fig. 7-7
Circumcision.

Transurethral Microwave Thermotherapy (Prostatron Treatment)

TUMT now offers physicians a new method for treating benign prostatic hypertrophy other than surgery or medications. A Prostatron (see Figure 7-8), which received U.S. Food and Drug Administration approval in May 1996, is used to deliver microwaves that heat the designated area for 1 hour, eliminating excess tissue. Anesthetic is not required. Improvement of symptoms continues for 3 to 6 weeks.

Practice saying each of these terms aloud. To assist you in pronunciation, obtain the audiotape designed for use with this text. Learn the definitions and spellings of the surgical terms by completing exercises 16 and 17.

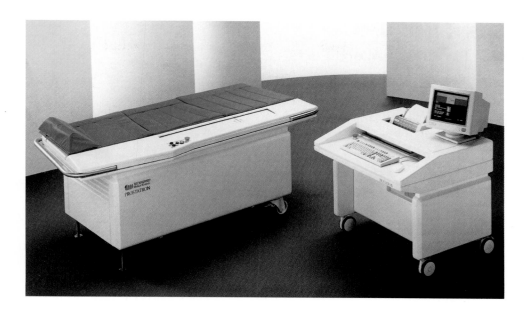

Fig. 7-8
The Prostatron® device is used to perform transurethral microwave thermotherapy (TUMT®), a noninvasive treatment for benign prostatic hyperplasia.

Exercise 16

Fill in the blanks with the correct term.

1. The surgery performed to remove the prostate gland is _____ _____ .

2. The surgical procedure performed to remove the prepuce is called a(n) _____ .

3. The surgery performed to correct erectile dysfunction of the penis is _____ _____.

4. Surgical removal of a hydrocele is _____ .

5. _____ _____ _____ is a treatment for benign prostatic hypertrophy.

6. A surgical procedure for BPH that widens the urethra by making small incisions is called _____ _____ of the _____ .

Exercise 17

Spell each of the surgical terms. Have someone dictate the terms on p. 190 to you, or say the words into a tape recorder; then spell the words from your recording. Study any words you have spelled incorrectly.

1. _____   4. _____

2. _____   5. _____

3. _____   6. _____

Procedural Terms
Not Built From Word Parts

Term	Definition
Diagnostic Imaging	
transrectal ultrasound . . . . (trans-REK-tal)	uses sound waves obtained by placing a probe into the rectum. The sound waves are transformed into an image of the prostate gland on a television screen where it is viewed by the physician.
Laboratory Procedures	
prostatic specific antigen (PSA) . . (PROS-tat-ik) (AN-ti-jen)	a test that measures the level of prostatic specific antigen in the blood. Elevated test results may indicate the presence of prostatic cancer.
Additional Procedural Terms	
digital rectal examination (DRE) . (DIJ-it-al) (REC-tal)	a physical examination in which the physician inserts a finger into the rectum and feels for the size and shape of the prostate gland through the rectal wall

Exercise 18

Fill in the blanks with the correct terms.

1. A procedure whereby the physician feels for the size and shape of the prostate gland through the rectal wall is called _____ _____

   _____ .

2. A blood test which, when elevated, may indicate the presence of prostatic cancer is called _____ _____ _____ .

3. A diagnostic ultrasound examination used to obtain images of the prostate gland is called _____ _____ .

Complementary Terms
Built From Word Parts

Term	Definition
andropathy . . . . (an-DROP-a-thē)	diseases of the male (that is, peculiar to the male, such as testitis)
aspermia . . . . (a-SPER-mē-a)	condition of absence of sperm
oligospermia . . . . (ol-i-gō-SPER-mē-a)	condition of scanty sperm (in the semen)
spermatolysis . . . . (sper-ma-TOL-i-sis)	dissolution (destruction) of sperm

Practice saying each of these terms aloud. To assist you in pronunciation, obtain the audiotape designed for use with this text. Exercises 19, 20, and 21 will help you learn the definitions and spellings of the complementary terms related to the male reproductive system.

Exercise 19 ....

Analyze and define the following complementary terms.

1. oligospermia _____

2. andropathy _____

3. spermatolysis _____

4. aspermia _____

Exercise 20 ....

Build the complementary terms for the following definitions by using the word parts you have learned.

1. dissolution (destruction) of sperm

   _____ / / _____
   WR   CV   S

2. diseases of the male

   _____ / / _____
   WR   CV   S

3. condition of the absence of sperm

   _____ / _____ / _____
   P   WR   S

4. condition of scanty sperm (in the semen)

   _____ / / _____ / _____
   WR   CV   WR   S

Exercise 21 ....

Spell each of the complementary terms. Have someone dictate the terms on p. 192 to you, or say the words into a tape recorder; then spell the words from your recording. Think about the word parts before attempting to write the word. Study any words you have spelled incorrectly.

1. _____   3. _____

2. _____   4. _____

Complementary Terms

Not Built From Word Parts

Term	Definition
acquired immune deficiency syndrome (AIDS)	a disease that affects the body's immune system, transmitted by exchange of body fluid during the sexual act, reuse of contaminated needles, or receiving contaminated blood transfusions
artificial insemination . . . . (ar-ti-FISH-al) (in-sem-i-NĀ-shun)	introduction of semen into the vagina by artificial means
chlamydia . . . . (klah-MID-ē-a)	a sexually transmitted disease, sometimes called "silent STD" because many are not aware they have the disease. Symptoms that occur when the disease becomes serious are painful urination and discharge from the penis in males and genital itching, vaginal discharge, and bleeding between menstrual periods in the female. The causative agent is *C. trachomatis.*
coitus . . . . (KO-i-tus)	sexual intercourse between male and female
condom . . . . (KON-dum)	cover for the penis worn during coitus
ejaculation . . . . (ē-jak-ū-LĀ-shun)	ejection of semen from the male urethra
genital herpes . . . . (JEN-i-tal) (HER-pēz)	sexually transmitted disease caused by *Herpesvirus hominis* type 2
gonads . . . . (GŌ-nads)	male and female sex glands
gonorrhea . . . . (gon-or-RĒ-a)	contagious, inflammatory sexually transmitted disease caused by a bacterial organism that affects the mucous membranes of the genitourinary system
heterosexual . . . . (*het*-er-ō-SEKS-shū-al)	person who is attracted to a member of the opposite sex
homosexual . . . . (*hō*-mō-SEKS-shū-al)	person who is attracted to a member of the same sex
human immunodeficiency virus (HIV) . . . . (im-ū-nō-de-FISH-en-sē)	a type of retrovirus that causes AIDS. HIV infects T-helper cells of the immune system, allowing for opportunistic infections such as candidiasis, *P. carinii* pneumonia, tuberculosis, and Kaposi's sarcoma.
human papilloma virus (HPV) . . .	a prevalent sexually transmitted disease causing benign or cancerous growths in male and female genitals (venereal warts)

orgasm . . . .   climax of sexual stimulation
(ŌR-gazm)

prosthesis . . . .   an artificial replacement of an absent body part
(pros-THĒ-sis)

puberty . . . .   period when secondary sex characteristics de-
(PŪ-ber-tē)   velop and the ability to reproduce sexually be-
                                              gins

sexually transmitted disease
(STD) . . . .   disease, such as syphilis, gonorrhea, and genital
                                              herpes, transmitted during sexual intercourse
                                              (also called *venereal disease*)

sterilization . . . .   process that renders an individual unable to
(stăr-il-i-ZĀ-shun)   produce offspring

syphilis . . . . infectious sexually transmitted disease having
(SIF-i-lis)   lesions that can affect any organ or tissue; a
                                              syphilitic mother may transmit the disease to
                                              her unborn infant, since the causative organ-
                                              ism is able to pass through the placenta

trichomoniasis . . . .   a sexually transmitted disease caused by a one-
(trik-ō-mō-NĪ-a-sis)   cell organism, *Trichomonas.* It infects the geni-
                                              tourinary tract. Males may be asymptomatic or
                                              may develop urethritis, an enlarged prostate
                                              gland, or epididymitis. Females experience
                                              itching, dysuria, and vaginal or urethral dis-
                                              charge.

List of Sexually Transmitted Diseases

acquired immunodeficiency syndrome

human immunodeficiency virus infections

syphilis

genital herpes

venereal warts (human papilloma virus)

gonorrhea

chlamydia

trichomoniasis

cytomegalovirus infections

(Sexually transmitted diseases may occur in both males and females.)

Venereal

is derived from **Venus,** the goddess of love. In ancient times it was noted that the disease was part of the misfortunes of love.

Practice saying each of these terms aloud. To assist you in pronunciation, obtain the audiotape designed for use with this text. Learn the definitions and spellings of the complementary terms by completing exercises 22, 23, 24, and 25.

Exercise 22

Write the definitions of the following terms.

1. puberty *period when secondary sex characteristics develop and the ability to sexually reproduce begins*

2. orgasm *climax of sexual stimulation*

3. gonorrhea *contagious, inflammatory venereal disease*

4. homosexual *person who is attracted to a member of the same sex*

5. coitus *sexual intercourse between male and female*

6. genital herpes *contagious venereal disease caused by the herpes hominus type 2 virus*

7. heterosexual *a person who is attracted to a member of the opposite sex*

8. syphilis *infectious venereal disease having lesions that can affect any organ or tissue*

9. ejaculation *ejection of semen from the male urethra*

10. gonads *male and female sex glands*

11. STD *Sexually transmitted disease; a disease transmitted during sexual intercourse*

12. sterilization *process rendering an individual unable to produce offspring*

13. human papilloma virus *an STD causing growths on the male & female genitalia*

14. acquired immune deficiency syndrome *a disease transmitted by exchange of body fluids during the sexual act.*

15. trichomoniasis *STD caused by a one-celled organism, Trichomonas, it affects the genitourinary system.*

16. artificial insemination *introduction of semen into the vagina by artificial means*

17. chlamydia *one of the more prevalent STDs, caused by bacterium, Chlamydia trachomatis*

18. condom *a cover for the penis worn during coitus*

19. prosthesis *an artificial replacement of an absent body part*

20. human immunodeficiency virus *a type of retrovirus that causes AIDS.*

reuse of contaminated needles and contaminated blood transfusions that affects the body's immune system

Exercise 23 ....

Match the terms in the first column with their correct definitions in the second column.

_____ 1. coitus

_____ 2. ejaculation

_____ 3. human papilloma virus

_____ 4. gonads

_____ 5. genital herpes

_____ 6. gonorrhea

_____ 7. heterosexual

_____ 8. orgasm

_____ 9. condom

_____ 10. prosthesis

a. male and female sex glands

b. climax of sexual stimulation

c. one who is attracted to a member of the opposite sex

d. STD caused by Herpesvirus hominis type 2

e. ejection of semen

f. an artificial replacement for an absent body part

g. sexual intercourse between man and woman

h. venereal warts

i. contagious and inflammatory STD

j. cover of the penis worn during coitus

k. one who is attracted to a member of the same sex

Exercise 24 ....

Match the terms in the first column with their correct definitions in the second column.

_____ 1. homosexual

_____ 2. STD

_____ 3. sterilization

_____ 4. syphilis

_____ 5. puberty

_____ 6. AIDS

_____ 7. trichomoniasis

_____ 8. artificial insemination

_____ 9. chlamydia

_____ 10. HIV

a. abbreviation for diseases such as syphilis, gonorrhea, and genital herpes

b. a disease that affects the body's immune system

c. a type of retrovirus that causes AIDS

d. sexually transmitted disease that can affect any organ and that can be transmitted to an unborn infant

e. introduction of semen into vagina by means other than intercourse

f. one who is attracted to members of the same sex

g. a prevalent STD caused by a bacterium, _C. trachomatis_ (silent STD)

h. process rendering an individual unable to produce offspring

i. an STD caused by a one-cell organism, _Trichomonas_

j. period when the ability to sexually reproduce begins

Exercise 25

Spell each of the complementary terms. Have someone dictate the terms on pp. 194 and 195 to you, or say the words into a tape recorder; then spell the words from your recording. Study any words you have spelled incorrectly.

1. _____   11. _____
2. _____   12. _____
3. _____   13. _____
4. _____   14. _____
5. _____   15. _____
6. _____   16. _____
7. _____   17. _____
8. _____   18. _____
9. _____   19. _____
10. _____   20. _____

Abbreviations

AIDS . . . .   acquired immune deficiency syndrome

BPH . . . .   benign prostatic hypertrophy (also called *benign prostatic hyperplasia*)

DRE . . . .   digital rectal examination

HIV . . . .   human immunodeficiency virus

HPV . . . .   human papilloma virus

PSA . . . .   prostatic specific antigen

STD . . . .   sexually transmitted disease

TUIP . . . .   transurethral incision of the prostate

TUMT . . . .   transurethral microwave thermotherapy

TURP . . . .   transurethral resection of the prostate gland

CHAPTER REVIEW

Exercises

Exercise 26

Complete the hospital report by writing the medical terms in the blanks. Use the list of definitions with the corresponding numbers.

Case History: This Asian man is a retired attorney who came into the emergency department at 3 AM complaining that he was in great pain and could not urinate. He had not been seen by a physician for several years but claimed to be in good health except for a "little high blood pressure."

Source of Information: This patient and his wife, both of whom are reliable historians.

CHIEF COMPLAINT: The patient is a 75-year-old retired gentleman who comes into the emergency department complaining of lower abdominal pain and inability to void for the past 12 hours.

MEDICAL HISTORY: States that several years ago he was told that he had high blood pressure and to decrease his sodium intake and lose 15 pounds, which he has done. Otherwise unremarkable.

PRESENT ILLNESS: The patient complains of urinary frequency, 1. _____ × 2, hesitancy, intermittency, diminished force and caliber of the urinary stream, a sensation of not having completely emptied the bladder and postvoid dribbling. Earlier today, he had 2. _____ at the end of urination. Abdomen shows a suprapubic mass approximately three fingerbreadths below the umbilicus, dull to percussion, and slightly tender.

IMPRESSION: 3. _____ bladder distension secondary to urinary outlet obstruction, probably secondary to 4. _____ _____ _____ .

PLAN:
1. Indwelling Foley catheter for relief of urine obstruction.
2. 5. _____ consult.

1. night urination
2. blood in the urine
3. pertaining to urine
4. nonmalignant excessive development of the prostate gland (pertaining to)
5. study of the male and female urinary systems and the reproductive system in the male

Exercise 27 ....

To test your understanding of the terms introduced in this chapter, circle the words that correctly complete the sentences. The italicized words refer to the correct answer.

1. A *discharge from the glans penis* is referred to medically as (balanorrhagia, balanorrhea, balanorrhaphy).
2. The surgical procedure circumcision is the removal of the *foreskin,* or (glans penis, testes, prepuce).
3. *A person who is attracted to a member of the opposite sex* is (heterosexual, homosexual).
4. The patient had a diagnosis of (aspermia, phimosis, impotence), or *a narrowing of the opening of the prepuce.*
5. The *operation for the surgical fixation of the testicle is* (orchidopexy, orchidotomy, orchioplasty).

6. An *artificial replacement* or (condom, prosthesis, artificial insemination) is used to correct erectile dysfunction of the penis.

7. Which of the following is a treatment for benign prostatic hypertrophy that uses a device called a *Prostatron?* (transurethral prostatectomy, suprapubic prostatectomy, transurethral microwave thermotherapy)

Exercise 28

Unscramble the following mixed-up terms. The words on the left hint at the meaning in each of the following.

1. vas deferens (duct)   / / / / / / / / /
                             t e s y a c v o m

2. glans penis   / / / / n / / r / / /
                            r a a l b e a r h o n

3. male   / / / / / p / / / /
                            t o d y h a p r n

4. prostate gland   / / / / / / / i / / /
                           a t t i s s t o i p r

5. testes   / / / / / / / t / / /
                           m o o c h y d o r i t

Exercise 29

The following terms did not appear in this chapter but are composed of word parts that have appeared in this chapter or previous chapters. Find their definitions by translating the word parts literally.

1. **autophagia** _____
   (*aw*-tō-FĀ-jē-a)

2. **bronchadenitis** _____
   (*bron*-kad-e-NĪ)-tis)

3. **necrospermia** _____
   (*nek*-rō-SPERM-ē-a)

4. **paracystitis** _____
   (*pār*-a-sis-TĪ-tis)

5. **pathosis** _____
   (pa-THŌ-sis)

6. **polyhydruria** _____
   (*pol*-ē-hī-DRŪ-rē-a)

7. **trachelomyitis** _____
   (*trā*-ke-lō-mī-YĪ-tis)

8. **viscerogenic** _____
   (*vis*-er-ō-JEN-ik)

Suffixes Chapters 2-4 Crossword Puzzle

Across Clues

2. instrument to measure
4. substance or agent that produces or causes
6. flow, excessive discharge
8. measurement
9. disease
10. surgical repair
11. sudden involuntary muscle contraction
13. pertaining to sound or voice
14. instrument to cut
15. instrument for visual examination
17. pertaining to
18. cell
19. pertaining to carbon dioxide
22. producing, originating, causing
24. chest
25. cut into or incision
28. abnormal condition
30. rapid flow of blood
32. inflammation
34. creation of an artificial opening
36. one who studies and practices
37. control, stop
38. process of recording

Down Clues

1. softening
3. a stretching out, dilatation
5. diseased state, abnormal state
7. surgical removal
10. eating, swallowing
11. visual examination
12. breathing
13. surgical fixation, suspension
16. hernia or protrusion
17. blood condition
19. surgical puncture to aspirate fluid
20. pain
21. constriction, narrowing
23. tumor, swelling
26. resembling
27. record, x-ray film
29. pertaining to
31. pertaining to
33. study of
34. pertaining to oxygen
35. to view

█ Review of Terms

Can you build, analyze, define, pronounce, and spell the following terms *built from word parts?*

Diseases and Disorders	Surgical	Complementary
anorchism	balanoplasty	andropathy
balanitis	epididymectomy	aspermia
balanocele	orchioplasty	oligospermia
balanorrhea	orchidectomy, or orchiectomy	spermatolysis
benign prostatic hypertrophy (BPH)	orchidopexy, or orchiopexy	
cryptorchidism	orchidotomy, or orchiotomy	
epididymitis	prostatectomy	
orchiepididymitis	prostatocystotomy	
orchitis, orchiditis, or testitis	prostatolithotomy	
prostatitis	prostatovesiculectomy	
prostatocystitis	transurethral resection of the prostate gland (TURP)	
prostatolith	vasectomy	
prostatorrhea	vasovasostomy	
prostatovesiculitis	vesiculectomy	

Can you define, pronounce, and spell the following terms *not built from word parts?*

Diseases and Disorders

erectile dysfunction

hydrocele

impotent

phimosis

priapism

prostatic cancer

testicular carcinoma

testicular torsion

varicocele

Surgical

circumcision

hydrocelectomy

penile implant

suprapubic
prostatectomy

transurethral incision
of the prostate
(TUIP)

transurethral
microwave
thermotherapy
(TUMT)

Procedural

digital rectal
examination (DRE)

prostatic specific
antigen (PSA)

transrectal ultrasound

Complementary

acquired immune
deficiency syndrome
(AIDS)

artificial insemination

chlamydia

coitus

condom

ejaculation

genital herpes

gonads

gonorrhea

heterosexual

homosexual

human immuno
deficiency virus
(HIV)

human papilloma
virus (HPV)

orgasm

prosthesis

puberty

sexually transmitted
disease (STD)

sterilization

syphilis

trichomoniasis

Female Reproductive System

Objectives............... **Upon completion of this chapter you will be able to:**
1. Identify the organs and other structures of the female reproductive system.
2. Define and spell the word parts presented in this chapter.
3. Build and analyze medical terms using word parts.
4. Define, pronounce, and spell the disease and disorder, procedural, surgical, and complementary terms for the female reproductive system.

ANATOMY

The female reproductive system produces the female sex cells and hormones and also provides for conception and pregnancy (Figures 8-1 and 8-2).

Internal Organs of the Female Reproductive System

ovaries	pair of almond-shaped organs located in the pelvic cavity. Sex cells are formed in the ovaries.
ovum (*pl.* ova)	female sex cell
graafian follicles	several thousand microscopic sacs that make up a large portion of the ovaries. Each follicle contains an immature ovum. The graafian follicles develop to maturity monthly between puberty and menopause. It moves to the surface of the ovary and releases the ovum, which passes into the fallopian tube.
fallopian, or uterine, tube	pair of 5-inch (12 cm) tubes, attached to the uterus, that provide a passageway for the ovum to move from the ovary to the uterus
fimbria (*pl.* fimbriae)	finger-like ends of the fallopian tubes
uterus	pear-sized and pear-shaped muscular organ that lies in the pelvic cavity, except during pregnancy. Its functions are menstruation, pregnancy, and labor.
endometrium	lining of the uterus

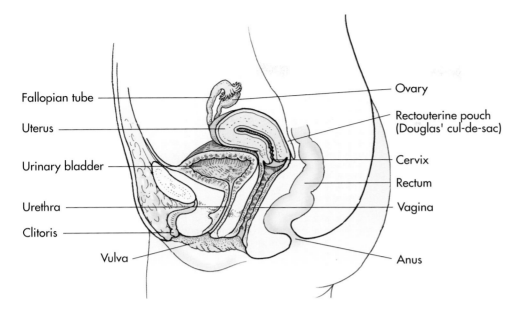

Fig. 8-1
Female reproductive organs and associated structures.

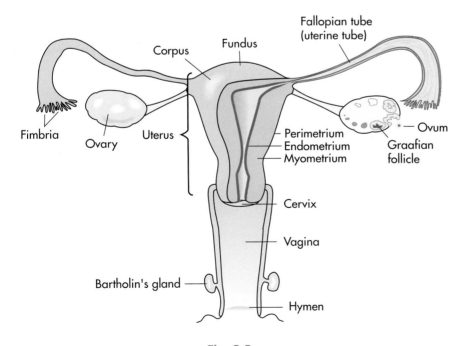

Fig. 8-2
Female reproductive system.

The fallopian tube

was named in honor of Gabriele Falloppio because he described it in his works. Falloppio also gave the **vagina** and the **placenta** their present names.

The graafian follicle

is named for Dutch anatomist Reinier de **Graaf,** who discovered the sac in 1672.

myometrium	muscular middle layer of the uterus
perimetrium	outer thin layer that covers the surface of the uterus
corpus, or body	large central portion of the uterus
fundus	rounded upper portion of the uterus
cervix	narrow lower portion of the uterus
vagina	a 3-inch (7-8 cm) tube that connects the uterus to the outside of the body
hymen	fold of membrane found near the opening of the vagina
rectouterine pouch	pouch between the posterior wall of the uterus and the anterior wall of the rectum (also called *Douglas' cul-de-sac*) (Figure 8-1)

Glands of the Female Reproductive System

Bartholin's glands
were described by Thomas Bartholinus, a Danish anatomist, in 1675.

Bartholin's glands	pair of mucus-producing glands located on each side of and just above the vaginal opening
mammary glands, or breasts	milk-producing glands of the female. Each breast consists of 15 to 20 divisions, or lobes (Figure 8-3).
mammary papilla	breast nipple
areola	dark area around the breast nipple

External Female Reproductive Structures

vulva, or external genitals	two pairs of lips that surround the vagina
clitoris	highly erogenous erectile body located anterior to the urethra
perineum	pelvic floor in both the male and female. In women it usually refers to the area between the vaginal opening and the anus.

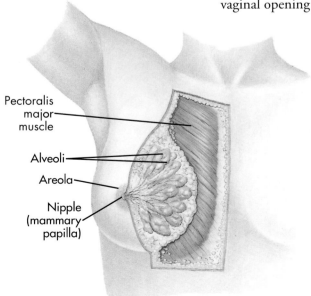

Pectoralis major muscle

Alveoli

Areola

Nipple (mammary papilla)

Fig. 8-3
Female breast.

Learn the anatomical terms by completing exercises 1 and 2.

Exercise 1 ....

Match the definitions in the first column with the anatomical terms in the second column.

_____ 1. organ in which sex
  cells are formed

_____ 2. lower portion of the
  uterus

_____ 3. lining of the uterus

_____ 4. upper portion of the
  uterus

_____ 5. pelvic floor

_____ 6. ends of fallopian tubes

_____ 7. large central portion
  of the uterus

_____ 8. layer that covers the
  uterus

_____ 9. muscle layer of the
  uterus

a. perimetrium

b. fundus

c. ovaries

d. perineum

e. fimbriae

f. cervix

g. endometrium

h. corpus

i. myometrium

j. ovum

Exercise 2 ....

Match the definitions in the first column with the anatomical terms in the second column.

_____ 1. connects the uterus
  to the outside of the
  body

_____ 2. located above the
  vaginal opening

_____ 3. breast

_____ 4. female sex cells

_____ 5. external genitals

_____ 6. passageway for
  ovum

_____ 7. colored area around
  the nipple

_____ 8. microscopic sacs in
  the ovaries

_____ 9. muscular organ

_____ 10. nipples

_____ 11. rectouterine pouch

a. ovary

b. vagina

c. Bartholin's glands

d. mammary gland

e. vulva

f. fallopian tube

g. areola

h. Douglas' cul-de-sac

i. uterus

j. mammary papillae

k. ova

l. graafian follicles

WORD PARTS

Combining Forms of the Female Reproductive System

Study the word parts and their definitions listed below. Completing the exercises that follow and Exercise Figures A and B will help you learn the terms.

Combining Form	Definition
arche/o	first, beginning
cervic/o (Cx)	cervix
colp/o, vagin/o	vagina
culd/o	cul-de-sac
episi/o, vulv/o	vulva
gynec/o, gyn/o	woman
hymen/o	hymen
hyster/o, metr/o, metr/i, uter/o . .	uterus
(NOTE: The combining vowel *i* or *o* may be used with metr/.)	
mamm/o, mast/o	breast
men/o	menstruation
oophor/o	ovary
perine/o	perineum
salping/o	fallopian tube (uterine tube)

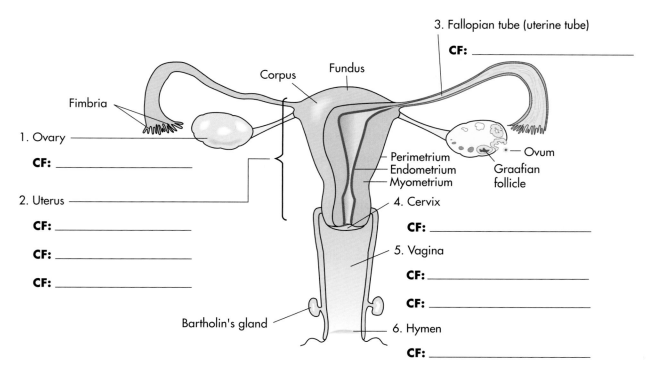

Exercise Fig. A

Fill in the blanks with combining forms in this diagram of the frontal view of the female reproductive system.

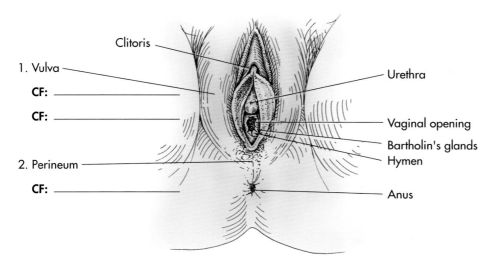

Clitoris

1. Vulva

CF: _____

CF: _____

Urethra

Vaginal opening

Bartholin's glands

Hymen

2. Perineum

CF: _____

Anus

Exercise Fig. B
Fill in the blanks with combining forms in this diagram showing the external reproductive organs.

Learn the anatomical locations and definitions of the combining forms by completing exercises 3 and 4.

Exercise 3 ....

Write the definitions of the following combining forms.

1. vagin/o _____

2. oophor/o _____

3. metr/o, metr/i _____

4. uter/o _____

5. hymen/o _____

6. hyster/o _____

7. men/o _____

8. episi/o _____

9. cervic/o _____

10. colp/o _____

11. gynec/o _____

12. mamm/o _____

13. perine/o _____

14. salping/o _____

15. vulv/o _____

16. mast/o _____

17. arche/o _____

18. culd/o _____

19. gyn/o _____

Exercise 4

Write the combining form for each of the following terms.

1. vulva

    a. _____

    b. _____

2. breast

    a. _____

    b. _____

3. menstruation _____

4. ovary _____

5. fallopian tube _____

6. perineum _____

7. vagina

    a. _____

    b. _____

8. uterus

    a. _____

    b. _____

    c. _____

9. woman

    a. _____

    b. _____

10. hymen _____

11. cul-de-sac _____

12. cervix _____

13. beginning _____

Prefix and Suffixes

Prefix	Definition
peri-	surrounding (outer)

Suffixes	Definition
-atresia	absence of a normal body opening; occlusion; closure
-ial	pertaining to
-salpinx	fallopian tube (Figure 8-4)

(NOTE: for learning purposes *salpinx* and *atresia* are presented as suffixes.)

Learn the prefix and suffixes by completing exercises 5 and 6.

> **Atresia**
>
> literally means no **perforation or hole.** It is composed of the Greek words **a,** meaning **without,** and **tresis,** meaning **perforation.** The term may be used alone as in "atresia of vagina" or combined with other word parts as in "gynatresia" meaning closure of a part of the female genital tract, usually the vagina.

Exercise 5

Write the word part for each of the following.

1. fallopian tube   _____

2. pertaining to   _____

3. surrounding   _____

4. absence of a normal body opening   _____

Exercise 6

Write the definitions of the following word parts.

1. -salpinx _____

2. peri- _____

3. -ial _____

4. -atresia _____

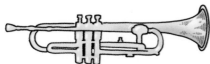

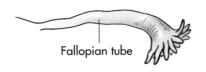

Fallopian tube

Fig. 8-4
Salpinx is derived from *salpingx,* the Greek term for *trumpet.* The term was used for the fallopian tubes because of their trumpet-like shape.

MEDICAL TERMS

The terms you need to learn to complete this chapter are listed below. The exercises following each list will help you learn the definition and the spelling of each word.

Disease and Disorder Terms

Built From Word Parts

Term	Definition
amenorrhea .... (ā-*men*-ō-RĒ-a)	absence of menstrual discharge (menostasis)
Bartholin's adenitis .... (BAR-tō-lins) (*ad*-e-NĪ-tis)	inflammation of Bartholin's gland
cervicitis .... (*ser*-vi-SĪ-tis)	inflammation of the cervix
colpitis, **vaginitis** .... (kol-PĪ-tis), (vaj-i-NĪ-tis)	inflammation of the vagina
dysmenorrhea .... (*dis*-men-ō-RĒ-a)	painful menstrual discharge
endocervicitis .... (*en*-dō-*ser*-vi-SĪ-tis)	inflammation of the inner (lining) of the cervix
endometritis .... (*en*-dō-mē-TRĪ-tis)	inflammation of the inner (lining) of the uterus (endometrium)
hematosalpinx .... (*hem*-a-tō-SAL-pinks)	blood in the fallopian tube
hydrosalpinx .... (hī-drō-SAL-pinks)	water in the fallopian tube
hysteratresia .... (his-ter-a-TRĒ-zē-a)	closure of the uterus (uterine cavity)
mastitis .... (*mas*-TĪ-tis)	inflammation of the breast
menometrorrhagia .... (*men*-ō-*met*-rō-RĀ-jē-a)	rapid flow of blood from the uterus at menstruation (and between menstrual cycles)
metrorrhea .... (me-trō-RĒ-a)	excessive discharge from the uterus
myometritis .... (*mī*-o-mē-TRĪ-tis)	inflammation of the uterine muscle (myometrium)
oophoritis .... (ō-of-ō-RĪ-tis)	inflammation of the ovary
perimetritis .... (*per*-i-mē-TRĪ-tis)	inflammation surrounding (outer layer) of the uterus (perimetrium)
pyosalpinx .... (pī-o-SAL-pinks)	pus in the fallopian tube
salpingitis .... (*sal*-pin-JĪ-tis)	inflammation of the fallopian tube (Exercise Figure C)

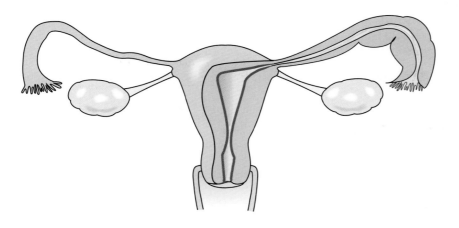

Exercise Fig. C

Fill in the blanks to label the diagram.

FALLOPIAN TUBE / INFLAMMATION

salpingocele . . . .   hernia of the fallopian tube
    (sal-PING-gō-sēl)

vulvovaginitis . . . .   inflammation of the vulva and vagina
    (*vul*-vō-VAJ-i-nī-tis)

Practice saying each of these terms aloud. To assist you in pronunciation, obtain the audiotape designed for use with this text. Learn the definitions and spellings of the disease and disorder terms by completing exercises 7, 8, and 9.

Exercise 7 . . . .

Analyze and define the following terms.

1. colpitis _____

2. cervicitis _____

3. hydrosalpinx _____

4. hematosalpinx _____

5. metrorrhea _____

6. oophoritis _____

7. (Bartholin's) adenitis _____

8. vulvovaginitis _____

9. salpingocele _____

10. menometrorrhagia _____

11. amenorrhea _____

12. dysmenorrhea _____

13. mastitis _____

14. perimetritis _____

15. myometritis _____

16. endometritis _____

17. endocervicitis _____

18. pyosalpinx _____

19. hysteratresia _____

20. salpingitis _____

21. vaginitis _____

Exercise 8 ....

Build disease and disorder terms for the following definitions using the word parts you have learned.

1. inflammation of the breast

_____ / _____
WR   S

2. excessive discharge from the uterus

_____ / _____
WR   S

3. inflammation of the fallopian tube

_____ / _____
WR   S

4. inflammation of the vulva and vagina

_____ / _____ / _____ / _____
WR   CV   WR   S

5. absence of menstrual discharge

_____ / _____ / _____
P   WR   S

6. inflammation of the cervix

_____ / _____
WR   S

7. inflammation of (Bartholin's) gland

_____ / _____
(Bartholin's)   WR   S

8. water in the fallopian tube

_____ / _____ / _____
WR   CV   S

9. painful menstrual discharge

_____ / _____ / _____
P   WR   S

10. blood in the fallopian tube

_____ / _____ / _____
WR   CV   S

11. inflammation of the vagina

a. _____ / _____   b. _____ / _____
WR   S   WR   S

12. rapid flow of blood from the uterus at menstruation (and between menstrual cycles)

_____ / ___ / _____ / ___
WR / CV / WR / S

13. inflammation of the ovary

_____ / ___
WR / S

14. hernia of the fallopian tube

_____ /__/__
WR /CV/ S

15. inflammation surrounding the uterus

___ / _____ / ___
P / WR / S

16. inflammation of the inner (lining) of the uterus

___ / _____ / ___
P / WR / S

17. inflammation of the inner (lining) of the cervix

___ / _____ / ___
P / WR / S

18. inflammation of the uterine muscle

_____ / ___ / _____ / ___
WR / CV / WR / S

19. pus in the fallopian tube

_____ /__/__
WR /CV/ S

20. closure of the uterus

_____ / ___
WR / S

Exercise 9 ....

Spell each of the disease and disorder terms. Have someone dictate the terms on pp. 212 and 213 to you, or say the words into a tape recorder; then spell the words from your recording. Think about the word parts before attempting to write the word. Study any words you have spelled incorrectly.

1. _____   12. _____

2. _____   13. _____

3. _____   14. _____

4. _____   15. _____

5. _____   16. _____

6. _____   17. _____

7. _____   18. _____

8. _____   19. _____

9. _____   20. _____

10. _____   21. _____

11. _____

Disease and Disorder Terms

Not Built From Word Parts

Term	Definition
adenomyosis . . . . (ad-e-nō-mī-Ō-sis)	growth of endometrium into the muscular portion of the uterus
endometriosis . . . . (*en*-dō-*mē*-trē-Ō-sis)	abnormal condition in which endometrial tissue occurs in various areas in the pelvic cavity (Figure 8-5)
fibrocystic breast disease . . . . (fī-bro-SIS-tik)	a disorder characterized by one or more benign tumors in the breast
fibroid tumor . . . . (FĪ-broyd)	benign fibroid tumor of the uterine muscle (also called *myoma of the uterus*) (Figure 8-6)
pelvic inflammatory disease (PID)	inflammation of the female pelvic organs
prolapsed uterus	downward displacement of the uterus in the vagina (also called *hysteroptosis*) (Exercise Figure D)
toxic shock syndrome (TSS)	a severe illness characterized by high fever, vomiting, diarrhea, and myalgia, followed by hypotension and, in severe cases, shock and death. Usually affects menstruating women using tampons.
vesicovaginal fistula . . . . (*ves*-i-kō-VAJ-i-nal) (FIS-tū-la)	opening between the bladder and the vagina (Exercise Figure E)

Practice saying each of these terms aloud. To assist you in pronunciation, obtain the audiotape designed for use with this text. Learn the definitions and spellings of the disease and disorder terms by completing exercises 10, 11, and 12.

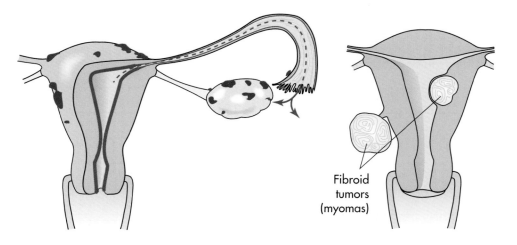

Fig. 8-5
Endometriosis.

Fig. 8-6
Fibroid tumors (myomas).

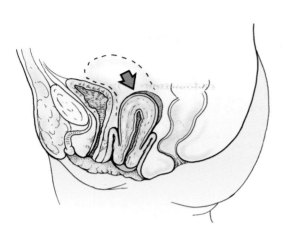

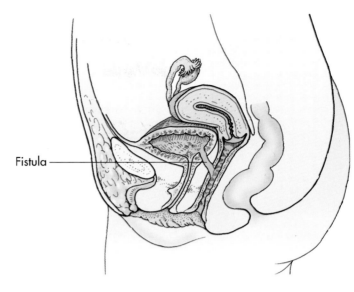

Fistula

Exercise Fig. D
Fill in the blanks to complete labeling of the diagram. Prolapsed uterus or

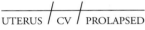

_____ / ___ / _____
UTERUS / CV / PROLAPSED

Exercise Fig. E

_____ / ___ / _____ / _____
A BLADDER / CV / VAGINA / PERTAINING TO **fistula**.

Exercise 10 ....

Fill in the blanks with the correct definitions.

1. prolapsed uterus _*downward displacement   of the uterus in the vagina*_

2. pelvic inflammatory disease _*inflammation of the female pelvic organs*_

3. vesicovaginal fistula _*opening between the bladder and the vagina*_

4. fibroid tumor _*benign fibroid tumor of the uterine muscle*_

5. endometriosis _*abnormal condition in which endometrial tissue occurs in various areas in the pelvic cavity*_

6. adenomyosis _*growth of endometrium into the muscular portion of the uterus*_

7. toxic shock syndrome _*a severe illness characterized by high fever, vomiting, diarrhea, and myalgia, followed by hypotension and, in severe cases, shock and death.*_

8. fibrocystic breast disease _*a disorder characterized by one or more benign tumors in the breast*_

Exercise 11 ....

Write the term for each of the following.

1. opening between the bladder and the vagina _*vesicovaginal fistula*_

2. benign fibroid tumor of the uterine muscle _*fibroid tumor*_

3. inflammation of the female pelvic organs _*pelvic inflammatory disease*_

4. downward displacement of the uterus in the vagina _prolapsed uterus_

5. endometrial tissue in the pelvic cavity _endometriosis_

6. growth of endometrium into the muscular portion of the uterus _adenomyosis_

7. affects menstruating women using tampons ~~adenomyo~~ _toxic shock syndrome_

8. one or more benign tumors in the breast _fibrocystic breast disease_

Exercise 12

Spell the disease and disorder terms. Have someone dictate the terms on p. 216 to you, or say the words into a tape recorder; then spell the words from your recording. Study any words you have spelled incorrectly.

1. _____   5. _____
2. _____   6. _____
3. _____   7. _____
4. _____   8. _____

Surgical Terms

Built From Word Parts

Term	Definition
cervicectomy .... (*ser*-vi-SEK-tō-mē)	excision of the cervix
colpoperineorrhaphy .... (*kōl*-pō-*pār*-i-nē- ŌR-a-fē)	suture of the vagina and perineum (performed to mend perineal vaginal tears)
colpoplasty .... (KOL-pō-*plas*-tē)	surgical repair of the vagina
colporrhaphy .... (*kōl*-PŌR-a-fē)	suture of the vagina
episioperineoplasty .... (e-*piz*-ē-ō-pār-i-nē-o-PLAST-ē)	surgical repair of the vulva and perineum
episiorrhaphy .... (e-*piz*-ē-ŌR-a-fē)	suture of (a tear in) the vulva
hymenectomy .... (*hī*-men-EK-tō-mē)	excision of the hymen
hymenotomy .... (*hī*-men-OT-ō-mē)	incision of the hymen
hysterectomy .... (*his*-te-REK-tō-mē)	excision of the uterus (Exercise Figure F)
hysteropexy .... (HIS-ter-ō-*pek*-sē)	surgical fixation of the uterus

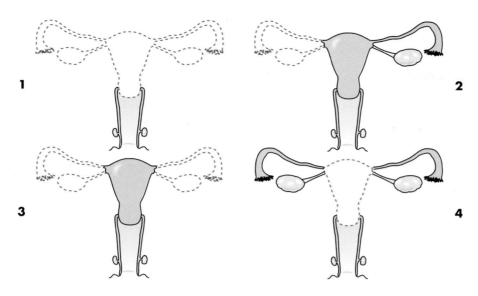

Exercise Fig. F

1, UTERUS / EXCISION, **bilateral** FALLOPIAN TUBE / CV / OVARY / EXCISION.

2, FALLOPIAN TUBE / CV / OVARY / EXCISION **3, Bilateral** OVARY / CV / FALLOPIAN TUBE / EXCISION.

4, UTERUS / EXCISION.

hysterosalpingo-oophorectomy . .   excision of the uterus, fallopian tubes, and ovaries
(*his*-ter-ō-sal-*ping*-gō-ō-of-ō-REK-tō-mē)   (Exercise Figure F)

mammoplasty . . . .   surgical repair of the breasts (performed to en-
(MAM-ō-*plas*-tē)   large or reduce in size, to lift, or to reconstruct
after removal of a tumor)

mammotome . . . .   instrument used to cut breast (tissue)
(MAM-ō-tōm)

mastectomy . . . .   surgical removal of a breast
(mas-TEK-tō-mē)

oophorectomy . . . .   excision of an ovary
(ō-of-ō-REK-tō-mē)

oophorosalpingectomy . . . .   excision of an ovary and a fallopian tube (Exer-
(ō-*of*-ō-rō-sal-pin-JEK-tō-mē)   cise Figure F)

perineorrhaphy . . . .   suture of (a tear in) the perineum
(*pār*-i-nē-ŌR-a-fē)

salpingectomy . . . .   excision of a fallopian tube
(*sal*-pin-JEK-tō-mē)

salpingostomy . . . .   creation of an artificial opening in a fallopian
(*sal*-ping-GOS-tō-mē)   tube (performed to restore patency)

vulvectomy . . . .   excision of the vulva
(vul-VEK-tō-mē)

Fig. 8-7
The Mammotome®, an instrument used for early diagnosis of breast cancer.

Types of Surgery Performed to Treat Malignant Breast Tumors

Halsted mastectomy—removal of breast tissue, nipple, underlying muscle, and lymph nodes. Also called *radical mastectomy*

Modified radical mastectomy—removal of breast tissue, nipple, and lymph nodes

Simple mastectomy—removal of breast tissue and usually the nipple, referred to as a *total mastectomy*

Subcutaneous mastectomy—removal of breast tissue, preserving the overlying skin, nipple, and areola, so that the breast may be reconstructed

Lumpectomy—removal of the cancerous lesion only, also called *tylectomy*

The mammotome is a new breast biopsy instrument. It is used to obtain the specimen for stereotactic breast biopsy procedure (see p. 223). The mammotome probe is inserted through a tiny incision that does not require sutures, thus minimizing scarring. It is useful in sampling difficult lesions and enables physicians to diagnose breast cancer at the earliest possible stage (Figure 8-7).

Practice saying each of these terms aloud. To assist you in pronunciation, obtain the audiotape designed for use with this text. Learn the definitions and spellings of the surgical terms by completing exercises 13, 14, and 15.

Exercise 13

Analyze and define the following surgical terms.

1. colporrhaphy _____

2. colpoplasty _____

3. episiorrhaphy _____

4. hymenotomy _____

5. hysteropexy _____

6. vulvectomy _____

7. perineorrhaphy _____

8. salpingostomy _____

9. oophorosalpingectomy _____

10. oophorectomy _____

11. mastectomy _____

12. salpingectomy _____

13. cervicectomy _____

14. colpoperineorrhaphy _____

15. episioperineoplasty _____

16. hymenectomy _____

17. hysterosalpingo-oophorectomy _____

18. hysterectomy _____

19. mammoplasty _____

20. mammotome _____

Exercise 14 ....

Build surgical terms for the following definitions by using the word parts you have learned.

1. suture of the vagina

_____ / _____
     WR   S

2. excision of the cervix

_____ / _____
     WR   S

3. suture of the vulva

_____ / _____
     WR   S

4. surgical repair of the vulva and perineum

_____ / _____ / _____ / _____ / _____
 WR   CV   WR   CV   S

5. surgical repair of the vagina

_____ / _____ / _____
     WR   CV   S

6. suture of the vagina and perineum

_____ / _____ / _____ / _____
 WR   CV   WR   S

7. excision of the uterus, ovaries, and fallopian tubes

_____ / _____ / _____ / _____ / _____ / _____
 WR   CV   WR   CV   WR   S

8. surgical fixation of the uterus

_____ / _____ / _____
     WR   CV   S

9. excision of the hymen

_____ / _____
     WR   S

10. incision of the hymen

_____ / _____
     WR   S

11. excision of the uterus

_____ / _____
     WR   S

12. excision of the ovary

_____ / _____
     WR   S

13. surgical removal of a breast

_____ / _____
     WR   S

14. excision of a fallopian tube   _____ / _____
                                              WR   S

15. suture of the perineum   _____ / _____
                                        WR   S

16. excision of the ovary and fal-
    lopian tube   _____ / ___ / _____ / _____
                                  WR   CV   WR   S

17. creation of an artificial
    opening in the fallopian tube   _____ / _____
                                              WR   S

18. excision of the vulva   _____ / _____
                                      WR   S

19. surgical repair of the breasts   _____ / ___ / _____
                                          WR   CV   S

20. instrument used to cut breast
    (tissue)   _____ / ___ / _____
                                WR   CV   S

Exercise 15 ....

Spell each of the surgical terms. Have someone dictate the terms on pp. 218-220 to you, or say the words into a tape recorder; then spell the words from your recording. Think about the word parts before attempting to write the word. Study any words you have spelled incorrectly.

1. _____   11. _____

2. _____   12. _____

3. _____   13. _____

4. _____   14. _____

5. _____   15. _____

6. _____   16. _____

7. _____   17. _____

8. _____   18. _____

9. _____   19. _____

10. _____   20. _____

Surgical Terms

Not Built From Word Parts

Term	Definition
anterior and posterior colporrhaphy (A & P repair)	when a weakened vaginal wall results in a cystocele (protrusion of the bladder against the anterior wall of the vagina) and a rectocele (protrusion of the rectum against the posterior wall of the vagina), an A & P repair corrects the condition (Exercise Figure G)

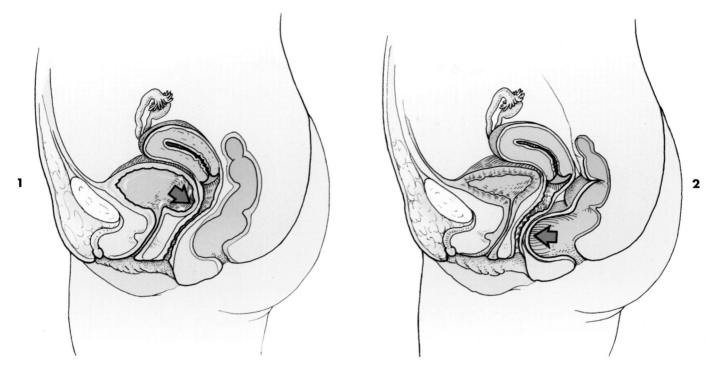

Exercise Fig. G

1, BLADDER / HERNIATION. **2**, Rectocele. Anterior and posterior colporrhaphies correct this condition.

dilatation and curettage (D & C) . (*dil*-a-TĀ-shun and kū-re-TAHZH)	dilatation of the cervix and scraping of the endometrium with an instrument called a *curette*. It is performed to diagnose disease, to correct bleeding, and to empty uterine contents.
laparoscopy or laparoscopic surgery . . . . (*lap*-a-ROS-kō-pē)	visual examination of the abdominal cavity, accomplished by insertion of a laparoscope through a tiny incision near the umbilicus. It is used for surgical procedures such as tubal sterilization (blocking of the fallopian tubes) or biopsy of the ovaries. It may also be used to diagnose endometriosis (Figure 8-8).
myomectomy . . . . (mī-ō-MEK-tō-mē)	excision of a fibroid tumor (myoma) from the uterus
stereotactic breast biopsy . . . . (ster-ē-ō-TAC-tic)	a new technique that combines mammography and computer assisted biopsy to obtain tissue from a breast lump
tubal ligation . . . . (lī-GĀ-shun)	closure of the fallopian tubes for sterilization

Practice saying each of these terms aloud. To assist you in pronunciation, obtain the audiotape designed for use with this text. Learn the definitions and spellings of the surgical terms by completing exercises 16, 17, and 18.

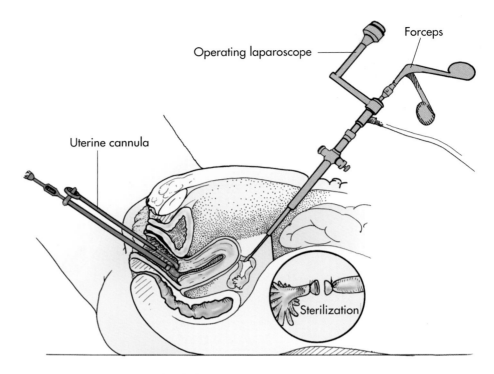

Operating laparoscope

Forceps

Uterine cannula

Sterilization

Fig. 8-8
Laparoscopic tubal sterilization.

Exercise 16

Fill in the blanks with the correct term.

1. Two procedures used for sterilization of the female are _laparoscopy_ and _tubal_ _ligation_.

2. The surgery used to repair a cystocele and rectocele is a(n) _anterior_ _and_ _posterior_ _colporrhaphy_.

3. D & C is the abbreviation for _dilation_ and _curettage_.

4. _Stereotactic_ _breast_ _biopsy_ is used to obtain tissue from a breast lump.

5. Excision of a fibroid tumor from the uterus is called _myomectomy_.

Exercise 17

Match the surgical procedures in the first column with the corresponding organs in the second column. You may use the answers in the second column more than once.

_C_ 1. dilatation and curettage   a. fallopian tubes

_a_ 2. laparoscopic sterilization   b. vagina

_a_ 3. tubal ligation   c. uterus

_b_ 4. Anterior and posterior   d. ovaries
       colporrhaphy repair
                                        e. vulva
_C_ 5. myomectomy
                                        f. mammary glands
_f_ 6. stereotactic breast biopsy

Exercise 18 ....

Spell each of the surgical terms. Have someone dictate the terms on pp. 222 and 223 to you, or say the words into a tape recorder; then spell the words from your recording. Study any words you have spelled incorrectly.

1. _____   4. _____

2. _____   5. _____

3. _____   6. _____

Procedural Terms

Built From Word Parts

Term	Definition

Diagnostic Imaging

hysterosalpingogram . . . .   x-ray film of the uterus and the fallopian tubes
(*his*-ter-ō-*sal*-PING-gō-gram)   (Exercise Figure H)

mammogram . . . .   x-ray film of the breast
(MAM-ō-gram)

mammography . . . .   process of x-ray filming the breast
(ma-MOG-ra-fē)

sonohysterography . . . .   process of recording the uterus by use of sound
(son-ō-HYST-er-og-ra-fē)   (an ultrasound procedure)

Endoscopy

colposcope . . . .   instrument used for visual examination of the
(KOL-pō-skōp)   vagina (and cervix)

colposcopy . . . .   visual examination (with a magnified view) of
(kol-POS-kō-pē)   the vagina (and cervix)

culdoscope . . . .   instrument used for visual examination of
(KUL-dō-skōp)   Douglas' cul-de-sac

> **Endoscopy**
>
> dates back to the time of Hippocrates II (460-375 BC) who mentions using a speculum to look into a rectum to see where it was affected. By the end of the nineteenth century, cystoscopy, proctoscopy, laryngoscopy, and esophagoscopy were well established. Use of the endoscope for surgery was not widely practiced in the United States until the 1970s when gynecologists started performing laparoscopic tubal sterilization. The first ectopic pregnancy was removed by laparoscopic surgery in 1973, the first laparoscopic appendectomy occurred in 1983, and the first laparoscopic cholecystectomy in 1989.

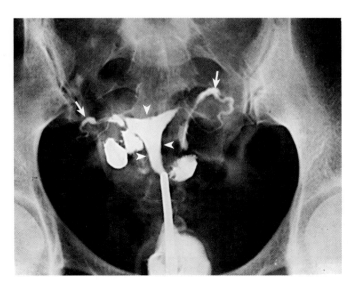

Exercise Fig. H

UTERUS / CV / FALLOPIAN TUBES / CV / X-RAY FILM. **Liquid** contrast material is injected through the vagina to outline the uterus and fallopian tubes before the x-ray film is made. This procedure is usually performed to determine whether an obstruction exists in the fallopian tubes that may cause sterility.

culdoscopy . . . .   visual examination of Douglas' cul-de-sac (Ex-
   (kul-DOS-kō-pē)   ercise Figure I)

hysteroscope . . . .   instrument used for visual examination of the
   (HIS-ter-ō-skōp)   uterus

hysteroscopy . . . .   visual examination of the uterus
   (*his*-ter-OS-kō-pē)

Additional Procedural Term

culdocentesis . . . .   surgical puncture to remove fluid from
   (*kul*-dō-sen-TĒ-sis)   Douglas' cul-de-sac (Exercise Figure I)

Sonohysterography is a new technique for evaluating the uterine cavity. Saline solution is injected into the uterine cavity, followed by transvaginal sonography. It is
used preoperatively to assess polyps, myomas, and adhesions.

Practice saying each of these words aloud. To assist you in pronunciation, obtain the
audiotape designed for use with this text. Learn the definitions and spellings of the
procedural terms by completing exercises 19, 20, and 21.

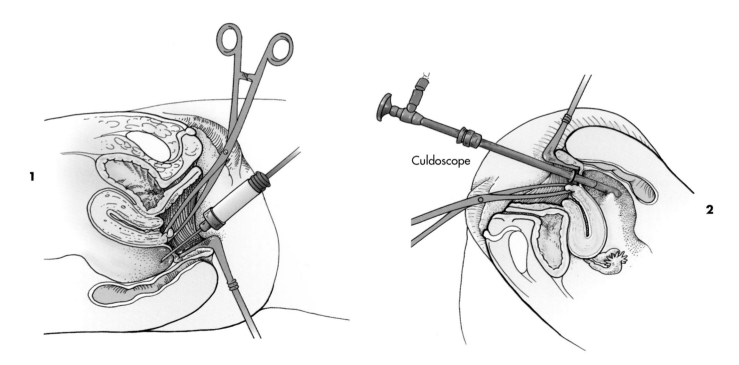

Culdoscope

Exercise Fig. I
Fill in the blanks to complete labeling of the diagram.

1, CUL-DE-SAC / CV / SURGICAL PUNCTURE TO REMOVE FLUID **performed to remove**

pus or other fluid from the rectouterine pouch. 2, CUL-DE-SAC / CV / VISUAL

EXAMINATION **performed to view the pelvic cavity and organs. It may be used to
diagnose ectopic pregnancy.**

Endoscopic Surgery

Endoscopic surgery includes the use of a slender, flexible fiberoptic endoscope that is inserted into a natural body cavity, such as the mouth, or into other body areas through a small incision. Three or four other tiny incisions may be made to accommodate visualization equipment that projects the patient's internal organs and structures onto a TV screen and to accommodate other instruments and devices needed to complete the surgery (Figure 8-9).

Because the surgeon performs endoscopic surgery, sometimes referred to as *videoscopic surgery,* by viewing a TV screen, the surgeon must master a new set of skills. Although it is thought that endoscopic surgery will not replace large incision surgery, its use is in demand because of the reduced trauma and medical cost to the patient. Continued advances in technology will improve and expand its use.

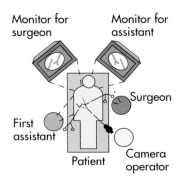

Fig. 8-9
Operative setup for laparoscopic hysterectomy.

Types of Endoscopic Surgery

Instrument	Procedure	Type of Surgery
arthroscope	arthroscopy or	biopsy
	arthroscopic surgery	meniscus repair
		synovectomy
		ligament repair
colonoscope	colonoscopy	polypectomy
hysteroscope	hysteroscopy	myomectomy
		polypectomy
laparoscope	laparoscopy or	tubal sterilization
	laparoscopic surgery	ovary biopsy
		adhesiolysis
		cholecystectomy
		appendectomy
		herniorrhaphy
		hysterectomy
pelviscope	pelviscopy	oophorectomy
		adhesiolysis
		myomectomy
		ovarian cystectomy
thoracoscope	thoracoscopy	biopsy
		wedge resection of the lung

Exercise 19 ···

Analyze and define the following procedural terms.

1. colposcopy _____

2. mammogram _____

3. colposcope _____

4. hysteroscopy _____

5. hysterosalpingogram _____

6. culdoscope _____

7. culdoscopy _____

8. culdocentesis _____

9. mammography _____

10. hysteroscope _____

11. sonohysterography _____

Exercise 20 ···

Build procedural terms that correspond to the following definitions by using the word parts you have learned.

1. x-ray film of the uterus and fallopian tubes

_____
WR / CV / WR / CV / S

2. visual examination of the vagina (and cervix)

_____
WR / CV / S

3. instrument used for visual examination of the vagina (and cervix)

_____
WR / CV / S

4. visual examination of the uterus

_____
WR / CV / S

5. x-ray film of the breast

_____
WR / CV / S

6. instrument used for visual examination of Douglas' cul-de-sac

_____
WR / CV / S

7. visual examination of Douglas'
   cul-de-sac

   ————————————— / / / —————————————
   WR   CV   S

8. surgical puncture to remove
   fluid from Douglas' cul-de-sac

   ————————————— / / / —————————————
   WR   CV   S

9. instrument used for visual examination of the uterus

   ————————————— / / / —————————————
   WR   CV   S

10. process of x-ray filming the breast   ————————————— / / / —————————————
    WR   CV   S

11. process of recording the uterus
    by use of sound

    ——————— / / / ——————— / / / ———————
    WR   CV   WR   CV   S

Exercise 21

Spell each of the procedural terms. Have someone dictate the terms on pp. 225 and
226 to you, or say the words into a tape recorder; then spell the words from your
recording. Think about the word parts before attempting to write the word. Study any
words you have spelled incorrectly.

1. _____   7. _____

2. _____   8. _____

3. _____   9. _____

4. _____   10. _____

5. _____   11. _____

6. _____

Complementary Terms
Built From Word Parts

Term | Definition
colpalgia . . . . | pain in the vagina
(kol-PAL-jē-a) |
gynecologist . . . . | physician who specializes in gynecology
(gīn-e-KOL-ō-jist) |
gynecology . . . . | branch of medicine dealing with diseases of the
(gīn-e-KOL-ō-jē) | female reproductive system
gynopathic . . . . | pertaining to disease of women
(gīn-ō-PATH-ik) |
leukorrhea . . . . | white discharge (from the vagina)
(lū-kō-RĒ-a) |

mastalgia . . . .   pain in the breast
  (mas-TAL-jē-a)

mastoptosis . . . .   sagging breast
  (mas-tō-TŌ-sis)

menarche . . . .   beginning of menstruation
  (me-NAR-kē)

oligomenorrhea . . . .   scanty menstrual flow
  (*ol*-i-gō-men-ō-RĒ-a)

vulvovaginal . . . .   pertaining to the vulva and vagina
  (*vul*-vō-VAJ-i-nal)

Practice saying each of these terms aloud. To assist you in pronunciation, obtain the audiotape designed for use with this text. Exercises 22, 23, and 24 will help you learn the definitions and spellings of the complementary terms related to the female reproductive system.

Exercise 22 . . . .

Analyze and define the following complementary terms.

  1. gynecologist _____

  2. gynecology _____

  3. colpalgia _____

  4. vulvovaginal _____

  5. mastalgia _____

  6. menarche _____

  7. leukorrhea _____

  8. oligomenorrhea _____

  9. gynopathic _____

 10. mastoptosis _____

Exercise 23 . . . .

Build complementary terms that correspond to the following definitions by using the word parts you have learned.

  1. scanty menstrual flow   _____ / ___ / ___ / ___
                                    WR   CV   WR   S

  2. white discharge (from the   _____ / ___
     vagina)   WR   S

3. beginning of menstruation

_____ / _____
         WR   /   WR

4. pain in the breast

_____ / _____
         WR   /   S

5. pertaining to the vulva and
    vagina

_____ / ___ / ___ / _____
      WR   / CV / WR /   S

6. pain in the vagina

_____ / _____
         WR   /   S

7. physician who specializes in
    gynecology

_____ / _____
         WR   /   S

8. branch of medicine dealing
    with diseases of the female re-
    productive system

_____ / _____
         WR   /   S

9. sagging breast

_____ / ___ / _____
      WR   / CV /   S

10. pertaining to disease of
    women

_____ / ___ / ___ / _____
      WR   / CV / WR /   S

Exercise 24

Spell each of the complementary terms. Have someone dictate the terms on pp. 229 and 230 to you, or say the words into a tape recorder; then spell the words from your recording. Think about the word parts before attempting to write the word. Study any words you have spelled incorrectly.

1. _____   6. _____

2. _____   7. _____

3. _____   8. _____

4. _____   9. _____

5. _____   10. _____

Fig. 8-10
Vaginal speculum.

Complementary Terms
Not Built From Word Parts

Term	Definition
dyspareunia . . . . (*dis*-pa-RŪ-nē-a)	difficult or painful intercourse
estrogen replacement therapy (ERT) . . . . (ES-trō-jen)	replacement of hormones to treat menopause, also called *hormone replacement therapy* (HRT)
fistula . . . . (FIS-tū-la)	abnormal passageway between two organs or between an internal organ and the body surface
menopause . . . . (MEN-o-pawz)	cessation of menstruation, usually around the ages of 48 to 50 years
Pap smear	method of examining stained exfoliative cells. It is used most commonly to detect cancers of the cervix.
premenstrual syndrome (PMS) . .	a syndrome involving physical and emotional symptoms occurring in the 10 days before menstruation. Symptoms include nervous tension, irritability, mastalgia, edema, and headache. Its cause is not fully understood.
speculum . . . . (SPEK-ū-lum)	instrument for opening a body cavity to allow visual inspection (Figure 8-10)

Practice saying each of these terms aloud. To assist you in pronunciation, obtain the audiotape designed for use with this text. Learn the definitions and spellings of the complementary terms by completing exercises 25, 26, and 27.

Exercise 25 . . . .

Write the definitions of the following terms.

1. menopause _____

2. dyspareunia _____

3. fistula _____

4. premenstrual syndrome _____

5. speculum _____

6. estrogen replacement therapy _____

7. Pap smear _____

Exercise 26 ....

Write the term for each of the following.

1. abnormal passageway   _____

2. painful intercourse   _____

3. cessation of menstruation   _____

4. syndrome involving physical _____   _____
   and emotional symptoms

5. instrument for opening a   _____
   body cavity

6. hormone replacement   _____ _____ _____

7. used to detect cervical cancer _____   _____

Exercise 27 ....

Spell each of the complementary terms. Have someone dictate the terms on p. 232 to you, or say the words into a tape recorder; then spell the words from your recording. Study any words you have spelled incorrectly.

1. _____   5. _____

2. _____   6. _____

3. _____   7. _____

4. _____

Abbreviations
....

A & P repair	anterior and posterior colporrhaphy
Cx	cervix
D & C	dilatation and curettage
ERT	estrogen replacement therapy
FBD	fibrocystic breast disease
GYN	gynecology
HRT	hormone replacement therapy
PID	pelvic inflammatory disease
PMS	premenstrual syndrome
TAH/BSO	total abdominal hysterectomy/bilateral salpingo oophorectomy
TSS	toxic shock syndrome

CHAPTER REVIEW

Exercises

Exercise 28

Complete the hospital report by writing the medical terms in the blanks. Use the list of definitions with the corresponding numbers.

Case History: A 48-year-old Puerto Rican woman is referred for follow-up after a suspicious mass in the left breast was discovered in routine 1. _____ . She has a positive family history (mother's sister) of 2. _____ of the breast. She also has had a(n) 3. _____ for 4. _____ and 5. _____ . She elects to have the biopsy in the outpatient surgery department.

Pathology Report: <u>GROSS DESCRIPTION</u>: Received labeled "breast biopsy" is an ovoid mass of predominantly adipose breast tissue measuring 4.5 × 3.0 × 1.3 cm. Sectioning reveals a focal area of suspicious 6. _____ . Frozen section reveals fat 7. _____ and evidence of invasive malignancy in an area measuring 0.25 cm in the center of the specimen. The surgeon is so informed.

<u>MICROSCOPIC DESCRIPTION</u>: Microscopic examination of the frozen section specimen confirms the presence of fat necrosis. There is a focal duct epithelial 8. _____ exhibiting a papillomatous pattern. In this area is found a well-differentiated adenocarcinoma. Occasional breast parenchymal fragments are also identified and show fibrocystic changes. These are predominantly nonproliferative, although in slide D, a small, radial scar containing ducts showing proliferative fibrocystic changes with significant atypia and adjacent sclerosis adenosis is identified.

<u>DIAGNOSIS</u>:   Left breast biopsy:

      1. radial scar

      2. nonproliferative and proliferative fibrocystic changes with significant atypia

      3. papillary duct adenocarcinoma

      4. focal sclerosing adenosis

---

1. process of x-ray filming of the breast
2. cancerous tumor
3. excision of the uterus
4. growth of endometrium into the muscular portion of the uterus
5. abdominal condition in which endometrial tissue occurs in various areas of the pelvic cavity
6. abnormal hard spot
7. abnormal condition of death (dead tissue because of disease)
8. excessive development (of cells)

Exercise 29

To test your understanding of the terms introduced in this chapter, circle the words that correctly complete the sentences. The italicized words refer to the correct answer.

1. The patient was diagnosed as having *painful menstruation,* or (oligomenorrhea, dysmenorrhea, amenorrhea).

2. *Inflammation of the inner lining of the uterus* is (endocervicitis, endometritis, endometriosis).

3. The patient is scheduled in surgery for a *salpingectomy,* which is the *excision* of the (fallopian tube, ovary, uterus).

4. An *episiorrhaphy* is a (suture of the vulva, discharge from the vulva, rapid discharge from the vulva).

5. A surgical procedure to *reduce breast size* is called (mammogram, mammography, mammoplasty).

6. A *hysterosalpingo-oophorectomy* is the excision of the (uterus, fallopian tubes, and ovaries; uterus, ovaries, and cervix; uterus, fallopian tubes, and vagina).

7. *Blood in the fallopian tube* is called (hematosalpinx, hydrosalpinx, pyosalpinx).

8. *Endometrial tissue occurring in various areas of the pelvic cavity* is called (adenomyosis, endometriosis, hysteratresia).

9. The doctor requested a (hysteroscope, colposcope, speculum) *to open the vagina for visual examination.*

Exercise 30

Unscramble the following mixed-up terms. The words on the left indicate the word root in each of the following.

1. uterus

/ / / s / / / / / / / /
x   e   p   r   o   y   e   t   h   s   y

2. white

/ / e / / / / / / / e / /
e   e   k   u   l   r   r   o   h   a

3. woman

/ / / / / / / / / / / /
y   o   g   o   g   y   c   e   n   l

4. breast

/ / / / / a / / / / /
g   l   a   a   s   t   m   a   i

5. menstruation

/ / / / / r / / / /
h   e   r   n   a   c   m   e

Exercise 31

The following exercise includes words and word parts introduced in previous chapters. Circle the letter of the correct answer in each of the following.

1. The term that means *excision of the nail* is
   a. onychectomy
   b. rhytidectomy
   c. pneumonectomy
   d. nephrectomy
   e. vesiculectomy

2. The patient was admitted to the hospital with a condition of a *kidney stone,* or

   a. nephroma   b. nephrohypertrophy   c. nephromegaly

   d. nephroptosis   e. nephrolithiasis

3. The patient was admitted to the hospital with possible lung cancer. To assist in confirming the diagnosis, the physician ordered an *x-ray film of the bronchi,* or

   a. bronchography   b. bronchogram   c. bronchoscopy

   d. bronchoplasty   e. bronchiectasis

4. The medical term for *pinpoint hemorrhages* is

   a. papule   b. purpura   c. pustules

   d. petechiae   e. pallor

5. The word root for the color *blue* is

   a. erythr   b. leuk   c. melan

   d. xanth   e. cyan

6. A *tumor composed of connective tissue* is called a(n)

   a. neuroma   b. sarcoma   c. epithelioma

   d. carcinoma   e. lipoma

Combining Forms—Chapters 7 and 8—Crossword Puzzle

Across Clues

1. vagina
2. prostate
5. vulva
8. cervix
9. fallopian tube
11. male
14. epididymis
17. uterus
18. ovary
22. sperm
23. abdomen
24. abbreviation for occupational medicine
26. vulva
27. glans penis
28. uterus

Down Clues

3. sperm
4. cul-de-sac
6. vessel, duct
7. menstruation
10. perineum
12. woman
13. seminal vesicles
15. testis
16. first, beginning
19. testis, testicle
20. uterus
21. testis
25. breast

Review of Terms

Can you build, analyze, define, pronounce, and spell the following terms *built from word parts?*

Diseases and Disorders	Surgical	Procedural	Complementary
amenorrhea	cervicectomy	colposcope	colpalgia
Bartholin's adenitis	colpoperineorrhaphy	colposcopy	gynecologist
cervicitis	colpoplasty	culdocentesis	gynecology (GYN)
colpitis	colporrhaphy	culdoscope	gynopathic
dysmenorrhea	episioperineoplasty	culdoscopy	leukorrhea
endocervicitis	episiorrhaphy	hysterosalpingogram	mastalgia
endometritis	hymenectomy	hysteroscope	mastoptosis
hematosalpinx	hymenotomy	hysteroscopy	menarche
hydrosalpinx	hysterectomy	mammogram	oligomenorrhea
hysteratresia	hysteropexy	mammography	vulvovaginal
mastitis	hysterosalpingo-oophorectomy	sonohysterography	
menometrorrhagia	mammoplasty		
metrorrhea	mammotome		
myometritis	mastectomy		
oophoritis	oophorectomy		
perimetritis	oophorosalpingectomy		
pyosalpinx	perineorrhaphy		
salpingitis	salpingectomy		
salpingocele	salpingostomy		
vaginitis	vulvectomy		
vulvovaginitis			

Can you define, pronounce, and spell the following terms *not built from word parts?*

Diseases and Disorders	Surgical	Complementary
adenomyosis	anterior and posterior colporrhaphy (A & P repair)	dyspareunia
endometriosis	dilatation and curettage (D & C)	estrogen replacement therapy (ERT)
fibrocystic breast disease (FBD)	laparoscopy	fistula
fibroid tumor	myomectomy	hormone replacement therapy (HRT)
pelvic inflammatory disease (PID)	stereotactic breast biopsy	menopause
prolapsed uterus	tubal ligation	premenstrual syndrome (PMS)
toxic shock syndrome (TSS)		speculum
vesicovaginal fistula		

Obstetrics and Neonatology

Upon completion of this chapter you will be able to:
1. Identify the organs and other structures relating to pregnancy.
2. Define and spell the word parts presented in this chapter.
3. Build and analyze medical terms using word parts.
4. Define, pronounce, and spell the disease and disorder, procedural, surgical, and complementary terms related to obstetrics and neonatology.

ANATOMY

Human life, or pregnancy, begins with the union of a mature female sex cell with a mature male sex cell. The duration of pregnancy in a human is 280 days, which is 9 calendar months, or 10 lunar months (a lunar month is 4 weeks or 28 days).

Terms Relating to Pregnancy

gamete	mature sex cell: sperm (male) or ovum (female)
ovulation	expulsion of an ovum from an ovary (Figure 9-1)
conception, or fertilization	beginning of pregnancy, when the sperm enters the ovum. Fertilization normally occurs in the fallopian tubes (Figure 9-1).
zygote	cell formed by the union of the sperm and the ovum (Figure 9-2)
gestation, pregnancy	development of a new individual from conception to birth
gestation period	duration of pregnancy
implantation, nidation	embedding of the zygote in the uterine lining. The process normally begins about 7 days after fertilization and continues for several days (Figure 9-1).
embryo	unborn offspring in the stage of development from implantation of the zygote to the second month of pregnancy. This period is characterized by rapid growth of the embryo (Figure 9-3).
fetus	unborn offspring from the second month of pregnancy until birth

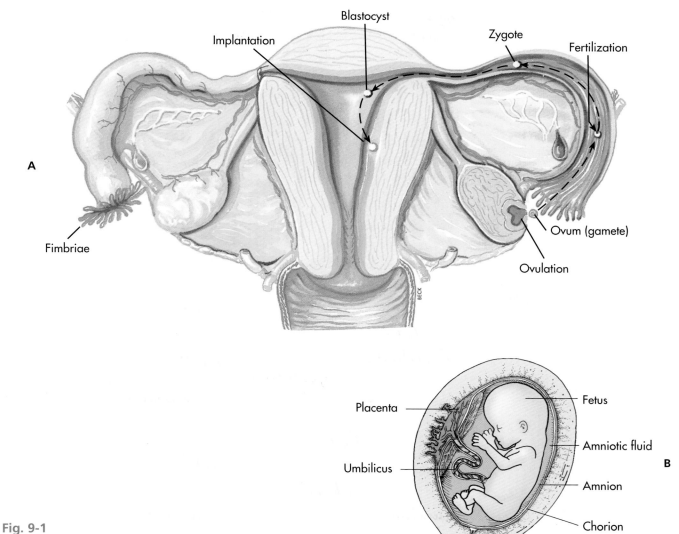

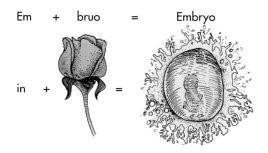

Fig. 9-1
A, Ovulation, fertilization, and implantation.
B, Development of the fetus.

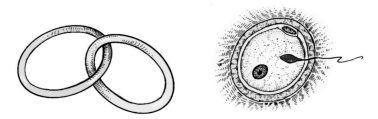

Fig. 9-2
Zygote is derived from the Greek *zygosis,* which means *yoking* or *joining together.*

Fig. 9-3
Embryo comes from the Greek *em,* meaning *in,* plus *bruo,* meaning *to bud* or *shoot.*

placenta, or afterbirth . . . .   a structure that grows on the wall of the uterus during pregnancy and allows for nourishment of the unborn child

amniotic, or amnionic, sac
(also known as *bag of waters*) . . . .   membranous bag that surrounds the fetus before delivery

chorion . . . .   outermost layer of the fetal membrane

amnion . . . .   innermost layer of the fetal membrane

amniotic fluid . . . .   fluid within the amniotic sac, which surrounds the fetus

Learn the anatomical terms by completing exercise 1.

Exercise 1 . . . .

Fill in the blanks with the correct terms.

1. The expulsion of a mature ovum, or __*gamete*__ , from an ovary is called __*ovulation*__ . When the male gamete enters the female gamete, __*fertilization*__ occurs, and a(n) __*zygote*__ is formed. This marks the beginning of the __*gestation*__ period.

2. Once the zygote is implanted, it becomes a(n) __*embryo*__ until the second month of gestation. The unborn offspring from the second month until birth is called a(n) __*fetus*__ .

3. The fetus is surrounded by a(n) __*amniotic*__ sac, which has an outermost layer, called the __*chorion*__ , and an innermost layer, called the __*amnion*__ . This sac contains the __*amniotic*__ fluid that surrounds the fetus.

▌ W O R D   P A R T S

▌ Combining Forms for Obstetrics and Neonatology

Study the word parts and their definitions listed below. Completing the exercises that follow and Exercise Figure A will help you to learn the terms.

Combining Form	Definition
amni/o, amnion/o	amnion, amniotic fluid
chori/o	chorion
embry/o	embryo, to be full
fet/o, fet/i . . . . (NOTE: both *i* and *o* may be used as combining vowels with *fet*.)	fetus, unborn child
gravid/o, cyes/o, cyes/i . . . . (NOTE: both *o* and *i* may be used as combining vowels with *cyes*.)	pregnancy

Puerper

is made up of two Latin word roots: **puer,** meaning **child,** and **per,** meaning **through.**

Exercise Fig. A
Fill in the blanks with combining forms in this diagram of fetal development.

lact/o . . . . milk
nat/o . . . . birth
omphal/o . . . . umbilicus, navel
par/o, part/o . . . . bear, give birth to; labor, childbirth
puerper/o . . . . childbirth

Learn the anatomical locations and definitions of the combining forms by completing exercises 2 and 3.

Exercise 2

Write the definitions of the following combining forms.

1. fet/o, fet/i _____

2. lact/o _____

3. par/o, part/o _____

4. omphal/o _____

5. amni/o, amnion/o _____

6. puerper/o _____

7. gravid/o, cyes/o, cyes/i _____

8. nat/o _____

9. chori/o _____

10. embry/o _____

Exercise 3

Write the combining form for each of the following terms.

1. milk   _____

2. fetus   _____

3. chorion   _____

4. amnion, amniotic fluid   a. _____

                                 b. _____

5. childbirth   _____

6. give birth to   a. _____

                                 b. _____

7. pregnancy   a. _____

                                 b. _____

8. embryo   _____

9. birth   _____

10. umbilicus, or navel   _____

Combining Forms Commonly Used In Obstetrics and Neonatology

Combining Form	Definition
cephal/o	head
esophag/o	esophagus (tube leading from the throat to the stomach) (see Figure 11-1, p. 317)
pelv/i, pelv/o . . . . (NOTE: both *i* and *o* may be used as the combining vowel with *pelv.*)	pelvic bone, pelvis (see Exercise Figures A and B, pp. 426 and 427)
prim/i . . . . (NOTE: the combining vowel is *i.*)	first
pseud/o	false
pylor/o	pylorus (pyloric sphincter) (see Figure 11-2, p. 318)

Learn the combining forms by completing exercises 4 and 5.

Exercise 4

Write the definition of the following combining forms.

1. prim/i _____

2. pylor/o _____

3. cephal/o _____

4. esophag/o _____

5. pseud/o _____

6. pelv/o, pelv/i _____

Exercise 5

Write the combining form for each of the following.

1. head   _____

2. pylorus   _____

3. false   _____

4. esophagus   _____

5. first   _____

6. pelvic bone, pelvis   _____

Prefixes

Prefix	Definition
ante-	before
micro-	small
multi-	many
nulli-	none
post-	after

Learn the prefixes by completing exercises 6 and 7.

Exercise 6

Write the definitions of the following prefixes.

1. post- _____

2. multi- _____

3. nulli- _____

4. micro- _____

5. ante- _____

Exercise 7 ....

Write the prefix for each of the following definitions.

1. none _____

2. small _____

3. many _____

4. before _____

5. after _____

Suffixes

Suffix	Definition
-orrhexis	rupture
-tocia	birth, labor

> **-Orrhexis**
>
> is the last of the four **-orrh-** suffixes to be learned. The other three introduced in earlier chapters are **-orrhea** (excessive flow or discharge), **-orrhagia** (rapid flow [of blood]), and **-orrhaphy** (suturing, repair).

Learn the suffixes by completing exercises 8 and 9.

Exercise 8 ....

Write the definitions of the following suffixes.

1. -orrhexis _____

2. -tocia _____

Exercise 9 ....

Write the suffix for each of the following definitions.

1. birth, labor _____

2. rupture _____

> Several terms introduced in this chapter end with the noun suffixes, **-a, -e, -is,** and **-us.** The suffixes have no special meaning but should be analyzed as suffixes.

MEDICAL TERMS

The terms you need to learn to complete this chapter are listed below. The exercises following each list will help you to learn the definition and the spelling of each word.

Obstetric Disease and Disorder Terms
Built From Word Parts

Term	Definition
amnionitis . . . . (*am*-nē-ō-NĪ-tis)	inflammation of the amnion
chorioamnionitis . . . . (*kō*-rē-ō-*am*-nē-ō-NĪ-tis)	inflammation of the chorion and amnion
choriocarcinoma . . . . (*kō*-rē-ō-*kar*-si-NŌ-ma)	cancerous tumor of the chorion
dystocia . . . . (dis-TŌ-sē-a)	difficult labor
embryotocia . . . . (*em*-brē-ō-TŌ-sē-a)	birth of an embryo (abortion)
hysterorrhexis . . . . (his-ter-ō-REK-sis)	rupture of the uterus
salpingocyesis . . . . (sal-PING-gō-sī-ē-sis)	pregnancy occurring in the fallopian tube (an ectopic pregnancy) (Exercise Figure B)

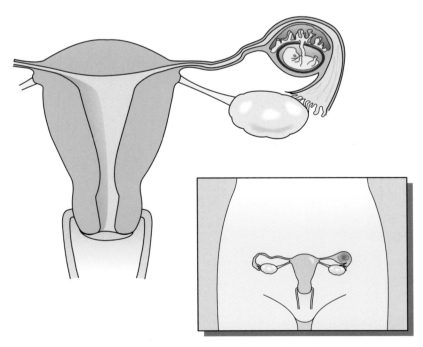

Exercise Fig. B

Fill in the blanks to complete labeling of the diagram. Ectopic pregnancy in the fal-

lopian tubes or ‾‾‾‾‾‾‾‾‾ / ‾‾‾ / ‾‾‾‾‾‾‾‾‾
FALLOPIAN TUBE   CV   PREGNANCY.

Practice saying each of these terms aloud. To assist you in pronunciation, obtain the audiotape designed for use with this text. Learn the definitions and spellings of the disease and disorder terms by completing exercises 10, 11, and 12.

Exercise 10

Analyze and define the following diagnostic terms.

1. chorioamnionitis _inflammation of the chorion and amnion_
2. choriocarcinoma _cancerous tumor of the chorion_
3. dystocia _difficult labor_
4. amnionitis _inflammation of the amnion_
5. hysterorrhexis _rupture of the uterus_
6. embryotocia _birth of an embryo, abortion_
7. salpingocyesis _pregnancy in a fallopian tube (ectopic pregnancy)_

Exercise 11

Build disease and disorder terms for the following definitions using the word parts you have learned.

1. cancerous tumor of the chorion
   _____/___/_____/___
   WR /CV/ WR / S

2. inflammation of the amnion
   _____/____
   WR / S

3. inflammation of the chorion and amnion
   _____/___/_____/___
   WR /CV/ WR / S

4. birth of an embryo (abortion)
   _____/___/___
   WR /CV/ S

5. difficult labor
   _____/_____
   P / S(WR)

6. rupture of the uterus
   _____/____
   WR / S

7. pregnancy occurring in the fallopian tube
   _____/___/_____/___
   WR /CV/ WR / S

Exercise 12 ....

Spell each of the disease and disorder terms. Have someone dictate the terms on p. 245 to you, or say the words into a tape recorder; then spell the words from your recording. Think about the word parts before attempting to write the word. Study any words you have spelled incorrectly.

1. _____   5. _____

2. _____   6. _____

3. _____   7. _____

4. _____

Obstetric Disease and Disorder Terms
Not Built From Word Parts

Term	Definition
abortion .... (ab-ŌR-shun)	termination of pregnancy by the expulsion from the uterus of an embryo or a nonviable fetus
abruptio placentae .... (ab-RUP-shē-ō) (pla-SEN-tē)	premature separation of the placenta from the uterine wall (Figure 9-4, *A*)

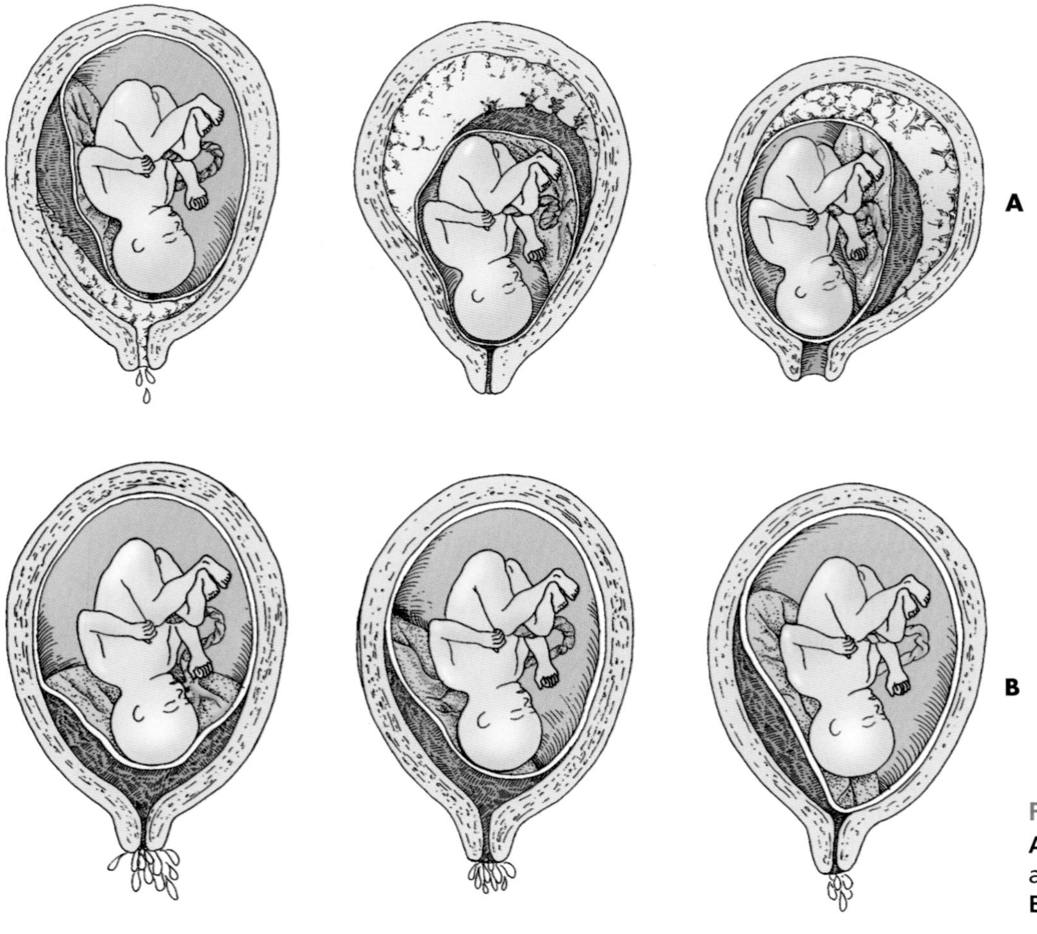

Fig. 9-4
A, Various stages of abruptio placentae.
B, Placenta previa.

**Cesarean Section
(C-Section)**

is the birth of a baby through an incision in the mother's abdomen and uterus. The origin of the term has no relation to the birth of Julius Caesar, as is commonly believed. One suggested etymology is that from 715 to 672 BC it was Roman law that the operation be performed on dying women in the last few months of pregnancy in the hope of saving the child. At that time the operation was called a **caeso matris utero,** which means **the cutting of the mother's uterus.**

eclampsia . . . .
(ē-KLAMP-sē-a)

severe complication and progression of preeclampsia characterized by convulsion and coma (see *preeclampsia* below)

ectopic pregnancy . . . .
(ek-TOP-ik)

pregnancy occurring outside the uterus, commonly in the fallopian tubes

placenta previa . . . .
(pla-SEN-ta) (PRĒV-ē-a)

abnormally low implantation of the placenta on the uterine wall. (Dilatation of the cervix can cause separation of the placenta from the uterine wall, resulting in bleeding. With severe hemorrhage, a cesarean section may be necessary to save the mother's life.) (Figure 9-4, *B*)

preeclampsia . . . .
(prē-ē-KLAMP-sē-a)

abnormal condition encountered during pregnancy or shortly after delivery, characterized by high blood pressure, edema, and proteinuria, and with no convulsions or coma

Practice saying each of these terms aloud. To assist you in pronunciation, obtain the audiotape designed for use with this text. Learn the definitions and spellings of the disease and disorder terms by completing exercises 13, 14, and 15.

Exercise 13

Write the definitions of the following terms.

1. abruptio placentae _____

2. abortion _____

3. placenta previa _____

4. eclampsia _____

5. ectopic pregnancy _____

6. preeclampsia _____

Exercise 14

Write the term for each of the following definitions.

1. premature separation of the
   placenta from the uterine wall   _____

2. severe complication and
   progression of preeclampsia   _____

3. termination of pregnancy by
   the expulsion from the uterus
   of an embryo or nonviable fetus   _____

4. pregnancy occurring outside the uterus

   _____

5. abnormally low implantation of the placenta on the uterine wall

   _____

6. abnormal condition encountered during pregnancy or shortly after delivery

   _____

Exercise 15

Spell the disease and disorder terms. Have someone dictate the terms on pp. 247-248 to you, or say the words into a tape recorder; then spell the words from your recording. Study any words you have spelled incorrectly.

1. _____   4. _____

2. _____   5. _____

3. _____   6. _____

Neonatology Disease and Disorder Terms

Built From Word Parts

Term	Definition
microcephalus .... (_mī_-krō-SEF-a-lus)	(fetus with a very) small head
omphalitis .... (_om_-fa-LĪ-tis)	inflammation of the umbilicus
omphalocele .... (om-FAL-ō-_sēl_)	(congenital) herniation (of part of intestine through the abdominal wall) at the umbilicus (Exercise Figure C)
pyloric stenosis .... (pī-LŌR-ik) (ste-NŌ-sis)	narrowing of the (pertaining to) pyloric sphincter. Congenital pyloric stenosis occurs in 1 of every 200 newborns.
tracheoesophageal fistula .... (TRĀ-kē-ō-ē-_sof_-a-_jē_-al) (FIS-tū-la)	abnormal passageway (between) pertaining to the esophagus and the trachea

Practice saying each of these terms aloud. To assist you in pronunciation, obtain the audiotape designed for use with this text. Learn the definitions and spellings of the disease and disorder terms by completing exercises 16, 17, and 18.

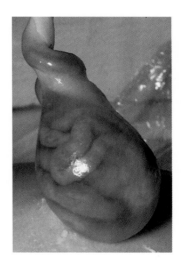

Exercise Fig. C
Fill in the blanks to label the diagram.

_____ / _____ / _____
UMBILICUS / CV / HERNIATION
containing liver.

Exercise 16

Analyze and define the following diagnostic terms.

1. pyloric stenosis _____

2. omphalocele _____

3. omphalitis _____

4. microcephalus _____

5. tracheoesophageal fistula _____

Exercise 17 ....

Build disease and disorder terms for the following definitions using the word parts you have learned.

1. hernia (of part of the intestine through the abdominal wall) at the umbilicus

   _____ / ___ / ___
   WR   CV   S

2. (fetus with a very) small head

   _____ / ___ / ___
   P   WR   S

3. narrowing of (pertaining to) the pyloric sphincter

   _____ / ___   stenosis
   WR   S

4. abnormal passageway (between) pertaining to the esophagus and the trachea

   ___ / ___ / ___ / ___   fistula
   WR   CV   WR   S

5. inflammation of the umbilicus

   _____ / ___
   WR   S

Exercise 18 ....

Spell each of the disease and disorder terms. Have someone dictate the terms on p. 249 to you, or say the words into a tape recorder; then spell the words from your recording. Think about the word parts before attempting to write the word. Study any words you have spelled incorrectly.

1. _____   4. _____

2. _____   5. _____

3. _____

Neonatology Disease and Disorder Terms

Not Built From Word Parts

Term	Definition
cleft lip and palate	congenital split of the lip and roof of the mouth (*cleft* indicates a fissure)
Down syndrome	congenital condition characterized by varying degrees of mental retardation and multiple defects (formerly called *mongolism*)

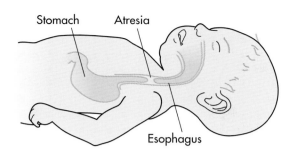

Fig. 9-5
Esophageal atresia.

erythroblastosis fetalis . . . . (e-*rith*-rō-blas-TŌ-sis) (fet-A-lis)	condition of the newborn characterized by he-molysis of the erythrocytes. The condition is usually caused by incompatibility of the in-fant's and mother's blood, occurring when the mother's blood is Rh negative and the infant's blood is Rh positive.
esophageal atresia . . . . (ē-sof-a-JĒ-al) (a-TRĒ-zē-a)	congenital absence of part of the esophagus. Food cannot pass from the baby's mouth to the stomach (Figure 9-5).
spina bifida (divided spine) . . . . . (SPĪ-na) (BIF-i-da)	congenital defect in the vertebral column caused by the failure of the vertebral arch to fuse
hyaline membrane disease **(HMD)** . . . . (HĪ-a-lin)	respiratory complication found especially in premature infants (also known as *respiratory distress syndrome of newborn* [RDS])

Practice saying each of these terms aloud. To assist you in pronunciation, obtain the audiotape designed for use with this text. Learn the definitions and spellings of the disease and disorder terms by completing exercises 19 and 20.

Exercise 19 . . . .

Match the terms in the first column with their correct definitions in the second col-umn.

_____ 1. Down syndrome

_____ 2. cleft lip and palate

_____ 3. spina bifida

_____ 4. erythroblastosis fetalis

_____ 5. hyaline membrane disease

_____ 6. esophageal atresia

a. defect of the vertebral column

b. respiratory complication

c. split of the lip and roof of the mouth

d. caused by incompatibility of the infant's and the mother's blood

e. congenital absence of part of the esophagus

f. congenital condition characterized by men-tal retardation

g. pregnancy occurring outside the uterus

Exercise 20

Spell the disease and disorder terms. Have someone dictate the terms on pp. 250 and 251 to you, or say the words into a tape recorder; then spell the words from your recording. Study any words you have spelled incorrectly.

1. _____   4. _____

2. _____   5. _____

3. _____   6. _____

Obstetric Surgical Terms

Built From Word Parts

Term	Definition
amniotomy . . . . (*am*-nē-OT-ō-mē)	incision into the amnion (rupture of the fetal membrane to induce labor)
episiotomy . . . . (e-*piz*-ē-OT-ō-mē)	incision of the vulva (perineum), usually done during delivery to prevent tearing of the perineum (also called *perineotomy*) (Figure 9-6)

Obstetric Procedural Terms

Built From Word Parts

Term	Definition
Diagnostic Imaging	
amniography . . . . (*am*-nē-OG-ra-fē)	x-ray filming of the amniotic fluid (contrast medium is injected into the amniotic fluid, outlining the amniotic cavity and fetus)
fetography . . . . (fē-TOG-ra-fē)	x-ray filming the fetus

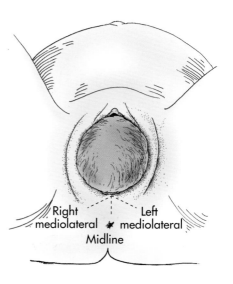

Fig. 9-6
Episiotomies.

Additional Obstetric Procedural Terms

amniocentesis . . . . (*am*-nē-ō-sen-TĒ-sis)	surgical puncture to aspirate amniotic fluid (the needle is inserted through the abdominal and uterine walls, utilizing ultrasound to guide the needle. The fluid is used for the assessment of fetal health and maturity to aid in diagnosing fetal abnormalities) (Exercise Figure D)
amnioscope . . . . (AM-nē-ō-skōp)	instrument used for visual examination of the amniotic fluid (and the fetus)
amnioscopy . . . . (*am*-nē-OS-kō-pē)	visual examination of amniotic fluid (and the fetus)
fetometry . . . . (fē-TOM-e-trē)	measurement of the fetus (for size)
pelvimetry . . . . (pel-VIM-e-trē)	measurement of the (mother's) pelvis (to determine ability of the fetus to pass through)

Practice saying each of these terms aloud. To assist you in pronunciation, obtain the audiotape designed for use with this text. Learn the definitions and spellings of the surgical and procedural terms by completing exercises 21, 22, and 23.

Exercise 21

Analyze and define the following surgical terms.

1. episiotomy _____

2. amniotomy _____

3. amnioscope _____

4. amniography _____

5. fetography _____

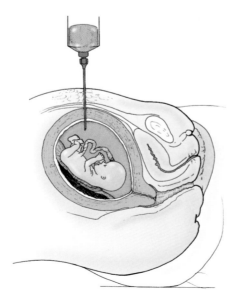

Exercise Fig. D
Fill in the blanks to label the
diagram. _____ / AMNIOTIC FLUID /
_____
CV / SURGICAL PUNCTURE TO ASPIRATE
FLUID

6. amniocentesis _____

7. amnioscopy _____

8. pelvimetry _____

9. fetometry _____

Exercise 22

Build surgical terms for the following definitions by using the word parts you have learned.

1. incision into the fetal membrane

   _____ / _____
   WR   S

2. incision of the vulva

   _____ / _____
   WR   S

3. x-ray filming of the amniotic fluid (cavity and fetus)

   _____ / ___ / _____
   WR   CV   S

4. visual examination of the amniotic fluid (and fetus)

   _____ / ___ / _____
   WR   CV   S

5. surgical puncture to aspirate amniotic fluid

   _____ / ___ / _____
   WR   CV   S

6. instrument used for visual examination of the amniotic fluid (and fetus)

   _____ / ___ / _____
   WR   CV   S

7. x-ray filming the fetus

   _____ / ___ / _____
   WR   CV   S

8. measurement of the (mother's) pelvis

   _____ / ___ / _____
   WR   CV   S

9. measurement of the fetus (for size)

   _____ / ___ / _____
   WR   CV   S

Exercise 23

Spell each of the surgical and procedural terms. Have someone dictate the terms on pp. 252 and 253 to you, or say the words into a tape recorder; then spell the words from your recording. Think about the word parts before attempting to spell the word. Study any words you have spelled incorrectly.

1. _____   3. _____

2. _____   4. _____

5. _____   8. _____

6. _____   9. _____

7. _____

Complementary Terms

Built From Word Parts

Term	Definition
amniochorial .... (*am*-nē-ō-KŌ-rē-al)	pertaining to the amnion and chorion
amniorrhea .... (*am*-nē-ō-RĒ-a)	discharge (escape) of amniotic fluid
amniorrhexis .... (*am*-nē-ō-REK-sis)	rupture of the amnion
antepartum .... (*an*-tē-PAR-tum)	occurring before childbirth
cyesiology .... (sī-*ē*-sē-OL-ō-jē)	study of pregnancy
cyesis .... (sī-Ē-sis)	pregnancy
embryogenic .... (*em*-brē-ō-JEN-ik)	producing an embryo
embryoid .... (EM-brē-oyd)	resembling an embryo
embryologist .... (*em*-brē-OL-ō-jist)	one who specializes in embryology
embryology .... (*em*-brē-OL-ō-jē)	study (or science of the development) of the embryo
fetal .... (FĒ-tal)	pertaining to the fetus
gravida .... (GRAV-i-da)	pregnant woman
gravidopuerperal .... (*grav*-i-dō-pū-ER-per-al)	pertaining to pregnancy and the puerperium
intrapartum .... (*in*-tra-PAR-tum)	occurring during labor and childbirth
lactic .... (LAK-tik)	pertaining to milk
lactogenic .... (*lak*-tō-JEN-ik)	producing milk (by stimulation)
lactorrhea .... (*lak*-tō-RĒ-a)	(spontaneous) discharge of milk
multigravida .... (*mul*-ti-GRAV-i-da)	woman who has been pregnant many (two or more) times
multipara (multip) .... (mul-TIP-a-ra)	woman who has given birth many (two or more viable offspring) times

natal . . . .   pertaining to birth
(NĀ-tal)

neonate . . . .   new birth (an infant from birth to 4 weeks of
(NĒ-ō-nāt)   age, synonymous with *newborn* [NB])

neonatology . . . .   branch of medicine that deals with diagnosis
(*nē*-ō-nā-TOL-ō-jē)   and treatment of disorders in newborns

nulligravida . . . .   woman who has never been pregnant
(*nul*-li-GRAV-i-da)

nullipara . . . .   woman who has not given birth (to a viable
(nu-LIP-a-ra)   offspring)

para . . . .   woman who has given birth (to a viable off-
(PAR-a)   spring)

postpartum . . . .   occurring after childbirth
(pōst-PAR-tum)

primigravida . . . .   woman in her first pregnancy
(prī-mi-GRAV-i-da)

primipara . . . .   woman who has borne one (viable offspring)
(prī-MIP-a-ra)

pseudocyesis . . . .   false pregnancy
(*sū*-dō-sī-Ē-sis)

puerpera . . . .   woman who has just given birth
(pū-ER-per-a)

puerperal . . . .   pertaining to (immediately after) childbirth
(pū-ER-per-al)

Practice saying each of these terms aloud. To assist you in pronunciation, obtain the audiotape designed for use with this text. Exercises 24, 25, and 26 will help you learn the definitions and spellings of the complementary terms related to the urinary system.

Exercise 24

Analyze and define the following complementary terms.

1. puerpera _woman who has just given birth_
2. amniorrhexis _rupture of the amnion_
3. antepartum _occurring before childbirth_
4. cyesiology _study of pregnancy_
5. pseudocyesis _false pregnancy_
6. cyesis _pregnancy_
7. lactic _pertaining to milk_
8. lactorrhea _(spontaneous) discharge of milk_
9. amniorrhea _discharge (escape) of amniotic fluid_

10. embryologist _____ one who specializes in embryology

11. multipara _____ woman who has given birth many times 2 or more

12. embryogenic _____ producing an embryo

13. embryoid _____ resembling an embryo

14. fetal _____ pertaining to the fetus

15. gravida _____ pregnant woman

16. embryology _____ study of the embryo

17. amniochorial _____ pertaining to the amnion and chorion

18. multigravida _____ woman who has been pregnant many times 2 or more

19. lactogenic _____ producing milk

20. natal _____ pertaining to birth

21. gravidopuerperal _____ pertaining to pregnancy and the puerperium

22. neonatology _____ branch of medicine that deals with diagnosis and treatment of disorders in newborns

23. nullipara _____ woman who has not given birth

24. para _____ woman who has given birth

25. primigravida _____ woman in her first pregnancy

26. postpartum _____ occurring after childbirth

27. neonate _____ new birth

28. primipara _____ woman who has born one

29. puerperal _____ pertaining to childbirth

30. nulligravida _____ woman who has never been pregnant

31. intrapartum _____ occurring during labor and childbirth

Exercise 25

Build the complementary terms for the following definitions by using the word parts you have learned.

1. pertaining to the amnion and chorion

   _____ / _____ / _____ / _____
   WR   CV   WR   S

2. before childbirth

   _____ / _____ / _____
   P   WR   S

3. producing an embryo

    WR / CV / S

4. study of pregnancy

    WR / CV / S

5. pertaining to the fetus

    WR / S

6. pregnancy

    WR / S

7. pertaining to milk

    WR / S

8. (spontaneous) discharge of milk

    WR / S

9. discharge (escape) of amniotic fluid

    WR / S

10. false pregnancy

    P / CV / WR / S

11. one who specializes in embryology

    WR / S

12. (stimulating) the production of milk

    WR / CV / S

13. study or science of the development of embryos

    WR / S

14. rupture of the amnion

    WR / S

15. resembling an embryo

    WR / S

16. pregnant woman

    WR / S

17. pertaining to pregnancy and the puerperium

    WR / CV / WR / S

18. woman who has given birth to many (two or more viable offspring)

    P / WR / S

19. pertaining to birth

    WR / S

20. new birth (an infant from birth to 4 weeks of age)

    P / WR / S

21. branch of medicine that deals with the newborn

_____ / _____ / _____
       P   WR   S

22. woman who has not given birth (to a viable offspring)

_____ / _____ / _____
       P   WR   S

23. woman who has given birth (to a viable offspring)

_____ / _____
        WR   S

24. woman in her first pregnancy

_____ / ___ / _____ / ____
  WR CV WR S

25. after childbirth

_____ / _____ / _____
       P   WR   S

26. woman who has borne one (viable offspring)

_____ / ___ / _____ / ____
  WR CV WR S

27. woman who has been pregnant many (two or more times)

_____ / _____ / ____
   P   WR   S

28. pertaining to (immediately after) childbirth

_____ / _____
        WR   S

29. woman who has never been pregnant

_____ / _____ / ____
   P   WR   S

30. woman who has just given birth

_____ / _____
        WR   S

31. during labor and childbirth

_____ / _____ / _____
       P   WR   S

Exercise 26

Spell each of the complementary terms. Have someone dictate the terms on pp. 255 and 256 to you, or say the words into a tape recorder; then spell the words from your recording. Think about the word parts before attempting to write the word. Study any words you have spelled incorrectly.

1. _____

2. _____

3. _____

4. _____

5. _____

6. _____

7. _____

8. _____

9. _____

10. _____

11. _____

12. _____

13. _____	23. _____
14. _____	24. _____
15. _____	25. _____
16. _____	26. _____
17. _____	27. _____
18. _____	28. _____
19. _____	29. _____
20. _____	30. _____
21. _____	31. _____
22. _____	

Complementary Terms

Not Built From Word Parts

Term	Definition
breech birth .... (brēch)	parturition in which the buttocks, feet, or knees emerge first
congenital anomaly .... (kon-JEN-i-tal) (a-NOM-a-lē)	abnormality present at birth
lochia .... (LŌ-kē-a)	vaginal discharge following childbirth
meconium .... (me-KŌ-nē-um)	first stool of the newborn (greenish black)
obstetrician .... (*ob*-ste-TRISH-an)	physician who specializes in obstetrics
obstetrics (OB) .... (ob-STET-riks)	medical specialty dealing with pregnancy, childbirth, and puerperium
parturition .... (*par*-tū-RISH-un)	act of giving birth
premature infant	infant born before completing 37 weeks of gestation
puerperium .... (pū-er-PĒ-rē-um)	period from delivery until the reproductive organs return to normal (about 6 weeks)

Practice saying each of these terms aloud. To assist you in pronunciation, obtain the audiotape designed for use with this text. Learn the definitions and spellings of the complementary terms by completing exercises 27, 28, and 29.

Exercise 27 ....

Match the definitions in the first column with the correct terms in the second column.

_____ 1. vaginal discharge

_____ 2. medical specialty

_____ 3. abnormality present at birth

_____ 4. period after delivery

_____ 5. giving birth

_____ 6. physician specializing in obstetrics

_____ 7. buttocks, feet, or knees first

_____ 8. first stool

_____ 9. born before completing 37 weeks of gestation

a. lochia

b. obstetrician

c. premature infant

d. meconium

e. obstetrics

f. parturition

g. puerperium

h. lactorrhea

i. congenital anomaly

j. breech birth

Exercise 28 ....

Write the definitions of the following terms.

1. meconium _____

2. obstetrics _____

3. premature infant _____

4. lochia _____

5. puerperium _____

6. parturition _____

7. obstetrician _____

8. congenital anomaly _____

9. breech birth _____

Exercise 29 ....

Spell each of the complementary terms. Have someone dictate the terms on p. 260 to you, or say the words into a tape recorder; then spell the words from your recording. Study any words you have spelled incorrectly.

1. _____   3. _____

2. _____   4. _____

5. _____   8. _____

6. _____   9. _____

7. _____

Abbreviations

C/S, C-section . . . .   cesarean section

EDD . . . .   expected (estimated) date of delivery

DOB . . . .   date of birth

HMD . . . .   hyaline membrane disease

LMP . . . .   last menstrual period

multip . . . .   multipara

NB . . . .   newborn

OB . . . .   obstetrics

RDS . . . .   respiratory distress syndrome

CHAPTER REVIEW

Exercises

Exercise 30

Complete the hospital report by writing the medical terms in the blanks. Use the list of definitions with the corresponding numbers.

> **Case   History**:   The   patient   is   a   24-year-old   married   Latina, 1. _____ III Para II, whose EDD is 1 week from today. She has received   prenatal   care   since   the   second   month   of   pregnancy.   This 2. _____ has been uncomplicated, with no spotting, albuminuria, hypertension, edema, or 3. _____ . She has gained 25 lb. Routine ultrasonography   revealed   a   single   4. _____ . 5. _____ indicates adequate pelvis for normal-sized fetus. When examined at the 6. _____ office this week, it was noted that fetus' presentation was cephalic. Patient has attended Lamaze classes with her husband.

1. pregnant woman
2. development of a new individual from conception to birth
3. sugar in the urine
4. unborn offspring from second month of pregnancy
5. measurement of the mother's pelvis
6. physician who specializes in obstetrics

Exercise 31

To test your understanding of the terms introduced in this chapter, circle the words that correctly complete the sentences. The italicized words refer to the correct answer.

1. The premature infant was diagnosed as having *hyaline membrane disease,* a disease of the (umbilicus, erythrocytes, lungs).
2. Because of inadequate uterine contractions, the patient was experiencing *difficult labor,* or (dysphasia, dystocia, dysuria).
3. Down syndrome was diagnosed prenatally by laboratory analysis of *amniotic fluid removed by surgical puncture,* or (amniocentesis, amniography, amnioscope).
4. The word that means *before childbirth* is (intrapartum, antepartum, antipartum).
5. *Nulligravida* is a woman who (has never been pregnant, has not given birth).
6. *Multipara* is a woman who has (borne two or more viable offspring, been pregnant two or more times).
7. *Primigravida* is a woman (in her first pregnancy, who has borne one child).
8. The word that means the *act of giving birth* is (parturition, puerperium, gravido-puerperal).
9. *Rupture of the uterus* is called (hysterorrhaphy, hysterorrhexis, hysteroptosis).

Exercise 32

Unscramble the following mixed-up terms. The word on the left indicates the word root in each of the following.

1. vulva

   / / / / s / / / t / / / /
   t e y m p o s i i o

2. umbilicus

   / / / p / / / / / c / / / /
   e e l l o o m a h p c

3. amnion

   / / / / / o / / / /
   m a n t i o c

4. pregnancy

   / / / / t / / / / a / / / /
   d a v i m t i g r a u l

Exercise 33

The following are words studied in previous chapters. Write the definitions of the italicized word parts.

1. *cyto*genic _____

2. *leuko*cyte _____

3. dermato*plasty* _____

4. *laryng*itis _____

5. *pneumon*ectomy _____

6. uretero*cele* _____

7. *nephr*osis _____

8. *cervic*itis _____

9. rhino*rrhagia* _____

10. prostat*orrhea* _____

11. colp*orrhaphy* _____

Combining Forms Crossword Puzzle

Across Clues
1. pregnancy
4. childbirth
5. pregnancy
6. first
8. amnion
11. umbilicus
12. bear, give birth
13. head

Down Clues
2. amnion
3. fetus, unborn child
4. pelvis
5. chorion
6. false
7. milk
9. embryo
10. birth

Review of Terms

Can you build, analyze, define, pronounce, and spell the following terms *built from word parts*?

Diseases and Disorders (Obstetrics)	Diseases and Disorders (Neonatology)	Surgical (Obstetrics)	Procedural (Obstetrics)	Complementary (Obstetrics and Neonatology)	
amnionitis	microcephalus	amniotomy	amniocentesis	amniochorial	lactogenic
chorioamnionitis	omphalitis	episiotomy	amniography	amniorrhea	lactorrhea
choriocarcinoma	omphalocele		amnioscope	amniorrhexis	multigravida
dystocia	pyloric stenosis		amnioscopy	antepartum	multipara (multip)
embryotocia	tracheoesophageal fistula		fetography	cyesiology	natal
hysterorrhexis			fetometry	cyesis	neonate
salpingocyesis			pelvimetry	embryogenic	neonatology
				embryoid	nulligravida
				embryologist	nullipara
				embryology	para
				fetal	postpartum
				gravida	primigravida
				gravidopuerperal	primipara
				intrapartum	pseudocyesis
				lactic	puerpera
					puerperal

Can you define, pronounce, and spell the following terms *not built from word parts*?

Diseases and Disorders (Obstetrics)	Diseases and Disorders (Neonatology)	Complementary
abortion	cleft lip and palate	breech birth
abruptio placentae	Down syndrome	congenital anomaly
eclampsia	erythroblastosis fetalis	lochia
ectopic pregnancy	esophageal atresia	meconium
placenta previa	spina bifida	obstetrician
preeclampsia	hyaline membrane disease (HMD)	obstetrics (OB)
		parturition
		premature infant
		puerperium

Cardiovascular and Lymphatic Systems

Objectives............. **Upon completion of this chapter you will be able to:**

1. Identify the organs and other structures of the cardiovascular and lymphatic systems.
2. Define and spell the word parts presented in this chapter.
3. Build and analyze medical terms using word parts.
4. Define, pronounce, and spell the disease and disorder, procedural, surgical, and complementary terms for the cardiovascular and lymphatic systems.

ANATOMY

The cardiovascular system is composed of the heart, blood vessels, and blood. The function of the system is to nourish the body by transporting nutrients and oxygen to the cells and removing carbon dioxide and other waste products (Figure 10-1).

Structures of the Cardiovascular System

heart . . . . muscular organ the size of a closed fist, located behind the breast bone between the lungs. The pumping action of the heart circulates blood throughout the body. The heart consists of two upper chambers, the *right atrium (pl.* atria*)* and the *left atrium,* and two lower chambers, the *right ventricle* and the *left ventricle*. Valves of the heart keep the blood flowing in one direction. The *cardiac septum* separates the right and left sides of the heart.

right
tricuspid valve . . . . located between the right atrium and right ventricle

left bicuspid valve . . . . located between the left atrium and left ventricle

semilunar valves . . . . located between the right ventricle and the pulmonary artery and between the left ventricle and the aorta

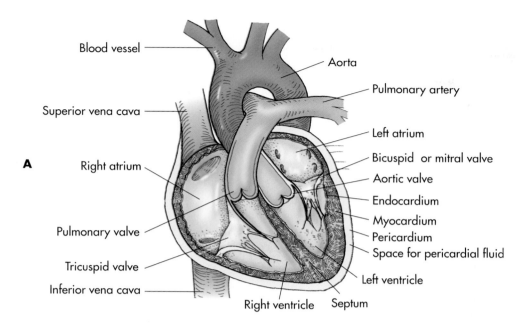

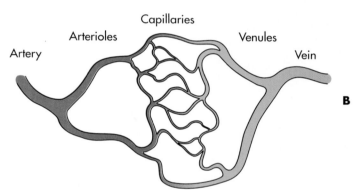

Fig. 10-1
A, Interior of the heart. **B,** Microcirculation.

three layers of the heart

pericardium	two-layer sac (*pericardial sac*) covering the heart (*pericardial fluid* allows the layers to move without friction)
visceral layer	lies closest to the myocardium
parietal layer	lines the pericardium
myocardium	middle, thick, muscular layer
endocardium	inner lining of the heart
blood vessels	tubelike structures that carry blood throughout the body
arteries	carry blood containing oxygen and other nutrients away from the heart to the body cells. The pulmonary artery is an exception: it carries carbon dioxide and other waste products to the lungs.

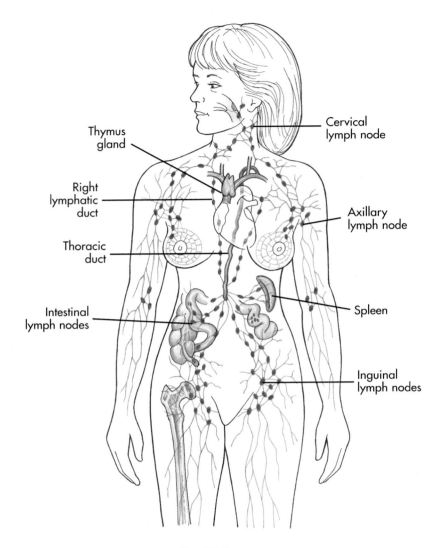

Fig. 10-2
Lymphatic system.

arterioles	smallest arteries
aorta	largest artery in the body
veins	carry blood containing carbon dioxide and other waste products back to the heart. The pulmonary veins are an exception: they carry oxygenated blood from the lungs to the heart.
venules	smallest veins
venae cavae	largest veins in the body. The *inferior vena cava* carries blood to the heart from body parts below the diaphragm, and the *superior vena cava* returns the blood to the heart from the upper part of the body
capillaries	connect arterioles with venules
blood	composed of *plasma* and *formed elements,* such as *cells*
plasma	liquid portion of blood in which cells float

cells

    erythrocytes . . . .   red blood cells that carry oxygen

    leukocytes . . . .   white blood cells that fight infection

    platelets (thrombocytes) . . . .   platelets for coagulation

Structures of the Lymphatic System

The lymphatic system has as its major function the removal of excessive tissue fluid, which develops from increased metabolic activity. Lymphatics, or lymph vessels, are found throughout the body (Figure 10-2).

lymph . . . .   transparent, usually colorless, tissue fluid

lymph nodes . . . .   small, spherical bodies made up of lymphoid tissue. They are found singularly or may be grouped together. The nodes act as filters in keeping substances such as bacteria from the blood.

spleen . . . .   located in the left side of the abdominal cavity between the stomach and the diaphragm. The spleen is the largest lymphatic organ in the body.

thymus gland . . . .   located behind the breast bone between the lungs. It plays an important role in the development of the body's immune system.

Learn the anatomical terms by completing exercises 1 and 2.

Exercise 1

Match the anatomical terms in the first column with the correct definitions in the second column.

_g_	1. aorta	a. white blood cell
_j_	2. artery	b. lies between the left atrium and left ventricle
_e_	3. arterioles	c. outer layer of the pericardial sac
_m_	4. atria	d. pumps blood throughout the body
_b_	5. bicuspid valve	e. smallest arteries
_k_	6. blood	f. inner lining of the heart
_i_	7. capillaries	g. largest artery in the body
_f_	8. endocardium	h. red blood cell
_l_	9. visceral layer	i. connects arterioles with venules
_h_	10. erythrocyte	j. carries blood away from the heart
_d_	11. heart	k. composed of plasma and cells
_a_	12. leukocyte	l. layer of the pericardial sac that lies closest to the myocardium
_n_	13. lymph	m. upper chambers of the heart
		n. colorless tissue fluid

Exercise 2

Match the anatomical terms in the first column with the correct definitions in the second column.

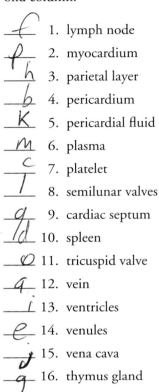

f 1. lymph node

p 2. myocardium

h 3. parietal layer

b 4. pericardium

K 5. pericardial fluid

m 6. plasma

c 7. platelet

l 8. semilunar valves

q 9. cardiac septum

d 10. spleen

o 11. tricuspid valve

a 12. vein

i 13. ventricles

e 14. venules

j 15. vena cava

g 16. thymus gland

a. carries blood back to the heart

b. two-layer sac covering the heart

c. thrombocyte

d. largest lymphatic organ in the body

e. smallest veins

f. acts as a filter to keep bacteria from the blood

g. plays an important role in the body's immune system

h. lines the pericardial sac

i. lower chambers of the heart

j. largest vein in the body

k. allows the double layer of the covering of the heart to move without friction

l. between the right ventricle and the pulmonary artery and between the left ventricle and the aorta

m. liquid portion of the blood

n. carries oxygenated blood away from the heart

o. between the right atrium and the right ventricle

p. muscular layer of the heart

q. separates heart into right and left sides

WORD PARTS

Combining Forms of the Cardiovascular and Lymphatic Systems

Study the word parts and their definitions listed below. Completing the exercises that follow will help you learn the terms.

Combining Form	Definition
angi/o	vessel (usually refers to blood vessel)
aort/o	aorta
arteri/o	artery
atri/o	atrium
cardi/o, coron/o	heart
(NOTE: *coron/o* is used for blood vessels of the heart, such as the coronary artery.)	
lymph/o	lymph
phleb/o	vein (another word root for vein is *ven/o,* covered in Chapter 6)
plasm/o	plasma
splen/o	spleen
thym/o	thymus gland
valv/o, valvul/o	valve
ventricul/o	ventricle

Learn the anatomical locations and meanings of the combining forms by completing exercises 3 and 4 and Exercise Figure A.

Vital Air

It was believed in ancient times that arteries carried air. Vital air, or **pneuma,** did not allow blood in the arteries. A cut in an artery allowed vital air to escape and blood to replace it. The Greek **arteria,** meaning **windpipe,** was given for this reason.

Coronary

is derived from the Latin **coronalis,** meaning **crown** or **wreath.** It describes the arteries encircling the heart.

Ventricle

is derived from the Latin **venter,** meaning **little belly.** It was first applied to the belly and then to the stomach. Later it was extended to mean any small cavity in an organ or body.

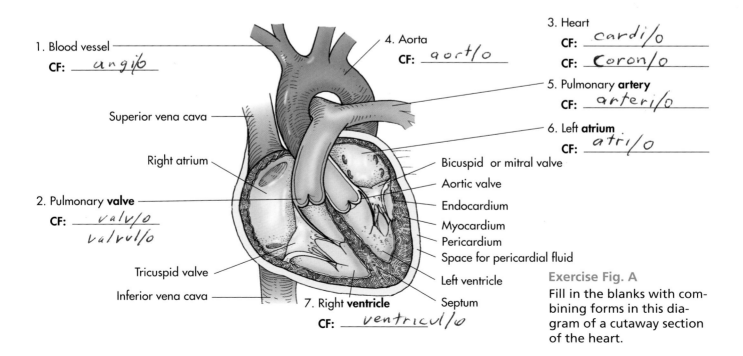

1. Blood vessel
   CF: _angi/o_

2. Pulmonary **valve**
   CF: _valv/o_
   valvul/o

4. Aorta
   CF: _aort/o_

3. Heart
   CF: _cardi/o_
   CF: _coron/o_

5. Pulmonary **artery**
   CF: _arteri/o_

6. Left **atrium**
   CF: _atri/o_

7. Right **ventricle**
   CF: _ventricul/o_

Superior vena cava
Right atrium
Tricuspid valve
Inferior vena cava
Bicuspid or mitral valve
Aortic valve
Endocardium
Myocardium
Pericardium
Space for pericardial fluid
Left ventricle
Septum

Exercise Fig. A
Fill in the blanks with combining forms in this diagram of a cutaway section of the heart.

Exercise 3

Write the definitions of the following combining forms.

1. cardi/o ___ *heart*
2. atri/o ___ ~~artery~~ *atrium*
3. plasm/o ___ *plasma*
4. angi/o ___ *vessel*
5. coron/o ___ *heart*
6. aort/o ___ *aorta*
7. valv/o ___ *valve*
8. splen/o ___ *spleen*
9. thym/o ___ *thymus gland*
10. phleb/o ___ *vein*
11. ventricul/o ___ *ventricle*
12. arteri/o ___ *artery*
13. valvul/o ___ *valve*
14. lymph/o ___ *lymph*

Exercise 4

Write the combining form for each of the following terms.

1. artery ___ *arteri/o*
2. vein ___ *phleb/o*
3. heart   a. ___ *cardi/o*
           b. ___ *coron/o*
4. atrium ___ *atri/o*
5. ventricle ___ *ventricul/o*
6. lymph ___ *lympho*
7. aorta ___ *aort/o*

8. vessel (usually blood vessel)   _angi/o_

9. valve   a. _valv/o_

       b. _valvul/o_

10. spleen   _splen/o_

11. plasma   _plasm/o_

12. thymus gland   _thym/o_

Combining Forms Commonly Used With the Cardiovascular and Lymphatic Systems

Combining Form	Definition
ather/o	yellowish, fatty plaque
bacteri/o	bacteria
ech/o	sound
electr/o	electricity, electrical activity
isch/o	deficiency, blockage
sphygm/o	pulse
steth/o	chest
therm/o	heat
thromb/o	clot

Learn the combining forms by completing exercises 5 and 6.

Exercise 5

Write the definition of the following combining forms.

1. ech/o _sound_

2. steth/o _chest_

3. thromb/o _clot_

4. isch/o _deficiency, blockage_

5. therm/o _heat_

6. sphygm/o _pulse_

7. ather/o _yellowish, fatty plaque_

8. electr/o _electricity, electrical activity_

9. bacteri/o _bacteria_

Exercise 6

Write the combining form for each of the following.

1. clot   _Thromb/o_

2. chest   _steth/o_

3. sound   _ech/o_

4. deficiency, blockage   _isch/o_

5. yellowish, fatty plaque   _ather/o_

6. heat   _therm/o_

7. bacteria   _bacteri/o_

8. electricity, electrical activity _electr/o_

9. pulse   _sphygm/o_

Prefixes

Prefix	Definition
brady-	slow
tachy-	fast, rapid

Learn the prefixes by completing exercises 7 and 8.

Exercise 7

Write the definitions of the following prefixes.

1. tachy- _fast, rapid_

2. brady- _slow_

Exercise 8

Write the prefix for each of the following.

1. fast, rapid   _tachy-_

2. slow   _brady-_

Suffixes

Suffix	Definition
-ac	pertaining to
-apheresis	removal
-crit	to separate
-graph	instrument used to record (see Chapter 5 for suffixes *-gram* and *-graphy*)
-odynia	pain
-penia	abnormal reduction in number
-poiesis	formation
-sclerosis	hardening

-graph is the instrument used to record, i.e., the machine, as in **telegraph** or **electrocardiograph**

-graphy is the process of recording, the act of setting down or registering a record, as in **photography** or **electroencephalography**

-gram is the record (the picture, the x-ray film, or tracing), as in **telegram** or **electrocardiogram**

Learn the suffixes by completing exercises 9 and 10.

Exercise 9

Write the definitions of the following suffixes.

1. -crit ___ to separate ___
2. -graph ___ instrument used to record ___
3. -penia ___ abnormal reduction in number ___
4. -sclerosis ___ hardening ___
5. -odynia ___ pain ___
6. -apheresis ___ removal ___
7. -poiesis ___ formation ___
8. -ac ___ pertaining to ___

Exercise 10

Write the suffix for each of the following.

1. formation   _-poiesis_

2. pertaining to   _-ac_

3. hardening   _-sclerosis_

4. instrument used to record   _-graph_

5. abnormal reduction in numbers   _-penia_

6. pain   _-odynia_

7. separate   _-crit_

8. removal   _-apheresis_

MEDICAL TERMS

The terms you need to learn to complete this chapter are listed below. The exercises following each list will help you learn the definition and the spelling of each word.

Disease and Disorder Terms

Built From Word Parts

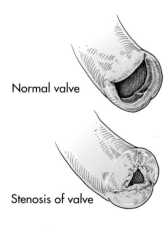

Normal valve

Stenosis of valve

Fig. 10-3
Aortic stenosis.

Term (Heart and Blood Vessels)	Definition
angiocarditis . . . . (*an*-jē-ō-kar-DĪ-tis) (NOTE: the *i* in cardi/o is dropped because the suffix begins with an *i*.)	inflammation of the blood vessels and heart
angioma . . . . (an-jē-Ō-ma)	tumor composed of blood vessels
angiospasm . . . . (AN-jē-ō-spazm)	spasm (contraction) of the blood vessels
angiostenosis . . . . (an-jē-ō-ste-NŌ-sis)	narrowing of a blood vessel
aortic stenosis . . . . (ā-ŌR-tik) (ste-NŌ-sis)	narrowing of the aorta (Figure 10-3)
arteriorrhexis . . . . (ar-*te*-rē-ō-REK-sis)	rupture of an artery

arteriosclerosis . . . .   hardening of the arteries
(ar-*te*-rē-ō-skle-*RŌ-sis*)

atherosclerosis . . . .   hardening of the ~~arteries~~ (in which yellowish,
(*ath*-er-ō-skle-RŌ-sis)   fatty plaque is deposited on the arterial wall)
(Exercise Figure B)

atrioventricular defect . . . .   defect pertaining to an atrium and ventricle
(*ā*-trē-ō-ven-TRIK-ū-lar)

bacterial endocarditis . . . .   inflammation of the inner lining of the heart
(bak-TE-rē-al)   caused by bacteria
(en-dō-kar-DĪ-tis)

bradycardia . . . .   condition of a slow heart rate (less than 60
(brād-ē-KAR-dē-a)   contractions per minute)
(NOTE: the *i* in cardi/o has
been dropped.)   *50-100 normal*

cardiodynia . . . .   pain in the heart
(*kar*-dē-ō-DIN-ē-a)

cardiomegaly . . . .   enlargement of the heart
(*kar*-dē-ō-MEG-a-lē)

cardiomyopathy . . . .   disease *process* of the heart muscle
(kar-dē-ō-mī-OP-a-thē)

cardiovalvulitis . . . .   inflammation of the valves of the heart
(kar-dē-ō-val-vū-LĪ-tis)

coronary ischemia . . . .   deficient supply of blood to the heart's blood
(KŌR-ō-na-rē) (is-KĒ-mē-a)   vessels

coronary thrombosis . . . .   abnormal condition of a clot in a blood vessel
(KŌR-ō-na-rē) (throm-BŌ-sis)   of the heart

endocarditis . . . .   inflammation of the inner lining of the heart
(*en*-dō-kar-DĪ-tis)

myocarditis . . . .   inflammation of the muscle of the heart
(*mī*-ō-kar-DĪ-tis)

pericarditis . . . .   inflammation of the outer (double layer of the)
(par-i-kar-DĪ-tis)   heart

polyarteritis . . . .   inflammation of many (sites) in the arteries
(pol-ē-ar-te-RĪ-tis)
(NOTE: the *i* in arteri/o has
been dropped.)

tachycardia . . . .   abnormal state of rapid heart rate (of over 100
(*tak*-i-KAR-dē-a)   beats per minute, which may be caused by ill-
(NOTE: the *i* in cardi/o has   ness or exercise)
been dropped.)

doctors don't want to be called until beyond 120

Term (Blood and Lymphatic Systems)

Definition

hematocytopenia . . . .   abnormal reduction in number of blood cells
(*hēm*-a-tō-sī-tō-PĒ-nē-a)

hematoma . . . .   tumor of blood (swelling caused by an accu-
(*hēm*-a-TŌ-ma)   mulation of clotted blood in the tissues)

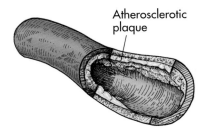

Atherosclerotic plaque

Exercise Fig. B
Fill in the blanks to label the diagram.
ather /o/ sclerosis
FATTY PLAQUE/CV/HARDENING

lymphadenitis . . . .   inflammation of the lymph glands
(*limf*-ad-en-Ī-tis)

lymphadenopathy . . . .   disease of the lymph glands. Lymphadenopa-
(lim-*fad*-e-NOP-a-thē)   thy syndrome (LAS) is a persistent, generalized
swelling of the lymph nodes often preceding
the development of AIDS.

lymphoma . . . .   tumor of lymphatic tissue
(limf-Ō-ma)

splenomegaly . . . .   enlargement of the spleen
(*sple*-nō-MEG-a-lē)

thymoma . . . .   tumor of the thymus gland
(thī-MŌ-ma)

Practice saying each of these terms aloud. To assist you in pronunciation, obtain the
audiotape designed for use with this text. Learn the definitions and spellings of the
disease and disorder terms by completing exercises 11, 12, and 13.

Exercise 11 . . . .

Analyze and define the following terms.

1. endocarditis _inflammation of the inner layer of the heart_
2. bradycardia _condition of slow heart rate_
3. cardiomegaly _enlargement of the heart_
4. arteriosclerosis _hardening of the arteries_
5. cardiovalvulitis _inflammation of the valve of the heart_
6. angiocarditis _inflammation of the blood vessels and heart_
7. arteriorrhexis _rupture of an artery_
8. tachycardia _abnormal state of rapid heart rate_
9. angiostenosis _narrowing of blood vessels_
10. atrioventricular defect _defect pertaining to the atrium and ventricles_
11. coronary ischemia _deficient supply of blood to the heart's blood vessels_
12. pericarditis _inflammation of outer layer of heart_
13. cardiodynia _pain in the heart_
14. aortic stenosis _narrowing of the aorta_
15. coronary thrombosis _abnormal condition of a clot in a blood vessel of the heart_
16. atherosclerosis _hardening of the yellowish fatty plaque deposited on the arterial wall_

17. myocarditis _____ inflammation of the muscle of the heart

18. angioma _____ tumor composed of blood vessels

19. thymoma _____ tumor of the thymus gland

20. hematocytopenia _____ abnormal reduction in the number of blood cells

21. lymphoma _____ tumor of lymphatic tissue

22. lymphadenitis _____ inflammation of lymph glands

23. splenomegaly _____ enlargement of the spleen

24. hematoma _____ tumor of blood

25. polyarteritis _____ inflammation of many (sites) in the arteries

26. cardiomyopathy _____ disease of the heart muscles

27. bacterial endocarditis _____ inflammation within the heart caused by bacteria

28. angiospasm _____ spasm of the blood vessels

29. lymphadenopathy _____ disease of the lymph glands

Exercise 12

Build disease and disorder terms for the following definitions using the word parts you have learned.

1. rupture of an artery

_____
WR / S

2. enlargement of the heart

_____
WR / CV / S

3. deficient supply of blood to the heart's blood vessels

_____
WR / S

_____
WR / S

4. inflammation of the blood vessels and the heart

_____
WR / CV / WR / S

5. inflammation of the inner layer of the heart

_____
P / WR / S

6. condition of slow heart rate

_____
P / WR / S

7. hardening of the arteries

    _____ / ___ / ___
                    WR   CV   S

8. abnormal condition of a clot in a blood vessel of the heart

    _____ / ___
                    WR   S

    _____ / ___
                    WR   S

9. pain in the heart

    _____ / ___
                    WR   S

10. inflammation of the muscle of the heart

    _____ / ___ / ___ / ___
                    WR   CV   WR   S

11. narrowing of blood vessels

    _____ / ___ / ___
                    WR   CV   S

12. abnormal state of a rapid heart rate

    _____ / ___ / ___
                    P   WR   S

13. hardening of the arteries (yellowish, fatty plaque is deposited on the arterial wall)

    _____ / ___ / ___
                    WR   CV   S

14. tumor composed of blood vessels

    _____ / ___
                    WR   S

15. inflammation of the valves of the heart

    _____ / ___ / ___ / ___
                    WR   CV   WR   S

16. narrowing of the aorta

    _____ / ___ _____ stenosis
                    WR   S

17. inflammation of the outer double layer of the heart

    _____ / ___ / ___
                    P   WR   S

18. defect pertaining to the atrium and ventricle of the heart

    _____ / ___ / ___ / ___ _____ defect
                    WR   CV   WR   S

19. abnormal reduction in number of blood cells

    _____ / ___ / ___ / ___ / ___
                    WR   CV   WR   CV   S

20. tumor of lymphatic tissue

    _____ / ___
                    WR   S

21. tumor of the thymus gland

    _____ / ___
                    WR   S

22. enlargement of the spleen

    _____ / ___ / ___
                    WR   CV   S

23. tumor of blood (accumulation of clotted blood in the tissues)

   _____ / _____
   WR   S

24. inflammation of lymph glands

   _____ / _____ / _____
   WR   WR   S

25. disease of the heart muscle

   _____ / __ / __ / __ / _____
   WR   CV   WR   CV   S

26. inflammation of many (sites) in the arteries

   _____ / _____ / _____
   P   WR   S

27. spasm of the blood vessels

   _____ / __ / _____
   WR   CV   S

28. inflammation of the inner lining of the heart caused by bacteria

   _____ / _____   _____ / _____ / _____
   WR   S   P   WR   S

29. disease of the lymph glands

   _____ / _____ / __ / _____
   WR   WR   CV   S

Exercise 13

Spell each of the disease and disorder terms. Have someone dictate the terms on pp. 276-278 to you, or say the words into a tape recorder; then spell the words from your recording. Think about the word parts before attempting to write the word. Study any words you have spelled incorrectly.

1. _____   16. _____

2. _____   17. _____

3. _____   18. _____

4. _____   19. _____

5. _____   20. _____

6. _____   21. _____

7. _____   22. _____

8. _____   23. _____

9. _____   24. _____

10. _____   25. _____

11. _____   26. _____

12. _____   27. _____

13. _____   28. _____

14. _____   29. _____

15. _____

Disease and Disorder Terms

Not Built From Word Parts

Term	Definition
anemia (a-NĒ-mē-a)	reduction in the amount of hemoglobin in the blood
aneurysm (AN-ū-rizm)	ballooning of a weakened portion of an arterial wall (Figure 10-4)
angina pectoris (an-JĪ-na) (PEK-to-ris)	chest pain, which may radiate to the left arm and jaw, that occurs when there is an insufficient supply of blood to the heart muscle
cardiac arrest (KAR-dē-ak) (a-REST)	sudden cessation of cardiac output and effective circulation, which requires cardiopulmonary resuscitation (CPR)
cardiac tamponade (KAR-dē-ak) (tam-pō-NĀD)	acute compression of the heart caused by fluid accumulation in the pericardial cavity
coarctation of the aorta (*kō*-ark-TĀ-shun)	congenital cardiac condition characterized by a narrowing of the aorta (Figure 10-5)
congenital heart disease (kon-JEN-i-tal)	heart abnormality present at birth
congestive heart failure (CHF) (kon-JES-tiv)	inability of the heart to pump enough blood through the body to supply the tissues and organs
coronary occlusion (KŌR-ō-na-rē) (o-KLŪ-zhun)	obstruction of an artery of the heart, usually from atherosclerosis (also called *heart attack*)
deep vein thrombosis (DVT)	condition of thrombus in a deep vein of the body. Iliac and femoral veins are commonly affected.
dysrhythmia (dis-RITH-mē-a)	any disturbance or abnormality in the heart's normal rhythmic pattern
embolus, *pl.* **emboli** (EM-bō-lus), (EM-bō-lī)	blood clot or foreign material, such as air or fat, which enters the bloodstream and moves until it lodges at another point in the circulation
fibrillation (fi-bril-Ā-shun)	rapid, quivering, noncoordinated contractions of the atria or ventricles
hemophilia (hē-mō-FIL-ē-a)	inherited bleeding disease caused by a deficiency of the coagulation factor VIII
hemorrhoid (HEM-ō-royd)	varicose vein in the rectal area, which may be internal or external
Hodgkin's disease (HOJ-kins)	malignant disorder of the lymphatic tissue characterized by progressive enlargement of the lymph nodes, usually beginning in the cervical nodes
hypertensive heart disease (HHD) (*hī*-per-TEN-siv)	disorder of the heart brought about by persistent high blood pressure

Angina Pectoris

was believed by the ancients to be a disorder of the breast. The Latin **angere,** meaning **to throttle,** was used to represent the sudden pain and was added to **pectus** for **breast.**

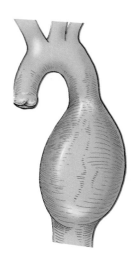

Fig. 10-4
 Aneurysm.

Hodgkin's Disease

was first described in 1832 by Thomas Hodgkin, a pathologist at Guy's Hospital in London. In 1865 the name **Hodgkin's disease** was given to the condition by another English physician, Sir Samuel Wilks.

intermittent claudication . . . .
(klaw-di-KĀ-shun)

pain and discomfort in calf muscles while walking. A condition seen in occlusive artery disease.

leukemia . . . .
(lū-KĒ-mē-a)

disease characterized by excessive increase in abnormal white blood cells formed in the bone marrow

mitral valve stenosis . . . .
(MĪ-tral)

a narrowing of the mitral valves from scarring, usually caused by episodes of rheumatic fever

myocardial infarction (MI) . . . . . .
(mī-ō-KAR-dē-al)
(in-FARK-shun)

death of a portion of the myocardial muscle caused by an interrupted blood supply (also called *heart attack*)

rheumatic fever . . . .
(rū-MAT-ik)

an inflammatory disease, usually occurring in children and often following an upper respiratory tract streptococcal infection

rheumatic heart disease . . . .
(rū-MAT-ik)

damage to the heart muscle or heart valves caused by one or more episodes of rheumatic fever

sickle cell anemia . . . .
(SIK-el) (sel) (a-NĒ-mē-a)

a hereditary, chronic hemolytic disease characterized by crescent or sickle-shaped red blood cells

thromboangiitis obliterans . . . . . .
(*throm*-bō-*an*-jē-Ī-tis)
(ob-LIT-er-anz)

vascular inflammatory disorder, usually affecting the lower extremities (also called *Buerger's disease*) *inflammation and clotting of vessel*

varicose veins (varicosities) . . . . . .
(VAR-i-kōs)

distended or tortuous veins usually found in the lower extremities

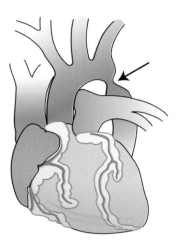

Fig. 10-5
Coarctation of the aorta.

Thromboangiitis obliterans

also known as **Buerger's disease,** still bears the name of Dr. Leo Buerger, a New York physician who differentiated the disease from another condition called **endarteritis obliterans.**

Varicose Veins and Current Treatment

Varicose veins usually occur in the superficial veins of the legs, which return about 15% of the blood back to the heart. One-way valves in the veins help move the blood upward. When these valves fail, or the veins lose their elasticity, the blood flows backward, pools, and forms varicose veins. Approximately 80 million Americans, mostly women, have varicose veins or small, shallow spider veins. Causes are heredity, obesity, pregnancy, illness, or injury. Ligation and stripping was the usual surgical procedure for treatment.

Current Treatment

Ambulatory phlebectomy—Tiny punctures are made in the skin through which the varicose veins are pulled out. Local anesthetic is used, and the procedure is minimally invasive.

Sclerotherapy—sclerotherapy takes less than an hour and requires no anesthesia. A solution is injected into the varicose vein and destroys it over several months. Sclerotherapy isn't effective on varicose veins that extend into the groin area.

Laser or intense pulsed light—This noninvasive technique is used to remove spider veins. The light causes the veins to shrink and collapse.

Practice saying each of these terms aloud. To assist you in pronunciation, obtain the audiotape designed for use with this text. Learn the definitions and spellings of the disease and disorder terms by completing exercises 14, 15, 16, and 17.

Exercise 14

Fill in the blanks with the correct terms.

1. A congenital cardiac condition characterized by a narrowing of the aorta is called ___coarctation___ of the aorta.

2. A blood clot or foreign material that enters the bloodstream and moves until it lodges at another point in the circulation is called a(n) ___embolus___.

3. Sudden cessation of cardiac output and effective circulation is referred to as a(n) ___cardiac___ ___arrest___.

4. ___Congenital___ heart disease is the name given to a heart abnormality present at birth.

5. Veins that are distended or tortuous are called ___varicose___ ___veins___.

6. Obstruction of an artery of the heart, usually from atherosclerosis is called a(n) ___coronary___ ___occlusion___.

7. ___aneurysm___ is the name given to the ballooning of a weakened portion of an artery wall.

8. ___Hodgkin's___ disease is the name given to a malignant disorder of lymphatic tissue characterized by enlarged lymph nodes.

9. Varicose veins in the rectal area are called ___hemorrhoids___

10. ___Angina___ ___pectoris___ is a cardiac condition characterized by chest pain caused by an insufficient blood supply to the cardiac muscle.

11. Death of a portion of myocardial muscle caused by an interrupted blood supply is called a(n) ___myocardial___ ___infarction___.

12. The condition in which the atria or ventricles have rapid, quivering, noncoordinated contractions is called ___fibrillation___.

13. Any disturbance or abnormality in the heart's normal rhythmic pattern is called a(n) ___dysrhythmia___

14. A disorder of the heart brought about by a persistently elevated blood pressure is called ___hypertensive___ heart disease.

15. ___Congestive___ ___heart___ ___failure___ is the inability of the heart to pump enough blood through the body to supply tissues and organs.

16. ___Thromboangiitis obliterans___ is the name given to an inflammatory vascular disorder affecting the lower extremities.

17. ___Hemophilia___ is an inherited bleeding disease caused by a deficiency of the coagulation factor VIII.

18. ___Leukemia___ is a disease in which the number of abnormal white blood cells formed in the bone marrow is excessively increased.

19. A reduction in the amount of hemoglobin in the blood results in a condition known as ___anemia___.

20. A hereditary, chronic hemolytic disease in which the red blood cells are crescent-shaped is called ___Sickle___ ___cell___ ___anemia___.

21. ___Intermittent claudication___ is a condition in which a patient suffers pain and discomfort in calf muscles while walking.

22. Acute compression of the heart caused by fluid accumulation in the pericardial cavity is known as ___Cardiac___ ___tamponade___

23. Episodes of rheumatic fever can cause ___mitral___ ___valve___ ___Stenosis___ and ___rheumatic___ ___heart___ ___disease___.

24. ___Deep___ ___vein___ ___Thrombosis___ usually affects the iliac and femoral veins.

25. An inflammatory disease usually occurring in children is ___rheumatic___ ___fever___.

Exercise 15

Match the terms in the first column with the correct definitions in the second column.

_____ 1. anemia

_____ 2. aneurysm

_____ 3. angina pectoris

_____ 4. dysrhythmia

_____ 5. cardiac arrest

_____ 6. cardiac tamponade

_____ 7. coarctation of the aorta

_____ 8. congenital heart disease

_____ 9. congestive heart failure

_____ 10. coronary occlusion

_____ 11. intermittent claudication

_____ 12. deep vein thrombosis

a. sudden cessation of cardiac output and effective circulation

b. obstruction of an artery of the heart, usually from atherosclerosis

c. ballooning or weakening of an artery wall

d. reduction of the amount of hemoglobin in the blood

e. any disturbance or abnormality in the heart's normal rhythmic pattern

f. chest pain occurring because of insufficient blood supply to the heart muscle

g. inability of heart to pump enough blood through the body to supply tissues or organs

h. pain in calf muscles while walking

i. congenital cardiac condition with narrowing of the aorta

j. acute compression of heart caused by fluid in the pericardial cavity

k. heart abnormality present at birth

l. commonly affects the iliac and femoral veins

m. rapid, quivering, noncoordinated contractions of the atria or ventricles

Exercise 16

Match the terms in the first column with the correct definitions in the second column.

_____ 1. embolus

_____ 2. fibrillation

_____ 3. hemophilia

_____ 4. hemorrhoids

_____ 5. Hodgkin's disease

_____ 6. hypertensive heart disease

_____ 7. leukemia

_____ 8. myocardial infarction

_____ 9. sickle cell anemia

_____ 10. thromboangiitis obliterans

_____ 11. varicose veins

_____ 12. mitral valve stenosis and rheumatic heart disease

_____ 13. rheumatic fever

a. inherited bleeding disease caused by a deficiency of the coagulation factor VIII

b. heart disorder brought on by persistent high blood pressure

c. distended or tortuous veins

d. excessive increase of abnormal white blood cells formed in the bone marrow

e. rapid, quivering, noncoordinated contractions of the atria or ventricles

f. caused by episodes of rheumatic fever

g. vascular inflammatory disorder usually affecting the lower extremities

h. varicose veins in the rectal area

i. blood clot or foreign material that enters the bloodstream and moves until it lodges at another point

j. malignant disorder of lymphatic tissue with enlargement of lymph nodes

k. death of a portion of myocardial muscle caused by an interrupted blood supply

l. chronic, hemolytic disease having crescent-shaped blood cells

m. often follows an upper respiratory streptococcal infection

Exercise 17

Spell the disease and disorder terms. Have someone dictate the terms on pp. 282-283 to you, or say the words into a tape recorder; then spell the words from your recording. Study any words you have spelled incorrectly.

1. _____

2. _____

3. _____

4. _____

5. _____

6. _____

7. _____

8. _____

9. _____

10. _____

11. _____

12. _____

13. _____   20. _____

14. _____   21. _____

15. _____   22. _____

16. _____   23. _____

17. _____   24. _____

18. _____   25. _____

19. _____   26. _____

Surgical Terms

Built From Word Parts

Term	Definition

angioplasty . . . . surgical repair of a blood vessel
(AN-jē-ō-plas-tē)

angiorrhaphy . . . . suturing of a blood vessel
(an-jē-OR-a-fē)

atherectomy . . . . surgical removal of plaque from a blocked
(ath-er-EK-tō-mē) | artery using a specialized catheter and a rotary cutter. Used to open blocked arteries.

endarterectomy . . . . excision within (of the thickened interior of an
(*end*-ar-ter-EK-tō-mē) | artery, usually named for the artery to be
(NOTE: the *o* from *endo-* is | cleaned out, such as *carotid endarterectomy*)
dropped for easier pronuncia- | (Exercise Figure C)
tion.)

pericardiostomy . . . . creation of an artificial opening in the outer
(*par*-i-kar-dē-OS-tō-mē) | (double) layer of the heart

phlebectomy . . . . excision of a vein
(fle-BEK-tō-mē)

phlebotomy . . . . incision into a vein (to remove blood or to give
(fle-BOT-ō-mē) | blood or intravenous fluids, also called
venipuncture)

splenectomy . . . . excision of the spleen
(sple-NEK-tō-mē)

splenopexy . . . . surgical fixation of the spleen
(SPLE-nō-*peks*-ē)

thymectomy . . . . excision of the thymus gland
(thī-MEK-tō-mē)

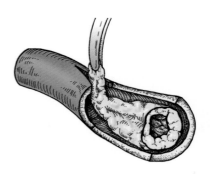

Exercise Fig. C
Fill in the blanks to label the diagram.

_____ / _____ /
WITHIN   ARTERY

_____
EXCISION

Practice saying each of these terms aloud. To assist you in pronunciation, obtain the audiotape designed for use with this text. Learn the definitions and spellings of the surgical terms by completing exercises 18, 19, and 20.

Exercise 18 ....

Analyze and define the following surgical terms.

1. pericardiostomy _____

2. thymectomy _____

3. angioplasty _____

4. splenopexy _____

5. angiorrhaphy _____

6. endarterectomy _____

7. phlebotomy _____

8. splenectomy _____

9. phlebectomy _____

10. atherectomy _____

Exercise 19 ....

Build surgical terms for the following definitions by using the word parts you have learned.

1. excision within (of the thick-
    ened interior of an artery)   _____ / _____ / _____
                                      P   WR   S

2. surgical fixation of the spleen   _____ / _____ / _____
                                          WR   CV   S

3. suturing of a blood vessel   _____ / _____
                                     WR   S

4. incision into a vein   _____ / _____
                               WR   S

5. excision of the thymus gland   _____ / _____
                                       WR   S

6. creation of an artificial
    opening in the outer layer of
    the heart   _____ / _____ / _____
                    P   WR   S

7. surgical repair of a blood
    vessel   _____ / _____ / _____
                 WR   CV   S

8. excision of a spleen   _____ / _____
                               WR   S

9. excision of a vein   _____ / _____
                              WR   S

10. surgical removal of plaque   _____ / _____
                                       WR   S

Exercise 20 ....

Spell each of the surgical terms. Have someone dictate the terms on p. 287 to you, or say the words into a tape recorder; then spell the words from your recording. Think about the word parts before attempting to write the word. Study any words you have spelled incorrectly.

1. _____   6. _____

2. _____   7. _____

3. _____   8. _____

4. _____   9. _____

5. _____   10. _____

Surgical Terms
Not Built From Word Parts

Term	Definition
aneurysmectomy . . . . (*an*-ū-riz-MEK-tō-mē)	surgical excision of an aneurysm (the ballooning of a weakened blood vessel wall)
bone marrow transplant	infusion of normal bone marrow cells from a donor with matching cells and tissue to a recipient with a certain type of leukemia or anemia
cardiac pacemaker	battery-powered or nuclear-powered apparatus implanted under the skin to regulate the heart rate (Figure 10-6)

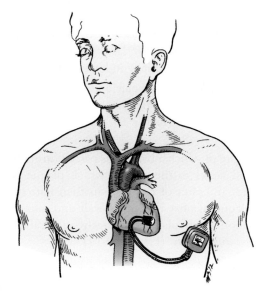

Fig. 10-6
Cardiac pacemaker.

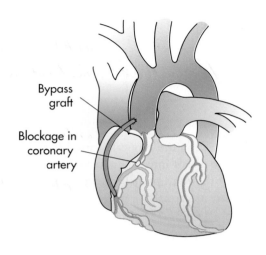

Bypass graft

Blockage in coronary artery

Fig. 10-7
Coronary artery bypass graft.

coronary artery bypass graft (CABG) . . . .
surgical technique to bring a new blood supply to heart muscles by detouring around blocked arteries (Figure 10-7)

coronary stent . . . .
(stent)
a supportive scaffold device implanted in the artery. Used to prevent closure of the artery after angioplasty or atherectomy (Figure 10-8).

defibrillation . . . .
(dē-fib-ri-LĀ-shun)
application of an electric shock to the myocardium through the chest wall to restore normal cardiac rhythm (Figure 10-9)

embolectomy . . . .
(em-bō-LEK-tō-mē)
surgical removal of an embolus or clot

femoropopliteal bypass . . . .
(FEM-or-ō-pop-li-TĒ-al)
surgery to establish an alternate route from femoral artery to popliteal artery to bypass obstructive portion (Figure 10-10)

hemorrhoidectomy . . . .
(hem-ō-royd-EK-tō-mē)
excision of hemorrhoids, the varicosed veins in the rectal region

intracoronary thrombolytic therapy . . . .
(in-tra-KOR-ō-na-rē)
(throm-bōl-I-tik)
an injection of a medication in a blocked coronary vessel to dissolve blood clots *Streptokinase*

laser angioplasty . . . .
(LĀ-zer) (AN-jē-ō-*plas*-tē)
the use of **l**ight **a**mplification by **s**timulated **e**mission of **r**adiation or laser beam to open blocked arteries, especially in lower extremities

mitral commissurotomy . . . .
(MĪ-tral) (*kom*-i-shūr-OT-ō-mē)
surgical procedure to repair a stenosed mitral valve by breaking apart the leaves (commissures) of the valve (Figure 10-11)

percutaneous transluminal coronary angioplasty (PTCA) . . .
(*per*-kū-TĀ-nē-us) (trans-LŪM-in-al) (KOR-ō-na-rē) (AN-jē-ō-*plas*-tē)
procedure in which a balloon is passed through a blood vessel to the area in which plaque is formed. Inflation of the balloon then flattens the plaque against the vessel wall and allows the blood to circulate more freely (also called *balloon angioplasty*) (Figure 10-12).

Stent

is the name of a supporting device, such as a stiff cylinder or a mold, fashioned to anchor a graft. It is used to preserve dilatation during healing or to provide support to keep a skin graft in place. Stent is not related to the term **stenosis.** Many believe that stent is probably a Scottish colloquialism of **stint,** meaning limitation or restraint. Another explanation is that the term originated from Charles Stent, a nineteenth-century English dentist who developed a dental prosthesis from a plastic resinous substance. The substance became known as **Stent's mass.**

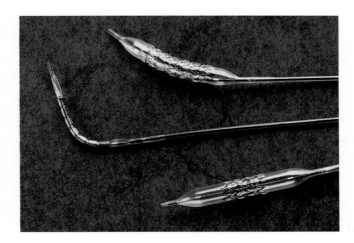

Fig. 10-8
Paragon® coronary stents used to prevent closure of the artery after angioplasty or atherectomy.

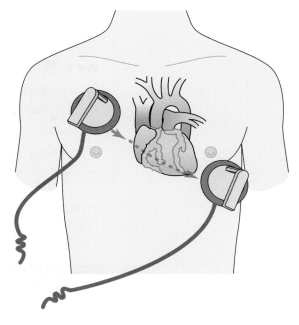

Fig. 10-9
Defibrillation being performed on a patient.

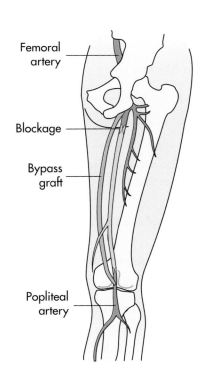

Femoral artery

Blockage

Bypass graft

Popliteal artery

Fig. 10-10
Femoropopliteal bypass.

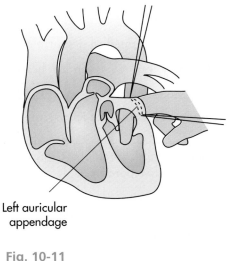

Left auricular appendage

Fig. 10-11
Mitral commissurotomy.

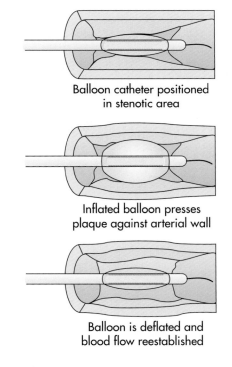

Balloon catheter positioned in stenotic area

Inflated balloon presses plaque against arterial wall

Balloon is deflated and blood flow reestablished

Fig. 10-12
Percutaneous transluminal coronary angioplasty.

> ### Thrombolytic Therapy for Myocardial Infarction
>
> Intracoronary thrombolytic therapy is the use of drugs in the treatment of myocardial infarction in which a blood clot has formed in the coronary artery. Drugs such as streptokinase, urokinase, and alteplase are administered intravenously to dissolve the clot (thrombolysis). The greatest benefit occurs when the drug is administered 3 to 6 hours after the myocardial infarction, before extensive anoxia or damage to the myocardium takes place. Thrombolytic therapy is known to reduce mortality, save myocardium, and restore ventricular function.

Practice saying each of these terms aloud. To assist you in pronunciation, obtain the audiotape designed for use with this text. Learn the definitions and spellings of these surgical terms by completing exercises 21, 22, and 23.

Exercise 21

1. Surgical excision of hemorrhoids is called a(n) _____ .

2. The procedure in which a balloon is passed through a blood vessel to flatten plaque against the vessel wall when the balloon is inflated is called

   _____ _____ _____

   _____ .

3. To regulate the heart rate, the physician may insert a(n) _____ _____ under the patient's skin.

4. A mitral _____ is the name of the surgery performed to repair a stenosed mitral valve.

5. The surgery performed to detour blood around a blocked artery so that a new blood supply can be given to heart muscles is called _____

   _____ _____ _____ .

6. The surgical excision of an aneurysm is called a(n) _____ .

7. A(n) _____ _____ is the name of the surgery performed to establish an alternate route from femoral artery to popliteal artery to bypass obstructive portion.

8. _____ _____ is the name of the procedure to open blocked arteries with a laser beam.

9. An injection of a medication into a blocked coronary vessel to dissolve blood clots is called _____ _____ therapy.

10. _____ is the application of electric shock to the myocardium through the chest wall to restore cardiac rhythm.

11. _____ _____ _____ is a procedure to transfuse bone marrow cells to recipient from donor with matching tissue and cells.

12. _____ is the surgical removal of an embolus, or clot.

13. A supportive scaffold device used to prevent closure of a coronary artery is called

    _____ _____ .

Exercise 22

Match the terms in the first column with their correct definitions in the second column.

_____ 1. aneurysmectomy

_____ 2. coronary artery bypass graft

_____ 3. femoropopliteal bypass

_____ 4. hemorrhoidectomy

_____ 5. cardiac pacemaker

_____ 6. mitral commissurotomy

_____ 7. percutaneous transluminal coronary angioplasty

_____ 8. defibrillation

_____ 9. laser angioplasty

_____ 10. bone marrow transplant

_____ 11. intracoronary thrombolytic therapy

_____ 12. embolectomy

_____ 13. coronary stent

a. pressing plaque against a blood vessel wall by inflating a balloon passed through the blood vessel

b. use of medication to dissolve blood clots in a blocked coronary vessel

c. application of electric shock to the myocardium through the chest wall to restore cardiac rhythm

d. apparatus implanted under the skin to regulate heartbeat

e. procedure performed to open blocked arteries using a laser beam

f. diverts blood past a blocked artery in the heart

g. supportive scaffold device implanted in an artery

h. excision of a weakened ballooning blood vessel wall

i. normal bone marrow cells infused from donor with matching tissues and cells into recipient with leukemia

j. surgical removal of an embolus

k. surgical procedure to establish an alternate route from femoral artery to popliteal artery to bypass obstructive portion

l. surgical excision of varicose veins in the rectal area

m. surgical procedure to break apart the leaves of the mitral valve

n. surgical removal of a thickened artery

Exercise 23

Spell each of the surgical terms. Have someone dictate the terms on pp. 289-290 to you, or say the words into a tape recorder; then spell the words from your recording. Study any words you have spelled incorrectly.

1. _____   4. _____

2. _____   5. _____

3. _____   6. _____

7. _____   11. _____

8. _____   12. _____

9. _____   13. _____

10. _____

Procedural Terms

Built From Word Parts
Heart and Blood Vessels

Diagnostic Imaging

angiography . . . .   x-ray filming of a blood vessel (after an injec-
(an-jē-OG-ra-fē)   tion of contrast medium; the procedure is
                    named for the vessel to be studied for example,
                    femoral angiography)

angioscope . . . .   instrument used for visual examination of a
(AN-jē-ō-skōp)   blood vessel

angioscopy . . . .   visual examination of a blood vessel
(an-jē-OS-kō-pē)

aortogram . . . .   x-ray film of the aorta (made after an injection
(ā-ŌR-tō-gram)   of contrast medium)

arteriogram . . . .   x-ray film of an artery (taken after an injection
(ar-TE-rē-ō-gram)   of contrast medium) (Figure 10-13)

phlebography . . . .   x-ray filming a vein (filled with contrast
(fle-BOG-ra-fē)   medium)

venogram . . . .   x-ray film of the veins (taken after an injection
(VĒ-nō-gram)   of dye)

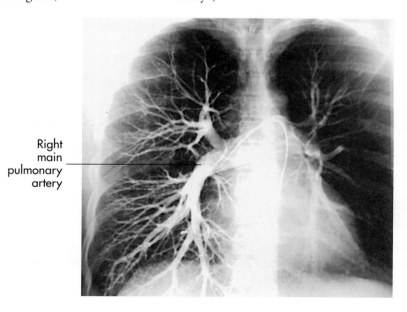

Right
main
pulmonary
artery

Fig.10-13

Arteriography. Visualization of the right main pulmonary artery is performed following injection of contrast material.

Lead II

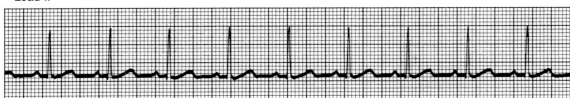

Exercise Fig. D

ELECTRICAL ACTIVITY / CV / HEART / CV / RECORD. **A normal sinus rhythm in lead II.**

Cardiovascular Diagnostic Procedures

echocardiogram . . . . — record of the heart using sound (structure and
(*ek*-ō-KAR-dē-ō-gram) — motion)

electrocardiogram (ECG, EKG) . . — record of the electrical activity of the heart (Ex-
(e-*lek*-trō-KAR-dē-ō-gram) — ercise Figure D)

electrocardiograph . . . . — instrument used to record the electrical activity
(e-*lek*-trō-KAR-dē-ō-graf) — of the heart

electrocardiography . . . . — recording the electrical activity of the heart
(e-*lek*-trō-*kar*-dē-OG-ra-fē)

phonocardiogram . . . . — graphic record of heart sound
(*fŏ*-nō-KAR-dē-ō-gram)

Additional Procedural Terms

sphygmocardiograph . . . . — instrument used to measure pulse waves and
(*sfĭg*-mō-KAR-dē-ō-graf) — heartbeat

stethoscope . . . . — instrument used to examine chest sounds (pro-
(STETH-ō-skōp) — duced by heart and lungs)

Blood and Lymphatic Systems

Laboratory

erythrocyte count . . . . — red (blood) cell (RBC) count (number of red
(e-RITH-rō-sīt) — blood cells per cubic millimeter of blood)

hematocrit (HCT) . . . . — separated blood (volume percentage of ery-
(he-MAT-ō-krit) — throcytes in whole blood after separation by
— centrifuge)

leukocyte count . . . . — white (blood) cell (WBC) count (number of
(LŪ-kō-sīt) — white blood cells per cubic millimeter of
— blood)

(handwritten note: 10,000+ is good, below that is bad)

(handwritten note: 7,000 – 11,000)

> ### Stethoscope
>
> is a term derived from the
> Greek **stethos**, meaning **chest**,
> and **scopeo**, meaning **to view**
> or **examine**. It means **to see**
> what is in the body by
> listening to the body sounds.
> The stethoscope was first
> called a **baton** or **cylinder**.

Diagnostic Imaging

lymphadenography . . . . — x-ray filming the lymph nodes and glands (af-
(lim-*fad*-e-NOG-ra-fē) — ter an injection of contrast medium)

lymphangiogram . . . . — x-ray film of the lymphatic vessels
(lim-FAN-jē-ō-gram)

lymphangiography . . . . — x-ray filming the lymphatic vessels (after an in-
(lim-*fan*-jē-OG-ra-fē) — jection of contrast medium)

Practice saying each of these words aloud. To assist you in pronunciation, obtain the audiotape designed for use with this text. Learn the definitions and spellings of the procedural terms by completing exercises 24, 25, and 26.

Exercise 24 ....

Analyze and define the following procedural terms.

1. electrocardiograph _____

2. sphygmocardiograph _____

3. venogram _____

4. angiography _____

5. echocardiogram _____

6. stethoscope _____

7. aortogram _____

8. electrocardiogram _____

9. phonocardiogram _____

10. arteriogram _____

11. electrocardiography _____

12. erythrocyte count _____

13. lymphangiogram _____

14. hematocrit _____

15. lymphadenography _____

16. leukocyte count _____

17. lymphangiography _____

18. angioscopy _____

19. phlebography _____

20. angioscope _____

Exercise 25 ....

Build procedural terms that correspond to the following definitions by using the word parts you have learned.

1. instrument used to record the electrical activity of the heart

   ————————— / / ——————— / / —————————
   WR CV WR CV S

2. instrument used to examine chest sounds

   ——————————————— / / —————————————
   WR CV S

3. x-ray film of an artery (taken after an injection of contrast medium)

   ——————————————— / / —————————————
   WR CV S

4. x-ray film of the veins (taken after an injection of contrast medium)

   ——————————————— / / —————————————
   WR CV S

5. x-ray filming of a blood vessel

   ——————————————— / / —————————————
   WR CV S

6. record of the electrical activity of the heart

   ————————— / / ——————— / / —————————
   WR CV WR CV S

7. record made of the structure and motion of the heart using sound waves

   ————————— / / ——————— / / —————————
   WR CV WR CV S

8. graphic record of heart sound

   ————————— / / ——————— / / —————————
   WR CV WR CV S

9. instrument used to measure pulse waves and heartbeat

   ————————— / / ——————— / / —————————
   WR CV WR CV S

10. x-ray film of the aorta (taken after an injection of contrast medium)

    ——————————————— / / —————————————
    WR CV S

11. recording the electrical activity of the heart

    ————————— / / ——————— / / —————————
    WR CV WR CV S

12. separated blood (volume percentage of erythrocytes in whole blood after separation by centrifuge)

    ——————————————— / / —————————————
    WR CV S

13. x-ray film of lymphatic vessels

_____ / _____ / ___ / ___
WR   WR   CV   S

14. white (blood) cell count
(number of white blood cells
per cubic millimeter of blood)

_____ / ___ / ___ _____ count
WR   CV   S

15. x-ray filming the lymph nodes
and glands

_____ / _____ / ___ / ___
WR   WR   CV   S

16. red (blood) cell count
(number of red blood cells per
cubic millimeter of blood)

_____ / ___ / ___ _____ count
WR   CV   S

17. x-ray filming the lymphatic
vessels

_____ / _____ / ___ / ___
WR   WR   CV   S

18. visual examination of a blood
vessel

_____ / ___ / ___
WR   CV   S

19. x-ray filming a vein

_____ / ___ / ___
WR   CV   S

20. instrument used for visual examination of a blood vessel

_____ / ___ / ___
WR   CV   S

Exercise 26 ....

Spell each of the procedural terms. Have someone dictate the terms on pp. 294-295 to you, or say the words into a tape recorder; then spell the words from your recording. Think about the word parts before attempting to write the word. Study any words you have spelled incorrectly.

1. _____   11. _____

2. _____   12. _____

3. _____   13. _____

4. _____   14. _____

5. _____   15. _____

6. _____   16. _____

7. _____   17. _____

8. _____   18. _____

9. _____   19. _____

10. _____   20. _____

Procedural Terms

Not Built From Word Parts
Heart and Blood Vessels

Cardiovascular Diagnostic Procedures

Terms	Definitions
cardiac catheterization (KAR-dē-ak) (*kath*-e-ter-ī-ZĀ-shun)	introduction of a catheter into the heart by way of a blood vessel for the purpose of determining cardiac disease (also called *angiocardiography* and *coronary arteriography*) (Figure 10-14)
cardiac scan	two-dimensional photographic representation of the heart taken after the introduction of radioactive material into the body
Doppler flow studies (DOP-ler)	study that uses ultrasound to determine the velocity of the flow of blood within the vessels (Figure 10-15)
impedance plethysmography (IPG) (im-PĒD-dans) (pleth-iz-MOG-ra-fē)	measuring venous flow to the limbs using a plethysmograph, which records electrical resistance (impedance) caused by venous occlusion. Used to detect deep vein thrombosis.
single-photon emission computed tomography (SPECT)	a nuclear medicine scan that visualizes the heart from several different angles. A trace of substance such as **sestamibi** or **thallium** is injected intravenously. The SPECT scanner creates images from the tracer absorbed by the body tissues. It is used to assess damage to cardiac tissue.
thallium stress testing (THAL-ē-um)	a nuclear medicine test used to determine blood flow to the myocardium while the patient is exercising. Used to diagnose coronary artery disease. The radioisotope thallium-201 is administered intravenously. Like thallium, sestamibi is also used in stress testing.

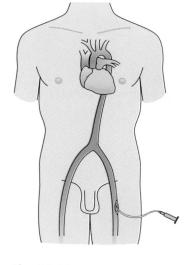

Fig. 10-14
Cardiac catheterization.

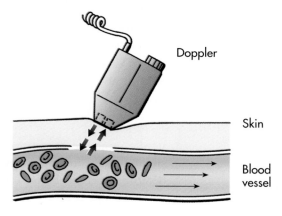

Fig. 10-15
Doppler flow effect showing the red blood cells reflecting sound.

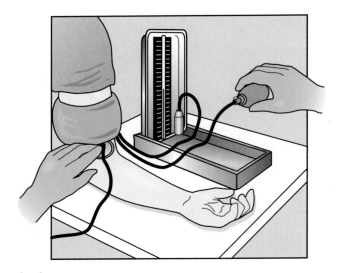

Fig. 10-16
Sphygmomanometer.

x **transesophageal echocar-**
diogram (TEE) . . . .   an ultrasound test that examines cardiac func-
  (trans-e-sof-a-JĒ-al)   tion and structure by using an ultrasound
  (ek-ō-KAR-dē-ō-gram)   probe placed in the esophagus, which provides
                                        views of the heart structures

treadmill stress test . . . .   test to assess the ability of the coronary circula-
                                        tion to handle the increased load placed on the
                                        heart by exercise

Additional Procedural Terms

sphygmomanometer . . . .   device used for measuring arterial blood pres-
  (sfig-mō-ma-NOM-e-ter)   sure (Figure 10-16)

Blood and Lymphatic System

Laboratory Procedures

Terms	Definitions
complete blood count (CBC)	basic blood screening that includes tests on he-moglobin, hematocrit, red blood cell morphology (size and shape), leukocyte count, and white blood cell differential (types of WBCs)
coagulation time . . . . (kō-ag-ū-LĀ-shun)	blood test to determine the time it takes for blood to form a clot
hemoglobin (Hgb) . . . . (HĒ-mō-glō-bin)	oxygen-carrying components in red blood cells, responsible for giving blood its color
prothrombin time (PT) . . . . (prō-THROM-bin)	test to determine certain coagulation activity defects; also used to monitor anticoagulation therapy

Additional Procedural Terms

bone marrow biopsy . . . .   needle puncture to remove bone marrow for
                                        study, usually from the sternum or ilium, to
                                        determine certain blood cell diseases, such as
                                        leukemia and anemia (Figure 10-17)

Practice saying each of these terms aloud. To assist you in pronunciation, obtain the
audiotape designed for use with this text. Learn the definitions and spellings of these
procedural terms by completing exercises 27, 28, and 29.

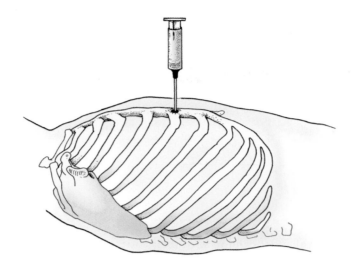

Fig. 10-17
Sternal puncture to remove bone marrow for diagnostic purposes.

Exercise 27 ....

Fill in the blanks with the correct terms.

1. A device for measuring blood pressure is called a(n) _____ .

2. _____ _____ is the name of the blood test that determines the time it takes for blood to form a clot.

3. A test to assess coronary circulation during exercise is a(n) _____ _____ test.

4. _____ _____ _____ is the name of a basic blood-screening test.

5. The study in which ultrasound is used to determine the velocity of flow of blood within vessels is called _____ _____ _____ .

6. Two-dimensional photographic representation of the heart taken after the introduction of radioactive material is called a(n) _____ _____ .

7. _____ _____ _____ is the name given to a procedure performed to determine certain blood diseases, such as leukemia.

8. A blood test performed to determine certain coagulation defects and to monitor anticoagulation therapy is called _____ _____ .

9. _____ _____ is the name given to a procedure in which a catheter is introduced into the heart to determine pathology in the heart or its vessels.

10. The oxygen-carrying component in the red blood cells is called _____ .

11. _____ _____ measures venous flow to the limbs.

12. A nuclear medicine test to determine the presence of coronary artery disease is

_____ _____ _____ .

13. _____ _____ is a test in which an ultrasound probe provides views of the heart structure from the esophagus.

14. A nuclear medicine test which uses a scanner and a tracer to produce images is called a(n) _____ _____ _____

_____ _____ .

Exercise 28 ....

Match the terms in the first column with their correct definitions in the second column.

_____ 1. cardiac catheterization

_____ 2. cardiac scan

_____ 3. complete blood count

_____ 4. coagulation time

_____ 5. hemoglobin

_____ 6. Doppler flow studies

_____ 7. prothrombin time

_____ 8. sphygmomanometer

_____ 9. bone marrow biopsy

_____ 10. treadmill stress test

_____ 11. impedance plethysmography

_____ 12. thallium stress testing

_____ 13. transesophageal echocardiogram

_____ 14. single-photon emission computed tomography

a. device used for measuring arterial blood pressure

b. test to assess coronary circulation during exercise

c. test to determine certain coagulation activity defects

d. passage of a tube into the heart to determine disease within the heart

e. visualizes the heart from several different angles

f. a nuclear medicine test

g. responsible for the red color of blood

h. basic blood-screening test

i. an ultrasound test that provides views of the heart from the esophagus

j. study in which ultrasound is used to determine the velocity of the flow of blood within the vessels

k. performed to determine certain blood cell diseases, such as leukemia

l. test to determine the number of red blood cells

m. measures venous flow to the limbs

n. two-dimensional photograph of the heart

o. determines the time it takes for blood to form a clot

Exercise 29

Spell each of the procedural terms. Have someone dictate the terms on pp. 299-300 to you, or say the words into a tape recorder; then spell the words from your recording. Study any words you have spelled incorrectly.

1. _____   8. _____

2. _____   9. _____

3. _____   10. _____

4. _____   11. _____

5. _____   12. _____

6. _____   13. _____

7. _____   14. _____

Complementary Terms

Built From Word Parts

Term	Definition
cardiac (KAR-dē-ak)	pertaining to the heart
cardiogenic (*kar*-dē-ō-JEN-ik)	originating in the heart
cardiologist (*kar*-dē-OL-ō-jist)	physician who studies and treats diseases of the heart
cardiology (*kar*-dē-OL-ō-jē)	study of the heart
hematologist (*hē*-ma-TOL-ō-jist)	physician who studies and treats diseases of the blood
hematology (*hē*-ma-TOL-ō-jē)	study of the blood
hematopoiesis (*hē*-ma-tō-poy-Ē-sis)	formation of blood cells
hemolysis (hē-MOL-i-sis)	dissolution of (red) blood cells
hemostasis (*hē*-mō-STĀ-sis)	stoppage of bleeding
hypothermia (*hī*-pō-THER-mē-a)	condition of (body) temperature that is below normal (sometimes induced for various surgical procedures, such as bypass surgery)
plasmapheresis (plaz-ma-fe-RĒ-sis)	removal of plasma (from withdrawn blood)
tachypnea (tak-IP-nē-a)	rapid breathing
thrombolysis (throm-BOL-i-sis)	dissolution of a clot

92-70

Practice saying each of these terms aloud. To assist you in pronunciation, obtain the audiotape designed for use with this text. Exercises 30, 31, and 32 will help you to learn the definitions and spellings of the complementary terms.

Exercise 30 ....

Analyze and define the following complementary terms.

1. hypothermia _____
2. hematopoiesis _____
3. cardiology _____
4. cardiologist _____
5. hemolysis _____
6. hematologist _____
7. cardiac _____
8. hematology _____
9. plasmapheresis _____
10. hemostasis _____
11. cardiogenic _____
12. tachypnea _____
13. thrombolysis _____

Exercise 31 ....

Build the complementary terms for the following definitions by using the word parts you have learned.

1. study of the heart

_____ / _____
WR   S

2. formation of blood cells

_____ / ___ / _____
WR   CV   S

3. condition of (body) temperature that is below normal

_____ / ___ / ___ / _____
P   WR   S

4. dissolution of (red) blood cells

_____ / ___ / _____
WR   CV   S

5. removal of plasma (from withdrawn blood)

_____ / _____
WR   S

6. physician who studies and
   treats diseases of the blood

   _____ / _____
         WR   S

7. pertaining to the heart

   _____ / _____
         WR   S

8. physician who studies and
   treats diseases of the heart

   _____ / _____
         WR   S

9. study of the blood

   _____ / _____
         WR   S

10. stoppage of bleeding

    _____ / ___ / _____
        WR   CV   S

11. rapid breathing

    _____ / _____
          P   S(WR)

12. originating in the heart

    _____ / ___ / _____
        WR   CV   S

13. dissolution of a clot

    _____ / ___ / _____
        WR   CV   S

Exercise 32

Spell each of the complementary terms. Have someone dictate the terms on p. 303 to you, or say the words into a tape recorder; then spell the words from your recording. Think about the word parts before attempting to write the word. Study any words you have spelled incorrectly.

1. _____   8. _____
2. _____   9. _____
3. _____   10. _____
4. _____   11. _____
5. _____   12. _____
6. _____   13. _____
7. _____

Complementary Terms
Not Built From Word Parts

Term	Definition
Heart and Blood Vessels	
auscultation .... (*aws*-kul-TĀ-shun)	hearing sounds within the body through a stethoscope
blood pressure (BP)	pressure exerted by the blood against the blood vessel walls

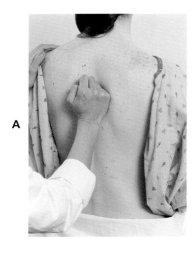

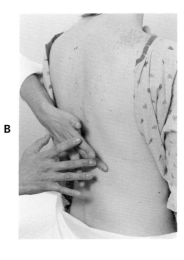

Fig. 10-18
Percussion technique. Percussion may be performed directly **(A)** or indirectly **(B)**.

cardiopulmonary resuscitation (CPR) . . . .
(*kar*-dē-ō-PUL-mō-nar-ē)
(rē-*sus*-i-TĀ-shun)

emergency procedure consisting of artificial ventilation and external cardiac massage

diastole . . . .
(dī-AS-tō-lē)

phase in the cardiac cycle in which the ventricles relax between contractions, i.e., the resistance of the blood vessel walls *resting period of heart*

extracorporeal . . . .
(*ek*-stra-kōr-PŌ-rē-al)

occurring outside the body (during open heart surgery extracorporeal circulation occurs when blood is diverted outside the body to a heart-lung machine)

extravasation . . . .
(eks-trav-a-SĀ-shun)

escape of blood from the blood vessel into the tissue

heart murmur . . . .
(MER-mer)

a short duration humming sound of cardiac or vascular origin

hypertension . . . .
(*hī*-per-TEN-shun)

blood pressure that is above normal (greater than 140/90) *systole diastole 9/50 120/80*

hypotension . . . .
(*hī*-pō-TEN-shun)

blood pressure that is below normal *80/60 some would be norm*

lumen . . . .
(LŪ-men)

space within a tubular part or organ, such as the space within a blood vessel

occlude . . . .
(o-KLŪD)

to close tightly

percussion . . . .
(per-KUSH-un)

tapping of a body surface with the fingers to determine the density of the part beneath (Figure 10-18)

peripheral vascular . . . .
(per-IF-er-al) (VAS-kū-lar)

referring to the blood vessels outside the heart and the lymphatic vessels

systole . . . .
(SIS-tō-lē)

phase in the cardiac cycle in which the ventricles contract *working period of heart*

vasoconstrictor . . . .
(*vās*-ō-kon-STRIK-tor)

agent or nerve that narrows the lumen of blood vessels

vasodilator . . . .
(*vās*-ō-DĪ-lā-tor)

agent or nerve that enlarges the lumen of blood vessels

venipuncture . . . .
(VEN-i-*punk*-chūr)

puncture of a vein to remove blood, instill a medication, or start an intravenous infusion

Blood and Lymphatic Systems

anticoagulant . . . .
(*an*-ti-kō-AG-ū-lant)

agent that slows down the clotting process

dyscrasia . . . .
(dis-KRĀ-zhē-a)

abnormal or pathological condition of the blood

hemorrhage . . . .
(HEM-or-ij)

rapid flow of blood

manometer . . . .
(ma-NOM-e-ter)

instrument used to measure the pressure of fluids

plasma . . . . liquid portion of the blood in which elements
(PLAZ-ma)   or cells are suspended, and which contains
some of the clotting factors

serum . . . . liquid portion of the blood without the clot-
(SĒR-um)   ting factors

Practice saying each of these terms aloud. To assist you in pronunciation, obtain the
audiotape designed for use with this text. Learn the definitions and spellings of these
complementary terms by completing exercises 33, 34 and 35.

Exercise 33

Write the term for each of the following definitions.

1. agent that narrows the
lumen of a blood vessel
_____

2. space within a tubelike
structure
_____

3. emergency procedure consisting
of artificial ventilation and
external cardiac massage
_____ _____

4. phase in the cardiac cycle in
which the ventricles relax
_____

5. pressure exerted by blood
against blood vessel walls
_____ _____

6. blood pressure that is
below normal
_____

7. escape of blood from the
blood vessel into the tissue
_____

8. puncture of a vein to remove
blood
_____

9. phase in the cardiac cycle in
which the ventricles contract
_____

10. agent that enlarges the lumen
of a blood vessel
_____

11. blood pressure that is above
normal
_____

12. referring to the blood vessels
outside the heart and the
lymphatic vessels
_____ _____

13. to close tightly   _____

14. tapping of a body surface   _____
    with the fingers to determine
    the density of the part beneath

15. listening to sounds within the   _____
    body through a stethoscope

16. liquid portion of the blood   _____
    that contains clotting factors

17. instrument used to measure   _____
    the pressure of fluids

18. rapid flow of blood   _____

19. agent that slows down the   _____
    clotting process

20. liquid portion of the blood   _____
    without the clotting factors

21. pathological condition of   _____
    the blood

22. a humming sound of cardiac   _____   _____
    or vascular origin

23. occurring outside the body   _____

Exercise 34

Write the definitions of the following terms.

1. lumen _____

2. extravasation _____

3. blood pressure _____

4. venipuncture _____

5. peripheral vascular _____

6. vasodilator _____

7. hypertension _____

8. cardiopulmonary resuscitation _____

9. systole _____

10. hypotension _____

11. vasoconstrictor _____

12. diastole _____

13. auscultation _____

14. occlude _____

15. percussion _____

16. serum _____

17. dyscrasia _____

18. manometer _____

19. plasma _____

20. hemorrhage _____

21. anticoagulant _____

22. extracorporeal _____

23. heart murmur _____

Exercise 35 ....

Spell each of the complementary terms. Have someone dictate the terms on pp. 305-307 to you, or say the words into a tape recorder; then spell the words from your recording. Study any words you have spelled incorrectly.

1. _____   13. _____

2. _____   14. _____

3. _____   15. _____

4. _____   16. _____

5. _____   17. _____

6. _____   18. _____

7. _____   19. _____

8. _____   20. _____

9. _____   21. _____

10. _____   22. _____

11. _____   23. _____

12. _____

Abbreviations

BP	blood pressure
CABG	coronary artery bypass graft
CAD	coronary artery disease
CBC	complete blood count
CCU	coronary care unit
CHF	congestive heart failure
CPR	cardiopulmonary resuscitation
DVT	deep vein thrombosis
ECG, EKG	electrocardiogram
HCT	hematocrit
Hgb	hemoglobin
HHD	hypertensive heart disease
IPG	impedance plethysmography
MI	myocardial infarction
PT	prothrombin time
PTCA	percutaneous transluminal coronary angioplasty
RBC	red blood cell (erythrocyte)
SPECT	single-photon emission computed tomography
WBC	white blood cell (leukocyte)

CHAPTER REVIEW

Exercises

Exercise 36

Complete the hospital report by writing the medical terms in the blanks. Use the list of definitions with the corresponding numbers.

1. chest pain, occurs when there is an insufficient supply of blood to the heart muscle

2. test to assess the ability of coronary circulation when increased load is placed on the heart

3. a nuclear medicine test used to determine blood flow to the myocardium

4. deficient supply of blood to the heart's blood vessels

5. x-ray filming a blood vessel

6. narrowing

7. surgical repair of a blood vessel

8. physician who studies and treats diseases of the heart

9. record of the electrical activity of the heart

10. introduction of a catheter into the heart by way of a blood vessel to determine cardiac disease

11. death of a portion of the myocardial muscle caused by an interrupted blood supply

---

Case History: This is the third hospitalization for this 76-year-old widowed Filipina who was admitted for recurrent angina.

History of Present Illness: The patient has a long history of stable 1. _____ _____ and had a positive 2. _____ _____ _____ in 1988. A(n) 3. _____ _____ _____ in 1991 showed reversible 4. _____ . In May of 1992 she underwent cataract surgery. She developed severe chest pain postoperatively. The ECG at that time showed ischemic ST changes in the anterior leads. A subsequent coronary 5. _____ revealed a 90% focal left anterior descending 6. _____ . The patient then underwent 7. _____ of this lesion. The 90% stenosis was dilated to a 20% stenosis. The patient had an uncomplicated course and was discharged home.

Over the last 10 days the patient has had at least five episodes of chest pain, all relieved by rest or a single nitroglycerin tablet. She had an episode yesterday while gardening, which lasted almost 20 minutes before subsiding after a second nitroglycerin tablet. She came to her 8. _____ office today. An 9. _____ was done, which showed marked anterior T wave inversion in the anterior leads, and she was immediately sent to this hospital for an evaluation.

Atherogenic risk factors include hypercholesterolemia, for which she is now taking lovastatin. She is also hypertensive and smokes one pack of cigarettes per day. She is not diabetic. Current medications are lovastatin 20 mg daily, enalapril 20 mg bid, nifedipine 10 mg tid, nitroglycerin prn.

Recommendations: Patient is being admitted on an urgent basis for emergency 10. _____ _____ and redilatation if necessary. Serial ECGs and enzymes will be obtained to rule out a(n) 11. _____ _____ .

Exercise 37

To test your understanding of the terms introduced in this chapter, circle the words that correctly complete the sentences. The italicized words refer to the correct answer.

1. *Yellowish, fatty plaque within the arteries* is (arteriosclerosis, atherosclerosis, aortosclerosis).

2. *Enlargement of the spleen* is (splenatrophy, spleniasis, splenomegaly).

3. *Inflammation of the middle muscular layer of the heart* is (endocarditis, myocarditis, pericarditis).

4. Another name for a *heart attack* is (myocardial infarction, coronary fibrillation, angina pectoris).

5. The *surgical excision of a thickened artery interior* is an (arteriorrhaphy, angioplasty, endarterectomy).

6. *Varicose veins in the rectal area* are (plasma, thrombi, hemorrhoids).

7. A *graphic record of heart sounds* is called a(n) (electrocardiogram, phonocardiogram, vectorcardiogram).

8. *Reduction of body temperature to a level below normal* results in a condition called (hypothermia, hypertension, hyperthermia).

9. (Impedance plethysmography, cardiac scan, aortogram) is used *to determine if a patient has a blood clot in the femoral vein.*

10. *A humming sound* or (hemorrhage, murmur, auscultation) *originating in the heart* is the result of many episodes of rheumatic fever, an inflammatory disease occurring in children.

11. The doctor uses an (echocardiograph, electrocardiogram, angioscope) *to visualize the blood vessel* and guide the laser beam to open blocked arteries; this procedure is called (echocardiography, angioscopy).

12. Which of the following is *a nuclear medicine test used to diagnose coronary artery disease* (coronary stent, thallium stress testing, transesophageal echocardiogram)?

Exercise 38

Unscramble the following mixed-up terms. The words on the left indicate the word root in each of the following.

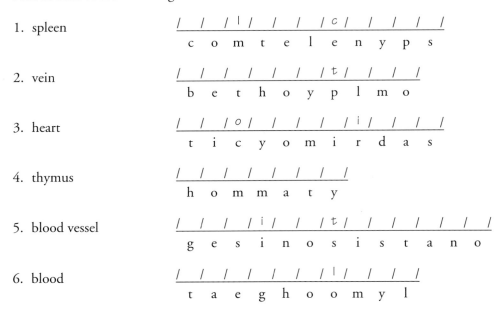

1. spleen — c o m t e l e n y p s

2. vein — b e t h o y p l m o

3. heart — t i c y o m i r d a s

4. thymus — h o m m a t y

5. blood vessel — g e s i n o s i s t a n o

6. blood — t a e g h o o m y l

Exercise 39

The following terms did not appear in this chapter but are composed of word parts that have appeared in this chapter or previous chapters. Find their definitions by translating the word parts literally.

1. **cytoscopy** _____
   (sī-TOS-kō-pē)

2. **dysphonia** _____
   (dis-FŌ-nē-a)

3. **electrotome** _____
   (ē-LEK-trō-tōm)

4. **lipemia** _____
   (li-PĒ-mē-a)

5. **nephropyosis** _____
   (*nef*-rō-pī-Ō-sis)

6. **oligomenorrhea** _____
   (*ol*-i-gō-*men*-ō-RĒ-a)

7. **oophoropexy** _____
   (ō-OF-ō-rō-pek-sē)

8. **pleurodynia** _____
   (*plūr*-ō-DIN-nē-a)

9. **pyelectasis** _____
   (pī-e-LEK-ta-sis)

10. **subungual** _____
    (sub-UNG-gwal)

Combining Forms Crossword Puzzle

Across Clues
1. heart
7. ventricle
15. clot
16. heart (refers to blood vessels)
20. blockage, deficiency
21. spleen
22. aorta

Down Clues
2. vessel
3. valve
4. artery
5. yellowish, fatty plaque
6. chest
8. electricity, electrical activity
10. plasma
12. pulse
17. valve
18. atrium
19. sound

Review of Terms

Can you build, analyze, define, pronounce, and spell the following terms *built from word parts?*

Diseases and Disorders
Heart and Blood Vessels

angiocarditis

angioma

angiospasm

angiostenosis

aortic stenosis

arteriorrhexis

arteriosclerosis

atherosclerosis

atrioventricular defect

bacterial endocarditis

bradycardia

cardiodynia

cardiomegaly

cardiomyopathy

cardiovalvulitis

coronary ischemia

coronary thrombosis

endocarditis

myocarditis

pericarditis

polyarteritis

tachycardia

Blood and Lymphatic System

hematocytopenia

hematoma

lymphadenitis

lymphadenopathy

lymphoma

splenomegaly

thymoma

Surgical

angioplasty

angiorrhaphy

atherectomy

endarterectomy

pericardiostomy

phlebectomy

phlebotomy

splenectomy

splenopexy

thymectomy

Procedural
Heart and Blood Vessels

angiography

angioscope

angioscopy

aortogram

arteriogram

echocardiogram

electrocardiogram ECG, EKG

electrocardiograph

electrocardiography

phlebography

phonocardiogram

sphygmocardiograph

stethoscope

venogram

Blood and Lymphatic Systems

erythrocyte count (RBC)

hematocrit (HCT)

leukocyte count (WBC)

lymphadenography

lymphangiogram

lymphangiography

Complementary

cardiac

cardiogenic

cardiologist

cardiology

hematologist

hematology

hematopoiesis

hemolysis

hemostasis

hypothermia

plasmapheresis

tachypnea

thrombolysis

Can you define, pronounce, and spell the following terms *not built from word parts?*

Diseases and Disorders

anemia

aneurysm

angina pectoris

cardiac arrest

cardiac tamponade

coarctation of the aorta

congenital heart disease

congestive heart failure (CHF)

coronary occlusion

deep vein thrombosis (DVT)

dysrhythmia

embolus, *pl.* emboli

fibrillation

hemophilia

hemorrhoid

Hodgkin's disease

hypertensive heart disease (HHD)

intermittent claudication

leukemia

mitral valve stenosis

myocardial infarction (MI)

rheumatic fever

rheumatic heart disease

sickle cell anemia

thromboangiitis obliterans

varicose veins

Surgical

aneurysmectomy

bone marrow transplant

cardiac pacemaker

coronary artery bypass graft (CABG)

coronary stent

defibrillation

embolectomy

femoropopliteal bypass

hemorrhoidectomy

intracoronary thrombolytic therapy

laser angioplasty

mitral commissurotomy

percutaneous transluminal coronary angioplasty (PTCA)

Procedural
Heart and Blood Vessels

cardiac catheterization

cardiac scan

Doppler flow studies

impedance plethysmography

single-photon emission computed tomography

sphygmomanometer

thallium stress test

treadmill stress test

transesophageal echocardiogram

Blood and Lymphatic Systems

complete blood count (CBC)

coagulation time

hemoglobin (Hgb)

prothrombin time (PT)

bone marrow biopsy

Complementary
Heart and Blood Vessels

auscultation

blood pressure (BP)

cardiopulmonary resuscitation (CPR)

diastole

extracorporeal

extravasation

heart murmur

hypertension

hypotension

lumen

occlude

percussion

peripheral vascular

systole

vasoconstrictor

vasodilator

venipuncture

Blood and Lymphatic Systems

anticoagulant

dyscrasia

hemorrhage

manometer

plasma

serum

Digestive System

Upon completion of this chapter you will be able to:
1. Identify the organs and other structures of the digestive system.
2. Define and spell the word parts presented in this chapter.
3. Build and analyze medical terms using word parts.
4. Define, pronounce, and spell the disease and disorder, procedural, surgical, and complementary terms for the digestive system.

ANATOMY

The digestive tract, also known as the *alimentary canal* or the *gastrointestinal tract,* is made up of several digestive organs. The organs connect to form a continuous passageway from the mouth to the anus (Figure 11-1). With the help of accessory organs, the digestive tract prepares ingested food for use by the body cells and eliminates the solid waste products from the body.

Organs of the Digestive Tract

mouth	opening through which food passes into the body
palate	forms the roof of the mouth
uvula	soft, V-shaped mass that hangs from the roof of the back of the mouth
pharynx, throat	performs the swallowing action that passes food from the mouth to the esophagus
esophagus	ten-inch (25 cm) tube that extends from the pharynx to the stomach
stomach	container for food (Figure 11-2)
antrum	lower bulge of the stomach
pyloric sphincter	ring of muscles that guards the opening between the stomach and the duodenum
small intestine	twenty-foot (6 m) canal extending from the pyloric sphincter to the large intestine (Figure 11-1)

[handwritten annotations: "10 in" next to esophagus; "20 ft" next to small intestine]

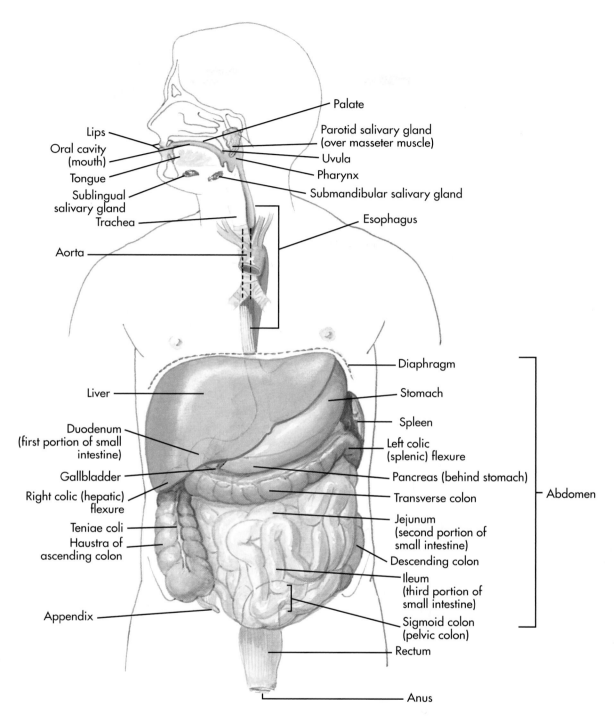

Fig.11-1
Organs of the digestive system and some associated structures.

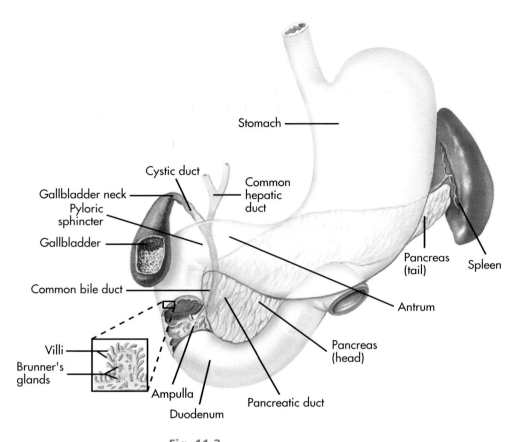

Fig. 11-2
Sources of intestinal secretions.

Duodenum

is derived from the Latin **duodeni,** meaning **twelve each,** a reference to its length. It was named in 240 BC by a Greek physician.

Jejunum is derived from the Latin **jejunus,** meaning **empty;** it was so named because the early anatomists always found it empty.

Ileum is derived from the Greek **eilein,** meaning **to roll,** a reference to the peristaltic waves that move food along the digestive tract. This term was first used in the early part of the seventeenth century.

10-12in

duodenum .... first 10 to 12 inches (25 cm) of the small intestine

8 ft.

jejunum .... second portion of the small intestine, approximately 8 feet (2.4 m) long

11 ft

ileum .... third portion of the small intestine, approximately 11 feet (3.3 m) long, which connects with the large intestine

5 ft

large intestine .... canal that is approximately 5 feet (1.5 m) long and extends from the ileum to the anus (Figure 11-3)

cecum .... first portion of the large intestine (Figure 11-3)

colon .... next portion of the large intestine. The colon is divided into four parts: ascending colon, transverse colon, descending colon, and sigmoid colon (Figure 11-3)

8-10in

rectum .... remaining portion of the large intestine, approximately 8 to 10 inches (20 cm) long, extends from the sigmoid colon to the anus

anus .... sphincter muscle (ringlike band of muscle fiber that keeps an opening tight) at the end of the digestive tract

Accessory Organs

salivary glands . . . . produce saliva, which flows into the mouth (Figure 11-1)

liver . . . . produces bile, which is necessary for the digestion of fats. The liver performs many other functions concerned with digestion.

bile ducts . . . . passageways that carry bile: the hepatic duct is a passageway for bile from the liver, and the cystic duct carries bile from the gallbladder. They join to form the common bile duct, which conveys bile to the duodenum.

gallbladder . . . . small, saclike structure that stores bile

pancreas . . . . located behind the stomach. It produces pancreatic juice, which helps digest all types of food and insulin for carbohydrate metabolism.

Other Structures

peritoneum . . . . lining of the abdominal and pelvic cavities

appendix . . . . small pouch, which has no known function, is attached to the cecum

abdomen . . . . portion of the body between the thorax and the pelvis

Learn the anatomical terms by completing exercises 1 and 2.

> ### Pancreas
>
> is derived from the Greek **pan,** meaning **all,** and **krea,** meaning **flesh.** The pancreas was first described in 300 BC. It was so named because of its fleshy appearance.

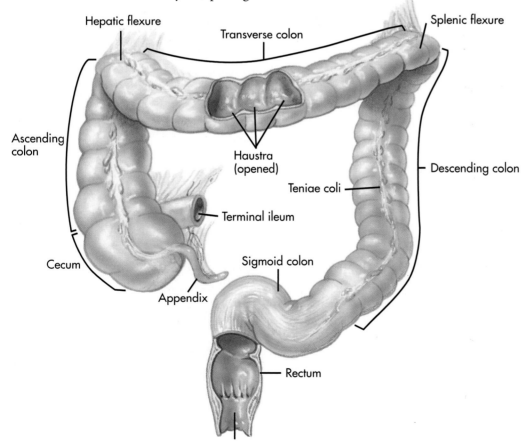

Fig. 11-3
Anatomy of the large intestine.

Exercise 1

Fill in the blanks with the correct terms.

The digestive tract, also known as the (1) _alimentary_ _canal_, and (2) _gastrointestinal tract_, begins with the mouth, connects with the throat, or (3) _pharynx_, and continues on to a 10-inch tube called the (4) _esophagus_; this connects with the (5) _stomach_, the container for food.

The small intestine, the next portion of the digestive tract, is made up of three portions. They are called the (6) _duodenum_, (7) _jejunum_, and (8) _ileum_. The small intestine connects with the first portion of the large intestine, the (9) _cecum_, and then connects with the colon, which is divided into four parts called (10) _ascending colon_ _transverse colon_, (11) _descending colon_, (12) _____ _____, and (13) _sigmoid_ _colon_. The (14) _rectum_ extends from the colon to the (15) _anus_.

Exercise 2

Match the definitions in the first column with the correct terms in the second column.

_l_ 1. lower bulge of the stomach

_d_ 2. hangs from the roof of the mouth

_g_ 3. produce saliva

h _e_ 4. produces bile

_f_ 5. forms the roof of the mouth

_j_ 6. guards the opening between the stomach and the duodenum

_b_ 7. located behind the stomach

_i_ 8. small pouch, which has no known function

_c_ 9. lining of the abdominal and pelvic cavities

_g_ 10. portion of the body between the pelvis and thorax

_e_ 11. stores bile

a. salivary glands

b. pancreas

c. peritoneum

d. uvula

e. gallbladder

f. palate

g. abdomen

h. liver

i. appendix

j. pyloric sphincter

k. cecum

l. antrum

WORD PARTS

Combining Forms for the Digestive Tract

Study the word parts and their definitions listed below. Completing the exercises that follow and Exercise Figure A will help you learn the terms.

Combining Form	Definition
an/o	anus
antr/o	antrum
cec/o	cecum
col/o	colon
duoden/o	duodenum
enter/o	*small* intestine
esophag/o	esophagus

(NOTE: *esophag/o* was covered in Chapter 9.)

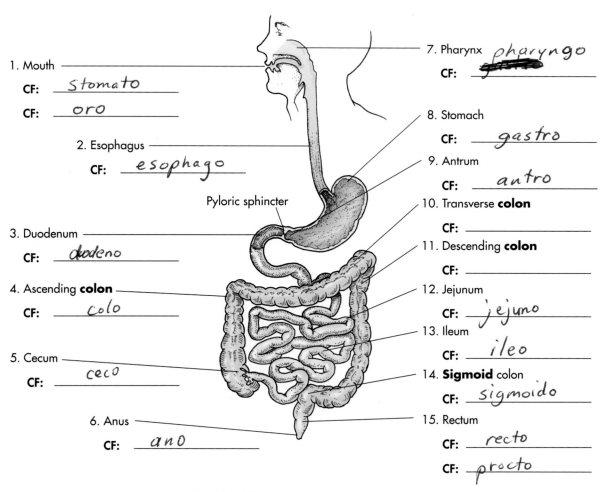

1. Mouth
   CF: _Stomato_
   CF: _oro_

2. Esophagus
   CF: _esophago_

Pyloric sphincter

3. Duodenum
   CF: _duodeno_

4. Ascending **colon**
   CF: _colo_

5. Cecum
   CF: _ceco_

6. Anus
   CF: _ano_

7. Pharynx _pharyngo_
   CF: ~~_____~~

8. Stomach
   CF: _gastro_

9. Antrum
   CF: _antro_

10. Transverse **colon**
    CF: _____

11. Descending **colon**
    CF: _____

12. Jejunum
    CF: _jejuno_

13. Ileum
    CF: _ileo_

14. **Sigmoid** colon
    CF: _sigmoido_

15. Rectum
    CF: _recto_
    CF: _procto_

Exercise Fig. A
Fill in the blanks with combining forms.

gastr/o	. . . .	stomach
ile/o	. . . .	ileum
jejun/o	. . . .	jejunum
(**proct/o**, **rect/o**	. . . .	rectum
sigmoid/o	. . . .	sigmoid colon
stomat/o, **or/o**	. . . .	mouth

Learn the anatomical locations and meanings of the combining forms by completing exercises 3 and 4.

Exercise 3 ....

Write the definitions of the following combining forms.

1. proct/o _____

2. gastr/o _____

3. an/o _____

4. cec/o _____

5. ile/o _____

6. stomat/o _____

7. duoden/o _____

8. col/o _____

9. or/o _____

10. enter/o _____

11. rect/o _____

12. antr/o _____

13. esophag/o _____

14. jejun/o _____

15. sigmoid/o _____

Exercise 4 ....

Write the combining form for each of the following terms.

1. cecum _____

2. stomach _____

3. ileum _____

4. jejunum _____

5. sigmoid colon _____

6. esophagus _____

7. rectum a. _____

 b. _____

8. intestines _____

9. duodenum _____

10. colon _____

11. mouth a. _____

 b. _____

12. anus _____

13. antrum _____

Combining Forms for the Accessory Organs/Combining Forms Commonly Used With Digestive System Terms

Combining Form	Definition
appendic/o	appendix
cheil/o	lip
chol/e (NOTE: the combining vowel is *e*.)	gall, bile
cholangi/o	bile duct
choledoch/o	common bile duct
diverticul/o	diverticulum, or blind pouch, extending from a hollow organ (*pl.* diverticula) (Figure 11-4)
gingiv/o	gum
gloss/o, lingu/o	tongue
hepat/o	liver
herni/o	hernia, or protrusion of an organ through a body wall. The layman's term for hernia is *rupture*. Types include abdominal, hiatal, or diaphragmatic, inguinal, and umbilical hernia (Figure 11-5).
lapar/o, abdomin/o, celi/o	abdomen (abdominal cavity)

palat/o	. . . .	palate
pancreat/o	. . . .	pancreas
peritone/o	. . . .	peritoneum
pylor/o	. . . .	pylorus, pyloric sphincter

(NOTE: *pylor/o* was covered in Chapter 9.)

polyp/o	. . . .	polyp, small growth
sial/o	. . . .	saliva, salivary gland
uvul/o	. . . .	uvula

Learn the anatomical locations and definitions of the combining forms by completing exercises 5 and 6, and Exercise Figure B.

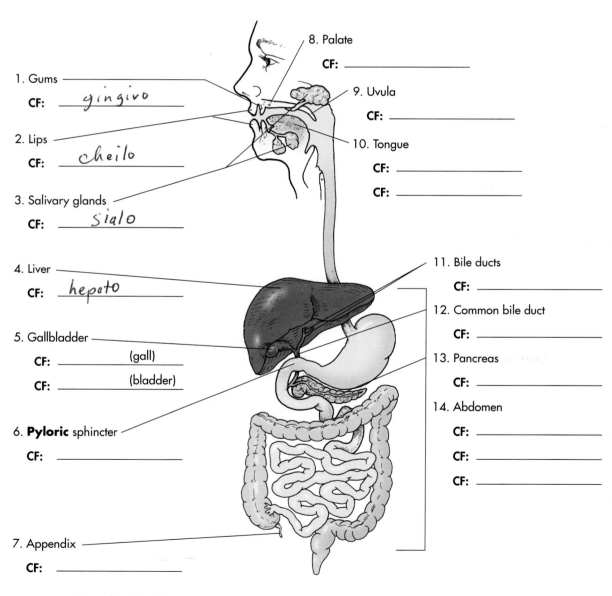

1. Gums
   CF: _gingivo_

2. Lips
   CF: _cheilo_

3. Salivary glands
   CF: _sialo_

4. Liver
   CF: _hepato_

5. Gallbladder
   CF: _____ (gall)
   CF: _____ (bladder)

6. **Pyloric** sphincter
   CF: _____

7. Appendix
   CF: _____

8. Palate
   CF: _____

9. Uvula
   CF: _____

10. Tongue
    CF: _____
    CF: _____

11. Bile ducts
    CF: _____

12. Common bile duct
    CF: _____

13. Pancreas
    CF: _____

14. Abdomen
    CF: _____
    CF: _____
    CF: _____

Exercise Fig. B
Fill in the blanks with combining forms in this diagram of the digestive system.

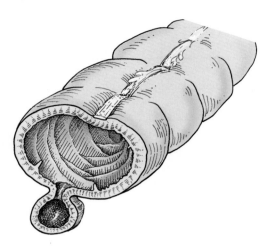

Fig. 11-4
Diverticulum of the large intestine.

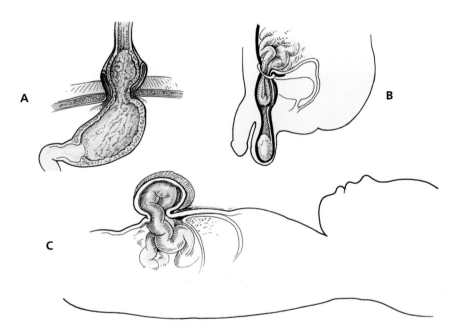

Fig. 11-5
Types of hernias. **A,** Hiatal. **B,** Inguinal. **C,** Umbilical.

Exercise 5 ....

Write the definitions of the following combining forms.

1. herni/o _____

2. abdomin/o _____

3. sial/o _____

4. chol/e _____

5. diverticul/o _____

6. gingiv/o _____

7. appendic/o _____

8. gloss/o _____

9. hepat/o _____

10. cheil/o _____

11. peritone/o _____

12. palat/o _____

13. pancreat/o _____

14. lapar/o _____

15. lingu/o _____

16. choledoch/o _____

17. pylor/o _____

18. uvul/o _____

19. cholangi/o _____

20. polyp/o _____

21. celi/o _____

Exercise 6 ....

Write the combining form for each of the following.

1. palate _____

2. saliva, salivary gland _____

3. pancreas _____

4. peritoneum _____

5. tongue   a. _____

                     b. _____

6. gum _____

7. pylorus, pyloric sphincter _____

8. liver   _____

9. gall, bile   _____

10. abdomen   a. _____

                 b. _____

                 c. _____

11. hernia   _____

12. diverticulum   _____

13. lip   _____

14. appendix   _____

15. uvula   _____

16. bile duct   _____

17. common bile duct   _____

18. small growth   _____

Suffix

Suffix	Definition
-pepsia	digestion

Learn the suffix by completing exercises 7 and 8.

Exercise 7

Write the definition of the following suffix.

1. -pepsia _____

Exercise 8

Write the suffix for the following definition.

1. digestion   _____

MEDICAL TERMS

The terms you need to learn to complete this chapter are listed below. The exercises following each list will help you learn the definition and the spelling of each word.

Disease and Disorder Terms

Built From Word Parts

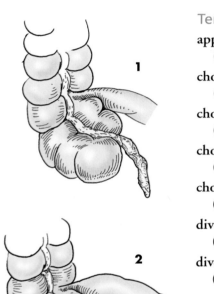

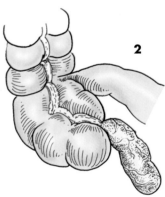

Exercise Fig. C

Fill in the blanks to label the diagram. **1,** Normal appendix.

2, APPENDIX / INFLAMMA-TION.

Term	Definition
appendicitis . . . . (ap-*pen*-di-SĪ-tis)	inflammation of the appendix (Exercise Figure C)
cholangioma . . . . (kō-lan-jē-Ō-ma)	tumor of the bile duct
cholecystitis . . . . (*kō*-lē-sis-TĪ-tis)	inflammation of the gallbladder
choledocholithiasis . . . . (kō-led-ō-kō-lith-Ī-a-sis)	condition of stones in the common bile duct (Exercise Figure D)
cholelithiasis . . . . (*kō*-lē-lith-Ī-a-sis)	condition of gallstones
diverticulitis . . . . (*dī*-ver-tik-ū-LĪ-tis)	inflammation of the diverticulum
diverticulosis . . . . (*dī*-ver-tik-ū-LŌ-sis)	abnormal condition of having diverticula
gastritis . . . . (gas-TRĪ-tis)	inflammation of the stomach
gastroenteritis . . . . (*gas*-trō-en-te-RĪ-tis)	inflammation of the stomach and intestines *small*
gastroenterocolitis . . . . (*gas*-trō-*en*-ter-ō-kō-LĪ-tis)	inflammation of the stomach, intestines, and colon
gingivitis . . . . (jin-ji-VĪ-tis)	inflammation of the gums
hepatitis . . . . (hep-a-TĪ-tis)	inflammation of the liver
hepatoma . . . . (hep-a-TŌ-ma)	tumor of the liver
palatitis . . . . (pal-a-TĪ-tis)	inflammation of the palate
pancreatitis . . . . (*pan*-krē-a-TĪ-tis)	inflammation of the pancreas
polyposis . . . . (pol-ē-PŌ-sis)	abnormal condition of (multiple) polyps (in the mucous membrane of the intestine, especially the colon, high potential for malignancy) (Figure 11-6)
proctoptosis . . . . (*prok*-top-TŌ-sis)	prolapse of the rectum

appear on mucus membranes

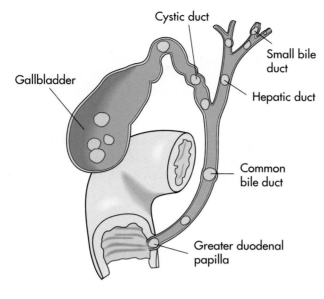

Exercise Fig. D

Common sites of $\overline{\text{GALL} \ / \ \text{CV} \ / \ \text{STONES} \ / \ \text{CONDITION OF}}$

$\overline{\text{COMMON SITE DUCT} \ / \ \text{CV} \ / \ \text{STONES} \ / \ \text{CONDITION OF.}}$

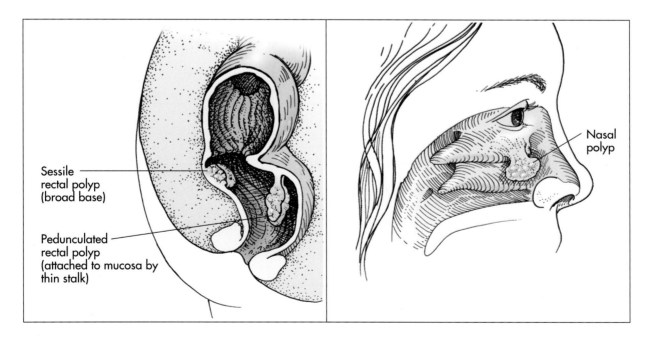

Fig. 11-6
Polyp is a general term used to describe a protruding growth from a mucous membrane. Polyps are commonly found in the nose, uterus, intestines, and bladder.

rectocele . . . . (REK-tō-sēl)	protrusion of the rectum
sialolith . . . . (sī-AL-ō-lith)	stone in the salivary gland
uvulitis . . . . (ū-vū-LĪ-tis)	inflammation of the uvula

Practice saying each of these terms aloud. To assist you in pronunciation, obtain the audiotape designed for use with this text. Learn the definitions and spellings of the disease and disorder terms by completing exercises 9, 10, and 11.

Exercise 9 . . . .

Analyze and define the following terms.

1. cholelithiasis _____

2. diverticulosis _____

3. sialolith _____

4. hepatoma _____

5. uvulitis _____

6. pancreatitis _____

7. proctoptosis _____

8. gingivitis _____

9. gastritis _____

10. rectocele _____

11. palatitis _____

12. hepatitis _____

13. appendicitis _____

14. cholecystitis _____

15. diverticulitis _____

16. gastroenteritis _____

17. gastroenterocolitis _____

18. choledocholithiasis _____

19. cholangioma _____

20. polyposis _____

Exercise 10 ....

Build disease and disorder terms for the following definitions using the word parts you have learned.

1. tumor of the liver

   _____ / _____
              WR   S

2. inflammation of the stomach

   _____ / _____
              WR   S

3. stone in the salivary gland

   _____ / ___ / _____
       WR   CV   WR

4. inflammation of the appendix

   _____ / _____
              WR   S

5. inflammation of the diverticulum

   _____ / _____
              WR   S

6. inflammation of the gallbladder

   _____ / ___ / _____ / _____
     WR   CV   WR   S

7. abnormal condition of having diverticula

   _____ / _____
              WR   S

8. inflammation of the stomach and intestines

   _____ / ___ / _____ / _____
     WR   CV   WR   S

9. prolapse of the rectum

   _____ / ___ / _____
       WR   CV   S

10. protrusion of the rectum

    _____ / ___ / _____
        WR   CV   S

11. inflammation of the uvula

    _____ / _____
               WR   S

12. inflammation of the gums

    _____ / _____
               WR   S

13. inflammation of the liver

    _____ / _____
               WR   S

14. inflammation of the palate

    _____ / _____
               WR   S

15. condition of gallstones

    _____ / ___ / _____ / _____
      WR   CV   WR   S

16. inflammation of the stomach, intestines, and colon

    _____ / ___ / _____ / ___ / _____ / _____
      WR   CV   WR   CV   WR   S

17. inflammation of the pancreas   _____ / _____
                                                          WR   S

18. tumor of the bile duct   _____ / _____
                                                          WR   S

19. condition of stones in the common bile duct   _____ / _____ / _____ / _____
                                    WR   CV   WR   S

20. abnormal condition of (multiple) polyps   _____ / _____
                                                           WR   S

Exercise 11

Spell each of the disease and disorder terms. Have someone dictate the terms on pp. 328, 330 to you, or say the words into a tape recorder; then spell the words from your recording. Think about the word parts before attempting to write the word. Study any words you have spelled incorrectly.

1. _____
2. _____
3. _____
4. _____
5. _____
6. _____
7. _____
8. _____
9. _____
10. _____

11. _____
12. _____
13. _____
14. _____
15. _____
16. _____
17. _____
18. _____
19. _____
20. _____

Disease and Disorder Terms

Not Built From Word Parts

Term	Definition
adhesion (ad-HĒ-zhun)	abnormal growing together of two surfaces that normally are separated. This may occur after abdominal surgery; surgical treatment is called *adhesiolysis* or *adhesiotomy* (Figure 11-7).
anorexia nervosa (*an*-ō-REK-sē-a) (ner-VŌ-sa)	psychoneurotic disorder characterized by a prolonged refusal to eat, resulting in emaciation, amenorrhea, and abnormal fear of becoming obese. It occurs primarily in adolescents.

bulimia . . . .   gorging with food, then inducing vomiting
(bū-LIM-ē-a)

cirrhosis . . . .   chronic disease of the liver with gradual de-
(ser-RŌ-sis)   struction of cells, most commonly caused by
alcoholism

[handwritten in margin: orange yellow liver]

Crohn's disease . . . .   chronic inflammation, usually affecting the
(krōnz)   ileum and sometimes the colon, characterized
by cobblestone ulcerations along the intestinal
wall and the formation of scar tissue. It may
cause obstruction. Also called *regional ileitis* or
regional enteritis.

[handwritten in margin: Ulcer starts by breaking open of mucus membrane bacteria gets in]

duodenal ulcer . . . .   ulcer in the duodenum (Figure 11-8)
(*dū*-o-DĒ-nal)

gastric ulcer . . . .   ulcer in the stomach (Figure 11-8)
(GAS-trik)

**gastroesophageal reflux
disease (GERD)** . . . .   the backward flow of the gastrointestinal con-
(gas-trō-ē-sof-a-JĒ-al) (RĒ-fluks)   tents into the esophagus, gradually breaking
down the mucous barrier of the esophagus

ileus . . . .   obstruction of the intestine, often caused by
(IL-ē-us)   failure of peristalsis

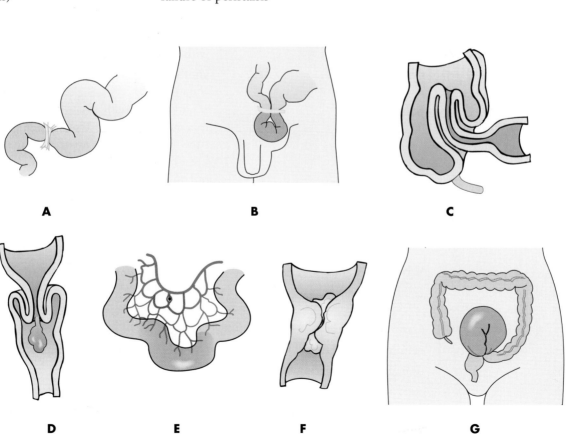

Fig. 11-7
Causes of intestinal obstruction. **A,** Adhesions. **B,** Strangulated inguinal hernia. **C,** Ileocecal intussusception.
D, Intussusception due to polyps. **E,** Mesenteric occlusion. **F,** Neoplasm. **G,** Volvulus of the sigmoid colon.

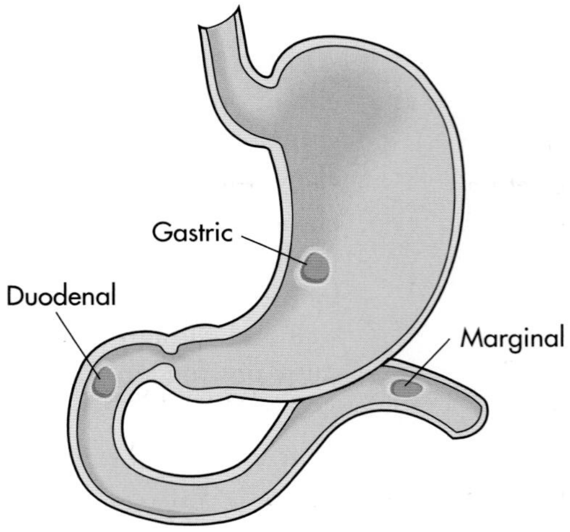

Fig. 11-8
Sites of peptic ulcers.

[handwritten: spastic colon]

[handwritten: at ileum / cecum]

[handwritten: caused by tumors most of time]

intussusception . . . .
(*in*-tus-sus-SEP-shun)

telescoping of a segment of the intestine (Figure 11-7)

irritable bowel syndrome (IBS) . .

periodic disturbances of bowel function (diarrhea and/or constipation) usually associated with abdominal pain

peptic ulcer . . . .
(PEP-tik)

another name for gastric or duodenal ulcer (Figure 11-8)

polyp . . . .
(POL-ip)

tumor-like growth extending outward from a mucous membrane. Usually benign, common sites are in the nose, throat, and intestines (Figure 11-6).

ulcerative colitis . . . .
(UL-ser-a-tiv) (kōl-LĪ-tis)

inflammation of the colon with the formation of ulcers. The main symptom is diarrhea—as many as 15 to 29 stools per day. An ileostomy may be performed in an attempt to cure the condition.

volvulus . . . .
(VOL-vū-lus)

twisting or kinking of the intestine, causing intestinal obstruction (Figure 11-7)

Gastroesophageal reflux disease (GERD) is estimated to be the most common gastrointestinal disorder. The acidity of the regurgitated stomach contents causes irritation and inflammation of the esophagus (reflux esophagitis).

Practice saying each of these terms aloud. To assist you in pronunciation, obtain the audiotape designed for use with this text. Learn the definitions and spellings of the disease and disorder terms by completing exercises 12, 13, and 14.

Exercise 12

Match the definitions in the first column with the correct terms in the second column.

_____ 1. prolonged refusal to eat

_____ 2. chronic disease of the liver

_____ 3. chronic inflammation of the intestines

_____ 4. abnormal growing together of two surfaces

_____ 5. twisted intestine

_____ 6. gastric or duodenal ulcer

_____ 7. telescoping of a segment of the intestine

_____ 8. tumor-like growth

_____ 9. formation of ulcers in the colon

_____ 10. gorging food, then inducing vomiting

_____ 11. obstruction of the intestine

_____ 12. periodic disturbance of bowel function

_____ 13. backward flow of the gastrointestinal contents into the esophagus

a. intussusception

b. cirrhosis

c. gastroesophageal reflux disease

d. volvulus

e. Crohn's disease

f. anorexia nervosa

g. peptic ulcer

h. ulcerative colitis

i. irritable bowel syndrome

j. bulimia

k. polyp

l. hernia

m. ileus

n. adhesion

Exercise 13

Write the definitions of the following terms.

1. peptic ulcer _____

2. anorexia nervosa _____

3. Crohn's disease _____

4. volvulus _____

5. adhesion _____

6. cirrhosis _____

7. intussusception _____

8. gastric ulcer _____

9. duodenal ulcer _____

10. ulcerative colitis _____

11. bulimia _____

12. polyp _____

13. irritable bowel syndrome _____

14. ileus _____

15. gastroesophageal reflux disease _____

Exercise 14

Spell the disease and disorder terms. Have someone dictate the terms on pp. 332-334 to you, or say the words into a tape recorder; then spell the words from your recording. Study any words you have spelled incorrectly.

1. _____   9. _____

2. _____   10. _____

3. _____   11. _____

4. _____   12. _____

5. _____   13. _____

6. _____   14. _____

7. _____   15. _____

8. _____

Surgical Terms

Built From Word Parts

Term	Definition
abdominoplasty (ab-DOM-i-nō-plas-tē)	surgical repair of the abdomen
anoplasty (Ā-nō-*plas*-tē)	surgical repair of the anus
antrectomy (an-TREK-tō-mē)	excision of the antrum
appendectomy (*ap*-en-DEK-tō-mē)	excision of the appendix

celiotomy . . . .   incision into the abdominal cavity
    (sē-lē-OT-ō-mē)

cheilorrhaphy . . . .   suture of the lip
    (kī-LOR-a-fē)

cholecystectomy . . . .   excision of the gallbladder
    (*kō*-lē-sis-TEK-tō-mē)

choledocholithotomy . . . .   incision into the common bile duct to remove
    (kō-led-ō-kō-li-THOT-ō-mē)   a stone

choledocholithotripsy . . . .   surgical crushing of a stone in the common
    (kō-led-ō-kō-LITH-ō-trip-sē)   bile duct

colectomy . . . .   excision of the colon
    (kō-LEK-tō-mē)

colostomy . . . .   artificial opening into the colon through the
    (kō-LOS-tō-mē)   abdominal wall. (Used for the passage of stool.
                                It is performed for cancer of the colon)

diverticulectomy . . . .   excision of a diverticulum
    (*dī*-ver-tik-ū-LEK-tō-mē)

enterorrhaphy . . . .   suture of the intestine
    (en-ter-OR-a-fē)

esophagogastroplasty . . . .   surgical repair of the esophagus and the stom-
    (e-*sof*-a-gō-GAS-trō-plas-tē)   ach

gastrectomy . . . .   excision of the stomach (Exercise Figure E)
    (gas-TREK-tō-mē)

gastrojejunostomy . . . .   creation of an artificial opening between the
    (*gas*-trō-je-jū-NOS-tō-mē)   stomach and jejunum

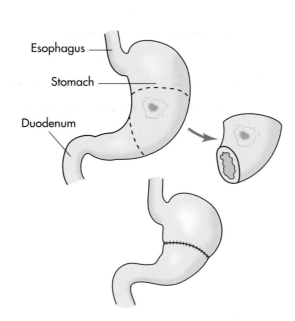

Exercise Fig. E

Fill in the blanks to complete the diagram. _____ / _____
STOMACH / SURGICAL REMOVAL

(Diagram labels: Esophagus, Stomach, Duodenum)

Percutaneous endoscopic gastrostomy (PEG)

was first described in 1980. It is an alternative to traditional gastrostomy. An endoscope is used to place a tube in the stomach. Cost and discomfort to the patient are reduced when PEG is used instead of traditional gastrostomy.

gastrostomy . . . .
(gas-TROS-tō-mē)

creation of an artificial opening into the stomach through the abdominal wall. (A tube is inserted through the opening for administration of food when swallowing is impossible) (Figure 11-9)

gingivectomy . . . .
(*jin*-ji-VEK-tō-mē)

surgical removal of gum (tissue)

glossorrhaphy . . . .
(glo-SŌR-a-fē)

suture of the tongue

herniorrhaphy . . . .
(*her*-nē-ŌR-a-fē)

suturing of a hernia (for repair)

ileostomy . . . .
(il-ē-OS-tō-mē)

creation of an artificial opening into the ileum through the abdominal wall. (Used for the passage of stool. It is performed for ulcerative colitis, Crohn's disease, or cancer) Exercise Figure F)

laparotomy . . . .
(*lap*-a-ROT-ō-mē)

incision into the abdomen

palatoplasty . . . .
(PAL-a-tō-*plas*-tē)

surgical repair of the palate

polypectomy . . . .
(pol-ē-PEK-tō-mē)

excision of a polyp

pyloromyotomy . . . .
(pī-*lor*-ō-mī-OT-ō-mē)

incision into the pyloric muscle

pyloroplasty . . . .
(pī-LOR-ō-plas-tē)

surgical repair of the pylorus

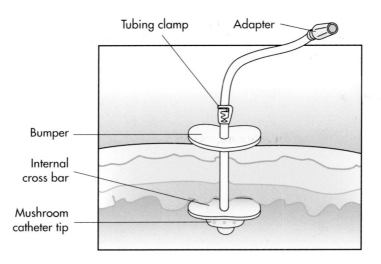

Tubing clamp   Adapter

Bumper

Internal cross bar

Mushroom catheter tip

Fig. 11-9
Percutaneous endoscopic gastrostomy (PEG).

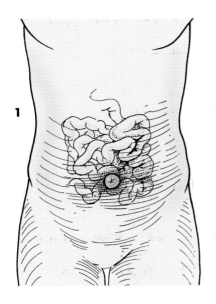 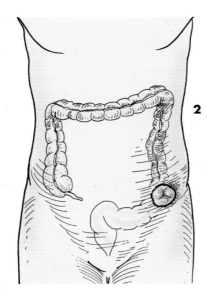

Exercise Fig. F

Fill in the blanks to label the diagram. **1,** ILEUM / ARTIFICIAL OPENING following

total colectomy. **2,** COLON / ARTIFICIAL OPENING following abdominal perineal
resection.

uvulectomy . . . .   excision of the uvula
   (ū-vū-LEK-tō-mē)

**uvulopalatopharyngoplasty
(UPPP)** . . . .   surgical repair of the uvula, palate, and pharynx
   (ū-vū-lō-*pal*-a-tō-*phar*-   (performed to correct obstructive sleep apnea)
   in-GŌ-plas-tē)

Practice saying each of these terms aloud. To assist you in pronunciation, obtain the
audiotape designed for use with this text. Learn the definitions and spellings of the
surgical terms by completing exercises 15, 16, and 17.

Exercise 15

Analyze and define the following surgical terms.

1. gastrectomy _____ *excision of the stomach* _____

2. esophagogastroplasty _____ *Surgical repair of the esophagus and the stomach*

3. diverticulectomy _____ *excision of a diverticulum* _____

4. antrectomy _____ *excision of the antrum* _____

5. palatoplasty — surgical repair of the palate

6. uvulectomy — excision of the uvula

7. gastrojejunostomy — creation of an artificial opening between the stomach and jejunum

8. cholecystectomy — excision of the gallbladder

9. colectomy — excision of the colon

10. colostomy — artificial opening into the colon through the abdominal wall

11. pyloroplasty — surgical repair of the pylorus

12. anoplasty — surgical repair of the anus

13. appendectomy — excision of the appendix

14. cheilorrhaphy — suture of the lip

15. gingivectomy — surgical removal of the gum

16. laparotomy — incision into the abdomen

17. ileostomy — creation of an artificial opening into the ileum through the abdominal wall

18. gastrostomy — creation of an artificial opening into the stomach through the abdominal wall.

19. herniorrhaphy — suturing of a hernia

20. glossorrhaphy — suture of the tongue

21. choledocholithotomy — incision into the common bile duct to remove a stone

22. choledocholithotripsy — surgical crushing of a stone in the common bile duct

23. polypectomy — excision of a polyp

24. enterorrhaphy — suture of the intestine

25. abdominoplasty — surgical repair of the abdomen

26. pyloromyotomy — incision into the pyloric muscle

27. uvulopalatopharyngoplasty — surgical repair of the uvula, palate and pharynx

28. celiotomy — incision into the abdominal cavity

Exercise 16

Build surgical terms for the following definitions by using the word parts you have learned.

1. excision of the appendix

   _____
           WR / S

2. suture of the tongue

   _____
           WR / S

3. surgical repair of the esophagus and stomach

   _____
   WR / CV /   WR / CV / S

4. excision of a diverticulum

   _____
           WR / S

5. artificial opening into the
   ileum

   _____
           WR / S

6. surgical removal of gum
   tissue

   _____
           WR / S

7. incision into the abdomen

   _____
           WR / S

8. surgical repair of the anus

   _____
         WR /CV/ S

9. excision of the antrum

   _____
           WR / S

10. excision of the gallbladder

    _____
    WR / CV / WR / S

11. excision of the colon

    _____
            WR / S

12. creation of an artificial
    opening into the colon

    _____
            WR / S

13. excision of the stomach

    _____
            WR / S

14. creation of an artificial
    opening into the stomach

    _____
            WR / S

15. creation of an artificial
    opening between the stomach
    and jejunum

    _____
    WR / CV / WR / S

16. excision of the uvula

_____
WR $/$ S

17. surgical repair of the palate

_____
WR $/$ CV $/$ S

18. surgical repair of the pylorus

_____
WR $/$ CV $/$ S

19. suture of a hernia

_____
WR $/$ S

20. suture of the lip

_____
WR $/$ S

21. surgical crushing of a stone in the common bile duct

_____
WR $/$ CV $/$ WR $/$ CV $/$ S

22. incision into the common bile duct to remove a stone

_____
WR $/$ CV $/$ WR $/$ S

23. excision of a polyp

_____
WR $/$ S

24. suture of the intestine

_____
WR $/$ S

25. surgical repair of the abdomen

_____
WR $/$ CV $/$ S

26. incision into the abdominal cavity

_____
WR $/$ S

27. incision into the pylorus muscle

_____
WR $/$ CV $/$ WR $/$ S

28. surgical repair of the uvula, palate, and pharynx

_____
WR $/$ CV $/$ WR $/$ CV $/$ WR $/$ CV $/$ S

Exercise 17

Spell each of the surgical terms. Have someone dictate the terms on pp. 336-339 to you, or say the words into a tape recorder; then spell the words from your recording. Think about the word parts before attempting to write the word. Study any words you have spelled incorrectly.

1. _____   3. _____

2. _____   4. _____

5. _____   17. _____

6. _____   18. _____

7. _____   19. _____

8. _____   20. _____

9. _____   21. _____

10. _____   22. _____

11. _____   23. _____

12. _____   24. _____

13. _____   25. _____

14. _____   26. _____

15. _____   27. _____

16. _____   28. _____

Surgical Terms

Not Built From Word Parts

Term	Definition
abdominoperineal resection (ab-*dom*-in-ō-*par*-i-NĒ-el)	removal of the colon and rectum through both abdominal and perineal approaches *will be permanent*
anastomosis (a-*nas*-tō-MŌ-sis)	surgical connection between two normally distinct structures
vagotomy (vā-GOT-ō-mē)	cutting of certain branches of the vagus nerve, performed with gastric surgery to reduce the amount of gastric acid produced and thus reduce the recurrence of ulcers

Exercise 18

Write the term for each of the following definitions.

1. cutting certain branches of the vagus nerve   _____

2. surgical connection between two structures   _____

3. removal of the colon and rectum   _____

Exercise 19

Spell each of the surgical terms. Have someone dictate the terms on p. 343 to you, or say the words into a tape recorder; then spell the words from your recording. Study any words you have spelled incorrectly.

1. _____   3. _____

2. _____

Procedural Terms

Built From Word Parts

Term	Definition
Diagnostic Imaging	
cholangiogram . . . . (kō-LAN-jē-ō-gram)	x-ray film of bile ducts. (An injection of radiopaque material is used to outline the ducts.)
cholecystogram (GB series) . . . . . (*kō*-lē-SIS-tō-gram)	x-ray film of the gallbladder. Cholecystograms are still in use; however, abdominal ultrasound is the more common diagnostic test for diagnosing cholelithiasis (Exercise Figure G).

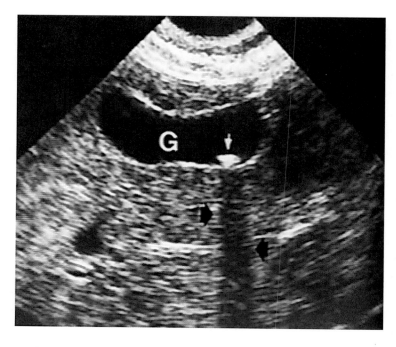

Exercise Fig. G

Abdominal ultrasound showing GALL / CV / STONE / CONDITION OF.

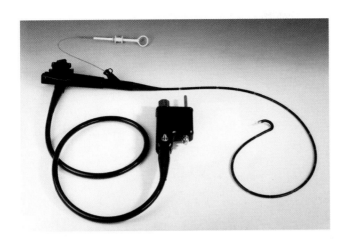

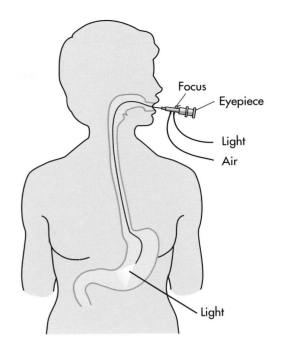

Focus
Eyepiece
Light
Air
Light

Exercise Fig. H

Fiberscope, a type of STOMACH / CV / INSTRUMENT USED FOR VISUAL EXAMINATION that has glass fibers in a flexible tube; this allows for light to be transmitted back to the examiner.

Endoscopy

colonoscope . . . . instrument used for visual examination of the
(kō-LON-ō-skōp)   colon

colonoscopy . . . . visual examination of the colon
(kō-lon-OS-kō-pē)

endoscope . . . . instrument used for visual examination within
(EN-dō-skōp)   a hollow organ

endoscopy . . . . visual examination within a hollow organ
(en-DOS-kō-pē)

esophagogastroduodenoscopy
(EGD) . . . . visual examination of the esophagus, stomach,
(e-*sof*-a-gō-*gas*-trō-dū-od-e-   and duodenum
NOS-kō-pē)

esophagoscope . . . . instrument for visual examination of the
(e-SOF-a-gō-skōp)   esophagus

esophagoscopy . . . . visual examination of the esophagus
(e-*sof*-a-GOS-kō-pē)

gastroscope . . . . instrument used for visual examination of the
(GAS-trō-skōp)   stomach (Exercise Figure H)

gastroscopy . . . . visual examination of the stomach
(gas-TROS-kō-pē)

laparoscope . . . . instrument used for visual examination of the
(LAP-a-rō-skōp)   abdominal cavity

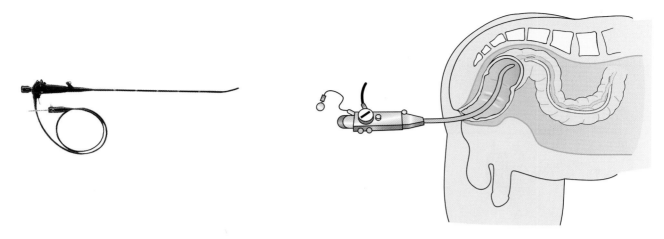

Exercise Fig. I

Flexible sigmoidoscopy used to perform a SIGMOID COLON / CV / VISUAL EXAMINATION.

laparoscopy . . . .   visual examination of the abdominal cavity
  (lap-a-ROS-kō-pē)

proctoscope . . . .   instrument used for visual examination of the
  (PROK-tō-skōp)   rectum

proctoscopy . . . .   visual examination of the rectum
  (prok-TOS-kō-pē)

sigmoidoscope . . . .   instrument used for visual examination of the
  (sig-MOY-dō-skōp)   sigmoid colon

sigmoidoscopy . . . .   visual examination of the sigmoid colon (Exer-
  (*sig*-moy-DOS-kō-pē)   cise Figure I)

> Operative and postoperative **cholangiography** use the injection of contrast medium
> into the common bile duct. The dye is inserted through the drainage T-tube to dis-
> cover any small remaining gallstones after surgery.

> The **laparoscope** is the instrument used to perform laparoscopic surgery, a modern
> method that replaces open abdominal incisional surgery. Surgeries performed using
> a laparoscope include laparoscopic cholecystectomy, laparoscopic herniorrhaphy,
> and laparoscopic appendectomy.

Practice saying each of these words aloud. To assist you in pronunciation, obtain the
audiotape designed for use with this text. Learn the definitions and spellings of the
procedural terms by completing exercises 20, 21, and 22.

Exercise 20

Analyze and define the following procedural terms.

1. esophagoscope _____

2. esophagoscopy _____

3. gastroscope _____

4. gastroscopy _____

5. proctoscope _____

6. proctoscopy _____

7. endoscope _____

8. endoscopy _____

9. sigmoidoscope _____

10. sigmoidoscopy _____

11. cholecystogram _____

12. cholangiogram _____

13. esophagogastroduodenoscopy _____

14. colonoscope _____

15. laparoscope _____

16. colonoscopy _____

17. laparoscopy _____

Exercise 21

Build procedural terms that correspond to the following definitions by using the word parts you have learned.

1. visual examination within a
    hollow organ
    _____ / _____
    P   S(WR)

2. instrument used for visual ex-
    amination of the stomach
    _____ / ___ / ___
    WR   CV   S

3. instrument used for visual ex-
    amination of the rectum
    _____ / ___ / ___
    WR   CV   S

4. instrument used for visual examination of the sigmoid colon

————————————————
WR / CV / S

5. x-ray film of the gallbladder

————————————————
WR / CV / WR / CV / S

6. instrument used for visual examination within a hollow organ

————————————————
P / S(WR)

7. instrument used for visual examination of the esophagus

————————————————
WR / CV / S

8. visual examination of the rectum

————————————————
WR / CV / S

9. visual examination of the esophagus

————————————————
WR / CV / S

10. visual examination of the sigmoid colon

————————————————
WR / CV / S

11. x-ray film of bile ducts

————————————————
WR / CV / S

12. visual examination of the stomach

————————————————
WR / CV / S

13. instrument used for visual examination of the abdominal cavity

————————————————
WR / CV / S

14. visual examination of the esophagus, stomach, and duodenum

————————————————
WR / CV / WR / CV / WR / CV / S

15. visual examination of the colon

————————————————
WR / CV / S

16. visual examination of the abdominal cavity

————————————————
WR / CV / S

17. instrument used for visual examination of the colon

————————————————
WR / CV / S

Exercise 22 ....

Spell each of the procedural terms. Have someone dictate the terms on pp. 344-346 to you, or say the words into a tape recorder; then spell the words from your recording. Think about the word parts before attempting to write the word. Study any words you have spelled incorrectly.

1. _____   10. _____
2. _____   11. _____
3. _____   12. _____
4. _____   13. _____
5. _____   14. _____
6. _____   15. _____
7. _____   16. _____
8. _____   17. _____
9. _____

Procedural Terms
Not Built From Word Parts

Term	Definition
Diagnostic Imaging	
lower GI (gastrointestinal) series	series of x-ray films taken of the large intestine after a barium enema has been administered (also called *barium enema*)
upper GI (gastrointestinal) series	series of x-ray films taken of the stomach and duodenum after barium has been swallowed (Figure 11-10)
Endoscopy	
endoscopic retrograde cholangiopancreatography (ERCP) .... (kō-lan-jē-ō-*pan*-krē-a-TOG-rah-fē)	radiographic (x-ray) examination of the bile and pancreatic ducts using contrast medium, fluoroscopy, and endoscopy (Figure 11-11)
endoscopic ultrasound (EUS)	a procedure using an endoscope fitted with an ultrasound probe that provides images of layers of the intestinal wall. Used to detect tumors and cystic growths and for staging of malignant tumors.

ERCP was first performed in 1968. ERCP is used to evaluate obstructions, pancreatic cancer, and unexplained pancreatitis. It is used to diagnose stone diseases, strictures, and pancreatic neoplasms.

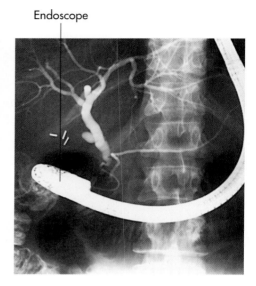

Endoscope

Fig. 11-10
Upper gastrointestinal series demonstrates the site of a small bowel obstruction.

Fig. 11-11
Endoscopic retrograde cholangiopancreatography (ERCP) is used to diagnose biliary and pancreatic pathologic conditions.

Laboratory Procedures

Helicobacter pylori
(H. pylori) **antibodies test** . . . . . .
(hēl-i-kō-BAK-ter)

a blood test to determine the presence of *H pylori* bacteria. The bacteria can be found in the lining of the stomach and can cause duodenal ulcers. Tests for *H pylori* also are done on biopsy specimens and by breath test.

occult blood test . . . .
(O-KULT)

a test to detect occult blood in feces. It is used to screen for bowel cancer. Occult blood refers to blood that is present but can only be viewed microscopically. Also called *Hema-Check* and *Colo-Rect.*

Abdominal ultrasound, which includes images of the liver, gallbladder, biliary tract, and pancreas, is a major diagnostic tool. It can detect liver cysts, abscesses, tumors, gallstones, an enlarged pancreas, and pancreatic tumors. High-frequency sound waves are used to visualize the size and structure of the internal organs. Abdominal ultrasound is replacing the use of the cholecystogram to diagnose the presence of cholelithiasis.

Exercise 23

Write definitions for the following terms.

1. upper GI series _____

2. lower GI series _____

3. endoscopic retrograde cholangiopancreatography _____

4. endoscopic ultrasound _____

5. *Helicobacter pylori* antibodies test _____

6. occult blood test _____

Exercise 24

Match the tests in the first column with their correct definitions in the second column.

_____ 1. occult blood test

_____ 2. lower GI series

_____ 3. *Helicobacter pylori* bacteria

_____ 4. upper GI series

_____ 5. endoscopic retrograde cholangiopancreatography

a. their presence can cause duodenal ulcers

b. x-ray film of the stomach and duodenum

c. examination of bile and pancreatic ducts

d. detects blood in feces

e. x-ray film of the esophagus

f. x-ray film of the large intestine

Exercise 25

Spell each of the procedural terms. Have someone dictate the terms on pp. 349-350 to you, or say the words into a tape recorder; then spell the words from your recording. Study any words you have spelled incorrectly.

1. _____   4. _____

2. _____   5. _____

3. _____   6. _____

Complementary Terms

Built From Word Parts

Term	Definition
abdominal . . . . (ab-DOM-i-nal)	pertaining to the abdomen
abdominocentesis . . . . (ab-*dom*-i-nō-sen-TĒ-sis)	surgical puncture to remove fluid from the abdominal cavity (also called *paracentesis*)
anal . . . . (Ā-nal)	pertaining to the anus
apepsia . . . . (ā-PEP-sē-a)	without (lack of) digestion
aphagia . . . . (a-FĀ-jē-a)	without the (inability) to swallow
bradypepsia . . . . (*brād*-ē-PEP-sē-a)	slow digestion
dyspepsia . . . . (dis-PEP-sē-a)	difficult digestion
dysphagia . . . . (dis-FĀ-jē-a)	difficult swallowing
gastrodynia . . . . (*gas*-trō-DIN-ē-a)	pain in the stomach
gastroenterologist . . . . (*gas*-trō-en-ter-OL-ō-jist)	a physician who specializes in diseeases of the stomach and intestines
gastroenterology . . . . (*gas*-tro-en-ter-OL-ō-jē)	study of the stomach and intestines
gastromalacia . . . . (*gas*-trō-ma-LĀ-shē-a)	softening of the stomach
glossopathy . . . . (glo-SOP-a-thē)	disease of the tongue
ileocecal . . . . (*il*-ē-ō-SĒ-kal)	pertaining to the ileum and cecum
nasogastric . . . . (*nā*-zō-GAS-trik)	pertaining to the nose and stomach
oral . . . . (Ō-ral)	pertaining to the mouth
pancreatic . . . . (*pan*-krē-AT-ik)	pertaining to the pancreas
peritoneal . . . . (*par*-i-tō-NĒ-al)	pertaining to the peritoneum
proctologist . . . . (prok-TOL-ō-jist)	physician who specializes in proctology
proctology . . . . (prok-TOL-ō-jē)	branch of medicine concerned with disorders of the rectum and anus
stomatogastric . . . . (*stō*-ma-tō-GAS-trik)	pertaining to the mouth and stomach
sublingual . . . . (sub-LING-gwal)	pertaining to under the tongue

Practice saying each of these terms aloud. To assist you in pronunciation, obtain the audiotape designed for use with this text. Exercises 26, 27, and 28 will help you learn the definitions and spellings of the complementary terms related to the digestive system.

Exercise 26

Analyze and define the following complementary terms.

1. aphagia _____ inability to swallow

2. dyspepsia _____ difficult digestion

3. anal _____ pertaining to the anus

4. dysphagia _____ difficult swallowing

5. glossopathy _____ disease process of the tongue

6. ileocecal _____ pertaining to the ileum and cecum

7. oral _____ pertaining to the mouth

8. stomatogastric _____ pertaining to the mouth and stomach

9. bradypepsia _____ slow digestion

10. abdominocentesis _____ surgical puncture to remove fluid from the abdominal cavity

11. apepsia _____ without digestion

12. gastromalacia _____ softening of the stomach

13. pancreatic _____ pertaining to the pancreas

14. gastrodynia _____ pain in the stomach

15. peritoneal _____ pertaining to the peritoneum

16. sublingual _____ pertaining to under the tongue

17. proctology _____ branch of medicine concerned with disorders of the rectum and anus

18. nasogastric _____ pertaining to the nose and stomach

19. abdominal _____ pertaining to the abdomen

20. proctologist _____ physician who specializes in proctology

21. gastroenterology _____ study of the stomach and small intestines

22. gastroenterologist _____ a physician who specializes in diseases of the stomach and small intestines

Exercise 27

Build the complementary terms for the following definitions by using the word parts you have learned.

1. disease of the tongue

   _____ / ___ / ___
                              WR   CV   S

2. without (inability) to swallow

   _____ / _____
                              P   S(WR)

3. pertaining to under the tongue

   _____ / ___ / ___
                              P   WR   S

4. pertaining to the nose and the stomach

   _____ / ___ / ___ / ___
                              WR   CV   WR   S

5. pertaining to the mouth and the stomach

   _____ / ___ / ___ / ___
                              WR   CV   WR   S

6. pertaining to the anus

   _____ / ___
                              WR   S

7. surgical puncture to remove fluid from the abdominal cavity

   _____ / ___ / ___
                              WR   CV   S

8. pertaining to the peritoneum

   _____ / ___
                              WR   S

9. pertaining to the abdomen

   _____ / ___
                              WR   S

10. difficult swallowing

    _____ / _____
                               P   S(WR)

11. pertaining to the ileum and cecum

    _____ / ___ / ___ / ___
                               WR   CV   WR   S

12. slow digestion

    _____ / _____
                               P   S(WR)

13. softening of the stomach

    _____ / ___ / ___
                               WR   CV   S

14. without (lack of) digestion

    _____ / _____
                               P   S(WR)

15. pain in the stomach

    _____ / ___
                               WR   S

16. physician who specializes in proctology

    _____ / ___
                               WR   S

17. difficult digestion

_____ / _____
P / S(WR)

18. pertaining to the pancreas

_____ / _____
WR / S

19. branch of medicine concerned
with disease of the rectum and
anus

_____ / _____
WR / S

20. pertaining to the mouth

_____ / _____
WR / S

21. physician who specializes in
diseases of the stomach and
intestines

_____ / _____ / _____ / _____
WR / CV / WR / S

22. study of the stomach and
intestines

_____ / _____ / _____ / _____
WR / CV / WR / S

Exercise 28

Spell each of the complementary terms. Have someone dictate the terms on p. 352
to you, or say the words into a tape recorder; then spell the words from your recording. Think about the word parts before attempting to write the word. Study any
words you have spelled incorrectly.

1. _____   12. _____
2. _____   13. _____
3. _____   14. _____
4. _____   15. _____
5. _____   16. _____
6. _____   17. _____
7. _____   18. _____
8. _____   19. _____
9. _____   20. _____
10. _____   21. _____
11. _____   22. _____

Complementary Terms

Not Built From Word Parts

Term	Definition
ascites . . . . (a-SĪ-tēz)	abnormal collection of fluid in the peritoneal cavity
diarrhea . . . . (dī-a-RĒ-a) (NOTE: diarrhea is composed of *dia*, meaning through, and *orrhea*, meaning flow. The *o* is dropped.)	frequent discharge of liquid stool

mainly caused by alcoholism or blockage of vessels in liver

danger— dehydration electrolyte imbalance

dysentery .... (DIS-en-ter-ē)	disorder that involves inflammation of the intestine associated with diarrhea and abdominal pain + bleeding
feces .... (FĒ-sēz)	waste from the digestive tract expelled through the rectum (also called a *bowel movement, stool, or fecal matter*)
flatus .... (FLĀ-tus)	gas in the digestive tract or expelled through the anus
gastric lavage .... (la-VOZH)	washing out of the stomach
gavage .... (ga-VOZH)	process of feeding a person through a nasogastric tube
hematemesis .... (hēm-a-TEM-e-sis)	vomiting of blood
nausea .... (NAW-zē-a)	urge to vomit
reflux .... (RĒ-fluks)	return of flow. In esophageal reflux, the stomach contents flow back into the esophagus.
vomit .... (VOM-it)	matter expelled from the stomach through the mouth (also called *vomitus* or *emesis*)

Practice saying each of these terms aloud. To assist you in pronunciation, obtain the audiotape designed for use with this text. Learn the definitions and spellings of the complementary terms by completing exercises 29, 30, and 31.

Exercise 29

Match the definitions in the first column with the correct terms in the second column.

_____ 1. abnormal collection of fluid

_____ 2. matter expelled from the stomach

_____ 3. feeding a person through a tube

_____ 4. washing out of the stomach

_____ 5. urge to vomit

_____ 6. frequent discharge of liquid stool

_____ 7. waste expelled from the rectum

_____ 8. vomiting of blood

_____ 9. return of flow

_____ 10. inflammation of the intestine

_____ 11. gas expelled through the anus

a. hematemesis
b. flatus
c. gastric lavage
d. reflux
e. vomit
f. gavage
g. ascites
h. dysentery
i. diarrhea
j. anastomosis
k. feces
l. nausea

Exercise 30

Write definitions for each of the following terms.

1. ascites _____
2. gavage _____
3. gastric lavage _____
4. feces _____
5. nausea _____
6. vomit _____
7. dysentery _____
8. diarrhea _____
9. flatus _____
10. reflux _____
11. hematemesis _____

Exercise 31

Spell each of the complementary terms. Have someone dictate the terms on pp. 355-356 to you, or say the words into a tape recorder; then spell the words from your recording. Study any words you have spelled incorrectly.

1. _____   7. _____
2. _____   8. _____
3. _____   9. _____
4. _____   10. _____
5. _____   11. _____
6. _____

Abbreviations

BE ...... B.q E Correct .... barium enema
EGD .... esophagogastroduodenoscopy
ERCP .... endoscopic retrograde cholangiopancreatography
EUS .... endoscopic ultrasound
GB series .... gallbladder series

GERD . . . .   gastroesophageal reflux disease

GI . . . .   gastrointestinal

H. pylori . . . .   *Helicobacter pylori*

IBS . . . .   irritable bowel syndrome

N & V . . . .   nausea and vomiting

PEG . . . .   percutaneous endoscopic gastrostomy

UGI . . . .   upper gastrointestinal

UPPP . . . .   uvulopalatopharyngoplasty

CHAPTER REVIEW

Exercises

Exercise 32

Complete the hospital report by writing the medical terms in the blanks. Use the list of definitions with the corresponding numbers.

> **Case History**: This is a 40-year-old African-American woman who was referred to 1. _____ clinic for evaluation. Patient complains of persistent 2. _____ and vomiting with upper abdominal pain. She has also had a problem with 3. _____ but denies any 4. _____ . She has not used any alcohol or salicylates. She is currently on several medications, but they do not appear to be ulcerogenic.

> 5. _____ : the patient was prepared for the procedure by being given 2 mg of intravenous Versed along with Hurricaine spray. After the patient was placed in the left lateral decubitus position, the Olympus 6. _____ was passed into the esophagus without any difficulty. The esophagus in its entirety was essentially free of mucosal abnormalities. No evidence of 7. _____ . The stomach was entered; some gastric juices were aspirated. The stomach, body, cardia, and antrum, proximally, were all free of mucosal abnormalities. In the distal antral area some mild erythematous changes were noted. The pylorus had normal peristaltic activity in the opening. The first part of the duodenum, however, revealed evidence of ulcerations, both anterosuperiorly as well as posteroinferiorly, with surrounding tissue irritation noted. These 8. _____ were less than 1 mm in size. The second part of the duodenum, however, was free of mucosal abnormalities. Withdrawing the scope confirmed the findings upon entry. The patient, in fact, tolerated the procedure quite well. Vital signs will be taken every half hour for the next 2 hours.
>
> Postop Diagnosis: 9. _____   10. _____

1. visual examination within a hollow organ

2. urge to vomit

3. difficult digestion

4. vomiting of blood

5. visual examination of the esophagus, stomach, and duodenum

6. instrument used for visual examination of the stomach

7. return of flow

8. eroded sore on the skin or mucous membrane

9. inflammation of the stomach

10. ulcer in the duodenum

Exercise 33

To test your understanding of the terms introduced in this chapter, circle the words that correctly complete the sentences. The italicized words refer to the correct answer.

1. Mr. E. was admitted to the hospital with a diagnosis of *gallstones,* or (cholelithiasis, cholecystitis, sialolithiasis).

2. An abdominal ultrasound confirmed the admitting diagnosis, and Mr. E. is now scheduled for an *excision of the gallbladder,* or (cholecystostomy, cholecystectomy, colectomy).

3. The patient was diagnosed with a condition the symptoms of which include *inflammation of the colon and formation of ulcers* called (cirrhosis, ulcerative colitis, peptic ulcer).

4. A *prolapse of the rectum* is (rectocele, intussusception, proctoptosis).

5. An *abnormal growing together of two surfaces* is (anastomosis, adhesion, amniocentesis).

6. Three surgical procedures are often performed on a patient with peptic ulcers. They are (1) *excision of the stomach,* or (gastrotomy, gastrostomy, gastrectomy); (2) *surgical repair of the pylorus,* or (pyloroplasty, cheilorrhaphy, gastrojejunostomy); and (3) *cutting of certain branches of the vagus nerve,* or (colostomy, vagotomy, gingivectomy).

7. *Difficult digestion* is (dyspepsia, bradypepsia, dysphagia).

8. *Feeding* a person *through a gastric tube* is called (lavage, gavage, gastrostomy).

9. The *surgical procedure to remove the colon and rectum and create an artificial opening into the colon* is (colectomy and colostomy; abdominal perineal resection and colostomy; abdominal perineal resection and ileostomy).

10. *Surgical crushing of a stone in the common bile duct* is (choledocholithotripsy, cholangiolithotripsy, cholecystolithotripsy).

11. To rule out cancer of the colon, the doctor performed a diagnostic procedure to *visually examine the colon* or (colonoscopy, colonoscope, colostomy).

12. The doctor diagnosed the patient as having *an obstruction of the intestine* or (polyp, irritable bowel syndrome, ileus).

13. Which of the following tests is used to screen for bowel cancer? (occult blood, *Helicobacter pylori* antibodies, upper GI series)

Exercise 34

Unscramble the following mixed-up terms. The words on the left indicate the *suffix* in each of the following.

1. suture

    / / / e / / / / / / / / / h / /
    i r y r c l p a h h h e o

2. creation of an artificial opening

    / / / l / / / / / / / /
    t i l m o y s o e

3. excision

    / / / n / / / v / / / / / /
    t g e v i n i g o y m c

4. softening

    / / / s / / / / m / / / / / /
    t s a g a i c l a r o m a

5. swallowing

    / / / s / / / / / /
    d a p g y i s a h

6. digestion

    / / p / / / / / /
    p s p a a e i

7. surgical repair

    / / v / / / / / / / / / o / / / / / / / / / / / / / / /
    y s n y h p p u v o l l a t o r a g p o l a a t u

Exercise 35

Test your knowledge on diagnostic procedural terms by circling the letter of each correct answer.

1. The physician did a visual examination of the vagina and cervix to note changes in the cells and capillary network. The procedure takes 10 minutes and is called a
    a. coloscopy
    b. colposcope
    c. sigmoidoscope
    d. colposcopy
    e. coloscope

2. The physician ordered x-ray films of the large intestine to rule out the presence of a tumor. This is called a(n)
    a. upper GI series
    b. mammogram
    c. cholecystogram
    d. intravenous pyelogram
    e. barium enema

3. The patient was experiencing hematuria. To locate and control the source of the bleeding, the doctor performed a
   a. bronchoscopy
   b. culdoscopy
   c. cystoscopy
   d. proctoscopy
   e. gastroscopy

4. The patient was scheduled for an x-ray film of a blood vessel, or
   a. arteriogram
   b. angiogram
   c. aortogram
   d. venogram
   e. nephrogram

5. A record of the electrical impulses of the heart is a(n)
   a. electrocardiogram
   b. echocardiogram
   c. electrocardiograph
   d. phonocardiograph
   e. electrocardiography

Combining Forms Crossword Puzzle

Across Clues
1. palate
3. abdomen
5. liver
9. peritoneum
11. intestine
13. ileum
14. cecum
16. diverticulum
19. pylorus
21. gum
24. jejunum
25. sigmoid
26. uvula

Down Clues
1. rectum
2. abdomen
4. tongue
5. hernia
6. stomach
7. antrum
8. appendix
9. pancreas
10. gall, bile
12. duodenum
15. lip
17. colon
18. mouth
20. rectum
21. tongue
22. saliva
23. anus

Review of Terms

Can you build, analyze, define, pronounce, and spell the following terms *built from word parts?*

Diseases and Disorders

appendicitis

cholangioma

cholecystitis

choledocholithiasis

cholelithiasis

diverticulitis

diverticulosis

gastritis

gastroenteritis

gastroenterocolitis

gingivitis

hepatitis

hepatoma

palatitis

pancreatitis

polyposis

proctoptosis

rectocele

sialolith

uvulitis

Surgical

abdominoplasty

anoplasty

antrectomy

appendectomy

celiotomy

cheilorrhaphy

cholecystectomy

choledocholithotomy

choledocholithotripsy

colectomy

colostomy

diverticulectomy

enterorrhaphy

esophagogastroplasty

gastrectomy

gastrojejunostomy

gastrostomy

gingivectomy

glossorrhaphy

herniorrhaphy

ileostomy

laparotomy

palatoplasty

polypectomy

pyloromyotomy

pyloroplasty

uvulectomy

uvulopalatopharyngoplasty
   (UPPP)

Procedural

cholangiogram

cholecystogram

colonoscope

colonoscopy

endoscope

endoscopy

esophagogastroduodenoscopy
   (EGD)

esophagoscope

esophagoscopy

gastroscope

gastroscopy

laparoscope

laparoscopy

proctoscope

proctoscopy

sigmoidoscope

sigmoidoscopy

Complementary

abdominal

abdominocentesis

anal

apepsia

aphagia

bradypepsia

dyspepsia

dysphagia

gastrodynia

gastroenterologist

gastroenterology

gastromalacia

glossopathy

ileocecal

nasogastric

oral

pancreatic

peritoneal

proctologist

proctology

stomatogastric

sublingual

Can you define, pronounce, and spell the following terms *not built from word parts?*

Diseases and Disorders	Surgical	Procedural	Complementary
adhesion	abdominoperineal resection	endoscopic retrograde cholangiopancreatography (ERCP)	ascites
anorexia nervosa	anastomosis		diarrhea
bulimia	vagotomy	endoscopic ultrasound (EUS)	dysentery
cirrhosis			feces
Crohn's disease		*Helicobacter pylori* antibodies test (H. pylori)	flatus
duodenal ulcer			gastric lavage
gastric ulcer		lower GI (gastrointestinal) series	gavage
gastroesophageal reflux disease (GERD)		occult blood test	hematemesis
ileus		upper GI (gastrointestinal) series	nausea
intussusception			reflux
irritable bowel syndrome (IBS)			vomit
peptic ulcer			
polyp			
ulcerative colitis			
volvulus			

Objectives .... **Upon completion of this chapter you will be able to:**
1. Identify the anatomy of the eye.
2. Define and spell the word parts presented in this chapter.
3. Build and analyze medical terms using word parts.
4. Define, pronounce, and spell the disease and disorder, procedural, surgical, and complementary terms for the eye.

ANATOMY

The eye is located in a bony protective cavity of the skull called the *orbit* (Figure 12-1).

Structures of the Eye

sclera	outer protective layer of the eye; anteriorly referred to as the *white of the eye*
cornea	transparent anterior part of the sclera, which is in front of the aqueous fluid and lies over the iris
choroid	middle layer of the eye, which is interlaced with many blood vessels
iris	muscular structure that gives the eye its color allowing light to pass through
pupil	opening in the center of the iris
lens	lies directly behind the pupil. Its function is to focus and bend light.
retina	innermost layer of the eye, which contains the vision receptors (Figure 12-2)
aqueous fluid	watery liquid found in the anterior cavity of the eye
vitreous fluid	jellylike liquid found behind the lens in the posterior cavity of the eye
meibomian glands	oil glands found in the upper and lower edges of the eyelids that help lubricate the eye
lacrimal glands and ducts	produce and drain tears
optic nerve	carries visual impulses from the retina to the brain
conjunctiva	mucous membrane lining the eyelids and covering the anterior portion of the sclera

Learn the anatomical terms by completing exercises 1 and 2.

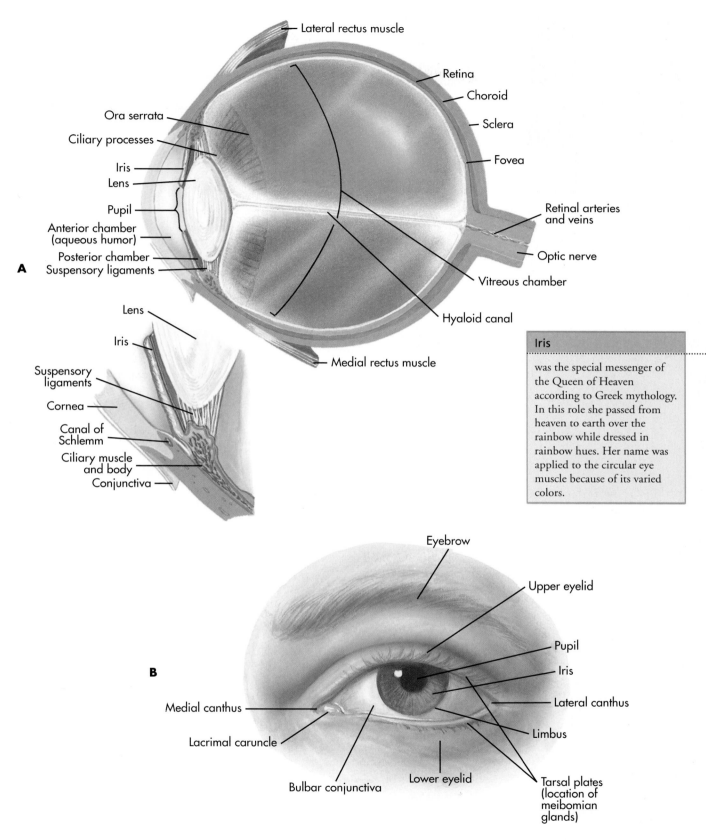

Lateral rectus muscle

Retina

Choroid

Sclera

Fovea

Ora serrata

Ciliary processes

Iris

Lens

Pupil

Anterior chamber
(aqueous humor)

Posterior chamber

Suspensory ligaments

Retinal arteries
and veins

Optic nerve

Vitreous chamber

Hyaloid canal

A

Medial rectus muscle

Lens

Iris

Suspensory
ligaments

Cornea

Canal of
Schlemm

Ciliary muscle
and body

Conjunctiva

> **Iris**
>
> was the special messenger of the Queen of Heaven according to Greek mythology. In this role she passed from heaven to earth over the rainbow while dressed in rainbow hues. Her name was applied to the circular eye muscle because of its varied colors.

Eyebrow

Upper eyelid

Pupil

Iris

Lateral canthus

Limbus

Tarsal plates
(location of
meibomian
glands)

B

Medial canthus

Lacrimal caruncle

Bulbar conjunctiva

Lower eyelid

Fig. 12-1
A, Anatomy of the eye. **B,** Visible surface of the eye.

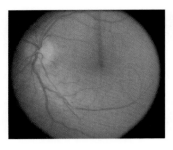

Fig. 12-2
Ophthalmoscopic view of the retina.

Exercise 1

Match the anatomical terms in the first column with the correct definitions in the second column.

_____ 1. aqueous fluid

_____ 2. choroid

_____ 3. conjunctiva

_____ 4. cornea

_____ 5. iris

_____ 6. lacrimal glands

_____ 7. lens

a. lies directly behind the pupil

b. gives the eye its color

c. middle layer of the eye

d. watery liquid found in the anterior cavity of the eye

e. produce tears

f. mucous membrane lining the eyelids

g. jellylike fluid behind the lens and in the posterior cavity

h. transparent anterior part of the sclera

Exercise 2

Match the anatomical terms in the first column with the correct definitions in the second column.

_____ 1. meibomian glands

_____ 2. optic nerve

_____ 3. orbit

_____ 4. pupil

_____ 5. retina

_____ 6. sclera

_____ 7. vitreous fluid

a. outer protective layer of the eye

b. innermost layer of the eye

c. jellylike liquid found behind the lens and in the posterior cavity of the eye

d. oil glands in eyelids that help lubricate the eye

e. opening in the center of the iris

f. carries visual impulses from the retina to the brain

g. middle layer of the eye

h. bony protective cavity of the skull in which the eye lies

WORD PARTS

Combining Forms for the Eye

Study the word parts and their definitions listed below. Completing the exercises that follow will help you learn the terms.

Combining Form	Definition
blephar/o	eyelid
conjunctiv/o	conjunctiva
cor/o, core/o, pupill/o	pupil

corne/o, kerat/o . . . .   cornea
   (NOTE: *kerat/o* also means *hard*
   or *horny tissue*, see Chapter 4.)

dacry/o, lacrim/o . . . .   tear, tear duct

irid/o, iri/o . . . .   iris

ophthalm/o, ocul/o . . . .   eye

opt/o . . . .   vision

retin/o . . . .   retina

scler/o . . . .   sclera *or hard*

Learn the anatomical locations and meanings of the combining forms by completing
exercises 3 and 4 and Exercise Figure A.

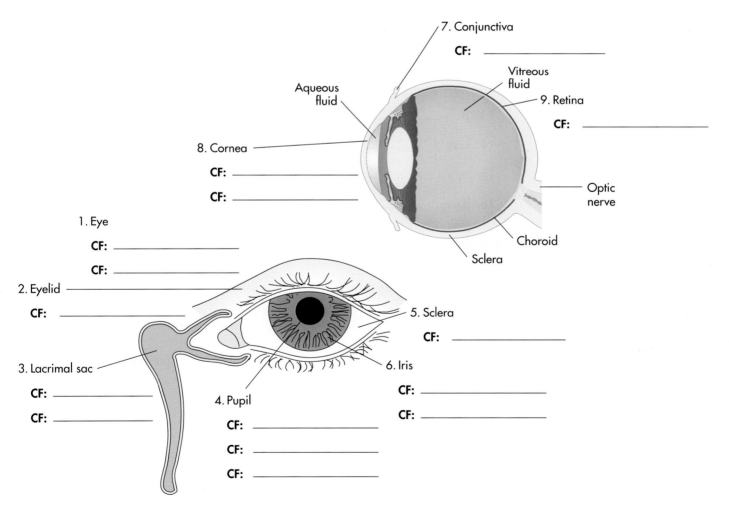

Exercise Fig. A
Diagram of the eye. Fill in the blanks with combining forms.

Exercise 3

Write the definitions of the following combining forms.

1. ocul/o _____

2. blephar/o _____

3. corne/o _____

4. lacrim/o _____

5. retin/o _____

6. pupill/o _____

7. scler/o _____

8. irid/o _____

9. conjunctiv/o _____

10. cor/o _____

11. ophthalm/o _____

12. kerat/o _____

13. iri/o _____

14. core/o _____

15. opt/o _____

16. dacry/o _____

Exercise 4

Write the combining form for each of the following terms.

1. eye   a. _____

                      b. _____

2. cornea   a. _____

                      b. _____

3. conjunctiva   _____

4. tear duct, tear   a. _____

                      b. _____

5. eyelid   _____

6. pupil
a. _____

b. _____

c. _____

7. sclera
_____

8. retina
_____

9. iris
a. _____

b. _____

10. vision
_____

Combining Forms Commonly Used With the Eye

Combining Form	Definition
cry/o	cold
dipl/o	two, double
phot/o	light
ton/o	tension, pressure

Learn the combining forms by completing exercises 5 and 6.

Exercise 5

Write the definitions of the following combining forms.

1. ton/o _____

2. phot/o _____

3. cry/o _____

4. dipl/o _____

Exercise 6

Write the combining form for each of the following.

1. cold
_____

2. tension, pressure
_____

3. two, double
_____

4. light
_____

Prefix and Suffixes

Prefix	Definition
bi-, bin-	two

Suffixes	Definitions
-ician	one who
-opia	vision (condition)
-phobia	abnormal fear of or aversion to specific things
-plegia	paralysis

Learn the prefix and suffixes by completing exercises 7 and 8.

Exercise 7

Write the definition of the following prefix and suffixes.

1. -opia _____

2. bi- _____

3. -plegia _____

4. -ician _____

5. -phobia _____

6. bin- _____

Exercise 8

Write the prefix or suffixes for each of the following definitions.

1. one who   _____

2. paralysis   _____

3. two   a. _____

                                   b. _____

4. abnormal fear of or
   aversion to specific things   _____

5. vision (condition)   _____

MEDICAL TERMS

The terms you need to learn to complete this chapter are listed below. The exercises following each list will help you learn the definition and the spelling of each word.

Disease and Disorder Terms

Built From Word Parts

Term	Definition
blepharitis .... (*blef*-a-RĪ-tis)	inflammation of the eyelid (Exercise Figure B)
blepharoptosis .... (*blef*-ar-op-TŌ-sis)	drooping of the eyelid (Exercise Figure C)
conjunctivitis .... (kon-*junk*-ti-VĪ-tis)	inflammation of the conjunctiva
corneoiritis .... (*kor*-nē-ō-ī-RĪ-tis)	inflammation of the cornea and the iris
dacryocystitis .... (*dak*-rē-ō-sis-TĪ-tis)	inflammation of the tear (lacrimal) sac (Exercise Figure D)
diplopia .... (di-PLŌ-pē-a)	double vision
endophthalmitis .... (en-dof-thal-MĪ-tis) (NOTE: the *o* in *endo* is dropped.)	inflammation within the eye
iridoplegia .... (*īr*-i-dō-PLĒ-jē-a)	paralysis of the iris

Exercise Fig. B
Fill in the blanks to label the

‾‾‾‾‾/‾‾‾‾‾
diagram. EYELID / INFLAMMATION.
Thickened lids with crusts around lashes.

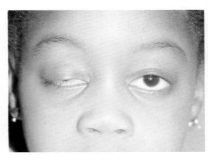

Exercise Fig. C
Fill in the blanks to label the diagram.

‾‾‾‾‾/‾‾‾‾‾
EYELID / DROOPING

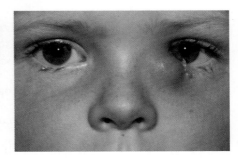

Exercise Fig. D
Fill in the blanks to label the diagram.

‾‾‾‾/‾‾‾/‾‾‾‾/‾‾‾‾‾
TEAR / CV / SAC / INFLAMMATION

iritis . . . . (ī-RĪ-tis)	inflammation of the iris
keratitis . . . . (kar-a-TĪ-tis)	inflammation of the cornea
leukocoria . . . . (lū-kō-KŌ-rē-a)	condition of white pupil
oculomycosis . . . . (*ok*-ū-lō-mī-KŌ-sis)	abnormal condition of the eye caused by a fungus
ophthalmalgia . . . . (*of*-thal-MAL-jē-a)	pain in the eye
ophthalmoplegia . . . . (of-thal-mō-PLĒ-jē-a)	paralysis of the eye (muscle)
ophthalmorrhagia . . . . (of-*thal*-mō-RĀ-jē-a)	rabid flow of blood from the eye (hemorrhage)
photophobia . . . . (*fŏ*-tō-FŌ-bē-a)	abnormal fear of (sensitivity to) light
photoretinitis . . . . (*fŏ*-tō-*ret*-i-NĪ-tis)	inflammation of the retina caused by (extreme) light
retinoblastoma . . . . (ret-i-nō-blas-TŌ-ma)	tumor arising from the developing retinal cell
sclerokeratitis . . . . (*skle*-rō-kar-a-TĪ-tis)	inflammation of the sclera and cornea
scleromalacia . . . . (*skle*-rō-ma-LĀ-shē-a)	softening of the sclera

Practice saying each of these terms aloud. To assist you in pronunciation, obtain the audiotape designed for use with this text. Learn the definitions and spellings of the disease and disorder terms by completing exercises 9, 10, and 11.

Exercise 9

Analyze and define the following terms.

1. sclerokeratitis _____

2. ophthalmalgia _____

3. corneoiritis _____

4. blepharoptosis _____

5. diplopia _____

6. ophthalmorrhagia _____

7. conjunctivitis _____

8. leukocoria _____

9. iridoplegia _____

10. scleromalacia _____

11. photophobia _____

12. blepharitis _____

13. oculomycosis _____

14. photoretinitis _____

15. dacryocystitis _____

16. endophthalmitis _____

17. iritis _____

18. retinoblastoma _____

19. keratitis _____

20. ophthalmoplegia _____

Exercise 10

Build disease and disorder terms for the following definitions using the word parts you have learned.

1. inflammation of the conjunctiva

   _____ / _____
        WR   /   S

2. abnormal eye condition
   caused by a fungus

   _____ / _____ / _____ / _____
     WR   /   CV /   WR   /   S

3. pain in the eye

   _____ / _____
        WR   /   S

4. inflammation of the retina
   caused by light

   _____ / _____ / _____ / _____
     WR   /   CV /   WR   /   S

5. double vision

   _____ / _____
        WR   /   S

6. inflammation of the eyelid

   _____ / _____
        WR   /   S

7. condition of white pupil

   _____ / _____ / _____ / _____
     WR   /   CV /   WR   /   S

8. paralysis of the iris

   _____ / _____ / _____
             WR   / CV /   S

9. inflammation of the cornea
   and the iris

   _____ / _____ / _____ / _____
     WR   /   CV /   WR   /   S

10. drooping of the eyelid

_____
WR / CV / S

11. inflammation of the iris

_____
WR / S

12. tumor arising from developing retinal cell

_____
WR / CV / WR / S

13. softening of the sclera

_____
WR / CV / S

14. inflammation of a tear (lacrimal) sac

_____
WR / CV / WR / S

15. rabid flow of blood from the eye (hemorrhage)

_____
WR / S

16. inflammation of the sclera and cornea

_____
WR / CV / WR / S

17. abnormal fear of (sensitivity to) light

_____
WR / CV / S

18. inflammation of the cornea

_____
WR / S

19. inflammation within the eye

_____
P / WR / S

20. paralysis of the eye (muscle)

_____
WR / CV / S

Exercise 11

Spell each of the disease and disorder terms. Have someone dictate the terms on pp. 371-372 to you, or say the words into a tape recorder; then spell the words from your recording. Think about the word parts before attempting to write the word. Study any words you have spelled incorrectly.

1. _____   11. _____

2. _____   12. _____

3. _____   13. _____

4. _____   14. _____

5. _____   15. _____

6. _____   16. _____

7. _____   17. _____

8. _____   18. _____

9. _____   19. _____

10. _____   20. _____

Disease and Disorder Terms

Not Built From Word Parts

Term	Definition
astigmatism (Ast) (a-STIG-ma-tizm)	defective curvature of the refractive surface of the eye
cataract (KAT-a-rakt)	clouding of the lens of the eye (Figure 12-3)
chalazion (ka-LĀ-zē-on)	obstruction of the oil gland of the eyelid also called *meibomian cyst* (Figure 12-4)
detached retina	separation of the retina from the choroid in back of the eye (Figure 12-5)
emmetropia (Em) (em-e-TRŌ-pē-a)	normal condition of the eye
glaucoma (glaw-KŌ-ma)	abnormally increased intraocular tension (Figure 12-6)

Cataract

is derived from the Greek **kato**, meaning **down**, and **raktos**, meaning **precipice**. Together, the words were interpreted as **waterfall**. The cataract sufferer sees things as through a watery veil of mist, or waterfall.

Glaucoma

is composed of the Greek **glaukos**, meaning **blue-gray** or **sea green**, and **oma**, meaning a morbid condition. The term was given to any condition in which gray or green replaced the black in the pupil.

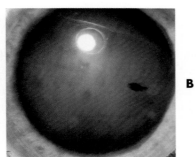

Fig. 12-3
A, Snowflake cataract. **B,** Senile cataract.

Fig. 12-4
Chalazion (right upper eyelid).

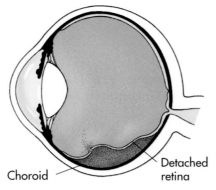

Fig. 12-5
Detached retina. Vitreous fluid has seeped through a break in the retina, causing the choroid coat and retina to separate.

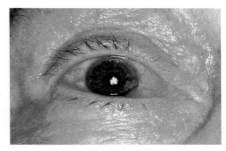

Fig. 12-6
Appearance of the eye in acute glaucoma.

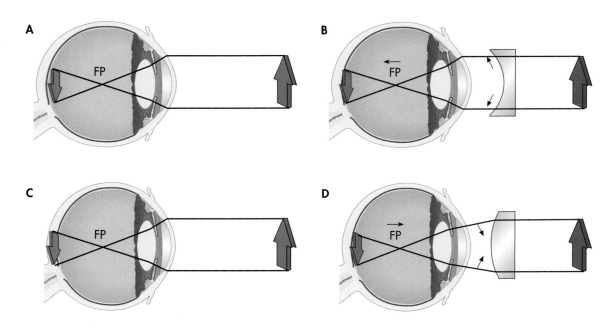

Fig. 12-7
Refraction disorders. **A** and **B,** abnormal and corrected refraction in myopia; and **C** and **D,** hyperopia. FP = focal point.

hyperopia		farsightedness (Figure 12-7)
(*hī*-per-Ō-pē-a)		
macular degeneration		a progressive deterioration of the portion of the retina called the *macula lutea*, resulting in loss of central vision
(MAC-ū-lar)		
myopia		nearsightedness (Figure 12-7)
(mī-Ō-pē-a)		
nyctalopia		poor vision at night or in faint light
(nik-ta-LŌ-pē-a)		
nystagmus		involuntary, rhythmic movements of the eyes
(nis-TAG-mus)		
presbyopia		impaired vision as a result of aging
(*pres*-bē-Ō-pē-a)		
pterygium		abnormal fold of membrane extending from conjunctiva to cornea
(te-RIJ-ē-um)		
retinitis pigmentosa		hereditary, progressive disease marked by night blindness with atrophy and retinal pigment changes
(ret-i-NĪ-tis) (pig-men-TŌ-sa)		
strabismus		abnormal condition of squint or crossed eyes caused by the visual axes not meeting at the same point
(stra-BIZ-mus)		
sty (hordeolum)		infection of the oil gland of the eyelid (Figure 12-8)
(stī) (hōr-DĒ-ō-lum)		

Age-related macular degeneration is the leading cause of blindness in persons over 65 years of age. Onset occurs between the ages of 50 and 60.

Fig. 12-8
Hordeolum (sty).

Practice saying each of these terms aloud. To assist you in pronunciation, obtain the audiotape designed for use with this text. Learn the definitions and spellings of the disease and disorder terms by completing exercises 12, 13, and 14.

Exercise 12

Fill in the blanks with the correct terms.

1. Another name for nearsightedness is _____ .

2. Impaired vision as a result of aging is _____ .

3. The abnormal condition of squint or crossed eyes caused by visual axes not meeting at the same point is called _____ .

4. An obstruction of the oil gland of the eyelid is called a(n) _____ .

5. A defective curvature of the refractive surface of the eye causes a condition known as _____ .

6. _____ is the name given to involuntary, rhythmic movements of the eye.

7. A clouding of the lens of the eye is called a(n) _____ .

8. _____ is the name given to an infection of the oil gland of the eyelids.

9. A condition of abnormally increased intraocular tension is _____ .

10. A(n) _____ _____ is a separation of the retina from the choroid in the back of the eye.

11. Another name for farsightedness is _____ .

12. Normal condition of the eye is called _____ .

13. _____ _____ is a hereditary, progressive disease causing night blindness with retinal pigment changes and atrophy.

14. Poor vision at night or in faint light is called _____ .

15. A _____ is an abnormal fold of membrane extending from conjunctiva to the cornea.

16. _____ _____ is the progressive deterioration of the macula lutea.

Exercise 13 ....

Match the terms in the first column with the correct definitions in the second column.

_____ 1. astigmatism

_____ 2. cataract

_____ 3. chalazion

_____ 4. detached retina

_____ 5. glaucoma

_____ 6. myopia

_____ 7. nystagmus

_____ 8. hyperopia

_____ 9. presbyopia

_____ 10. strabismus

_____ 11. sty

_____ 12. pterygium

_____ 13. retinitis pigmentosa

_____ 14. nyctalopia

_____ 15. emmetropia

_____ 16. macular degeneration

a. infection of the oil gland of the eyelid

b. deterioration of the macula lutea

c. crossed eyes or squint caused by visual axes not meeting at the same point

d. involuntary, rhythmic movements of the eye

e. impaired vision caused by aging

f. defective curvature of the refractive surface of the eye

g. normal condition of the eye

h. clouding of a lens of the eye

i. hereditary progressive disease marked by night blindness

j. nearsightedness

k. obstruction of the oil gland of the eye

l. abnormal fold of membrane extending from the conjunctiva to the cornea

m. increased intraocular tension

n. separation of the retina from the choroid in the back of the eye

o. poor vision at night or in faint light

p. farsightedness

q. double vision

Exercise 14 ....

Spell the disease and disorder terms. Have someone dictate the terms on pp. 375 and 376 to you, or say the words into a tape recorder; then spell the words from your recording. Study any words you have spelled incorrectly.

1. _____   9. _____

2. _____   10. _____

3. _____   11. _____

4. _____   12. _____

5. _____   13. _____

6. _____   14. _____

7. _____   15. _____

8. _____   16. _____

Surgical Terms

Built From Word Parts

Term	Definition
blepharoplasty . . . . (BLEF-a-rō-plast-tē)	surgical repair of the eyelid
cryoretinopexy . . . . (krī-ō-re-tin-ō-PEK-sē)	surgical fixation of the retina by extreme cold (liquid nitrogen)
dacryocystorhinostomy . . . . (dak-rē-ō-sis-tō-rī-NOS-tō-mē)	creation of an artificial opening between the tear (lacrimal) sac and the nose (to restore drainage into the nose when the nasolacrimal duct is obstructed or obliterated)
dacryocystotomy . . . . (dak-rē-ō-sis-TOT-ō-mē)	incision into the tear sac
iridectomy . . . . (ir-i-DEK-tō-mē)	excision (of part) of the iris
iridosclerotomy . . . . (ir-i-dō-skle-ROT-tō-mē)	incision (into the edge) of the iris and into the sclera
keratoplasty . . . . (KAR-a-tō-plas-tē)	surgical repair of the cornea (corneal transplant)
sclerotomy . . . . (skle-ROT-ō-mē)	incision into the sclera

Practice saying each of these terms aloud. To assist you in pronunciation, obtain the audiotape designed for use with this text. Learn the definitions and spellings of the surgical terms by completing exercises 15, 16, and 17.

Exercise 15

Analyze and define the following surgical terms.

1. keratoplasty _____

2. sclerotomy _____

3. dacryocystotomy _____

4. cryoretinopexy _____

5. iridosclerotomy _____

6. blepharoplasty _____

7. iridectomy _____

8. dacryocystorhinostomy _____

Exercise 16 ....

Build surgical terms for the following definitions by using the word parts you have learned.

1. creation of an artificial opening between the tear (lacrimal) sac and the nose (to restore drainage when the nasolacrimal duct is obstructed)

WR / CV / WR / CV / WR / S

2. excision of the iris

──────────────────────
WR / S

3. surgical repair of the cornea

──────────────────────
WR / CV / S

4. incision of the sclera

──────────────────────
WR / S

5. surgical repair of the eyelid

──────────────────────
WR / CV / S

6. surgical fixation of the retina by a method using extreme cold

──────────────────────
WR / CV / WR / CV / S

7. incision into the tear sac

──────────────────────
WR / CV / WR / S

8. incision (into the edge) of the iris and into the sclera

WR / CV / WR / S

Exercise 17 ....

Spell each of the surgical terms. Have someone dictate the terms on p 379 to you, or say the words into a tape recorder; then spell the words from your recording. Think about the word parts before attempting to write the word. Study any words you have spelled incorrectly.

1. _____   5. _____

2. _____   6. _____

3. _____   7. _____

4. _____   8. _____

Surgical Terms

Not Built From Word Parts

Term	Definition
cryoextraction of the lens . . . . (*krī*-ō-eks-TRAK-shun)	procedure in which a cataract is lifted from the eye with an extremely cold probe (cryoprobe) (Figure 12-9)
enucleation . . . . (e-*nū*-klē-Ā-shun)	surgical removal of the eye (also, the removal of any organ that comes out clean and whole)
phacoemulsification . . . . (*fa*-kō-ē-*mul*-si-fi-KĀ-shun)	method to remove cataracts in which an ultrasonic needle probe breaks up the lens, which is then aspirated
photorefractive keratectomy (PRK) (fō-tō-rē-FRAK-tiv) (ker-a-TEK-tō-mē)	a procedure for the treatment of nearsightedness in which an excimer laser is used to reshape (flatten) the corneal surface
radial keratotomy (RK) . . . . (ker-a-TOT-ō-mē)	surgery in which spoke-like incisions are made to flatten the cornea, thus correcting nearsightedness
retinal photocoagulation . . . . (RET-in-al) (*fō*-tō-kō-*ag*-ū-LĀ-shun)	procedure to repair tears in the retina by use of an intense, precisely focused light beam, which causes coagulation of the tissue protein; used to repair retinal detachment
scleral buckling . . . . (SKLE-ral) (BUK-ling)	repair of a detached retina. A strip of sclera is resected, or a fold is made in the sclera. An implant is inserted with sutures to hold and buckle the sclera (Figure 12-10).
strabotomy . . . . (stra-BOT-ō-mē)	incision into the tendon of an extrinsic muscle of the eye to relieve strabismus
trabeculectomy . . . . (tra-bek-ū-LEK-tō-mē)	surgical creation of a drain to reduce intraocular pressure
vitrectomy . . . . (vi-TREK-tō-mē)	surgical removal of all or part of the vitreous fluid

Practice saying each of these terms aloud. To assist you in pronunciation, obtain the audiotape designed for use with this text. Learn the definitions and spellings of the surgical terms by completing exercises 18, 19, and 20.

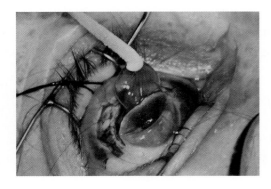

Fig. 12-9
Cryoextraction of the lens. Cryoprobe freezes to surface of cataract and makes it easy to remove.

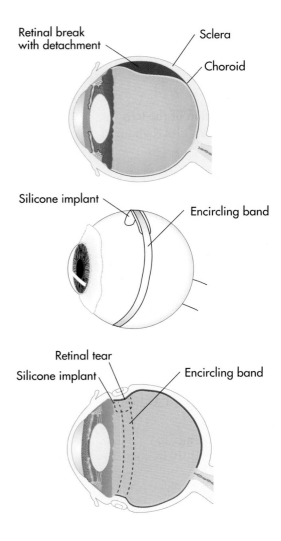

Fig. 12-10
Scleral buckling.

Exercise 18

Fill in the blank with the correct terms.

1. The procedure performed to repair tears in the retina is called
    _____ _____ .

2. _____ of the lense is the name given to the procedure in which the cataract is lifted from the eye by an extremely cold probe.

3. Surgical removal of an eye is called a(n) _____ .

4. _____ is the name given to the procedure that breaks up the lens with ultrasound and then aspirates it.

5. An incision into the tendon of the extrinsic muscle to relieve a cross-eyed condition is a(n) _____ .

6. _____ is the surgical creation of a drain to reduce intraocular pressure.

7. An operation to repair a detached retina in which the sclera is folded or resected, an implant inserted, and sutures made to hold the sclera is called
    _____ _____ .

8. Surgery in which spoke-like incisions are made to flatten the cornea, thus correcting nearsightedness is called a _____ _____ .

9. Surgery to remove vitreous fluid from the eye is called _____ .

10. _____ _____ is a procedure for the treatment of
nearsightedness in which an excimer laser is used to reshape the cornea.

Exercise 19

Match the terms in the first column with their correct definitions in the second column.

_____ 1. strabotomy

_____ 2. enucleation

_____ 3. trabeculectomy

_____ 4. retinal photocoagulation

_____ 5. cryoextraction of lens

_____ 6. phacoemulsification

_____ 7. scleral buckling

_____ 8. radial keratotomy

_____ 9. vitrectomy

_____ 10. photorefractive
keratectomy

a. surgery to flatten the cornea, thus correcting nearsightedness

b. surgical creation of a permanent drain to reduce intraocular pressure

c. procedure for the treatment of nearsightedness in which an excimer laser is used to reshape the cornea

d. procedure in which the lens is broken up by
ultrasound and aspirated

e. incision into the extrinsic muscle to relieve
crossed eyes

f. surgical removal of an eye

g. surgical removal of vitreous fluid

h. operation in which a cataract is lifted from
the eye with an extremely cold probe

i. detached retina surgery in which the sclera
is folded, an implant inserted, and sutures
made to hold the sclera

j. surgical incision of the sclera

k. procedure to repair tears in the retina

Exercise 20

Spell each of the surgical terms. Have someone dictate the terms on p. 381 to you, or
say the words into a tape recorder; then spell the words from your recording. Study
any words you have spelled incorrectly.

1. _____

2. _____

3. _____

4. _____

5. _____

6. _____

7. _____

8. _____

9. _____

10. _____

Procedural Terms

Built From Word Parts

Term	Definition
Diagnostic Imaging	
fluorescein angiography .... (flō-RES-ē-in) (an-jē-OG-ra-fē)	x-ray filming of blood vessels (of the eye using fluorescing dye)
Ophthalmic Evaluation	
keratometer .... (*kar*-a-TOM-e-ter)	instrument used to measure (the curvature of) the cornea (used for fitting contact lenses)
ophthalmoscope .... (of-THAL-mō-skōp)	instrument used for visual examination of (the interior) of the eye (Figure 12-11)
ophthalmoscopy .... (*of*-thal-MOS-kō-pē)	visual examination of the eye
optometer .... (op-TOM-e-ter)	instrument used to measure (power and range of) vision
optometry .... (op-TOM-e-trē)	measurement of vision (acuity and the prescribing of corrective lenses)
optomyometer .... (*op*-tō-mī-OM-e-ter)	instrument used to measure (the power of) the muscles of vision
pupillometer .... (pū-pil-OM-e-ter)	instrument used to measure (the width and diameter of) the pupil
pupilloscope .... (pū-PIL-ō-skōp)	instrument used for visual examination of the pupil
tonometer .... (ton-OM-e-ter)	instrument used to measure pressure (within the eye, used to diagnose glaucoma) (Figure 12-12)
tonometry .... (ton-OM-e-trē)	measurement of pressure (within the eye)

Practice saying each of these words aloud. To assist you in pronunciation, obtain the audiotape designed for use with this text. Learn the definitions and spellings of the procedural terms by completing exercises 21, 22, and 23.

Fig. 12-11
Ophthalmoscope used to view the retina.

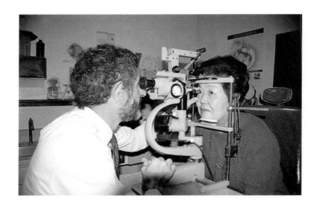

Fig. 12-12
Tonometry.

Exercise 21 ....

Analyze and define the following procedural terms.

1. optometer _____

2. pupilloscope _____

3. optometry _____

4. ophthalmoscope _____

5. tonometry _____

6. pupillometer _____

7. optomyometer _____

8. tonometer _____

9. keratometer _____

10. ophthalmoscopy _____

11. fluorescein angiography _____

Exercise 22 ....

Build procedural terms that correspond to the following definitions by using the word parts you have learned.

1. instrument used to measure (the power and range of) vision

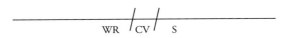

2. measurement of pressure (within the eye)

3. instrument used to measure (the width and diameter of) the pupil

4. instrument used to measure (the curvature of) the cornea

5. measurement of vision (acuity and the prescribing of corrective lenses)

6. instrument used to measure (the power of) the muscles of vision

_____ / CV / WR / CV / S
         WR

7. instrument used for visual examination of (the interior) of the eye

_____ / CV / S
         WR   CV

8. instrument used to measure pressure (within the eye)

_____ / CV / S
         WR   CV

9. instrument used for visual examination of the pupil

_____ / CV / S
         WR   CV

10. visual examination of the eye

_____ / CV / S
         WR   CV

11. x-ray filming of blood vessels (of the eye, using fluorescing dye)

fluorescein _____ / CV / S
                    WR   CV

Exercise 23

Spell each of the procedural terms. Have someone dictate the terms on p. 384 to you, or say the words into a tape recorder; then spell the words from your recording. Think about the word parts before attempting to write the word. Study any words you have spelled incorrectly.

1. _____   7. _____

2. _____   8. _____

3. _____   9. _____

4. _____   10. _____

5. _____   11. _____

6. _____

Complementary Terms

Built From Word Parts

Term	Definition
binocular . . . . (bin-OK-ū-lar)	pertaining to two or both eyes
corneal . . . . (KŌR-nē-al)	pertaining to the cornea
intraocular . . . . (*in*-tra-OK-ū-lar)	pertaining to within the eye
lacrimal . . . . (LAK-ri-mal)	pertaining to tears or tear ducts
nasolacrimal . . . . (*nā*-zō-LAK-ri-mal)	pertaining to the nose and tear ducts
ophthalmic . . . . (of-THAL-mik)	pertaining to the eye
ophthalmologist . . . . (*of*-thal-MOL-ō-jist)	physician who specializes in ophthalmology
ophthalmology (ophth) . . . . (*of*-thal-MOL-ō-jē)	study of diseases and treatment of the eye
ophthalmopathy . . . . (*of*-thal-MOP-a-thē)	(any) disease of the eye
optic . . . . (OP-tik)	pertaining to vision
optician . . . . (op-TISH-in)	one who is skilled in filling prescriptions for lenses
pupillary . . . . (PŪ-pi-lar-ē)	pertaining to the pupil
retinal . . . . (RET-i-nal)	pertaining to the retina
retinopathy . . . . (*ret*-i-NOP-a-thē)	(any noninflammatory) disease of the retina (such as diabetic retinopathy)

Practice saying each of these terms aloud. To assist you in pronunciation, obtain the audiotape designed for use with this text. Exercises 24, 25, and 26 will help you learn the definitions and spellings of the complementary terms related to the eye.

Exercise 24

Analyze and define the following complementary terms.

1. ophthalmology _____

2. binocular _____

3. optician _____

4. lacrimal _____

5. pupillary _____

6. retinopathy _____

7. ophthalmologist _____

8. corneal _____

9. ophthalmic _____

10. nasolacrimal _____

11. optic _____

12. intraocular _____

13. retinal _____

14. ophthalmopathy _____

Exercise 25 ....

Build the complementary terms for the following definitions by using the word parts you have learned.

1. study of diseases and treatment of the eye

   _____ / _____
           WR   S

2. pertaining to two or both eyes

   _____ / _____ / _____
     P   WR   S

3. pertaining to the retina

   _____ / _____
           WR   S

4. pertaining to within the eye

   _____ / _____ / _____
     P   WR   S

5. physician who specializes in
   ophthalmology

   _____ / _____
           WR   S

6. pertaining to tears or tear
   ducts

   _____ / _____
           WR   S

7. pertaining to vision

   _____ / _____
           WR   S

8. one who is skilled in filling
   prescriptions for lenses

   _____ / _____
           WR   S

9. (any noninflammatory) disease of the retina

     _____ / ___ / ___
           WR   CV   S

10. pertaining to the cornea

     _____ / ___
           WR   S

11. pertaining to the nose and tear ducts

     _____ / ___ / ___ / ___
           WR   CV   WR   S

12. any disease of the eye

     _____ / ___ / ___
           WR   CV   S

13. pertaining to the pupil

     _____ / ___
           WR   S

Exercise 26

Spell each of the complementary terms. Have someone dictate the terms on p. 387 to you, or say the words into a tape recorder; then spell the words from your recording. Think about the word parts before attempting to write the word. Study any words you have spelled incorrectly.

1. _____   8. _____
2. _____   9. _____
3. _____   10. _____
4. _____   11. _____
5. _____   12. _____
6. _____   13. _____
7. _____   14. _____

Complementary Terms

Not Built From Word Parts

Term	Definition
miotic . . . . (mī-OT-ik)	agent that constricts the pupil
mydriatic . . . . (*mid*-rē-AT-ik)	agent that dilates the pupil
oculus dexter (OD) . . . . (OK-ū-lus) (DEX-ter)	medical term for right eye
oculus sinister (OS) . . . . (OK-ū-lus) (sin-IS-ter)	medical term for left eye

Optometrist

is derived from the Greek
optikos, meaning **sight,** and
metron, meaning **measure.**
Literally, an optometrist is a
person who measures sight.

oculus uterque (OU) . . . .   medical term for each eye
  (OK-ū-lus) (ū-TERK)

optometrist . . . .   a health professional who prescribes corrective
  (op-TOM-e-trist)   lenses and/or eye exercises

visual acuity (VA) . . . .   sharpness of vision for either distance or near-
  (VIZH-ū-al) (a-KŪ-i-tē)   ness

Practice saying each of these terms aloud. To assist you in pronunciation, obtain the
audiotape designed for use with this text. Learn the definitions and spellings of the
complementary terms by completing exercises 27, 28, and 29.

Exercise 27

Write the definitions for the following complementary terms.

1. oculus sinister _____

2. optometrist _____

3. mydriatic _____

4. oculus uterque _____

5. visual acuity _____

6. miotic _____

7. oculus dexter _____

Exercise 28

Fill in the blanks with the correct terms.

1. The medical term for the left eye is _____ _____ .

2. An agent that dilates a pupil is a(n) _____ .

3. _____ _____ means each eye.

4. An agent that constricts a pupil is a(n) _____ .

5. The medical term for the right eye is _____ _____ .

6. A health professional who prescribes corrective lenses and/or eye exercises is a(n)
   _____ .

7. Another term for sharpness of vision is _____ _____ .

Exercise 29

Spell each of the complementary terms. Have someone dictate the terms on pp. 389-390 to you, or say the words into a tape recorder; then spell the words from your recording. Study any words you have spelled incorrectly.

1. _____   5. _____

2. _____   6. _____

3. _____   7. _____

4. _____

Abbreviations

ARMD	age-related macular degeneration
Ast	astigmatism
ECCE	extracapsular cataract extraction
Em	emmetropia
ICCE	intracapsular cataract cryoextraction
IOP	intraocular pressure
OD	right eye (oculus dexter)
ophth	ophthalmology
OS	left eye (oculus sinister)
OU	both eyes (oculus uterque)
PERRLA	pupils equal, round, reactive to light and accommodation
PRK	photorefractive keratectomy
REM	rapid eye movement
RK	radial keratotomy
VA	visual acuity
VF	visual field

CHAPTER REVIEW

Exercises

Exercise 30

Complete the hospital report by writing the medical terms in the blanks. Use the list of definitions with the corresponding numbers.

Case History: This is a 66-year-old Chicano, hypertensive and diabetic, on oral medication: Micronase and Lopressor. History of a 1. _____ , excised without complication. Family history of 2. _____ (brother).

EXAMINATION

Visual Acuities: Aided: OD 20/25-2 OS 20/30-1 OU 20/25

Unaided: OD 20/100 OS 20/80-1 OU 20/80

Externals: 2 mm 3. _____ OD PERRLA (pupils equal, round, reactive to light and accommodation)

Ocular motility normal

Ophthalmoscopic: Lens: OS showed early cortical spokes

Disk: margins normal

Cup to disk ratio: 0.2 OU

Fundus: copper wire appearance to arteries along with marked arteriovenous compression. Pronounced narrowing of the arterioles. A-V ratio 1 to 2. Several punctate hemorrhages and hard yellow exudates noted in macular area of both eyes.

Refraction: OD $-1.00 -0.50 \times 90$ 20/20

OS $-0.75 -0.50 \times 85$ 20/25

Tonometry: 14 mm/Hg OD 13 mm/Hg OS

Visual Field: Negative OU

Diagnosis: Patient is a compound myopic 4. _____ and 5. _____ with stage 1 diabetic 6. _____ and grade II 7. _____ and 8. _____. He also shows an early 9. _____ in the left eye.

Treatment: Provide prescription for corrective lenses. See patient for follow-up visit in 6 months to reevaluate diabetic retinopathy and cataract. Counsel patient to report any sudden changes in vision.

---

1. abnormal fold of membrane extending from conjunctiva to cornea
2. abnormally increased intraocular tension
3. drooping of eyelid

4. defective curvature of the refractive surface of the eye

5. impaired vision as a result of aging

6. (any noninflammatory) disease of the retina

7. blood pressure that is above normal

8. hardening of the arteries

9. clouding of the lens of the eye

Exercise 31

To test your understanding of the terms introduced in this chapter, circle the words that correctly complete the sentences. The italicized words refer to the correct answer.

1. The patient's *pupils* needed to be *dilated,* therefore the doctor requested that a (miotic, mydriatic, miopic) medication be placed in each eye.

2. A person with a *defective curvature of the refractive surface* of the eye has a(n) (astigmatism, glaucoma, strabismus).

3. The doctor diagnosed the patient with the *clouded lens* of the eye as having a(n) (nystagmus, astigmatism, cataract).

4. To *measure the pressure within the patient's eye,* the physician used a(n) (optomyometer, pupillometer, tonometer).

5. A person who is *farsighted* has (hyperopia, myopia, diplopia).

6. An *obstruction of the oil gland of the eyelid* is called a(n) (sty, chalazion, conjunctivitis).

7. A patient with an *involuntary rhythmic movement of the eyes* has a condition known as (astigmatism, strabismus, nystagmus).

8. The name of the *surgery performed to create a permanent drain to reduce intraocular pressure* is (trabeculectomy, strabotomy, phacoemulsification).

9. The doctor ordered an *x-ray filming of the blood vessels of the eye* or a(n) (ophthalmoscopy, fluorescein angiography, optometer).

Exercise 32

Unscramble the following mixed-up terms. The word on the left gives a hint about the word root in each of the scrambled words.

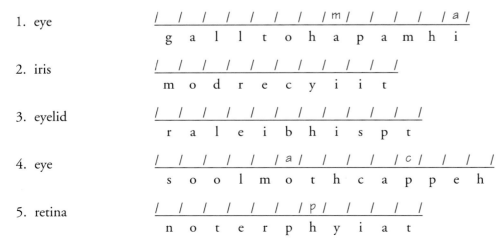

1. eye   / / / / / / / /m/ / / / /a/
          g a l l t o h a p a m h i

2. iris   / / / / / / / / / /
          m o d r e c y i i t

3. eyelid   / / / / / / / / / / /
          r a l e i b h i s p t

4. eye   / / / / / /a/ / / / /c/ / /
          s o o l m o t h c a p p e h

5. retina   / / / / / / /p/ / / / /
          n o t e r p h y i a t

Exercise 33

The following terms did not appear in this chapter but are composed of word parts that have appeared in this chapter or previous chapters. Find their definitions by translating the word parts literally.

1. **endonasal** _____
   (*en*-dō-NĀ-zal)

2. **erythropoiesis** _____
   (e-*rith*-rō-poy-Ē-sis)

3. **esophagocele** _____
   (e-SOF-a-gō-sēl)

4. **fibrogenic** _____
   (*fi*-brō-JEN-ik)

5. **glomerulosclerosis** _____
   (glō-*mer*-u-lō-skle-RŌ-sis)

6. **hematorrhea** _____
   (*hēm*-a-tō-RĒ-a)

7. **hepatolith** _____
   (HEP-a-tō-lith)

8. **histolysis** _____
   (his-TOL-i-sis)

9. **hydropyonephrosis** _____
   (*hī*-drō-*pī*-ō-ne-FRŌ-sis)

10. **hypermyotrophy** _____
    (hī-per-mī-OT-rō-fē)

Review of Terms

Can you build, analyze, define, pronounce, and spell the following terms *built from word parts?*

Diseases and Disorders

blepharitis

blepharoptosis

conjunctivitis

corneoiritis

dacryocystitis

diplopia

endophthalmitis

iridoplegia

iritis

keratitis

leukocoria

oculomycosis

ophthalmalgia

ophthalmoplegia

ophthalmorrhagia

photophobia

photoretinitis

retinoblastoma

sclerokeratitis

scleromalacia

Surgical

blepharoplasty

cryoretinopexy

dacryocystorhinostomy

dacryocystotomy

iridectomy

iridosclerotomy

keratoplasty

sclerotomy

Procedural

fluorescein angiography

keratometer

ophthalmoscope

ophthalmoscopy

optometer

optometry

optomyometer

pupillometer

pupilloscope

tonometer

tonometry

Complementary

binocular

corneal

intraocular

lacrimal

nasolacrimal

ophthalmic

ophthalmologist

ophthalmology (ophth)

ophthalmopathy

optic

optician

pupillary

retinal

retinopathy

Can you define, pronounce, and spell the following terms *not built from word parts?*

Diseases and
Disorders

astigmatism (Ast)

cataract

chalazion

detached retina

emmetropia (Em)

glaucoma

hyperopia

macular degeneration

myopia

nyctalopia

nystagmus

presbyopia

pterygium

retinitis pigmentosa

strabismus

sty (hordeolum)

Surgical

cryoextraction of the lens

enucleation

phacoemulsification

photorefractive keratectomy
    (PRK)

radial keratotomy (RK)

retinal photocoagulation

scleral buckling

strabotomy

trabeculectomy

vitrectomy

Complementary

miotic

mydriatic

oculus dexter (OD)

oculus sinister (OS)

oculus uterque (OU)

optometrist

visual acuity (VA)

Objectives .... **Upon completion of this chapter you will be able to:**
1. Identify the anatomy of the ear.
2. Define and spell the word parts presented in this chapter.
3. Build and analyze medical terms using word parts.
4. Define, pronounce, and spell the disease and disorder, procedural, surgical, and complementary terms for the ear.

ANATOMY

The two functions of the ear are to hear and to provide the sense of balance. The ear is made up of three parts: the *external* ear, the *middle* ear, and the *inner* ear (Figure 13-1). We hear because sound waves vibrate through the ear, where they are transformed into nerve impulses that are then carried to the brain.

Structures of the Ear

external ear

auricle, pinna . . . . located on both sides of the head. The auricle directs sound waves into the external auditory meatus.

external auditory meatus . . . . . short tube that ends at the tympanic membrane. The inner part lies within the temporal bone of the skull and contains the glands that secrete earwax (cerumen).

middle ear

tympanic membrane, eardrum . semitransparent membrane that separates the external auditory meatus and the middle ear cavity (Figure 13-2)

eustachian tube . . . . connects the middle ear and the pharynx. It equalizes air pressure on both sides of the eardrum.

ossicles . . . . bones of the middle ear that carry sound vibrations. The ossicles comprise the malleus (hammer), incus (anvil), and stapes (stirrup). The stapes connects to the *oval window,* which carries the sound vibrations to the inner ear.

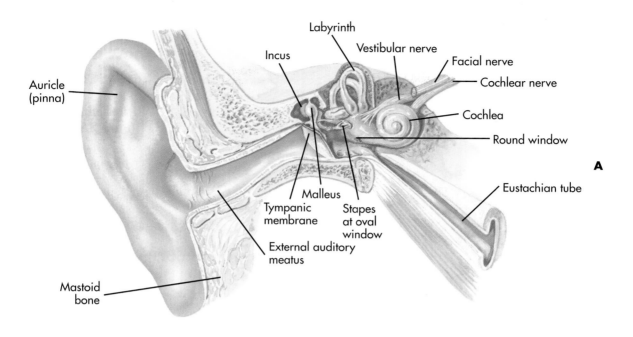

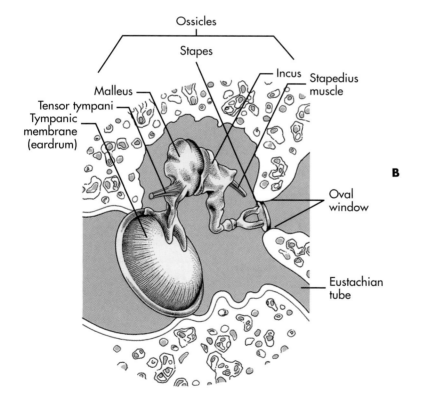

Tympanic Membrane

is derived from the Greek **tympanon,** meaning **drum,** because of its resemblance to a drum or tambourine.

Stapes

is Latin for **stirrup.** The anatomical stapes was so named for its stirrup-like shape.

Fig. 13-1

A, Gross anatomy of the ear. **B,** The middle ear.

Fig. 13-2
Normal tympanic membrane.

inner ear, labyrinth . . . .   bony spaces within the temporal bone of the skull. It contains the following:

cochlea . . . .   is snail-shaped and contains the organ of hearing. The cochlea connects to the oval window in the middle ear.

**semicircular canals
and vestibule** . . . .   contains receptors and endolymph that help the body maintain its sense of balance (equilibrium).

mastoid bone and cells . . . .   located in the skull bone behind the external auditory meatus

Learn the anatomical terms by completing exercise 1.

Exercise 1 . . . .

Match the anatomical terms in the first column with the correct definitions in the second column.

_____ 1. auricle

_____ 2. cochlea

_____ 3. eustachian tube

_____ 4. external auditory meatus

_____ 5. labyrinth

_____ 6. mastoid bone

_____ 7. ossicles

_____ 8. oval window

_____ 9. semicircular canals

_____ 10. tympanic membrane

a. contains receptors and endolymph, which help maintain equilibrium

b. equalizes air pressure on both sides of the eardrum

c. separates the external auditory meatus and middle ear cavity

d. malleus, incus, and stapes

e. carries sound vibration to the inner ear

f. contains glands that secrete earwax

g. one located on each side of the head

h. bony spaces in the inner ear

i. relays messages to the brain

j. contains the organ of hearing

k. located in the skull behind the external auditory meatus

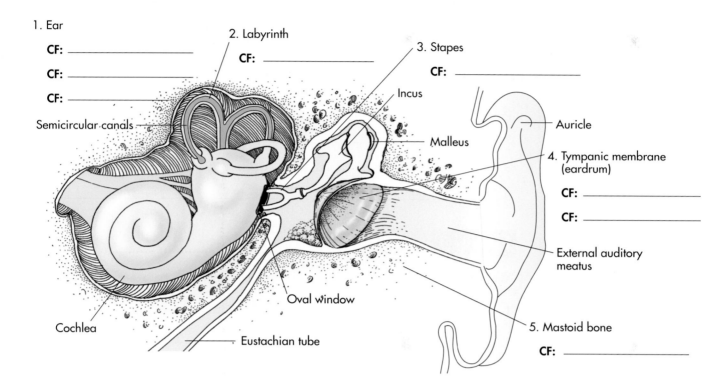

1. Ear

   CF: _____

   CF: _____

   CF: _____

   Semicircular canals

2. Labyrinth

   CF: _____

3. Stapes

   CF: _____

   Incus

   Malleus

   Auricle

4. Tympanic membrane
   (eardrum)

   CF: _____

   CF: _____

   External auditory
   meatus

5. Mastoid bone

   CF: _____

Cochlea

Oval window

Eustachian tube

Exercise Fig. A
Fill in the blanks with
combining forms in this
diagram of the ear.

WORD PARTS

Combining Forms for the Ear

Study the word parts and their definitions listed below. Completing the exercises that follow will help you learn the terms.

Combining Form	Definition
acou/o, audi/o	hearing
aur/i, aur/o	ear
labyrinth/o	labyrinth
mastoid/o	mastoid bone
myring/o	tympanic membrane (eardrum)
ot/o	ear
staped/o	stapes (middle ear bone)
tympan/o	tympanic membrane (eardrum), middle ear

Learn the anatomical locations and meanings of the combining forms by completing exercises 2 and 3 and Exercise Figure A.

Exercise 2

Write the definitions of the following combining forms.

1. staped/o _____

2. mastoid/o _____

3. audi/o _____

4. ot/o _____

5. tympan/o _____

6. aur/o, aur/i _____

7. acou/o _____

8. labyrinth/o _____

9. myring/o _____

Exercise 3

Write the combining form for each of the following terms.

1. ear   a. _____

                                          b. _____

                                          c. _____

2. mastoid bone   _____

3. stapes   _____

4. tympanic membrane (eardrum),   _____
   middle ear

5. labyrinth   _____

6. hearing   a. _____

                                          b. _____

7. tympanic membrane   _____
   (eardrum)

MEDICAL TERMS

The terms you need to learn to complete this chapter are listed below. The exercises following each list will help you learn the definition and the spelling of each word.

Disease and Disorder Terms

Built From Word Parts

Term	Definition
labyrinthitis . . . . (*lab*-i-rin-THĪ-tis)	inflammation of the labyrinth (in the inner ear)
mastoiditis . . . . (*mas*-toyd-Ī-tis)	inflammation of the mastoid bone (and cells)

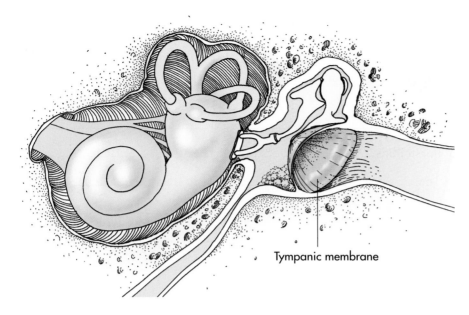

Fig. 13-3
Otitis media. Bulging, perforated, reddened, or retracted tympanic membrane.

myringitis . . . . (mir-in-JĪ-tis)	inflammation of the tympanic membrane (eardrum)
otalgia . . . . (ō-TAL-jē-a)	pain in the ear
otomastoiditis . . . . (ō-tō-*mas*-toyd-Ī-tis)	inflammation of the ear and the mastoid bone
otomycosis . . . . (ō-tō-mī-KŌ-sis)	abnormal condition of fungus in the ear (it usually affects the external auditory meatus)
otopyorrhea . . . . (ō-tō-pī-ō-RĒ-a)	discharge of pus from the ear
otosclerosis . . . . (ō-tō-skle-RŌ-sis)	hardening of the ear (stapes) (caused by irregular bone development and resulting in hearing loss)
tympanitis . . . . (tim-pan-Ī-tis)	inflammation of the middle ear (also called *otitis media*) (Figure 13-3)

Practice saying each of these terms aloud. To assist you in pronunciation, obtain the audiotape designed for use with this text. Learn the definitions and spellings of the disease and disorder terms by completing exercises 4, 5, and 6.

Exercise 4

Analyze and define the following terms.

1. otomycosis _____

2. tympanitis _____

3. otomastoiditis _____

4. otalgia _____

5. labyrinthitis _____

6. myringitis _____

7. otosclerosis _____

8. mastoiditis _____

9. otopyorrhea _____

Exercise 5

Build disease and disorder terms for the following definitions using the word parts you have learned.

1. inflammation of the tympanic
   membrane

   _____ / _____
            WR   S

2. discharge of pus from the ear

   _____ / _____ / _____ / _____
     WR   CV   WR   S

3. inflammation of the mastoid
   bone

   _____ / _____
            WR   S

4. pain in the ear

   _____ / _____
            WR   S

5. hardening of the (ear) stapes

   _____ / ____ / _____
          WR   CV   S

6. abnormal condition of fungus
   in the ear

   _____ / _____ / _____ / _____
     WR   CV   WR   S

7. inflammation of the ear and the
   mastoid bone

   _____ / _____ / _____ / _____
     WR   CV   WR   S

8. inflammation of the labyrinth

   _____ / _____
              WR   S

9. inflammation of the middle ear

   _____ / _____
              WR   S

Exercise 6

Spell each of the disease and disorder terms. Have someone dictate the terms on pp. 400-401 to you, or say the words into a tape recorder; then spell the words from your recording. Think about the word parts before attempting to write the word. Study any words you have spelled incorrectly.

1. _____   6. _____

2. _____   7. _____

3. _____   8. _____

4. _____   9. _____

5. _____

Disease and Disorder Terms

Not Built From Word Parts

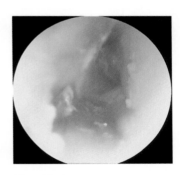

Fig. 13-4
Otitis externa.

Term	Definition
acoustic neuroma . . . . (a-KOOS-tik) (nū-RŌ-ma)	benign tumor within the auditory canal growing from the acoustic nerve. May cause hearing loss
ceruminoma . . . . (*se*-roo-mi-NŌ-ma) (NOTE: although *cerumen* is spelled with an *e,* the word root is *cerumin/o.*)	tumor of the glands that secrete earwax (cerumen)
Ménière's disease . . . . (MEN-ē-ārz)	chronic disease of the inner ear characterized by dizziness and ringing in the ear
otitis externa . . . . (ō-TĪ-tis) (ex-TER-na)	inflammation of the outer ear (Figure 13-4)
otitis media (OM) . . . . (ō-TĪ-tis) (MĒ-dia)	inflammation of the middle ear (Figure 13-3)
presbycusis . . . . (prez-bē-KŪ-sis)	hearing impairment in old age
tinnitus . . . . (tin-NĪ-tus)	ringing in the ears
vertigo . . . . (VER-tig-ō)	dizziness

Practice saying each of these terms aloud. To assist you in pronunciation, obtain the audiotape designed for use with this text. Learn the definitions and spellings of the disease and disorder terms by completing exercises 7, 8, and 9.

Exercise 7

Fill in the blanks with the correct terms.

1. The patient complained of dizziness, or _____ , and ringing in the ears, or _____ .

2. A chronic ear disease characterized by dizziness and ringing in the ears is called _____ disease.

3. Inflammation of the middle ear is called _____
_____ .

4. _____ is the name given to a tumor of the glands that secrete earwax.

5. _____ _____ means inflammation of the outer ear.

6. A benign tumor arising from the acoustic nerve is called a(n) _____
_____ .

7. _____ is hearing impairment in old age.

Exercise 8

Match the terms in the first column with the correct definitions in the second column.

_____ 1. vertigo

_____ 2. ceruminoma

_____ 3. tinnitus

_____ 4. Ménière's disease

_____ 5. otitis externa

_____ 6. acoustic neuroma

_____ 7. otitis media

_____ 8. presbycusis

a. inflammation of the middle ear

b. tumor of the glands that secrete earwax

c. chronic ear problem characterized by vertigo and tinnitus

d. benign tumor arising from the acoustic nerve

e. dizziness

f. hardening of the oval window

g. ringing in the ears

h. inflammation of the outer ear

i. hearing impairment in old age

Exercise 9

Spell the disease and disorder terms. Have someone dictate the terms on p. 403 to you, or say the words into a tape recorder; then spell the words from your recording. Study any words you have spelled incorrectly.

1. _____

2. _____

3. _____

4. _____

5. _____

6. _____

7. _____

8. _____

Surgical Terms

Built From Word Parts

Term	Definition
labyrinthectomy . . . . (*lab*-i-rin-THEK-tō-mē)	excision of the labyrinth
mastoidectomy . . . . (*mas*-toy-DEK-tō-mē)	excision of the mastoid bone
mastoidotomy . . . . (*mas*-toy-DOT-ō-mē)	incision into the mastoid bone
myringoplasty . . . . (mi-RING-gō-*plas*-tē)	surgical repair of the tympanic membrane
myringotomy . . . . (mir-in-GOT-ō-mē)	incision of the tympanic membrane (performed to release pus and relieve pressure in the middle ear) (Exercise Figure B)
tympanoplasty . . . . (tim-pan-ō-PLAS-tē)	surgical repair of the eardrum

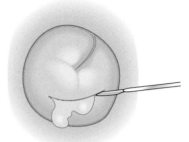

Exercise Fig. B
Fill in the blanks to complete the diagram.

TYMPANIC MEMBRANE / INCISION:
incision to release pus from
the tympanic membrane in
acute otitis media.

Practice saying each of these terms aloud. To assist you in pronunciation, obtain the audiotape designed for use with this text. Learn the definitions and spellings of the surgical terms by completing exercises 10, 11, and 12.

Exercise 10

Analyze and define the following surgical terms.

1. mastoidectomy _____

2. myringotomy _____

3. labyrinthectomy _____

4. mastoidotomy _____

5. tympanoplasty _____

6. myringoplasty _____

Exercise 11

Build surgical terms for the following definitions by using the word parts you have learned.

1. incision into the mastoid
   $$\overline{}_{\text{WR}} \,/\, \overline{}_{\text{S}}$$

2. excision of the labyrinth
   $$\overline{}_{\text{WR}} \,/\, \overline{}_{\text{S}}$$

3. surgical repair of the middle ear   _____ / __ / __
                                                        WR CV   S

4. excision of the mastoid bone   _____ / __
                                                        WR   S

5. incision into the tympanic   _____ / __
   membrane   WR   S

6. surgical repair of the eardrum   _____ / __ / __
                                                        WR CV   S

Exercise 12 ....

Spell each of the surgical terms. Have someone dictate the terms on p. 405 to you, or say the words into a tape recorder; then spell the words from your recording. Think about the word parts before attempting to write the word. Study any words you have spelled incorrectly.

1. _____   4. _____

2. _____   5. _____

3. _____   6. _____

Procedural Terms
Built From Word Parts

Exercise Fig. C

_____ / __ / _____
HEARING   CV   MEASUREMENT
One earphone emits a test sound while the other emits a masking noise. The patient is asked to signal when the test sound occurs.

Term	Definition
acoumeter (a-KOO-mē-ter)	instrument used to measure (acuteness of) hearing
audiogram (AW-dē-ō-gram)	(graphic) record of hearing
audiometer (*aw*-dē-OM-e-ter)	instrument used to measure hearing
audiometry (*aw*-dē-OM-e-trē)	measurement of hearing (Exercise Figure C)
otoscope (Ō-tō-skōp)	instrument used for visual examination of the ear
otoscopy (ō-TOS-kō-pē)	visual examination of the ear
tympanometer (tim-pa-NOM-e-ter)	instrument to measure middle ear function
tympanometry (tim-pa-NOM-e-trē)	measurement (of the movement) of the tympanic membrane

Practice saying each of these terms aloud. To assist you in pronunciation, obtain the audiotape designed for use with this text. Learn the definitions and spellings of the procedural terms by completing exercises 13, 14, and 15.

Exercise 13 ···

Analyze and define the following procedural terms.

1. otoscope _____

2. audiometry _____

3. audiogram _____

4. otoscopy _____

5. audiometer _____

6. tympanometry _____

7. acoumeter _____

8. tympanometer _____

Exercise 14 ···

Build procedural terms that correspond to the following definitions by using the word parts you have learned.

1. measurement (of movement) of the tympanic membrane

   _____ / ___ / ___
   WR   CV   S

2. instrument used to measure hearing

   _____ / ___ / ___
   WR   CV   S

3. visual examination of the ear

   _____ / ___ / ___
   WR   CV   S

4. (graphic) record of hearing

   _____ / ___ / ___
   WR   CV   S

5. instrument used for visual examination of the ear

   _____ / ___ / ___
   WR   CV   S

6. measurement of hearing

   _____ / ___ / ___
   WR   CV   S

7. instrument used to measure (acuteness of) hearing

   _____ / ___
   WR   S

8. instrument to measure middle ear (function)

   _____ / ___ / ___
   WR   CV   S

Exercise 15 ....

Spell each of the procedural terms. Have someone dictate the terms on p. 406 to you, or say the words into a tape recorder; then spell the words from your recording. Think about the word parts before attempting to write the word. Study any words you have spelled incorrectly.

1. _____   5. _____

2. _____   6. _____

3. _____   7. _____

4. _____   8. _____

Complementary Terms

Built From Word Parts

Term	Definition
audiologist . . . . (aw-dē-OL-ō-jist)	one who is skilled in and specializes in audiology
audiology . . . . (aw-dē-OL-ō-jē)	study of hearing
aural . . . . (AW-rul)	pertaining to the ear
otologist . . . . (ō-TOL-ō-jist)	physician who studies and treats diseases of the ear
otology (Oto) . . . . (ō-TOL-ō-jē)	study of the ear
otorhinolaryngologist (ENT) . . . . (ō-tō-*rī*-nō-*lar*-in-GOL-ō-jist)	physician who studies and treats diseases and disorders of the ear, nose, and throat, also called *otolaryngologist*

Practice saying each of these terms aloud. To assist you in pronunciation, obtain the audiotape designed for use with this text. Exercises 16, 17, and 18 will help you learn the definitions and spellings of the complementary terms related to the ear.

Exercise 16 ....

Analyze and define the following complementary terms.

1. otology _____

2. audiologist _____

3. otorhinolaryngologist _____

4. audiology _____

5. otologist _____

6. aural _____

Exercise 17 ....

Build the complementary terms for the following definitions by using the word parts you have learned.

1. study of hearing

_____ / _____
                        WR   S

2. physician who studies and treats diseases and disorders of the ear, nose, and throat

_____ / ____ / _____ / ____ / _____ / _____
 WR   CV   WR   CV   WR   S

3. study of the ear

_____ / _____
                        WR   S

4. one who is skilled in audiology

_____ / _____
                        WR   S

5. physician who studies and treats diseases of the ear

_____ / _____
                        WR   S

6. pertaining to the ear

_____ / _____
                        WR   S

Exercise 18 ....

Spell each of the complementary terms. Have someone dictate the terms on p. 408 to you, or say the words into a tape recorder; then spell the words from your recording. Think about the word parts before attempting to write the word. Study any words you have spelled incorrectly.

1. _____   4. _____

2. _____   5. _____

3. _____   6. _____

Abbreviations

AD	right ear (auris dexter)
AS	left ear (auris sinister)
AU	both ears (aures unitas)
ENT	ear, nose, throat
EENT	eye, ear, nose, and throat
OM	otitis media
Oto	otology

CHAPTER REVIEW

Exercises

Exercise 19

Complete the hospital report by writing the medical terms in the blanks. Use the list of definitions with the corresponding numbers.

> **Case History**: This 62-year-old American Indian man, appearing younger than his age, was brought into the ENT clinic by his daughter who states that he is unable to hear what is being said to him by family members. She states that this problem has existed for at least 30 years but that it appears to be getting markedly worse. Patient states that he had several episodes of ear infection as a child and young adult. He denies any change in hearing. 1. _____ reveals there is scarring of tympanic membranes bilaterally. Both auditory canals are normal. He will be referred for 2. _____ .

> **Results of Audiometry**: Auditory acuity at 500 Hz, 1000 Hz, 2000 Hz, and 4000 Hz c/s in both right and left ears is markedly diminished. The patient is hearing at only 40 and 60 dB at both 1000 and 500 c/s. He did not hear anything at 4000 or 2000 c/s.
>
> Impression: Severe loss of hearing bilaterally, probably secondary to 3. _____ _____ as a child. Some loss may be attributable to 4. _____ .

1. visual examination of the ear
2. measurement of hearing
3. inflammation of the middle ear
4. hearing impairment in old age

Exercise 20

To test your understanding of the terms introduced in this chapter, circle the words that correctly complete the sentences. The italicized phrase is the definition of the term.

1. *Inflammation of the eardrum* is (labyrinthitis, mastoiditis, myringitis).
2. The patient complained of *ringing in the ears,* or (tinnitus, vertigo, tympanitis).
3. The patient seeking a *specialist for his labyrinthitis* consulted an (optometrist, audiologist, otologist).
4. The physician planned to release the pus from the middle ear by making an *incision in the tympanic membrane,* or performing a (mastoidotomy, myringotomy, labyrinthectomy).

Exercise 21

Unscramble the following mixed-up terms. The word on the left indicates a word part in each of the following.

1. instrument
   / / / / s / / / / /
   c o o s t e p o

2. pain
   / / t / / / / / /
   g i o l a a t

3. fungus
   / / / o / / / / / / / /
   y o c o o t m i s s

4. pus
   / / / / p / / / / / / e / /
   r y e t o p a o r o h

Exercise 22

The following terms did not appear in this chapter but are composed of word parts that have appeared in this chapter or previous chapters. Find their definitions by translating the word parts literally.

1. **aglycemia** _____
   (*ā*-glī-SĒ-mē-a)

2. **cardionephric** _____
   (*kar*-dē-ō-NEF-rik)

3. **cholecystogastric** _____
   (*kō*-lē-*sis*-tō-GAS-trik)

4. **chromogenic** _____
   (*krō*-mō-JEN-ic)

5. **cystoplegia** _____
   (*sis*-tō-PLĒ-jē-a)

6. **dacryosinusitis** _____
   (*dak*-rē-ō-sī-nus-Ī-tis)

7. **gastroenterocolitis** _____
   (*gas*-trō-*en*-ter-ō-kō-LĪ-tis)

8. **hemocytolysis** _____
   (hē-mō-sī-TOL-i-sis)

9. **hysteroptosis** _____
   (*his*-ter-op-TŌ-sis)

10. **osteofibroma** _____
    (*os*-tē-ō-fī-BRŌ-ma)

11. **parasalpingeal** _____
    (*par*-a-sal-PIN-jē-al)

12. **pericephalic** _____
    (par-i-se-FAL-ik)

Combining Forms Crossword Puzzle

Across Clues

1. hearing
4. cornea
6. light
9. abbreviation for Medical Corps
12. labyrinth
14. by mouth (medical abbreviation)
15. abbreviation for aortic regurgitation
17. abbreviation for number
18. conjunctiva
20. mastoid
22. tear duct
24. cornea
25. retina
27. double
28. vision

Down Clues

2. ear
3. cold
5. eardrum, middle ear
7. tension
8. eyelid
10. pupil
11. eardrum
13. eye
16. sclera
19. stapes
21. tear
23. hearing
25. respiratory therapist (abbreviation)
26. abbreviation for ethylene oxide

Review of Terms

Can you build, analyze, define, pronounce, and spell the following terms *built from word parts?*

Diseases and Disorders	Surgical	Procedural	Complementary
labyrinthitis	labyrinthectomy	acoumeter	audiologist
mastoiditis	mastoidectomy	audiogram	audiology
myringitis	mastoidotomy	audiometer	aural
otalgia	myringoplasty	audiometry	otologist
otomastoiditis	myringotomy	otoscope	otology (Oto)
otomycosis	tympanoplasty	otoscopy	otorhinolaryngologist (ENT)
otopyorrhea		tympanometer	
otosclerosis		tympanometry	
tympanitis			

Can you define, pronounce, and spell the following terms *not built from word parts?*

Diseases and Disorders

acoustic neuroma

ceruminoma

Ménière's disease

otitis externa

otitis media (OM)

presbycusis

tinnitus

vertigo

Musculoskeletal System

Upon completion of this chapter you will be able to:
1. Identify the anatomy of the musculoskeletal system.
2. Define and spell the word parts presented in this chapter.
3. Build and analyze medical terms using word parts.
4. Define, pronounce, and spell the disease and disorder, procedural, surgical, and complementary terms for the musculoskeletal system.

ANATOMY

The musculoskeletal system is made up of bones, muscles, and joints. The body contains 206 bones, which are the framework of the body, and more than 500 muscles, which are responsible for movement. Joints are any place in the body at which two or more bones meet.

Bone Structure

periosteum	outermost layer of the bone, made up of fibrous tissue (Figures 14-1)
compact bone	dense, hard layers of bone tissue that lie underneath the periosteum
cancellous (spongy) bone	contains little spaces like a sponge and is encased in the layers of compact bone
endosteum	membranous lining of the hollow cavity of the bone
diaphysis	shaft of the long bones (Figure 14-1)
epiphysis	ends of the long bones
bone marrow	material found in the cavities of bones
red marrow	thick, blood-like material found in flat bones and the ends of long bones. Location of blood cell formation
yellow marrow	soft, fatty material found in the medullary cavity of long bones

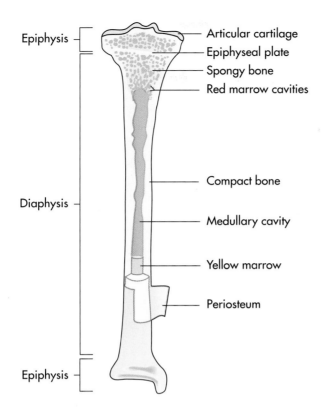

Fig. 14-1
Bone Structure.

Epiphysis — Articular cartilage
Epiphyseal plate
Spongy bone
Red marrow cavities

Compact bone

Diaphysis — Medullary cavity

Yellow marrow

Periosteum

Epiphysis

Periosteum

is composed of the prefix **peri,** meaning **surrounding,** and the word root **oste,** meaning **bone.**

Endosteum

is composed of the prefix **endo,** meaning **within,** and the word root **oste,** meaning **bone.**

Diaphysis

comes from the Greek **diaphusis,** meaning **state of growing between.**

Epiphysis

has been used in the English language since the 1600s and retains the meaning given to it by a Greco-Roman physician. It means a portion of bone attached for a time to another bone by a cartilage, but which later combines with the principal bone. During the period of growth, the epiphysis is separated from the main portion of the bone by cartilage.

Skeletal Bones

maxilla . . . . upper jawbones (Figure 14-2, *A*)

mandible . . . . lower jawbone

vertebral column . . . . made up of bones called *vertebrae (pl.)* or *vertebra (sing.)* (Figure 14-2, *A*)

   cervical vertebrae (C1 to C7) . . first set of seven bones, forming the neck

   thoracic vertebrae (T1 to T12) second set of 12 vertebrae; they articulate with the 12 pairs of ribs to form the outward curve of the spine

   lumbar vertebrae (L1 to L5) . . . third set of five larger vertebrae, which forms the inward curve of the spine

   sacrum . . . . next four vertebrae, which fuse together in the young child

   coccyx . . . . five vertebrae fused together to form the tailbone (Figures 14-2, *B* and 14-3)

   lamina (*pl.* laminae) . . . . part of the vertebral arch

clavicle . . . . collarbone (Figure 14-2, *A*)

scapula . . . . shoulder blade

   acromion . . . . extension of the scapula, which forms the high point of the shoulder

sternum . . . . breastbone (Figure 14-2, *A*)

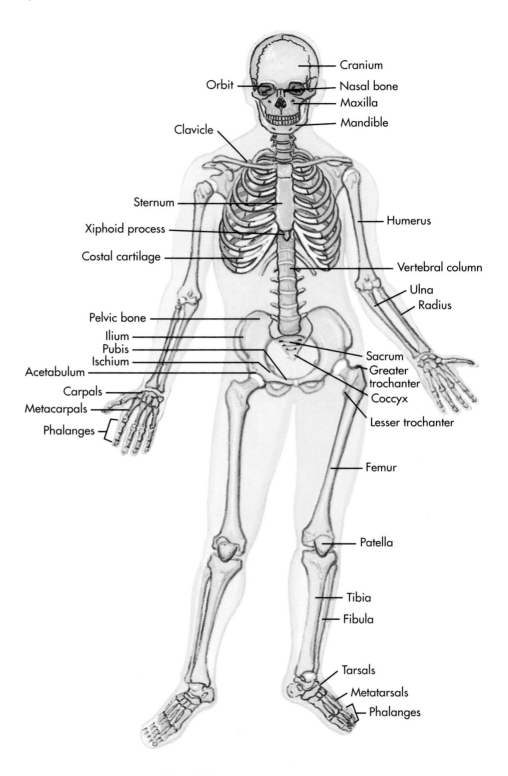

Fig. 14-2
A, Anterior view of the skeleton.

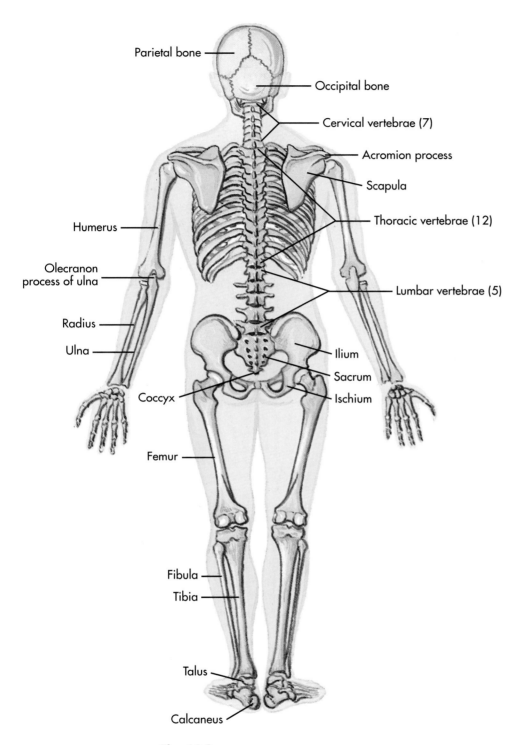

Fig. 14-2
B, Posterior view of the skeleton.

Parietal bone

Occipital bone

Cervical vertebrae (7)

Acromion process

Scapula

Thoracic vertebrae (12)

Humerus

Olecranon
process of ulna

Lumbar vertebrae (5)

Radius

Ulna

Ilium

Coccyx

Sacrum

Ischium

Femur

Fibula

Tibia

Talus

Calcaneus

xiphoid process	lower portion of the sternum
humerus	upper arm bone (Figure 14-2, *A* and *B*)
ulna and radius	lower arm bones (Figure 14-2, *A* and *B*)
carpal bones	wrist bones (Figure 14-2, *A*)
metacarpal bones	hand bones (Figure 14-2, *A*)
phalanges (*sing.* **phalanx**)	finger and toe bones (Figure 14-2, *A*)
pelvic bone, hip bone	made up of three bones fused together (Figure 14-2, *A*)
ischium	lower, rear portion on which one sits
ilium	upper, wing-shaped part on each side
pubis	anterior portion of the pelvic bone
acetabulum	large socket in the pelvic bone for the head of the femur
femur	upper leg bone (Figure 14-2, *A* and *B*)
tibia and fibula	lower leg bones (Figure 14-2, *A* and *B*)
patella	kneecap (Figure 14-2, *A*)
tarsal bones	ankle bones (Figure 14-2, *A*)
calcaneus	heel bone
metatarsal bones	foot bones (Figure 14-2, *A*)

Joints

Joints, also called *articulations,* hold our bones together and make movement possible (Figure 14-4).

articular cartilage	smooth layer of gristle covering the contacting surface of joints
meniscus	crescent-shaped cartilage found in the knee
intervertebral disk	cartilaginous disk found between each vertebra in the spine

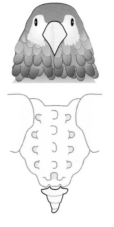

Metacarpus

literally means **beyond the wrist**. It is composed of the prefix **meta-**, meaning **beyond**, and **carpus**, meaning **wrist**.

Fig. 14-3

Coccyx is derived from the Greek word for *cuckoo* because of its resemblance to a cuckoo's beak.

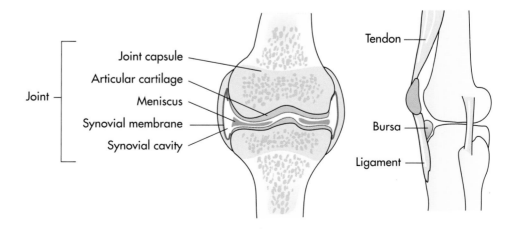

Fig. 14-4
Joint.

symphysis pubis	cartilaginous joint at which two pubic bones fuse together
synovia	fluid secreted by the synovial membrane and found in joint cavities
bursa (*pl.* bursae)	small, fluid-filled sac that allows for easy movement of one part of a joint over another
ligament	flexible, tough band of fibrous connective tissue that attaches one bone to another at a joint
tendon	band of fibrous connective tissue that attaches muscle to bone
aponeurosis	strong sheet of tissue that acts as a tendon to attach muscles to bone

Muscles

skeletal muscles (also known as *striated*)	attached to bones by tendons and make body movement possible. Skeletal muscles produce action by pulling and by working in pairs. Also known as *voluntary muscles* because we have control over these muscles (Figure 14-5, *A* and *B*).
smooth muscles (also known as *unstriated*)	located in internal organs such as the walls of blood vessels and the digestive tract. They are also called *involuntary muscles* because they respond to impulses from the autonomic nerves and are not controlled voluntarily.
cardiac muscle	forms most of the wall of the heart. Its involuntary contraction produces the heartbeat.

Learn the anatomical terms by completing exercises 1, 2, and 3.

Exercise 1

Match the definitions in the first column with the correct terms in the second column.

_____ 1. shaft of a long bone   a. skeletal muscle

_____ 2. hard layer of bone tissue   b. cancellous bone

_____ 3. outermost layer of bone   c. smooth muscle

_____ 4. found in bone cavities   d. diaphysis

_____ 5. lining of the bone cavity   e. endometrium

_____ 6. end of each long bone   f. cardiac muscle

_____ 7. contains little spaces   g. epiphysis

_____ 8. produces heartbeats   h. periosteum

_____ 9. voluntary muscles   i. compact bone

_____ 10. located in internal organs   j. endosteum

   k. bone marrow

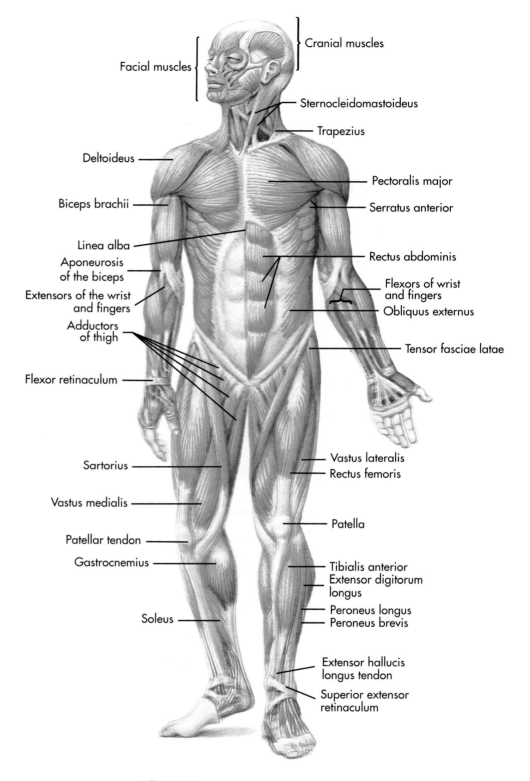

Cranial muscles

Facial muscles

Sternocleidomastoideus

Trapezius

Deltoideus

Pectoralis major

Biceps brachii

Serratus anterior

Linea alba

Rectus abdominis

Aponeurosis
of the biceps

Flexors of wrist
and fingers

Extensors of the wrist
and fingers

Obliquus externus

Adductors
of thigh

Tensor fasciae latae

Flexor retinaculum

Vastus lateralis

Sartorius

Rectus femoris

Vastus medialis

Patella

Patellar tendon

Tibialis anterior

Gastrocnemius

Extensor digitorum
longus

Peroneus longus

Peroneus brevis

Soleus

Extensor hallucis
longus tendon

Superior extensor
retinaculum

Fig. 14-5

A, Anterior view of the muscular system.

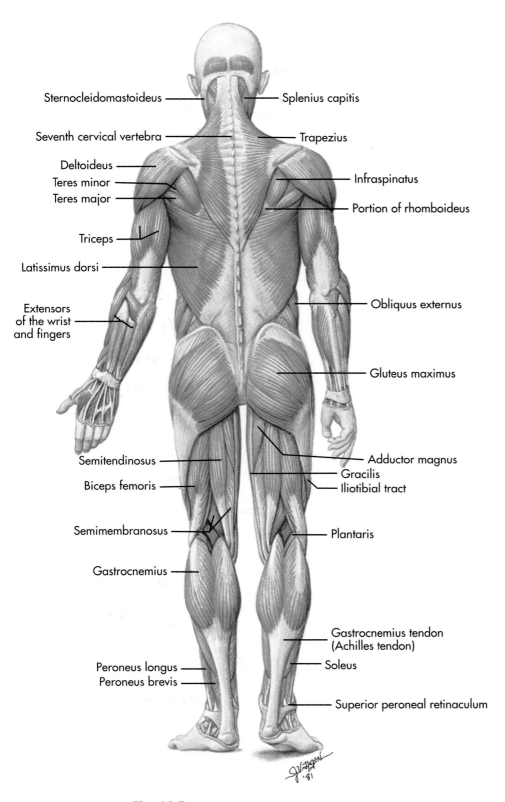

Sternocleidomastoideus

Seventh cervical vertebra

Deltoideus

Teres minor

Teres major

Triceps

Latissimus dorsi

Extensors
of the wrist
and fingers

Semitendinosus

Biceps femoris

Semimembranosus

Gastrocnemius

Peroneus longus
Peroneus brevis

Splenius capitis

Trapezius

Infraspinatus

Portion of rhomboideus

Obliquus externus

Gluteus maximus

Adductor magnus
Gracilis
Iliotibial tract

Plantaris

Gastrocnemius tendon
(Achilles tendon)
Soleus

Superior peroneal retinaculum

Fig. 14-5
B, Posterior view of the muscular system.

Exercise 2 ....

Write the name of the bone to match the definition.

1. shoulder blade   _scapula_

2. breastbone   _sternum_

3. lower jawbone   _mandible_

4. collarbone   _clavicle_

5. upper arm bone   _humerus_

6. lower arm bones   a. _radius_

                         b. _ulna_

7. ankle bones   _tarsals_

8. finger, toe bones   _phalanges_

9. foot bones   _metatarsals_

10. hand bones   _metacarpals_

11. upper leg bone   _femur_

12. lower leg bones   a. _fibula_

                         b. _tibia_

13. kneecap   _patella_

14. neck   _cervical   vertebrae_

15. third set of vertebrae _lumbar   vertebrae_

16. anterior portion of the pelvic bone   _pubis_

17. four vertebrae fused together   _sacrum_

18. lower rear portion of the pelvic bone   _ischium_

19. tailbone   _coccyx_

20. upper, wing-shaped part of the pelvic bone   _ilium_

21. wrist bones   _carpals_

Exercise 3

Match the definitions in the first column with the correct terms in the second column.

_____ 1. attaches muscle to bone

_____ 2. fluid-filled sac

_____ 3. smooth layer of gristle

_____ 4. socket in the pelvic bone

_____ 5. fluid

_____ 6. heel bone

_____ 7. attaches bone to bone

_____ 8. cartilage found in the knee

_____ 9. pubic bone joint

_____ 10. acts as a tendon

_____ 11. found between each vertebra

_____ 12. part of the arch of the vertebra

a. acetabulum

b. aponeurosis

c. bursa

d. calcaneus

e. cartilage

f. intervertebral disk

g. lamina

h. ligament

i. meniscus

j. periosteum

k. symphysis pubis

l. synovia

m. tendon

Actions of Muscles

Term	Definition
adduction (ad-DUK-shun)	movement of drawing toward the middle (Figure 14-6)
abduction (ab-DUK-shun)	movement of drawing away from the middle

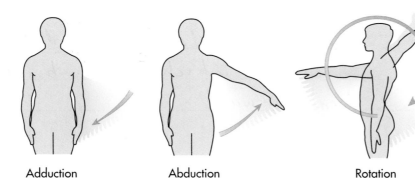

Adduction   Abduction   Rotation

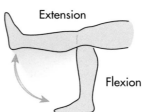

Supination

Pronation   Eversion   Inversion

Extension

Flexion

Fig. 14-6
Actions of muscles.

eversion . . . . (ē-VER-zhun)	turning outward
inversion . . . . (in-VER-zhun)	turning inward
extension . . . . (ek-STEN-shun)	movement in which a limb is placed in a straight position *increase L*
flexion . . . . (FLEK-shun)	movement in which a limb is bent *decrease L*
pronation . . . . (prō-NĀ-shun)	movement that turns the palm down
supination . . . . (sū-pi-NĀ-shun)	movement that turns the palm up
rotation . . . . (rō-tā-shun)	turning around its own axis

elbow AP = 180°

Learn the terms that describe the actions of muscles by completing exercises 4 and 5.

Exercise 4

Write the definitions of the following terms.

1. abduction ___ *movement of drawing away from the midline* ___

2. pronation ___ *movement that turns the palm down* ___

3. supination ___ *movement that turns the palm up* ___

4. rotation ___ *turning around its own axis* ___

5. extension ___ *movement in which a limb is placed in a straight position* ___

6. eversion ___ *turning outward* ___

7. adduction ___ *movement of drawing toward the midline* ___

NO, 8. flexion ___ *movement in which a limb is bent* ___

9. inversion ___ *turning inward* ___

Exercise 5

Match the terms in the first column with the correct definitions in the second column.

_____ 1. abduction

_____ 2. adduction

_____ 3. pronation

_____ 4. rotation

_____ 5. eversion

_____ 6. extension

_____ 7. flexion

_____ 8. inversion

_____ 9. supination

a. movement in which the limb is placed in a straight position

b. movement that turns the palm up

c. turning outward

d. drawing toward the middle

e. conveying toward the center

f. turning inward

g. movement in which the limb is bent

h. drawing away from the middle

i. movement that turns the palm down

j. turning around its own axis

WORD PARTS

Combining Forms of the Musculoskeletal System

At first glance the number of word parts introduced in this chapter may seem overwhelming to you, but notice that many of them are names for bones already learned in the anatomical section. The definitions of the word parts include both anatomical terms and commonly used words. For example, both *carpal* and *wrist bone* are given as the definition of the word root *carp/o*. Learn the anatomical locations and definitions of the combining forms of the musculoskeletal system by completing Exercise Figures A and B.

Combining Form	Definition
carp/o	carpals (wrist bones)
clavic/o, clavicul/o	clavicle (collarbone)
cost/o	rib
crani/o	cranium (skull)
femor/o	femur (upper leg bone)
fibul/o	fibula (lower leg bone)
humer/o	humerus (upper arm bone)
ili/o	ilium
ischi/o	ischium
lumb/o	loin, lumbar region of the spine
mandibul/o	mandible (lower jawbone)
maxill/o	maxilla (upper jawbone)

> **Disk**
>
> is from the Greek **diskos,** meaning flat plate. A variant spelling, **disc,** is also used, though chiefly in ophthalmology.

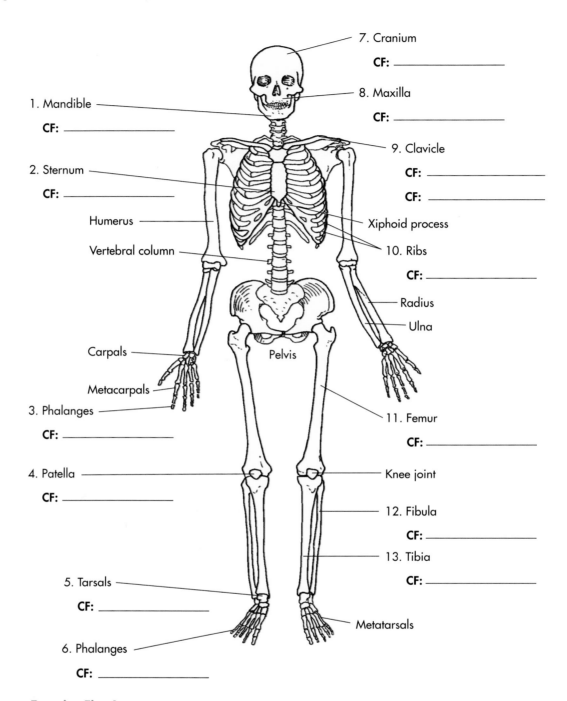

7. Cranium
CF: _____

1. Mandible
CF: _____

8. Maxilla
CF: _____

2. Sternum
CF: _____

9. Clavicle
CF: _____
CF: _____

Humerus

Vertebral column

Xiphoid process

10. Ribs
CF: _____

Radius

Ulna

Carpals

Pelvis

Metacarpals

3. Phalanges
CF: _____

11. Femur
CF: _____

4. Patella
CF: _____

Knee joint

12. Fibula
CF: _____

13. Tibia
CF: _____

5. Tarsals
CF: _____

Metatarsals

6. Phalanges
CF: _____

Exercise Fig. A
Fill in the blanks with combining forms in this diagram of the skeleton, anterior view.

patell/o	patella (kneecap)
phalang/o	phalanges (finger or toe bones)
pub/o	pubis
rachi/o	spine, vertebral column
radi/o	radius (lower arm bone)
sacr/o	sacrum

scapul/o . . . .   scapula (shoulder blade)

stern/o . . . .   sternum (breastbone)

tars/o . . . .   tarsals (ankle bones)

tibi/o . . . .   tibia (lower leg bone)

uln/o . . . .   ulna (lower arm bone)

vertebr/o, spondyl/o . . . .   vertebra

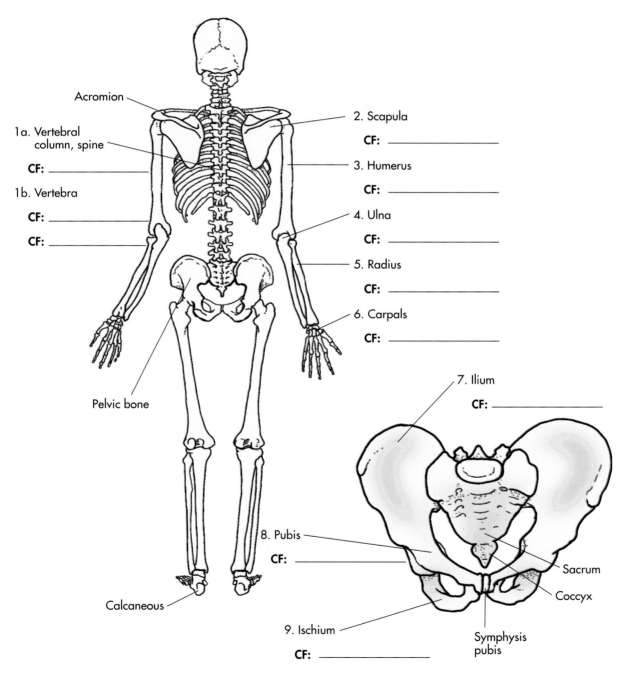

Exercise Fig. B

Fill in the blanks with combining forms in this diagram of the skeleton, posterior view, and the pelvis.

Learn the anatomical locations and definitions of the combining forms by completing exercises 6, 7, 8, and 9, and Exercise Figure C.

Exercise 6 ....

Write the definitions of the following combining forms.

1. clavic/o _____

2. cost/o _____

3. crani/o _____

4. femor/o _____

5. clavicul/o _____

6. humer/o _____

7. ili/o _____

8. ischi/o _____

9. carp/o _____

10. fibul/o _____

11. mandibul/o _____

12. lumb/o _____

Exercise 7 ....

Write the combining form for each of the following terms.

1. clavicle   a. _____

                     b. _____

2. rib   _____

3. cranium   _____

4. femur   _____

5. humerus   _____

6. carpals   _____

7. ischium   _____

8. fibula _____

9. ilium _____

10. mandible _____

11. loin, lumbar region _____

Exercise 8 ....

Write the definitions of the following combining forms.

1. rachi/o _____

2. patell/o _____

3. spondyl/o _____

4. maxill/o _____

5. phalang/o _____

6. uln/o _____

7. radi/o _____

8. tibi/o _____

9. pub/o _____

10. tars/o _____

11. scapul/o _____

12. stern/o _____

13. vertebr/o _____

14. sacr/o _____

Exercise 9 ....

Write the combining form for each of the following terms.

1. maxilla _____

2. ulna _____

3. radius _____

4. tibia _____

5. pubis   _____

6. tarsals   _____

7. vertebra   a.   _____

                               b.   _____

8. sternum   _____

9. scapula   _____

10. patella   _____

11. phalanges   _____

12. sacrum   _____

13. vertebral column, spine   _____

Combining Forms for Joints

Combining Form	Definitions
aponeur/o	aponeurosis
arthr/o	joint
burs/o	bursa (cavity)
chondr/o	cartilage
disk/o	intervertebral disk
menisc/o	meniscus (crescent)
synovi/o	synovia, synovial membrane
ten/o, tend/o, tendin/o	tendon

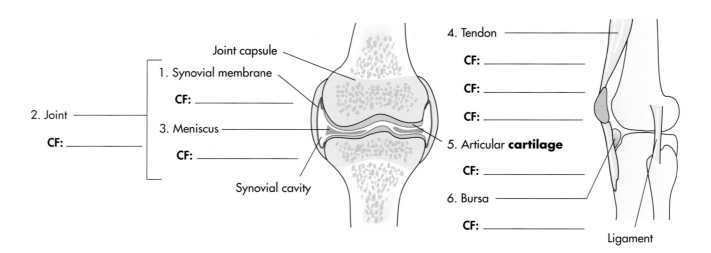

Exercise Fig. C
Fill in the blanks to label this diagram of the joint.

Learn the anatomical locations and definitions of the combining forms by completing exercises 10 and 11.

Exercise 10

Write the definitions of the following combining forms.

1. arthr/o _____

2. aponeur/o _____

3. menisc/o _____

4. tendin/o _____

5. chondr/o _____

6. ten/o _____

7. burs/o _____

8. tend/o _____

9. synovi/o _____

10. disk/o _____

Exercise 11

Write the combining form for each of the following terms.

1. meniscus   _____

2. aponeurosis   _____

3. joint   _____

4. cartilage   _____

5. tendon   a. _____

                               b. _____

                               c. _____

6. bursa   _____

7. synovia, synovial membrane   _____

8. intervertebral disk   _____

Combining Forms Commonly Used With Musculoskeletal System Terms

Combining Form	Definition
ankyl/o	crooked, stiff, bent *fixed*
kinesi/o	movement, motion
kyph/o	hump
lamin/o	lamina (thin, flat plate or layer)
lord/o	bent forward *at lumbar region*
myel/o, myelon/o	bone marrow
my/o, myos/o . . . . (NOTE: *my/o* was introduced in Chapter 2.)	muscle
oste/o	bone
petr/o . . . . (NOTE: *lith/o,* also a combining form for *stone,* was introduced in Chapter 6.)	stone
scoli/o	crooked, curved

Learn the anatomical locations and definitions of the combining forms by completing exercises 12 and 13.

Exercise 12

Write the definitions of the following combining forms.

1. my/o _____

2. petr/o _____

3. kinesi/o _____

4. oste/o _____

5. lamin/o _____

6. myel/o _____

7. kyph/o _____

8. ankyl/o _____

9. scoli/o _____

10. myelon/o _____

11. myos/o _____

12. lord/o _____

Exercise 13

Write the combining form for each of the following.

1. muscle
   a. _____
   b. _____

2. stone _____

3. movement, motion _____

4. bone _____

5. lamina _____

6. bone marrow
   a. _____
   b. _____

7. hump _____

8. crooked, stiff, bent _____

9. crooked, curved _____

10. bent forward _____

Prefixes

Prefix	Definition
inter-	between
supra-	above
syn-, sym-	together, joined

Learn the prefixes by completing exercises 14 and 15.

Exercise 14

Write the definition of the following prefixes.

1. supra- _____

2. syn-, sym- _____

3. inter- _____

Exercise 15

Write the prefix for each of the following definitions.

1. together, joined _____

2. between _____

3. above _____

Suffixes

Suffix	Definition
-asthenia	weakness
-clasis, -clast, -clasia	break
-desis	surgical fixation, fusion
-physis	growth
-schisis	split, fissure

Learn the suffixes by completing exercises 16 and 17.

Exercise 16

Write the definitions of the following suffixes.

1. -physis _____

2. -clasis _____

3. -desis _____

4. -clast _____

5. -schisis _____

6. -clasia _____

7. -asthenia _____

Exercise 17

Write the suffix for each of the following definitions.

1. growth   _____

2. weakness   _____

3. break   a. _____

                                 b. _____

                                 c. _____

4. surgical fixation, fusion   _____

5. split, fissure   _____

MEDICAL TERMS

The terms you need to learn to complete this chapter are listed below. The exercises following each list will help you learn the definition and spelling of each word.

Disease and Disorder Terms

Built From Word Parts

Term	Definition
ankylosis .... (an-kil-Ō-sis)	abnormal condition of stiffness (often referring to a joint, such as the result of chronic rheumatoid arthritis)
arthritis .... (ar-THRĪ-tis)	inflammation of a joint (the two most common forms of arthritis are rheumatoid arthritis and osteoarthritis)
arthrochondritis .... (*ar*-thrō-kon-DRĪ-tis)	inflammation of joint cartilages
bursitis .... (ber-SĪ-tis)	inflammation of a bursa
bursolith .... (BER-sō-lith)	stone in a bursa
carpoptosis .... (*kar*-pō-TŌ-sis)	drooping wrist (wristdrop)
chondromalacia .... (kon-drō-ma-LĀ-shē-a)	softening of cartilage
cranioschisis .... (*krā*-nē-OS-ki-sis)	(congenital) fissure of the skull
diskitis .... (dis-KĪ-tis)	inflammation of an intervertebral disk
kyphosis .... (kī-FŌ-sis)	abnormal hump (of the thoracic spine); also called *hunchback* *or humpback*
lordosis .... (lōr-DŌ-sis)	abnormal condition of bending forward (forward curvature of the lumbar spine) *swayback*
maxillitis .... (*mak*-si-LĪ-tis)	inflammation of the maxilla
meniscitis .... (*men*-i-SĪ-tis)	inflammation of a meniscus
myasthenia .... (*mī*-as-THĒ-nē-a)	muscle weakness
myeloma .... (*mī*-e-LŌ-ma)	(malignant) tumor in the bone marrow
osteitis .... (*os*-tē-Ī-tis)	inflammation of the bone

osteoarthritis (OA) . . . .   inflammation of the bone and joint (Exercise
(*os*-tē-ō-ar-THRĪ-tis)   Figure D)

osteocarcinoma . . . .   cancerous tumor of the bone
(*os*-tē-ō-*kar*-si-NŌ-ma)

osteochondritis . . . .   inflammation of the bone and cartilage
(*os*-tē-ō-kon-DRĪ-tis)

osteofibroma . . . .   tumor of the bone and fibrous tissue
(*os*-tē-ō-fī-BRŌ-ma)

osteomalacia . . . .   softening of bones
(*os*-tē-ō-ma-LĀ-shē-a)

osteomyelitis . . . .   inflammation of the bone and bone marrow
(*os*-tē-ō-*mī*-e-LĪ-tis)

osteopetrosis . . . .   abnormal condition of stonelike bones (mar-
(*os*-tē-ō-pe-TRŌ-sis)   blelike bones caused by increased formation of
bone)

osteosarcoma . . . .   malignant tumor of the bone
(os-tē-ō-sar-KŌ-ma)

polymyositis . . . .   inflammation of many muscles
(*pol*-ē-mī-ō-SĪ-tis)

rachischisis . . . .   (congenital) fissure of the vertebral column
(ra-KIS-kis-is)   (also called *spina bifida*) (Exercise Figure C in
Chapter 15, p. 480)

scoliosis . . . .   abnormal (lateral) curve (of the spine) (Exer-
(*skō*-lē-Ō-sis)   cise Figure E)

spondylarthritis . . . .   inflammation of the vertebral joints
(*spon*-dil-ar-THRĪ-tis)

synoviosarcoma . . . .   a malignant tumor of the synovial membrane
(si-nō-vē-ō-sar-KŌ-ma)

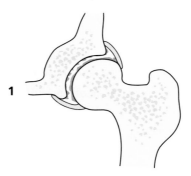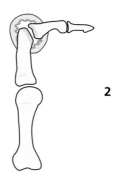

Exercise Fig. D
Fill in the blanks to label the diagram.

1, Example of BONE / CV / JOINT / INFLAMMATION, a degenerative disease of the joints, with deterioration of articular cartilage. Osteoarthritis is generally a disease of later life and affects the spine and weight-bearing joints, especially the hips. **2,** Example of rheumatoid arthritis, a chronic systemic disease, which may lead to ankylosis and deformity. Small joints of the hands and feet are commonly affected. Most often it affects people between 36 and 50 years of age and is more commonly found in women.

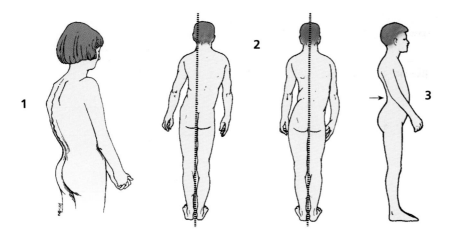

Exercise Fig. E

Fill in the blanks to label the diagram. **1,** HUMP / ABNORMAL.

2, CURVE (OF THE SPINE) / ABNORMAL. **3,** BENDING FORWARD / ABNORMAL CONDITION.

tendinitis . . . .   inflammation of a tendon
   (*ten*-di-NĪ-tis)

tenodynia . . . .   pain in a tendon
   (*ten*-ō-DIN-ē-a)

tenosynovitis . . . .   inflammation of the tendon and synovial
   (ten-ō-sin-ō-VĪ-tis)   membrane
   (NOTE: the *i* in *synovi* is
   dropped because the suffix begins with an *i*.)

Practice saying each of these terms aloud. To assist you in pronunciation, obtain the audiotape designed for use with this text. Learn the definitions and spellings of the disease and disorder terms by completing exercises 18, 19, and 20.

Exercise 18 ....

Analyze and define the following disease and disorder terms.

1. osteitis _____

2. osteomyelitis _____

3. osteopetrosis _____

4. osteomalacia _____

5. osteocarcinoma _____

6. osteochondritis _____

7. osteofibroma _____

8. arthritis _____

9. arthrochondritis _____

10. myeloma _____

11. tendinitis _____

12. tenodynia _____

13. carpoptosis _____

14. bursitis _____

15. spondylarthritis _____

16. ankylosis _____

17. kyphosis _____

18. scoliosis _____

19. cranioschisis _____

20. maxillitis _____

21. meniscitis _____

22. rachischisis _____

23. bursolith _____

24. myasthenia _____

25. osteosarcoma _____

26. chondromalacia _____

27. synoviosarcoma _____

28. tenosynovitis _____

29. polymyositis _____

30. diskitis _____

31. lordosis _____

32. osteoarthritis _____

Exercise 19

Build disease and disorder terms for the following definitions using the word parts you have learned.

1. cancerous tumor of the bone

   _____ / ___ / _____ / ___
   WR   CV   WR   S

2. inflammation of the bone and cartilage

   _____ / ___ / _____ / ___
   WR   CV   WR   S

3. tumor of the bone and fibrous tissue

_____
WR / CV / WR / S

4. inflammation of a joint

_____
WR / S

5. inflammation of joint cartilage

_____
WR / CV / WR / S

6. tumor of the bone marrow

_____
WR / S

7. inflammation of a tendon

_____
WR / S

8. pain in a tendon

_____
WR / S

9. drooping wrist (wristdrop)

_____
WR / CV / S

10. inflammation of the bursa

_____
WR / S

11. inflammation of the vertebral joints

_____
WR / WR / S

12. abnormal condition of stiffness

_____
WR / S

13. abnormal hump (of the thoracic spine)

_____
WR / S

14. abnormal (lateral) curve of the spine

_____
WR / S

15. fissure of the skull

_____
WR / CV / S

16. inflammation of the maxilla

_____
WR / S

17. inflammation of the meniscus

_____
WR / S

18. fissure of the vertebral column

_____
WR / S

19. stone in the bursa

_____
WR / CV / S

20. muscle weakness

_____
WR / S

21. inflammation of the bone

_____
WR / S

22. inflammation of the bone and
    bone marrow

    _____
         WR / CV / WR / S

23. abnormal condition of stone-
    like bones (marblelike bones)

    _____
         WR / CV / WR / S

24. softening of bones

    _____
         WR / CV / S

25. inflammation of the tendon
    and synovial membrane

    _____
         WR / CV / WR / S

26. malignant tumor of the sy-
    novial membrane

    _____
         WR / CV / S

27. malignant tumor of the bone

    _____
         WR / CV / S

28. softening of cartilage

    _____
         WR / CV / S

29. inflammation of an interverte-
    bral disk

    _____
         WR / S

30. inflammation of many
    muscles

    _____
         P / WR / S

31. abnormal condition of
    bending forward

    _____
         WR / S

32. inflammation of the bone and
    joint

    _____
         WR / CV / WR / S

Exercise 20

Spell each of the disease and disorder terms. Have someone dictate the terms on pp.
435-437 to you, or say the words into a tape recorder; then spell the words from your
recording. Think about the word parts before attempting to write the word. Study any
words you have spelled incorrectly.

1. _____   5. _____

2. _____   6. _____

3. _____   7. _____

4. _____   8. _____

9. _____   21. _____

10. _____   22. _____

11. _____   23. _____

12. _____   24. _____

13. _____   25. _____

14. _____   26. _____

15. _____   27. _____

16. _____   28. _____

17. _____   29. _____

18. _____   30. _____

19. _____   31. _____

20. _____   32. _____

Disease and Disorder Terms
Not Built From Word Parts

Term	Definition
ankylosing spondylitis . . . . (an-kil-Ō-sing) (*spon*-di-LĪ-tis)	form of arthritis that first affects the spine and adjacent structures, and which, as it progresses, causes a forward bend of the spine. Also called *Strümpell-Marie arthritis* or *disease,* and *rheumatoid spondylitis.*
bunion . . . . (BUN-yun)	abnormal enlargement of the joint at the base of the great toe, commonly caused by poorly fitted shoes (Figure 14-7)

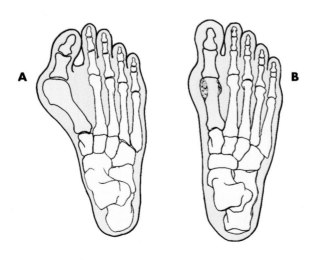

Fig. 14-7
A, Bunion. **B,** Bunionectomy.

carpal tunnel syndrome (CTS) . . . a common, painful disorder of the wrist caused by compression of a nerve

Colles' fracture . . . . a type of wrist fracture (the fracture is at the
(KOL-ēz)   lower end of the radius, the distal fragment being displaced backward) (Figure 14-8)

exostosis . . . . abnormal benign growth on the surface of a
(*ex*-sos-TŌ-sis)   bone (also called *spur*)

fracture (fx) . . . . broken bone (Figure 14-9)
(FRAK-chūr)

gout . . . . disease in which an excessive amount of uric
(gowt)   acid in the blood causes sodium urate crystals (*tophi*) to be deposited in the joints, especially that of the great toe (Figure 14-10)

herniated disk . . . . rupture of the intervertebral disk cartilage,
(HER-nē-āt-ed)   which allows the contents to protrude through it, putting pressure on the spinal nerve roots (also called *slipped disk, ruptured disk,* or *herniated nucleus pulposus* [HNP]) (Figure 14-11)

muscular dystrophy (MD) . . . . . . group of hereditary diseases characterized by
(DIS-trō-fē)   degeneration of muscle and weakness

myasthenia gravis (MG) . . . . chronic disease characterized by muscle weak-
(*mī*-as-THĒ-nē-a) (GRA-vis)   ness and thought to be caused by a defect in the transmission of impulses from nerve to muscle cell. The face, larynx, and throat are frequently affected; there is no true paralysis of the muscles.

osteoporosis . . . . abnormal loss of bone density occurring fre-
(*os*-tē-ō-po-RŌ-sis)   quently in postmenopausal women

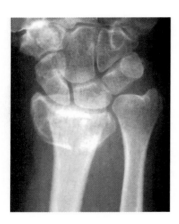

Fig. 14-8
X-ray showing a typical Colles' fracture.

Palmar uniportal endoscopic carpal tunnel release, also called *Mirza technique,* is an endoscopic technique for carpal tunnel release surgery. Previously carpal tunnel release was done with open surgery.

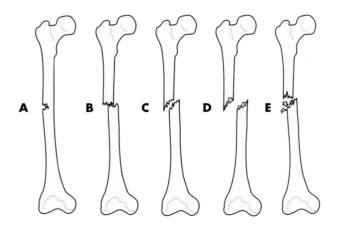

Fig. 14-9
Types of fractures. **A,** Greenstick. **B,** Transverse. **C,** Oblique. **D,** Spiral. **E,** Comminuted.

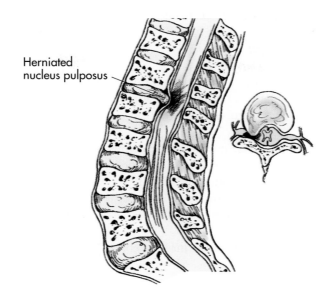

Herniated
nucleus pulposus

Fig. 14-11
Herniated disk.

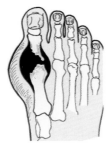

Fig. 14-10
Gout.

Repetitive motion syndrome is an increasingly common and somewhat controversial diagnosis in which pain develops in the hand and forearm in the course of normal work activities. Permanent injury is not common.

Practice saying each of these terms aloud. To assist you in pronunciation, obtain the audiotape designed for use with this text. Learn the definitions and spellings of the disease and disorder terms by completing exercises 21, 22, and 23.

Exercise 21 ....

Write the term for each of the following definitions.

1. abnormal benign growth
   on the surface of the bone   _____

2. group of hereditary diseases
   characterized by degeneration   _____ _____
   of muscle and weakness

3. chronic disease characterized
   by muscle weakness and
   thought to be caused by a   _____ _____
   defect in the transmission
   of impulses from nerve to
   muscle cell

4. abnormal enlargement of the joint at the base of the great toe

_____

5. form of arthritis that first affects the spine and adjacent structures

_____ _____

6. disease in which an excessive amount of uric acid in the blood causes sodium urate crystals (tophi) to be deposited in the joints

_____

7. rupture of the intervertebral disk cartilage, which allows the contents to protrude through it, putting pressure on the spinal nerve roots

a. _____ _____

b. _____ _____

c. _____ _____

8. broken bone

_____

9. abnormal loss of bone density

_____

10. a disorder of the wrist caused by compression of a nerve

_____ _____ _____

11. a type of fractured wrist

_____ _____

Exercise 22

Write the definitions of the following terms.

1. exostosis _____

2. muscular dystrophy _____

3. myasthenia gravis _____

4. bunion _____

5. ankylosing spondylitis _____

6. osteoporosis _____

7. gout _____

8. herniated disk, slipped disk, ruptured disk _____

9. fracture _____

10. carpal tunnel syndrome _____

11. Colles' fracture _____

Exercise 23

Spell the disease and disorder terms. Have someone dictate the terms on pp. 441-442 to you, or say the words into a tape recorder; then spell the words from your recording. Study any words you have spelled incorrectly.

1. _____   7. _____

2. _____   8. _____

3. _____   9. _____

4. _____   10. _____

5. _____   11. _____

6. _____

Surgical Terms

Built From Word Parts

Term	Definition
aponeurorrhaphy (*ap*-ō-nū-ROR-a-fē)	suture of an aponeurosis
arthroclasia (*ar*-thrō-KLĀ-zhē-a)	(surgical) breaking of a (stiff) joint
arthrodesis (*ar*-thrō-DĒ-sis)	surgical fixation of a joint
arthroplasty (AR-thrō-plas-tē)	surgical repair of a joint
arthrotomy (ar-THROT-ō-mē)	incision of a joint
bursectomy (bur-SEK-tō-mē)	excision of a bursa
bursotomy (bur-SOT-ō-mē)	incision of a bursa

carpectomy . . . .   excision of a carpal bone
(kar-PEK-tō-mē)

chondrectomy . . . .   excision of a cartilage
(kon-DREK-tō-me)

chondroplasty . . . .   surgical repair of a cartilage
(KON-drō-plas-tē)

costectomy . . . .   excision of a rib
(kos-TEK-tō-mē)

cranioplasty . . . .   surgical repair of the skull
(KRĀ-nē-ō-plas-tē)

craniotomy . . . .   incision of the skull (as for surgery of the
(*krā*-nē-OT-ō-mē)   brain)

diskectomy . . . .   excision of an intervertebral disk
(dis-KEK-tō-mē)

laminectomy . . . .   excision of a lamina (often done to relieve the
(*lam*-i-NEK-tō-mē)   symptoms of a ruptured disk)

maxillectomy . . . .   excision of the maxilla
(*mak*-si-LEK-tō-mē)

meniscectomy . . . .   excision of the meniscus (performed for a torn
(*men*-i-SEK-tō-mē)   cartilage)

myoplasty . . . .   surgical repair of a muscle
(MĪ-ō-plas-tē)

myorrhaphy . . . .   suture of a muscle
(mī-OR-a-fē)

ostectomy . . . .   excision of bone
(os-TEK-tō-mē)
(NOTE: one *e* is dropped.)

osteoclasis . . . .   (surgical) breaking of a bone (to correct a de-
(*os*-tē-OK-la-sis)   formity)

osteoplasty . . . .   surgical repair of the bone
(OS-tē-ō-plas-tē)

osteotome . . . .   instrument used to cut the bone
(OS-tē-ō-tōm)

osteotomy . . . .   incision of the bone
(*os*-tē-OT-ō-mē)

patellectomy . . . .   excision of the patella
(*pat*-e-LEK-tō-mē)

phalangectomy . . . .   excision of a finger or toe bone
(fal-an-JEK-tō-mē)

rachiotomy . . . .   incision into the vertebral column
(*ra*-kē-OT-ō-mē)

spondylosyndesis . . . .   fusing together of the vertebrae (spinal fusion)
(*spon*-di-lō-SIN-dē-sis)
(NOTE: the prefix *syn*- appears
in the middle of the term.)

synovectomy . . . .   excision of the synovial membrane (of a joint)
(sin-ō-VEK-tō-mē)
(NOTE: the *i* in *synovi* is
dropped because the suffix begins with a vowel.)

tarsectomy . . . .   excision of (one or more) tarsal bones
(tar-SEK-tō-mē)

tenomyoplasty . . . .   surgical repair of the tendon and muscle
(*ten*-ō-MĪ-ō-plas-tē)

tenorrhaphy . . . .   suture of a tendon
(ten-ŌR-a-fē)

tenotomy . . . .   incision of the tendon
(ten-OT-ō-mē)

Total hip replacement arthroplasty is indicated for degenerative joint disease or
rheumatoid arthritis. The operation commonly involves replacement of the hip
joint with a metallic femoral head and a plastic-coated acetabulum.

Total knee joint replacement arthroplasty is designed to replace worn surfaces of
the knee joint. Various prostheses are used.

Metatarsal arthroplasty is used to treat deformities associated with rheumatoid
arthritis or hallux valgus (deformity of the great toe), and to treat painful or un-
stable joints.

Percutaneous diskectomy is a surgical procedure that uses fluoroscopy to guide insertion of a nucleotome into the affected spinal disk and remove the thick, sticky nucleus of the disk. This allows the disk to soften and contract, relieving the severe low
back and leg pain.

Practice saying each of these terms aloud. To assist you in pronunciation, obtain the
audiotape designed for use with this text. Learn the definitions and spellings of the
surgical terms by completing exercises 24, 25, and 26.

Exercise 24

Analyze and define the following surgical terms.

1. osteoclasis _____
2. ostectomy _____
3. osteoplasty _____
4. osteotomy _____

5. osteotome _____

6. arthroclasia _____

7. arthrodesis _____

8. arthroplasty _____

9. arthrotomy _____

10. chondrectomy _____

11. chondroplasty _____

12. myoplasty _____

13. myorrhaphy _____

14. tenomyoplasty _____

15. tenotomy _____

16. tenorrhaphy _____

17. costectomy _____

18. patellectomy _____

19. aponeurorrhaphy _____

20. carpectomy _____

21. phalangectomy _____

22. meniscectomy _____

23. spondylosyndesis _____

24. laminectomy _____

25. bursectomy _____

26. bursotomy _____

27. craniotomy _____

28. cranioplasty _____

29. maxillectomy _____

30. rachiotomy _____

31. tarsectomy _____

32. synovectomy _____

33. diskectomy _____

Exercise 25

Build surgical terms for the following definitions by using the word parts you have learned.

1. (surgical) breaking of a bone (to correct a deformity)

   _____ / ___ / ___
   WR   CV   S

2. excision of bone

   _____ / ___
   WR   S

3. surgical repair of the bone

   _____ / ___ / ___
   WR   CV   S

4. incision of the bone

   _____ / ___
   WR   S

5. instrument used to cut the bone

   _____ / ___ / ___
   WR   CV   S

6. (surgical) breaking of a (stiff) joint

   _____ / ___ / ___
   WR   CV   S

7. surgical fixation of a joint

   _____ / ___ / ___
   WR   CV   S

8. surgical repair of a joint

   _____ / ___ / ___
   WR   CV   S

9. incision of a joint

   _____ / ___
   WR   S

10. excision of cartilage

   _____ / ___
   WR   S

11. surgical repair of cartilage

   _____ / ___ / ___
   WR   CV   S

12. surgical repair of a muscle

   _____ / ___ / ___
   WR   CV   S

13. suture of a muscle

   _____ / ___
   WR   S

14. surgical repair of a tendon and muscle

_____ / / / / / /
WR CV WR CV S

15. incision of the tendon

_____ /
WR   S

16. suture of a tendon

_____ /
WR   S

17. excision of a rib

_____ /
WR   S

18. excision of the patella

_____ /
WR   S

19. suture of an aponeurosis

_____ /
WR   S

20. excision of a carpal bone

_____ /
WR   S

21. excision of a finger or toe bone

_____ /
WR   S

22. excision of a meniscus

_____ /
WR   S

23. fusing together of the vertebrae

_____ / / /
WR CV P S

24. excision of a lamina

_____ /
WR   S

25. excision of a bursa

_____ /
WR   S

26. incision of a bursa

_____ /
WR   S

27. incision of the skull

_____ /
WR   S

28. surgical repair of the skull

_____ / /
WR CV S

29. excision of the maxilla

_____ /
WR   S

30. incision of the vertebral column

_____ /
WR   S

31. excision of (one or more) tarsal bones

_____ /
WR   S

32. excision of the synovial mem-
    brane

$\dfrac{\qquad\qquad}{\text{WR}}\Big/\dfrac{\qquad\qquad}{\text{S}}$

33. excision of an intervertebral
    disk

$\dfrac{\qquad\qquad}{\text{WR}}\Big/\dfrac{\qquad\qquad}{\text{S}}$

Exercise 26

Spell each of the surgical terms. Have someone dictate the terms on pp. 445-447 to you, or say the words into a tape recorder; then spell the words from your recording. Think about the word parts before attempting to write the word. Study any words you have spelled incorrectly.

1. _____
2. _____
3. _____
4. _____
5. _____
6. _____
7. _____
8. _____
9. _____
10. _____
11. _____
12. _____
13. _____
14. _____
15. _____
16. _____
17. _____

18. _____
19. _____
20. _____
21. _____
22. _____
23. _____
24. _____
25. _____
26. _____
27. _____
28. _____
29. _____
30. _____
31. _____
32. _____
33. _____

Procedural Terms

Built From Word Parts

Term	Definition
Diagnostic Imaging	
arthrogram · · · · · · · · · · · · · · · · · ·	x-ray film of a joint
(AR-thrō-gram)	
Endoscopy	
arthroscopy · · · · · · · · · · · · · · · ·	visual examination inside a joint (Exercise Figure F)
(ar-THROS-kō-pē)	
Additional Procedural Terms	
arthrocentesis · · · · · · · · · · · · · · ·	surgical puncture of a joint to aspirate fluid
(*ar*-thrō-sen-TĒ-sis)	
electromyogram (EMG) · · · · · · · ·	record of the (intrinsic) electric activity in a (skeletal) muscle
(ē-*lek*-trō-MĪ-ō-gram)	

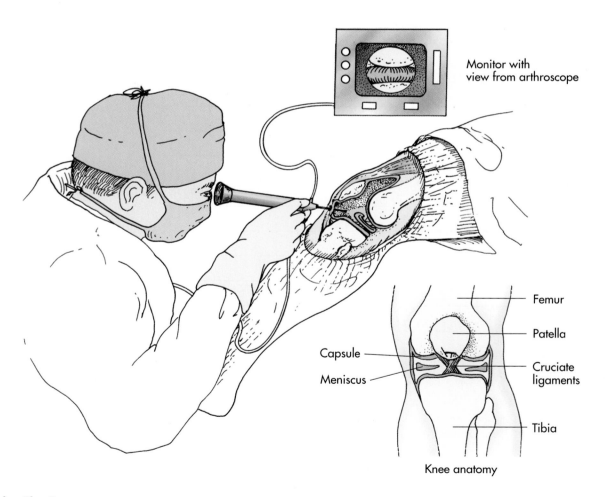

Monitor with view from arthroscope

Femur
Patella
Capsule
Meniscus
Cruciate ligaments
Tibia

Knee anatomy

Exercise Fig. F

Fill in the blanks to label the diagram. JOINT / CV / VISUAL EXAMINATION of the knee, performed for diagnostic purposes or for surgical repair of ligaments of meniscus.

Practice saying each of these words aloud. To assist you in pronunciation, obtain the audiotape designed for use with this text. Learn the definitions and spellings of the procedural terms by completing exercises 27, 28, and 29.

Exercise 27 ....

Analyze and define the following procedural terms.

1. electromyogram _____

2. arthrogram _____

3. arthroscopy _____

4. arthrocentesis _____

Exercise 28 ....

Build procedural terms for the following definitions using word parts you have learned.

1. x-ray film of a joint   _____
                                             WR / CV / S

2. visual examination inside a
   joint   _____
                                             WR / CV / S

3. surgical puncture of a joint to
   aspirate fluid   _____
                                             WR / CV / S

4. record of the electrical activity
   of a muscle   _____
                                             WR / CV / WR / CV / S

Exercise 29 ....

Spell each of the procedural terms. Have someone dictate the terms on p. 452 to you, or say the words into a tape recorder; then spell the words from your recording. Think about the word parts before attempting to write the word. Study any words you have spelled incorrectly.

1. _____   3. _____

2. _____   4. _____

The following diagnostic imaging procedures are commonly used for diagnosing diseases, fractures, strain, and other conditions of the musculoskeletal system.

Radiography (x-ray) of the bones and joints is used to identify fractures or tumors, monitor healing, or identify abnormal structures.

Computed tomography (CT) of the bone and joints gives accurate definition of bone structure and demonstrates subtle changes such as linear fractures (Figure 14-12).

Magnetic resonance imaging (MRI) of the bones is used to evaluate the ligaments of the knee, spinal stenosis, and degenerative disk changes (Figure 14-13).

Bone scan (nuclear medicine test) is used to detect the presence of metastatic disease of the bone and to monitor degenerative bone disease (Figure 14-14).

Single-photon emission computed tomography (SPECT) of the bone is an even more sensitive nuclear method for detecting bone abnormalities.

Bone densitometry is a method of determining the density of bone by radiographic techniques used to diagnose osteoporosis.

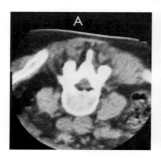
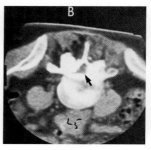
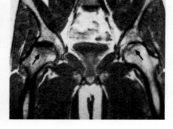

Fig. 14-12
Normal **(A)** and abnormal **(B)** computerized axial tomographic scans of the lumbar spine.

Fig. 14-13
MRI showing avascular necrosis of the femoral heads.

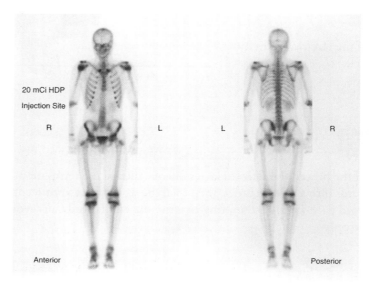

Fig. 14-14
Whole body bone scan.

Complementary Terms
Built From Word Parts

Term	Definition
arthralgia (ar-THRAL-jē-a)	pain in the joint
atrophy (AT-rō-fē)	without development (wasting)
bradykinesia (*brād*-ē-kin-Ē-zhē-a)	slow movement
carpal (CAR-pal)	pertaining to the wrist
cranial (KRĀ-nē-al)	pertaining to the cranium
dyskinesia (dis-ki-NĒ-zhē-a)	difficult movement
dystrophy (DIS-trō-fē)	abnormal development
femoral (FEM-ō-ral)	pertaining to the femur
humeral (HŪ-mer-al)	pertaining to the humerus
hyperkinesia (*hī*-per-kin-Ē-zhē-a)	excessive movement (overactive)
hypertrophy (hī-PER-trō-fē)	excessive development
iliofemoral (*il*-ē-ō-FEM-ō-ral)	pertaining to the ilium and femur
intercostal (in-ter-KOS-tal)	pertaining to between the ribs
intervertebral (*in*-ter-VER-te-bral)	pertaining to between the vertebrae
intracranial (*in*-tra-KRĀ-nē-al)	pertaining to within the cranium
ischiofibular (*is*-kē-ō-FIB-ū-lar)	pertaining to the ischium and fibula
ischiopubic (*is*-kē-ō-PŪ-bik)	pertaining to the ischium and pubis
lumbar (LUM-bar)	pertaining to the loins (the part of the back between the thorax and pelvis)
lumbocostal (lum-bō-KOS-tal)	pertaining to the loins and the ribs
lumbosacral (lum-bō-SĀ-kral)	pertaining to the lumbar region (loin) and the sacrum
osteoblast (OS-tē-ō-blast)	developing bone cell

osteocyte		bone cell
(OS-tē-ō-sīt)		
osteonecrosis		(abnormal) death of bone (tissues)
(*os*-tē-ō-ne-KRŌ-sis)		
pubofemoral		pertaining to the pubis and femur
(*pŭ*-bō-FEM-ō-ral)		
sacral		pertaining to the sacrum
(SĀ-kral)		
sacrovertebral		pertaining to the sacrum and vertebrae
(sā-krō-VER-te-bral)		
sternoclavicular		pertaining to the sternum and clavicle
(*ster*-nō-kla-VIK-ū-lar)		
sternoid		resembling the sternum
(STER-noyd)		
subcostal		pertaining to below the rib
(sub-KOS-tal)		
submandibular		pertaining to below the mandible
(*sub*-man-DIB-ū-lar)		
submaxillary		pertaining to below the maxilla
(sub-MAK-si-lar-ē)		
subscapular		pertaining to below the scapula
(sub-SKAP-ū-lar)		
substernal		pertaining to below the sternum
(sub-STER-nal)		
suprascapular		pertaining to above the scapula
(*sŭ*-pra-SKAP-ū-lar)		
suprapatellar		pertaining to above the patella
(sū-pra-pa-TEL-ar)		
symphysis		growing together
(SIM-fi-sis)		
vertebrocostal		pertaining to the vertebrae and ribs
(*ver*-te-brō-KOS-tal)		

Practice saying each of these terms aloud. To assist you in pronunciation, obtain the audiotape designed for use with this text. Exercises 30, 31, and 32 will help you learn the definitions and spellings of the complementary terms related to the musculoskeletal system.

Exercise 30

Analyze and define the following complementary terms.

1. symphysis _____

2. femoral _____

3. humeral _____

4. intervertebral _____

5. hyperkinesia _____

6. dyskinesia _____

7. bradykinesia _____

8. intracranial _____

9. sternoclavicular _____

10. iliofemoral _____

11. ischiofibular _____

12. submaxillary _____

13. ischiopubic _____

14. submandibular _____

15. pubofemoral _____

16. suprascapular _____

17. subcostal _____

18. vertebrocostal _____

19. subscapular _____

20. osteoblast _____

21. osteocyte _____

22. osteonecrosis _____

23. sternoid _____

24. arthralgia _____

25. carpal _____

26. lumbar _____

27. lumbocostal _____

28. lumbosacral _____

29. sacral _____

30. sacrovertebral _____

31. substernal _____

32. suprapatellar _____

33. dystrophy _____

34. atrophy _____

35. hypertrophy _____

36. intercostal _____

37. cranial _____

Exercise 31 ....

Build the complementary terms for the following definitions by using the word parts you have learned.

1. growing together

_____ / _____
P   S(WR)

2. pertaining to the femur

_____ / _____
WR   S

3. pertaining to the humerus

_____ / _____
WR   S

4. pertaining to between the ver-
    tebrae

_____ / _____ / _____
P   WR   S

5. excessive movement (overac-
    tivity)

_____ / _____ / _____
P   WR   S

6. difficult movement

_____ / _____ / _____
P   WR   S

7. slow movement

_____ / _____ / _____
P   WR   S

8. pertaining to within the
    cranium

_____ / _____ / _____
P   WR   S

9. pertaining to the sternum and
    clavicle

_____ / _____ / _____ / _____
WR   CV   WR   S

10. pertaining to the ilium and
    femur

_____ / _____ / _____ / _____
WR   CV   WR   S

11. pertaining to the ischium and
    fibula

_____ / _____ / _____ / _____
WR   CV   WR   S

12. pertaining to below the maxilla

P / WR / S

13. pertaining to the ischium and pubis

WR / CV / WR / S

14. pertaining to below the mandible

P / WR / S

15. pertaining to the pubis and femur

WR / CV / WR / S

16. pertaining to above the scapula

P / WR / S

17. pertaining to below the rib

P / WR / S

18. pertaining to the vertebrae and ribs

WR / CV / WR / S

19. pertaining to below the scapula

P / WR / S

20. developing bone cell

WR / CV / WR

21. bone cell

WR / CV / S

22. (abnormal) death of bone (tissues)

WR / CV / WR / S

23. resembling the sternum

WR / S

24. pain in the joint

WR / S

25. pertaining to the wrist

WR / S

26. pertaining to the sacrum

WR / S

27. pertaining to the loins

WR / S

28. pertaining to the sacrum and vertebrae

WR / CV / WR / S

29. pertaining to the lumbar region (loin) and the sacrum

    WR / CV /   WR / S

30. pertaining to the loins and ribs

    WR / CV /   WR / S

31. pertaining to below the sternum

    P / WR / S

32. pertaining to above the patella

    P / WR / S

33. abnormal development

    P / S(WR)

34. without development

    P / S(WR)

35. excessive development

    P / S(WR)

36. pertaining to the cranium

    WR / S

37. pertaining to between the ribs

    P / WR / S

Exercise 32 ....

Spell each of the complementary terms. Have someone dictate the terms on pp. 455-456 to you, or say the words into a tape recorder; then spell the words from your recording. Think about the word parts before attempting to write the word. Study any words you have spelled incorrectly.

1. _____ 13. _____

2. _____ 14. _____

3. _____ 15. _____

4. _____ 16. _____

5. _____ 17. _____

6. _____ 18. _____

7. _____ 19. _____

8. _____ 20. _____

9. _____ 21. _____

10. _____ 22. _____

11. _____ 23. _____

12. _____ 24. _____

25. _____   32. _____

26. _____   33. _____

27. _____   34. _____

28. _____   35. _____

29. _____   36. _____

30. _____   37. _____

31. _____

Complementary Terms
Not Built From Word Parts

Term	Definition
chiropodist, podiatrist .... (ki-ROP-ō-dist) (pō-DĪ-a-trist)	specialist in treating and diagnosing foot disease and disorders such as corns and ingrown toenails
chiropractic .... (*kī*-rō-PRAK-tik)	system of therapy that consists of manipulation of the vertebral column
chiropractor .... (*kī*-rō-PRAK-tor)	specialist in chiropractic
orthopedics (ortho) .... (*or*-thō-PĒ-diks)	branch of medicine dealing with the study and treatment of diseases and abnormalities of the musculoskeletal system
orthopedist .... (*or*-thō-PĒ-dist)	physician who specializes in orthopedics
orthotics .... (or-THOT-iks)	making and fitting of orthopedic appliances, such as arch supports, used to support, align, prevent, or correct deformities
orthotist .... (ŌR-thō-tist)	one who is skilled in orthotics
osteopathy .... (*os*-tē-OP-a-thē)	system of medicine that uses the usual forms of diagnosis and treatment but places greater emphasis on the role of the relationship between body organs and the musculoskeletal system; manipulation may be used in addition to other treatments
osteopath .... (OS-tē-ō-path)	physician who specializes in osteopathy
prosthesis .... (pros-THĒ-sis)	an artificial substitute for a missing body part such as a leg or an eye

don't believe in a lot of meds (handwritten annotation)

Practice saying each of these terms aloud. To assist you in pronunciation, obtain the audiotape designed for use with this text. Learn the definitions and spellings of the complementary terms by completing exercises 33, 34, and 35.

Chiropodist

is made up of the Greek word roots **chir**, meaning **hand**, and **pod**, meaning **foot**, plus **ist**, meaning **one who practices.** The term was probably applied to persons who manually, or by using their hands, treat disorders of the feet.

Chiropractic

is composed of the Greek **chir** and the English **practice.** Chiropractic was discovered in 1895 by D.D. Palmer, and the school bearing his name was later founded by his son, B.J. Palmer. The degree, Doctor of Chiropractic, or D.C., is awarded for completion of 2 years of premedical study followed by 4 years of training in an approved school.

Orthopedic

is a term devised by French physician Dr. Nicolas Andry in 1741. **Orthopedic** comes from the Greek **orthos,** meaning **straight** and **ped,** meaning **child.** The word implies **to straighten a child.** During this time rickets, osteomyelitis, poliomyelitis, and tuberculosis were main causes of orthopedic problems. All left their victims with severe deformities.

Osteopathy

was founded in 1874 by American physician Dr. Andrew Taylor Still. It was the first system to treat disease by adjustment. Still believed that bones, ligaments, and muscles that are out of adjustment cause disease. He named the system **osteopathy,** from the word parts **oste,** meaning **bone,** and **path,** meaning **disease.** The practice of osteopathy is currently similar to conventional medical practice.

Exercise 33

Match the definitions in the first column with the correct terms in the second column. The terms in the second column may be used more than once.

_____ 1. specialist in manipulation of the vertebral
column

_____ 2. branch of medicine
dealing with treatment
of diseases of the
musculoskeletal system

_____ 3. physician

_____ 4. foot specialist

_____ 5. substitute for a body
part

_____ 6. system of therapy

_____ 7. system of medicine

_____ 8. making of orthopedic
appliances

_____ 9. skilled in orthotics

a. chiropodist

b. chiropractic

c. chiropractor

d. osteopath

e. osteopathy

f. orthopedics

g. orthopedist

h. podiatrist

i. orthotics

j. prosthesis

k. orthotist

Exercise 34

Write the definitions of the following.

1. chiropractor _____

2. chiropractic _____

3. orthopedics _____

4. orthopedist _____

5. chiropodist _____

6. podiatrist _____

7. osteopath _____

8. osteopathy _____

9. orthotics _____

10. prosthesis _____

11. orthotist _____

Exercise 35 ....

Spell each of the complementary terms. Have someone dictate the terms on p. 461 to you, or say the words into a tape recorder; then spell the words from your recording. Study any words you have spelled incorrectly.

1. _____   7. _____
2. _____   8. _____
3. _____   9. _____
4. _____   10. _____
5. _____   11. _____
6. _____

▌Abbreviations

ACL	anterior cruciate ligament
C1-C7	cervical vertebrae
CTS	carpal tunnel syndrome
EMG	electromyogram
fx	fracture
HNP	herniated nucleus pulposus
IM	intramuscular
L1-L5	lumbar vertebrae
MD	muscular dystrophy
MG	myasthenia gravis
MRI	magnetic resonance imaging
OA	osteoarthritis
ortho	orthopedics
RA	rheumatoid arthritis
ROM	range of motion
THA	total hip arthroplasty
THR	total hip replacement
TKA	total knee arthroplasty
TKR	total knee replacement
T1-T12	thoracic vertebrae

CHAPTER REVIEW

Exercises

Exercise 36

Complete the hospital report by writing the medical terms in the blanks. Use the list of definitions with the corresponding numbers.

> **Case History:** This 37-year-old married African-American man was admitted to the 1. _____ service of the hospital. He complains of pain when walking and golfing. He says that his knees have "been painful" for many years since he quit playing semiprofessional football, but the pain has become severe in the last 6 months. He is scheduled for 2. _____ . His preoperative diagnosis is 3. _____ , left knee, with possible tear, 4. _____ meniscus.

> **Operative Report:** After induction of spinal anesthetic, the patient was positioned on the operating table, and a tourniquet was applied over the upper left thigh. Following positioning of the leg in a circumferential holder, the end of the table was flexed to allow the leg to hang freely. The patient's left leg was prepped and draped in the usual manner. Following exsanguination of the leg with an Esmarch bandage, the tourniquet was inflated to 300 mm Hg. The knee was inspected using anterolateral and anteromedial parapatellar portholes.
>
> **Findings:** The synovium in the 5. _____ pouch showed moderate to severe inflammatory changes with villi formation and hyperemia. The undersurface of the patella showed loss of normal articular cartilage on the lateral patellar facet with exposed bone in that area and moderate to severe 6. _____ of the medial facet. Similar changes were noted in the intercondylar groove. In the medial compartment, the patient had smooth articular cartilage on the femur and moderate chondromalacia of the tibial plateau. The 7. _____ meniscus appeared normal with no evidence of tears and a smooth articular surface on the femoral condyle. The examination and probing were repeated with no additional 8. _____ being identified. The tourniquet was then released and the knee flushed with lactated Ringer's solution until the bleeding slowed. The wounds were Steri-stripped closed, a sterile bandage with an external Ace wrap applied, and the patient returned to the postoperative recovery area in stable condition.

1. branch of medicine dealing with the study and treatment of diseases and abnormalities of the musculoskeletal system
2. visual examination of the inside of a joint
3. inflammation of a joint
4. toward the middle or midline
5. pertaining to above the patella
6. softening of the cartilage
7. toward the side
8. study of body changes caused by disease

Exercise 37

To test your understanding of the terms introduced in this chapter, circle the words that correctly complete the sentences. The italicized words refer to the correct answer.

1. The medical term for *hunchback* is (kyphosis, ankylosis, scoliosis).
2. Surgical treatment for a degenerative, painful hip joint may be total hip replacement, or (arthroplasty, arthrodesis, arthroclasia).
3. The medical term for *excision of cartilage* is (carpectomy, chondrectomy, costectomy).
4. *Difficult movement* is (hyperkinesia, bradykinesia, dyskinesia).
5. Vitamin D deficiency in adults may cause *osteomalacia,* or (muscle weakness, marblelike bones, softening of bones).
6. The *surgical breaking of a bone* to correct a deformity is called (osteoclasis, arthroclasia, osteoplasty).
7. The medical term that means *pertaining to below the rib* is (subscapular, subcostal, substernal).
8. The medical term for *growing together* is (diaphysis, epiphysis, symphysis).
9. A(n) (orthopedist, podiatrist, chiropractor) is *competent to treat* a person with a *fractured femur.*
10. (Osteoporosis, osteopetrosis, osteomyelitis) is the *abnormal loss of bone density.*
11. A common *disorder of the wrist caused by compression of a nerve* is called (lordosis, carpal tunnel syndrome, synoviosarcoma).

Exercise 38

Fill in the blanks with the correct terms.

1. An ankle fracture several years ago still causes pain for the patient. To reduce the pain, the doctor recommended a surgical procedure to fuse the joint. This procedure is called _____ .
2. While playing soccer, Jimmy Smith tore the meniscus in his left knee. The orthopedic surgeon will use an endoscopic procedure to repair the meniscus. The procedure is called _____ .
3. Mrs. Brown severed her tendon by accidentally walking into a patio door, breaking the glass and causing injury. Surgery was required to suture the tendon back together. This surgical procedure is called _____ .
4. Learning about the electrical impulses of muscles can assist the physician in diagnosing muscular dystrophy. What test will the doctor order to obtain information? _____ . Patients with muscular dystrophy often have _____ or muscle wasting.
5. Adjective forms of medical terms are often used by health care providers to indicate areas of the body to describe the location of pain, the sites of injections, lesions and so forth. Below are some examples. Fill in the blank with the correct medical term.
   a. _____ laceration (pertaining to the cranium)
   b. _____ muscles (pertaining to between the ribs)

c. pain in the left _____ region (pertaining to below the ribs)

d. herniation of the _____ disk (pertaining to between the vertebrae)

e. _____ pressure (pertaining to within the cranium)

f. _____ artery (pertaining to the femur)

g. strain of the _____ area (pertaining to the ischium and pubis)

h. degenerative disease of the _____ joint (pertaining to the sternum and the clavicle)

i. a growth was detected in the left _____ region (pertaining to below the mandible)

Exercise 39

Unscramble the following mixed-up terms. The word on the left indicates the prefix in each of the following.

1. within

/ / / / /a/ / / / / /a/ /
r a n l a i n a c t r i

2. above

/ / / / /a/ / /a/ / / / /
r a c p u l s a r s u p a

3. together

/ / / / / /y/ / / /
m i s s y p y h

4. below

/ / / / /o/ / / /
b a c t u s o s l

5. many

/ / / / /m/ / / / / / / /
m p i s i y o y l o s t

Exercise 40

The following terms did not appear in this chapter but are composed of word parts that have appeared in this or the previous chapters. Find their definitions by translating the word parts literally.

1. **craniorachischisis** _____
   (_krā_-nē-ō-ra-KIS-ki-sis)

2. **humeroradial** _____
   (_hū_-mer-ō-RĀ-dē-al)

3. **interpubic** _____
   (_in_-ter-PŪ-bik)

4. **intrasternal** _____
   (_in_-tra-STERN-al)

5. **myokinesis** _____
   (_mī_-ō-ki-NĒ-sis)

6. **osteoarthropathy** _____
   (_os_-tē-ō-ar-THROP-a-thē)

7. **osteolysis** _____
   (os-tē-OL-i-sis)

8. **osteoma** _____
   (os-tē-Ō-ma)

9. **osteometry** _____
   (_os_-tē-OM-e-trē)

10. **osteosclerosis** _____
    (os-tē-ō-skle-RŌ-sis)

11. **polyarthritis** _____
    (*pol*-ē-ar-THRĪ-tis)

12. **spondylodynia** _____
    (*spon*-di-lō-DĪN-ē-a)

13. **tenalgia** _____
    (ten-AL-jē-a)

14. **vertebrosternal** _____
    (*ver*-te-brō-STERN-al)

Combining Forms Crossword Puzzle

Across Clues
1. cartilage
2. ulna
6. scapula
9. tendon
10. developing cell
12. bursa
14. clavicle
16. maxilla
19. ischium
18. vertebra
22. tibia
26. stone
28. aponeurosis
29. crooked
31. fibula
32. tarsals
37. spine, vertebral column
38. joint

Down Clues
1. skull
3. movement, motion
4. mandible
5. pubis
7. finger or toe bone
8. hump
11. rib
13. kneecap
15. meniscus
17. ilium
20. wrist bone
21. bone marrow
23. spinal column
24. sternum
25. radius
27. bone
30. lamina
33. abbreviation for alarm reaction
34. abbreviation for rheumatoid arthritis
35. abbreviation for science
36. abbreviation for occupational history

Review of Terms

Can you build, analyze, define, pronounce, and spell the following terms *built from word parts?*

Diseases and Disorders

ankylosis

arthritis

arthrochondritis

bursitis

bursolith

carpoptosis

chondromalacia

cranioschisis

diskitis

kyphosis

lordosis

maxillitis

meniscitis

myasthenia

myeloma

osteitis

osteoarthritis (OA)

osteocarcinoma

osteochondritis

osteofibroma

osteomalacia

osteomyelitis

osteopetrosis

osteosarcoma

polymyositis

rachischisis

scoliosis

spondylarthritis

synoviosarcoma

tendinitis

tenodynia

tenosynovitis

Surgical

aponeurorrhaphy

arthroclasia

arthrodesis

arthroplasty

arthrotomy

bursectomy

bursotomy

carpectomy

chondrectomy

chondroplasty

costectomy

cranioplasty

craniotomy

diskectomy

laminectomy

maxillectomy

meniscectomy

myoplasty

myorrhaphy

ostectomy

osteoclasis

osteoplasty

osteotome

osteotomy

patellectomy

phalangectomy

rachiotomy

spondylosyndesis

synovectomy

tarsectomy

tenomyoplasty

tenorrhaphy

tenotomy

Procedural

arthrocentesis

arthrogram

arthroscopy

electromyogram (EMG)

Complementary

arthralgia

atrophy

bradykinesia

carpal

cranial

dyskinesia

dystrophy

femoral

humeral

hyperkinesia

hypertrophy

iliofemoral

intercostal

intervertebral

intracranial

ischiofibular

ischiopubic

lumbar

lumbocostal

lumbosacral

osteoblast

osteocyte

osteonecrosis

pubofemoral

sacral

sacrovertebral

sternoclavicular

sternoid

subcostal

submandibular

submaxillary

subscapular

substernal

suprascapular

suprapatellar

symphysis

vertebrocostal

Can you define, pronounce, and spell the following terms *not built from word parts?*

Diseases and Disorders	Complementary
ankylosing spondylitis	chiropodist
bunion	chiropractic
carpal tunnel syndrome (CTS)	chiropractor
Colles' fracture	orthopedics (ortho)
exostosis	orthopedist
fracture (fx)	orthotics
gout	orthotist
herniated disk	osteopathy
muscular dystrophy (MD)	osteopath
myasthenia gravis (MG)	podiatrist
osteoporosis	prosthesis

Nervous System

CHAPTER

15

Objectives .... **Upon completion of this chapter you will be able to:**
1. Identify the organs and other structures of the nervous system.
2. Define and spell the word parts presented in this chapter.
3. Build and analyze medical terms using word parts.
4. Define, pronounce, and spell the disease and disorder, procedural, surgical, and complementary terms for the nervous system.

ANATOMY

The nervous system and the endocrine system cooperate in regulating and controlling the activities of the other body systems.

The nervous system may be divided into two parts: the *central nervous system* (CNS) and the peripheral nervous system (PNS) (Figure 15-1). The central nervous system consists of the brain and spinal cord. The peripheral nervous system is made up of cranial nerves, which carry impulses between the brain and neck and head, and spinal nerves, which carry messages between the spinal cord and abdomen, limbs, and chest.

Organs of the Central Nervous System

brain	major portion of the central nervous system (Figure 15-2)
cerebrum	largest portion of the brain, divided into left and right hemispheres. The cerebrum controls the skeletal muscles, interprets general senses (such as temperature, pain, and touch), and contains centers for sight and hearing. Intellect, memory, and emotional reactions also take place in the cerebrum.
ventricles	spaces within the cerebrum that contain a fluid called *cerebrospinal fluid.* The cerebrospinal fluid flows through the subarachnoid space around the brain and spinal cord.
cerebellum	sometimes referred to as the *hindbrain.* It is located under the posterior portion of the cerebrum. Its function is to assist in the coordination of skeletal muscles and to maintain balance.
brainstem	stemlike portion of the brain, which connects with the spinal cord

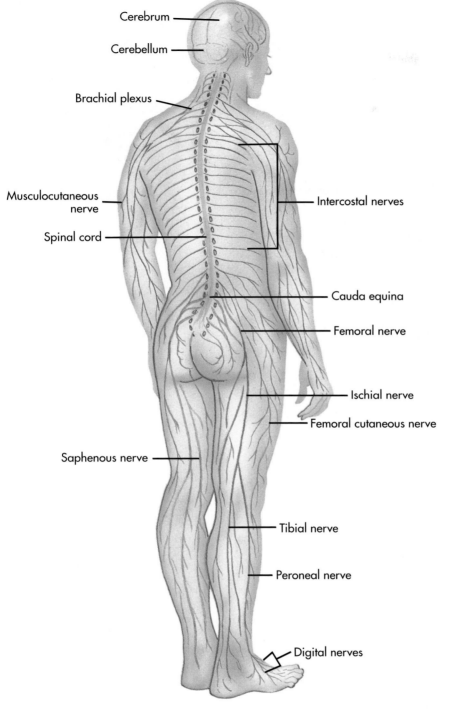

Fig. 15-1
Simplified view of the nervous system.

Cerebellum

was named in the third century BC by Erasistratus, who also named the cerebrum. **Cerebellum** literally means **little brain** and is the diminutive of **cerebrum,** meaning **brain.** Although it was named long ago, its function was not understood until the nineteenth century.

pons . . . .   literally mean *bridge.* It connects the cerebrum with the cerebellum and brainstem.

medulla oblongata . . . .   located between the pons and spinal cord. It contains centers that control respiration, heart rate, and the muscles in the blood vessel walls, which assist in determining blood pressure.

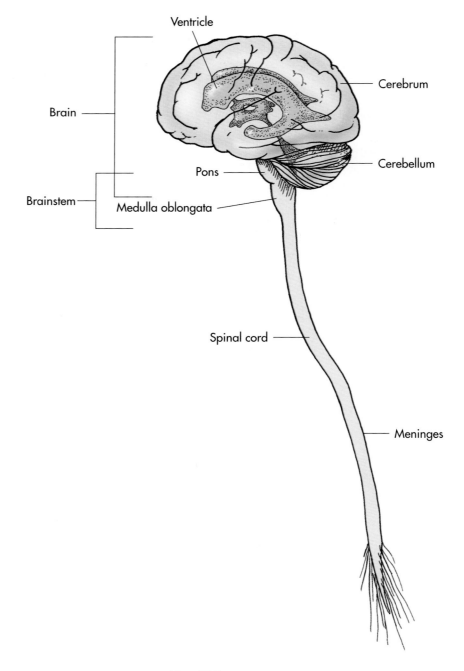

Ventricle

Cerebrum

Brain

Cerebellum

Pons

Medulla oblongata

Brainstem

Spinal cord

Meninges

Fig. 15-2
Brain and spinal cord.

Meninges

were first named by a Persian physician in the tenth century. When translated into Latin, they became **dura mater,** meaning **hard mother** (because it is a tough membrane), and **pia mater,** meaning **soft mother** (because it is a delicate membrane). **Mater** was used because the Arabians believed that the meninges were the mother of all other body membranes.

---

spinal cord . . . . passes through the vertebral canal extending from the medulla oblongata to the level of the second lumbar vertebra. The spinal cord conducts nerve impulses to and from the brain and initiates reflex action to sensory information without input from the brain.

meninges . . . . three layers of membrane that cover the brain and spinal cord (Figure 15-3)

dura mater . . . . tough outer layer of the meninges

arachnoid . . . . delicate middle layer of the meninges. The arachnoid membrane is loosely attached to the pia mater by weblike fibers, which allow for the *subarachnoid space.*

pia mater . . . . thin inner layer of the meninges

Organs of the Peripheral Nervous System

nerve . . . . cordlike structure that carries impulses from one part of the body to another. There are 12 pairs of cranial nerves and 31 pairs of spinal nerves (Figures 15-1 and 15-3).

ganglion (*pl.*, ganglia) . . . . group of nerve cell bodies located outside the central nervous system

Learn the anatomical terms by completing exercises 1 and 2.

Exercise 1

Fill in the blanks with the correct terms.

The layer of membrane that covers the brain and spinal cord is called the

(1) _____ . It is composed of three layers called (2) _____

_____ , (3) _____ , and (4) _____

_____ . Below the middle layer is a space called the

(5) _____ _____ through which the (6) _____

_____ flows around the brain and spinal cord.

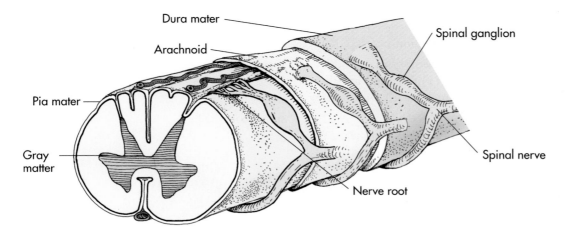

Fig. 15-3
Layers of meninges.

Exercise 2 ....

Match the definitions in the first column with the correct terms in the second column.

_____ 1. maintains balance

_____ 2. connects the cerebrum with the cerebellum and brainstem

_____ 3. spaces within the cerebrum

_____ 4. contains the control center for respiration

_____ 5. carries impulses from one part of the body to another

_____ 6. conducts impulses to and from the brain

_____ 7. group of nerve cell bodies outside the CNS

a. nerve

b. ganglion

c. pia mater

d. cerebellum

e. medulla oblongata

f. pons

g. ventricles

h. spinal cord

WORD PARTS

Combining Forms of the Nervous System

Study the word parts and their definitions listed below. Completing the exercises that follow will help you learn the terms.

Combining Form	Definition
cerebell/o	cerebellum
cerebr/o	cerebrum, brain
dur/o	hard, dura mater
encephal/o	brain
gangli/o, ganglion/o	ganglion
mening/i, mening/o .... (NOTE: both *i* and *o* are used as combining vowels with *mening*.)	meninges
myel/o .... (NOTE: *myel/o* also means *bone marrow;* see Chapter 14).	spinal cord
neur/o .... (NOTE: *neur/o* was introduced in Chapter 2.)	nerve
radic/o, radicul/o, rhiz/o	nerve root (proximal end of a peripheral nerve, closest to the spinal cord)

Learn the anatomical locations and meanings of the combining forms by completing exercises 3 and 4 and Exercise Figures A and B.

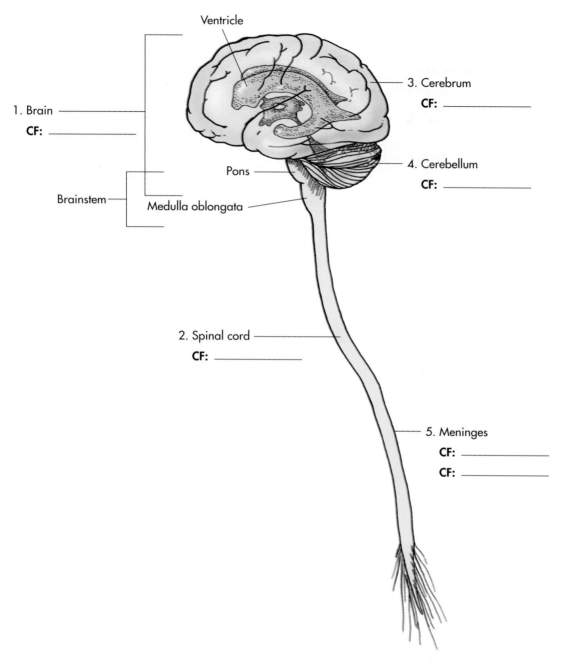

Ventricle

1. Brain

CF: _____

3. Cerebrum

CF: _____

4. Cerebellum

CF: _____

Pons

Brainstem

Medulla oblongata

2. Spinal cord

CF: _____

5. Meninges

CF: _____

CF: _____

Exercise Fig. A
Fill in the blanks to label this diagram of the brain and spinal cord.

Exercise 3 ....

Write the definitions of the following combining forms.

1. cerebell/o _____

2. neur/o _____

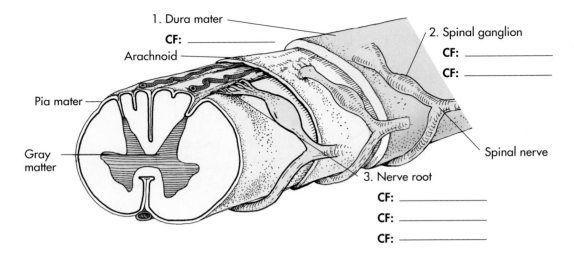

Exercise Fig. B
Fill in the blanks to label this diagram of the layers of meninges.

3. myel/o _____

4. mening/o, mening/i _____

5. encephal/o _____

6. cerebr/o _____

7. radicul/o _____

8. gangli/o _____

9. radic/o _____

10. dur/o _____

11. ganglion/o _____

12. rhiz/o _____

Exercise 4

Write the combining form for each of the following terms.

1. cerebellum   _____

2. nerve   _____

3. spinal cord   _____

4. meninges   a. _____

b. _____

5. brain   _____

6. cerebrum, brain   _____

7. nerve root   a. _____

b. _____

c. _____

8. hard, dura mater   _____

9. ganglion   a. _____

b. _____

Combining Forms Commonly Used With Nervous System Terms

Combining Form	Definition
esthesi/o	sensation, sensitivity, feeling
mon/o	one
phas/o	speech
poli/o	gray matter
psych/o, ment/o, phren/o	mind
quadr/i	four

(NOTE: an *i* is the combining vowel in *quadr/i*.)

Learn the combining forms by completing exercises 5 and 6.

Exercise 5

Write the definitions of the following combining forms.

1. mon/o _____

2. psych/o _____

3. quadr/i _____

4. ment/o _____

5. phas/o _____

6. esthesi/o _____

7. phren/o _____

8. poli/o _____

Exercise 6 ....

Write the combining form for each of the following.

1. four   _____

2. one   _____

3. mind   a. _____

                                b. _____

                                c. _____

4. speech   _____

5. gray matter   _____

6. sensation, sensitivity, feeling   _____

Prefixes

Prefix	Definition
hemi-	half
pre-	before
tetra-	four

Learn the prefixes by completing exercises 7 and 8.

Exercise 7 ....

Write the definition of the following prefixes.

1. tetra- _____

2. hemi- _____

3. pre- _____

Exercise 8

Write the prefix for each of the following definitions.

1. half _____

2. four _____

3. before _____

Suffixes

Suffix	Definition
-iatry	treatment, specialty
-iatrist	specialist, physician (*-ologist* also means special-ist)
-ictal	seizure, attack
-paresis	slight paralysis

Learn the suffixes by completing exercises 9 and 10.

Exercise 9

Write the definitions of the following suffixes.

1. -paresis _____

2. -iatry _____

3. -ictal _____

4. -iatrist _____

Exercise 10

Write the suffix for each of the following.

1. slight paralysis _____

2. treatment, specialty _____

3. seizure _____

4. specialist, physician _____

MEDICAL TERMS

The terms you need to learn to complete this chapter are listed below. The exercises following each list will help you learn the definition and spelling of each word.

Disease and Disorder Terms

Built From Word Parts

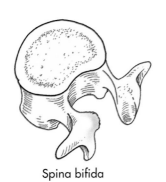

Spina bifida

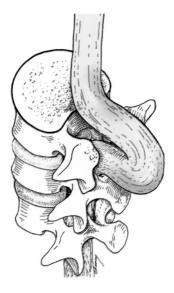

Exercise Fig. C

Fill in the blanks to label the diagram. Spina bifida and

<u>MENINGES</u> / CV /

<u>SPINAL CORD</u> / CV / PROTRU-
SION.

Term	Definition
cerebellitis . . . . (ser-e-bel-Ī-tis)	inflammation of the cerebellum
cerebral thrombosis . . . . (se-RĒ-bral) (throm-BŌ-sis)	abnormal condition of a clot in the cerebrum (pertaining to)
duritis . . . . (dū-RĪ-tis)	inflammation of the dura mater
encephalitis . . . . (*en*-sef-a-LĪ-tis)	inflammation of the brain
encephalomalacia . . . . (en-*sef*-a-lō-ma-LĀ-shē-a)	softening of the brain
encephalomyeloradiculitis . . . . . . (en-*sef*-a-lō-*mī*-e-lō-ra-*dik*-ū-LĪ-tis)	inflammation of the brain, spinal cord, and nerve roots
gangliitis . . . . (*gang*-glē-Ī-tis)	inflammation of the ganglion
meningitis . . . . (*men*-in-JĪ-tis)	inflammation of the meninges
meningocele . . . . (me-NING-gō-sēl)	protrusion of the meninges (through a defect in the skull or vertebral column)
meningomyelocele . . . . (me-*ning*-gō-MĪ-e-lō-*sēl*)	protrusion of the meninges and spinal cord (through the vertebral column) (Exercise Figure C)
neuralgia . . . . (nū-RAL-jē-a)	pain in a nerve
neuroarthropathy . . . . (*nūr*-ō-ar-THROP-a-thē)	disease of nerves and joints
neurasthenia . . . . (*nū*-ras-THĒ-nē-a)	nerve weakness (nervous exhaustion, fatigue, and weakness)
neuritis . . . . (nū-RĪ-tis)	inflammation of the nerve
neuroblast . . . . (NŪ-rō-blast)	developing nerve cell
neuroma . . . . (nū-RŌ-ma)	tumor made up of nerve (cells)

poliomyelitis . . . .   inflammation of the gray matter of the spinal
  (pō-lē-ō-*mī*-e-LĪ-tis)   cord. (This infectious disease, commonly re-
ferred to as *polio,* is caused by one of three po-
lioviruses.)

polyneuritis . . . .   inflammation of many nerves
  (*pol*-ē-nū-RĪ-tis)

radiculitis . . . .   inflammation of the nerve roots
  (ra-*dik*-ū-LĪ-tis)

rhizomeningomyelitis . . . .   inflammation of the nerve root, meninges, and
  (rī-zō-men-ning-gō-mī-e-LĪ-tis)   spinal cord

subdural hematoma . . . .   blood tumor pertaining to below the dura
  (sub-DŪ-ral) (*hēm*-a-TŌ-ma)   mater (*hematoma,* literally translated, means
blood tumor; however, a hematoma is a tumor-
like mass produced by the collection of blood
in a tissue or cavity)

Practice saying each of these terms aloud. To assist you in pronunciation, obtain the
audiotape designed for use with this text. Learn the definitions and spellings of the
disease and disorder terms by completing exercises 11 and 12.

Exercise 11

Analyze and define the following terms.

1. neuritis _____

2. neuroma _____

3. neuralgia _____

4. neuroarthropathy _____

5. neuroblast _____

6. neurasthenia _____

7. encephalomalacia _____

8. encephalitis _____

9. encephalomyeloradiculitis _____

10. meningitis _____

11. meningocele _____

12. meningomyelocele _____

13. radiculitis _____

14. cerebellitis _____

15. gangliitis _____

16. duritis _____

17. polyneuritis _____

18. poliomyelitis _____

19. cerebral thrombosis _____

20. subdural hematoma _____

21. rhizomeningomyelitis _____

Exercise 12

Build disease and disorder terms for the following definitions using the word parts you have learned.

1. inflammation of the nerve   _____ / _____
                                         WR   S

2. tumor made up of nerve (cells)   _____ / _____
                                              WR   S

3. pain in a nerve   _____ / _____
                             WR   S

4. disease of nerves and joints   _____ / ___ / _____ / ___ / _____
                                      WR   CV   WR   CV   S

5. developing nerve cell   _____ / ___ / _____
                              WR   CV   WR

6. nerve weakness (nervous exhaustion, fatigue, and weakness)   _____ / _____
                   WR   S

7. softening of the brain   _____ / ___ / _____
                               WR   CV   S

8. inflammation of the brain   _____ / _____
                                       WR   S

9. inflammation of the brain,
   spinal cord, and nerve roots   _____ / ___ / _____ / ___ / _____ / ___
                                     WR   CV   WR   CV   WR   S

10. inflammation of the meninges   _____ / _____
                                           WR   S

11. protrusion of the meninges
    (through a defect in the skull
    or vertebral column)   _____ / ___ / _____
                              WR   CV   S

12. protrusion of the meninges
    and spinal cord (through the
    vertebral column)

    ————————————————————
    WR ╱CV╱ WR ╱CV╱ S

13. inflammation of the (spinal)
    nerve roots

    ————————————————————
    WR ╱ S

14. inflammation of the cerebel-
    lum

    ————————————————————
    WR ╱ S

15. inflammation of the ganglion

    ————————————————————
    WR ╱ S

16. inflammation of the dura
    mater

    ————————————————————
    WR ╱ S

17. inflammation of many nerves

    ————————————————————
    P ╱ WR ╱ S

18. inflammation of the gray
    matter of the spinal cord

    ————————————————————
    WR ╱CV╱ WR ╱ S

19. abnormal condition of a clot in
    the cerebrum (pertaining to)

    ——————————   ——————————
    WR ╱ S   WR ╱ S

20. blood tumor pertaining to
    below the dura mater

    ——————————   ——————————
    P ╱ WR╱ S   WR ╱ S

21. inflammation of the nerve
    root, meninges, and spinal
    cord

    ————————————————————
    WR ╱CV╱ WR ╱CV╱ WR ╱ S

Exercise 13

Spell each of the disease and disorder terms. Have someone dictate the terms on pp. 480 and 481 to you, or say the words into a tape recorder; then spell the words from your recording. Think about the word parts before attempting to write the word. Study any words you have spelled incorrectly.

1. _____   7. _____

2. _____   8. _____

3. _____   9. _____

4. _____   10. _____

5. _____   11. _____

6. _____   12. _____

13. _____   18. _____

14. _____   19. _____

15. _____   20. _____

16. _____   21. _____

17. _____

Disease and Disorder Terms

Not Built From Word Parts

Bell's Palsy
is named after Sir Charles Bell, a Scottish physician (1774-1842) who demonstrated sensory function of the fifth cranial nerve and the cause of facial palsy.

Epilepsy
was written about by Hippocrates, in 400 BC, in a book titled **Sacred Disease.** It was believed at one time that epilepsy was a punishment for offending the gods. The Greek **epilepsia** meant **seizure** and is derived from **epi,** meaning **upon,** and **lambaneia,** meaning **to seize.** The term literally means **seized upon** (by the gods).

Hydrocephalus
literally means **water in the head** and is made of the word parts **hydro,** meaning **water** and **cephal,** meaning **head.** The condition was first described around AD 30 in the book **De Medicina.**

Parkinson's Disease
is also called **parkinsonism, paralysis agitans,** and **shaking palsy.** Since Dr. James Parkinson, an English professor, described the disease in 1817 in his **Essay on the Shaking Palsy,** it has often been referred to as **Parkinson's disease.**

Term	Definition
Alzheimer's disease (AD) (AHLTS-*hī*-merz)	disease characterized by early senility, confusion, loss of recognition of persons or familiar surroundings, and restlessness
amyotrophic lateral sclerosis (ALS) (a-mī-ō-TROF-ik) (LAT-er-al) (skle-RŌ-sis)	progressive muscle atrophy caused by hardening of nerve tissue on the lateral columns of the spinal cord. Also called *Lou Gehrig disease*
Bell's palsy (belz)	paralysis of muscles on one side of the face, usually a temporary condition. Symptoms include a sagging mouth on the affected side and nonclosure of the eyelid (Figure 15-4).
cerebral aneurysm (se-RĒ-bral) (AN-ū-rizm)	aneurysm in the cerebrum (see aneurysm, p. 282)
cerebral palsy (CP) (se-RĒ-bral) (PAWL-zē)	condition characterized by lack of muscle control and partial paralysis, caused by a brain defect or lesion present at birth or shortly after
cerebrovascular accident (CVA) (se-rē-brō-VAS-kū-lar)	interruption of blood supply to the brain caused by a cerebral thrombosis, cerebral embolism, or cerebral hemorrhage. The patient may experience mild to severe paralysis. Also called *stroke,* or *brain attack* (Figure 15-5)
epilepsy (EP-i-lep-sē)	disorder in which the main symptom is recurring seizures
hydrocephalus (*hī*-drō-SEF-a-lus)	increased amount of cerebrospinal fluid in the ventricles of the brain, which causes enlargement of the cranium
multiple sclerosis (MS) (skle-RŌ-sis)	degenerative disease characterized by sclerotic patches along the brain and spinal cord
neurosis (nū-RŌ-sis)	emotional disorder that involves an ineffective way of coping with anxiety or inner conflict
Parkinson's disease	chronic degenerative disease of the central nervous system. Symptoms include muscular tremors, rigidity, expressionless face, and shuffling gait. It usually occurs after the age of 50 years.

psychosis . . . .
(sī-KŌ-sis)

major mental disorder characterized by extreme derangement, often with delusions and hallucinations

Reye's syndrome . . . .
(RĪZ)

disease of the brain and other organs such as the liver. Affects children and adolescents. The cause is unknown, but it typically follows a viral infection.

sciatica . . . .
(sī-AT-i-ka)

inflammation of the sciatic nerve, causing pain that travels from the thigh through the leg to the foot and toes

shingles . . . .

viral disease that affects the peripheral nerves and causes blisters on the skin that follow the course of the affected nerves. Also called *herpes zoster*

transient ischemic attack (TIA) . .
(is-KĒM-ik)

sudden deficient supply of blood to the brain lasting a short time (see coronary ischemia, p. 277)

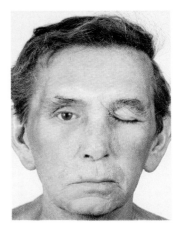

Fig. 15-4
Bell's palsy.

Cerebrovascular accident is the most common disease of the nervous system. It is the third-highest cause of death in the United States, claiming 200,000 lives every year.

Practice saying each of these terms aloud. To assist you in pronunciation, obtain the audiotape designed for use with this text. Learn the definitions and spellings of the disease and disorder terms by completing exercises 14, 15, and 16.

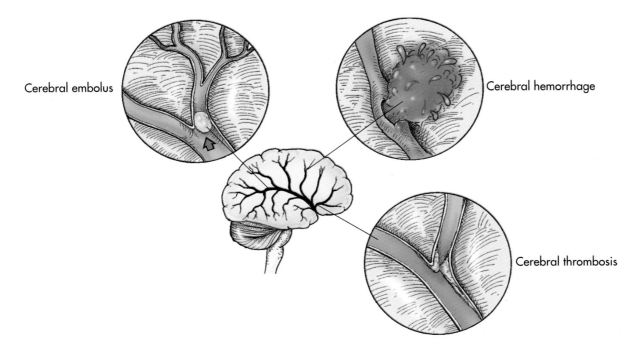

Cerebral embolus

Cerebral hemorrhage

Cerebral thrombosis

Fig. 15-5
Cerebrovascular accident, which may be caused by a cerebral embolism, a cerebral thrombosis, or a cerebral hemorrhage.

Exercise 14 ....

Many of the disease and disorder terms include word parts you have studied in this chapter or previous chapters. To become familiar with the terms, write the definition of the italicized word part in each of the following.

1. *cerebro*vascular accident _____

2. *psych*osis _____

3. *epi*lepsy _____

4. multiple *sclerosis* _____

5. hydro*cephalus* _____

6. *neur*osis _____

7. *cerebral* palsy _____

Exercise 15 ....

Match the diseases in the first column with the corresponding symptoms in the second column.

_____ 1. psychosis

_____ 2. sciatica

_____ 3. transient ischemic attack

_____ 4. Parkinson's disease

_____ 5. cerebral palsy

_____ 6. hydrocephalus

_____ 7. neurosis

_____ 8. cerebrovascular accident

_____ 9. Alzheimer's disease

_____ 10. Reye's syndrome

_____ 11. epilepsy

_____ 12. multiple sclerosis

_____ 13. shingles

_____ 14. amyotrophic lateral sclerosis

_____ 15. Bell's palsy

_____ 16. cerebral aneurysm

a. causes pain from the thigh to the toes

b. derangement, possibly including delusions and hallucinations

c. paralysis of muscles on one side of the face

d. hardened patches scattered along the brain and spinal cord

e. inability to cope with anxiety or inner conflict

f. aneurysm in the cerebrum

g. mild to severe paralysis

h. blisters on the skin

i. early senility

j. muscle tremors and rigidity

k. inflammation of the spinal cord

l. lack of muscle control

m. affects children and adolescents, typically following viral infections

n. deficient supply of blood to the brain

o. also called Lou Gehrig disease

p. enlargement of the cranium

q. recurring seizures

Exercise 16 ....

Spell the disease and disorder terms. Have someone dictate the terms on pp. 484-485 to you, or say the words into a tape recorder; then spell the words from your recording. Study any words you have spelled incorrectly.

1. _____   9. _____
2. _____   10. _____
3. _____   11. _____
4. _____   12. _____
5. _____   13. _____
6. _____   14. _____
7. _____   15. _____
8. _____   16. _____

Surgical Terms

Built From Word Parts

Term	Definition
ganglionectomy . . . . (*gang*-glē-on-EK-tō-mē)	excision of a ganglion (also called *gangliectomy*)
neurectomy . . . . (nū-REK-tō-mē)	excision of a nerve
neurolysis . . . . (nū-ROL-i-sis)	separating a nerve (from adhesions)
neuroplasty . . . . (NŪ-rō-plas-tē)	surgical repair of a nerve
neurorrhaphy . . . . (nū-RŌR-a-fē)	suture of a nerve
neurotomy . . . . (nū-ROT-ō-mē)	incision into a nerve
radicotomy, rhizotomy . . . . (*rad*-i-KOT-ō-mē) (rī-ZOT-ō-mē)	incision into a nerve root (Exercise Figure D)

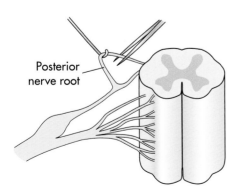

Posterior
nerve root

Exercise Fig. D
Fill in the blanks to complete the dia-

gram. $\dfrac{\text{NERVE ROOT}}{}$ / INCISION after laminectomy. Posterior nerve root identified for incision.

Practice saying each of these terms aloud. To assist you in pronunciation, obtain the audiotape designed for use with this text. Learn the definitions and spellings of the surgical terms by completing exercises 17, 18, and 19.

Exercise 17 ....

Analyze and define the following surgical terms.

1. radicotomy _____

2. neurectomy _____

3. neurorrhaphy _____

4. ganglionectomy _____

5. neurotomy _____

6. neurolysis _____

7. neuroplasty _____

8. rhizotomy _____

Exercise 18 ....

Build surgical terms for the following definitions by using the word parts you have learned.

1. incision into a nerve root   a. _____ / _____
                                            WR   S

                                 b. _____ / _____
                                            WR   S

2. excision of a nerve   _____ / _____
                                            WR   S

3. suture of a nerve   _____ / _____
                                            WR   S

4. excision of a ganglion   _____ / _____
                                            WR   S

5. incision into a nerve   _____ / _____
                                            WR   S

6. separating a nerve (from adhe-
   sions)   _____ / ____ / _____
                                       WR   CV   S

7. surgical repair of a nerve   _____ / ____ / _____
                                       WR   CV   S

Exercise 19 ....

Spell each of the surgical terms. Have someone dictate the terms on p. 487 to you, or say the words into a tape recorder; then spell the words from your recording. Think about the word parts before attempting to write the word. Study any words you have spelled incorrectly.

1. _____   5. _____

2. _____   6. _____

3. _____   7. _____

4. _____   8. _____

▌Procedural Terms
Built From Word Parts

Term   Definition
Diagnostic Imaging

cerebral angiography . . . .   x-ray filming of the blood vessels in the brain
 (se-RĒ-bral) (an-jē-OG-ra-fē)   (after an injection of contrast medium)

myelogram . . . .   x-ray film of the spinal cord (after an injection
 (MĪ-e-lō-gram)   of dye into the spinal fluid that surrounds the
                                            spinal cord) (Exercise Figure E)

Neurodiagnostic Procedures

**echoencephalography
(EchoEG)** . . . .   process of recording the brain (structures) by
 (*ek*-ō-en-*sef*-a-LOG-ra-fē)   use of sound (also called *ultrasonography*)

electroencephalogram (EEG) . . . .   record of the electrical impulses of the brain
 (e-*lek*-trō-en-SEF-a-lō-gram)

electroencephalograph . . . .   instrument used to record the electrical im-
 (e-*lek*-trō-en-SEF-a-lō-graf)   pulses of the brain

electroencephalography . . . .   process of recording the electrical impulses of
 (e-*lek*-trō-en-*sef*-a-LOG-ra-fē)   the brain

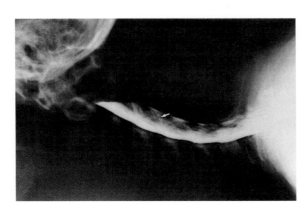

Exercise Fig. E

$$\overline{}\ /\ \overline{}\ /$$
SPINAL CORD / CV /

X-RAY FILM. **Prone, lateral view shows posterior nerve roots.**

Practice saying each of these words aloud. To assist you in pronunciation, obtain the audiotape designed for use with this text. Learn the definitions and spellings of the procedural terms by completing exercises 20, 21 and 22.

Exercise 20 ....

Analyze and define the following procedural terms.

1. electroencephalogram _____

2. electroencephalograph _____

3. electroencephalography _____

4. echoencephalography _____

5. myelogram _____

6. cerebral angiography _____

Exercise 21 ....

Build procedural terms that correspond to the following definitions by using the word parts you have learned.

1. process of recording brain (structures) by use of sound

   _____ / __ / _____ / __ / __
   WR / CV / WR / CV / S

2. record of the electrical impulses of the brain

   _____ / __ / _____ / __ / __
   WR / CV / WR / CV / S

3. instrument used for recording the electrical impulses of the brain

   _____ / __ / _____ / __ / __
   WR / CV / WR / CV / S

4. process of recording the electrical impulses of the brain

   _____ / __ / _____ / __ / __
   WR / CV / WR / CV / S

5. x-ray film of the spinal cord

   _____ / __ / __
   WR / CV / S

6. x-ray filming of the blood vessels in the brain

   _____ / __   _____ / __ / __
   WR / S   WR / CV / S

Exercise 22 ....

Spell each of the procedural terms. Have someone dictate the terms on p. 489 to you, or say the words into a tape recorder; then spell the words from your recording. Think about the word parts before attempting to write the word. Study any words you have spelled incorrectly.

1. _____   4. _____

2. _____   5. _____

3. _____   6. _____

Procedural Terms
Not Built From Word Parts

Term	Definition
Diagnostic Imaging	
computed tomography of the brain (CT scan) . . . . (tō-MOG-ra-fē)	process that includes the use of a computer to produce a series of images of the tissues of the brain at any desired depth. The procedure is noninvasive, painless, and particularly useful in diagnosing brain tumors (Figures 15-6 and 15-7).
magnetic resonance imaging of the brain (MRI) . . . . (mag-NET-ik) (re-zo-NANCE) (IM-a-jing)	a noninvasive technique that produces cross-sectional and vertical images of soft tissues of the brain by use of magnetic waves. Unlike CT scan, MRI produces images without use of radiation or contrast medium. It is used to visualize tumors, edema, and multiple sclerosis (Figure 15-8).

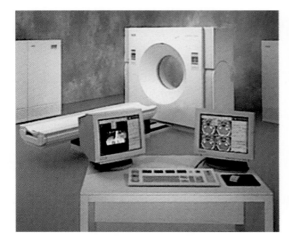

Fig. 15-6
CT scanner.

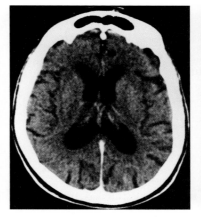

Fig. 15-7
CT scan of the brain shows enlargement of ventricular system.

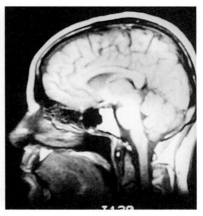

Fig. 15-8
Sagittal MRI section through the brain.

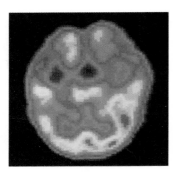

Fig. 15-9
Positron emission tomography (PET) scan.

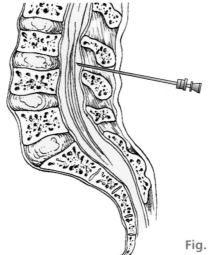

Fig. 15-10
Lumbar puncture with needle in place.

**positron emission tomography
of the brain (PET scan)** . . . .
   (POS-i-tron) (e-MI-shun)
   (tō-MOG-ra-fē)

a new technique that permits viewing of a slice of the brain and gives information about brain function such as blood flow. The patient is injected with radioactive material. A special camera records the radioactive decay within the brain. The information is transmitted to a computer which projects images onto a television screen (Figure 15-9).

Neurodiagnostic Procedures

**evoked potential studies
(EP studies)** . . . .

a group of diagnostic tests that measure changes and responses in brain waves elicited by visual, auditory, or somatosensory stimuli. Visual evoked response (VER) is a response to visual stimuli. Auditory evoked response (AER) is a response to auditory stimuli.

Additional Procedural Terms

lumbar puncture (LP) . . . .

insertion of a needle into the subarachnoid space between the third and fourth lumbar vertebrae. It is performed for many reasons, including the removal of cerebrospinal fluid for diagnostic purposes (Figure 15-10).

The first full-scale CT unit for head scanning was installed in a hospital in Wimbledon, United Kingdom in 1971. Its ability to provide neurological diagnostic information gained rapid recognition. The first units in the United States were used in 1973. The first scanner for visualizing sections of the body other than the brain was developed in 1974 by Dr. Robert Ledly at Georgetown University Medical Center.

A magnetic resonance imaging scanner was first used in the United States in 1981. The scanner was developed in England and installed there in 1975.

Stereotactic radiosurgery is used for patients with inoperable tumors or arteriovenous malformations (AVMs). A special frame is mounted on the patient's head. A computer-guided grid system produces a three-dimensional image of the brain. A high-powered computer designs a plan for high-intensity radiation that matches the exact size and shape of the tumor. Radiation is then delivered directly to the tumor only, sparing surrounding tissue.

Exercise 23

Fill in the blanks with the correct terms.

1. A computer is used to produce images during _____ _____ of the brain.

2. A needle is inserted into the subarachnoid space during a (n) _____ _____ .

3. Produces images reflecting brain function: _____ _____ _____ of the brain.

4. Uses magnetic waves to produce images: _____ _____ _____ of the brain.

5. Measures responses in brain waves from stimuli: _____ _____ _____ .

Exercise 24

Write the definitions of the following terms.

1. lumbar puncture _____

2. computed tomography of the brain _____

3. magnetic resonance imaging _____

4. positron emission tomography of the brain _____

5. evoked potential studies _____

Exercise 25

Spell each of the procedural terms. Have someone dictate the terms on pp. 491-492 to you, or say the words into a tape recorder; then spell the words from your recording. Study any words you have spelled incorrectly.

1. _____   4. _____

2. _____   5. _____

3. _____

▌Complementary Terms

Built From Word Parts

Term	Definition
anesthesia (*an*-es-THĒ-zē-a)	without (loss of) feeling or sensation
aphasia (a-FĀ-zē-a)	condition of without speaking (loss or impairment of the ability to speak)
cephalalgia (*sef*-el-AL-jē-a)	pain in the head (headache)
cerebral (se-RĒ-bral)	pertaining to the cerebrum
craniocerebral (*krā*-nē-ō-sar-Ē-bral)	pertaining to the cranium and cerebrum
dysphasia (dis-FĀ-zē-a)	condition of difficulty speaking
encephalosclerosis (en-*sef*-a-lō-skle-RŌ-sis)	hardening of the brain
hemiparesis (*hem*-i-pa-RĒ-sis)	slight paralysis of half (right or left side of the body)
hemiplegia (*hem*-i-PLĒ-jē-a)	paralysis of half (right or left side) of the body; cerebrovascular accident is the most common cause of hemiplegia (Exercise Figure F)
hyperesthesia (hī-per-es-THĒ-zē-a)	excessive sensitivity (to stimuli)
interictal (in-ter-IK-tal)	(occurring) between seizures or attacks
monoparesis (mon-ō-pa-RĒ-sis)	slight paralysis of one (limb)
monoplegia (*mon*-ō-PLĒ-jē-a)	paralysis of one (limb)
myelomalacia (*mī*-e-lō-ma-LĀ-shē-a)	softening of the spinal cord
neuroid (NŪ-royd)	resembling a nerve
neurologist (nū-ROL-ō-jist)	physician who specializes in neurology
neurology (nū-ROL-ō-jē)	branch of medicine dealing with the nervous system's function and disorders
panplegia (pan-PLĒ-jē-a)	total paralysis (also spelled *pamplegia*)
phrenic (FREN-ik)	pertaining to the mind
phrenopathy (fre-NOP-a-thē)	disease of the mind
postictal (pōst-IK-tal)	(occurring) after a seizure or attack

preictal . . . . (prē-IK-tal)	(occurring) before a seizure or attack
psychiatrist . . . . (sī-KĪ-a-trist)	a physician who treats mental disorders
psychiatry . . . . (sī-KĪ-a-trē)	branch of medicine that deals with the treatment of mental disorders
psychogenic . . . . (sī-kō-JEN-ik)	originating in the mind
psychologist . . . . (sī-KOL-ō-jist)	specialist in the study of psychology
psychology . . . . (sī-KOL-ō-jē)	study of the mind (mental processes and behavior)
psychopathy . . . . (sī-KOP-a-thē)	(any) disease of the mind
psychosomatic . . . . (*sī*-kō-sō-MAT-ik)	pertaining to the mind and body (interrelations of)
quadriplegia . . . . (*kwod*-ri-PLĒ-jē-a)	paralysis of four (limbs) (Exercise Figure F)
subdural . . . . (sub-DŪ-ral)	pertaining to below the dura mater
tetraplegia . . . . (*te*-tra-PLĒ-jē-a)	paralysis of four (limbs) (synonymous with *quadriplegia*) (Exercise Figure F)

Practice saying each of these terms aloud. To assist you in pronunciation, obtain the audiotape designed for use with this text. Exercises 26, 27, and 28 will help you learn the definitions and spellings of the complementary terms related to the nervous system.

Exercise 26

Analyze and define the following complementary terms.

1. hemiplegia _____

2. tetraplegia _____

3. neurologist _____

4. neurology _____

5. neuroid _____

6. quadriplegia _____

7. cerebral _____

8. monoplegia _____

9. aphasia _____

10. dysphasia _____

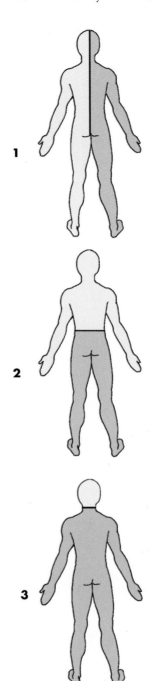

Exercise Fig. F

Fill in the blanks to label this diagram of types of paralysis.

_____ / _____
1, HALF / PARALYSIS.

2, Paraplegia.

_____ / _____
3, FOUR / PARALYSIS **or**

_____ / _____
FOUR / PARALYSIS.

11. hemiparesis _____

12. anesthesia _____

13. hyperesthesia _____

14. subdural _____

15. cephalalgia _____

16. psychosomatic _____

17. psychopathy _____

18. psychology _____

19. psychiatry _____

20. psychologist _____

21. psychogenic _____

22. phrenic _____

23. phrenopathy _____

24. craniocerebral _____

25. myelomalacia _____

26. encephalosclerosis _____

27. postictal _____

28. panplegia _____

29. interictal _____

30. monoparesis _____

31. preictal _____

32. psychiatrist _____

Exercise 27

Build the complementary terms for the following definitions by using the word parts you have learned.

1. slight paralysis of half (right or
   left side of the body)

   _____ / _____

   P   S(WR)

2. without (loss of) feeling or
   sensation

   _____ / _____ / _____

   P   WR   S

3. excessive sensitivity (to stimuli)

_____ / _____ / ____
P   WR   S

4. below the dura mater

_____ / _____ / ____
P   WR   S

5. pain in the head (headache)

_____ / ____
WR   S

6. pertaining to the mind and body (interrelations of)

_____ / __ / _____ / ____
WR   CV   WR   S

7. (any) disease of the mind

_____ / __ / ____
WR   CV   S

8. study of the mind

_____ / ____
WR   S

9. branch of medicine that deals with the treatment of mental disorders

_____ / ____
WR   S

10. specialist in the study of psychology

_____ / ____
WR   S

11. originating in the mind

_____ / __ / ____
WR   CV   S

12. pertaining to the mind

_____ / ____
WR   S

13. disease of the mind

_____ / __ / ____
WR   CV   S

14. pertaining to the cranium and cerebrum

_____ / __ / _____ / ____
WR   CV   WR   S

15. softening of the spinal cord

_____ / __ / ____
WR   CV   S

16. hardening of the brain

_____ / __ / ____
WR   CV   S

17. paralysis of half (left or right side) of the body

_____ / _____
P   S(WR)

18. paralysis of four (limbs)

_____ / _____
P   S(WR)

19. physician who specializes in neurology

_____ / ____
WR   S

20. branch of medicine dealing with the nervous system's function and disorders

_____ / ____
WR   S

21. resembling a nerve

_____
WR / S

22. paralysis of four (limbs)

_____
WR /CV/ S

23. pertaining to the cerebrum

_____
WR / S

24. paralysis of one (limb)

_____
WR /CV/ S

25. condition of without speaking
(loss or impairment of the
ability to speak)

_____
P / WR / S

26. condition of difficulty speaking

_____
P / WR / S

27. (occurring) before a seizure or
attack

_____
P /S(WR)

28. slight paralysis of one (limb)

_____
WR /CV/ S

29. (occurring) after a seizure

_____
P /S(WR)

30. total paralysis

_____
P /S(WR)

31. (occurring) between seizures
or attacks

_____
P /S(WR)

32. a physician who treats mental
disorders

_____
WR / S

Exercise 28

Spell each of the complementary terms. Have someone dictate the terms on pp. 494-495 to you, or say the words into a tape recorder; then spell the words from your recording. Think about the word parts before attempting to write the word. Study any words you have spelled incorrectly.

1. _____   7. _____

2. _____   8. _____

3. _____   9. _____

4. _____   10. _____

5. _____   11. _____

6. _____   12. _____

13. _____   23. _____
14. _____   24. _____
15. _____   25. _____
16. _____   26. _____
17. _____   27. _____
18. _____   28. _____
19. _____   29. _____
20. _____   30. _____
21. _____   31. _____
22. _____   32. _____

Complementary Terms
Not Built From Word Parts

Term	Definition
afferent (AF-er-ent)	conveying toward a center (for example, afferent nerves carry impulses to the central nervous system)
ataxia (a-TAK-sē-a)	lack of muscle coordination
cognitive (COG-ni-tiv)	pertaining to the mental processes of comprehension, judgment, memory, and reason
coma (KŌ-ma)	state of profound unconsciousness
concussion (kon-KUSH-un)	jarring or shaking that results in an injury. Brain concussions are caused by slight or severe head injury; symptoms include vertigo and loss of consciousness.
conscious (KON-shus)	awake, alert, aware of one's surroundings
convulsion (kun-VUL-zhun)	sudden, involuntary contraction of a group of muscles
dementia (de-MEN-shē-a)	mental decline
disorientation (dis-ō-rē-en-TĀ-shun)	a state of mental confusion as to time, place, or identity
efferent (EF-er-ent)	conveying away from the center (for example, efferent nerves carry information away from the central nervous system)
gait (gāt)	a manner or style of walking
incoherent (in-kō-HĒR-ent)	unable to express one's thoughts or ideas in an orderly, intelligible manner

Paraplegia

is composed of the Greek **para,** meaning **beside,** and **plegia,** meaning **paralysis.** It has been used since Hippocrates' time and at first meant paralysis of any limb or side of the body. Since the nineteenth century, it has been used to mean paralysis from the waist down.

paraplegia . . . .   paralysis from the waist down caused by dam-
(*par*-a-PLĒ-jē-a)   age to the lower level of the spinal cord

seizure . . . .   sudden attack with an involuntary series of
(SĒ-zher)   contractions (synonymous with convulsion)

shunt . . . .   tube implanted in the body to redirect the flow
                                                  of a fluid

syncope . . . .   fainting or sudden loss of consciousness caused
(SIN-cō-pē)   by lack of blood supply to the cerebrum

unconsciousness . . . .   state of being unaware of surroundings and in-
(un-KON-shus-nes)   capable of responding to stimuli as a result of
                                                  injury, shock, or illness

Practice saying each of these terms aloud. To assist you in pronunciation, obtain the audiotape designed for use with this text. Learn the definitions and spellings of the complementary terms by completing exercises 29, 30, and 31.

Exercise 29

Write the term for each of the following definitions.

1. jarring or shaking that   _____
   results in an injury

2. state of being unaware of   _____
   surroundings and incapable
   of responding to stimuli as a
   result of injury, shock, or
   illness

3. awake, alert, aware of one's   _____
   surroundings

4. sudden attack with involun-   _____
   tary contractions

5. sudden, involuntary contrac-   _____
   tion of a group of muscles

6. tube implanted in the body to   _____
   redirect the flow of a fluid

7. paralysis from the waist down   _____
   caused by damage to the
   lower level of the spinal cord

8. state of profound unconscious-   _____
   ness

9. fainting   _____

10. lack of muscle coordination   _____

11. a manner or style of walking _____

12. mental decline _____

13. unable to express one's thoughts or ideas in an orderly, intelligible manner _____

14. a state of mental confusion as to time, place, or identity _____

15. pertaining to the mental processes of comprehension, judgment, memory, and reason _____

16. conveying toward the center _____

17. conveying away from the center _____

Exercise 30 ....

Write the definitions for the following terms.

1. shunt _____

2. paraplegia _____

3. coma _____

4. concussion _____

5. unconsciousness _____

6. conscious _____

7. seizure _____

8. convulsion _____

9. syncope _____

10. ataxia _____

11. dementia _____

12. gait _____

13. cognitive _____

14. disorientation _____

15. incoherent _____

16. efferent _____

17. afferent _____

Exercise 31

Spell each of the complementary terms. Have someone dictate the terms on pp. 499-500 to you, or say the words into a tape recorder; then spell the words from your recording. Study any words you have spelled incorrectly.

1. _____   10. _____

2. _____   11. _____

3. _____   12. _____

4. _____   13. _____

5. _____   14. _____

6. _____   15. _____

7. _____   16. _____

8. _____   17. _____

9. _____

Abbreviations

AD	Alzheimer's disease
AER	auditory evoked response
ALS	amyotrophic lateral sclerosis
AZM	artereovenous malformation
CNS	central nervous system
CSF	cerebrospinal fluid
CP	cerebral palsy
CVA	cerebrovascular accident
EchoEG	echoencephalography
EEG	electroencephalogram
EP studies	evoked potential studies
LP	lumbar puncture
MRI	magnetic resonance imaging
MS	multiple sclerosis
PET scan	positron emission tomography
PNS	peripheral nervous system
TIA	transient ischemic attack
VER	visual evoked response

CHAPTER REVIEW

Exercises

Exercise 32

Complete the hospital report by writing the medical terms in the blanks. Use the list of definitions with the corresponding numbers.

Case History: An 85-year-old white man was admitted to the hospital because of fever and confusion. He was in his usual state of good health until 3 days before admission, when he began to show signs of confusion and 1. _____ accompanied by a fever of 38.5° C. His fever continued, and he showed a steady decline in 2. _____ function. He developed expressive 3. _____ . On physical examination the patient was 4. _____ and alert but disoriented to time and place. Blood pressure was 160/80 mmHg, pulse 96, respiration 20, temperature 38.8° C. There were no focal neurological deficits. Chest x-ray examination, urinalysis, and blood cultures were negative. A(n) 5. _____ consultation was obtained. 6. _____ _____ _____ of the brain was performed, which disclosed inflammatory changes in the left temporal lobe, consistent with herpes simplex 7. _____ . A(n) 8. _____ was markedly abnormal for his age. The patient was given acyclovir intravenous infusion. On the second hospital day, the patient developed a generalized 9. _____ . He was placed on intravenous Dilantin and lorazepam. He later lapsed into a semicomatose state. He responded to tactile and verbal stimuli but was completely 10. _____ . A nasogastric tube was placed, and enteral feedings were begun. Following 14 days of IV acyclovir, the patient slowly began to improve, and by the third week of his illness, he was talking normally and taking nourishment. He is expected to make a complete recovery.

1. a state of mental confusion as to time, place, or identity
2. pertaining to the mental processes of comprehension, judgment, memory, and reason
3. loss of the ability to speak
4. awake, alert, and aware of one's surroundings
5. branch of medicine dealing with the nervous system
6. noninvasive technique that produces cross-sectional and vertical images of the brain by magnetic waves
7. inflammation of the brain
8. record of electrical impulses of the brain
9. sudden attack with involuntary series of contractions
10. unable to express one's thoughts or ideas in an orderly, intelligible manner

Exercise 33

To test your understanding of the terms introduced in this chapter, circle the words that correctly complete the sentences. The italicized words refer to the correct answer.

1. *Tetraplegia* is synonymous with (paraplegia, monoplegia, hemiplegia, quadriplegia).

2. The *inability to speak* or (aphagia, aphasia, dysphasia, dysphagia) may be an after-effect of cerebrovascular accident.

3. A symptom of brain concussion is vertigo, or dizziness, and may cause a patient to be *unaware of his or her surroundings* and *unable to respond to stimuli,* that is, to be (subconscious, unconscious, convulsive).

4. The newborn had *meninges protruding through a defect in his skull,* or a (meningocele, myelomeningocele, myelomalacia).

5. *The branch of medicine that deals with the treatment of mental disorders* is (neurology, psychology, psychiatry).

6. *Multiple sclerosis* is a common disease of the nervous system and generally occurs in young adults. It is characterized by (seizures, hardened patches along the brain and spinal cord, muscular tremors).

7. *The recording of electrical impulses of the brain,* or (echoencephalogram, electroencephalogram, electroencephalograph, electroencephalography), is used to study brain function and is valuable for diagnosing epilepsy, tumors, and other brain diseases.

8. Cerebral *thrombosis,* or (blood clot, infection, hardened patches), may cause a stroke.

9. The patient was admitted to the neurology unit of the hospital with a diagnosis of cerebrovascular accident. The physician ordered *a diagnostic procedure that would give information about brain function* or (computed tomography, positron emission tomography, magnetic resonance imaging).

Exercise 34

Unscramble the following mixed-up terms. The word on the left indicates the organs affected by the disease process named by the scrambled word.

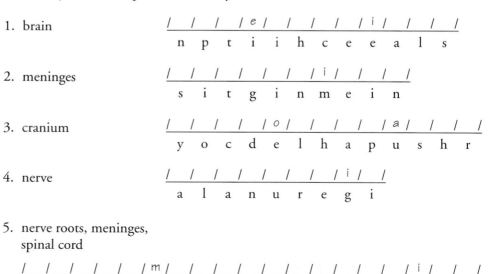

1. brain

/ / / / e / / / / / i / / / /
n p t i i h c e e a l s

2. meninges

/ / / / / / / i / / / /
s i t g i n m e i n

3. cranium

/ / / / o / / / / a / / / /
y o c d e l h a p u s h r

4. nerve

/ / / / / / / i / /
a l a n u r e g i

5. nerve roots, meninges, spinal cord

/ / / / / m / / / / / / / / / / i / / /
l n i n i t i s i y m e m h r z o g o e

Exercise 35

The following definitions are of medical terms that did not appear in this chapter or previous chapters; but they are made up of word parts you have studied. Test your knowledge by building the term to match the definition.

1. paralysis of one muscle

   _____

2. many pregnancies (the word has an *-is* suffix)

   _____

3. inflammation of many carti-lages of the body

   _____

4. disease of the gray matter of the spinal cord

   _____

5. surgical removal of the colon and rectum

   _____

6. suture of the muscle

   _____

7. excision of half of the colon

   _____

8. excision of the ovaries and uterus

   _____

Combining Forms Crossword Puzzle

Across Clues

2. mind
4. cerebellum
6. abbreviation for diabetes insipidus
7. abbreviation for undetermined origin
8. brain
13. nerve root
14. mind
15. ganglion
16. speech

Down Clues

1. four
2. spinal cord
3. gray matter
5. sensation
6. dura mater
9. cerebrum
10. meninges
11. one
12. mind

Review of Terms

Can you build, analyze, define, pronounce, and spell the following terms *built from word parts?*

Diseases and Disorders

cerebellitis

cerebral thrombosis

duritis

encephalitis

encephalomalacia

encephalomyeloradiculitis

gangliitis

meningitis

meningocele

meningomyelocele

neuralgia

neuroarthropathy

neurasthenia

neuritis

neuroblast

neuroma

poliomyelitis

polyneuritis

radiculitis

rhizomeningomyelitis

subdural hematoma

Surgical

ganglionectomy

neurectomy

neurolysis

neuroplasty

neurorrhaphy

neurotomy

radicotomy

rhizotomy

Procedural

cerebral angiography

echoencephalography
  (EchoEG)

electroencephalogram (EEG)

electroencephalograph

electroencephalography

myelogram

Complementary

anesthesia

aphasia

cephalalgia

cerebral

craniocerebral

dysphasia

encephalosclerosis

hemiparesis

hemiplegia

hyperesthesia

interictal

monoparesis

monoplegia

myelomalacia

neuroid

neurologist

neurology

panplegia

phrenic

phrenopathy

postictal

preictal

psychiatrist

psychiatry

psychogenic

psychologist

psychology

psychopathy

psychosomatic

quadriplegia

subdural

tetraplegia

Can you define, pronounce, and spell the following terms *not built from word parts?*

Diseases and Disorders

Alzheimer's disease (AD)

amyotrophic lateral sclerosis (ALS)

Bell's palsy

cerebral aneurysm

cerebral palsy (CP)

cerebrovascular accident (CVA)

epilepsy

hydrocephalus

multiple sclerosis (MS)

neurosis

Parkinson's disease

psychosis

Reye's syndrome

sciatica

shingles

transient ischemic attack (TIA)

Procedural

computed tomography of the brain (CT)

evoked potential studies (EP)

lumbar puncture (LP)

magnetic resonance imaging (MRI)

positron emission tomography of the brain (PET)

Complementary

afferent

ataxia

cognitive

coma

concussion

conscious

convulsion

dementia

disorientation

efferent

gait

incoherent

paraplegia

seizure

shunt

syncope

unconsciousness

Endocrine System

Objectives .... **Upon completion of this chapter you will be able to:**
1. Identify the organs and other structures of the endocrine system.
2. Define and spell the word parts presented in this chapter.
3. Build and analyze medical terms using word parts.
4. Define, pronounce, and spell the disease and disorder, procedural, surgical, and complementary terms for the endocrine system.

ANATOMY

The endocrine system is composed of a series of glands located in various parts of the body (Figure 16-1). These glands are called *ductless glands,* because they have no ducts or tubes to carry the secretions they produce to other body parts. Their secretions, called *hormones,* are secreted directly into the blood. Only those terms related to the major endocrine glands—pituitary, thyroid, parathyroid, adrenals, and the islets of Langerhans in the pancreas—are presented in this chapter. The thymus and the male and female sex glands were discussed in previous chapters.

Endocrine Glands

pituitary gland, hypophysis
   cerebri .... is approximately the size of a pea and is located at the base of the brain. The pituitary is divided into two lobes (Figure 16-2).

   anterior lobe,
   adenohypophysis .... produces and secretes the following hormones:

     growth hormone (GH) ..... regulates the growth of the body

     adrenocorticotropic
     hormone (ACTH) .... stimulates the adrenal cortex

     thyroid-stimulating
     hormone (TSH) .... stimulates the thyroid gland

     gonadotropic hormones .... affect the male and female reproductive systems

       follicle-stimulating hormone
       (FSH), luteinizing
       hormone (LH) .... regulate development, growth, and function of the ovaries and testes

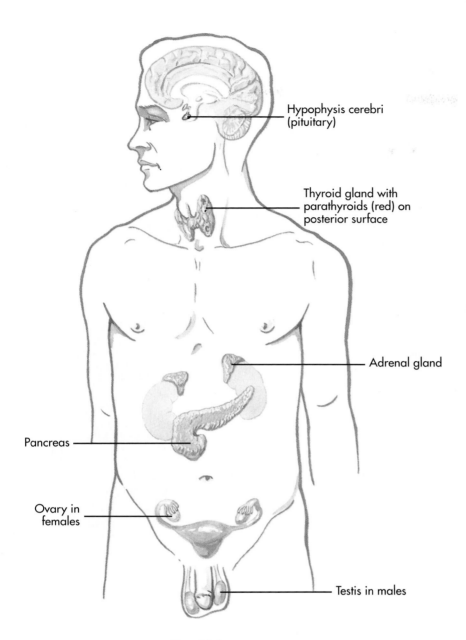

Fig. 16-1
The endocrine system.

prolactin or lactogenic hormone (PRL) . . . .   promotes development of glandular tissue during pregnancy and produces milk after birth of an infant

posterior lobe, neurohypophysis . . . .   stores and releases the following hormones:

antidiuretic hormone (ADH) . . . .   stimulates the kidney to reabsorb water

oxytocin . . . .   stimulates uterine contractions during labor and postpartum

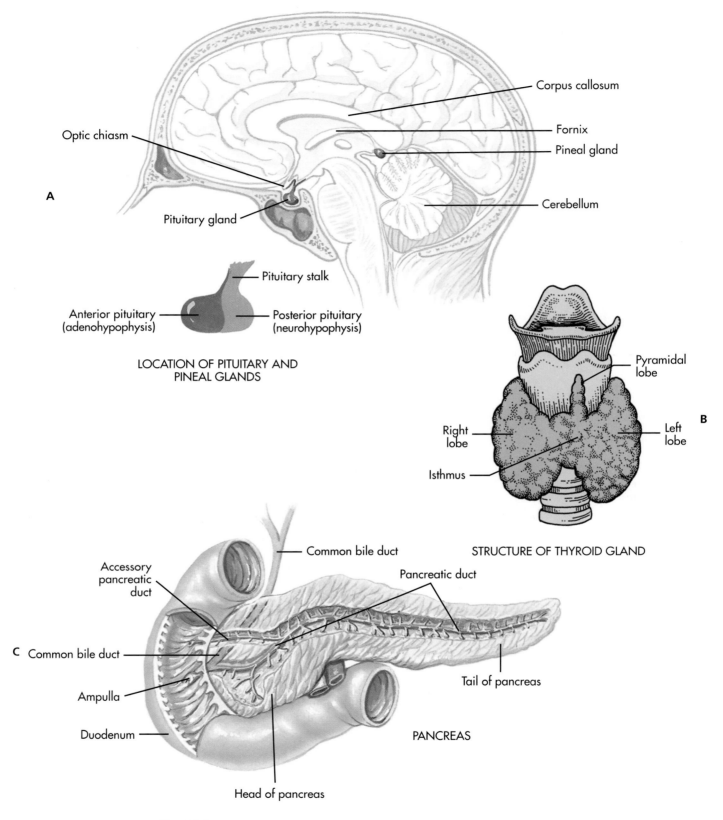

Fig. 16-2
A, Pituitary and pineal glands. **B,** Thyroid gland. **C,** Pancreatic gland.

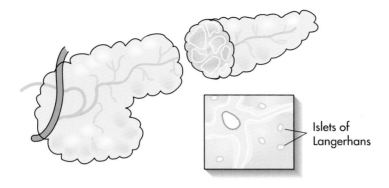

Fig. 16-3
Pancreas, with islets of Langerhans.

thyroid gland	largest endocrine gland. It is located in the neck in the area of the larynx and comprises bilateral lobes connected by an isthmus (Figure 16-2). The thyroid gland secretes the hormone *thyroxine,* which requires iodine for its production. Thyroxine is necessary for body cell metabolism.
parathyroid glands	four small bodies lying directly behind the thyroid. *Parathormone,* the hormone produced by the glands, helps to maintain the level of calcium in the blood.
islets of Langerhans	cellular clusters found throughout the pancreas that secrete the insulin necessary to control carbohydrate metabolism. Different cells found throughout the pancreas perform nonendocrine functions such as digestion (Figure 16-3).
adrenal glands, suprarenals	located one above each kidney. The outer portion is called the *cortex,* and the inner portion is called the *medulla.* The following hormones are secreted by the adrenal glands:
cortisol	secreted by the cortex. It aids the body during stress and in the metabolism of food.
aldosterone	secreted by the cortex. Electrolytes (mineral salts) that are necessary for normal body function are regulated by this hormone.
epinephrine (adrenaline), and norepinephrine	secreted by the medulla. These hormones help the body to deal with stress by increasing the blood pressure, heartbeat, and respirations.

Learn the anatomical terms by completing exercises 1 and 2.

Exercise 1

Match the terms in the first column with the correct definitions in the second column.

_____ 1. adrenal cortex

_____ 2. adrenal glands

_____ 3. adrenaline

_____ 4. adrenal medulla

_____ 5. adrenocorticotropic hormone

_____ 6. adenohypophysis

_____ 7. aldosterone

a. stimulates the adrenal cortex

b. secretes cortisol and aldosterone

c. anterior lobe of pituitary that secretes growth hormone and thyroid-stimulating hormone

d. another name for epinephrine

e. assists in regulating body electrolytes

f. another name for norepinephrine

g. located above each kidney

h. secretes epinephrine and norepinephrine

Exercise 2

Match the terms in the first column with the correct definitions in the second column.

_____ 1. antidiuretic hormone

_____ 2. islets of Langerhans

_____ 3. neurohypophysis

_____ 4. parathyroid glands

_____ 5. pituitary gland

_____ 6. thyroid gland

a. secrete insulin

b. maintain the blood calcium level

c. located in the neck, secretes thyroxine

d. secreted by posterior lobe of the pituitary

e. stores and releases antidiurectic hormone and oxytocin

f. another name for the anterior lobe of the pituitary

g. located at the base of the brain

WORD PARTS

Combining Forms of the Endocrine System

Study the word parts and their definitions listed below. Completing the exercises that follow will help you learn the terms.

Combining Form	Definition
adren/o, adrenallo	adrenal glands
cortic/o	cortex (the outer layer of a body organ)
endocrin/o	endocrine
parathyroid/o	parathyroid glands
thyroid/o, thyr/o	thyroid glands

Learn the anatomical locations and meanings of the combining forms by completing exercises 3 and 4 and Exercise Figures A and B.

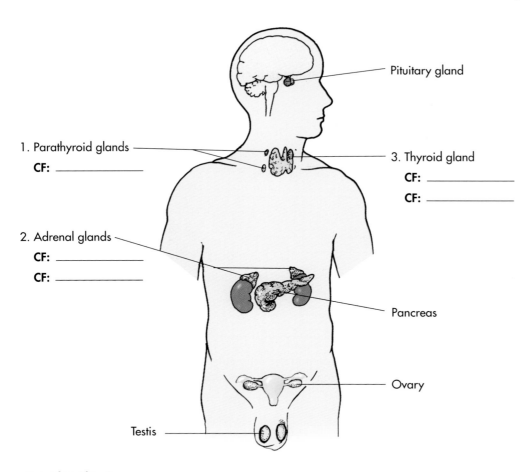

Pituitary gland

1. Parathyroid glands

CF: _____

3. Thyroid gland

CF: _____

CF: _____

2. Adrenal glands

CF: _____

CF: _____

Pancreas

Ovary

Testis

Exercise Fig. A
Fill in the blanks with combining forms in this diagram of endocrine glands in the human body.

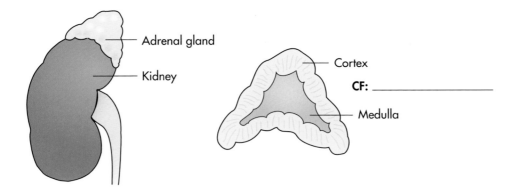

Adrenal gland

Kidney

Cortex

CF: _____

Medulla

Exercise Fig. B
Fill in the blanks with combining forms in this diagram of adrenal glands (with interior view).

Exercise 3

Write the definitions of the following combining forms.

1. cortic/o _____

2. adren/o _____

3. parathyroid/o _____

4. thyroid/o _____

5. adrenal/o _____

6. thyr/o _____

7. endocrin/o _____

Exercise 4

Write the combining form for each of the following terms.

1. adrenal gland   a. _____

                         b. _____

2. thyroid gland   a. _____

                         b. _____

3. endocrine   _____

4. cortex   _____

5. parathyroid gland   _____

Combining Forms Commonly Used With Endocrine System Terms

Combining Form	Definition
acr/o	extremities, height
calc/i . . . . (NOTE: the combining vowel is *i*.)	calcium
dips/o	thirst
kal/i . . . . (NOTE: the combining vowel is *i*.)	potassium
natr/o	sodium
toxic/o	poison

Learn the combining forms by completing exercises 5 and 6.

Exercise 5

Write the definitions of the following combining forms.

1. dips/o _____

2. toxic/o _____

3. kal/i _____

4. calc/i _____

5. acr/o _____

6. natr/o _____

Exercise 6

Write the combining form for each of the following.

1. poison _____

2. extremities, height _____

3. calcium _____

4. thirst _____

5. potassium _____

6. sodium _____

Prefixes and Suffix

Prefixes	Definition
ex-, exo-	outside, outward

Suffix	Definition
-drome	run, running

Learn the prefixes and suffix by completing exercises 7 and 8.

Exercise 7

Write the definitions of the following word parts.

1. ex-, exo- _____

2. -drome _____

Exercise 8 ....

Write the prefix and suffix in the following:

1. run, running   _____

2. outside, outward   a. _____

                                        b. _____

MEDICAL TERMS
....

The terms you need to learn to complete this chapter are listed below. The exercises following each list will help you learn the definition and spelling of each word.

Disease and Disorder Terms
....

Built From Word Parts

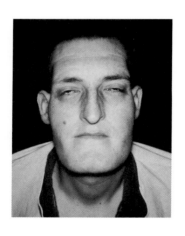

Exercise Fig. C
Fill in the blanks to complete the diagram.

_____ / ___ /
EXTREMITIES / CV /

_____
ENLARGEMENT, a metabolic disorder characterized by marked enlargement of the bones of the face, jaw, and extremities.

Term	Definition
acromegaly . . . . (*ak*-rō-MEG-a-lē)	enlargement of the extremities (and bones of the face caused by excessive production of the growth hormone) (Exercise Figure C)
adrenalitis . . . . (ad-*rēn*-al-Ī-tis)	inflammation of the adrenal gland
adrenomegaly . . . . (ad-*rēn*-ō-MEG-a-lē)	enlargement (of one or both) of the adrenal glands
hypercalcemia . . . . (*hī*-per-kal-SĒ-mē-a)	excessive calcium (Ca) in the blood
hyperglycemia . . . . (*hī*-per-glī-SĒ-mē-a)	excessive sugar in the blood
hyperkalemia . . . . (*hī*-per-ka-LĒ-mē-a)	excessive potassium (K) in the blood
hyperthyroidism . . . . (*hī*-per-THĪ-royd-izm)	state of excessive thyroid gland activity
hypocalcemia . . . . (*hī*-pō-kal-SĒ-mē-a)	deficient level of calcium in the blood
hypoglycemia . . . . (*hī*-pō-glī-SĒ-mē-a)	deficient level of sugar in the blood
hypokalemia . . . . (*hī*-pō-ka-LĒ-mē-a)	deficient level of potassium in the blood
hyponatremia . . . . (*hī*-pō-na-TRĒ-mē-a)	deficient level of sodium (Na) in the blood
hypothyroidism . . . . (*hī*-pō-THĪ-royd-izm)	state of deficient thyroid gland activity

parathyroidoma . . . .   tumor of a parathyroid gland
  (*par*-a-THĪ-roy-*dō*-ma)

thyrotoxicosis . . . .   abnormal condition of poisoning caused by
  (*thī*-rō-*tok*-si-KŌ-sis)   (excessive) activity of the thyroid gland (also
                    called *hyperthyroidism*)

Practice saying each of these terms aloud. To assist you in pronunciation, obtain the
audiotape designed for use with this text. Learn the definitions and spellings of the
disease and disorder terms by completing exercises 9, 10, and 11.

Exercise 9

Analyze and define the following terms.

1. adrenalitis _____

2. hypocalcemia _____

3. hyperthyroidism _____

4. hyperkalemia _____

5. thyrotoxicosis _____

6. hyperglycemia _____

7. adrenomegaly _____

8. hypothyroidism _____

9. hypokalemia _____

10. parathyroidoma _____

11. acromegaly _____

12. hypoglycemia _____

13. hypercalcemia _____

14. hyponatremia _____

Exercise 10

Build disease and disorder terms for the following definitions using the word parts
you have learned.

1. enlargement of the adrenal
    gland   _____
                         WR   CV   S

2. state of deficient thyroid gland
    activity   _____
                         P   WR   S

3. enlargement of the extremities   _____ / ___ / ___
                                                      WR   CV   S

4. deficient level of sugar in the
   blood   _____ / _____ / ___
              P   WR   S

5. excessive potassium in the
   blood   _____ / _____ / ___
              P   WR   S

6. deficient level of calcium in
   the blood   _____ / _____ / ___
                  P   WR   S

7. state of excessive production
   of the thyroid gland   _____ / _____ / ___
                             P   WR   S

8. excessive calcium in the blood   _____ / _____ / ___
                                       P   WR   S

9. abnormal condition of poisoning caused by excessive activity
   of the thyroid gland   ___ / ___ / _____ / ___
                           WR   CV   WR   S

10. tumor of a parathyroid   _____ / ___
                                          WR   S

11. excessive sugar in the blood   _____ / _____ / ___
                                      P   WR   S

12. deficient level of potassium in
    the blood   _____ / _____ / ___
                   P   WR   S

13. inflammation of the adrenal
    gland   _____ / ___
                      WR   S

14. deficient level of sodium in
    the blood   _____ / _____ / ___
                   P   WR   S

Exercise 11

Spell each of the disease and disorder terms. Have someone dictate the terms on pp.
516 and 517 to you, or say the words into a tape recorder; then spell the words from
your recording. Think about the word parts before attempting to write the word.
Study any words you have spelled incorrectly.

1. _____   4. _____

2. _____   5. _____

3. _____   6. _____

7. _____   11. _____

8. _____   12. _____

9. _____   13. _____

10. _____   14. _____

Disease and Disorder Terms
Not Built From Word Parts

Term	Definition
acidosis .... (*as*-i-DŌ-sis)	condition brought about by an abnormal accumulation of acid products of metabolism, seen frequently in uncontrolled diabetes mellitus (see discussion of diabetes mellitus that follows)
Addison's disease	chronic syndrome resulting from a deficiency in the hormonal secretion of the adrenal cortex. Symptoms may include weakness, darkening of skin, loss of appetite, depression, and other emotional problems.
cretinism .... (KRĒ-tin-izm)	condition caused by congenital absence or atrophy (wasting away) of the thyroid gland, resulting in hypothyroidism. The disease is characterized by puffy features, mental deficiency, large tongue, and dwarfism.
Cushing's syndrome	group of symptoms that are attributed to the excessive production of cortisol by the adrenal cortices (*pl.* of cortex). This syndrome may be the result of a pituitary tumor. Symptoms include abnormally pigmented skin, "moon face," pads of fat on the chest and abdomen, and wasting away of muscle (Figure 16-4).
diabetes insipidus (DI) .... (*dī*-a-BĒ-tēz) (in-SIP-i-dus)	result of decreased activity of the antidiuretic hormone of the posterior lobe of the pituitary gland. Patients complain of excessive thirst (*polydipsia*) and pass large amounts of urine (*polyuria*).
diabetes mellitus (DM) .... (*dī*-a-BĒ-tēz) (mel-LĪ-tus)	chronic disease involving a disorder of carbohydrate metabolism. Diabetes mellitus is caused by underactivity of the islets of Langerhans in the pancreas, which results in insufficient production of insulin. When the disease is not controlled or is untreated, the patient may develop ketosis, acidosis, and finally coma.
gigantism .... (jī-GAN-tizm)	condition brought about by overproduction of the pituitary growth hormone

Addison's disease

was named in 1855 for Thomas Addison, an English physician and pathologist. He described the disease as a "morbid state with feeble heart action, anemia, irritability of the stomach, and a peculiar change in the color of the skin."

Cushing's syndrome

was named for an American neurosurgeon, Harvey Williams Cushing (1869-1939), after he described adrenal cortical hyperfunction.

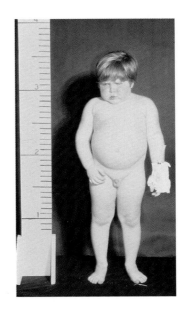

Fig. 16-4
Cushing's syndrome.

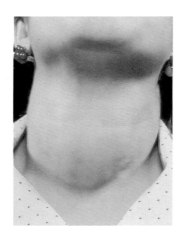

Fig. 16-5
Enlargement of the thyroid gland in goiter.

goiter .... enlargement of the thyroid gland (Figure 16-5)
  (GOY-ter)

ketosis .... condition resulting from uncontrolled diabetes
  (kē-TŌ-sis)   mellitus, in which the body has an abnormal
                          concentration of ketone bodies (compounds
                          that are a normal product of fat metabolism)

myxedema .... condition resulting from a deficiency of the
  (*mik*-se-DĒ-ma)   thyroid hormone, thyroxine (Figure 16-6)

tetany .... condition resulting in spasms of the nerves and
  (TET-a-nē)   muscles, which result from low amounts of cal-
                          cium in the blood caused by a deficiency of the
                          parathyroid hormone

Practice saying each of these terms aloud. To assist you in pronunciation, obtain the audiotape designed for use with this text. Learn the definitions and spellings of the disease and disorder terms by completing exercises 12, 13, and 14.

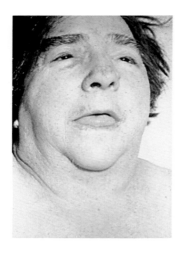

Fig. 16-6
Myxedema.

Exercise 12

Match the terms in the first column with the correct definitions in the second column.

_____ 1. acidosis

_____ 2. Addison's disease

_____ 3. cretinism

_____ 4. Cushing's syndrome

_____ 5. diabetes insipidus

_____ 6. diabetes mellitus

_____ 7. gigantism

_____ 8. goiter

_____ 9. ketosis

_____ 10. myxedema

_____ 11. tetany

a. results from a deficiency in the hormonal secretion of the adrenal cortex

b. attributed to the excessive production of cortisol

c. caused by underactivity of the islets of Langerhans

d. abnormal accumulation of acid products of metabolism

e. enlargement of the thyroid gland

f. results from low blood calcium

g. caused by an excessive amount of parathormone

h. result of a decreased activity of antidiuretic hormone

i. caused by deficiency of the thyroid hormone

j. caused by a wasting away of the thyroid gland

k. abnormal concentration of compounds resulting from fat metabolism

l. caused by overproduction of the pituitary growth hormone

Exercise 13

Write the name of the endocrine gland responsible for each of the following conditions.

1. myxedema _____
2. tetany _____
3. ketosis _____
4. gigantism _____
5. goiter _____
6. Addison's disease _____
7. diabetes mellitus _____
8. cretinism _____
9. acidosis _____
10. Cushing's syndrome _____
11. diabetes insipidus _____

Exercise 14

Spell the disease and disorder terms. Have someone dictate the terms on pp. 519-520 to you, or say the words into a tape recorder; then spell the words from your recording. Study any words you have spelled incorrectly.

1. _____   7. _____
2. _____   8. _____
3. _____   9. _____
4. _____   10. _____
5. _____   11. _____
6. _____

Surgical Terms
Built From Word Parts

Term	Definition
adrenalectomy (ad-*rē*-nal-EK-tō-mē)	excision of an adrenal gland
parathyroidectomy (*par*-a-*thī*-royd-EK-tō-mē)	excision of a parathyroid gland

thyroidectomy . . . .   excision of the thyroid gland
(*thī*-royd-EK-tō-mē)

thyroidotomy . . . .   incision of the thyroid gland
(*thī*-royd-OT-ō-mē)

thyroparathyroidectomy . . . .   excision of the thyroid and parathyroid glands
(*thī*-rō-par-a-*thī*-royd-EK-tō-
mē)

Practice saying each of these terms aloud. To assist you in pronunciation, obtain the audiotape designed for use with this text. Learn the definitions and spellings of the surgical terms by completing exercises 15, 16, and 17.

Exercise 15 ....

Analyze and define the following surgical terms.

1. thyroidotomy _____

2. adrenalectomy _____

3. thyroparathyroidectomy _____

4. thyroidectomy _____

5. parathyroidectomy _____

Exercise 16 ....

Build surgical terms for the following definitions by using the word parts you have learned.

1. excision of the thyroid gland

   _____/_____
   WR   S

2. excision of the thyroid and
   parathyroid glands

   _____/____/_____/____
   WR   CV   WR   S

3. excision of the adrenal gland

   _____/_____
   WR   S

4. excision of a parathyroid
   gland

   _____/_____
   WR   S

5. incision of the thyroid gland

   _____/_____
   WR   S

Exercise 17 ....

Spell each of the surgical terms. Have someone dictate the terms on pp. 521-522 to you, or say the words into a tape recorder; then spell the words from your recording. Think about the word parts before attempting to write the word. Study any words you have spelled incorrectly.

1. _____   4. _____

2. _____   5. _____

3. _____

Procedural Terms
Not Built From Word Parts

Term	Definition
Diagnostic Imaging	
radioactive iodine uptake (RAIU) . . . . (rā-dē-ō-ak-tiv) (ī-ō-dīn)	a nuclear medicine scan that measures thyroid function. Radioactive iodine is given to the patient orally, after which its uptake into the thyroid gland is measured.
thyroid scan . . . . (thī-royd)	a nuclear medicine test that shows the size, shape, and position of the thyroid gland. The patient is given a radioactive substance to visualize the thyroid gland. An image is recorded as the scanner is passed over the neck area. Used to detect tumors and nodules.
Laboratory Procedures	
fasting blood sugar (FBS)	a test to determine the amount of glucose (sugar) in the blood after fasting for 8 to 10 hours. Elevation indicates diabetes mellitus.
glucose tolerance test (GTT) . . . . (GLOO-kōs)	performed to determine abnormalities in glucose metabolism and is used to confirm the diagnosis of diabetes mellitus. After blood is drawn for an FBS, the patient is given glucose (sugar) either intravenously or orally. Timed urine and blood specimens are drawn at intervals and the glucose level in each specimen is measured.
thyroxine level (T$_4$) . . . . (thī-ROK-sin)	a direct measurement of the amount of thyroxine in the blood. A greater-than-normal amount indicates hyperthyroidism; a less-than-normal amount indicates hypothyroidism.

thyroid-stimulating hormone level (TSH) (thyrotropin level) (thī-royd)   a blood test that measures the amount of thyroid-stimulating hormone in the blood. Used to diagnose hyperthyroidism and to monitor patients on thyroid replacement therapy

> Ultrasound and computed tomography (CT scanning) are also used to diagnose various other conditions of the endocrine system. Examples are CT of the adrenal glands and thyroid echogram using ultrasound.

Exercise 18

Match the terms in the first column with their correct definitions in the second column.

_____ 1. glucose tolerance test

_____ 2. fasting blood sugar

_____ 3. thyroid scan

_____ 4. thyroxine level

_____ 5. radioactive iodine uptake

_____ 6. thyroid-stimulating hormone level

a. a nuclear medicine test used to determine the size, shape, and position of the thyroid gland

b. determines the amount of glucose in the blood

c. determines abnormalities in glucose metabolism

d. uses radioactive iodine to measure thyroid function

e. used to diagnose hyperthyroidism and to monitor thyroid replacement therapy

f. measures the amount of thyroxine in the blood

g. used to determine hypernatremia

Exercise 19

Write the name of the procedure that measures the following:

1. thyroid function   _____

2. the amount of glucose in the blood   _____

3. amount of thyroid-stimulating hormone in the blood   _____

4. amount of thyroxine in the blood   _____

5. the size, shape, and position of the thyroid gland   _____

6. abnormalities in glucose metabolism   _____

Exercise 20

Spell each of the procedural terms. Have someone dictate the terms on pp. 523-524 to you, or say the words into a tape recorder; then spell the words from your recording. Study any words you have spelled incorrectly.

1. _____   4. _____

2. _____   5. _____

3. _____   6. _____

Complementary Terms

Built From Word Parts

Term	Definition
adrenocorticohyperplasia (a-*drē*-nō-*kōr*-ti-kō-*hī*-per-PLĀ-zhē-a) (NOTE: *hyper*, a prefix, appears within this word.)	excessive development of the adrenal cortex
adrenopathy (*ad*-rēn-OP-a-thē)	disease of the adrenal gland
calcipenia (kal-si-PĒ-nē-a)	deficiency of calcium (also called *hypocalcemia*)
cortical (KŌR-ti-kal)	pertaining to the cortex
corticoid (KŌR-ti-koyd)	resembling the cortex
endocrinologist (en-dō-kri-NOL-ō-jist)	a physician who specializes in endocrinology
endocrinology (en-dō-kri-NOL-ō-jē)	the study of the endocrine glands
endocrinopathy (en-dō-kri-NOP-a-thē)	(any) disease of the endocrine system
euthyroid (ū-THĪ-royd)	resembling a normal thyroid
exophthalmic (*ek*-sof-THAL-mik)	pertaining to eyes (bulging) outward (abnormal protrusion of the eyeball) (Exercise Figure D)
polydipsia (*pol*-ē-DIP-sē-a)	abnormal state of much thirst
syndrome (SIN-drōm)	(set of symptoms that) run (occur) together

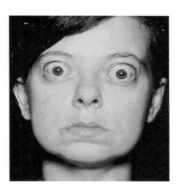

Exercise Fig. D
Protrusion of eyes, a characteristic of

$\underline{}$ / $\underline{}$ /
OUTWARD / EYES /

$\underline{}$
PERTAINING TO **thyroid disease.**

Exophthalmic

is derived from the Greek **ex**, meaning **outward**, and **ophthalmos**, meaning **eye**. Protrusion of the eyeball is sometimes a symptom of hyperthyroidism, which was first described by Dr. Robert Graves in 1835 and is frequently called **Graves' disease.**

Practice saying each of these terms aloud. To assist you in pronunciation, obtain the audiotape designed for use with this text. Exercises 21, 22, and 23 will help you learn the definitions and spellings of the complementary terms related to the endocrine system.

Exercise 21

Analyze and define the following complementary terms.

1. corticoid _____

2. exophthalmic _____

3. syndrome _____

4. adrenopathy _____

5. endocrinologist _____

6. polydipsia _____

7. calcipenia _____

8. endocrinopathy _____

9. adrenocorticohyperplasia _____

10. euthyroid _____

11. cortical _____

12. endocrinology _____

Exercise 22

Build the complementary terms for the following definitions by using the word parts you have learned.

1. pertaining to eyes bulging out   _____ / _____ / _____
                                        P   WR   S

2. (any) disease of the endocrine
   system   _____ /_/_____
                                        WR   CV   S

3. resembling the cortex   _____ / _____
                                        WR   S

4. (set of symptoms that) run
   (occur) together   _____ / _____
                                        P   S(WR)

5. excessive development of the
   adrenal cortex   _____/_/_____/_/___/_____
                                      WR CV WR CV P S(WR)

6. the study of endocrine glands   _____ / _____
                                        WR   S

7. abnormal state of much thirst   _____ / _____ / _____
                                        P   WR   S

8. disease of the adrenal gland   _____ /_/_____
                                        WR   CV   S

9. deficiency of calcium   _____ /_/_____
                                        WR   CV   S

10. resembling normal thyroid

           _____ / _____ / _____
             P   WR   S

11. pertaining to the cortex

           _____ / _____
             WR   S

12. a physician who specializes in endocrinology

           _____ / _____
             WR   S

Exercise 23

Spell each of the complementary terms. Have someone dictate the terms on p. 525 to you, or say the words into a tape recorder; then spell the words from your recording. Think about the word parts before attempting to write the word. Study any words you have spelled incorrectly.

1. _____   7. _____

2. _____   8. _____

3. _____   9. _____

4. _____   10. _____

5. _____   11. _____

6. _____   12. _____

Complementary Terms

Not Built From Word Parts

Term	Definition
hormone . . . . (HOR-mōn)	a secretion of an endocrine gland (carried in the blood plasma)
isthmus . . . . (IS-mus)	narrow strip of tissue connecting two large parts in the body, such as the isthmus that connects the two lobes of the thyroid gland (Figure 16-2, *B*)
metabolism . . . . (me-TAB-ō-lizm)	sum total of all the chemical processes that take place in a living organism

Practice saying each of these terms aloud. To assist you in pronunciation, obtain the audiotape designed for use with this text. Learn the definitions and spellings of the complementary terms by completing exercises 24, 25, and 26.

Exercise 24

Fill in the blanks with the correct terms.

1. The total of all the chemical processes that take place in a living organism is called its _____ .

2. The secretion from an endocrine gland is called a(n) _____ .

3. A narrow strip of tissue connecting large parts in the body is called a(n) _____ .

Exercise 25

Write the definitions of the following terms.

1. isthmus _____

2. metabolism _____

3. hormone _____

Exercise 26

Spell each of the complementary terms. Have someone dictate the terms on p. 527 to you, or say the words into a tape recorder; then spell the words from your recording. Study any words you have spelled incorrectly.

1. _____   3. _____

2. _____

Abbreviations

ACTH	adrenocorticotropic hormone
ADH	antidiuretic hormone
Ca	calcium
DI	diabetes insipidus
DM	diabetes mellitus
FBS	fasting blood sugar
GH	growth hormone
GTT	glucose tolerance test
K	potassium
Na	sodium
RAIU	radioactive iodine uptake
T$_4$	thyroxine
TSH	thyroid-stimulating hormone

CHAPTER REVIEW

Exercises

Exercise 27

Complete the hospital report by writing the medical terms in the blanks. Use the list of definitions with the corresponding numbers.

Case History: This 53-year-old female executive secretary presents to the clinic with complaints of excessive urination and thirst for the last month. She has also lost about 10 pounds.

History and Physical Examination: Chief Complaint: 1. _____,
2. _____ History of Present Illness: This patient presented to the emergency department following an episode of syncope at work. She was oriented ×3, but responses to questions were sluggish. Routine lab work was ordered. Blood sugar was discovered to be over 600 mg/dl. Urinalysis showed moderate ketonuria. For the past 4 weeks she had been experiencing polyuria and polydipsia, drinking 3-4 quarts of water daily for the past 10 days. This has also resulted in nocturia. She denies anorexia, nausea, vomiting, or any abdominal pain.

Medical History: No allergies; no previous hospitalizations. Does not smoke or drink. She has no recent illnesses.

Family History; Social History: Mother died of a 3. _____ at age 78. Father is still living at the age of 85, but has had 4. _____ _____ for 20 years. She has two brothers, no sisters. She has no children and has never been married.

Review of Systems: Essentially unremarkable, except for occasional headaches and blurred vision. No chest pain, no awareness of cardiac palpitations or irregularities. Denies nausea, vomiting, or 5. _____, although has lost 10 pounds in the past month.

Admission Physical Examination: A 53-year-old woman in no acute distress. BP 120/84 mm/Hg, respiratory rate of 22, pulse rate of 76.

HEENT: Clear, nonicteric sclerae. Pupils equal, round, reactive to light; funduscopic examination is benign.

CHEST: Clear to auscultation and percussion.

HEART: JVD is flat; PMI fifth left intercostal space, left midclavicular line; S1 and S2 are appreciated, no S3 or S4. No murmurs, lifts, heaves, or thrills. Sinus rhythm.

EXTREMITIES: Negative for clubbing, 6. _____, or edema. Pulses intact.

ABDOMEN: Soft, nontender; bowel sounds normal, without evidence of organomegaly.

RECTAL: Unremarkable, guaiac negative.

NEUROLOGIC: Alert, oriented to time, person, and place; cranial nerves II through XII are grossly within normal limits.

ASSESSMENT: Diabetic 7. _____, cause needs to be ascertained. Most likely adult onset diabetes mellitus.

1. excessive urine
2. excessive thirst
3. interruption of blood supply to the brain caused by cerebral thrombosis, cerebral embolism, or cerebral hemorrhage
4. chronic disease involving disorder of carbohydrate metabolism caused by underactivity of islets of Langerhans in the pancreas, which results in insufficient production of insulin
5. vomiting of blood

6. abnormal condition of blue (bluish discoloration of skin) caused by inadequate supply of oxygen in the blood

7. abnormal concentration of ketone bodies

Exercise 28

To test your understanding of the terms introduced in this chapter, circle the words that correctly complete the sentences. The italicized words refer to the correct answer.

1. A patient who has an *enlargement of the thyroid gland* has (myxedema, tetany, goiter).

2. A condition that results from *uncontrolled diabetes mellitus* is (calcipenia, ketosis, tetany).

3. *Addison's disease* is caused by an *underfunctioning* of the (adrenal, pituitary, thyroid) gland.

4. *Decreased activity* of the (thyroid, antidiuretic hormone, adrenals) may cause diabetes insipidus.

5. *Cushing's syndrome* is caused by (overactivity, underactivity) of the *adrenal cortices*.

6. A *wasting away of the thyroid gland* may result in (cretinism, myxedema, tetany).

Exercise 29

Unscramble the following mixed-up terms. The word on the left hints at the condition named by the scrambled term.

1. thyroid

   / / / / / / /
   r   o   i   g   e   t

2. potassium

   / / / /e/ / / / /e/ / /
   p   a   y   m   e   h   r   l   a   i   e   k

3. thirst

   / / / / / /i/ / / /
   y   o   p   p   l   i   d   i   a   s

4. adrenal

   / / / /e/ / / /e/ / / /
   o   n   g   e   m   a   a   y   l   e   r   d

5. calcium

   / / / /o/ / / / /e/ / /
   l   o   a   m   p   e   c   a   y   h   i   c

Exercise 30

The following terms did not appear in this chapter but are composed of word parts that have appeared in this chapter or previous chapters. Find their definitions by translating the word parts literally.

1. **acrodermatitis** _____
   (*ak*-rō-der-ma-TĪ-tis)

2. **calciuria** _____
   (*kal*-sē-Ū-rē-a)

3. **interalveolar** _____
(*in*-ter-al-VĒ-ō-lar)

4. **kalemia** _____
(ka-LĒ-mē-a)

5. **neurotripsy** _____
(NŪ-rō-trip-sē)

6. **ophthalmomalacia** _____
(of-*thal*-mō-ma-LĀ-shē-a)

7. **pancreatography** _____
(*pan*-krē-a-TOG-ra-fē)

8. **phlebosclerosis** _____
(*fleb*-ō-skle-RŌ-sis)

9. **pneumomelanosis** _____
(*nū*-mō-mel-a-NŌ-sis)

10. **rectoscope** _____
(REK-tō-skōp)

▌ Review of Terms

Can you build, analyze, define, pronounce, and spell the following terms *built from word parts?*

Diseases and Disorders	Surgical	Complementary
acromegaly	adrenalectomy	adrenocorticohyperplasia
adrenalitis	parathyroidectomy	adrenopathy
adrenomegaly	thyroidectomy	calcipenia
hypercalcemia	thyroidotomy	cortical
hyperglycemia	thyroparathyroidectomy	corticoid
hyperkalemia		endocrinologist
hyperthyroidism		endocrinology
hypocalcemia		endocrinopathy
hypoglycemia		euthyroid
hypokalemia		exophthalmic
hyponatremia		polydipsia
hypothyroidism		syndrome
parathyroidoma		
thyrotoxicosis		

Can you define, pronounce, and spell the following terms *not built from word parts?*

Diseases and Disorders	Procedural	Complementary
acidosis	fasting blood sugar (FBS)	hormone
Addison's disease	glucose tolerance test (GTT)	isthmus
cretinism	radioactive iodine uptake (RAIU)	metabolism
Cushing's syndrome	thyroid scan	
diabetes insipidus (DI)	thyroid-stimulating hormone level (TSH)	
diabetes mellitus (DM)	thyroxine level (T_4)	
gigantism		
goiter		
ketosis		
myxedema		
tetany		

APPENDIX A

Combining Forms	Definition	Chapter
abdomin/o	abdomen	11
acou/o	hearing	13
acr/o	extremities, height	16
adenoid/o	adenoids	5
aden/o	gland	4
adrenal/o	adrenal gland	16
adren/o	adrenal gland	16
albumin/o	albumin	6
alveol/o	alveolus	5
amni/o	amnion	9
amnion/o	amnion	9
andr/o	male	7
angi/o	vessel	10
ankyl/o	crooked, stiff, bent	14
anter/o	front	3
antr/o	antrum	11
an/o	anus	11
aort/o	aorta	10
aponeur/o	aponeurosis	14
appendic/o	appendix	11
arche/o	first, beginning	8
arteri/o	artery	10
arthr/o	joint	14
atel/o	imperfect, incomplete	5
ather/o	yellowish, fatty plaque	10
atri/o	atrium	10
aur/i	ear	13
aur/o	ear	13
aut/o	self	4
azot/o	urea, nitrogen	6

Combining Forms	Definition	Chapter
bacteri/o	bacteria	10
balan/o	glans penis	7
bi/o	life	4
blast/o	developing cell	6
blephar/o	eyelid	12
bronch/i	bronchus	5
bronch/o	bronchus	5
burs/o	bursa (cavity)	14
calc/i	calcium	16
cancer/o	cancer	2
carcin/o	cancer	2
cardi/o	heart	10
carp/o	carpals (wrist bones)	14
caud/o	tail (downward)	3
cec/o	cecum	11
celi/o	abdomen (abdominal cavity)	11
cephal/o	head	3, 9
cerebell/o	cerebellum	15
cerebr/o	cerebrum, brain	15
cervic/o	cervix	8
cheil/o	lip	11
cholangi/o	bile duct	11
chol/e	gall, bile	11
choledoch/o	common bile duct	11
chondr/o	cartilage	14
chori/o	chorion	9
chrom/o	color	2
clavic/o	clavicle (collarbone)	14
clavicul/o	clavicle (collarbone)	14
col/o	colon	11
colp/o	vagina	8
coni/o	dust	4
conjunctiv/o	conjunctiva	12
core/o	pupil	12
corne/o	cornea	12
coron/o	heart	10
cortic/o	cortex (outer layer of body organ)	16
cor/o	pupil	12
cost/o	rib	14
crani/o	cranium (skull)	14
cry/o	cold	12

Combining Forms	Definition	Chapter
crypt/o	hidden	4
culd/o	cul-de-sac	8
cutane/o	skin	4
cyan/o	blue	2
cyes/i	pregnancy	9
cyes/o	pregnancy	9
cyst/o	bladder, sac	6
cyt/o	cell	2
dacry/o	tear, tear duct	12
dermat/o	skin	4
derm/o	skin	4
diaphragmat/o	diaphragm	5
dipl/o	two, double	12
dips/o	thirst	16
disk/o	intervertebral disk	14
dist/o	away (from the point of reference)	3
diverticul/o	diverticulum	11
dors/o	back	3
duoden/o	duodenum	11
dur/o	hard, dura mater	15
ech/o	sound	10
electr/o	electricity, electrical activity	10
embry/o	embryo, to be full	9
encephal/o	brain	15
endocrin/o	endocrine	16
enter/o	intestine	11
epididym/o	epididymis	7
epiglott/o	epiglottis	5
episi/o	vulva	8
epitheli/o	epithelium	2
erythr/o	red	2
esophag/o	esophagus	9, 11
esthesi/o	sensation, sensitivity, feeling	15
eti/o	cause (of disease)	2
femor/o	femur (upper leg bone)	14
fet/i	fetus, unborn child	9
fet/o	fetus, unborn child	9
fibr/o	fibrous tissue	2
fibul/o	fibula (lower leg bone)	14
gangli/o	ganglion	15
ganglion/o	ganglion	15

Combining Forms	Definition	Chapter
gastr/o	stomach	11
gingiv/o	gum	11
glomerul/o	glomerulus	6
gloss/o	tongue	11
glyc/o	sugar	6
glycos/o	sugar	6
gnos/o	knowledge	2
gravid/o	pregnancy	9
gynec/o	woman	8
gyn/o	woman	8
hem/o	blood	5
hemat/o	blood	5
hepat/o	liver	11
herni/o	hernia	11
heter/o	other	4
hidr/o	sweat	4
hist/o	tissue	2
humer/o	humerus (upper arm bone)	14
hydr/o	water	6
hymen/o	hymen	8
hyster/o	uterus	8
iatr/o	medicine, physician	2
ile/o	ileum	11
ili/o	ilium	14
infer/o	below	3
irid/o	iris	12
iri/o	iris	12
ischi/o	ischium	14
isch/o	deficiency, blockage	10
jejun/o	jejunum	11
kal/i	potassium	16
kary/o	nucleus	2
kerat/o	cornea	12
kerat/o	horny tissue, hard	4
kinesi/o	movement, motion	14
kyph/o	hump	14
labyrinth/o	labyrinth	13
lacrim/o	tear duct, tear	12
lact/o	milk	9
lamin/o	lamina (thin, flat plate or layer)	14
lapar/o	abdomen	11

Combining Forms	Definition	Chapter
laryng/o	larynx	5
later/o	side	3
lei/o	smooth	2
leuk/o	white	2
lingu/o	tongue	11
lip/o	fat	2
lith/o	stone, calculus	6
lob/o	lobe	5
lord/o	bent forward	14
lumb/o	loin (or lumbar region of the spine)	14
lymph/o	lymph	10
mamm/o	breast	8
mandibul/o	mandible (lower jawbone)	14
mast/o	breast	8
mastoid/o	mastoid	13
maxill/o	maxilla (upper jawbone)	14
meat/o	meatus (opening)	6
melan/o	black	2
mening/i	meninges	15
mening/o	meninges	15
menisc/o	meniscus (crescent)	14
men/o	menstruation	8
ment/o	mind	15
metr/i	uterus	8
metr/o	uterus	8
mon/o	one	15
muc/o	mucus	5
myc/o	fungus	4
myel/o	bone marrow	14
myel/o	spinal cord	15
myelon/o	bone marrow	14
myos/o	muscle	14
myring/o	eardrum	13
my/o	muscle	2, 14
nas/o	nose	5
nat/o	birth	9
necr/o	death (cells, body)	4
nephr/o	kidney	6
neur/o	nerve	2, 15
noct/i	night	6
ocul/o	eye	12

Combining Forms	Definition	Chapter
olig/o	scanty, few	6
omphal/o	umbilicus, navel	9
onc/o	tumor	2
onych/o	nail	4
oophor/o	ovary	8
ophthalm/o	eye	12
opt/o	vision	12
orchid/o	testis, testicle	7
orchi/o	testis, testicle	7
orch/o	testis, testicle	7
organ/o	organ	2
or/o	mouth	11
orth/o	straight	5
oste/o	bone	14
ot/o	ear	13
ox/i	oxygen	5
ox/o	oxygen	5
pachy/o	thick	4
palat/o	palate	11
pancreat/o	pancreas	11
parathyroid/o	parathyroid gland	16
par/o	bear, give birth to, labor	9
patell/o	patella (kneecap)	14
path/o	disease	2
part/o	bear, give birth to, labor	9
pelv/i	pelvis, pelvic bone	9
pelv/o	pelvis, pelvic bone	9
perine/o	perineum	8
peritone/o	peritoneum	11
petr/o	stone	14
phalang/o	phalanx (finger or toe bone)	14
pharyng/o	pharynx	5
phas/o	speech	15
phleb/o	vein	10
phot/o	light	12
phren/o	mind	15
plasm/o	plasma	10
pleur/o	pleura	5
pneumat/o	lung, air	5
pneum/o	lung, air	5
pneumon/o	lung, air	5
poli/o	gray matter	15

Combining Forms	Definition	Chapter
polyp/o	polyp, small growth	11
poster/o	back, behind	3
prim/i	first	9
proct/o	rectum	11
prostat/o	prostate gland	7
proxim/o	near (the point of reference)	3
pseud/o	false	9
psych/o	mind	15
pub/o	pubis	14
puerper/o	childbirth	9
pulmon/o	lung	5
pupill/o	pupil	12
pyel/o	renal pelvis	6
pylor/o	pylorus (pyloric sphincter)	9, 11
py/o	pus	5
quadr/i	four	15
rachi/o	spinal or vertebral column	14
radic/o	nerve root	15
radicul/o	nerve root	15
radi/o	radius (lower arm bone)	14
rect/o	rectum	11
ren/o	kidney	6
retin/o	retina	12
rhabd/o	rod-shaped, striated	2
rhin/o	nose	5
rhytid/o	wrinkles	4
rhiz/o	nerve root	15
salping/o	fallopian (uterine) tube	8
sacr/o	sacrum	14
sarc/o	flesh, connective tissue	2
scapul/o	scapula (shoulder bone)	14
scler/o	sclera or hard	12
scoli/o	crooked, curved	14
seb/o	sebum (oil)	4
sept/o	septum	5
sial/o	saliva	11
sigmoid/o	sigmoid	11
sinus/o	sinus	5
somat/o	body	2
son/o	sound	6
spermat/o	spermatozoan, sperm	7
sperm/o	spermatozoan, sperm	7

Combining Forms	Definition	Chapter
sphygm/o	pulse	10
spir/o	breathe, breathing	5
splen/o	spleen	10
spondyl/o	vertebra	14
staped/o	stapes (middle ear bone)	13
staphyl/o	grape-like clusters	4
stern/o	sternum (breastbone)	14
steth/o	chest	10
stomat/o	mouth	11
strept/o	twisted chains	4
super/o	above	3
synovi/o	synovia, synovial membrane	14
system/o	system	2
tars/o	tarsals (ankle bones)	14
tendin/o	tendon	14
tend/o	tendon	14
ten/o	tendon	14
test/o	testis, testicle	7
therm/o	heat	10
thorac/o	thorax (chest)	5
thromb/o	clot	10
thym/o	thymus gland	10
thyroid/o	thyroid gland	16
thyr/o	thyroid gland	16
tibi/o	tibia (lower leg bone)	14
tom/o	cut, section	6
ton/o	tension, pressure	12
tonsill/o	tonsils	5
toxic/o	poison	16
trachel/o	neck, neck like	6
trache/o	trachea	5
trich/o	hair	4
tympan/o	eardrum, middle ear	13
uln/o	ulna (lower arm bone)	14
ungu/o	nail	4
ureter/o	ureter	6
urethr/o	urethra	6
urin/o	urine, urinary tract	6
ur/o	urine, urinary tract	6
uter/o	uterus	8
uvul/o	uvula	11
vagin/o	vagina	8

Combining Forms	Definition	Chapter
valv/o	valve	10
valvul/o	valve	10
vas/o	vessel, duct	7
ven/o	vein	6
ventricul/o	ventricle	10
ventr/o	belly, front,	3
vertebr/o	vertebra	14
vesic/o	bladder, sac	6
vesicul/o	seminal vesicles	7
viscer/o	internal organs	2
vulv/o	vulva	8
xanth/o	yellow	2
xer/o	dry	4

Prefix	Definition	Chapter
a-	without, absence of	5
an-	without, absence of	5
ante-	before	9
bi-	two	3, 12
bin-	two	12
brady-	slow	10
dia-	through, complete	2
dys-	difficult, labored, painful, abnormal	2
endo-	within	5
epi-	on, upon, over	4
eu-	normal, good	5
ex-	outside, outward	16
exo-	outside, outward	16
hemi-	half	15
hyper-	above, excessive	2
hypo-	below, incomplete, deficient	2
inter-	between	14
intra-	within	4
meta-	after, beyond, change	2
micro-	small	9
multi-	many	9
neo-	new	2
nulli-	none	9
pan-	all, total	5
para-	beside, beyond, around	4
per-	through	4

Prefix	Definition	Chapter
peri-	surrounding (outer)	8
poly-	many, much	6
post-	after	9
pre-	before	15
pro-	before	2
sub-	under, below	4
supra-	above	14
sym-	together, joined	14
syn-	together, joined	14
tachy-	fast, rapid	10
tetra-	four	15
trans-	through, across, beyond	7
uni-	one	3

Suffix	Definition	Chapter
-ac	pertaining to	10
-ad	toward	3
-al	pertaining to	2
-algia	pain	5
-apheresis	removal	10
-ar	pertaining to	5
-ary	pertaining to	5
-asthenia	weakness	14
-atresia	absence of a normal body opening, occlusion, closure	8
-capnia	carbon dioxide	5
-cele	hernia, protrusion	5
-centesis	surgical puncture to aspirate fluid	5
-clasia	break	14
-clasis	break	14
-clast	break	14
-coccus (*pl.* cocci)	berry-shaped (a form of bacterium)	4
-crit	to separate	10
-cyte	cell	2
-desis	surgical fixation, fusion	14
-drome	run, running	16
-eal	pertaining to	5
-ectasis	stretching out, dilatation, expansion	5
-ectomy	excision, surgical removal	4
-emia	blood condition	5

Suffix	Definition	Chapter
-esis	condition	6
-gen	substance or agent that produces or causes	2
-genesis	origin, cause	2
-genic	pertaining to producing, originating, causing	2
-gram	record, x-ray film	5
-graph	instrument used to record	10
-graphy	process of recording, x-ray filming	5
-ia	condition of diseased or abnormal state	4
-ial	pertaining to	8
-iasis	condition	6
-iatrist	specialist, physician	15
-iatry	treatment specialty	15
-ic	pertaining to	2
-ician	one who	12
-ictal	seizure, attack	15
-ior	pertaining to	3
-ism	state of	7
-itis	inflammation	4
-lysis	loosening, dissolution, separating	6
-malacia	softening	4
-megaly	enlargement	6
-meter	instrument used to measure	5
-metry	measurement	5
-odynia	pain	10
-oid	resembling	2
-ologist	one who studies and practices (specialist)	2
-ology	study of	2
-oma	tumor, swelling	2
-opia	vision (condition)	12
-opsy	view of, viewing	4
-orrhagia	rapid flow of blood	5
-orrhaphy	suturing, repairing	6
-orrhea	flow, excessive discharge	4
-orrhexis	rupture	9
-osis	abnormal condition (means increased when used with blood cell word roots)	2
-ostomy	creation of an artificial opening	5

Suffix	Definition	Chapter
-otomy	cut into or incision	5
-ous	pertaining to	2
-oxia	oxygen	5
-paresis	slight paralysis	15
-pathy	disease	2
-penia	abnormal reduction in number	10
-pepsia	digestion	11
-pexy	surgical fixation, suspension	5
-phagia	eating, swallowing	4
-phobia	abnormal fear of or aversion to specific objects or things	12
-phonia	sound or voice	5
-physis	growth	14
-plasia	condition of formation, development, growth	2
-plasm	a growth, a substance, a formation	2
-plasty	surgical repair	4
-plegia	paralysis	12
-pnea	breathing	5
-poiesis	formation	10
-ptosis	dropping, sagging, prolapse	6
-salpinx	fallopian tube	8
-sarcoma	malignant tumor	2
-schisis	split, fissure	14
-sclerosis	hardening	10
-scope	instrument used for visual examination	5
-scopic	pertaining to visual examination	5
-scopy	visual examination	5
-sis	state of	2
-spasm	sudden involuntary muscle contraction	5
-stasis	control, stop, standing	2
-stenosis	constriction, narrowing	5
-thorax	chest	5
-tocia	birth, labor	9
-tome	instrument used to cut	4
-tripsy	surgical crushing	6
-trophy	nourishment, development	6
-uria	urine, urination	6

APPENDIX B

Definition	Combining Form	Chapter
black	melan/o	2
bladder, sac	cyst/o	6
bladder, sac	vesic/o	6
blood	hemat/o	5
blood	hem/o	5
blue	cyan/o	2
body	somat/o	2
bone	oste/o	14
bone marrow	myelon/o	14
bone marrow	myel/o	14
brain	encephal/o	15
breast	mamm/o	8
breast	mast/o	8
breathe, breathing	spir/o	5
bronchus bronch/i,	bronch/o	5
bursa (cavity)	burs/o	14
calcium	calc/i	16
cancer	cancer/o	2
cancer	carcin/o	2
carpus (wrist bone)	carp/o	14
cartilage	chondr/o	14
cause (of disease)	eti/o	2
cecum	cec/o	11
cell	cyt/o	2
cerebellum	cerebell/o	15
cerebrum, brain	cerebr/o	15
cervix	cervic/o	8
chest	steth/o, pector/o	10
childbirth	puerper/o	9
chorion	chori/o	9
clavicle (collar bone)	clavic/o	14
clavicle (collar bone)	clavicul/o	14
clot	thromb/o	10
cold	cry/o	12
colon	col/o	11
color	chrom/o	2
common bile duct	choledoch/o	11
conjunctiva	conjunctiv/o	12
cornea	corne/o	12
cornea	kerat/o	12
cortex	cortic/o	16

Definition	Combining Form	Chapter
cranium, skull	crani/o	14
crooked, curved	scoli/o	14
crooked, stiff, bent	ankyl/o	14
cul-de-sac	culd/o	8
cut, section	tom/o	6
death (cells, body)	necr/o	4
deficiency, blockage	isch/o	10
developing cell	blast/o	6
diaphragm	diaphragmat/o	5
disease	path/o	2
diverticulum	diverticul/o	11
dry	xer/o	4
duodenum	duoden/o	11
dust	coni/o	4
ear	ot/o	13
ear	aur/i, aur/o	13
eardrum	myring/o	13
eardrum, middle ear	tympan/o	13
electricity, electrical activity	electr/o	10
embryo, to be full	embry/o	9
endocrine	endocrin/o	16
epididymis	epididym/o	7
epiglottis	epiglott/o	5
epithelium	epitheli/o	2
esophagus	esophag/o	9, 11
extremities, height	acr/o	16
eye	opthalm/o	12
eye	ocul/o	12
eyelid	blephar/o	12
fallopian tube	salping/o	8
false	pseud/o	9
fat	lip/o	2
femur (upper leg bone)	femor/o	14
fetus, unborn child	fet/o, fet/i	9
fibrous tissue	fibr/o	2
fibula (lower leg bone)	fibul/o	14
first	prim/i	9
first, beginning	arche/o	8
flesh, connective tissue	sarc/o	2
four	quadr/i	15
fungus	myc/o	3

Definition	Combining Form	Chapter
gall, bile	chol/e	11
ganglion	gangli/o	15
ganglion	ganglion/o	15
gland	aden/o	4
glans penis	balan/o	7
glomerulus	glomerul/o	6
grape-like clusters	staphyl/o	4
gray matter	poli/o	15
gum	gingiv/o	11
hair	trich/o	4
hard, dura mater	dur/o	15
head	cephal/o	9
hearing	audi/o	13
hearing	acou/o	13
heart	cardi/o, coron/o	10
heat	therm/o	10
hernia	herni/o	11
hidden	crypt/o	4
horny tissue, hard	kerat/o	4
humerus (upper arm bone)	humer/o	14
hump	kyph/o	14
hymen	hymen/o	8
ileum	ile/o	11
ilium	ili/o	14
imperfect, incomplete	atel/o	5
internal organs	viscer/o	2
intervertebral disk	disk/o	14
intestine	enter/o	11
iris	irid/o	12
iris	iri/o	12
ischium	ischi/o	14
jejunum	jejun/o	11
joint	arthr/o	14
kidney	nephr/o	6
kidney	ren/o	6
knowledge	gnos/o	2
labyrinth	labyrinth/o	13
lamina (thin flat plate or layer)	lamin/o	14
larynx	laryng/o	5
life	bi/o	4
light	phot/o	12

Definition	Combining Form	Chapter
lip	cheil/o	11
liver	hepat/o	11
lobe	lob/o	5
lung	pulmon/o	5
lung, air	pneumat/o	5
lung, air	pneum/o	5
lung, air	pneumon/o	5
lymph	lymph/o	10
male	andr/o	7
mandible (lower jaw bone)	mandibul/o	14
mastoid	mastoid/o	13
maxilla (upper jaw bone)	maxill/o	14
meatus (opening)	meat/o	6
medicine	iatr/o	2
meninges	mening/o, mening/i	15
meniscus (crescent)	**menisc/o**	**14**
menstruation	men/o	8
middle	medi/o	3
mind	ment/o	15
mind	psych/o	15
mind	phren/o	15
mouth	or/o	11
mouth	stomat/o	11
movement, motion	kinesi/o	14
mucus	muc/o	5
muscle	my/o	2, 14
muscle	myos/o	14
nail	ungu/o	4
nail	onych/o	4
near (the point of reference)	proxim/o	3
neck, necklike	trachel/o	6
nerve	neur/o	2, 15
nerve root	radicul/o	15
nerve root	radic/o	15
nerve root	rhiz/o	15
night	noct/i	6
nose	rhin/o	5
nose	nas/o	5
nucleus	kary/o	2
one	mon/o	15
organ	organ/o	2

Definition	Combining Form	Chapter
other	heter/o	4
ovary	oophor/o	8
oxygen	ox/o, ox/i	5
palate	palat/o	11
pancreas	pancreat/o	11
parathyroid gland	parathyroid/o	16
patella (kneecap)	patell/o	14
pelvis, pelvic bone	pelv/i, pelv/o	9
perineum	perine/o	8
peritoneum	peritone/o	11
phalanx, finger or toe bone	phalang/o	14
pharynx	pharyng/o	5
physician	iatr/o	2
plasma	plasm/o	10
pleura	pleur/o	5
poison	toxic/o	16
potassium	kal/i	16
pregnancy	cyes/o, cyes/i	9
pregnancy	gravid/o	9
prostate gland	prostat/o	7
pubis	pub/o	14
pulse	sphygm/o	10
pupil	core/o, cor/o	12
pupil	pupill/o	12
pus	py/o	5
pylorus, pyloric sphincter	pylor/o	9, 11
radius (lower arm bone)	radi/o	14
rectum	proct/o	11
rectum	rect/o	11
red	erythr/o	2
renal pelvis	pyel/o	6
retina	retin/o	12
rib	cost/o	14
rod-shaped, striated	rhabd/o	2
sacrum	sacr/o	14
saliva	sial/o	11
scanty, few	olig/o	6
scapula (shoulder bone)	scapul/o	14
sclera	scler/o	12
sebum (oil)	seb/o	4
self	aut/o	4

Definition	Combining Form	Chapter
seminal vesicles	vesicul/o	7
sensation, sensitivity, feeling	esthesi/o	14
septum	sept/o	5
sigmoid	sigmoid/o	11
side	later/o	3
sinus	sinus/o	5
skin	cutane/o	4
skin	dermat/o	4
skin	derm/o	4
small growth	polyp/o	11
smooth	lei/o	2
sound	son/o	6
sound	ech/o	10
speech	phas/o	15
spermatozoa, sperm	sperm/o	7
spermatozoa, sperm	spermat/o	7
spinal cord	myel/o	15
spleen	splen/o	10
stapes	staped/o	13
sternum (breast bone)	stern/o	14
stomach	gastr/o	11
stone	petr/o	14
stone, calculus	lith/o	6
straight	orth/o	5
sugar	glycos/o	6
sugar	glyc/o	6
sweat	hidr/o	4
synovia, synovial membrane	synovi/o	14
system	system/o	2
tail (downward)	caud/o	3
tarsus (ankle bone)	tars/o	14
tear duct, tear	lacrim/o	12
tear, tear duct	dacry/o	12
tendon	ten/o	14
tendon	tendin/o	14
tendon	tend/o	14
tension, pressure	ton/o	12
testis, testicle	orch/o	7
testis, testicle	test/o	7
testis, testicle	orchi/o	7
testis, testicle	orchid/o	7

Definition	Combining Form	Chapter
thick	pachy/o	4
thorax (chest)	thorac/o	5
thirst	dips/o	16
thymus gland	thym/o	10
thyroid gland	thyroid/o	16
thyroid gland	thyr/o	16
tibia (lower leg bone)	tibi/o	14
tissue	hist/o	2
tongue	lingu/o	11
tongue	gloss/o	11
tonsils	tonsill/o	5
trachea	trache/o	5
tumor	onc/o	2
twisted chains	strept/o	4
two, double	dipl/o	12
ulna (lower arm bone)	uln/o	14
umbilicus, navel	omphal/o	9
urea, nitrogen	azot/o	6
ureter	ureter/o	6
urethra	urethr/o	6
urinary bladder	vesic/o, cyst/o	6
urine, urinary tract	urin/o	6
urine, urinary tract	ur/o	6
uterus	uter/o	8
uterus	metr/o, metr/i	8
uterus	hyster/o	8
uvula	uvul/o	11
vagina	vagin/o	8
vagina	colp/o	8
valve	valv/o	10
valve	valvul/o	10
vein	phleb/o	10
vein	ven/o	6
ventricle	ventricul/o	10
vertebra	vertebr/o	14
vertebral or spinal column	rachi/o	14
vessel	angi/o	10
vessel, duct	vas/o	7
vision	opt/o	12
vulva	vulv/o	8
vulva	episi/o	8

Definition	Combining Form	Chapter
water	hydr/o	6
white	leuk/o	2
woman	gyn/o	8
woman	gynec/o	8
wrinkles	rhytid/o	4
yellow	xanth/o	2
yellowish, fatty plaque	ather/o	10

Definition	Prefix	Chapter
above	supra-	14
above, excessive	hyper-	2
after	post-	9
after, beyond, change	meta-	2
all, total	pan-	5
before	ante-	9
before	pro-	2
below, incomplete, deficient	hypo-	2
beside, beyond, around	para-	4
between	inter-	14
difficult, labored, painful, abnormal	dys-	2
fast, rapid	tachy-	10
four	tetra-, quadri-	14
half	hemi-, semi-	14
many	multi-	9
many, much	poly-	6
new	neo-	2
none	nulli-	9
normal	eu-	5
on, upon, over	epi-	4
one	uni-	3
outside, outward	ex-, exo-	16
slow	brady-	10
small	micro-	9
surrounding (outer)	peri-	8
through, complete	per-	4
through	dia-	2
through, across, beyond	trans-	7
together, joined	sym-	14
together, joined	syn-	14
two	bin-	14
two	bi-	2, 14

Definition	Prefix	Chapter
under, below	sub-	4
within	intra-	4
within	endo-	5
without, absence of	a-, an-	5

Definition	Suffix	Chapter
abnormal fear of or aversion to specific objects or things	-phobia	12
abnormal condition (means increased when used with blood cell word roots)	-osis	2
abnormal reduction in number	-penia	10
absence of a normal opening, occlusion, closure	-atresia	8
berry-shaped (a form of bacterium)	-coccus (*pl.* cocci)	4
birth, labor	-tocia	9
blood condition	-emia	5
break	-clasis	14
break	-clasia	14
break	-clast	14
breathing	-pnea	5
carbon dioxide	-capnia	5
cell	-cyte	2
chest	-thorax	5
condition	-iasis	6
condition	-esis	6
constriction, narrowing	-stenosis	5
control, stop, standing	-stasis	2
creation of an artificial opening	-ostomy	5
cut into, incision	-otomy	5
digestion	-pepsia	11
disease	-pathy	2
diseased or abnormal state	-ia	4
drooping, sagging, prolapse	-ptosis	6
eating, swallowing	-phagia	4
enlargement	-megaly	6
excision, surgical removal	-ectomy	4
fallopian tube	-salpinx	7
flow, excessive discharge	-orrhea	4
formation	-poiesis	10

Definition	Suffix	Chapter
formation, development, growth (pertaining to)	-plasia	2
growth	-physis	14
a growth, a substance, a formation	-plasm	2
hardening	-sclerosis	10
hernia, protrusion	-cele	5
inflammation	-itis	4
instrument for visual examination	-scope	5
instrument to measure	-meter	5
instrument used to cut	-tome	4
instrument used to record	-graph	10
loosening, dissolution, separating	-lysis	6
malignant tumor	-sarcoma	2
measurement	-metry	5
nourishment, development	-trophy	6
one who	-ician	12
one who studies and practices (specialist)	-ologist	2
origin, cause	-genesis	2
oxygen	-oxia	5
pain	-odynia	10
pain	-algia	5
paralysis	-plegia	12
pertaining to	-ac	10
pertaining to	-ous	2, 6
pertaining to	-ar	5
pertaining to	-ic	2
pertaining to	-ial	8
pertaining to	-ior	3
pertaining to	-eal	5
pertaining to	-ary	5
pertaining to	-al	2
pertaining to sound or voice	-phonia	5
pertaining to visual examination	-scopic	5
physician, specialist	-iatrist	15
process of recording, x-ray filming	-graphy	5
producing, originating, causing (pertaining to)	-genic	2
rapid flow of blood	-orrhagia	5
record, x-ray	-gram	5

Definition	Suffix	Chapter
removal	-apheresis	10
resembling	-oid	2
run, running	-drome	16
rupture	-orrhexis	9
seizure, attack	-ictal	15
slight paralysis	-paresis	15
softening	-malacia	4
split, fissure	-schisis	14
state	-ism	7
state of	-sis	2
stretching out, dilatation, expansion	-ectasis	5
study of	-ology	2
substance or agent that produces or causes	-gen	2
sudden, involuntary muscle contraction	-spasm	5
surgical crushing	-tripsy	6
surgical fixation, fusion	-desis	14
surgical fixation, suspension	-pexy	5
surgical puncture to aspirate fluid	-centesis	5
surgical repair	-plasty	4
suturing, repairing	-orrhaphy	6
to separate	-crit	10
toward	-ad	3
treatment	-iatry	15
tumor, swelling	-oma	2
urine, urination	-uria	6
view of, viewing	-opsy	4
vision (condition)	-opia	12
visual examination	-scopy	5
weakness	-asthenia	14

APPENDIX C

▌ Additional Combining Forms, Prefixes, and Suffixes

The following word parts were not included in the text. They are listed here for your easy reference.

Combining Form	Definition
acanth/o	thorny, spiny
acetabul/o	acetabulum (hip socket)
actin/o	ray, radius
aer/o	air, gas
algesi/o	pain
ambly/o	dull, dim
amyl/o	starch
anis/o	unequal, dissimilar
arteriol/o	arteriole (small artery)
articul/o	joint
axill/o	armpit
bil/i	bile
brachi/o	arm
bucc/o	cheek
cerumin/o	cerumen (earwax)
chir/o	hand
dactyl/o	fingers or toes
dent/i	tooth
dextr/o	right
diaphor/o	sweat
dynam/o	power, strength
ectop/o	located away from usual place
emmetr/o	a normal measure
faci/o	face
ger/o	old age, aged
geront/o	old age, aged
gluc/o	sweetness, sugar

Combining Form	Definition
gnath/o	jaw
gon/o	seed
home/o	sameness, unchanging
hom/o	same
hypn/o	sleep
ichthy/o	fish
immun/o	immune
is/o	equal, same
kin/e	movement
labi/o	lips
macr/o	abnormal largeness
morph/o	form, shape
narc/o	stupor
nyct/o	night
nyctal/o	night
oo/o	egg, ovum
ov/i	egg
ov/o	egg
papill/o	nipple
pector/o	chest
ped/o	child, foot
phac/o	lens of the eye
phag/o	eat, swallow
phak/o	lens of the eye
physi/o	nature
pod/o	foot
poikil/o	varied, irregular
pyr/o	fever, heat

Combining Form	Definition
somn/i	sleep
tars/o	edge of the eyelid, tarsal (instep of foot)
top/o	place

Prefix	Definition
ab-	from, away from
ana-	up, again, backward
anti-	against
apo-	upon
cata-	down
con-	together
contra-	against
de-	from, down from, lack of
dis-	to undo, free from
ecto-	outside, outer
eso-	inward
extra-	outside of, beyond
in-	in, into, not
infra-	under, below
mal-	bad
meso-	middle
pre-	in front of, before
re-	back
retro-	back, behind
semi-	half
super-	over, above
tri-	three
ultra-	beyond, excess

Suffix	Definition
-agra	excessive pain
-ase	enzyme
-cidal	killing
-clysis	irrigating, washing
-crine	separate, secrete
-ectopia	displacement
-emesis	vomiting
-er	one who
-lepsy	seizure
-lytic	destroy, reduce
-mania	madness, insane desire
-morph	form, shape
-odia	smell
-opia	vision
-philia	love
-phily	love
-phoria	feeling
-porosis	passage
-prandial	meal
-praxia	in front of, before
-ptysis	spitting
-sepsis	infection
-stalsis	contraction
-ule	little

APPENDIX D

Abbreviations

These abbreviations are written as they appear most commonly in physician's orders and on patient charts. Some may also appear in both capital and small letters and with or without periods.

Common Medical Abbreviations	Definitions
@	at
ā ā	of each
AA	Alcoholics Anonymous
ab	abortion
abd	abdomen
ABG	arterial blood gases
ac	before meals
ACTH	adrenocorticotropic hormone
AD	right ear
ADH	antidiuretic hormone
ADL	activities of daily living
ad lib	as desired
adm	admission
ADT	admission, discharge, transfer
AFB	acid-fast bacilli
AgNO$_3$	silver nitrate
alb	albumin
alka phos	alkaline phosphatase
alt dieb	alternate days (every other day)
alt hor	alternate hours
alt noct	alternate nights
AM	between midnight and noon
AMA	against medical advice

Common Medical Abbreviations	Definitions
amb	ambulate, ambulatory
amp	ampule
amt	amount
ant	anterior
AP	anteroposterior
A&P	auscultation and percussion
aq	aqueous
ARM	artificial rupture of membranes
AS	left ear
ASA	aspirin
ASAP	as soon as possible
as tol	as tolerated
AV	arteriovenous
ax	axillary
BE	barium enema
bid	twice a day
BK	below knee
BM	bowel movement
BP	blood pressure
BR	bedrest
BRP	bathroom privileges
BS	blood sugar, bowel sounds, breath sounds
BUN	blood urea nitrogen
Bx	biopsy

Common Medical Abbreviations	Definitions
c̄	with
C	Celsius
C_1–C_7	cervical vertebrae
Ca	calcium
cal	calorie
cap	capsule
CAPD	continuous ambulatory peritoneal dialysis
cath	catheterization
CBC	complete blood count
CBR	complete bed rest
cc	cubic centimeter
CC	chief complaint
CC	colony count
CCU	coronary care unit
CEA	carcinoma embryonic antigen
CHO	carbohydrate
chemo	chemotherapy
chol	cholesterol
CIP	computerized impedance plethysmography
circ	circumcision
cl	clinic
Cl	chloride
cl liq	clear liquid
cm	centimeter
CMV	cytomegalovirus
CNS	central nervous system
c/o	complains of
CO	carbon monoxide
CO_2	carbon dioxide
comp	compound
cond	condition
CPK	creatine phosphokinase
CPR	cardiopulmonary resuscitation
CRNA	certified registered nurse-anesthetist
C&S	culture and sensitivity
CSF	cerebrospinal fluid

Common Medical Abbreviations	Definitions
CT	computed tomography
Cu	copper
CVP	central venous pressure
cx	cervix
CXR	chest x-ray
DAT	diet as tolerated
DC	discontinued
del	delivery
diff	differential (part of complete blood count)
disch	discharge
DNA	deoxyribonucleic acid
DOA	dead on arrival
DOB	date of birth
dr	dram
DRG	diagnosis-related groupings
D/S	dextrose in saline
DW	distilled water
D/W	dextrose in water
Dx	diagnosis
E	enema
EBL	estimated blood loss
ECG	electrocardiogram
EchoEG	echoencephalography
ECT	electroconvulsive therapy
ED	emergency department
EDD	estimated date of delivery
EEG	electroencephalogram
EENT	eye, ear, nose, and throat
EGD	esophagogastroduo-denoscopy
EKG	electrocardiogram
elix	elixir
EMG	electromyogram
ENG	electronystagmography
ENT	ear, nose, and throat
EP studies	evoked potential studies
ER	emergency room

Common Medical Abbreviations	Definitions
ERCP	endoscopic retrograde-cholangiopancreatography
ERT	estrogen replacement therapy
ESR	erythrocyte sedimentation rate
ESWL	extracorporeal shock-wave lithotripsy
etiol	etiology
exam	examination
ext	extract
ext	external
F	Fahrenheit
FBS	fasting blood sugar
Fe	iron
FHT	fetal heart tones
flu	influenza
Fr	French (catheter size)
FSH	follicle-stimulating hormone
FTT	failure to thrive
Fx	fracture
g	gram
GB series	gall bladder series
GERD	gastroesophageal reflux disease
GI	gastrointestinal
gtt	drop
GTT	glucose tolerance test
GU	genitourinary
Gyn	gynecology
h	hour
H	hypodermic
HD	hemodialysis
H&H	hemoglobin and hematocrit
HCl	hydrochloric acid
HCO_3	bicarbonate
Hct	hematocrit
Hg	mercury
hgb	hemoglobin

Common Medical Abbreviations	Definitions
HIV	human immunodeficiency virus
H_2O	water
H_2O_2	hydrogen peroxide (hydrogen dioxide)
HOB	head of bed
H&P	history and physical examination
H. pylori	*Helicobacter pylori*
HRT	hormone replacement therapy
hs	hour of sleep (bedtime)
ht	height
Hx	history
hypo	hypodermic
ICU	intensive care unit
IM	intramuscular
inf	inferior
I&O	intake and output
IPG	impedance plethysmography
IPPB	intermittent positive-pressure breathing
irrig	irrigation
isol	isolation
IUD	intrauterine device
IV	intravenous
IVC	intravenous cholangiogram
IVP	intravenous pyelogram
K	potassium
KCl	potassium chloride
kg	kilogram
KO	keep open
KUB	kidney, ureter, bladder
KVO	keep vein open
L	liter
L_1–L_5	lumbar vertebrae
lab	laboratory
lac	laceration
lat	lateral
L&D	labor and delivery
LDH	lactic dehydrogenase

Common Medical Abbreviations	Definitions
lg	large
LLL	left lower lobe
LLQ	left lower quadrant
LMP	last menstrual period
LP	lumbar puncture
LPN	licensed practical nurse
LR	lactated Ringer's (IV solution)
lt	left
LUL	left upper lobe
LUQ	left upper quadrant
mcg	microgram
mets	metastasis
MCH	mean corpuscular hemoglobin
MCV	mean corpuscular volume
mEq	milliequivalent
mg	milligram
mL	milliliter
mm	millimeter
MOM	milk of magnesia
MR	may repeat
MRI	magnetic resonance imaging
MS	morphine sulfate
Na	sodium
NA	nursing assistant
NaCl	sodium chloride (salt)
NAS	no added salt
NB	newborn
neg	negative
neuro	neurology
NG	nasogastric
NICU	neurological intensive care unit, neonatal intensive care unit
noc	night
noct	night
NPO	nothing by mouth
NS	normal saline
NSR	normal sinus rhythm

Common Medical Abbreviations	Definitions
N&V	nausea and vomiting
NVS	neurovital signs
O_2	oxygen
OB	obstetrics
OD	right eye
OD	overdose
oint	ointment
OOB	out of bed
OP	outpatient
Ophth	ophthalmic
OR	operating room
Ortho	orthopedics
OS	left eye
OT	occupational therapy
oto	otology
OU	both eyes, each eye
oz	ounce
p̄	after
P	phosphorus
PA	physician's assistant
PA	posteroanterior
pc	after meals
PCU	progressive care unit
PCV	packed cell volume
PDR	*Physician's Desk Reference*
Peds	pediatrics
PEEP	positive end expiratory pressure
PEG	percutaneous endoscopic gastrostomy
per	by
PERRLA	pupils equal, round, reactive to light and accommodation
PET scan	positron emission tomography
PFT	pulmonary function tests
PICU	pediatric intensive care unit
PKU	phenylketonuria
PMS	premenstrual syndrome

Common Medical Abbreviations	Definitions
PM	between noon and midnight
PNS	peripheral nervous system
po	orally
po	postoperative
po	phone order
post-op	postoperatively
PP	postpartum
PP	postprandial (after meals)
PPD	purified protein derivative
pr	per rectum
PRBC	packed red blood cells
PRN	whenever necessary
PSA	prostatic specific antigen
PT	prothrombin time
pt	patient
pt	pint
PT	physical therapy
PTT	partial thromboplastin time
Px	prognosis
q	every
qd	every day
q_h	every [number] hour (example: q2h)
qid	four times a day
qn	every night
qod	every other day
qoh	every other hour
qt	quart
R	rectal
RAIU	radioactive iodine uptake
RBC	red blood cell count
reg	regular
REM	rapid eye movement
resp	respirations
RLL	right lower lobe
RLQ	right lower quadrant
RN	registered nurse
R/O	rule out
ROM	range of motion

Common Medical Abbreviations	Definitions
RR	recovery room
rt	right
rt	routine
RT	respiratory therapy
RUL	right upper lobe
Rx	prescription
$\bar{s}$	without
sc	subcutaneous
SICU	surgical intensive care unit
SMAC	sequential multiple analysis computer
ss	one-half
SSE	soapsuds enema
staph	staphylococcus
stat	immediately
STD	sexually transmitted disease
strep	streptococcus
subling	sublingual
subq	subcutaneously
sup	superior
supp	suppository
surg	surgical
SVN	small-volume nebulizer
T_1-T_{12}	thoracic vertebrae
T_4	thyroxine
tab	tab
TAT	tetanus antitoxin
TCDB	turn, cough, deep breathe
TCT	thrombin clotting time
temp	temperature
TIA	transient ischemic attack
tid	three times a day
tinct	tincture
TLC	tender loving care
TO	telephone order
TPN	total parenteral nutrition
tr	tincture
trach	tracheostomy
TSH	thyroid-stimulating hormone
TWE	tap water enema

Common Medical Abbreviations | Definitions

Abbreviation	Definition
Tx	traction
U	unit
UA	urinalysis
UGI	upper gastrointestinal
Ung	ointment
UPPP	uvulopalatopharyngoplasty
vag	vaginal
VCUG	voiding cystourethrogram
VDRL	Venereal Disease Research Laboratory
VPS	ventilation/perfusion scanning
VS	vital signs
WA	while awake
WBC	white blood cell count
W/C	wheelchair
wt	weight
XRT	radiotherapy, radiation therapy

Abbreviations of Diagnoses or Surgical Procedures | Definitions

Abbreviation	Definition
ABE	acute bacterial endocarditis
AD	Alzheimer's disease
AFIB	atrial fibrillation
AHD	arteriosclerotic heart disease
AI	aortic insufficiency
AIDS	acquired immune deficiency syndrome
AKA	above-knee amputation
ALL	acute lymphocytic leukemia
ALS	amyotrophic lateral sclerosis
AMI	acute myocardial infarction
AML	acute myelocytic leukemia
AOD	adult-onset diabetes

Abbreviations of Diagnoses or Surgical Procedures | Definitions

Abbreviation	Definition
A&P	anterior and posterior colporrhaphy
AP	angina pectoris
ARDS	adult respiratory distress syndrome
ARMD	age-related macular degeneration
ASCVD	arteriosclerotic cardiovascular disease
ASD	atrial septal defect
ASHD	arteriosclerotic heart disease
Ast	astigmatism
AUL	acute undifferentiated leukemia
AVR	aortic valve replacement
BA	bronchial asthma
BBB	bundle branch block
BKA	below-knee amputation
BOM	bilateral otitis media
BPH	benign prostatic hypertrophy, benign prostatic hyperplasia
BSO	bilateral salpingo-oophorectomy
CA	cancer, carcinoma
CABG	coronary artery bypass graft
CAD	coronary artery disease
CBS	chronic brain syndrome
CDH	congenital dislocation of the hip
CF	cystic fibrosis
CHB	complete heart block
CHD	coronary heart disease
CHF	congestive heart failure
CI	coronary insufficiency
CLD	chronic liver disease
CLL	chronic lymphocytic leukemia
CML	chronic myelogenous leukemia

Abbreviations of Diagnoses or Surgical Procedures	Definitions
COLD	chronic obstructive lung disease
COPD	chronic obstructive pulmonary disease
CP	cerebral palsy
CPD	cephalopelvic disproportion
CPN	chronic pyelonephritis
CRD	chronic respiratory disease
C/S, CS, C-section	cesarean section
CTS	carpal tunnel syndrome
CVA	cerebrovascular accident
D&C	dilatation and curettage
DI	diabetes insipidus
DIC	diffuse intravascular coagulation
DLE	discoid lupus erythematosus
DM	diabetes mellitus
DT	delirium tremens
DVT	deep vein thrombosis
EM	emmetropia
EP	ectopic pregnancy
ESWL	extracorporeal shock-wave lithotripsy
FBD	fibrocystic breast disease
FUO	fever of undetermined origin
GC	gonorrhea
GERD	gastroesophageal reflux disease
GSW	gunshot wound
HB	heart block
HCVD	hypertensive cardiovascular disease
HHD	hypertensive heart disease
HMD	hyaline membrane disease
HNP	herniated nucleus pulposus

Abbreviations of Diagnoses or Surgical Procedures	Definitions
IBS	irritable bowel syndrome
IDDM	insulin dependent diabetes mellitus
I&D	incision and drainage
IHD	ischemic heart disease
LAP	laparotomy
LE	lupus erythematosus
LTB	laryngotracheobronchitis
MD	muscular dystrophy
MG	myasthenia gravis
MI	myocardial infarction
MM	multiple myeloma
MS	multiple sclerosis
MVP	mitral valve prolapse
OD	overdose
OM	otitis media
OSA	obstructive sleep apnea
PAC	premature atrial contractions
PAT	paroxysmal atrial tachycardia
PCP	*Pneumocystis carinii* pneumonia
PD	Parkinson's disease
PDA	patent ductus arteriosus
PE	pulmonary embolism
PID	pelvic inflammatory disease
PKU	phenylketonuria
PTCA	percutaneous transluminal coronary angioplasty
PUL	percutaneous ultrasound lithotripsy
PVC	premature ventricular contractions
PVD	peripheral vascular disease
RA	rheumatoid arthritis
RDS	respiratory distress syndrome

Abbreviations of Diagnoses or Surgical Procedures	Definitions
RHD	rheumatic heart disease
SBE	subacute bacterial endocarditis
SIDS	sudden infant death syndrome
SLE	systemic lupus erythematosus
SMR	submucous resection
SO	salpingo-oophorectomy
STAPH	staphylococcus
STD	sexually transmitted disease
STREP	streptococcus
SVD	spontaneous vaginal delivery
T&A	tonsillectomy and adenoidectomy
TAH	total abdominal hysterectomy
TAH-BSO	total abdominal hysterectomy—bilateral salpingo-oophorectomy

Abbreviations of Diagnoses or Surgical Procedures	Definitions
TB	tuberculosis
THA	total hip arthroplasty
TIA	transient ischemic attack
TKA	total knee arthroplasty
TUIP	transurethral incision of the prostate
TUMP	transurethral microwave thermotherapy
TUR	transurethral reaction
TURP	transurethral resection of the prostate
TSS	toxic shock syndrome
TVH	total vaginal hysterectomy
UGI	upper gastrointestinal
UPPP	uvulopalatopharyngo-plasty
URI	upper respiratory infection
UTI	urinary tract infection
VD	venereal disease

APPENDIX E

Common Plural Endings for Medical Terms

In the English language, plurals are often formed by adding *s* or *es* to the word. Forming plurals in the language of medicine is not so simple. Use the table below to learn the standard plural formation of medical terms.

Singular Ending	Plural Ending	Example Singular	Plural
-a	-ae	vertebra	vertebrae
-ax	-aces	thorax	thoraces
-ex	-ices	apex	apices
-is	-es	pubis	pubes
-ix	-ixes	appendix	appendixes
-ma	-mata	sarcoma	sarcomata
-on	-a	ganglion	ganglia
-um	-a	ovum	ova
-us	-i	alveolus	alveoli
-y	-ies	biopsy	biopsies

APPENDIX F

Pharmacology Terms

Term	Definition
absorption	the process whereby a drug moves from the site of entry into the body toward the circulatory system and the target organ or tissue
ACE inhibitors	one of the categories of antihypertensive drugs. Angiotensin-converting enzyme inhibitors suppress the action of the renin-angiotensin-aldosterone system
action	the chemical changes or effects that a drug has on body cells. Drugs are usually classified on the basis of their actions.
administration	the giving by a nurse or other authorized person of a drug to a patient
adverse reaction	any harmful or unintended reaction to a drug administered at a normal dosage
ampoule	a small, sterile glass or plastic container that usually holds a single dose of a solution to be administered parenterally
analgesic	it acts on the nervous system to reduce the perception of pain. A *narcotic analgesic* is used for severe pain but can result in dependence and tolerance. A *nonnarcotic analgesic* is used for mild-to-moderate pain and is less likely to cause dependence and tolerance.
anesthetic	a drug or agent that is capable of producing a complete or partial loss of feeling
antacid	a drug or dietary substance that buffers, neutralizes, or absorbs hydrochloric acid in the stomach
antiinflammatory agent (NSAIDs)	a drug or agent that counteracts or reduces inflammation. The nonsteroidal antiinflammatory drugs (NSAIDs) are aspirin-like drugs that are used to treat inflammation, fever, and pain and are not glucocorticoid in nature.
antianemic agent	an agent used to treat or prevent anemia
antianxiety agent	a sedative or minor tranquilizer used to treat feelings of anxiety such as apprehension, worry, and fear
antiarrhythmic	an agent used to treat a cardiac arrhythmia
antibiotic	an antimicrobial agent, derived from cultures of a microorganism or produced semisynthetically, is used to treat bacterial infections
anticoagulant	a drug that is used to prevent or delay coagulation of the blood

Term	Definition
anticonvulsants	drugs that prevent or reduce the severity of epileptic or other convulsive seizures
antidepressants	drugs that are used to prevent or relieve depression
antidiabetics (hypoglycemics)	drugs that are prescribed to decrease the amount of glucose circulating in the blood
antidiarrheal drugs	drugs that relieve the symptoms of diarrhea. Antidiarrheals work by absorbing water from the digestive tract, by altering intestinal motility, by altering electrolyte transport, or by absorption of toxins or microorganisms.
antiemetic	a drug or agent used to prevent or alleviate nausea and vomiting
antihistamines	drugs capable of reducing the physiologic and pharmacologic effects of histamine by preventing it from reaching its site of action (receptor site)
antihyperlipidemic drugs	drugs prescribed to reduce the amount of lipids in the serum and thereby to reduce the risk of atherosclerotic cardiovascular disease
antihypertensives	drugs that are used to reduce high blood pressure. The five major categories of antihypertensives are: diuretics, adrenergic inhibitors, vasodilators, angiotensin-converting enzyme (ACE) inhibitors, and calcium antagonists.
antineoplastics	drugs that are used to control or kill cancer cells. Most anticancer drugs prevent the proliferation of cells by inhibiting the synthesis of deoxyribonucleic acid (DNA).
antipsychotics	drugs that are prescribed to counteract or diminish the symptoms of psychoses, i.e., schizophrenia and major affective disorders
antiseptic	a substance that inhibits the growth of microorganisms
antispasmodic	a drug or other agent that prevents smooth muscle spasms, as in the uterus, digestive system, or urinary tract
bactericidal	a drug or agent that is destructive to bacteria
barbiturate	a derivative of barbituric acid that acts as a sedative or hypnotic. Barbiturates act by depressing the respiratory rate, blood pressure, temperature, and central nervous system.
beta-blockers	agents that decrease the rate and force of heart contractions by blocking the beta-adrenergic receptors
bioavailability	the percentage of an administered drug that becomes available to affect the target organ or tissue
biotransformation	the chemical changes a substance undergoes in the body
calcium channel blockers	drugs that inhibit the flow of calcium ions across the membranes of smooth muscle cells. Calcium channel blockers are used primarily in the treatment of heart diseases marked by coronary artery spasms.
capsule (cap)	a small, soluble container, usually made of gelatin, used for enclosing a dose of medication for swallowing
cardiotonic	a pharmacologic agent that increases the force and efficiency of the heart's contractions
chemical name	the exact designation of the chemical structure of a drug

Term	Definition
chemotherapy	the treatment of infection and other diseases with chemical agents. The term *chemotherapeutic agent* usually refers to a medication used to treat cancer because it can alter the growth of cells.
contraindications	factors that prohibit administration of a drug
disinfectant	a chemical that can be applied to objects to destroy microorganisms
distribution	the pattern of absorption of drug molecules by various tissues after the chemical enters the circulatory system
diuretic	a drug that promotes the formation and excretion of urine. Diuretics are prescribed to reduce the volume of extracellular fluid in the treatment of many disorders, including hypertension, congestive heart failure, and edema.
dose	the amount of a drug or other substance to be administered at one time
drug	any substance taken by mouth, injected into a muscle, the skin, a blood vessel, or a cavity of the body, or applied topically to treat or prevent a disease or condition
drug clearance	the elimination of a drug from the body. It is commonly excreted by the kidneys, liver, lungs, and other routes. The rate of clearance helps determine the size and frequency of a medication's dosage.
drug-drug interaction	a modification of the effect of a drug when administered with another drug. The effect may be an increase or a decrease in the action of either substance, or it may be an adverse effect that is not normally associated with either drug.
effect (local, systemic)	the result of (or biologic response to) administration of a drug. Drug effects may be *local* (if confined to the administration site) or *systemic*. Drugs are prescribed for their therapeutic, prophylactic, or diagnostic effects, but they may also produce undesirable responses (adverse effects).
enteral	refers to the use of oral ingestion as a mode of drug administration. The enteral route is the most commonly used method of giving drugs.
Food and Drug Administration (FDA)	a federal agency responsible for the enforcement of federal regulations regarding the manufacture and distribution of food, drugs, and cosmetics as protection against the sale of impure or dangerous substances
formulary	a listing of drugs and drug information used by health practitioners to prescribe treatment that is medically appropriate
generic name	the official, established nonproprietary name assigned to a drug, often a simpler form of the chemical name
hormones (androgens, estrogens)	a complex chemical substance produced in one part or organ of the body that initiates or regulates the activity of an organ or a group of cells in another part of the body. *Androgens,* steroid hormones that increase male characteristics, may be administered orally or parenterally. Pharmaceutic preparations of *estrogen,* a hormonal steroidal compound that promotes development of female secondary sex characteristics, are used in oral contraceptives and for the relief of the discomforts of menopause.

Term	Definition
hypnotics	a class of drugs often used to produce sleep, may be used as sedatives
infusion	the introduction of a substance directly into a vein by means of gravity flow
inhalation	a method of drug administration that involves the breathing in of spray or vapor. The medication is absorbed into the circulation through the mucous membrane of the nasal passages.
intramuscular (IM)	the introduction of a hypodermic needle into a muscle to administer medication
intravenous (IV)	the delivery of nutrients or medication directly into the bloodstream via a vein
laxative	an agent that promotes bowel evacuation by increasing the bulk of the feces, by softening the stool, or by lubricating the intestinal wall
mechanism of action	the means by which a drug exerts a desired effect
muscle relaxant	a chemotherapeutic agent that reduces the contractility of muscle fibers
narcotic	a natural or synthetic product prescribed for pain relief
nonprescription drugs, over-the-counter (OTC)	a drug that may be purchased without a prescription
official name	the official established nonproprietary name assigned to a drug often a simpler form of the chemical name
ointment	a semisolid, externally applied preparation, usually containing a drug
oral	refers to the use of oral ingestion as a mode of drug administration
parenteral	the administration of medication or nutrients by a route other than the digestive tract
pharmacist	a person formally trained to formulate and dispense medications
pharmacodynamics	the study of the action of a drug on a living organism
pharmacokinetics	the study of the action of drugs within the body
pharmacology	the study of the preparation, properties, uses, and actions of drugs
pharmacy	*a.* the study of preparing and dispensing drugs, *b.* a place for preparing and dispensing drugs
placebo	an inactive substance, prescribed as if it were an effective dose of a needed medication
potency	the absolute amount of a drug required to produce a desired effect. When similar medications of the same dosage are compared, the drug that produces the maximal effect is said to be the most potent.
pregnancy safety	FDA-assigned risk categories relating to the documented problems with the use of a drug during pregnancy
prescription	an order for medication, therapy, or a therapeutic device given by a properly authorized person to a person properly authorized to dispense or perform the order
routes of administration	any one of the ways in which a drug may be administered, such as intramuscularly, intranasally, intravenously, orally, rectally, subcutaneously, sublingually, topically, or vaginally
sedative	a drug that reversibly depresses the central nervous system and is used chiefly to allay anxiety

Term	Definition
side effects	any reaction or consequence that results from a medication or therapy. This can be an effect carried beyond the desired limit or a reaction unrelated to the primary object of therapy. Usually, although not necessarily, the effect is undesirable.
solution	a mixture of one or more substances dissolved into another substance. The molecules of each of the substances disperse homogeneously and do not change chemically.
stimulants	any agent that increases the rate of activity of a body system
subcutaneous (sc, sq, subq)	the introduction of a medication into the subcutaneous tissue beneath the skin
suppository	an easily melted medicated mass for insertion in the rectum, urethra, or vagina
suspension	a liquid in which particles of a solid are dispersed, but not dissolved, and in which the dispersal is maintained by stirring or shaking the mixture
tablet	a small, solid dosage form of a medication. Most tablets are intended to be swallowed whole, but some may be dissolved in the mouth, chewed, or dissolved in liquid before swallowing; some may be placed in a body cavity.
thyroid supplements	prescribed to treat disorders of the thyroid gland, such as hypothyroidism, goiter, and thyroid carcinoma
topical	a method of drug administration by which the medication is applied directly to the skin
toxicity	refers to the level at which a drug's concentration within the body produces serious adverse effects
trade name	a proprietary name, assigned to a drug by its manufacturer, which is registered as part of the drug's identity
tranquilizers	a drug prescribed to reduce anxiety or agitation, ideally without decreasing consciousness
transdermal	a method of applying a drug to unbroken skin. The drug is absorbed continuously through the skin, producing a systemic effect.
United States Pharmacopeia (USP)	a compendium, recognized officially by the Federal Food, Drug and Cosmetic Act, that contains descriptions, uses, strengths, and standards of purity for selected drugs and for all of their forms of dosage
vasoconstrictors	an agent that promotes constriction of the blood vessels. Also called *vasopressors*
vasodilators	an agent that causes relaxation of the smooth muscle of the vascular system. Used in the treatment of acute heart failure in myocardial infarction, in cases associated with severe mitral insufficiency, and in failure resulting from myocardial disease.
vitamins	an organic compound essential in small quantities for normal physiologic and metabolic functioning. Vitamin deficiency diseases produce specific symptoms usually alleviated by the administration of the appropriate vitamin. Vitamins are classified according to their fat or water solubility, their physiologic effects, or their chemical structures.

APPENDIX G

▌Health Care Delivery/Managed Care Terms

Term	Definition
accreditation	a formal recognition that an organization conforms to a set of industry-specific, qualifying standards
activities of daily living (ADL)	activities performed as part of a person's daily routine of self-care
administrative costs	the costs assumed by a managed care plan for administrative services
accepting assignment	providers of medical services agreeing that the receipt of payment from Medicare for a professional service will constitute full payment for that service
alternative delivery system	all forms of health care delivery systems other than traditional fee-for-service indemnity health care
ambulatory setting	environment in which health care services are provided on an outpatient basis
ancillary care	health care services performed by clinical personnel other than physicians and nurses
appeal process	a mechanism by which patients, practitioners, or providers may request a reconsideration of a decision made by a medical review board
attrition rate	the disenrollment of members from a health maintenance organization, expressed as a percentage of total plan enrollment
basic health services	benefits that all federally qualified HMOs must offer as defined in the Federal HMO Regulations
benefit schedule	a summary of covered services, limitations, and applicable co-payments provided to a covered group of individuals
capitation	a per member, monthly payment to a provider that covers contracted health care services and is paid in advance of its delivery. It exists for a specific length of time regardless of the number of times a member uses the service.
carve out	a health benefit that is removed from a larger benefit package and is contracted for separately by a managed care organization
case management	the process whereby a health care professional supervises the administration of medical and ancillary services to a patient
case mix	the number, frequency, and severity of hospital admissions or managed care services utilized

Term	Definition
coinsurance	the percentage of the costs of medical services paid by the patient
concurrent review	a screening method by which a health care provider reviews the performance of a procedure or a hospital admission to assess its necessity
Consolidated Omnibus Budget Reconciliation Act (COBRA)	a law that requires employers to offer continued health insurance coverage to employees who have had their health insurance terminated
copayment	a nominal fee charged to HMO members for each medical visit or prescription filled
cost-effectiveness	usually considered as a ratio, the cost of a drug or procedure compared with the health care benefits resulting from it
cost shifting	the redistribution of payment sources. When one payer obtains a discount and the providers of care increase the costs to another payer to make up the difference.
deductible	a fixed amount of health care dollars a person must pay before payment from an insurer begins
diagnosis-related groups (DRG)	a classification system used to determine payments from Medicare based on assigning a standard flat rate to major diagnostic categories. This flat rate is paid to hospitals regardless of the full cost of the services provided.
direct costs	costs fully attributable to the provision of specific health care services
Employee Retirement Income Security Act of 1974 (ERISA)	a law that mandates reporting and disclosure requirements for health plans
exclusive provider organizations (EPO, EPA)	a preferred provider arrangement by which patient members of a health care plan must choose from a list of selected health care providers
fee for service (FFS)	traditional provider reimbursement by which a patient receives a bill from a physician that includes all professional services performed
first dollar coverage	a type of insurance plan in which there is no deductible and the insurer pays the full amount of the provided services
formulary	the panel or list of drugs chosen by a hospital or managed care organization that is available to be used by physicians for their patients
gatekeeper	a primary care physician in an HMO who is the initial provider of health care and who controls and authorizes referrals to other specialists as needed
Health Care Financing Administration (HCFA)	the federal agency responsible for administering Medicare and Medicaid
health maintenance organization (HMO)	an organization that provides the delivery of hospital, physician, and other health care services to an enrolled population for a fixed sum of money, paid in advance, for a specified period

Term	Definition
health maintenance organization-staff model	the purest form of managed care in which physicians are employees of the HMO and work in clinical facilities managed by the HMO. The physicians do not practice on a traditional fee-for-service basis and do not have their own private practice.
health maintenance organization-group model	the HMO organization contracts with an established physician group that is paid a fixed amount per patient to provide specific medical services. These physicians do not have traditional fee-for-service patients.
health maintenance organization-Individual Practice Association (IPA) model	the managed care organization contracts with independent physicians who work in their own private offices and see fee-for-service patients as well as HMO enrollees. They are paid by capitation for the HMO patients, and the physician assumes the responsibility for keeping the treatment cost low.
health maintenance organization-point-of-service model	sometimes referred to as an *open-ended HMO;* the patient can receive care either within the HMO network or by going outside to a physician not contracting with the HMO. Patients decide where they wish to go at the time the service is needed, knowing fuller insurance coverage is provided if they stay within the HMO physician network.
home care	medical care administered at a patient's residence by a health care professional
hospital alliance	a group of hospitals that have joined together to improve their competitive positions and buying powers
indemnity insurance	traditional fee-for-service medical plan under which patients are billed for each medical service performed
inpatient care	admission to a hospital, for at least 24 hours, under the care of a physician
managed health care	the use of a planned and systematic approach to providing health care, with the goal of offering quality care at the lowest possible cost
mandated benefits	health care benefits that health care plans are required by state or federal law to provide to members
Medicaid benefits	an entitlement program run by both the state and federal governments designed to provide health care coverage to patients who cannot afford to pay for private health insurance
Medicare	an entitlement program run by the Health Care Financing Administration of the federal government by which people age 65 and older receive health care insurance. Part A covers hospitalization and Part B covers outpatient and physician services.
nonparticipating provider	a health care provider who has not contracted with an insurance company or HMO to provide health care
open access	arrangement that allows members to see participating providers, usually specialists, without referral from a primary physician gatekeeper
open enrollment	a period during which a managed care organization allows persons not previously enrolled to apply for plan membership
out-of-pocket costs	the share of health services costs paid by the individual enrollee

Term	Definition
outpatient care	the provision of health care services outside of a hospital setting
Physicians Current Procedural Terminology (CPT)	a guide used for the billing and payment of physicians' services
physician-hospital organization (PHO)	an organization owned by both a hospital and its medical staff of physicians that contracts with HMOs and assumes responsibility for providing health care services to an identified group of individuals
preferred providers	physicians, hospitals, and other health care providers who contract to provide health care services to persons covered by a particular health plan
primary care physician (PCP)	sometimes referred to as *gatekeepers,* these general practitioners are the first physicians to see a patient for an illness
prospective payment	payment that is received before care is actually needed or rendered. It gives providers an incentive to utilize fewer resources as they get to keep the difference between what is prepaid and what is actually used.
provider	any licensed or approved supplier of medical services
reimbursement	payment to a medical provider in exchange for the performance of medical services
risk	the probability of loss, due to expenditure for medical services, for a defined patient population
third-party payer	an organization that pays for health-care expenses
utilization management	a process for measuring the optimal use of medical resources, based on medical necessity and cost-effectiveness
utilization review (UR)	a systematic, retrospective review designed to determine the medical necessity and economic appropriateness of medical services performed

Additional Health Care Delivery/Managed Care Abbreviations and Acronyms

Abbreviation/Acronym	Definition
AAAHC	Accreditation Association for Ambulatory Health Care
AAPPO	American Association of Preferred Provider Associations
ADS	Alternative Delivery System
AMCPA	American Managed Care Pharmacy Association
AMCRA	American Managed Care and Review Association
APT	admission per thousand
CEA	cost-effective analysis
CHO	Comprehensive Health Organization
CQI	continuous quality improvement
DME	durable medical equipment

Abbreviation/Acronym	Definition
DOS	date of service
FP	family practice
HBO	health benefits organization
LTC	long-term care
LOS	length of stay
MGMA	Medical Group Management Association
PCN	Primary care network
PMPM	per member, per month
POS	point of service
PPO	preferred provider organization
PPS	prospective payment system

APPENDIX H

▌Alternative Health Care Terms

Term	Definition
acupressure	the digital stimulation of anatomic pressure points on the body to preserve and restore health
acupuncture	the ancient practice of inserting very thin needles into acupoints just under the skin to treat disease, increase immune response, or relieve pain
Alexander technique	the use of movement and exercises to affect physiologic structure, posture, movement, and breathing
apiotherapy	the medicinal use of honeybee venom to treat inflammatory and degenerative diseases
applied kinesiology	noninvasive manipulative treatments to stimulate or relax key muscles, allowing for the diagnosis or resolution of health problems
aromatherapy	the therapeutic use of essential concentrated oils expressed from aromatic herbs, flowers, and trees. Both the aroma and external skin applications are used as therapy in treating infections, immune deficiencies, and stress.
autosuggestion	a mild form of self-hypnosis in which an individual sits quietly, breathes deeply, and relaxes to a desired state
Ayurvedic medicine	a centuries' old system of alternative medicine that includes herbs, aromatherapy, music therapy, massage, yoga, and other alternative medicine therapies. It places equal emphasis on mind, body, and spirit in achieving the harmony of wellness.
biofeedback therapy	a method for learned self-control of physiologic responses using electronic devices to reduce the symptoms of medical problems
bodywork	a general term that applies to a wide variety of manipulative therapies, emphasizing skillful touch, which affect posture, function, and behavior
chelation therapy	the use of oral and intravenous agents and exercise to prevent, halt, or reverse artery disease and draw toxins and metabolic wastes from the bloodstream. It is used as an alternative to bypass surgery and angioplasty.
Chinese medicine	an ancient system of medicine that balances the body's flow of energy (chi), thus curing disease, through the use of acupuncture and herbal remedies. Some practitioners of Chinese medicine use qigong (p. 579), a powerful technique of direct manipulation of chi to facilitate healing.
clay therapy	the use of the mineral composition of clay, both internally and externally, as an elixir or a poultice
colon therapy	self-cleansing of the intestines to remove waste matter that interferes with healthy function and the proper assimilation and absorption of nutrients
enzyme therapy	plant and pancreatic enzymes are ingested by mouth to improve digestion and the absorption of essential nutrients

Term	Definition
Feldenkrais method	a general system of neuromotor teaching and reconditioning that uses soft tissue manipulation to improve functional integration. The technique emphasizes specific gentle body movements to increase ease and range of motion and improve flexibility and coordination.
guided imagery	a technique by which imagination and directed mental activity are used to acquire self-control of responses to life and health situations and to reduce stress
herbal medicine	herbal remedies used internally or externally to maintain or restore health
holistic practitioner	a general term for any practitioner who considers the body as a functioning whole and approaches treatment in that manner. Although a holistic orientation most often may be associated with alternative types of treatment, many who practice traditional Western medicine use holistic principles.
homeopathy	a system of medical treatment based on the theory that certain diseases can be cured by giving minute doses of drugs that, in a healthy person, would produce symptoms like those of the disease. The very small doses administered by the homeopathist stimulate the body's own healing processes.
hydrotherapy	the use of hot or cold water, ice, and steam, both internally and externally, to maintain and restore health
hypnotherapy	using the power of suggestion and trance-like states to access deep levels of the mind in order to treat a wide range of health conditions
light therapy	the therapeutic use of ultraviolet, colored, and laser lights to reestablish the body's natural rhythm and reduce pain, depression, and other health conditions
massage therapy	a general term for a discipline that involves stroking of the body with hands to increase blood supply, relax muscle fibers, and relieve tension
meditation	a mental activity focusing attention on a single activity such as breathing, an image, or a sound, in order to calm and still the mind and stay pleasantly anchored in the present. This is used to identify and control reactions to stress situations.
movement therapy	a method of teaching more efficient ways to move, creating correct posture and effective use of the body. It facilitates new patterns of balanced movement
moxibustion	similar to acupuncture and acupressure, but instead of needling or pressing the acupoint, a particular herb is ignited and burned on or near that point on the skin
myofascial release	gentle release, through soft tissue manipulation, of the body's fascial system to restore proper function and biomechanics
naturopathic medicine	an array of healing practices based on the patient's individual needs and using the body's inherent ability to heal. It focuses on treating the underlying causes of disease with nontoxic therapies to restore the body's natural balance and health.
neurolinguistic programming	activities aimed at helping individuals detect and reprogram unconscious patterns of thought and behavior that are negatively affecting their health or recovery from illness
neuromuscular therapy	a specific type of massage therapy designed to relieve traumatized neuropathways, reduce hyperconstriction in the tissues, and restore proper biomechanical function
osteopathy	a form of physical medicine that helps restore the structural balance of the musculoskeletal system using joint manipulation, physical therapy, and postural reeducation
oxygen therapy	using oxygen in various forms to promote healing and destroy disease-producing organisms in the body. Oxygen may be inhaled, ingested, inserted in body orifices, given intravenously, or absorbed through the skin.

Term	Definition
qigong	a set of physical activities that combine movement, meditation, and breath regulation to enhance the flow of the body's energy, improve blood circulation, and strengthen immune system responses
Pilates	a method of physical and mental training designed to improve neuromuscular synchronicity
reflexology	stimulation of certain points or reflex areas on the hands, face, and feet to direct invisible nerve currents (and nervous energy) to specific organs
reiki	a deeply relaxing ancient spiritual massage technique. The client lies on a table, and energy is transferred from the practitioner, whose hands are placed in a sequence of standardized positions on the client's body.
rolfing	a type of treatment, offered in 10-hour cycles, in which the practitioner manually stretches and loosens connective tissue, allowing muscles and joints to move more freely
shiatsu	a Japanese style of massage using the noninvasive touch and pressure of finger, hand, and foot techniques to release physical and emotional tension. Involves extensive soft tissue manipulation and both active and passive exercises
sports massage	a form of bodywork designed with an athlete's specific needs in mind. It can improve performance, speed post-workout recovery, and aid in injury rehabilitation
tai chi chuan	an ancient Chinese discipline of meditative, dance-like movements that help to relax and strengthen the muscles and joints
vibration massage therapy	a form of massage on joints and other body structures to relieve tension and stress
watsu	a form of aquatic bodywork that takes place in chest-high warm water and involves both a series of flowing, dance-like movements and a body massage by a Watsu practitioner
yoga	a series of practices that use physical posture, breathing exercises, and meditation to reduce stress, lower blood pressure, regulate heart rate, reduce the aging process, and restore mind/body unity

APPENDIX I

Psychiatry Terms

The following psychiatric terminology is not meant to be inclusive but is designed to give the student an overview of the medical language used on a psychiatric unit.

Term	Definition
abstract thinking	a stage in the development of cognitive thought. The ability to understand relationships and to categorize objects based upon their essential characteristics. Abstract thinking requires flexibility, adaptability, and the use of concepts and generalizations.
acting out	indirect expression of feeling through behavior that attracts the attention of others and may be dangerous or destructive
adaptation	the process of changing to achieve equilibrium between an individual and the environment
adjustment disorder	a maladaptive reaction to an identifiable, transient situation
affect	the outward expression of a subjectively experienced feeling state. *Blunted* affect is characterized by a severe reduction in the intensity of expression; *flat* affect refers to a loss of expression; *inappropriate* affect describes a discordance between emotional expression and the content of speech; affect is *labile* when it is characterized by marked variability.
akathisia	motor restlessness that is one of the possible complications of treatment with antipsychotic medications
amnesia	loss of memory usually as a consequence of physical illness or injury or psychological trauma
antisocial personality	a disorder characterized by repetitive failure to abide by social and legal norms and to accept responsibility for one's own behavior
anxiety disorder	emotional illness characterized by feelings of apprehension, tension, or uneasiness arising, typically, from the anticipation of unreal or imagined danger
anorexia	an eating disorder, occurring predominantly in young women, which is characterized by a pathologic fear of weight gain, a distorted body image, and amenorrhea
apraxia	impairment of the ability to execute purposeful movements, even though adequate muscle strength and coordination are present

Term	Definition
attention deficit hyperactivity disorder (ADHD)	a syndrome of learning and behavioral problems characterized by developmentally inappropriate and marked inattention, impulsivity, and excessive motor activity
autism	a mental disorder, the features of which include onset during infancy or childhood, preoccupation with subjective mental activity, inability to interact socially, impaired communication, and repetitive body movements
behavior modification	a type of psychotherapy, based on principles of learning, which seeks to change maladaptive, observable behavior by substituting a new set of responses by the use of techniques such as reward and reinforcement
bipolar disorder (BMD)	a major psychologic disorder typified by a disturbance in mood. The disorder is manifested by manic and depressive episodes that may alternate or may occur simultaneously.
body language	a form of nonverbal communication; expression of a physical, mental, or emotional state by means of body position or movement
borderline personality disorder	a pervasive personality pattern, the features of which include instability of self-image, interpersonal relationships, and mood
bulimia	a mental disorder, occurring predominantly in young women, manifested by an insatiable craving for food, often resulting in episodes of binge eating, followed by purging; an awareness that the binges are abnormal; and a depressed mood
chemical dependence	a cluster of cognitive, behavioral, and physiologic symptoms that indicate impaired control of psychoactive substance use and continued use of the substance (often in larger amounts) despite adverse consequences
cognition	the mental process characterized by knowing, thinking, learning, and judging
commitment	involuntary hospital admission for treatment of psychiatric illness, usually sought after a patient has been deemed a danger to self or to others
confabulation	the fabrication of experiences or situations, often in a detailed and plausible way, to fill in and cover up gaps in memory
coping mechanism	the factors that enable an individual to regain emotional equilibrium after a stressful experience
cue	a stimulus that determines or may prompt the nature of a person's response
deinstitutionalization	transfer to a community setting of a patient who has been hospitalized for an extended period
delusion	a persistent false belief that is held despite evidence to the contrary. A delusion may be persecutory, grandiose, or somatic in nature
defense mechanism	an unconscious, intrapsychic reaction that offers protection to the self from a stressful situation. Examples of defense mechanisms are denial, displacement, isolation, projection, reaction formation, repression, substitution, and rationalization.

Term	Definition
dementia	a progressive, organic mental disorder characterized by chronic personality disintegration, confusion, disorientation, deterioration of intellectual capacity and function, and impaired memory, judgment, and control of impulses
depression	a mood disturbance characterized by feelings of sadness, despair, and discouragement. Depression ranges from normal feelings of sadness (resulting from and proportional to personal loss or tragedy), through dysthymia (depressive neurosis), to major depression.
developmental disorders	a disturbance in the acquisition of cognitive, language, motor, or social skills. Developmental disorders have an onset during childhood and tend to be chronic in nature.
disorientation	a state of mental confusion characterized by inadequate or incorrect perceptions of place, time, or identity. Disorientation may occur in organic mental disorders, in drug and alcohol intoxication, and after severe stress.
dyskinesia	an impairment of the ability to execute voluntary movements
dysphoria	a disorder of affect characterized by sadness and anguish
electroconvulsive therapy (ECT)	the induction of a brief convulsion by passing electric current through the brain for the treatment of affective disorders
euphoria	a feeling of well-being or elation. An exaggerated or abnormal sense of well-being commonly is seen during the manic stages of bipolar disorder, in some forms of schizophrenia, in organic mental disorders, and in toxic and drug-induced states.
flight of ideas	a continuous stream of talk marked by a rapid and abrupt shift from one topic to another, each subject being incoherent and not related to the preceding one or stimulated by environmental circumstances. The condition is frequently a symptom of acute manic states and schizophrenia.
gender identity disorder	a condition characterized by a persistent discomfort and sense of inappropriateness concerning one's anatomic sex
grandiose	an exaggerated belief of one's importance or identity
group therapy	the application of psychotherapeutic techniques within a small group of people who experience similar difficulties. Generally, a group leader (facilitator) directs the discussion of problems in an attempt to promote individual psychologic growth and favorable personality change.
hallucination	a sensory perception that does not result from external stimuli and that occurs in the waking state
insanity	a severe mental disorder; a legal rather than a medical term denoting a condition that is so severe as to interfere with the capability of functioning within the legal limits of society

Term	Definition
learning disabled (LD)	a disorder characterized by the inadequate development, usually in children of normal or above-average intelligence, of specific academic, language, speech, and motor skills. The disorder is not the result of demonstrable physical or neurologic disorders or deficient educational opportunities.
loose association	a disturbance of thinking in which the expressed ideas appear to lack any logical sequence or relationship to one another
magical thinking	a belief that merely thinking about an event in the external world can cause it to occur
maladaptive behavior	behavior that does not adjust to the environment or situation and interferes with mental health
malingering	the willful, deliberate, and fraudulent feigning or exaggeration of the symptoms of an illness
manic depressive illness (MDI)	a mood disturbance characterized by alternating attacks of mania (expansiveness, elation, and agitation) and depression, as in bipolar disorder
mental retardation (MR)	a disorder characterized by below average general intellectual function
mental status examination (MSE)	a diagnostic procedure in which a trained interviewer asks a set of standard questions to evaluate a person's psychologic competence
neurotransmitter	chemical compounds that transmit impulses from one neuron to another
neurosis	any one of the group of mental disorders characterized by anxiety symptoms and in which reality testing is intact (in contrast to psychosis)
obsessive-compulsive disorder (OCD)	a disorder characterized by or related to the tendency to perform repetitive acts or rituals, usually as a means of releasing tension or relieving anxiety
panic disorder	an anxiety state characterized by discrete, unpredictable, and recurring periods of intense fear or discomfort
paranoid disorder	any of a large group of mental disorders characterized by an impaired sense of reality and persistent delusions
personality disorder	a disruption in relatedness manifested in any of a large group of mental disorders. Symptoms of personality disorder include rigid, inflexible, and maladaptive behavior patterns that impair a person's ability to function in society.
phobia	an anxiety disorder marked by an obsessive, irrational, and intense fear of a specific object, activity, or physical situation
psychoanalysis	a branch of psychiatry, founded by Sigmund Freud, from which developed a system of psychotherapy based on the concepts of a dynamic unconscious
psychologic tests	any of a group of standardized tests designed to measure characteristics such as intelligence, aptitudes, and personality traits
psychopharmacology	the scientific study of the effects of drugs on behavior
psychosis	any major mental disorder of organic or emotional origin characterized by a gross impairment in reality testing

Term	Definition
psychotherapy	any of a large number of methods of treating mental and emotional disorders by psychologic techniques rather than by physical means
schizophrenia	any one of a large group of psychotic disorders characterized by gross distortion of reality, disturbances of language and communication, withdrawal from social interaction, and the disorganization and fragmentation of thought, perception, and emotional reaction
seasonal affective disorder (SAD)	a mood disorder associated with the decrease in sunlight during the autumn and winter and the effect of the lessened exposure on melatonin secretion. Symptoms include lethargy, depression, social withdrawal, and work difficulties.
somatoform disorders	any of a group of neurotic disorders, characterized by symptoms suggesting physical illness or disease, for which there are no demonstrable organic causes or physiologic dysfunctions
substance abuse	the overindulgence in and dependence on a stimulant, depressant, or other chemical substance, leading to effects that are detrimental to the individual's physical or mental health or the welfare of others
therapeutic community	use of a treatment setting as a community, with the immediate aim of full participation of all clients and the eventual goal of preparing clients for life outside the treatment setting
tolerance	the need for increasing amounts of a psychoactive substance to achieve intoxication or the desired effect
transference	an unconscious mechanism whereby feelings and attitudes originally associated with important people and events in one's early life are attributed to others in current interpersonal relationships
withdrawal	the avoidance of social interaction; also, the occurrence of specific physical symptoms when intake of a psychoactive substance is reduced or discontinued

Additional Psychiatry Abbreviations

Abbreviation	Definition
ADD	attention deficit disorder
AWOL	absent without leave/unauthorized
COT	court-ordered treatment
DSM	*Diagnostic and Statistical Manual*
DTO	danger to others
DTS	danger to self
EE	expressed emotion
EPS	extrapyramidal symptoms
GD	gravely disabled
GEI	guilty except insane
NGRI	not guilty by reason of insanity
PAD	persistently acutely disabled
RTC	residential treatment center

Abbreviation	Definition
RTU	restricted to unit
S	seclusion
S&R	seclusion & restraint
TO	time out
UALRU	unauthorized leave return urgent

ANSWERS

CHAPTER 1

Exercise Figures

Exercise Figure A. osteoarthr/itis

Exercise 1

1. b 2. a 3. d 4. e 5. c

Exercise 2

1. *F,* a medical term may begin with the root and have no prefix.
2. *F,* if the suffix begins with a vowel, the combining vowel is usually not used.
3. *T*
4. *T*
5. *F, O* is the combining vowel most often used.
6. *T*
7. *F,* a combining vowel is used between two word roots or between a word root and a suffix to ease pronunciation.
8. *F,* a combining form is not a word part.

Exercise 3

1. WR S
   arthr/itis

   inflammation of the joint

2. WR S
   hepat/itis

   inflammation of the liver

3. P WR S
   sub/hepat/ic

   pertaining to under the liver

4. P WR S
   intra/ven/ous

   pertaining to within the vein

5. WR CV S
   arthr/o/pathy
      CF

   disease of the joint

6. WR S
   oste/itis

   inflammation of the bone

Exercise 4

1. arthr/itis
2. hepat/ic
3. sub/hepat/ic

4. intra/ven/ous
5. oste/itis
6. hepat/itis
7. oste/o/arthr/o/pathy

CHAPTER 2

Exercise Figures
Exercise Figure
A. 1. neur/o
   2. sarc/o
   3. epitheli/o
   4. my/o

Exercise Figure
B. 1. carcinoma
   2. melanoma
   3. sarcoma

Exercise Figure C. hyperplasia
Exercise Figure
D. 1. erythrocyte
   2. leukocyte

Exercise 1

1. h   6. f
2. e   7. c
3. d   8. a
4. k   9. b
5. g   10. j

Exercise 2

1. h   5. g
2. b   6. a
3. c   7. f
4. e

Exercise 3

1. flesh, connec-   7. muscle
   tive tissue   8. nerve
2. fat   9. organ
3. nucleus   10. system
4. internal organs 11. epithelium
5. cell   12. fibrous tissue
6. tissue

Exercise 4

1. viscer/o   4. kary/o
2. epitheli/o   5. cyt/o
3. organ/o   6. hist/o

7. neur/o   10. system/o
8. my/oneur/o   11. sarc/o
9. lip/o   12. fibr/o

Exercise 5

1. tumor, mass
2. cancer
3. cause (of disease)
4. disease
5. body
6. cancer
7. rod-shaped, striated
8. smooth
9. knowledge
10. physician, medicine

Exercise 6

1. path/o   5. somat/o
2. onc/o   6. lei/o
3. eti/o   7. rhabd/o
4. a. cancer/o   8. gno/o
   b. carcin/o   9. iatr/o

Exercise 7

1. blue   4. yellow
2. red   5. color
3. white   6. black

Exercise 8

1. cyan/o   4. melan/o
2. erythr/o   5. xanth/o
3. leuk/o   6. chrom/o

Exercise 9

1. new
2. above, excessive
3. after, beyond, change
4. below, incomplete, deficient
5. difficult, labored, painful, abnormal
6. through, complete
7. before

Exercise 10

1. neo-   5. dys-
2. hyper-   6. dia-
3. hypo-   7. pro-
4. meta-

Exercise 11
1. i
2. l
3. e
4. f
5. g
6. j
7. h
8. b
9. p
10. c
11. n
12. k
13. q
14. m
15. a
16. o

Exercise 12
1. specialist
2. disease
3. study of
4. pertaining to
5. control, stop, standing
6. cell
7. abnormal condition
8. pertaining to
9. a growth, a substance, a formation
10. pertaining to
11. condition of formation, development, growth
12. resembling
13. substance or agent that produces or causes
14. producing, originating, causing
15. tumor, swelling
16. origin, cause
17. malignant tumor
18. state of

Exercise 13
1. WR S
   sarc/oma
   tumor composed of connective tissue
2. WR S
   melan/oma
   black tumor
3. WR S
   epitheli/oma
   tumor composed of epithelium
4. WR S
   lip/oma
   tumor containing fat
5. P S(WR)
   neo/plasm
   new growth
6. WR S
   my/oma
   tumor formed of muscle
7. WR S
   neur/oma
   tumor made up of nerve
8. WR S
   carcin/oma
   cancerous tumor

Exercise 14
1. melan/oma
2. carcin/oma
3. neo/plasm
4. epitheli/oma
5. sarc/oma
6. melan/o/carcin/oma
7. neur/oma
8. my/oma
9. rhabd/o/my/o/sarcoma
10. lei/o/my/oma
11. rhabd/o/my/oma
12. lei/o/my/o/sarcoma
13. lip/o/sarcoma
14. fibr/oma
15. fibr/o/sarcoma

Exercise 15
Spelling exercise; see text, p. 24.

Exercise 16
1. not malignant, nonrecurrent, favorable for recovery
2. tending to become progressively worse and to cause death, as in cancer
3. improvement or absence of signs of disease

9. WRCV WR CV S
   lei/o/my/o/sarcoma
   CF   CF
   malignant tumor of smooth muscle
10. WR CV WR CV S
    rhabd/o/my/o/sarcoma
    CF   CF
    malignant tumor of striated muscle
11. WRCV WR S
    lei/o/my/oma
    CF
    tumor of smooth muscle
12. WR CV WR S
    rhabd/o/my/oma
    CF
    tumor of striated muscle
13. WR S
    fibr/oma
    tumor composed of fibrous tissue
14. WRCV S
    lip/o/sarcoma
    CF
    malignant tumor composed of fat
15. WR CV S
    fibr/o/sarcoma
    CF
    malignant tumor composed of fibrous tissue

4. disease of unknown origin
5. response to injury or destruction of tissue; signs are redness, swelling, and pain
6. treatment of cancer by using drugs
7. treatment of cancer using radioactive substance (x-ray or radiation)
8. enclosed in a capsule, as in benign tumors
9. within a glass, observable within a test tube
10. within the living body
11. cancer in the early stage prior to invading the surrounding tissue

Exercise 17
Spelling exercise; see text, p. 26.

Exercise 18
1. WR S
   cyt/ology
   study of cells
2. WR S
   hist/ology
   study of tissue
3. WR S
   path/ology
   study of (body changes caused by) disease
4. WR S
   path/ologist
   specialist in pathology
5. WR S
   viscer/al
   pertaining to internal organs
6. P S(WR)
   meta/stasis
   beyond control (transfer of disease)
7. WR CV S
   onc/o/genic
   CF
   causing tumors
8. WR S
   onc/ology
   study of tumors
9. WR CV S
   kary/o/cyte
   CF
   cell with a nucleus
10. P S(WR)
    neo/pathy
    new disease
11. WR CV S
    kary/o/plasm
    CF
    substance of a nucleus

12. WR CV S
cyt/o/genic
CF
producing cells

13. WR S
system/ic
pertaining to a body system

14. WR S
cancer/ous
pertaining to cancer

15. WR CV S
cyt/o/plasm
CF
cell substance

16. WR CV S
carcin/o/genic
CF
producing cancer

17. WR S
somat/ic
pertaining to the body

18. WR CV S
somat/o/genic
CF
originating in the body

19. WR CV S
somat/o/plasm
CF
body substance

20. WR CV S
somat/o/pathy
CF
disease of the body

21. WR S
neur/oid
resembling a nerve

22. WR CV S
my/o/pathy
CF
disease of the muscle

23. WR CV S
erythr/o/cyte
CF
red (blood) cell

24. WR CV S
leuk/o/cyte
CF
white (blood) cell

25. WR S
cyan/osis
abnormal condition of blue (bluish discoloration of the skin)

26. WR S
epitheli/al
pertaining to epithelium

27. WR S
lip/oid
resembling fat

28. WR S
eti/ology
study of causes (of disease)

29. WR S
xanth/osis
abnormal condition of yellow

30. WR CV WR S
xanth/o/chrom/ic
CF
pertaining to yellow color

31. P S(WR)
hyper/plasia
excessive development (of cells)

32. WR CV WR S
erythr/o/cyt/osis
CF
increase in the number of red (blood) cells

33. WR CV WR S
leuk/o/cyt/osis
CF
increase in the number of white (blood) cells

34. WR CV S
carcin/o/gen
CF
substance that causes cancer

35. P S(WR)
hypo/plasia
incomplete development (of an organ or tissue)

36. WR S
cyt/oid
resembling a cell

37. WR S
onc/ologist
physician who specializes in oncology

38. P S(WR)
dys/plasia
abnormal development

39. WR CV S
path/o/genic
CF
producing disease

40. P WR S
pro/gno/sis
state of before knowledge

41. P WR S
dia/gno/sis
state of complete knowledge

42. WR CV S
iatr/o/genic
CF
produced by a physician (adverse condition)

43. WR S
iatr/ology
study of medicine

Exercise 19
1. cyt/o/plasm
2. xanth/o/chrom/ic
3. meta/stasis
4. neo/pathy
5. eti/ology
6. kary/o/plasm
7. onc/ology
8. path/ology
9. somat/ic
10. path/ologist
11. my/o/pathy
12. somat/o/plasm
13. xanth/osis
14. viscer/al
15. onc/o/genic
16. somat/o/genic
17. somat/o/pathy
18. erythr/o/cyte
19. neur/oid
20. system/ic
21. leuk/o/cyte
22. kary/o/cyte
23. lip/oid
24. cancer/ous
25. cyt/ology
26. hyper/plasia
27. cyt/oid
28. epitheli/al
29. cyan/osis
30. carcin/o/genic
31. path/o/genic
32. hist/ology
33. erythr/o/cyt/osis
34. hypo/plasia
35. leuk/o/cyt/osis
36. carcin/o/gen
37. onc/ologist
38. dys/plasia
39. iatr/ology
40. dia/gno/sis
41. iatr/o/genic
42. pro/gno/sis

Exercise 20
Spelling exercise; see text, p. 33.

Exercise 21
1. sarcoma, malignant
2. erythrocytosis
3. visceral

4. lipoma, nonrecurrent
5. carcinogenic
6. causes of disease
7. neoplasm
8. somatogenic
9. myopathy
10. dysplasia
11. iatrogenic
12. melanoma, pathology, prognosis
13. in vivo
14. liposarcoma

Exercise 22
1. oncology
2. somatic
3. carcinoma
4. melanoma
5. cytoid
6. iatrology

Exercise 23
1. resembling epithelium
2. pertaining to the nerves
3. agent that produces disease
4. resembling muscle
5. pertaining to white (blood) cells
6. pertaining to a physician or medicine

Answers

CHAPTER 3
Exercise Figures
Exercise Figure
A. 1. cephal/o
   2. anter/o
   3. ventr/o
   4. dors/o
   5. poster/o
   6. caud/o
   7. super/o
   8. later/o
   9. medi/o
   10. proxim/o
   11. dist/o
   12. infer/o

Exercise Figure
B. 1. super/ior
   2. dors/al, poster/ior
   3. anter/ior
   4. caud/al
   5. infer/ior
   6. cephal/ic
   7. medi/al
   8. later/al
   9. ventr/al
   10. proxim/al
   11. dist/al

Exercise Figure C. 1. poster/o/anter/ior;
                    2. anter/o/poster/ior

Exercise Figure
D. 1. coronal, or frontal plane
   2. midsagittal plane
   3. transverse

Exercise Figure
E. 1. umbilical
   2. epigastric
   3. hypogastric
   4. hypochondriac
   5. lumbar
   6. iliac

Exercise 1
1. belly (front)
2. head
3. side
4. middle
5. below
6. near (point of reference)
7. above
8. away (from the point of reference)
9. back
10. tail
11. front
12. back, behind

Exercise 2
1. later/o   7. dors/o
2. super/o   8. ventr/o
3. cephal/o   9. caud/o
4. dist/o   10. infer/o
5. anter/o   11. poster/o
6. medi/o   12. proxim/o

Exercise 3
1. c 2. b 3. d 4. a

Exercise 4
1. pertaining to   3. two
2. toward   4. one

Exercise 5
1. WR   S
    cephal/ad
    toward the head

2. WR   S
    cephal/ic
    pertaining to the head

3. WR   S
    caud/al
    pertaining to the tail

4. WR   S
    anter/ior
    pertaining to the front

5. WR   S
    poster/ior
    pertaining to the back

6. WR   S
    dors/al
    pertaining to the back

7. WR   S
    super/ior
    pertaining to above

8. WR   S
    infer/ior
    pertaining to below

9. WR   S
    proxim/al
    pertaining to the near

10. WR   S
    dist/al
    pertaining to away

11. WR   S
    later/al
    pertaining to a side

12. WR   S
    medi/al
    pertaining to the middle

13. WR   S
    medi/ad
    toward the middle

14. WR   S
    ventr/al
    pertaining to the belly (front)

15. WR CV WR   S
    poster/o/anter/ior
          CF
    pertaining to the back and to the front

16. P   WR   S
    uni/later/al
    pertaining to one side

17. WR CV WR   S
    medi/o/later/al
         CF
    pertaining to the middle and to the
    side

18. WR CV WR   S
    anter/o/poster/ior
          CF
    pertaining to the front and to the back

19. P WR S
bi/later/al

pertaining to two sides

Exercise 6
1. cephal/ad
2. cephal/ic
3. caud/al
4. anter/ior
5. poster/ior, dors/al
6. super/ior
7. infer/ior
8. proxim/al
9. dist/al
10. later/al
11. medi/al
12. medi/ad
13. ventr/al
14. poster/o/anter/ior
15. medi/o/later/al
16. uni/later/al
17. anter/o/poster/ior
18. bi/later/al

Exercise 7
Spelling exercise; see text, p. 45.

Exercise 8
1. transverse
2. midsagittal
3. coronal, or frontal

Exercise 9
Spelling exercise; see text, p. 46.

Exercise 10
1. iliac
2. epigastric
3. hypogastric
4. hypochondriac
5. umbilical
6. lumbar

Exercise 11
1. b 2. d 3. a 4. e 5. c 6. g

Exercise 12
Spelling exercise; see text, p. 49.

Exercise 13
1. distal
2. anterior
3. medial
4. superior
5. anteroposterior, frontal
6. epigastric
7. sagittal, lateral
8. bilateral

Exercise 14
1. pertaining to the front and to the side
2. pertaining to the front and to the middle
3. pertaining to the front and above
4. pertaining to the head and to the tail
5. toward the back of the head
6. pertaining to above and to the side
7. pertaining to the belly (front) and to the back

Answers

T	R	A	N	S	V	E	R	S	E					D		
														O		
V	E	N	T	R	A	L			L	U	M	B	A	R		
														S		
L	A	T	E	R	A	L			C	A	U	D	A	L		
												M		L		
C				E							B					
E	H	Y	P	O	C	H	O	N	D	R	I	A	C			
P			I							L						
H	Y	P	O	G	A	S	T	R	I	C						
A			A							C		M				
L	I		S			C	O	R	O	N	A	L	E			
I	L		T							L		D				
C	I		R									I				
	S	A	G	I	T	T	A	L				A				
	C		C									D				

CHAPTER 4
Exercise Figures
Exercise Figure
A. 1. horny tissue: kerat/o
   2. sweat: hidr/o
   3. hair: trich/o
   4. skin: cutane/o, dermat/o, derm/o
   5. sebum: seb/o

Exercise Figure B. nail: onych/o, ungu/o
Exercise Figure C. paronychia
Exercise Figure D. staphylococci
Exercise Figure E. streptococci

Exercise 1
1. c 2. d 3. g 4. b
5. f 6. h 7. a

Exercise 2
1. sweat
2. skin
3. nail
4. hair
5. horny tissue, hard
6. skin
7. sebum (oil)
8. nail
9. skin

Exercise 3
1. trich/o
2. hidr/o
3. a. onych/o
   b. ungu/o
4. seb/o
5. a. derm/o
   b. dermat/o
   c. cutane/o
6. kerat/o

Exercise 4
1. death
2. grapelike clusters
3. hidden
4. thick
5. dust
6. fungus
7.
8.
9.
10. chains
11.
12.
13.

Exercise 5
1. myc/o
2. necr/o
3. heter/o
4. xer/o
5. pachy/o
6. strept/o
7. rhytid/o
8. /o
9.
10.
11.
12.
13.

Exercise 6
1. under, below
2. beside, beyond, arou
3. on, upon, over
4. within
5. through

Exercise 7
1. intra-
2. sub-
3. epi-

Exercise 8
1. c
2. e
3. a
4. j
5. i

Exercise 9
1. surgical repair
2. excision or surgic
3. softening
4. inflammation
5. instrument used
6. eating, swallowin
7. excessive dischar
8. berry-shaped
9. view of, viewing
10. diseased or abno condition of

Exercise 10
1. WR CV WR
   dermat/o/coni/
   CF

   abnormal cond the skin caused by dust

2. WR WR S
   hidr/aden/itis

   inflammation at glands

3. WR S
dermat/itis
inflammation

4. WR WR S
pachy/derm/
thickening o

5. WR CV
onych/o/ma
  CF
softening o

6. WR CV WR
trich/o/my
  CF
abnormal _____ of a _____ the hair

7. WR CV
dermat/o
  CF
fibrous t

8. P WR
par/onyc
diseased

9. WR CV
onych/o/
  CF
abnorm _____ n nail

10. WR S
seb/orrhea
excessive discharge of sebum

11. WR CV S
onych/o/phagia
  CF
eating the nails, nail biting

12. WR CV WR S
xer/o/derm/a
  CF
dry skin

13. WRCV WR S
lei/o/derm/ia
  CF
condition of smooth skin

Exercise 11
1. pachy/derm/a
2. onych/o/myc/osis
3. seb/orrhea
4. dermat/itis
5. dermat/o/fibr/oma
6. onych/o/malacia
7. hidr/aden/itis
8. onych/o/crypt/osis
9. dermat/o/coni/osis
10. onych/o/phagia
11. par/onych/ia

12. xer/o/derm/a
13. lei/o/derm/ia

Exercise 12
Spelling exercise; see text, p. 63.

Exercise 13
1. systemic lupus erythematosus
2. abscess
3. fissure
4. abrasion
5. psoriasis
6. herpes
7. pediculosis
8. tinea
9. contusion
10. gangrene
11. lesion
12. Kaposi's sarcoma
13. actinic keratosis
14. carbuncle
15. acne
16. laceration
17. furuncle
18. squamous cell
19. cellulitis
20. impetigo
21. eczema
22. scabies
23. urticaria
24. basal cell
25. scleroderma
26. candidiasis

Exercise 14
1. f
2. j
3. g
4. l
5. m
6. c
7. i
8. k
9. e
10. b
11. h
12. a
13. d

Exercise 15
1. d
2. i
3. f
4. h
5. l
6. k
7. c
8. a
9. m
10. e
11. b
12. g
13. j

Exercise 16
Spelling exercise; see text, p. 68.

Exercise 17
1. WR S
rhytid/ectomy
excision of wrinkles

2. WR S
bi/opsy
view of life (removal of living tissue)

3. WR CV WR CV S
dermat/o/aut/o/plasty
  CF   CF
surgical repair using one's own skin for the skin graft

4. WR S
onych/ectomy
excision of a nail

5. WR CV S
rhytid/o/plasty
  CF
surgical repair of wrinkles

6. WR CV WR CV S
dermat/o/heter/o/plasty
  CF   CF
surgical repair using skin from others for the skin graft

Exercise 18
1. rhytid/ectomy
2. bi/opsy
3. dermat/o/heter/o/plasty
4. onych/ectomy
5. rhytid/o/plasty
6. dermat/o/plasty

Exercise 19
Spelling exercise; see text, p. 70.

Exercise 20
1. WR S
ungu/al
pertaining to the nail

2. WR S
derma/tome
instrument used to cut skin

3. WR CV S
strept/o/coccus
  CF
berry-shaped (bacteria) in twisted chains

4. P WR S
hypo/derm/ic
pertaining to under the skin

5. WR S
dermat/ology
study of the skin

6. P WR S
sub/cutane/ous
pertaining to under the skin

7. WR CV S
staphyl/o/coccus
  CF
berry-shaped (bacteria) in grape-like clusters

8. WR CV S
kerat/o/genic
  CF
originating in horny tissue

9. WR S
dermat/ologist
physician who specializes in skin diseases

10. WR   S
necr/osis
abnormal condition of death

11. P   WR   S
epi/derm/al
pertaining to upon the skin

12. WR CV WR   S
xanth/o/derm/a
‿‿
CF
yellow skin

13. WR CV WR   S
erythr/o/derm/a
‿‿
CF
red skin

14. WR CV WR   S
leuk/o/derm/a
‿‿
CF
white skin

15. P   WR   S
per/cutane/ous
pertaining to through the skin

Exercise 21
1. dermat/ology
2. necr/osis
3. derma/tome
4. ungu/al
5. staphyl/o/cocci
6. dermat/ologist
7. intra/derm/al
8. epi/derm/al
9. sub/cutane/ous, hypo/derm/ic
10. strept/o/cocci
11. kerat/o/genic
12. leuk/o/derm/a
13. erythr/o/derm/a
14. xanth/o/derm/a
15. per/cutane/ous

Exercise 22
Spelling exercise; see text, p. 73.

Exercise 23
1. cicatrix
2. diaphoresis
3. emollient
4. verruca
5. macule
6. jaundice
7. leukoplakia
8. petechiae
9. ulcer
10. keloid
11. pallor
12. ecchymosis
13. albino
14. decubitus ulcer
15. adipose
16. disseminated
17. pruritus
18. erythema
19. purpura
20. nevus
21. debridement
22. alopecia
23. allergy
24. papule
25. wheal
26. pustule
27. vesicle
28. dermabrasion

29. virus
30. induration
31. edema
32. cytomegalovirus

Exercise 24
1. m
2. o
3. h
4. a
5. j
6. e
7. n
8. l
9. g
10. d
11. b
12. f
13. k
14. c
15. q
16. i

Exercise 25
1. g
2. d
3. j
4. a
5. l
6. k
7. n
8. b
9. e
10. f
11. o
12. c
13. h
14. i
15. m
16. q

Exercise 26
Spelling exercise; see text, p. 79.

Exercise 27
1. dermatologist
2. nevus
3. medial
4. lesion
5. actinic keratosis
6. eczema
7. bilateral
8. biopsy
9. basal cell carcinoma
10. superior
11. dermis
12. pathology

Exercise 28
1. contusion
2. staphylococci
3. xeroderma
4. intradermal
5. softening of the nails
6. petechiae
7. diaphoresis
8. trichomycosis
9. vesicle
10. dermatoheteroplasty
11. induration
12. xanthoderma
13. smooth

Exercise 29
1. onychophagia
2. biopsy
3. xeroderma
4. rhytidectomy
5. onychocryptosis
6. cytomegalovirus

Exercise 30
1. pertaining to skin disease
2. tumor composed of fibrous tissue
3. abnormal condition of horny tissue
4. fat cell

5. resembling a nail
6. resembling hair

Answers

CHAPTER 5
Exercise Figures
Exercise Figure
A. 1. adenoids: adenoid/o
   2. pharynx: pharyng/o
   3. lung: pneum/o, pneumat/o, pneumon/o, pulmon/o
   4. bronchus: bronch/i, bronch/o
   5. alveolus: alveol/o
   6. sinus: sinus/o
   7. nose: nas/o, rhin/o
   8. tonsils: tonsill/o
   9. epiglottis: epiglott/o
   10. larynx: laryng/o
   11. trachea: trache/o
   12. pleura: pleur/o
   13. lobe: lob/o
   14. diaphragm: diaphragmat/o

Exercise Figure B. bronchiectasis
Exercise Figure C. pneumothorax
Exercise Figure D. thoracocentesis
Exercise Figure E. tracheostomy
Exercise Figure F. bronchoscopy, bronchoscope
Exercise Figure G. oximeter
Exercise Figure H. adenoidectomy, adenotome
Exercise Figure I. endotracheal, laryngoscope

Exercise 1
1. h
2. a
3. g
4. c
5. f
6. d
7. e
8. b

Exercise 2

1. nasal septum
2. epiglottis
3. bronchioles
4. nose
5. diaphragm
6. mediastinum
7. tonsils

Exercise 3

1. larynx
2. bronchus
3. pleura
4. air, lung
5. tonsil
6. lung
7. diaphragm
8. trachea
9. alveolus
10. air, lung
11. thorax (chest)
12. adenoids
13. pharynx
14. nose
15. sinus
16. lobe
17. epiglottis
18. air, lung
19. nose
20. septum

Exercise 4

1. a. nas/o
   b. rhin/o
2. laryng/o
3. a. pneum/o
   b. pneumat/o
   c. pneumon/o
4. pulmon/o
5. tonsill/o
6. trache/o
7. adenoid/o
8. pleur/o
9. diaphragmat/o
10. sinus/o
11. thorac/o
12. alveol/o
13. pharyng/o
14. a. bronch/o
    b. bronch/i
15. lob/o
16. epiglott/o
17. sept/o

Exercise 5

1. oxygen
2. breathe, breathing
3. mucus
4. imperfect, incomplete
5. straight
6. pus
7. blood

Exercise 6

1. spir/o
2. a. ox/o
   b. ox/i
3. atel/o
4. orth/o
5. py/o
6. muc/o
7. a. hem/o
   b. hemat/o

Exercise 7

1. within
2. without, absence of
3. all, total
4. normal, good

Exercise 8

1. endo-
2. eu-
3. a. a-
   b. an-
4. pan-

Exercise 9

1. k
2. f
3. m
4. g
5. c
6. b

7. j
8. a
9. l
10. h
11. d
12. e

Exercise 10

1. c
2. f
3. a
4. i
5. k
6. e
7. j
8. b
9. m
10. g
11. d
12. h

Exercise 11

1. chest
2. pertaining to
3. constriction, narrowing
4. hernia, protrusion
5. creation of an artificial opening
6. surgical fixation or suspension
7. instrument used to measure
8. sudden, involuntary muscle contraction
9. pain
10. visual examination
11. surgical puncture to aspirate fluid
12. cut into, incision
13. instrument used for visual examination
14. rapid flow of blood
15. stretching out, dilatation, expansion
16. record, x-ray film
17. breathing
18. process of recording, x-ray filming
19. measurement
20. blood condition
21. oxygen
22. carbon dioxide
23. sound or voice
24. pertaining to visual examination

Exercise 12

1. WR   S
    pleur/itis
    inflammation of the pleura

2. WR CV   WR   S
    nas/o/pharyng/itis
         CF
    inflammation of the nose and pharynx

3. WR CV   S
    pneum/o/thorax
         CF
    air in the chest

4. P   WR   S
    pan/sinus/itis
    inflammation of all sinuses

5. WR   S
    atel/ectasis
    incomplete expansion (or collapsed lung)

6. WR CV WR   S
    rhin/o/myc/osis
         CF
    abnormal condition of fungus in the nose

7. WR CV   S
    trache/o/stenosis
         CF
    narrowing of the trachea

8. WR   S
    epiglott/itis
    inflammation of the epiglottis

9. WR   S
    thorac/algia
    pain in the chest

10. WR   S   P   S(WR)
    pulmon/ary neo/plasm
    new growth (tumor) in the lung

11. WR CV S
    bronch/i/ectasis
         CF
    dilatation of the bronchi

12. WR   S
    tonsill/itis
    inflammation of the tonsils

13. WR CV WR   S
    pneum/o/coni/osis
         CF
    abnormal condition of dust in the lungs

14. WR CV   WR   S
    bronch/o/pneumon/ia
             CF
    diseased state (inflammation) of bronchi and lungs

15. WR   S
    pneumon/itis
    inflammation of the lung

16. WR   S
    laryng/itis
    inflammation of the larynx

17. WR CV S
    pneumat/o/cele
         CF
    hernia of the lung

18. WRCV S
    py/o/thorax
       CF
    pus in the chest (pleural space)

19. WR   S
    rhin/orrhagia
    rapid flow of blood from nose (nosebleed)

20.   WR   S
bronch/itis

inflammation of the bronchi

21.   WR   S
pharyng/itis

inflammation of the pharynx

22.   WR   S
trache/itis

inflammation of the trachea

23.   WR CV WR CV WR   S
laryng/o/trache/o/bronch/itis
　　　 CF 　　　 CF

inflammation of the larynx, trachea, and bronchi

24.   WR   S
adenoid/itis

inflammation of the adenoids

25.   WR CV   S
hem/o/thorax
　　　 CF

blood in the chest (pleural space)

26. WR S   WR   S
lob/ar pneumon/ia

diseased state of the lobe(s) of a lung

27.   WR   S
rhin/itis

inflammation of the nose

28.   WR CV   S   WR   S
bronch/o/genic carcin/oma
　　　 CF

cancerous tumor originating in a bronchus

29.   WR   S
pneumon/ia

diseased state of the lung

Exercise 13
1. thorac/algia
2. rhin/o/myc/osis
3. pneumat/o/cele
4. pulmon/ary neo/plasm
5. laryng/itis
6. atel/ectasis
7. adenoid/itis
8. laryng/o/trache/o/bronch/itis
9. bronch/i/ectasis
10. pleur/itis (or pleurisy)
11. pneum/o/coni/osis
12. pneumon/itis
13. pan/sinus/itis
14. trache/o/stenosis
15. nas/o/pharyng/itis
16. py/o/thorax
17. epiglott/itis
18. diaphragmat/o/cele
19. pneum/o/thorax

20. bronch/o/pneumon/ia
21. rhin/orrhagia
22. pharyng/itis
23. hem/o/thorax
24. trache/itis
25. bronch/itis
26. lob/ar pneumon/ia
27. rhin/itis
28. bronch/o/genic carcin/oma
29. pneumon/ia

Exercise 14
Spelling exercise; see text, p. 101.

Exercise 15
1. emphysema
2. pleural effusion
3. cor pulmonale
4. coccidioidomycosis
5. cystic fibrosis
6. influenza
7. chronic obstructive pulmonary disease
8. pertussis
9. croup
10. asthma
11. pulmonary edema
12. upper respiratory infection
13. pulmonary embolism
14. epistaxis
15. Legionnaire's disease
16. *Pneumocystis carinii* pneumonia
17. deviated septum
18. obstructive sleep apnea
19. tuberculosis
20. adult respiratory distress syndrome

Exercise 16
1. h		11. g
2. t		12. d
3. o		13. f
4. k		14. i
5. n		15. l
6. e		16. q
7. a		17. s
8. j		18. m
9. b		19. u
10. p		20. c

Exercise 17
Spelling exercise; see text, p. 106.

Exercise 18
1.   WR   S
trache/otomy

incision of the trachea

2.   WR   S
laryng/ostomy

creation of an artificial opening into the larynx

3.   WR   S
adenoid/ectomy

excision of the adenoids

4.   WR CV   S
rhin/o/plasty
　　　 CF

surgical repair of the nose

5.   WR CV   S
pleur/o/centesis
　　　 CF

surgical puncture to aspirate fluid from the pleural space

6.   WR   S
trache/ostomy

creation of an artificial opening into the trachea

7.   WR   S
sinus/otomy

incision of a sinus

8.   WR CV   S
laryng/o/plasty
　　　 CF

surgical repair of the larynx

9.   WR CV WR   S
pneum/o/bronch/otomy
　　　 CF

incision of lung and bronchus

10.   WR CV   S
bronch/o/plasty
　　　 CF

surgical repair of a bronchus

11.   WR   S
lob/ectomy

excision of a lobe of the lung

12.   WR CV WR   S
laryng/o/trache/otomy
　　　 CF

incision of larynx and trachea

13.   WR CV   S
trache/o/plasty
　　　 CF

surgical repair of the trachea

14.   WR   S
thorac/otomy

incision into the chest cavity

15.   WR   S
laryng/ectomy

excision of the larynx

16.   WR CV   S
thorac/o/centesis
　　　 CF

surgical puncture to aspirate fluid from the chest cavity

17. WR   S
 tonsill/ectomy

 excision of the tonsils

18. WR CV   S
 laryng/o/centesis
  ⌣
  CF

 surgical puncture to aspirate fluid from
 the larynx

19. WR CV   S
 pleur/o/pexy
  ⌣
  CF

 surgical fixation of the pleura

20. WR CV   S
 sept/o/plasty
  ⌣
  CF

 surgical repair of the septum

21. WR   S
 sept/otomy

 incision into the septum

Exercise 19
1. trache/o/plasty
2. laryng/o/trache/otomy
3. pleur/o/centesis
4. thorac/otomy
5. trache/ostomy
6. tonsill/ectomy
7. trache/otomy
8. bronch/o/plasty
9. laryng/ectomy
10. laryng/o/centesis
11. rhin/o/plasty
12. sinus/otomy
13. thorac/o/centesis or thora/centesis
14. adenoid/ectomy
15. laryng/o/plasty
16. lob/ectomy
17. pneum/o/bronch/otomy
18. laryng/ostomy
19. pneumon/ectomy
20. sept/otomy
21. sept/o/plasty

Exercise 20
Spelling exercise; see text, p. 111.

Exercise 21
1. WR CV   S
 spir/o/meter
  ⌣
  CF

 instrument used to measure breathing

2. WR CV   S
 laryng/o/scope
  ⌣
  CF

 instrument used for visual examination
 of the larynx

3. WR CV   S
 bronch/o/gram
  ⌣
  CF

 x-ray film of the bronchi

4. WR CV   S
 spir/o/metry
  ⌣
  CF

 measurement of breathing

5. WRCV S
 ox/i/meter
  ⌣
  CF

 instrument used to measure oxygen

6. WR CV   S
 bronch/o/graphy
  ⌣
  CF

 process of x-ray filming the bronchi

7. WR CV   S
 laryng/o/scopy
  ⌣
  CF

 visual examination of the larynx

8. WR CV   S
 bronch/o/scope
  ⌣
  CF

 instrument used for visual examination
 of the bronchi

9. WR CV   S
 thorac/o/scope
  ⌣
  CF

 instrument used for visual examination
 of the thorax

10. P   S(WR)
 endo/scope

 instrument used for visual examination
 of a hollow organ or body cavity

11. WR CV   S
 thorac/o/scopy
  ⌣
  CF

 visual examination of the thorax

12. P   S(WR)
 endo/scopic

 pertaining to visual examination of a
 hollow organ or body cavity

13. P   S(WR)
 endo/scopy

 visual examination of a hollow organ
 or body cavity

Exercise 22
1. laryng/o/scopy
2. spir/o/meter
3. bronch/o/gram
4. laryng/o/scope
5. bronch/o/scopy
6. spir/o/metry
7. bronch/o/scope
8. bronch/o/graphy
9. endo/scopy
10. thorac/o/scope

11. endo/scope
12. thorac/o/scopy
13. endo/scopic

Exercise 23
Spelling exercise; see text, p. 116.

Exercise 24
1. ventilation/perfusion scanning
2. chest CT scan
3. chest x-ray
4. arterial blood gases
5. pulse oximetry
6. acid-fast bacilli stain
7. pulmonary function tests

Exercise 25
1. f   5. b
2. e   6. c
3. a   7. g
4. d

Exercise 26
Spelling exercise; see text, p. 118.

Exercise 27
1. WR   S
 laryng/eal

 pertaining to the larynx

2. P S(WR)
 eu/pnea

 normal breathing

3. WR   S
 muc/oid

 resembling mucus

4. P S(WR)
 a/pnea

 absence of breathing

5. P   S(WR)
 hyp/oxia

 deficient oxygen to tissues

6. WR CV   S
 laryng/o/spasm
  ⌣
  CF

 spasmodic contraction of the larynx

7. P   WR   S
 endo/trach/eal

 pertaining to within the trachea

8. P S(WR)
 an/oxia

 absence of oxygen

9. P   S(WR)
 dys/phonia

 difficulty in speaking (voice)

10.   WR CV WR   S
bronch/o/alveol/ar
‾‾‾‾‾‾‾
CF

pertaining to the bronchi and alveoli

11.   P S(WR)
dys/pnea

difficult breathing

12.   P S(WR)
hypo/capnia

deficient in carbon dioxide

13.   WR CV   S
bronch/o/spasm
‾‾‾‾
CF

spasmodic contraction in the bronchus(i)

14.   WR CV   S
orth/o/pnea
‾‾‾‾
CF

able to breathe only in a straight position

15.   P   S(WR)
hyper/pnea

excessive breathing

16.   P S(WR)
a/capnia

absence of carbon dioxide

17.   P   S(WR)
hypo/pnea

deficient breathing

18.   P WR   S
hyp/ox/emia

deficient oxygen in the blood

19.   P S(WR)
a/phonia

absence of voice

20.   WR   S
rhin/orrhea

discharge from the nose

21.   WR CV S
aden/o/tome
‾‾‾
CF

surgical instrument used to cut the adenoids

22.   WR   S
muc/ous

pertaining to mucus

23.   WR CV   WR   S
nas/o/pharyng/eal
‾‾‾
CF

pertaining to the nose and pharynx

24.   WR   S
diaphragmat/ic

pertaining to the diaphragm

Exercise 28

1. hyp/oxia
2. muc/oid
3. orth/o/pnea
4. endo/trache/al
5. an/oxia
6. dys/pnea
7. laryng/eal
8. hyper/capnia
9. eu/pnea
10. a/phonia
11. laryng/o/spasm
12. hypo/capnia
13. nas/o/pharyng/eal
14. diaphragmat/ic
15. a/pnea
16. hyp/ox/emia
17. hyper/pnea
18. bronch/o/spasm
19. hypo/pnea
20. a/capnia
21. dys/phonia
22. rhin/orrhea
23. muc/ous
24. aden/o/tome

Exercise 29
Spelling exercise; see text, p. 123.

Exercise 30

1. hyperventilation
2. nebulizer
3. bronchodilator
4. ventilator
5. asphyxia
6. sputum
7. aspirate
8. airway
9. hiccup (hiccough)
10. cough
11. mucopurulent
12. hypoventilation
13. nosocomial
14. pulmonary
15. paroxysm
16. patent
17. bronchoconstrictor
18. mucus

Exercise 31

1. b   6. a
2. j   7. d
3. h   8. g
4. c   9. f
5. i

Exercise 32

1. e   6. a
2. h   7. b
3. i   8. d
4. c   9. f
5. j

Exercise 33
Spelling exercise; see text, p. 127.

Exercise 34

1. cough
2. dyspnea
3. pulmonary
4. chest x-ray
5. bronchus
6. laryngoscopy
7. arterial blood gases
8. hypoventilation
9. hypoxemia
10. bronchogenic carcinoma
11. pulmonary function tests
12. cor pulmonale

Exercise 35

1. epitaxis
2. laryngoplasty
3. orthopnea
4. arterial blood gases, hypoxia
5. thoracalgia
6. hyperventilation
7. nebulizer
8. hemothorax
9. pulmonary embolism
10. coccidioidomycosis
11. chest x-ray, nosocomial

Exercise 36

1. rhinomycosis
2. tonsillectomy
3. atelectasis
4. pansinusitis
5. lobectomy
6. bronchogram
7. endotracheal

Exercise 37

1. originating in the skin
2. instrument used for measuring or counting red blood cells
3. abnormal state of black nail
4. study of fungi
5. softening of a muscle
6. death of muscle tissue
7. abnormal condition of fungus in the tonsils
8. pertaining to the body and internal organs

Answers

```
P L E U R O . . P . . . . .
U . . . . . T O N S I L L O
L . . . . . E . . . . . A .
M U C O . S I N U S O . P Y O
N A S O . . M . . O L . N .
O . P H A R Y N G O . G O .
. . . D . . O . B O . . .
T R A C H E O . . O . . S
. . . N . . . . . . . P
A L V E O L O . . . P I
. . . I . X . . . . I R
. . . D . O . . . . R
O R T H O . . R H I N O
```

CHAPTER 6

Exercise Figures

Exercise Figure
A. 1. kidney: nephr/o, ren/o
   2. meatus: meat/o
   3. ureter: ureter/o
   4. bladder: cyst/o, vesic/o
   5. urethra: urethr/o

Exercise Figure
B. 1. renal pelvis: pyel/o
   2. glomerulus: glomerul/o

Exercise Figure C. cystolith
Exercise Figure D. cystostomy
Exercise Figure E. lithotripsy
Exercise Figure F. nephrostomy
Exercise Figure G. pyelolithotomy
Exercise Figure H. ureterostomy
Exercise Figure I. renogram
Exercise Figure J. pyelogram
Exercise Figure K. urinometer
Exercise Figure L. urinary

Exercise 1
1. g   5. a
2. d   6. b
3. f   7. e
4. c

Exercise 2
1. glomerulus   6. sac, bladder
2. sac, bladder   7. urethra
3. kidney   8. kidney
4. renal pelvis   9. meatus
5. ureter

Exercise 3
1. a. nephr/o   4. pyel/o
   b. ren/o   5. glomerul/o
2. a. cyst/o   6. urethr/o
   b. vesic/o   7. meat/o
3. ureter/o

Exercise 4
1. water   10. sound
2. vein   11. sugar
3. urea, nitrogen   12. developing cell,
4. neck, necklike   germ cell
5. night   13. scanty, few
6. stone, calculus 14. urine, urinary
7. cut, section   tract
8. albumin   15. sugar
9. urine, urinary
   tract

Exercise 5
1. a. glyc/o   7. tom/o
   b. glycos/o   8. albumin/o
2. trachel/o   9. noct/i
3. son/o   10. azot/o
4. a. urin/o   11. lith/o
   b. ur/o   12. ven/o
5. hydr/o   13. olig/o
6. blast/o

Exercise 6
1. many, much

Exercise 7
1. poly-

Exercise 8
1. c   5. g
2. i   6. e
3. d   7. a
4. f   8. b

Exercise 9
1. suturing, repairing
2. loosening, dissolution, separating
3. condition
4. nourishment, development
5. urine, urination
6. enlargement
7. drooping, sagging, prolapse
8. surgical crushing

Exercise 10
1. WR   S
   nephr/oma
   tumor of the kidney

2. WR CV WR
   cyst/o/lith
        CF
   stone in the bladder

3. WR CV WR   S
   nephr/o/lith/iasis
        CF
   condition of stone(s) in the kidney

4. WR   S
   ur/emia
   condition of urine in the blood

5. WR CV   S
   nephr/o/ptosis
        CF
   a drooping kidney

6. WR CV S
   cyst/o/cele
        CF
   protrusion of the bladder

7. WR CV P   S
   nephr/o/hyper/trophy
        CF
   excessive development of the kidney

8. WR CV WR S
   trachel/o/cyst/itis
          CF
   inflammation of the neck of the
   bladder

9. WR   S
   cyst/itis
   inflammation of the bladder

10. WR   S
    pyel/itis
    inflammation of the renal pelvis

11. WR CV S
    ureter/o/cele
          CF
    protrusion of a ureter

12. WR CV WR   S
    hydr/o/nephr/osis
          CF
    abnormal condition of water in the
    kidney

13. WR CV   S
    nephr/o/megaly
          CF
    enlargement of a kidney

14. WR CV WR   S
    ureter/o/lith/iasis
            CF
    condition of stone(s) in the ureters

15. WR CV WR   S
    pyel/o/nephr/itis
          CF
    inflammation of the renal pelvis and
    the kidney

16. WR   S
    ureter/itis
    inflammation of a ureter

17. WR   S
    nephr/itis
    inflammation of a kidney
```
```

18. WR CV WR S
urethr/o/cyst/itis
CF

inflammation of the urethra and bladder

19. WR CV S
ureter/o/stenosis
CF

narrowing of the ureter

20. WR CV WR S
nephr/o/blast/oma
CF

kidney tumor containing developing cell (tissue)

Exercise 11
1. nephr/o/megaly
2. cyst/itis
3. nephr/o/hyper/trophy
4. urethr/o/cyst/itis
5. cyst/o/cele
6. trachel/o/cyst/itis
7. hydr/o/nephr/osis
8. cyst/o/lith
9. glomerul/o/nephr/itis
10. nephr/oma
11. nephr/o/ptosis
12. nephr/itis
13. nephr/o/lith/iasis
14. ureter/o/cele
15. pyel/itis
16. ur/emia
17. ureter/o/stenosis
18. pyel/o/nephr/itis
19. ureter/o/lith/iasis
20. nephr/o/blast/oma

Exercise 12
Spelling exercise; see text, p. 147.

Exercise 13
1. renal calculi
2. urinary retention
3. polycystic kidney
4. hypospadias
5. renal hypertension
6. urinary suppression
7. epispadias
8. urinary tract infection

Exercise 14
1. c   5. a
2. f   6. e
3. d   7. b
4. h   8. g

Exercise 15
Spelling exercise; see text, p. 149.

Exercise 16
1. WR S
vesic/otomy
incision of the bladder

2. WR S
nephr/ostomy
creation of an artificial opening into the kidney

3. WR CV S
nephr/o/lysis
CF
separating the kidney

4. WR S
cyst/ectomy
excision of the bladder

5. WR S
ureter/otomy
incision of a ureter

6. WR CV WR S
pyel/o/lith/otomy
CF
incision of the renal pelvis to remove a stone

7. WR CV WR S
cyst/o/trachel/otomy
CF
incision of the neck of the bladder

8. WR CV S
nephr/o/pexy
CF
surgical fixation of the kidney

9. WR S
ureter/ostomy
creation of an artificial opening in the ureter

10. WR CV WR S
cyst/o/lith/otomy
CF
incision of the bladder to remove a stone

11. WR S
nephr/ectomy
excision of a kidney

12. WR S
pyel/ostomy
creation of an artificial opening in the renal pelvis

13. WR CV S
urethr/o/pexy
CF
surgical fixation of the urethra

14. WR S
ureter/ectomy
excision of a ureter

15. WR S
cyst/ostomy
creation of an artificial opening into the bladder

16. WR CV S
pyel/o/plasty
CF
surgical repair of the renal pelvis

17. WR S
cyst/orrhaphy
suturing of the bladder

18. WR S
urethr/ostomy
creation of an artificial opening into the urethra

19. WR CV S
cyst/o/plasty
CF
surgical repair of the bladder

20. WR S
meat/otomy
incision of the meatus

21. WR CV S
lith/o/tripsy
CF
surgical crushing of a stone

22. WR S
cyst/otomy
incision of the bladder

23. WR CV S
urethr/o/plasty
CF
surgical repair of the urethra

24. WR CV WR S
vesic/o/urethr/al suspension
CF
surgical suspension pertaining to the urethra and bladder

Exercise 17
1. urethr/otomy
2. nephr/ectomy
3. pyel/o/lith/otomy
4. urethr/o/pexy
5. cyst/orrhaphy
6. nephr/o/lysis
7. nephr/ostomy
8. ureter/otomy
9. urethr/o/plasty
10. cyst/ectomy
11. meat/otomy
12. urethr/ostomy
13. a. cyst/otomy
    b. vesic/otomy
14. pyel/o/plasty
15. cyst/o/trachel/otomy

16. ureter/ectomy
17. nephr/o/pexy
18. pyel/ostomy
19. cyst/o/lith/otomy
20. ureter/ostomy
21. cyst/o/plasty
22. lith/o/tripsy
23. vesic/o/urethr/al suspension
24. cyst/ostomy

Exercise 18
Spelling exercise; see text, p. 154.

Exercise 19
1. renal transplant
2. lithotrite
3. fulguration

Exercise 20
1. b 2. c 3. a

Exercise 21
Spelling exercise; see text, p. 157.

Exercise 22
1. WR CV S
    urethr/o/meter
        CF

    instrument used to measure the
    urethra

2. WR CV WR CV S
    cyst/o/urethr/o/gram
        CF   CF

    x-ray film of the bladder and the
    urethra

3. WR CV S
    meat/o/scope
        CF

    instrument used for visual examination
    of a meatus

4. WR CV WR CV S
    cyst/o/pyel/o/gram
        CF   CF

    x-ray film of the bladder and the renal
    pelvis

5. WR CV   S
    cyst/o/graphy
        CF

    x-ray filming the bladder

6. WR CV S
    urethr/o/scope
        CF

    instrument used for visual examination
    of the urethra

7. WR CV WR CV   S
    nephr/o/son/o/graphy
        CF   CF

    process of recording the kidney using
    (ultra) sound

8. WR CV S
    cyst/o/scope
        CF

    instrument used for visual examination
    of the bladder

9. WR CV S
    pyel/o/gram
        CF

    x-ray film of the renal pelvis

10. WR CV WR CV S
    nephr/o/tom/o/gram
         CF   CF

    sectional x-ray film of the kidney

11. WR CV   S
    cyst/o/gram
        CF

    x-ray film of the bladder

12. WR CV WR CV S
    cyst/o/ureter/o/gram
        CF   CF

    x-ray film of the bladder and ureters

13. WR CV   S
    meat/o/scopy
        CF

    visual examination of a meatus

14. WR CV S
    nephr/o/gram
         CF

    x-ray film of the kidney

15. WR CV S
    ureter/o/gram
         CF

    x-ray film of the ureters

16. WR CV   S
    cyst/o/scopy
        CF

    visual examination of the bladder

17. WR CV   S
    nephr/o/graphy
         CF

    x-ray filming the kidney

18. WR CV S
    urin/o/meter
        CF

    instrument used to measure urine

19.   P   WR S   WR CV   S
    intra/ven/ous pyel/o/gram
                       CF

    x-ray film of the renal pelvis with
    contrast medium injected within
    the vein

20.   WR CV   S
    retrograde pyel/o/gram
                   CF

    x-ray film of the renal pelvis (contrast
    medium injected in a direction
    opposite from normal through the
    urethra)

21. WR CV WR CV   S
    cyst/o/pyel/o/graphy
        CF   CF

    x-ray filming the bladder and the renal
    pelvis

22. WR CV   S
    ren/o/gram
        CF

    (graphic) record of the kidney

23. WR CV S
    nephr/o/scopy
         CF

    visual examination of the kidney

24. WR S WR S
    ren/al bi/opsy
    view of a portion of living kidney
    tissue

Exercise 23
1. cyst/o/scopy
2. cyst/o/ureter/o/gram
3. urethr/o/meter
4. nephr/o/tom/o/gram
5. cyst/o/pyel/o/gram
6. intra/ven/ous pyel/o/gram
7. meat/o/scope
8. urethr/o/scope
9. nephr/o/son/o/graphy
10. cyst/o/gram
11. meat/o/scopy
12. ureter/o/gram
13. pyel/o/gram
14. cyst/o/scope
15. cyst/o/urethr/o/gram
16. cyst/o/graphy
17. nephr/o/gram
18. urin/o/meter
19. ren/o/gram

20. cyst/o/pyel/o/graphy
21. nephr/o/graphy
22. retrograde pyel/o/gram
23. ren/al bi/opsy
24. nephr/o/scopy

Exercise 24
Spelling exercise; see text, p. 162.

Exercise 25
1. kidney, ureter, bladder
2. specific gravity
3. blood urea nitrogen
4. urinalysis

Exercise 26
1. c 2. b 3. d 4. a

Exercise 27
Spelling exercise; see text, p. 163.

Exercise 28
1. WR   S
   noct/uria

   night urination

2. WR   S
   ur/ologist

   physician who specializes in the diagnosis and treatment of diseases of the male and female urinary systems and in the reproductive system of the male

3. WR   S
   olig/uria

   scanty urination

4. WR   S
   azot/uria

   (excessive) urea and nitrogenous substances in the urine

5. WR   S
   hemat/uria

   blood in the urine

6. WR   S
   ur/ology

   study of the male and female urinary systems and the reproductive system of the male

7. P   S(WR)
   poly/uria

   much (excessive) urine

8. WR   S
   albumin/uria

   albumin in the urine

9. P   S(WR)
   an/uria

   absence of urine

10. P WR S
    di/ur/esis

    condition of urine passing through (increased excretion of urine)

11. WR   S
    py/uria

    pus in the urine

12. WR   S
    urin/ary

    pertaining to urine

13. WR   S
    glycos/uria

    sugar in the urine

14. WR   S
    meat/al

    pertaining to the meatus

15. P   S(WR)
    dys/uria

    difficult or painful urination

Exercise 29
1. noct/uria
2. olig/uria
3. py/uria
4. ur/ologist
5. poly/uria
6. azot/uria
7. urin/ary
8. hemat/uria
9. ur/ology
10. di/ur/esis
11. an/uria
12. glycos/uria
13. dys/uria
14. albumin/uria
15. meat/al

Exercise 30
Spelling exercise; see text, p. 166.

Exercise 31
1. urinal
2. hemodialysis
3. distended
4. catheter
5. incontinence
6. urinary catheterization
7. peritoneal dialysis
8. evacuate waste material
9. stricture
10. diuretic
11. enuresis
12. micturate
13. urodynamics

Exercise 32
1. e
2. g
3. f
4. a
5. d
6. c
7. h

Exercise 33
1. a
2. e
3. g
4. b
5. f
6. c

Exercise 34
Spelling exercise; see text, p. 169.

Exercise 35
1. nephrolithiasis
2. urology
3. kidney, ureter, and bladder
4. calculi
5. hematuria
6. intravenous pyelogram or intravenous urogram
7. hydronephrosis
8. cystoscopy
9. pyelogram
10. pyelolithotomy
11. catheter
12. voiding

Exercise 36
1. nephroptosis
2. ureterolithiasis
3. pyelogram
4. polyuria
5. nephropexy
6. urinary suppression
7. cystogram
8. enuresis
9. urinary tract infection

Exercise 37
1. cystoscopy
2. anuria
3. pyelitis
4. nephroma
5. uremia
6. ureterocele

Exercise 38
1. excessive fat in the blood
2. below normal amount of glucose in the blood
3. condition of white nail
4. pertaining to the nerves and skin
5. incision of a tumor
6. record of sound
7. pain in the body
8. study of hair

Answers

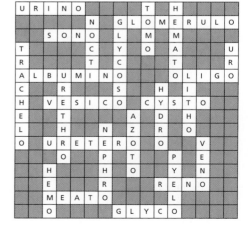

CHAPTER 7
Exercise Figures
Exercise Figure
A. 1. vas, or ductus, deferens: vas/o
   2. glans penis: balan/o
   3. seminal vesicles: vesicul/o
   4. prostate gland: prostat/o
   5. epididymis: epididym/o
   6. testis: orchid/o, orchi/o, orch/o, test/o

Exercise Figure B. cryptorchidism
Exercise Figure C. prostatic
Exercise Figure D. vasectomy

Exercise 1
1. c
2. i
3. e
4. j
5. f
6. a
7. k
8. g
9. b
10. l
11. h
12. n
13. d

Exercise 2
1. testis, testicle
2. vessel, duct
3. glans penis
4. prostate gland
5. testis, testicle
6. seminal vesicle
7. testis, testicle
8. epididymis
9. testis, testicle

Exercise 3
1. vas/o
2. prostat/o
3. balan/o
4. vesicul/o
5. epididym/o
6. a. orchid/o
   b. orchi/o
   c. orch/o
   d. test/o

Exercise 4
1. sperm
2. male
3. sperm

Exercise 5
1. a. sperm/o
   b. spermat/o
2. andr/o

Exercise 6
1. state of
2. through, across, beyond

Exercise 7
1. WR CV S
   prostat/o/lith
   CF
   stone in the prostate

2. WR S
   balan/itis
   inflammation of the glans penis

3. a. WR S
      orch/itis
   b. WR S
      orchid/itis

c. WR S
   test/itis
   inflammation of the testis

4. WR CV WR S
   prostat/o/vesicul/itis
   CF
   inflammation of the prostate gland and seminal vesicles

5. WR CV WR S
   prostat/o/cyst/itis
   CF
   inflammation of the prostate gland and bladder

6. WR WR S
   orchi/epididym/itis
   inflammation of the testis and epididymis

7. WR S
   prostat/orrhea
   excessive discharge from the prostate gland

8. WR S
   epididym/itis
   inflammation of the epididymis

9. WR S P S(WR)
   benign prostat/ic hyper/trophy
   nonmalignant excessive development of the prostate gland (pertaining to)

10. WR CV S
    balan/o/cele
    CF
    protrusion of the glans penis

11. WR WR S
    crypt/orchid/ism
    state of hidden testis

12. WR S
    balan/orrhea
    excessive discharge from the glans penis

13. WR S
    prostat/itis
    inflammation of the prostate

14. P WR S
    an/orch/ism
    state of absence of testis

Exercise 8
1. prostat/o/cyst/itis
2. prostat/o/lith
3. a. orchid/itis
   b. orch/itis
   c. test/itis
4. benign prostat/ic hyper/trophy
5. crypt/orchid/ism
6. prostat/o/vesicul/itis
7. an/orch/ism, or an/orchid/ism

8. balan/o/cele
9. prostat/itis
10. orchi/epididym/itis
11. balan/orrhea
12. epididym/itis
13. balan/itis
14. prostat/orrhea

Exercise 9
Spelling exercise; see text, p. 182.

Exercise 10
1. testicular carcinoma
2. phimosis
3. impotent
4. varicocele
5. hydrocele
6. prostatic cancer
7. erectile dysfunction
8. priapism
9. testicular torsion

Exercise 11
1. d
2. c
3. e
4. b
5. a
6. f
7. j
8. i
9. h

Exercise 12
Spelling exercise; see text, p. 186.

Exercise 13
1. WR S
   vas/ectomy
   excision of a duct

2. WR CV WR S
   prostat/o/cyst/otomy
   CF
   incision into the bladder and prostate gland

3. a. WR S
      orchid/otomy
   b. WR S
      orchi/otomy
      incision into a testis

4. WR S
   epididym/ectomy
   excision of an epididymis

5. a. WR CV S
      orchid/o/pexy
      CF
   b. WR CV S
      orchi/o/pexy
      CF
      surgical fixation of a testicle

6. WR CV WR S
   prostat/o/vesicul/ectomy
   CF
   excision of the prostate gland and seminal vesicles

7.   WR CV S
   orchi/o/plasty
        CF

   surgical repair of testis

8.   WR   S
   vesicul/ectomy

   excision of the seminal vesicle(s)

9.   WR   S
   prostat/ectomy

   excision of the prostate gland

10.   WR CV S
   balan/o/plasty
        CF

   surgical repair of the glans penis

11.   P   WR   S
   trans/urethr/al resection

   resection (of prostate gland) through
   the urethra

12.   WR CV WR   S
   vas/o/vas/ostomy
        CF

   creation of artificial opening between
   ducts

13. a.   WR   S
     orchid/ectomy
     b.   WR   S
     orchi/ectomy

     excision of one or both testes

14.   WR CV WR   S
   prostat/o/lith/otomy
          CF

   incision into prostate gland to remove
   a stone

Exercise 14
1. a. orchid/ectomy
    b. orchi/ectomy
2. balan/o/plasty
3. prostat/o/cyst/otomy
4. vesicul/ectomy
5. prostat/o/lith/otomy
6. a. orchid/otomy
    b. orchi/otomy
7. trans/urethr/al resection
8. epididym/ectomy
9. orchi/o/plasty
10. prostat/ectomy
11. vas/ectomy
12. prostat/o/vesicul/ectomy
13. a. orchid/o/pexy
    b. orchi/o/pexy
14. vas/o/vas/ostomy

Exercise 15
Spelling exercise; see text, p. 189.

Exercise 16
1. suprapubic prostatectomy, transurethral
    prostatectomy

2. circumcision
3. penile implant
4. hydrocelectomy
5. transurethral microwave therapy
6. transurethral incision of the prostate

Exercise 17
Spelling exercise; see text, p. 191.

Exercise 18
1. digital rectal exam
2. prostatic specific antigen
3. transrectal ultrasound

Exercise 19
1.   WR CV WR   S
   olig/o/sperm/ia
        CF

   condition of scanty sperm

2.   WR CV   S
   andr/o/pathy
        CF

   diseases of the male

3.   WR   CV S
   spermat/o/lysis
          CF

   dissolution of sperm

4.   P   WR   S
   a/sperm/ia

   condition of the absence of sperm

Exercise 20
1. spermat/o/lysis   3. a/sperm/ia
2. andr/o/pathy   4. olig/o/sperm/ia

Exercise 21
Spelling exercise; see text, p. 193.

Exercise 22
1. period when secondary sex
    characteristics develop and the ability to
    sexually reproduce begins
2. climax of sexual stimulation
3. contagious, inflammatory venereal
    disease
4. person who is attracted to a member of
    the same sex
5. sexual intercourse between male and
    female
6. contagious venereal disease caused by
    the herpes hominis type 2 virus
7. person who is attracted to a member of
    the opposite sex
8. infectious venereal disease having
    lesions that can affect any organ or
    tissue
9. ejection of semen from the male
    urethra

10. male and female sex glands
11. sexually transmitted disease; a disease
    transmitted during sexual intercourse
12. process rendering an individual unable
    to produce offspring
13. an STD causing growths on the male
    and female genitalia
14. a disease transmitted by exchange of
    body fluids during the sexual act, reuse
    of contaminated needles, and
    contaminated blood transfusions that
    affects the body's immune system
15. sexually transmitted disease caused by
    a one-cell organism, *Trichomonas;* it
    affects the genitourinary system.
16. introduction of semen into the vagina
    by artificial means
17. one of the more prevalent STDs.
    Caused by bacterium, *Chlamydia
    trachomatis*
18. a cover for the penis worn during
    coitus
19. an artificial replacement of an absent
    body part
20. a type of retrovirus that causes AIDS

Exercise 23
1. g   6. i
2. e   7. c
3. h   8. b
4. a   9. j
5. d   10. f

Exercise 24
1. f   6. b
2. a   7. i
3. h   8. e
4. d   9. g
5. j   10. c

Exercise 25
Spelling exercise; see text, p. 198.

Exercise 26
1. nocturia   4. benign prostatic
2. hematuria   hypertrophy
3. urinary   5. urology

Exercise 27
1. balanorrhea   4. phimosis
2. prepuce   5. orchidopexy
3. heterosexual   6. prosthesis
                  7. transurethral
                     microwave
                     thermotherapy

Exercise 28
1. vasectomy   4. prostatitis
2. balanorrhea   5. orchidotomy
3. andropathy

Exercise 29

1. eating or biting self
2. inflammation of the bronchial glands
3. abnormal state of dead sperm
4. inflammation around the (urinary) bladder
5. abnormal condition of disease
6. excessive amount of water in the urine
7. inflammation of the muscles of the neck
8. originating in the internal organs

Answers: Suffixes—Chapters 2 to 4

CHAPTER 8
Exercise Figures

Exercise Figure
A. 1. ovary: oophor/o
   2. uterus: hyster/o, metr/o (metr/i), uter/o
   3. fallopian, or uterine, tube: salping/o
   4. cervix: cervic/o
   5. vagina: colp/o, vagin/o
   6. hymen: hymen/o

Exercise Figure
B. 1. vulva: episi/o, vulv/o
   2. perineum: perine/o

Exercise Figure C. salpingitis
Exercise Figure D. hysteroptosis
Exercise Figure E. vesicovaginal
Exercise Figure F. *1*, hysterectomy, salpingo-oophorectomy. *2*, salpingo-oophorectomy. *3*, oophorosalpingectomy. *4*, hysterectomy.
Exercise Figure G. *1*, cystocele.

Exercise Figure H. hysterosalpingogram
Exercise Figure I. *1*, culdocentesis. *2*, culdoscopy.

Exercise 1

1. c
2. f
3. g
4. b
5. d
6. e
7. h
8. a
9. i

Exercise 2

1. b
2. c
3. d
4. k
5. e
6. f
7. g
8. l
9. i
10. j
11. h

Exercise 3

1. vagina
2. ovary
3. uterus
4. uterus
5. hymen
6. uterus
7. menstruation
8. vulva
9. cervix
10. vagina
11. woman
12. breast
13. perineum
14. fallopian tube
15. vulva
16. breast
17. beginning, first
18. cul-de-sac
19. woman

Exercise 4

1. a. episi/o
   b. vulv/o
2. a. mamm/o
   b. mast/o
3. men/o
4. oophor/o
5. salping/o
6. perine/o
7. a. vagin/o
   b. colp/o
8. a. uter/o
   b. metr/i, metr/o
   c. hyster/o
9. a. gynec/o
   b. gyn/o
10. hymen/o
11. culd/o
12. cervic/o
13. arche/o

Exercise 5

1. -salpinx
2. -ial
3. peri-
4. -atresia

Exercise 6

1. fallopian tube
2. surrounding
3. pertaining to
4. absence of a normal body opening

Exercise 7

1. WR S
   colp/itis
   inflammation of the vagina

2. WR S
   cervic/itis
   inflammation of the cervix

3. WR CV S
   hydr/o/salpinx
        CF
   water in the fallopian tube

4. WR CV S
   hemat/o/salpinx
         CF
   blood in the fallopian tube

5. WR S
   metr/orrhea
   excessive discharge from the uterus

6. WR S
   oophor/itis
   inflammation of the ovary

7. WR S
   Bartholin's aden/itis
   inflammation of Bartholin's gland

8. WR CV WR S
   vulv/o/vagin/itis
        CF
   inflammation of the vulva and vagina

9. WR CV S
   salping/o/cele
          CF
   hernia of the fallopian tube

10. WR CV WR S
    men/o/metr/orrhagia
         CF
    rapid flow of blood from the uterus (and between menstrual cycles)

11. P WR S
    a/men/orrhea
    absence of menstrual discharge

12. P WR S
    dys/men/orrhea
    painful menstrual discharge

13. WR S
    mast/itis
    inflammation of the breast

14. P WR S
    peri/metr/itis
    inflammation surrounding the uterus

15. WR CV WR S
    my/o/metr/itis
         CF
    inflammation of the uterine muscle

16. P WR S
    endo/metr/itis
    inflammation of the inner (lining) of the uterus

17. P WR S
    endo/cervic/itis
    inflammation of the inner (lining) of the cervix

18. WR CV   S
    py/o/salpinx
        ⌣
        CF

    pus in the fallopian tube

19. WR   S
    hyster/atresia

    closure of the uterus

20. WR   S
    salping/itis

    inflammation of the fallopian tube

21. WR   S
    vagin/itis

    inflammation of the vagina

Exercise 8
1. mast/itis
2. metr/orrhea
3. salping/itis
4. vulv/o/vagin/itis
5. a/men/orrhea
6. cervic/itis
7. Bartholin's aden/itis
8. hydr/o/salpinx
9. dys/men/orrhea
10. hemat/o/salpinx
11. a. colp/itis
    b. vagin/itis
12. men/o/metr/orrhagia
13. oophor/itis
14. salping/o/cele
15. peri/metr/itis
16. endo/metr/itis
17. endo/cervic/itis
18. my/o/metr/itis
19. py/o/salpinx
20. hyster/atresia

Exercise 9
Spelling exercise; see text, p. 215.

Exercise 10
1. downward placement of the uterus in the vagina
2. inflammation of the female pelvic organs
3. opening between the bladder and vagina
4. benign fibroid tumor of the uterine muscle
5. abnormal condition in which endometrial tissue occurs in various areas of the pelvic cavity
6. growth of endometrium into the muscular portion of the uterus
7. a severe illness characterized by high fever, vomiting, diarrhea, and myalgia
8. a disorder characterized by one or more benign tumors

Exercise 11
1. vesicovaginal fistula
2. fibroid tumor

3. pelvic inflammatory disease
4. prolapsed uterus
5. endometriosis
6. adenomyosis
7. toxic shock syndrome
8. fibrocystic breast disease

Exercise 12
Spelling exercise; see text, p. 218.

Exercise 13
1. WR   S
   colp/orrhaphy

   suture of the vagina

2. WR CV   S
   colp/o/plasty
       ⌣
       CF

   surgical repair of the vagina

3. WR   S
   episi/orrhaphy

   suture of the vulva (tear)

4. WR   S
   hymen/otomy

   incision of the hymen

5. WR CV   S
   hyster/o/pexy
        ⌣
        CF

   surgical fixation of the uterus

6. WR   S
   vulv/ectomy

   excision of the vulva

7. WR   S
   perine/orrhaphy

   suture of the perineum (tear)

8. WR   S
   salping/ostomy

   creation of an artificial opening in the fallopian tube

9. WR CV WR   S
   oophor/o/salping/ectomy
         ⌣
         CF

   excision of the ovary and fallopian tube

10. WR   S
    oophor/ectomy

    excision of the ovary

11. WR   S
    mast/ectomy

    surgical removal of a breast

12. WR   S
    salping/ectomy

    excision of a fallopian tube

13. WR   S
    cervic/ectomy

    excision of the cervix

14. WR CV WR   S
    colp/o/perine/orrhaphy
        ⌣
        CF

    suture of the vagina and perineum

15. WR CV WR CV   S
    episi/o/perine/o/plasty
         ⌣   ⌣
         CF   CF

    surgical repair of the vulva and perineum

16. WR   S
    hymen/ectomy

    excision of the hymen

17. WR CV WR CV WR   S
    hyster/o/salping/o/-oophor/ectomy
          ⌣   ⌣
          CF   CF

    excision of the uterus, fallopian tubes, and ovaries

18. WR   S
    hyster/ectomy

    excision of the uterus

19. WR CV   S
    mamm/o/plasty
         ⌣
         CF

    surgical repair of the breast

20. WR CV   S
    mamm/o/tome
         ⌣
         CF

    instrument used to cut breast (tissue)

Exercise 14
1. colp/orrhaphy
2. cervic/ectomy
3. episi/orrhaphy
4. episi/o/perine/o/plasty
5. colp/o/plasty
6. colp/o/perine/orrhaphy
7. hyster/o/salping/o/-oophor/ectomy
8. hyster/o/pexy
9. hymen/ectomy
10. hymen/otomy
11. hyster/ectomy
12. oophor/ectomy
13. mast/ectomy
14. salping/ectomy
15. perine/orrhaphy
16. oophor/o/salping/ectomy
17. salping/ostomy
18. vulv/ectomy
19. mamm/o/plasty
20. mamm/o/tome

Exercise 15
Spelling exercise; see text, p. 222.

Exercise 16
1. laparoscopy (sterilization); tubal ligation
2. anterior and posterior colporrhaphy (A & P repair)

3. dilatation and curettage
4. stereotactic breast biopsy
5. myomectomy

Exercise 17
1. c   4. b
2. a   5. c
3. a   6. f

Exercise 18
Spelling exercise; see text, p. 225.

Exercise 19
1. WR CV S
   colp/o/scopy
      CF
   visual examination of the vagina

2. WR CV S
   mamm/o/gram
        CF
   x-ray film of the breast

3. WR CV S
   colp/o/scope
      CF
   instrument used for visual examination of the vagina

4. WR CV S
   hyster/o/scopy
        CF
   visual examination of the uterus

5. WR CV WR CV S
   hyster/o/salping/o/gram
        CF   CF
   x-ray film of the uterus and fallopian tube

6. WR CV S
   culd/o/scope
      CF
   instrument used for visual examination of the Douglas cul-de-sac

7. WR CV S
   culd/o/scopy
      CF
   visual examination of the Douglas cul-de-sac

8. WR CV S
   culd/o/centesis
      CF
   surgical puncture to remove fluid from the Douglas cul-de-sac

9. WR CV S
   mamm/o/graphy
        CF
   process of x-ray filming the breast

10. WR CV S
    hyster/o/scope
         CF
    instrument used for visual examination of the uterus

11. WR CV WR CV S
    son/o/hyster/o/graphy
       CF   CF
    process of recording the uterus by use of sound

Exercise 20
1. hyster/o/salping/o/gram
2. colp/o/scopy
3. colp/o/scope
4. hyster/o/scopy
5. mamm/o/gram
6. culd/o/scope
7. culd/o/scopy
8. culd/o/centesis
9. hyster/o/scope
10. mamm/o/graphy
11. son/o/hyster/o/graphy

Exercise 21
Spelling exercise; see text, p. 229.

Exercise 22
1. WR S
   gynec/ologist
   physician who specializes in gynecology

2. WR S
   gynec/ology
   branch of medicine dealing with diseases of the female reproductive system

3. WR S
   colp/algia
   pain in the vagina

4. WR CV WR S
   vulv/o/vagin/al
        CF
   pertaining to the vulva and vagina

5. WR S
   mast/algia
   pain in the breast

6. WR WR
   men/arche
   beginning of menstruation

7. WR S
   leuk/orrhea
   white discharge (from the vagina)

8. WR CV WR S
   olig/o/men/orrhea
        CF
   scanty menstrual flow

9. WR CV WR S
   gyn/o/path/ic
      CF
   pertaining to disease of women

10. WR CV S
    mast/o/ptosis
         CF
    sagging breast

Exercise 23
1. olig/o/men/orrhea
2. leuk/orrhea
3. men/arche
4. mast/algia
5. vulv/o/vagin/al
6. colp/algia
7. gynec/ologist
8. gynec/ology
9. mast/o/ptosis
10. gyn/o/path/ic

Exercise 24
Spelling exercise; see text, p. 231.

Exercise 25
1. cessation of menstruation
2. painful intercourse
3. abnormal passageway between two organs or between an internal organ and the body surface
4. a syndrome involving physical and emotional symptoms occurring during the 10 days prior to menstruation
5. instrument for opening a body cavity to allow for visual inspection
6. replacement of hormones in the treatment of menopause
7. method of examining stained exfoliative cells used to detect cancers of the cervix

Exercise 26
1. fistula
2. dyspareunia
3. menopause
4. premenstrual syndrome
5. speculum
6. estrogen replacement therapy
7. Pap smear

Exercise 27
Spelling exercise; see text, p. 233.

Exercise 28
1. mammography   5. endometriosis
2. carcinoma   6. induration
3. hysterectomy   7. necrosis
4. adenomyosis   8. hyperplasia

Exercise 29
1. dysmenorrhea
2. endometritis
3. fallopian tube
4. suture of the vulva
5. mammoplasty
6. uterus, fallopian tubes, and ovaries
7. hematosalpinx
8. endometriosis
9. speculum

Exercise 30
1. hysteropexy
2. leukorrhea
3. gynecology
4. mastalgia
5. menarche

Exercise 31
1. a 2. e 3. b 4. d 5. e 6. b

Answers: Combining Forms— Chapters 7 and 8

		V	A	G	I	N	O		P	R	O	S	T	A	T	O	
	C								P								
V	U	L	V	O			M			C	E	R	V	I	C	O	
	L						E			R							
	D		S	A	L	P	I	N	G	O							
	O		O			E	O			A	N	D	R	O			
	G		V			R				T							
	Y		E	P	I	D	I	D	Y	M	O						
	N		S		N						T			A			
	E		I		E					M	E	T	R	O			
	C		C	O	O	P	H	O	R	O			S				
O		O		U		R		Y					T			H	
R			L			C		S	P	E	R	M	O			E	
C	E	L	I	O		H		T								O	M
H						I			E	P	I	S	I	O			A
O					D		R										M
		B	A	L	A	N	O										M
									H	Y	S	T	E	R	O		

CHAPTER 9
Exercise Figures
Exercise Figure
A. 1. umbilicus: omphal/o
   2. fetus: fet/o, fet/i
   3. amnion: amni/o, amnion/o
   4. chorion: chori/o

Exercise Figure B. salpingocyesis
Exercise Figure C. omphalocele
Exercise Figure D. amniocentesis

Exercise 1
1. gamete; ovulation; fertilization; zygote; gestation
2. embryo; fetus
3. amniotic; chorion; amnion; amniotic

Exercise 2
1. fetus, unborn child
2. milk
3. give birth to, bear, labor, child birth
4. umbilicus, navel
5. amnion, amniotic fluid
6. childbirth
7. pregnancy
8. birth
9. chorion
10. embryo, to be full

Exercise 3
1. lact/o
2. fet/o, fet/i
3. chori/o
4. a. amni/o
   b. amnion/o
5. puerper/o
6. a. par/o
   b. part/o
7. a. gravid/o
   b. cyes/o, cyes/i
8. embry/o
9. nat/o
10. omphal/o

Exercise 4
1. first
2. pylorus
3. head
4. esophagus
5. false
6. pelvic bone, pelvis

Exercise 5
1. cephal/o
2. pylor/o
3. pseud/o
4. esophag/o
5. prim/i
6. pelv/i, pelv/o

Exercise 6
1. after
2. many
3. none
4. small
5. before

Exercise 7
1. nulli-
2. micro-
3. multi-
4. ante-
5. post-

Exercise 8
1. rupture
2. birth, labor

Exercise 9
1. -tocia
2. -orrhexis

Exercise 10
1. WR CV WR S
   chori/o/amnion/itis
        CF
   inflammation of the chorion and amnion

2. WR CV WR S
   chori/o/carcin/oma
        CF
   cancerous tumor of the chorion

3. P S(WR)
   dys/tocia
   difficult labor

4. WR S
   amnion/itis
   inflammation of the amnion

5. WR S
   hyster/orrhexis
   rupture of the uterus

6. WR CV S
   embry/o/tocia
        CF
   birth of an embryo, abortion

7. WR CV WR S
   salping/o/cyes/is
        CF
   pregnancy in a fallopian tube (ectopic pregnancy)

Exercise 11
1. chori/o/carcin/oma
2. amnion/itis
3. chori/o/amnion/itis
4. embry/o/tocia
5. dys/tocia
6. hyster/orrhexis
7. salping/o/cyes/is

Exercise 12
Spelling exercise; see text, p. 247.

Exercise 13
1. premature separation of the placenta from the uterine wall
2. termination of pregnancy by the expulsion from the uterus of an embryo or nonviable fetus
3. abnormally low implantation of the placenta on the uterine wall
4. severe complication and progression of preeclampsia
5. pregnancy occurring outside the uterus
6. abnormal condition, encountered during pregnancy or shortly after delivery, of high blood pressure, edema, and proteinuria

Exercise 14
1. abruptio placentae
2. eclampsia
3. abortion
4. ectopic pregnancy
5. placenta previa
6. preeclampsia

Exercise 15
Spelling exercise; see text, p. 249.

Exercise 16
1. WR S
   pylor/ic stenosis
   narrowing of (pertaining to) the pyloric sphincter

2. WR CV S
    omphal/o/cele
          └CF┘
    hernia at the umbilicus

3. WR   S
    omphal/itis
    inflammation of the umbilicus

4. P   WR   S
    micro/cephal/us
    (fetus with a very) small head

5. WR CV WR   S
    trache/o/esophag/eal fistula
          └CF┘
    abnormal passageway (between)
    pertaining to the esophagus and the
    trachea

Exercise 17
1. omphal/o/cele
2. micro/cephal/us
3. pylor/ic stenosis
4. trache/o/esophag/eal fistula
5. omphal/itis

Exercise 18
Spelling exercise; see text, p. 250.

Exercise 19
1. f 2. c 3. a 4. d 5. b 6. e

Exercise 20
Spelling exercise; see text, p. 252.

Exercise 21
1. WR   S
    episi/otomy
    incision of the vulva (perineum)

2. WR   S
    amni/otomy
    incision into the amnion (rupture of the
    fetal membrane to induce labor)

3. WR CV S
    amni/o/scope
         └CF┘
    instrument for visual examination of
    amniotic fluid (and fetus)

4. WR CV S
    amni/o/graphy
         └CF┘
    x-ray filming of the amniotic fluid
    (cavity and fetus)

5. WR CV S
    fet/o/graphy
        └CF┘
    x-ray filming of the fetus

6. WR CV   S
    amni/o/centesis
         └CF┘
    surgical puncture to aspirate amniotic
    fluid

7. WR CV S
    amni/o/scopy
         └CF┘
    visual examination of amniotic fluid
    (and fetus)

8. WR CV S
    pelv/i/metry
        └CF┘
    measurement of the mother's pelvis to
    determine the ability of the fetus to pass
    through

9. WR CV S
    fet/o/metry
        └CF┘
    measurement of the fetus (for size)

Exercise 22
1. amni/otomy   6. amni/o/scope
2. episi/otomy   7. fet/o/graphy
3. amni/o/graphy   8. pelv/i/metry
4. amni/o/scopy   9. fet/o/metry
5. amni/o/centesis

Exercise 23
Spelling exercise; see text, p. 254.

Exercise 24
1. WR   S
    puerper/a
    woman who has just given birth

2. WR   S
    amni/orrhexis
    rupture of the amnion

3. P   WR   S
    ante/part/um
    occurring before childbirth

4. WR CV S
    cyes/i/ology
        └CF┘
    study of pregnancy

5. WR CV WR S
    pseud/o/cyes/is
         └CF┘
    false pregnancy

6. WR S
    cyes/is
    pregnancy

7. WR S
    lact/ic
    pertaining to milk

8. WR   S
    lact/orrhea
    (spontaneous) discharge of milk

9. WR   S
    amni/orrhea
    discharge (escape) of amniotic fluid

10. WR   S
    embry/ologist
    one who specializes in embryology

11. P   WR S
    multi/par/a
    woman who has given birth to many
    (two or more viable offspring)

12. WR CV S
    embry/o/genic
         └CF┘
    producing an embryo

13. WR   S
    embry/oid
    resembling an embryo

14. WR S
    fet/al
    pertaining to the fetus

15. WR S
    gravid/a
    pregnant woman

16. WR   S
    embry/ology
    study (or science of the development)
    of the embryo

17. WR CV WR S
    amni/o/chori/al
         └CF┘
    pertaining to the amnion and chorion

18. P   WR   S
    multi/gravid/a
    woman who has been pregnant many
    (two or more) times

19. WR CV S
    lact/o/genic
         └CF┘
    producing milk (by stimulation)

20. WR S
    nat/al
    pertaining to birth

21. WR CV WR   S
    gravid/o/puerper/al
          └CF┘
    pertaining to pregnancy and the
    puerperium

22. P WR S
    neo/nat/ology
    branch of medicine that deals with diagnosis and treatment of disorders in newborns

23. P WR S
    nulli/par/a
    woman who has not given birth (to a viable offspring)

24. WR S
    par/a
    woman who has given birth (to a viable offspring)

25. WR CV WR S
    prim/i/gravid/a
    ‿
    CF
    woman in her first pregnancy

26. P WR S
    post/part/um
    occurring after childbirth

27. P WR S
    neo/nat/e
    new birth (an infant from birth to 4 weeks of age, synonymous with newborn)

28. WR CVWR S
    prim/i/par/a
    ‿
    CF
    woman who has borne one (viable offspring)

29. WR S
    puerper/al
    pertaining to (immediately after) childbirth

30. P WR S
    nulli/gravid/a
    woman who has never been pregnant

31. P WR S
    intra/part/um
    occurring during labor and childbirth

Exercise 25
1. amni/o/chori/al
2. ante/part/um
3. embry/o/genic
4. cyes/i/ology
5. fet/al
6. cyes/is
7. lact/ic
8. lact/orrhea
9. amni/orrhea
10. pseud/o/cyes/is
11. embry/ologist
12. lact/o/genic
13. embry/ology
14. amni/orrhexis
15. embry/oid
16. gravid/a

17. gravid/o/puerper/al
18. multi/par/a
19. nat/al
20. neo/nat/e
21. neo/nat/ology
22. nulli/par/a
23. par/a
24. prim/i/gravid/a
25. post/part/um
26. prim/i/par/a
27. multi/gravid/a
28. puerper/al
29. nulli/gravid/a
30. puerper/a
31. intra/part/um

Exercise 26
Spelling exercise; see text, p. 259.

Exercise 27
1. a
2. e
3. i
4. g
5. f
6. b
7. j
8. d
9. c

Exercise 28
1. first stool of the newborn
2. medical specialty dealing with pregnancy, childbirth, and puerperium
3. infant born before completing 37 weeks of gestation
4. vaginal discharge following childbirth
5. period after delivery until the reproductive organs return to normal
6. act of giving birth
7. physician who specializes in obstetrics
8. abnormality present at birth
9. parturition in which the buttocks, feet, or knees emerge first

Exercise 29
Spelling exercise; see text, p. 261.

Exercise 30
1. gravida
2. gestation
3. glycosuria
4. fetus
5. pelvimetry
6. obstetrician's

Exercise 31
1. lungs
2. dystocia
3. amniocentesis
4. antepartum
5. has never been pregnant
6. borne two or more viable offspring
7. in her first pregnancy
8. parturition
9. hysterorrhexis

Exercise 32
1. episiotomy
2. omphalocele
3. amniotic
4. multigravida

Exercise 33
1. cell
2. white
3. surgical repair
4. larynx
5. lung
6. hernia, protrusion
7. kidney
8. cervix
9. rapid flow (of blood)
10. excessive discharge, flow
11. suture

Answers

CHAPTER 10
Exercise Figures
Exercise Figure
A. 1. blood vessel: angi/o
   2. valve: valv/o, valvul/o
   3. heart: cardi/o, coron/o
   4. aorta: aort/o
   5. artery: arteri/o
   6. atrium: atri/o
   7. ventricle: ventricul/o

Exercise Figure B. atherosclerosis
Exercise Figure C. endarterectomy
Exercise Figure D. electrocardiogram

Exercise 1
1. g
2. j
3. e
4. m
5. b
6. k
7. i
8. f
9. l
10. h
11. d
12. a
13. n

Exercise 2
1. f
2. p
3. h
4. b
5. k
6. m
7. c
8. l
9. q
10. d
11. o
12. a

13. i

15. j

14. e

16. g

Exercise 3

1. heart
2. atrium
3. plasma
4. vessel
5. heart
6. aorta
7. valve
8. spleen
9. thymus gland
10. vein
11. ventricle
12. artery
13. valve
14. lymph

Exercise 4

1. arteri/o
2. phleb/o
3. a. cardi/o
   b. coron/o
4. atri/o
5. ventricul/o
6. lymph/o
7. aort/o
8. angi/o
9. a. valv/o
   b. valvul/o
10. splen/o
11. plasm/o
12. thym/o

Exercise 5

1. sound
2. chest
3. clot
4. deficiency, blockage
5. heat
6. pulse
7. yellowish, fatty plaque
8. electricity, electrical activity
9. bacteria

Exercise 6

1. thromb/o
2. steth/o
3. ech/o
4. isch/o
5. ather/o
6. therm/o
7. bacteri/o
8. electr/o
9. sphygm/o

Exercise 7

1. fast, rapid
2. slow

Exercise 8

1. tachy-
2. brady-

Exercise 9

1. to separate
2. instrument used to record
3. abnormal reduction in number
4. hardening
5. pain
6. removal
7. formation
8. pertaining to

Exercise 10

1. -poiesis
2. -ac
3. -sclerosis
4. -graph
5. -penia
6. -odynia
7. -crit
8. -apheresis

Exercise 11

1.   P   WR   S
   endo/card/itis

   inflammation of the inner layer of the heart

2.   P   WR   S
   brady/card/ia

   condition of slow heart rate

3.   WR CV   S
   cardi/o/megaly
        CF

   enlargement of the heart

4.   WR CV   S
   arteri/o/sclerosis
          CF

   hardening of the arteries

5.   WR CV WR   S
   cardi/o/valvul/itis
        CF

   inflammation of the valves of the heart

6.   WR CV WR   S
   angi/o/card/itis
        CF

   inflammation of the heart and blood vessels and heart

7.   WR   S
   arteri/orrhexis

   rupture of an artery

8.   P   WR   S
   tachy/card/ia

   abnormal state of rapid heart rate

9.   WR CV   S
   angi/o/stenosis
        CF

   narrowing of blood vessels

10. WR CV   WR   S
   atri/o/ventricul/ar defect
        CF

   defect pertaining to the atrium and ventricles

11. WR   S WR   S
   coron/ary isch/emia

   deficient supply of blood to the heart's blood vessels

12.   P   WR   S
   peri/card/itis

   inflammation of outer layer of heart

13. WR   S
   cardi/odynia

   pain in the heart

14. WR S
   aort/ic stenosis

   narrowing of the aorta

15. WR   S   WR   S
   coron/ary thromb/osis

   abnormal condition of a clot in a blood vessel of the heart

16. WR CV   S
   ather/o/sclerosis
         CF

   hardening of the arteries, in which fatty plaque is deposited on the arterial wall

17. WR CV WR   S
   my/o/card/itis
        CF

   inflammation of the muscle of the heart

18. WR   S
   angi/oma

   tumor composed of blood vessels

19. WR   S
   thym/oma

   tumor of the thymus gland

20. WR   CV WR CV   S
   hemat/o/cyt/o/penia
          CF   CF

   abnormal reduction in the number of blood cells

21. WR   S
   lymph/oma

   tumor of lymphatic tissue

22. WR   WR   S
   lymph/aden/itis

   inflammation of lymph glands (nodes)

23. WR CV   S
   splen/o/megaly
          CF

   enlargement of the spleen

24. WR   S
   hemat/oma

   tumor of blood (swelling caused by an accumulation of clotted blood in the tissues)

25.   P   WR   S
   poly/arter/itis

   inflammation of many (sites) in the arteries

26. WR CV WR CV   S
   cardi/o/my/o/pathy
        CF   CF

   disease of the heart muscles

27. WR   S   P   WR   S
   bacteri/al endo/card/itis

   inflammation within the heart caused by bacteria

28. WR CV   S
   angi/o/spasm
         CF

   spasm of the blood vessels

29. WR   WR CV   S
   lymph/aden/o/pathy
               CF

   disease of the lymph glands

Exercise 12

1. arteri/orrhexis
2. cardi/o/megaly
3. coron/ary isch/emia
4. angi/o/card/itis
5. endo/card/itis
6. brady/card/ia
7. arteri/o/sclerosis
8. coron/ary thromb/osis
9. cardi/odynia
10. my/o/card/itis
11. angi/o/stenosis
12. tachy/card/ia
13. ather/o/sclerosis
14. angi/oma
15. cardi/o/valvul/itis
16. aort/ic stenosis
17. peri/card/itis
18. atri/o/ventricul/ar defect
19. hemat/o/cyt/o/penia
20. lymph/oma
21. thym/oma
22. splen/o/megaly
23. hemat/oma
24. lymph/aden/itis
25. cardi/o/my/o/pathy
26. poly/arter/itis
27. angi/o/spasm
28. bacteri/al endo/card/itis
29. lymph/aden/o/pathy

Exercise 13

Spelling exercise; see text, p. 281.

Exercise 14

1. coarctation
2. embolus
3. cardiac arrest
4. congenital
5. varicose veins
6. coronary occlusion
7. aneurysm
8. Hodgkin's
9. hemorrhoids
10. angina pectoris
11. myocardial infarction
12. fibrillation
13. dysrhythmia
14. hypertensive
15. congestive heart failure
16. thromboangiitis obliterans (Buerger's disease)
17. hemophilia
18. leukemia
19. anemia
20. sickle cell anemia
21. intermittent claudication
22. cardiac tamponade
23. mitral valve stenosis and rheumatic heart disease
24. deep vein thrombosis
25. rheumatic fever

Exercise 15

1. d
2. c
3. f
4. e
5. a
6. j
7. i
8. k
9. g
10. b
11. h
12. l

Exercise 16

1. i
2. e
3. a
4. h
5. j
6. b
7. d
8. k
9. l
10. g
11. c
12. f
13. m

Exercise 17

Spelling exercise; see text, p. 286.

Exercise 18

1. P   WR   S
    peri/cardi/ostomy

    creation of an artificial opening in the outer (double) layer of the heart

2. WR   S
    thym/ectomy

    excision of the thymus gland

3. WR CV S
    angi/o/plasty
        CF

    surgical repair of a blood vessel

4. WR CV S
    splen/o/pexy
        CF

    surgical fixation of the spleen

5. WR   S
    angi/orrhaphy

    suturing of a blood vessel

6. P   WR   S
    end/arter/ectomy

    excision within an artery of the thickened interior

7. WR   S
    phleb/otomy

    incision into a vein

8. WR   S
    splen/ectomy

    excision of the spleen

9. WR   S
    phleb/ectomy

    excision of a vein

10. WR   S
    ather/ectomy

    surgical removal of plaque

Exercise 19

1. end/arter/ectomy
2. splen/o/pexy
3. angi/orrhaphy
4. phleb/otomy
5. thym/ectomy
6. peri/cardi/ostomy
7. angi/o/plasty
8. splen/ectomy
9. phleb/ectomy
10. arther/ectomy

Exercise 20

Spelling exercise; see text, p. 289.

Exercise 21

1. hemorrhoidectomy
2. percutaneous transluminal coronary angioplasty
3. cardiac pacemaker
4. commissurotomy
5. coronary artery bypass graft
6. aneurysmectomy
7. femoropopliteal bypass
8. laser angioplasty
9. intracoronary thrombolytic
10. defibrillation
11. bone marrow transplant
12. embolectomy
13. coronary stent

Exercise 22

1. h
2. f
3. k
4. l
5. d
6. m
7. a
8. c
9. e
10. i
11. b
12. j
13. g

Exercise 23

Spelling exercise; see text, p. 293.

Exercise 24

1. WR CV WR CV S
    electr/o/cardi/o/graph
        CF   CF

    instrument used to record the electrical activity of the heart

2. WR CV WR CV S
    sphygm/o/cardi/o/graph
        CF   CF

    instrument used to measure pulse waves and heartbeat

3. WR CV S
    ven/o/gram
        CF

    x-ray film of the veins (taken after an injection of contrast medium)

4. WR CV   S
    angi/o/graphy
           CF
    process of x-ray filming a blood vessel

5. WR CV WR CV S
    ech/o/cardi/o/gram
        CF   CF
    record made of the structure and
    motion of the heart using sound waves

6. WR CV S
    steth/o/scope
         CF
    instrument to examine chest sounds

7. WR CV S
    aort/o/gram
         CF
    x-ray film of the aorta (taken after an
    injection of contrast medium)

8. WR CV WR CV S
    electr/o/cardi/o/gram
         CF   CF
    record of the electrical activity of the
    heart

9. WR CV WR CV S
    phon/o/cardi/o/gram
        CF   CF
    (graphic) record of heart sounds

10. WR CV S
    arteri/o/gram
          CF
    x-ray film of an artery (after an
    injection of contrast medium)

11. WR CV WR CV   S
    electr/o/cardi/o/graphy
         CF   CF
    process of recording the electrical
    activity of the heart

12. WR CV S
    erythr/o/cyte count
          CF
    red (blood) cell count (number of red
    blood cells per cubic millimeter of
    blood)

13. WR   WR CV S
    lymph/angi/o/gram
             CF
    x-ray film of lymphatic vessels

14. WR CV S
    hemat/o/crit
         CF
    separated blood (volume percentage of
    erythrocytes in whole blood)

15. WR   WR CV   S
    lymph/aden/o/graphy
             CF
    an x-ray filming of the lymph nodes
    and glands (after an injection of
    contrast medium)

16. WR CV S
    leuk/o/cyte count
        CF
    white (blood) cell count (number of
    white blood cells per cubic millimeter
    of blood)

17. WR   WR CV   S
    lymph/angi/o/graphy
             CF
    an x-ray filming of the lymphatic
    vessels (after an injection of the
    contrast medium)

18. WR CV   S
    angi/o/scopy
         CF
    visual examination of a blood vessel

19. WR CV   S
    phleb/o/graphy
          CF
    x-ray filming a vein

20. WR CV   S
    angi/o/scope
         CF
    instrument used for visual examination
    of a blood vessel

Exercise 25

1. electr/o/cardi/o/graph
2. steth/o/scope
3. arteri/o/gram
4. ven/o/gram
5. angi/o/graphy
6. electr/o/cardi/o/gram
7. ech/o/cardi/o/gram
8. phon/o/cardi/o/gram
9. sphygm/o/cardi/o/graph
10. aort/o/gram
11. electr/o/cardi/o/graphy
12. hemat/o/crit
13. lymph/angi/o/gram
14. leuk/o/cyte
15. lymph/aden/o/graphy
16. erythr/o/cyte
17. lymph/angi/o/graphy
18. angi/o/scopy
19. phleb/o/graphy
20. angi/o/scope

Exercise 26
Spelling exercise; see text, p. 298.

Exercise 27

1. sphygmomanometer
2. coagulation time
3. treadmill stress
4. complete blood count
5. Doppler flow studies
6. cardiac scan
7. bone marrow biopsy
8. prothrombin time
9. cardiac catheterization
10. hemoglobin
11. impedance plethysmography
12. thallium stress test
13. transesophageal echocardiogram
14. single-photon emission computed
    tomography

Exercise 28

1. d   8. a
2. n   9. k
3. h   10. b
4. o   11. m
5. g   12. f
6. j   13. i
7. c   14. e

Exercise 29
Spelling exercise; see text, p. 303.

Exercise 30

1. P   WR   S
    hypo/therm/ia
    condition of (body) temperature that
    is below normal

2. WR CV   S
    hemat/o/poiesis
         CF
    formation of blood cells

3. WR   S
    cardi/ology
    study of the heart

4. WR   S
    cardi/ologist
    physician who studies and treats
    diseases of the heart

5. WR CV S
    hem/o/lysis
        CF
    dissolution of blood cells

6. WR   S
    hemat/ologist
    physician who studies and treats
    diseases of the blood

7. WR   S
    cardi/ac
    pertaining to the heart

8. WR   S
    hemat/ology
    study of the blood

9. WR   S
    plasm/apheresis
    removal of plasma (from withdrawn blood)

10. WR CV S
    hem/o/stasis
         CF
    stoppage of bleeding

11. WR CV S
    cardi/o/genic
         CF
    originating in the heart

12. P   S(WR)
    tachy/pnea
    rapid breathing

13. WR   CV   S
    thromb/o/lysis
          CF
    dissolution of a clot

Exercise 31
1. cardi/ology
2. hemat/o/poiesis
3. hypo/therm/ia
4. hem/o/lysis
5. plasm/apheresis
6. hemat/ologist
7. cardi/ac
8. cardi/ologist
9. hemat/ology
10. hem/o/stasis
11. tachy/pnea
12. cardi/o/genic
13. thromb/o/lysis

Exercise 32
Spelling exercise; see text, p. 303.

Exercise 33
1. vasoconstrictor
2. lumen
3. cardiopulmonary resuscitation
4. diastole
5. blood pressure
6. hypotension
7. extravasation
8. venipuncture
9. systole
10. vasodilator
11. hypertension
12. peripheral vascular
13. occlude
14. percussion
15. auscultation
16. plasma
17. manometer
18. hemorrhage
19. anticoagulant
20. serum
21. dyscrasia
22. heart murmur
23. extracorporeal

Exercise 34
1. space within a tube-like structure
2. escape of blood from the blood vessel into the tissues
3. pressure exerted by the blood against the vessel walls
4. puncture of a vein to remove blood, start an intravenous infusion, or instill medication
5. referring to blood vessels outside the heart and lymphatic vessels
6. agent or nerve that enlarges the lumen of blood vessels
7. blood pressure that is above normal
8. emergency procedure consisting of artificial ventilation and external cardiac massage
9. phase in the cardiac cycle in which ventricles contract
10. blood pressure that is below normal
11. agent or nerve that narrows the lumen of blood vessels
12. cardiac cycle phase in which ventricles relax
13. hearing of sounds within the body through a stethoscope
14. to close tightly
15. tapping of a body surface with fingers to determine the density of parts beneath
16. liquid portion of the blood without clotting factors
17. abnormal or pathological condition of the blood
18. instrument used to measure the pressure of fluids
19. liquid portion of the blood in which the elements or cells are suspended and which contains the clotting factors
20. rapid flow of blood
21. agent that slows down the clotting process
22. occurring outside the body
23. humming sound of cardiac or vascular origin

Exercise 35
Spelling exercise; see text, p. 309.

Exercise 36
1. angina pectoris
2. treadmill stress test
3. thallium stress test
4. ischemia
5. angiography
6. stenosis
7. angioplasty
8. cardiologist
9. electrocardiogram
10. cardiac catheterization
11. myocardial infarction

Exercise 37
1. atherosclerosis
2. splenomegaly
3. myocarditis
4. myocardial infarction
5. endarterectomy
6. hemorrhoids
7. phonocardiogram
8. hypothermia
9. impedance plethysmography
10. murmur
11. angioscope, angioscopy
12. thallium stress testing

Exercise 38
1. splenectomy
2. phlebectomy
3. myocarditis
4. thymoma
5. angiostenosis
6. hematology
7. thallium stress test

Exercise 39
1. visual examination of a cell
2. difficulty in speaking
3. electrical cutting instrument
4. blood containing fat
5. abnormal condition of pus in the kidney
6. scanty menstrual discharge
7. surgical fixation of an ovary
8. pain in the pleura
9. dilatation of the renal pelvis
10. pertaining to under the nail

Answers

C	A	R	D	I	O		A					
							N			V		A
A				S		G			A		R	
T		V	E	N	T	R	I	C	U	L	O	T
H	P		L	E		O		V			E	
E	L		E	T			S	U		R		
R	A		C	H		P	L		I			
O	S		T	O		T	H	R	O	M	B	O
	M		R			Y						
C	O	R	O	N	O		G		V		A	
				E		M		A		T		
			I	S	C	H	O	L		A	R	
				H			V		I			
S	P	L	E	N	O		A	O	R	T	O	

CHAPTER 11
Exercise Figures
Exercise Figure
A. 1. mouth: stomat/o, or/o
   2. esophagus: esophag/o
   3. duodenum: duoden/o
   4. ascending colon: col/o
   5. cecum: cec/o
   6. anus: an/o
   7. pharynx: pharyng/o
   8. stomach: gastr/o

9. antrum: antr/o
10. transverse colon: col/o
11. descending colon: col/o
12. jejunum: jejun/o
13. ileum: ile/o
14. sigmoid colon: sigmoid/o
15. rectum: proct/o, rect/o

Exercise Figure
B. 1. gums: gingiv/o
2. lips: cheil/o
3. salivary glands: sial/o
4. liver: hepat/o
5. gallbladder: chol/e (gall), cyst/o (bladder)
6. pyloric sphincter: pylor/o
7. appendix: appendic/o
8. palate: palat/o
9. uvula: uvul/o
10. tongue: gloss/o, lingu/o
11. bile duct: cholangi/o
12. common bile duct: choledoch/o
13. pancreas: pancreat/o
14. abdomen: lapar/o, abdomin/o, celi/o

Exercise Figure C. appendicitis
Exercise Figure D. cholelithiasis, choledocholithiasis
Exercise Figure E. gastrectomy
Exercise Figure F. ileostomy, colostomy
Exercise Figure G. cholelithiasis
Exercise Figure H. gastroscope
Exercise Figure I. sigmoidoscopy

Exercise 1
1. alimentary canal
2. gastrointestinal tract
3. pharynx
4. esophagus
5. stomach
6. duodenum
7. jejunum
8. ileum
9. cecum
10. ascending colon
11. transverse colon
12. descending colon
13. sigmoid colon
14. rectum
15. anus

Exercise 2
1. l
2. d
3. a
4. h
5. f
6. j
7. b
8. i
9. c
10. g
11. e

Exercise 3
1. rectum
2. stomach
3. anus
4. cecum
5. ileum
6. mouth
7. duodenum
8. colon
9. mouth
10. intestines
11. rectum
12. antrum
13. esophagus
14. jejunum
15. sigmoid colon

Exercise 4
1. cec/o
2. gastr/o
3. ile/o
4. jejun/o
5. sigmoid/o
6. esophag/o
7. a. rect/o
   b. proct/o
8. enter/o
9. duoden/o
10. col/o
11. a. or/o
    b. stomat/o
12. an/o
13. antr/o

Exercise 5
1. hernia
2. abdomen
3. saliva
4. gall, bile
5. diverticulum
6. gum
7. appendix
8. tongue
9. liver
10. lip
11. peritoneum
12. palate
13. pancreas
14. abdomen
15. tongue
16. common bile duct
17. pylorus, pyloric sphincter
18. uvula
19. bile duct
20. polyp, small growth
21. abdomen

Exercise 6
1. palat/o
2. sial/o
3. pancreat/o
4. peritone/o
5. a. lingu/o
   b. gloss/o
6. gingiv/o
7. pylor/o
8. hepat/o
9. chol/e
10. a. abdomin/o
    b. lapar/o
    c. celi/o
11. herni/o
12. diverticul/o
13. cheil/o
14. appendic/o
15. uvul/o
16. cholangi/o
17. choledoch/o
18. polyp/o

Exercise 7
1. digestion

Exercise 8
1. -pepsia

Exercise 9
1. WR CV WR S
    chol/e/lith/iasis
         CF
    condition of gallstones

2. WR   S
    diverticul/osis
    abnormal condition of having diverticula

3. WR CV WR
    sial/o/lith
        CF
    stone in the salivary gland

4. WR   S
    hepat/oma
    tumor of the liver

5. WR   S
    uvul/itis
    inflammation of the uvula

6. WR   S
    pancreat/itis
    inflammation of the pancreas

7. WR CV S
    proct/o/ptosis
         CF
    prolapse of the rectum

8. WR   S
    gingiv/itis
    inflammation of the gums

9. WR S
    gastr/itis
    inflammation of the stomach

10. WR CV S
    rect/o/cele
         CF
    protrusion of the rectum

11. WR   S
    palat/itis
    inflammation of the palate

12. WR   S
    hepat/itis
    inflammation of the liver

13. WR   S
    appendic/itis
    inflammation of the appendix

14. WR CV WR S
    chol/e/cyst/itis
        CF
    inflammation of the gallbladder

15. WR   S
    diverticul/itis
    inflammation of a diverticulum

16. WR CV WR S
    gastr/o/enter/itis
          CF
    inflammation of the stomach and intestines

17. WR CV WR CV WR S
    gastr/o/enter/o/col/itis
          CF   CF
    inflammation of the stomach, intestines, and colon

18. WR   CV WR   S
     choledoch/o/lith/iasis
     ‿‿‿‿‿‿‿
         CF

     condition of stones in the common
     bile duct

19. WR   S
     cholangi/oma

     tumor of the bile duct

20. WR   S
     polyp/osis

     abnormal condition of (multiple)
     polyps

Exercise 10
1. hepat/oma
2. gastr/itis
3. sial/o/lith
4. appendic/itis
5. diverticul/itis
6. chol/e/cyst/itis
7. diverticul/osis
8. gastr/o/enter/itis
9. proct/o/ptosis
10. rect/o/cele
11. uvul/itis
12. gingiv/itis
13. hepat/itis
14. palat/itis
15. chol/e/lith/iasis
16. gastr/o/enter/o/col/itis
17. pancreat/itis
18. cholangi/oma
19. choledoch/o/lith/iasis
20. polyp/osis

Exercise 11
Spelling exercise; see text, p. 332.

Exercise 12
1. f
2. b
3. e
4. n
5. d
6. g
7. a
8. k
9. h
10. j
11. m
12. i
13. c

Exercise 13
1. another name for gastric or duodenal ulcer
2. psychoneurotic disorder characterized by a prolonged refusal to eat
3. chronic inflammation of the small and/or large intestines
4. twisting or kinking of the intestine
5. abnormal growing together of two surfaces that normally are separated
6. chronic disease of the liver with gradual destruction of cells
7. telescoping of segment of the intestine

8. ulcer in the stomach
9. ulcer in the duodenum
10. inflammation of the colon with the formation of ulcers
11. gorging food then inducing vomiting
12. tumor-like growth extending out from a mucous membrane
13. disturbance of bowel function
14. obstruction of the intestine, often caused by failure of peristalsis
15. backward flow of the gastrointestinal contents into the esophagus

Exercise 14
Spelling exercise; see text, p.336.

Exercise 15
1. WR   S
    gastr/ectomy

    excision of the stomach

2. WR   CV WR CV S
    esophag/o/gastr/o/plasty
    ‿‿‿‿‿ ‿‿‿‿‿
        CF   CF

    surgical repair of the esophagus and
    the stomach

3. WR   S
    diverticul/ectomy

    excision of a diverticulum

4. WR   S
    antr/ectomy

    excision of the antrum

5. WR CV S
    palat/o/plasty
    ‿‿‿
      CF

    surgical repair of the palate

6. WR   S
    uvul/ectomy

    excision of the uvula

7. WR CV WR   S
    gastr/o/jejun/ostomy
    ‿‿‿
      CF

    creation of an artificial opening
    between the stomach and the jejunum

8. WR CV WR   S
    chol/e/cyst/ectomy
    ‿‿‿
      CF

    excision of the gallbladder

9. WR   S
    col/ectomy

    excision of the colon

10. WR   S
    col/ostomy

    creation of an artificial opening into
    the colon

11. WR CV S
    pylor/o/plasty
    ‿‿‿
      CF

    surgical repair of the pylorus

12. WR CV S
    an/o/plasty
    ‿
     CF

    surgical repair of the anus

13. WR   S
    append/ectomy

    excision of the appendix

14. WR   S
    cheil/orrhaphy

    suture of the lips

15. WR   S
    gingiv/ectomy

    surgical removal of gum tissue

16. WR   S
    lapar/otomy

    incision into the abdomen

17. WR   S
    ile/ostomy

    creation of an artificial opening into
    the ileum

18. WR   S
    gastr/ostomy

    creation of an artificial opening into
    the stomach

19. WR   S
    herni/orrhaphy

    suturing of a hernia

20. WR   S
    gloss/orrhaphy

    suture of the tongue

21. WR   CV WR   S
    choledoch/o/lith/otomy
    ‿‿‿‿‿‿‿
        CF

    incision into the common bile duct to
    remove a stone

22. WR   CV WR CV S
    choledoch/o/lith/o/tripsy
    ‿‿‿‿‿‿‿ ‿‿‿
        CF   CF

    surgical crushing of a stone in the
    common bile duct

23. WR   S
    polyp/ectomy

    excision of a polyp

24. WR   S
    enter/orrhaphy

    suture of the intestine

25. WR   CV S
    abdomin/o/plasty
    ‿‿‿‿‿
        CF

    surgical repair of the abdomen

26. WR CV WR   S
  pylor/o/my/otomy
        CF
  incision into the pylorus muscle

27. WR CV WR CV   WR CV S
  uvul/o/palat/o/pharyng/o/plasty
     CF   CF   CF
  surgical repair of the uvula, palate, and pharynx

28. WR   S
  celi/otomy
  incision into the abdominal cavity

Exercise 16
1. append/ectomy
2. gloss/orrhaphy
3. esophag/o/gastr/o/plasty
4. diverticul/ectomy
5. ile/ostomy
6. gingiv/ectomy
7. lapar/otomy
8. an/o/plasty
9. antr/ectomy
10. chol/e/cyst/ectomy
11. col/ectomy
12. col/ostomy
13. gastr/ectomy
14. gastr/ostomy
15. gastr/o/jejun/ostomy
16. uvul/ectomy
17. palat/o/plasty
18. pylor/o/plasty
19. herni/orrhaphy
20. cheil/orrhaphy
21. choledoch/o/lith/o/tripsy
22. choledoch/o/lith/otomy
23. polyp/ectomy
24. enter/orrhaphy
25. abdomin/o/plasty
26. celi/otomy
27. pylor/o/my/otomy
28. uvul/o/palat/o/pharyng/o/plasty

Exercise 17
Spelling exercise; see text, p. 342.

Exercise 18
1. vagotomy
2. anastomosis
3. abdominoperineal resection

Exercise 19
Spelling exercise; see text, p. 346.

Exercise 20
1. WR CV S
  esophag/o/scope
        CF
  instrument used for visual examination of the esophagus

2. WR CV S
  esophag/o/scopy
        CF
  visual examination of the esophagus

3. WR CV S
  gastr/o/scope
       CF
  instrument used for visual examination of the stomach

4. WR CV S
  gastr/o/scopy
       CF
  visual examination of the stomach

5. WR CV S
  proct/o/scope
       CF
  instrument used for visual examination of the rectum

6. WR CV S
  proct/o/scopy
       CF
  visual examination of the rectum

7. P   S(WR)
  endo/scope
  instrument used for visual examination within a hollow organ.

8. P   S(WR)
  endo/scopy
  visual examination within a hollow organ

9. WR   CV S
  sigmoid/o/scope
          CF
  instrument used for visual examination of the sigmoid colon

10. WR   CV S
  sigmoid/o/scopy
          CF
  visual examination of the sigmoid colon

11. WR CV WR CV S
  chol/e/cyst/o/gram
       CF   CF
  x-ray film of the gallbladder

12. WR   CV S
  cholangi/o/gram
          CF
  x-ray film of bile ducts

13. WR   CV WR CV WR CV S
  esophag/o/gastr/o/duoden/o/scopy
          CF   CF   CF
  visual examination of the esophagus, stomach, and duodenum

14. WR CV S
  colon/o/scope
        CF
  instrument used for visual examination of the colon

15. WR CV S
  lapar/o/scope
        CF
  instrument used for visual examination of the abdominal cavity

16. WR CV S
  colon/o/scopy
        CF
  visual examination of the colon

17. WR CV S
  lapar/o/scopy
        CF
  visual examination of the abdominal cavity

Exercise 21
1. endo/scopy
2. gastr/o/scope
3. proct/o/scope
4. sigmoid/o/scope
5. chol/e/cyst/o/gram
6. endo/scope
7. esophag/o/scope
8. proct/o/scopy
9. esophag/o/scopy
10. sigmoid/o/scopy
11. cholangi/o/gram
12. gastr/o/scopy
13. lapar/o/scope
14. esophag/o/gastr/o/duoden/o/scopy
15. colon/o/scopy
16. lapar/o/scopy
17. colon/o/scope

Exercise 22
Spelling exercise; see text, p. 349.

Exercise 23
1. series of x-ray films taken of the stomach and duodenum after barium has been swallowed
2. series of x-ray films taken of the large intestine after a barium enema has been administered
3. x-ray examination of the bile and pancreatic ducts
4. an endoscope fitted with an ultrasound probe providing images of layers of the intestinal wall
5. a blood test to determine the presence of *Helicobacter pylori* bacteria, a cause of duodenal ulcers
6. a test to detect occult blood in feces

Exercise 24

1. d
2. f
3. a

4. b
5. c

Exercise 25

Spelling exercise; see text, p. 351.

Exercise 26

1. P S(WR)
   a/phagia
   without (inability) to swallow

2. P   S(WR)
   dys/pepsia
   difficult digestion

3. WR S
   an/al
   pertaining to the anus

4. P   S(WR)
   dys/phagia
   difficult swallowing

5. WR CV S
   gloss/o/pathy
   CF
   disease of the tongue

6. WR CV WR S
   ile/o/cec/al
   CF
   pertaining to the ileum and cecum

7. WR S
   or/al
   pertaining to the mouth

8. WR CV WR S
   stomat/o/gastr/ic
   CF
   pertaining to the mouth and stomach

9. P   S(WR)
   brady/pepsia
   slow digestion

10. WR   CV   S
    abdomin/o/centesis
    CF
    surgical puncture to remove fluid from
    the abdominal cavity

11. P S(WR)
    a/pepsia
    without (lack of) digestion

12. WR CV S
    gastr/o/malacia
    CF
    softening of the stomach

13. WR   S
    pancreat/ic
    pertaining to the pancreas

14. WR   S
    gastr/odynia
    pain in the stomach

15. WR   S
    peritone/al
    pertaining to the peritoneum

16. P   WR S
    sub/lingu/al
    pertaining to under the tongue

17. WR   S
    proct/ology
    branch of medicine concerned with
    disorders of the rectum and anus

18. WR CV WR S
    nas/o/gastr/ic
    CF
    pertaining to the nose and stomach

19. WR   S
    abdomin/al
    pertaining to the abdomen

20. WR   S
    proct/ologist
    physician who specializes in proctology

21. WR CV WR   S
    gastr/o/enter/ology
    CF
    study of the stomach and intestines

22. WR CV WR   S
    gastr/o/enter/ologist
    CF
    physician who specializes in diseases of
    the stomach and intestines

Exercise 27

1. gloss/o/pathy
2. a/phagia
3. sub/lingu/al
4. nas/o/gastr/ic
5. stomat/o/gastr/ic
6. an/al
7. abdomin/o/centesis
8. peritone/al
9. abdomin/al
10. dys/phagia
11. ile/o/cec/al
12. brady/pepsia
13. gastr/o/malacia
14. a/pepsia
15. gastr/odynia
16. proct/ologist
17. dys/pepsia

18. pancreat/ic
19. proct/ology
20. or/al
21. gastr/o/enter/ologist
22. gastr/o/enter/ology

Exercise 28

Spelling exercise; see text, p. 355.

Exercise 29

1. g
2. e
3. f
4. c
5. l
6. i

7. k
8. a
9. d
10. h
11. b

Exercise 30

1. abnormal collection of fluid in the
   peritoneal cavity
2. process of feeding a person through a
   nasogastric tube
3. washing out of the stomach
4. waste from the digestive tract expelled
   through the rectum
5. urge to vomit
6. matter expelled from the stomach
   through the mouth
7. disorder that involves inflammation of
   the intestine
8. frequent discharge of liquid stool
9. gas expelled through the anus
10. return of flow
11. vomiting of blood

Exercise 31

Spelling exercise; see text, p. 357.

Exercise 32

1. endoscopy
2. nausea
3. dyspepsia
4. hematemesis
5. esophagogastroduodenoscopy
6. gastroscope
7. reflux
8. ulcers
9. gastritis
10. duodenal ulcer

Exercise 33

1. cholelithiasis
2. cholecystectomy
3. ulcerative colitis
4. proctoptosis
5. adhesion
6. gastrectomy; pyloroplasty; vagotomy
7. dyspepsia
8. gavage

9. abdominal perineal resection and colostomy
10. choledocholithotripsy
11. colonoscopy
12. ileus
13. occult blood test

Exercise 34
1. cheilorrhaphy
2. ileostomy
3. gingivectomy
4. gastromalacia
5. dysphagia
6. apepsia
7. uvulopalatopharyngoplasty

Exercise 35
1. d   4. b
2. e   5. a
3. c

Answers

CHAPTER 12
Exercise Figures
Exercise Figure
A. 1. eye: ocul/o, ophthalm/o
2. eyelid: blephar/o
3. lacrimal sac: dacry/o, lacrim/o
4. pupil: cor/o, core/o, pupill/o
5. sclera: scler/o
6. iris: irid/o, iri/o
7. conjunctiva: conjunctiv/o
8. cornea: corne/o, kerat/o
9. retina: retin/o

Exercise Figure B. blepharitis
Exercise Figure C. blepharoptosis
Exercise Figure D. dacryocystitis

Exercise 1
1. d   5. b
2. c   6. e
3. f   7. a
4. h

Exercise 2
1. d   5. b
2. f   6. a
3. h   7. c
4. e

Exercise 3
1. eye   9. conjunctiva
2. eyelid   10. pupil
3. cornea   11. eye
4. tear, tear duct   12. cornea
5. retina   13. iris
6. pupil   14. pupil
7. sclera   15. vision
8. iris   16. tear, tear duct

Exercise 4
1. a. ocul/o   6. a. cor/o
   b. ophthalm/o   b. core/o
2. a. corne/o   c. pupill/o
   b. kerat/o   7. scler/o
3. conjunctiv/o   8. retin/o
4. a. lacrim/o   9. a. iri/o
   b. dacry/o   b. irid/o
5. blephar/o   10. opt/o

Exercise 5
1. tension, pressure   3. cold
2. light   4. two, double

Exercise 6
1. cry/o   3. dipl/o
2. ton/o   4. phot/o

Exercise 7
1. vision (condition)   5. abnormal fear of
2. two   or aversion to
3. paralysis   specific things
4. one who   6. two

Exercise 8
1. -ician   4. -phobia
2. -plegia   5. -opia
3. a. bi-
   b. bin-

Exercise 9
1. WR CV WR   S
   scler/o/kerat/itis
        CF

inflammation of the sclera and the cornea

2.   WR   S
   ophthalm/algia
   pain in the eye

3.   WR CVWR S
   corne/o/ir/itis
        CF

inflammation of the cornea and the iris

4.   WR CV S
   blephar/o/ptosis
        CF

drooping of the eyelid

5.   WR   S
   dipl/opia
   double vision

6.   WR   S
   ophthalm/orrhagia
   rapid flow of blood (hemorrhage) from the eye

7.   WR   S
   conjunctiv/itis
   inflammation of the conjunctiva

8. WR CV WR S
   leuk/o/cor/ia
        CF
   condition of white pupil

9. WR CV S
   irid/o/plegia
        CF
   paralysis of the iris

10. WR CV   S
    scler/o/malacia
         CF
    softening of the sclera

11. WR CV   S
    phot/o/phobia
         CF
    abnormal fear of (sensitivity to) light

12. WR   S
    blephar/itis
    inflammation of the eyelid

13. WR CV WR S
    ocul/o/myc/osis
         CF
    abnormal condition of the eye caused by a fungus

14. WR CV WR S
    phot/o/retin/itis
    ‾‾‾‾ CF ‾‾

    inflammation of the retina caused by light

15. WR CV WR S
    dacry/o/cyst/itis
    ‾‾‾‾ CF ‾‾

    inflammation of the tear (lacrimal) sac

16. P WR S
    end/ophthalm/itis

    inflammation within the eye

17. WR S
    ir/itis

    inflammation of the iris

18. WR CV WR S
    retin/o/blast/oma
    ‾‾‾‾ CF ‾‾

    tumor arising from developing retinal cell

19. WR S
    kerat/itis

    inflammation of the cornea

20. WR CV S
    ophthalm/o/plegia
    ‾‾‾‾ CF ‾‾

    paralysis of the eye (muscles)

Exercise 10
1. conjunctiv/itis
2. ocul/o/myc/osis
3. ophthalm/algia
4. phot/o/retin/itis
5. dipl/opia
6. blephar/itis
7. leuk/o/cor/ia
8. irid/o/plegia
9. corne/o/ir/itis
10. blephar/o/ptosis
11. ir/itis
12. retin/o/blast/oma
13. scler/o/malacia
14. dacry/o/cyst/itis
15. ophthalm/orrhagia
16. scler/o/kerat/itis
17. phot/o/phobia
18. kerat/itis
19. end/ophthalm/itis
20. ophthalm/o/plegia

Exercise 11
Spelling exercise; see text, p. 374.

Exercise 12
1. myopia
2. presbyopia
3. strabismus
4. chalazion
5. astigmatism

6. nystagmus
7. cataract
8. sty (hordeolum)
9. glaucoma
10. detached retina
11. hyperopia
12. emmetropia
13. retinitis pigmentosa
14. nyctalopia
15. pterygium
16. macular degeneration

Exercise 13
1. f	9. e
2. h	10. c
3. k	11. a
4. n	12. l
5. m	13. i
6. j	14. o
7. d	15. g
8. p	16. b

Exercise 14
Spelling exercise; see text, p. 378.

Exercise 15
1. WR CV S
   kerat/o/plasty
   ‾‾‾‾ CF

   surgical repair of the cornea

2. WR S
   scler/otomy

   incision into the sclera

3. WR CV WR S
   dacry/o/cyst/otomy
   ‾‾‾‾ CF

   incision into the tear sac

4. WR CV WR CV S
   cry/o/retin/o/pexy
   ‾‾ CF ‾‾ ‾‾ CF ‾‾

   surgical fixation of the retina by extreme cold

5. WR CV WR S
   irid/o/scler/otomy
   ‾‾‾‾ CF

   incision into (the edge of) the iris and into the sclera

6. WR CV S
   blephar/o/plasty
   ‾‾‾‾ CF

   surgical repair of the eyelid

7. WR S
   irid/ectomy

   excision of part of the iris

8. WR CV WR CV WR S
   dacry/o/cyst/o/rhin/ostomy
   ‾‾‾ CF ‾‾   ‾‾ CF ‾‾

creation of an artificial opening between the tear (lacrimal) sac and the nose

Exercise 16
1. dacry/o/cyst/o/rhin/ostomy
2. irid/ectomy
3. kerat/o/plasty
4. scler/otomy
5. blephar/o/plasty
6. cry/o/retin/o/pexy
7. dacry/o/cyst/otomy
8. irid/o/scler/otomy

Exercise 17
Spelling exercise; see text, p. 380.

Exercise 18
1. retinal photocoagulation
2. cryoextraction of the lens
3. enucleation
4. phacoemulsification
5. strabotomy
6. trabeculectomy
7. scleral buckling
8. radial keratotomy
9. vitrectomy
10. photorefractive keratectomy

Exercise 19
1. e	6. d
2. f	7. i
3. b	8. a
4. k	9. g
5. h	10. c

Exercise 20
Spelling exercise; see text, p. 383.

Exercise 21
1. WR CV S
   opt/o/meter
   ‾‾ CF ‾‾

   instrument used to measure vision (power and range)

2. WR CV S
   pupill/o/scope
   ‾‾‾ CF ‾‾

   instrument for visual examination of the pupil

3. WR CV S
   opt/o/metry
   ‾‾ CF ‾‾

   measurement of vision (visual acuity and the prescribing of corrective lenses)

4. WR   CV   S
ophthalm/o/scope
     CF

instrument used for visual examination of the eye (interior)

5. WR CV   S
ton/o/metry
      CF

measurement of pressure within the eye

6. WR   CV   S
pupill/o/meter
        CF

instrument that measures the pupil (width and diameter)

7. WR CV WR CV   S
opt/o/my/o/meter
    CF   CF

instrument used to measure the muscles of vision (power of)

8. WR CV   S
ton/o/meter
      CF

instrument used to measure pressure (within the eye)

9. WR CV   S
kerat/o/meter
       CF

instrument that measures (the curvature of) the cornea

10. WR   CV   S
ophthalm/o/scopy
          CF

visual examination of the eye

11. WR CV   S
angi/o/graphy
      CF

x-ray filming of blood vessels (of the eye using fluorescing dye)

Exercise 22
1. opt/o/meter
2. ton/o/metry
3. pupill/o/meter
4. kerat/o/meter
5. opt/o/metry
6. opt/o/my/o/meter
7. ophthalm/o/scope
8. ton/o/meter
9. pupill/o/scope
10. ophthalm/o/scopy
11. fluorescein angi/o/graphy

Exercise 23
Spelling exercise; see text, p. 386.

Exercise 24
1. WR   S
ophthalm/ology

study of diseases and treatment of the eye

2. P   WR   S
bin/ocul/ar

pertaining to two or both eyes

3. WR   S
opt/ician

one who is skilled in filling prescriptions for lenses

4. WR   S
lacrim/al

pertaining to tears or tear ducts

5. WR   S
pupill/ary

pertaining to the pupil of the eye

6. WR CV   S
retin/o/pathy
      CF

(any noninflammatory) disease of the retina

7. WR   S
ophthalm/ologist

physician who specializes in ophthalmology

8. WR   S
corne/al

pertaining to the cornea

9. WR   S
ophthalm/ic

pertaining to the eye

10. WR CV   WR   S
nas/o/lacrim/al
      CF

pertaining to the nose and tear ducts

11. WR   S
opt/ic

pertaining to vision

12. P   WR   S
intra/ocul/ar

pertaining to within the eye

13. WR   S
retin/al

pertaining to the retina

14. WR   CV   S
ophthalm/o/pathy
          CF

(any) disease of the eye

Exercise 25
1. ophthalm/ology
2. bin/ocul/ar

3. retin/al
4. intra/ocul/ar
5. ophthalm/ologist
6. lacrim/al
7. opt/ic
8. opt/ician
9. retin/o/pathy
10. corne/al
11. nas/o/lacrim/al
12. ophthalm/o/pathy
13. pupill/ary

Exercise 26
Spelling exercise; see text, p. 389.

Exercise 27
1. left eye
2. a health professional who prescribes corrective lenses and/or eye exercises
3. agent that dilates the pupil
4. each eye
5. sharpness of vision
6. agent that constricts the pupil
7. right eye

Exercise 28
1. oculus sinister   5. oculus dexter
2. mydriatic   6. optometrist
3. oculus uterque   7. visual acuity
4. miotic

Exercise 29
Spelling exercise; see text, p. 391.

Exercise 30
1. pterygium   6. retinopathy
2. glaucoma   7. hypertension
3. blepharoptosis   8. arteriosclerosis
4. astigmatism   9. cataract
5. presbyopia

Exercise 31
1. mydriatic   6. chalazion
2. astigmatism   7. nystagmus
3. cataract   8. trabeculectomy
4. tonometer   9. fluorescein
5. hyperopia   angiography

Exercise 32
1. ophthalmalgia   4. ophthalmoscope
2. iridectomy   5. retinopathy
3. blepharitis

Exercise 33
1. pertaining to within the nose
2. formation of red (blood cells)
3. hernia of the esophagus
4. producing fibers
5. hardening (caused by scarring) of the glomeruli
6. excessive flow of blood

7. stone in the liver
8. dissolution or breaking down of tissue
9. abnormal condition of water and pus in the kidney
10. excessive development of muscle tissue

CHAPTER 13
Exercise Figures
Exercise Figure
A. 1. ear: aur/i, aur/o, ot/o
   2. labyrinth: labyrinth/o
   3. stapes: staped/o
   4. tympanic membrane: tympan/o, myring/o
   5. mastoid bone: mastoid/o

Exercise Figure B. myringotomy
Exercise Figure C. audiometry

Exercise 1
1. g   6. k
2. j   7. d
3. b   8. e
4. f   9. a
5. h   10. c

Exercise 2
1. stapes   6. ear
2. mastoid   7. hearing
3. hearing   8. labyrinth
4. ear   9. tympanic
5. tympanic mem-   membrane
   brane (eardrum),
   middle ear

Exercise 3
1. a. aur/o   4. tympan/o
   b. aur/i   5. labyrinth/o
   c. ot/o   6. a. acou/o
2. mastoid/o   b. audi/o
3. staped/o   7. myring/o

Exercise 4
1. WRCV WR   S
   ot/o/myc/osis
      CF

   abnormal condition of fungus in the ear

2.   WR   S
   tympan/itis

   inflammation of the middle ear

3. WRCV   WR   S
   ot/o/mastoid/itis
      CF

   inflammation of the ear and the mastoid bone

4. WR   S
   ot/algia

   pain in the ear

5.   WR   S
   labyrinth/itis

   inflammation of the labyrinth

6.   WR   S
   myring/itis

   inflammation of the tympanic membrane

7. WRCV   S
   ot/o/sclerosis
      CF

   hardening of the ear (stapes) (caused by irregular bone development)

8.   WR   S
   mastoid/itis

   inflammation of the mastoid bone

9. WRCVWR   S
   ot/o/py/orrhea
      CF

   discharge of pus from the ear

Exercise 5
1. myring/itis   6. ot/o/myc/osis
2. ot/o/py/orrhea   7. ot/o/mastoid/itis
3. mastoid/itis   8. labyrinth/itis
4. ot/algia   9. tympan/itis
5. ot/o/sclerosis

Exercise 6
Spelling exercise; see text, p. 403.

Exercise 7
1 vertigo, tinnitus   5. otitis externa
2. Meniere's disease   6. acoustic neuroma
3. otitis media   7. presbycusis
4. ceruminoma

Exercise 8
1. e   5. h
2. b   6. d
3. g   7. a
4. c   8. i

Exercise 9
Spelling exercise; see text, p. 404.

Exercise 10
1.   WR   S
   mastoid/ectomy
   excision of the mastoid bone

2.   WR   S
   myring/otomy
   incision into the tympanic membrane

3.   WR   S
   labyrinth/ectomy
   excision of the labyrinth

4.   WR   S
   mastoid/otomy
   incision into the mastoid bone

5. WR   CV   S
   tympan/o/plasty
        CF
   surgical repair of the eardrum

6.   WR   CV   S
   myring/o/plasty
          CF
   surgical repair of the tympanic membrane

Exercise 11
1. mastoid/otomy   4. mastoid/ectomy
2. labyrinth/ectomy   5. myring/otomy
3. tympan/o/plasty   6. myring/o/plasty

Exercise 12
Spelling exercise; see text, p. 406.

Exercise 13
1. WRCV   S
   ot/o/scope
      CF

   instrument used for the visual examination of the ear

2.   WR CV   S
   audi/o/metry
        CF

   measurement of hearing

3.   WR CV   S
   audi/o/gram
        CF

   (graphic) record of hearing

4. WRCV   S
   ot/o/scopy
      CF

   visual examination of the ear

5.   WR CV   S
   audi/o/meter
        CF

   instrument used to measure hearing

6.   WR   CV   S
   tympan/o/metry
          CF

   measurement (of movement) of the tympanic membrane

7.   WR   S
   acou/meter

   instrument used to measure (acuteness of) hearing

8. WR CV S
<u>tympan/o/meter</u>
       CF

instrument used to measure middle ear (function)

Exercise 14
1. tympan/o/metry
2. audi/o/meter
3. ot/o/scopy
4. audi/o/gram
5. ot/o/scope
6. audi/o/metry
7. acou/meter
8. tympan/o/meter

Exercise 15
Spelling exercise; see text, p. 408.

Exercise 16
1. WR   S
ot/ology
study of the ear

2. WR   S
audi/ologist
one who is skilled in and specializes in audiology

3. WRCV WR CV WR   S
ot/o/rhin/o/laryng/ologist
     CF   CF
physician who studies and treats diseases of the ear, nose, and throat

4. WR   S
audi/ology
study of hearing

5. WR   S
ot/ologist
physician who studies and treats diseases of the ear

6. WR S
aur/al
pertaining to the ear

Exercise 17
1. audi/ology
2. ot/o/rhin/o/laryng/ologist
3. ot/ology
4. audi/ologist
5. ot/ologist
6. aur/al

Exercise 18
Spelling exercise; see text, p. 409.

Exercise 19
1. otoscopy
2. audiometry
3. otitis media
4. presbycusis

Exercise 20
1. myringitis
2. tinnitus
3. otologist
4. myringotomy

Exercise 21
1. otoscope
2. otalgia
3. otomycosis
4. otopyorrhea

Exercise 22
1. absence of sugar in the blood
2. pertaining to the heart and the kidney
3. pertaining to the gallbladder and the stomach
4. producing color
5. paralysis of the bladder
6. inflammation of the tear sac and the sinuses
7. inflammation of the stomach, small intestine, and colon
8. dissolution of blood cells
9. prolapse of the uterus
10. tumor of the bone and fibrous tissue
11. pertaining to around (or in the wall of) the fallopian tube
12. pertaining to surrounding the head

Answers

CHAPTER 14
Exercise Figures
Exercise Figure
A. 1. mandible: mandibul/o
   2. sternum: stern/o
   3. phalanges: phalang/o
   4. patella: patell/o
   5. tarsals: tars/o
   6. phalanges: phalang/o
   7. cranium: crani/o
   8. maxilla: maxill/o
   9. clavicle: clavic/o, clavicul/o
   10. ribs: cost/o
   11. femur: femor/o
   12. fibula: fibul/o
   13. tibia: tibi/o

Exercise Figure
B. 1. a. vertebral column, spine: rachi/o,
      b. vertebra: spondyl/o, vertebr/o
   2. scapula: scapul/o
   3. humerus: humer/o
   4. ulna: uln/o
   5. radius: radi/o
   6. carpals: carp/o
   7. ilium: ili/o
   8. pubis: pub/o
   9. ischium: ischi/o

Exercise Figure
C. 1. synovial membrane: synovi/o
   2. joint: arthr/o
   3. meniscus: menisc/o
   4. tendon: ten/o, tend/o, tendin/o
   5. cartilage: chondr/o
   6. bursa: burs/o

Exercise Figure D. osteoarthritis
Exercise Figure E. *A*, kyphosis. *B*, scoliosis. *C*, lordosis.
Exercise Figure F. arthroscopy

Exercise 1
1. d
2. i
3. h
4. k
5. j
6. g
7. b
8. f
9. a
10. c

Exercise 2
1. scapula
2. sternum
3. mandible
4. clavicle
5. humerus
6. a. ulna
   b. radius
7. tarsals
8. phalanges
9. metatarsals
10. metacarpals
11. femur
12. fibula, tibia
13. patella
14. cervical vertebrae
15. lumbar
16. pubis
17. sacrum
18. ischium
19. coccyx
20. ilium
21. carpals

Exercise 3
1. m
2. c
3. e
4. a
5. l
6. d
7. h
8. i
9. k
10. b
11. f
12. g

Exercise 4
1. movement of drawing away from the middle
2. movement that turns the palm down
3. movement that turns the palm up
4. turning around its own axis

5. movement in which a limb is placed in a straight position
6. movement of turning outward
7. movement of drawing toward the middle
8. movement in which a limb is bent
9. movement of turning inward

Exercise 5

1. h	6. a
2. d	7. g
3. i	8. f
4. j	9. b
5. c	

Exercise 6

1. clavicle	7. ilium
2. rib	8. ischium
3. (skull), cranium	9. carpals
4. femur	10. fibula
5. clavicle	11. mandible
6. humerus	12. loin, lumbar region

Exercise 7

1. a. clavicul/o	6. carp/o
b. clavic/o	7. ischi/o
2. cost/o	8. fibul/o
3. crani/o	9. ili/o
4. femor/o	10. mandibul/o
5. humer/o	11. lumb/o

Exercise 8

1. vertebral column, spine	8. tibia
2. patella	9. pubis
3. vertebra	10. tarsals
4. maxilla	11. scapula
5. phalanges	12. sternum
6. ulna	13. vertebra
7. radius	14. sacrum

Exercise 9

1. maxill/o	8. stern/o
2. uln/o	9. scapul/o
3. radi/o	10. patell/o
4. tibi/o	11. phalang/o
5. pub/o	12. sacr/o
6. tars/o	13. rachi/o
7. a. vertebr/o	
b. spondyl/o	

Exercise 10

1. joint	8. tendon
2. aponeurosis	9. synovia, synovial membrane
3. meniscus	
4. tendon	
5. cartilage	10. intervertebral disk
6. tendon	
7. bursa	

Exercise 11

1. menisc/o	6. burs/o
2. aponeur/o	7. synovi/o
3. arthr/o	8. disk/o
4. chondr/o	
5. a. tendin/o	
b. ten/o	
c. tend/o	

Exercise 12

1. muscle	7. hump
2. stone	8. crooked, stiff, bent
3. movement, motion	9. crooked, curved
4. bone	10. bone marrow
5. lamina	11. muscle
6. bone marrow	12. bent forward

Exercise 13

1. my/o, myos/o	7. kyph/o
2. petr/o	8. ankyl/o
3. kinesi/o	9. scoli/o
4. oste/o	10. lord/o
5. lamin/o	
6. a. myel/o	
b. myelon/o	

Exercise 14

1. above	3. between
2. together, joined	

Exercise 15

1. syn-, sym-	3. supra-
2. inter-	

Exercise 16

1. growth	4. break
2. break	5. fissure, split
3. fusion, surgical fixation	6. break
	7. weakness

Exercise 17

1. -physis	4. -desis
2. -asthenia	5. -schisis
3. a. -clasis	
b. -clast	
c. -clasia	

Exercise 18

1. WR S
   oste/itis

   inflammation of the bone

2. WR CV WR S
   oste/o/myel/itis
        CF

   inflammation of the bone and bone marrow

3. WR CV WR S
   oste/o/petr/osis
        CF

   abnormal condition of stonelike bones (marblelike bones)

4. WR CV S
   oste/o/malacia
        CF

   softening of bones

5. WR CV WR S
   oste/o/carcin/oma
        CF

   cancerous tumor of the bone

6. WR CV WR S
   oste/o/chondr/itis
        CF

   inflammation of the bone and cartilage

7. WR CV WR S
   oste/o/fibr/oma
        CF

   tumor of the bone and fibrous tissue

8. WR S
   arthr/itis

   inflammation of a joint

9. WR CV WR S
   arthr/o/chondr/itis
        CF

   inflammation of the joint cartilages

10. WR S
    myel/oma

    tumor in the bone marrow

11. WR S
    tendin/itis

    inflammation of a tendon

12. WR S
    ten/odynia

    pain in a tendon

13. WR CV S
    carp/o/ptosis
        CF

    drooping wrist (wrist drop)

14. WR S
    burs/itis

    inflammation of the bursa

15. WR WR S
    spondyl/arthr/itis

    inflammation of the vertebral joints

16. WR S
    ankyl/osis

    abnormal condition of stiffness

17. WR S
    kyph/osis

    abnormal hump (of the thoracic spine, also called *hunchback*)

18. WR   S
scoli/osis
abnormal (lateral) curve (of the spine)

19. WR CV S
crani/o/schisis
____
CF
fissure of the skull

20. WR   S
maxill/itis
inflammation of the maxilla

21. WR   S
menisc/itis
inflammation of the meniscus

22. WR   S
rachi/schisis
fissure of the vertebral column

23. WR CV WR
burs/o/lith
____
CF
stone in the bursa

24. WR   S
my/asthenia
muscle weakness

25. WR CV   S
oste/o/sarcoma
____
CF
malignant tumor of the bone

26. WR   CV   S
chondr/o/malacia
____
CF
softening of cartilage

27. WR   CV   S
synovi/o/sarcoma
____
CF
a malignant tumor of the synovial
membrane

28. WR CV WR   S
ten/o/synov/itis
____
CF
inflammation of the tendon and
synovial membrane

29. P   WR   S
poly/myos/itis
inflammation of many muscles

30. WR   S
disk/itis
inflammation of an intervertebral disk

31. WR   S
lord/osis
abnormal condition of bending
forward

32. WR CV WR   S
oste/o/arthr/itis
____
CF
inflammation of bone and joint

Exercise 19
1. oste/o/carcin/oma
2. oste/o/chondr/itis
3. oste/o/fibr/oma
4. arthr/itis
5. arthr/o/chondr/itis
6. myel/oma
7. tendin/itis
8. ten/odynia
9. carp/o/ptosis
10. burs/itis
11. spondyl/arthr/itis
12. ankyl/osis
13. kyph/osis
14. scoli/osis
15. crani/o/schisis
16. maxill/itis
17. menisc/itis
18. rachi/schisis
19. burs/o/lith
20. my/asthenia
21. oste/itis
22. oste/o/myel/itis
23. oste/o/petr/osis
24. oste/o/malacia
25. ten/o/synov/itis
26. synovi/o/sarcoma
27. oste/o/sarcoma
28. chondr/o/malacia
29. disk/itis
30. poly/myos/itis
31. lord/osis
32. oste/o/arthr/itis

Exercise 20
Spelling exercise; see text, p. 440.

Exercise 21
1. exostosis
2. muscular dystrophy
3. myasthenia gravis
4. bunion
5. ankylosing spondylitis
6. gout
7. a. herniated disk
   b. slipped disk
   c. ruptured disk
8. fracture
9. osteoporosis
10. carpal tunnel syndrome
11. Colles' fracture

Exercise 22
1. abnormal benign growth on the
   surface of a bone
2. group of hereditary diseases
   characterized by degeneration of
   muscle and weakness
3. chronic disease characterized by
   muscle weakness and thought to be
   caused by a defect in the transmission
   of impulses from nerve to muscle cell
4. abnormal enlargement of the joint at
   the base of the great toe
5. form of arthritis that first affects the
   spine and adjacent structures
6. abnormal loss of bone density
7. disease in which an excessive amount
   of uric acid in the blood causes sodium
   urate crystals (tophi) to be deposited
   in the joints
8. rupture of the intervertebral disk
   cartilage, which allows the contents to
   protrude through it, putting pressure
   on the spinal nerve roots
9. broken bone
10. a disorder of the wrist caused by
    compression of the nerve
11. a type of fractured wrist

Exercise 23
Spelling exercise; see text, p. 445.

Exercise 24
1. WR CV   S
oste/o/clasis
____
CF
(surgical) breaking of a bone

2. WR   S
ost/ectomy
excision of bone

3. WR CV   S
oste/o/plasty
____
CF
surgical repair of the bone

4. WR   S
oste/otomy
incision of the bone

5. WR CV   S
oste/o/tome
____
CF
instrument used to cut the bone

6. WR CV   S
arthr/o/clasia
____
CF
(surgical) breaking of a (stiff) joint

7. WR CV S
    arthr/o/desis
       CF

    surgical fixation of a joint

8. WR CV S
    arthr/o/plasty
       CF

    surgical repair of a joint

9. WR S
    arthr/otomy

    incision of a joint

10. WR S
    chondr/ectomy

    excision of a cartilage

11. WR CV S
    chondr/o/plasty
        CF

    surgical repair of a cartilage

12. WR CV S
    my/o/plasty
       CF

    surgical repair of a muscle

13. WR S
    my/orrhaphy

    suture of a muscle

14. WR CV WR S
    ten/o/my/o/plasty
       CF   CF

    surgical repair of the tendon and
    muscle

15. WR S
    ten/otomy

    incision of the tendon

16. WR S
    ten/orrhaphy

    suture of a tendon

17. WR S
    cost/ectomy

    excision of a rib

18. WR S
    patell/ectomy

    excision of the patella

19. WR S
    aponeur/orrhaphy

    suture of an aponeurosis

20. WR S
    carp/ectomy

    excision of a carpal bone

21. WR S
    phalang/ectomy

    excision of a finger or toe bone

22. WR S
    menisc/ectomy

    excision of the meniscus

23. WR CV P S
    spondyl/o/syn/desis
          CF

    fusing together of the vertebrae

24. WR S
    lamin/ectomy

    excision of the lamina

25. WR S
    burs/ectomy

    excision of a bursa

26. WR S
    burs/otomy

    incision of a bursa

27. WR S
    crani/otomy

    incision into the skull

28. WR CV S
    crani/o/plasty
        CF

    surgical repair of the skull

29. WR S
    maxill/ectomy

    excision of the maxilla

30. WR S
    rachi/otomy

    incision into the vertebral column

31. WR S
    tars/ectomy

    excision of (one or more) tarsal bones

32. WR S
    synov/ectomy

    excision of the synovial membrane

33. WR S
    disk/ectomy

    excision of an intervertebral disk

Exercise 25
1. oste/o/clasis
2. ost/ectomy
3. oste/o/plasty
4. oste/otomy
5. oste/o/tome
6. arthr/o/clasia
7. arthr/o/desis
8. arthr/o/plasty
9. arthr/otomy
10. chondr/ectomy
11. chondr/o/plasty
12. my/o/plasty
13. my/orrhaphy
14. ten/o/my/o/plasty
15. ten/otomy

16. ten/orrhaphy
17. cost/ectomy
18. patell/ectomy
19. aponeur/orrhaphy
20. carp/ectomy
21. phalang/ectomy
22. menisc/ectomy
23. spondyl/o/syn/desis
24. lamin/ectomy
25. burs/ectomy
26. burs/otomy
27. crani/otomy
28. crani/o/plasty
29. maxill/ectomy
30. rachi/otomy
31. tars/ectomy
32. synov/ectomy
33. disk/ectomy

Exercise 26
Spelling exercise; see text, p. 451.

Exercise 27
1. WR CV WR CV S
    electr/o/my/o/gram
       CF   CF

    record of the electrical activity in a
    muscle

2. WR CV S
    arthr/o/gram
       CF

    x-ray film of a joint

3. WR CV S
    arthr/o/scopy
       CF

    visual examination inside a joint

4. WR CV S
    arthr/o/centesis
       CF

    surgical puncture of a joint to aspirate
    fluid

Exercise 28
1. arthr/o/gram
2. arthr/o/scopy
3. arthr/o/centesis
4. electr/o/my/o/-
   gram

Exercise 29
Spelling exercise; see text, p. 453.

Exercise 30
1. P S(WR)
    sym/physis

    growing together

2. WR S
    femor/al

    pertaining to the femur

3.   WR S
humer/al

pertaining to the humerus

4.   P   WR S
inter/vertebr/al

pertaining to between the vertebrae

5.   P   WR S
hyper/kinesi/a

excessive movement (overactivity)

6.   P   WR S
dys/kinesi/a

difficult movement

7.   P   WR S
brady/kinesi/a

slow movement

8.   P   WR S
intra/crani/al

pertaining to within the cranium

9.   WR CV WR   S
stern/o/clavicul/ar
    CF

pertaining to the sternum and clavicle

10. WR CV WR   S
ili/o/femor/al
   CF

pertaining to the ilium and femur

11. WR CV WR S
ischi/o/fibul/ar
    CF

pertaining to the ischium and fibula

12.   P   WR   S
sub/maxill/ary

pertaining to below the maxilla

13.   WR CV WR S
ischi/o/pub/ic
    CF

pertaining to the ischium and pubis

14.   P   WR   S
sub/mandibul/ar

pertaining to below the mandible

15.   WR CV WR   S
pub/o/femor/al
    CF

pertaining to the pubis and femur

16.   P   WR   S
supra/scapul/ar

pertaining to above the scapula

17.   P   WR S
sub/cost/al

pertaining to below the rib

18.   WR CV WR S
vertebr/o/cost/a/l
    CF

pertaining to the vertebrae and ribs

19.   P   WR   S
sub/scapul/ar

pertaining to below the scapula

20. WR CV WR
oste/o/blast
    CF

developing bone cell

21.   WR CV S
oste/o/cyte
    CF

bone cell

22.   WR CV WR   S
oste/o/necr/osis
    CF

abnormal death of bone tissues

23.   WR   S
stern/oid

resembling the sternum

24.   WR   S
arthr/algia

pain in the joint

25.   WR   S
carp/al

pertaining to the wrist

26.   WR   S
lumb/ar

pertaining to the loins

27.   WR CV WR S
lumb/o/cost/al
    CF

pertaining to the loins and to the ribs

28.   WR CV WR S
lumb/o/sacr/al
    CF

pertaining to the lumbar region (loin) and the sacrum

29.   WR S
sacr/al

pertaining to the sacrum

30.   WR CV WR   S
sacr/o/vertebr/al
    CF

pertaining to the sacrum and vertebrae

31.   P   WR   S
sub/stern/al

pertaining to below the sternum

32.   P   WR   S
supra/patell/ar

pertaining to above the patella

33.   P   S(WR)
dys/trophy

abnormal development

34.   P   S(WR)
a/trophy

without development

35.   P   S(WR)
hyper/trophy

excessive development

36.   P   WR S
inter/cost/al

pertaining to between the ribs

37.   WR S
crani/al

pertaining to the cranium

Exercise 31

1. sym/physis
2. femor/al
3. humer/al
4. inter/vertebr/al
5. hyper/kinesi/a
6. dys/kinesi/a
7. brady/kinesi/a
8. intra/crani/al
9. stern/o/clavicul/ar
10. ili/o/femor/al
11. ischi/o/fibul/ar
12. sub/maxill/ary
13. ischi/o/pub/ic
14. sub/mandibul/ar
15. pub/o/femor/al
16. supra/scapul/ar
17. sub/cost/al
18. vertebr/o/cost/al
19. sub/scapul/ar
20. oste/o/blast
21. oste/o/cyte
22. oste/o/necr/osis
23. stern/oid
24. arthr/algia
25. carp/al
26. sacr/al
27. lumb/ar
28. sacr/o/vertebr/al
29. lumb/o/sacr/al
30. lumb/o/cost/al
31. sub/stern/al
32. supra/patell/ar
33. dys/trophy
34 a/trophy
35. hyper/trophy
36. crani/al
37. inter/cos/tal

Exercise 32
Spelling exercise; see text, p. 460.

Exercise 33
1. c
2. f
3. d, g, k
4. a, h
5. j
6. b
7. e
8. i
9. k

Exercise 34
1. specialist in chiropractic
2. system of therapy that consists of manipulation of the vertebral column
3. branch of medicine dealing with the study and treatment of diseases and abnormalities of the musculoskeletal system
4. physician who specializes in orthopedics
5. specialist in treating and diagnosing foot diseases and disorders
6. specialist in treating and diagnosing foot diseases and disorders
7. physician who specializes in osteopathy
8. system of medicine in which emphasis is on the relationship between body organs and the musculoskeletal system
9. making and fitting of orthopedic appliances
10. an artificial substitute for a missing body part
11. one who is skilled in orthotics

Exercise 35
Spelling exercise; see text, p. 463.

Exercise 36
1. orthopedic
2. arthroscopy
3. arthritis
4. medial
5. suprapatellar
6. chondromalacia
7. lateral
8. pathology

Exercise 37
1. kyphosis
2. arthroplasty
3. chondrectomy
4. dyskinesia
5. softening of the bones
6. osteoclasis
7. subcostal
8. symphysis
9. orthopedist
10. osteoporosis
11. carpal tunnel syndrome

Exercise 38
1. arthrodesis
2. arthroscopy
3. tenorrhaphy
4. electromyogram, atrophy
5. a. cranial
   b. intercostal
   c. subcostal
   d. intervertebral
   e. intracranial
   f. femoral
   g. ischiopubic
   h. sternoclavicular
   i. submandibular

Exercise 39
1. intracranial
2. suprascapular
3. symphysis
4. subcostal
5. polymyositis

Exercise 40
1. (congenital) fissure of the skull and vertebral column
2. pertaining to the humerus and radius
3. between the pubic bones
4. pertaining to within the sternum
5. muscular movement
6. (any) disease of the joints and bones
7. dissolution of bone
8. tumor composed of bone
9. measurement of bone
10. hardening of the bone
11. inflammation of many joints
12. pain in the vertebra
13. pain in the tendon
14. pertaining to the vertebrae and sternum

Answers

CHAPTER 15
Exercise Figures
Exercise Figure
A. 1. brain: encephal/o
   2. spinal cord: myel/o
   3. cerebrum: cerebr/o
   4. cerebellum: cerebell/o
   5. meninges: mening/i, mening/o

Exercise Figure
B. 1. dura mater: dur/o
   2. ganglion: gangli/o, ganglion/o
   3. nerve root: radic/o, radicul/o, rhiz/o

Exercise Figure C. meningomyelocele
Exercise Figure D. rhizotomy, radicotomy
Exercise Figure E. myelogram

Exercise Figure F. 1, hemiplegia
                    2, quadriplegia
                    3, tetraplegia

Exercise 1
1. meninges
2. dura mater
3. arachnoid
4. pia mater
5. subarachnoid space
6. cerebrospinal fluid

Exercise 2
1. d
2. f
3. g
4. e
5. a
6. h
7. b

Exercise 3
1. cerebellum
2. nerve
3. spinal cord
4. meninges
5. brain
6. cerebrum, brain
7. nerve root
8. ganglion
9. nerve root
10. hard, dura mater
11. ganglion
12. nerve root

Exercise 4
1. cerebell/o
2. neur/o
3. myel/o
4. a. mening/o, b. mening/i
5. encephal/o
6. cerebr/o
7. a. radicul/o b. radic/o, rhiz/o
8. dur/o
9. a. gangli/o, b. ganglion/o

Exercise 5
1. one
2. mind
3. four
4. mind
5. speech
6. sensation, sensitivity, feeling
7. mind
8. gray matter

Exercise 6
1. quadr/i
2. mon/o
3. a. phren/o b. psych/o c. ment/o
4. phas/o
5. poli/o
6. esthesi/o

Exercise 7
1. four
2. half
3. before

Exercise 8
1. hemi-
2. tetra-
3. pre-

Exercise 9
1. slight paralysis
2. specialty, treatment
3. seizure, attack
4. specialist, physician

Exercise 10
1. -paresis   3. -ictal
2. -iatry   4. -iatrist

Exercise 11
1. WR   S
   neur/itis
   inflammation of the nerve

2. WR   S
   neur/oma
   tumor made up of nerve (cells)

3. WR   S
   neur/algia
   pain in a nerve

4. WR CV WR CV S
   neur/o/arthr/o/pathy
      CF   CF
   disease of nerves and joints

5. WR CV WR
   neur/o/blast
      CF
   developing nerve cell

6. WR   S
   neur/asthenia
   nerve weakness (nervous exhaustion, fatigue, and weakness)

7. WR   CV   S
   encephal/o/malacia
        CF
   softening of the brain

8. WR   S
   encephal/itis
   inflammation of the brain

9. WR   CV WR CV WR   S
   encephal/o/myel/o/radicul/itis
        CF   CF
   inflammation of the brain, spinal cord, and nerve roots

10. WR   S
    mening/itis
    inflammation of the meninges

11. WR   CV   S
    mening/o/cele
        CF
    protrusion of the meninges

12. WR   CV WR CV S
    mening/o/myel/o/cele
         CF   CF
    protrusion of the meninges and spinal cord

13. WR   S
    radicul/itis
    inflammation of the nerve roots

14. WR   S
    cerebell/itis
    inflammation of the cerebellum

15. WR   S
    gangli/itis
    inflammation of the ganglion

16. WR   S
    dur/itis
    inflammation of the dura mater

17. P   WR   S
    poly/neur/itis
    inflammation of many nerves

18. WR CV WR   S
    poli/o/myel/itis
         CF
    inflammation of the gray matter of the spinal cord

19. WR   S   WR   S
    cerebr/al thromb/osis
    abnormal condition of a clot in the cerebrum

20. P   WR S   WR   S
    sub/dur/al hemat/oma
    blood tumor pertaining to below the dura mater

21. WR CV   WR   CV WR   S
    rhiz/o/mening/o/myel/itis
        CF   CF
    inflammation of the nerve root, meninges, and spinal cord

Exercise 12
1. neur/itis
2. neur/oma
3. neur/algia
4. neur/o/arthr/o/pathy
5. neur/o/blast
6. neur/asthenia
7. encephal/o/malacia
8. encephal/itis
9. encephal/o/myel/o/radicul/itis
10. mening/itis
11. mening/o/cele
12. mening/o/myel/o/cele
13. radicul/itis
14. cerebell/itis
15. gangli/itis
16. dur/itis
17. poly/neur/itis
18. poli/o/myel/itis
19. cerebr/al thromb/osis
20. sub/dur/al hemat/oma
21. rhiz/o/mening/o/myel/itis

Exercise 13
Spelling exercise; see text, p. 483.

Exercise 14
1. cerebrum (brain)   5. head
2. mind   6. nerve
3. upon   7. cerebrum (brain)
4. hardening

Exercise 15
1. b   9. i
2. a   10. m
3. n   11. q
4. j   12. d
5. l   13. h
6. p   14. o
7. e   15. c
8. g   16. f

Exercise 16
Spelling exercise; see text, p. 487.

Exercise 17
1. WR   S
   radic/otomy
   incision into a nerve root

2. WR   S
   neur/ectomy
   excision of a nerve

3. WR   S
   neur/orrhaphy
   suture of a nerve

4. WR   S
   ganglion/ectomy
   excision of a ganglion

5. WR   S
   neur/otomy
   incision into a nerve

6. WR CV   S
   neur/o/lysis
   separating a nerve (from adhesions)

7. WR CV   S
   neur/o/plasty
   surgical repair of a nerve

8. WR   S
   rhiz/otomy
   incision into a nerve root

Exercise 18
1. a. radic/otomy   4. ganglion/ectomy
   b. rhiz/otomy   5. neur/otomy
2. neur/ectomy   6. neur/o/lysis
3. neur/orrhaphy   7. neur/o/plasty

Exercise 19
Spelling exercise; see text, p. 489.

Exercise 20

1. WR CV WR CV S
   electr/o/encephal/o/gram
       CF   CF

   record of the electrical impulses of the brain

2. WR CV WR CV S
   electr/o/encephal/o/graph
       CF   CF

   instrument used to record the electrical impulses of the brain

3. WR CV WR CV S
   electr/o/encephal/o/graphy
       CF   CF

   process of recording the electrical impulses of the brain

4. WR CV WR CV S
   ech/o/encephal/o/graphy
     CF   CF

   process of recording the brain (structures) by use of sound

5. WR CV S
   myel/o/gram
     CF

   x-ray film of the spinal cord

6. WR S WR CV S
   cerebr/al angi/o/graphy
           CF

   process of x-ray filming of the blood vessels in the brain

Exercise 21

1. ech/o/encephal/o/graphy
2. electr/o/encephal/o/gram
3. electr/o/encephal/o/graph
4. electr/o/encephal/o/graphy
5. myel/o/gram
6. cerebr/al angi/o/graphy

Exercise 22

Spelling exercise; see text, p. 491.

Exercise 23

1. computed tomography
2. lumbar puncture
3. positron emission tomography
4. magnetic resonance imaging
5. evoked potential studies

Exercise 24

1. insertion of a needle into the subarachnoid space
2. process that includes the use of a computer to produce a series of images of the brain tissues at any desired depth
3. produces cross-sectional images of brain by use of magnetic waves
4. a technique that gives information about brain function
5. a group of diagnostic tests that measure changes and responses in brain waves from stimuli

Exercise 25

Spelling exercise; see text, p. 493.

Exercise 26

1. P S(WR)
   hemi/plegia

   paralysis of half (left or right side of the body)

2. P S(WR)
   tetra/plegia

   paralysis of four (limbs)

3. WR S
   neur/ologist

   physician who specializes in neurology

4. WR S
   neur/ology

   branch of medicine dealing with the nervous system's function and disorders

5. WR S
   neur/oid

   resembling a nerve

6. WR CV S
   quadr/i/plegia
     CF

   paralysis of four (limbs)

7. WR S
   cerebr/al

   pertaining to the cerebrum

8. WR CV S
   mon/o/plegia
     CF

   paralysis of one (limb)

9. P WR S
   a/phas/ia

   condition of without speaking (loss or impairment of the ability to speak)

10. P WR S
    dys/phas/ia

    condition of difficulty speaking

11. P S(WR)
    hemi/paresis

    slight paralysis of half (right or left side of the body)

12. P WR S
    an/esthesi/a

    without (loss of) feeling or sensation

13. P WR S
    hyper/esthesi/a

    excessive sensitivity (to stimuli)

14. P WR S
    sub/dur/al

    pertaining to below the dura mater

15. WR S
    cephal/algia

    pain in the head (headache)

16. WR CV WR S
    psych/o/somat/ic
      CF

    pertaining to the mind and body

17. WR CV S
    psych/o/pathy
      CF

    (any) disease of the mind

18. WR S
    psych/ology

    study of the mind (mental processes and behavior)

19. WR S
    psych/iatry

    branch of medicine that deals with the treatment of mental disorders

20. WR S
    psych/ologist

    specialist in the study of psychology

21. WR CV S
    psych/o/genic
      CF

    originating in the mind

22. WR S
    phren/ic

    pertaining to the mind

23. WR CV S
    phren/o/pathy
      CF

    disease of the mind

24. WR CV WR S
    crani/o/cerebr/al
      CF

    pertaining to the cranium and cerebrum

25. WR CV S
    myel/o/malacia
      CF

    softening of the spinal cord

26. WR CV S
    encephal/o/sclerosis
      CF

    hardening of the brain

27. P   S(WR)
    post/ictal
    (occurring) after a seizure or attack

28. P   S(WR)
    pan/plegia
    total paralysis

29. P   S(WR)
    inter/ictal
    (occurring) between seizures or attacks

30. WR CV S
    mon/o/paresis
        CF
    slight paralysis of one (limb)

31. P   S(WR)
    pre/ictal
    (occurring) before a seizure or attack

32. WR   S
    psych/iatrist
    a physician who treats mental
    disorders

Exercise 27
1. hemi/paresis
2. an/esthesi/a
3. hyper/esthesi/a
4. sub/dur/al
5. cephal/algia
6. psych/o/somat/ic
7. psych/o/pathy
8. psych/ology
9. psych/iatry
10. psych/ologist
11. psych/o/genic
12. phren/ic
13. phren/o/pathy
14. crani/o/cerebr/al
15. myel/o/malacia
16. encephal/o/sclerosis
17. hemi/plegia
18. tetra/plegia, quadr/i/plegia
19. neur/ologist
20. neur/ology
21. neur/oid
22. quadr/i/plegia, tetra/plegia
23. cerebr/al
24. mon/o/plegia
25. a/phas/ia
26. dys/phas/ia
27. pre/ictal
28. mon/o/paresis
29. post/ictal
30. pan/plegia
31. inter/ictal
32. psych/iatrist

Exercise 28
Spelling exercise; see text, p. 498.

Exercise 29
1. concussion
2. unconsciousness
3. conscious
4. seizure
5. convulsion
6. shunt
7. paraplegia
8. coma
9. syncope
10. ataxia
11. gait
12. dementia
13. incoherent
14. disorientation
15. cognitive
16. afferent
17. efferent

Exercise 30
1. tube implanted in the body to redirect the flow of a fluid
2. paralysis from the waist down caused by damage to the lower level of the spinal cord
3. state of profound unconsciousness
4. jarring or shaking that results in injury
5. state of being unaware of surroundings and incapable of responding to stimuli as a result of injury, shock, or illness
6. awake, alert, aware of one's surroundings
7. sudden attack
8. sudden involuntary contraction of a group of muscles
9. fainting, or sudden loss of consciousness
10. lack of muscle coordination
11. mental decline
12. a manner or style of walking
13. pertaining to the mental processes of comprehension, judgment, memory, and reasoning
14. a state of mental confusion as to time, place, and identity
15. unable to express one's thoughts or ideas in an orderly, intelligible manner
16. conveying away from the center
17. conveying toward the center

Exercise 31
Spelling exercise; see text, p. 502.

Exercise 32
1. disorientation
2. cognitive
3. aphasia
4. conscious
5. neurology
6. magnetic resonance imaging
7. encephalitis
8. electroencephalogram
9. seizure
10. incoherent

Exercise 33
1. quadriplegia
2. aphasia
3. unconscious
4. meningocele
5. psychiatry
6. hardened patches along brain and spinal cord
7. electroencephalography
8. blood clot
9. positron emission tomography

Exercise 34
1. encephalitis
2. meningitis
3. hydrocephalus
4. neuralgia
5. rhizomeningomyelitis

Exercise 35
1. monomyoplegia
2. polycyesis
3. polychondritis
4. poliomyelopathy
5. coloproctectomy
6. myorrhaphy
7. hemicolectomy
8. oophorohysterectomy

Answers

Q					M	E	N	T	O			P
U					Y							O
A			C	E	R	E	B	E	L	L	O	L
D			S		L					D	I	
R			T		O					U	O	
I			H						R			
			E	N	C	E	P	H	A	L	O	
M			S		E						M	
E	P	I	R	A	D	I	C	U	L	O	
N	H	O	E							N	
I	R	E	B		P	S	Y	C	H	O	
N	E		R							N	
G	A	N	G	L	I	O	N	O			
O	O					P	H	A	S	O	

CHAPTER 16
Exercise Figures
Exercise Figure
A. 1. parathyroid glands: parathyroid/o
   2. adrenal glands: adren/o, adrenal/o
   3. thyroid gland: thyroid/o, thyr/o

Exercise Figure B. cortex: cortic/o
Exercise Figure C. acromegaly
Exercise Figure D. exophthalmic

Exercise 1
1. b
2. g
3. d
4. h
5. a
6. c
7. e

Exercise 2

1. d
2. a
3. e
4. b
5. g
6. c

Exercise 3

1. cortex
2. adrenal gland
3. parathyroid gland
4. thyroid gland
5. adrenal gland
6. thyroid gland
7. endocrine

Exercise 4

1. a. adren/o
   b. adrenal/o
2. a. thyroid/o
   b. thyr/o
3. endocrin/o
4. cortic/o
5. parathyroid/o

Exercise 5

1. thirst
2. poison
3. potassium
4. calcium
5. extremities, height
6. sodium

Exercise 6

1. toxic/o
2. acr/o
3. calc/i
4. dips/o
5. kal/i
6. natr/o

Exercise 7

1. outside, outward
2. run, running

Exercise 8

1. -drome
2. a. ex-
   b. exo-

Exercise 9

1. WR   S
   adrenal/itis

   inflammation of an adrenal gland

2. P   WR   S
   hypo/calc/emia

   deficient level of calcium in the blood

3. P   WR   S
   hyper/thyroid/ism

   state of excessive thyroid gland activity

4. P   WR   S
   hyper/kal/emia

   excessive potassium in the blood

5. WR CV WR   S
   thyr/o/toxic/osis
        CF

   abnormal condition of poisoning caused by (excessive activity) of the thyroid gland

6. P   WR   S
   hyper/glyc/emia

   excessive sugar in the blood

7. WR CV   S
   adren/o/megaly
        CF

   enlargement of the adrenal gland

8. P   WR   S
   hypo/thyroid/ism

   state of deficient thyroid gland activity

9. P   WR S
   hypo/kal/emia

   deficient level of potassium in the blood

10. WR   S
    parathyroid/oma

    tumor of a parathyroid gland

11. WR CV   S
    acr/o/megaly
        CF

    enlargement of the extremities (and facial bones)

12. P   WR   S
    hypo/glyc/emia

    deficient level of sugar in the blood

13. P   WR   S
    hyper/calc/emia

    excessive calcium in the blood

14. P   WR   S
    hypo/natr/emia

    deficient level of sodium in the blood

Exercise 10

1. adren/o/megaly
2. hypo/thyroid/ism
3. acr/o/megaly
4. hypo/glyc/emia
5. hyper/kal/emia
6. hypo/calc/emia
7. hyper/thyroid/ism
8. hyper/calc/emia
9. thyr/o/toxic/osis
10. parathyroid/oma
11. hyper/glyc/emia
12. hypo/kal/emia
13. adrenal/itis
14. hypo/natr/emia

Exercise 11

Spelling exercise; see text, p. 518.

Exercise 12

1. d
2. a
3. j
4. b
5. h
6. c
7. l
8. e
9. k
10. i
11. f

Exercise 13

1. thyroid
2. parathyroid
3. islets of Langerhans (pancreas)
4. pituitary
5. thyroid
6. adrenal
7. islets of Langerhans (pancreas)
8. thyroid
9. islets of Langerhans (pancreas)
10. adrenal
11. pituitary

Exercise 14

Spelling exercise; see text, p. 521.

Exercise 15

1. WR   S
   thyroid/otomy

   incision into the thyroid gland

2. WR   S
   adrenal/ectomy

   excision of the adrenal gland

3. WR CV   WR   S
   thyr/o/parathyroid/ectomy
        CF

   excision of the thyroid and parathyroid glands

4. WR   S
   thyroid/ectomy

   excision of the thyroid gland

5. WR   S
   parathyroid/ectomy

   excision of the parathyroid gland

Exercise 16

1. thyroid/ectomy
2. thyr/o/parathyroid/ectomy
3. adrenal/ectomy
4. parathyroid/ectomy
5. thyroid/otomy

Exercise 17

Spelling exercise; see text, p. 523.

Exercise 18

1. c   2. b   3. a   4. f   5. d   6. e

Exercise 19

1. radioactive iodine uptake
2. fasting blood sugar
3. thyroid-stimulating hormone
4. thyroxine
5. thyroid scan
6. glucose tolerance test

Exercise 20

Spelling exercise; see text, p. 525.

Exercise 21

1. WR   S
    cortic/oid

    resembling the cortex

2. P   WR   S
    ex/ophthalm/ic

    pertaining to eyes (bulging) outward

3. P   S(WR)
    syn/drome

    set of symptoms that run together

4. WR CV S
    adren/o/pathy
        CF

    disease of the adrenal gland

5. WR   S
    endocrin/ologist

    a physician who specializes in
    endocrinology

6. P   WR   S
    poly/dips/ia

    abnormal state of much thirst

7. WR CV S
    calc/i/penia
        CF

    deficiency of calcium

8. WR   CV   S
    endocrin/o/pathy
            CF

    any disease of the endocrine system

9. WR CV WR CV P   S(WR)
    adren/o/cortic/o/hyper/plasia
        CF   CF

    excessive development of the adrenal
    cortex

10. P   WR   S
    eu/thyr/oid

    resembling normal thyroid

11. WR   S
    cortic/al

    pertaining to the cortex

12. WR   S
    endocrin/ology

    the study of endocrine glands

Exercise 22

1. ex/ophthalm/ic
2. endocrin/o/pathy
3. cortic/oid
4. syn/drome
5. adren/o/cortic/o/hyper/plasia
6. endocrin/ology
7. poly/dips/ia
8. adren/o/pathy
9. calc/i/penia
10. eu/thyr/oid
11. cortic/al
12. endocrin/ologist

Exercise 23

Spelling exercise; see text, p. 527.

Exercise 24

1. metabolism   3. isthmus
2. hormone

Exercise 25

1. narrow strip of tissue connecting large
    parts in the body
2. total of all chemical processes that take
    place in living organisms
3. a secretion of an endocrine gland

Exercise 26

Spelling exercise; see text, p. 528.

Exercise 27

1. polyuria   4. diabetes mellitus
2. polydipsia   5. hematemesis
3. cerebrovascular   6. cyanosis
    accident   7. ketosis

Exercise 28

1. goiter   5. overactivity
2. ketosis   6. cretinism
3. adrenal
4. antidiuretic
    hormone

Exercise 29

1. goiter   4. adrenomegaly
2. hyperkalemia   5. hypocalcemia
3. polydipsia

Exercise 30

1. inflammation of the skin of the
    extremities
2. calcium in the urine
3. pertaining to between the alveoli
4. potassium in the blood
5. surgical crushing of a nerve
6. softening of the eye
7. x-ray filming of the pancreas
8. hardening of a vein
9. abnormal condition of a black lung
10. instrument used to examine the
    rectum

BIBLIOGRAPHY

Alternative Medicine, The Burton Goldberg Group, Puyallup, Washington, 1994, Future Medicine Publishing.

Applegate EJ: *The anatomy and physiology learning system,* Philadelphia, 1995, WB Saunders.

Asperheim MK: *Pharmacology: an introductory text,* ed 8, Philadelphia, 1996, WB Saunders.

Austrin MG, Austrin HR: *Young's learning medical terminology,* ed 8, St. Louis, 1995, Mosby.

Davis NM: *Medical abbreviations: 4200 convenience at the expense of communications and safety,* ed 2, Huntingdon Valley, Pa, 1985, Neil M Davis Associates.

Ehrlich A: *Medical terminology for health professionals,* ed 3, Albany, 1997, Delmar Publishers.

Gylys BA, Wedding ME: *Medical terminology: a systems approach,* ed 3, Philadelphia, 1995, FA Davis Company.

Grimaldi PL: Managed care primer, *Nurse Management* (Suppl) pp. 4, 7, 8, Oct, 1996.

Haubrich WS: *Medical meanings: a glossary of word origins,* Philadelphia, 1997, American College of Physicians.

Ignatavicius et al: *Medical surgical nursing: a nursing process approach,* ed 2, 1995, WB Saunders.

LaFleur Brooks M: *Health unit coordinating,* ed 4, Philadelphia, 1997, WB Saunders.

LaFleur Brooks M, LaFleur D: *Programmed medical language,* St. Louis, 1996, Mosby.

Langford R, Thompson JM: *Mosby's handbook of diseases,* St. Louis, 1996, Mosby.

Lewis SM et al: *Medical surgical nursing,* St. Louis, 1996, Mosby.

Lilley LL et al: *Pharmacology and the nursing process,* St. Louis, 1997, Mosby.

Malarkey LM, McMorrow ME: *Nurse's manual of laboratory tests and diagnostic procedures,* Philadelphia, 1996, WB Saunders.

Managed care terms A thru Z, New York, Medicom International.

McKenry LM, Salerno E: *Mosby's pharmacology in nursing,* St. Louis, 1995, Mosby.

Mercier LM: *Practical orthopedics,* ed 4, St. Louis, 1995, Mosby.

New endoscopic technique for carpal tunnel speeds recovery and lessens risk of complication, *Modern Medicine,* vol 65, p 24, Apr 1997.

Otto SE: *Oncology nursing,* ed 3, St. Louis, 1997, Mosby.

Pagana KD, Pagana TJ: *Mosby's diagnostic and laboratory test reference,* ed 3, St. Louis, Mosby.

Potter PA, Perry AG: *Fundamentals of nursing: concepts, process, and practice,* ed 4, St. Louis, 1997, Mosby.

Rice J: *Medical terminology with human anatomy,* ed 3, Norfolk, Conn, 1995, Appleton and Lange.

Seidel HM et al: *Mosby's guide to physical examination,* ed 3, St. Louis, 1995, Mosby.

Sorrentino SA: *Essentials for nursing assistants,* St. Louis, 1997, Mosby.

Springhouse diagnostic nurse's reference library, ed 3, Springhouse, Pa, 1989, Springhouse Corp.

The Merck manual of diagnosis and therapy, Rathway, NJ, 1992, Merck Research Laboratories.

Thibodeau GA, Patton KT: *Anatomy and physiology,* ed 3, St. Louis, 1996, Mosby.

Watanabe H et al: Endoscopic ultrasonography for colorectal cancer using submucosal saline solution injection, *Gastrointestinal Endoscopy,* 45(6):508, 1997.

Williams SJ, Torrens PR: *Introduction to health services,* ed 4, York, Pa, 1993, Delmar Publishers.

ILLUSTRATION CREDITS

Chapter 1

Figure 1-2 courtesy Tribune Media Services.

Chapter 5

Figure 5-8 (A and B) from Gruber RP, Peck GC: *Rhinoplasty: State of the art,* St. Louis, 1993, Mosby.

Figures 5-9, 5-10, 5-11, 5-13, and Exercise Figures D and G from Lewis SM, Collier IC, Heitkemper MM: *Medical surgical nursing: Assessment and management of clinical problems,* ed 4, St. Louis, 1996, Mosby.

Figure 5-12 courtesy Nelcor Puritan Bennett.

Chapter 6

Exercise Figure I redrawn from Gillenwater JY et al: *Adult and pediatric urology,* ed 3, St. Louis, 1996, Mosby.

Exercise Figure J from Ballinger PW: *Merrill's atlas of radiographic positions and radiologic procedures,* ed 8, St. Louis, 1995, Mosby.

Exercise Figure K courtesy Fisher Scientific.

Chapter 7

Figure 7-8 courtesy EDAP Technomed, Inc.

Chapter 8

Figure 8-7 courtesy Biopsys Medical, Inc.

Figure 8-10 courtesy Richard Wolf Medical Instruments Corporation.

Exercise Figure H from Ballinger PW: *Merrill's atlas of radiographic positions and radiologic procedures,* ed 8, St. Louis, 1995, Mosby.

Chapter 9

Exercise Figure C from Zitelli BJ, Davis HW: *Atlas of pediatric physical diagnosis,* ed 2, St. Louis, 1992, Mosby.

Chapter 10

Figure 10-8 courtesy Paragon, Supplier: Vascular Therapy, Division of U.S. Surgical Corp.

Figure 10-13 from Ballinger PW: *Merrill's atlas of radiographic positions and radiologic procedures,* ed 8, St. Louis, 1995, Mosby.

Figure 10-18 from Seidel H et al: *Mosby's guide to physical examination,* ed 3, St. Louis, 1995, Mosby.

Exercise Figure D from Lounsbury P, Frye SJ: *Cardiac rhythm disorders,* ed 2, St. Louis, 1992, Mosby.

Chapter 11

Figure 11-10 and Exercise Figure G from Eisenberg RL, Dennis CA: *Radiographic pathology,* ed 2, St. Louis, 1995, Mosby.

Figure 11-11 from Ballinger PW: *Merrill's atlas of radiographic positions and radiologic procedures,* ed 8, St. Louis, 1995, Mosby.

Exercise Figures H and I courtesy Pentax Corporation.

Chapter 12

Figure 12-2 and Exercise Figures B and D from Zitelli BJ, Davis HW: *Atlas of pediatric physical diagnosis,* ed 2, St. Louis, 1992, Mosby.

Figure 12-3 (A and B) and Exercise Figure C from Seidel H et al: *Mosby's guide to physical examination,* ed 3, St. Louis, 1995, Mosby.

Figures 12-4, 12-8, and 12-11 from Thompson J, Wilson S: *Health assessment for nursing practice,* St. Louis, 1996, Mosby.

Figure 12-6 from *Mosby's medical, nursing, & allied health dictionary,* ed 4, St. Louis, 1994, Mosby.

Figure 12-12 from Lewis SM, Collier IC, Heitkemper MM: *Medical surgical nursing: Assessment and management of clinical problems,* ed 4, St. Louis, 1996, Mosby.

Chapter 13

Figure 13-2 from Seidel H et al: *Mosby's guide to physical examination,* ed 3, St. Louis, 1995, Mosby.

Figure 13-4 from Zitelli BJ, Davis HW: *Atlas of pediatric physical diagnosis,* ed 2, St. Louis, 1992, Mosby.

Exercise Figure C courtesy Micro Audiometrics.

Chapter 14

Figures 14-13, 14-17, 14-18, and 14-19 from Mercier LR: *Practical orthopedics,* ed 4, St. Louis, 1995, Mosby.

Chapter 15

Figure 15-4 from Perkin GD, Hotchberg FH, Miller D: *The atlas of clinical neurology,* St. Louis, 1986, Mosby.

Figure 15-6 courtesy Siemens Medical Systems.

Figure 15-7 from Eisenberg RL, Dennis CA: *Radiographic pathology,* ed 2, St. Louis, 1995, Mosby.

Figure 15-8 and Exercise Figure E from Ballinger PW: *Merrill's atlas of radiographic positions and radiologic procedures,* ed 8, St. Louis, 1995, Mosby.

Figure 15-9 from Thibodeau GA, Patton KT: *Anatomy & physiology,* ed 3, St. Louis, 1996, Mosby.

Chapter 16

Figure 16-4 from Zitelli BJ, Davis HW: *Atlas of pediatric physical diagnosis,* ed 2, St. Louis, 1992, Mosby.

Figure 16-5 courtesy Custom Medical Stock Photo, Inc., Chicago, Ill.

Figure 16-6 from Seidel H et al: *Mosby's guide to physical examination,* ed 3, St. Louis, 1995, Mosby.

Exercise Figure C from Kerth DA, Thibodeau GA, Anthony WA: *Anatomy & physiology,* St. Louis, 1997, Mosby.

Exercise Figure D courtesy Paul W. Ladenson, MD, The Johns Hopkins University and Hospital, Baltimore.

INDEX

SYSTEM REQUIREMENTS

Windows

486/25 MHz or faster processor
8 MB RAM
Sound card
SVGA 640 × 480 × 256 colors
2X or faster CD-ROM drive
Windows 3.1 or later

Macintosh

68030 or faster processor
8 MB free RAM
Sound card
SVGA 640 × 480 × 256 colors
2X or faster CD-ROM drive
System 7.1 or higher

CD INSTALLATION INSTRUCTIONS

Windows 95

Insert the *Exploring Medical Language* CD into your CD-ROM drive.
Click on the Start icon from the Taskbar. Select Run.
Type D:\terms95 (where D: is the drive designated for the CD-ROM) and press Enter.
The program will start automatically.

Windows 3.1

Insert the *Exploring Medical Language* CD into your CD-ROM drive.
If Windows is not running, type WIN at the DOS prompt.
Select Run from the File menu.
Type D:\terms31 (where D: is the drive designated for the CD-ROM) and press Enter.
The program will start automatically.

Macintosh

Insert the *Exploring Medical Language* CD into your CD-ROM drive.
Double-click on the *Exploring Medical Language* icon on the desktop.
Double-click on the *Exploring Medical Language* icon in the folder.
The program will start automatically.

Technical Support

Technical support for this product is available at no charge by calling Mosby's Technical Support Hotline between 9 a.m. and 6 p.m. CST, Monday through Friday. Inside the United States, call: 1-800-692-9010. Outside the United States, call: 314-872-8370.

You may also contact Mosby Technical Support through e-mail: technical.support@mosby.com